THE PLATONIC *political art*

THE PLATONIC *political art*

A Study of Critical Reason *and* Democracy

JOHN R. WALLACH

The Pennsylvania State University Press, University Park, Pennsylvania

Library of Congress Cataloging-in-Publication Data

Wallach, John R.
    The platonic political art : a study of critical reason
and democracy / John R. Wallach.

        p.   cm.
    Includes bibliographical references and index.
    ISBN 0-271-02075-X (cloth : alk. paper)
    ISBN 0-271-02076-8 (pbk. : alk. paper)
    1. Plato—Contributions in political science.
    2. Plato—Views on democracy. 3. Democracy.
    4. Reason. I. Title.
    JC75.D36 W35 2001
    320'.01—dc21

                                            00-031376

It is the policy of The Pennsylvania State University
Press to use acid-free paper for the first printing of all
clothbound books. Publications on uncoated stock sat-
isfy the minimum requirements of American National
Standard for Information Sciences—Permanence of
Paper for Printed Library Materials, ANSI Z39.48−1992.

FOR

AMANDA

CONTENTS

PREFACE AND
ACKNOWLEDGMENTS

The following seasoned convictions animate this book and motivated me to write it. Contemporary ethical and political thought does not address many of the most important questions about politics, deliberation, justice, and democracy today, while ancient Greek political thought—and particularly Plato's dialogues—explore these questions deeply and comprehensively (albeit indirectly). Linking these questions and occupying the gravitational center of ancient Greek ethical and political thought, particularly Plato's, is the notion of the political art, while any discussion of that notion is conspicuously absent in contemporary political theory. There has been no systematic study of the Platonic political art, and scant attention has been paid to it since the 1940s, while it was central to prewar scholarship on Plato. Why? On a more personal level, reading and trying to understand fully ancient Greek literature, particularly in its original language, is an energizing and clarifying intellectual experience. Hence it seemed worthwhile to undertake a thorough analysis and interpretation of the Platonic political art both as an intrinsically valuable project and for its possible reflections on contemporary ethical and political thought.

Genealogically speaking, the headwaters of this book primarily sprang from the extraordinarily vital and invigorating intellectual and political environs of the University of California at Santa Cruz and Princeton University in the 1970s and early 1980s. My distinguished teachers at these institutions manifested long-loving yet relentlessly critical relations to the major works in the history of Western political theory, philosophy, and literature—more particularly, ancient Greek thought and, most pointedly, Plato's dialogues. They helped to promote and sustain my belief that Plato's dialogues provide invaluable resources for critical political thought today. I cannot be thankful enough in this regard to Harry Berger Jr., Norman O. Brown, Raymond Geuss, John P. Lynch, Maurice Natanson, Dennis F. Thompson, and, most directly, J. Peter Euben, Michael Frede, and Sheldon Wolin.

It does me honor to mention the following individuals who contributed to the project that resulted in this book. During the 1980s, I had exchanges with three persons who cannot read these acknowledgments but who I would like to think can hear them. They pivotally affected the direction and destination of this project: Eric Havelock, Moses Finley, and Gregory Vlastos. (While carrying my bicycle up steps one morning on the way to the NEH Summer Seminar led by Professor Vlastos in 1987 at his home in Berkeley, my approach to understanding Plato's political thought crystallized.) During the writing of the book itself, I learned much about Plato from dialectical conversations with Julia Annas, Thomas Cole, Mitchell Miller, Josiah Ober, Gerald Press, and Christopher Rowe. Thomas Cole, Peter Euben, Mona Harrington, Melissa Lane, David Roochnik, Sheldon Wolin, Harvey Yunis, and an anonymous reviewer read all or parts of early or later drafts of this book and provided trenchant, helpful comments and criticisms. Friends and mentors who fueled the work and creative energy that made this book possible, and who deserve note here, are Harry Beskind, Peter Euben, Mona Harrington, Dori Laub, Rosalind Petchesky, Andrew Polsky, Michele Press, Molly Shanley, Ken Sherrill, Rogers Smith, Joan Tronto, Barbara Welter, and Sheldon Wolin. I also would like to thank the editors of *History of Political Thought,* especially Janet Coleman, for validating crucial parts of this book's argument by deciding to publish two of my articles. In so doing, they surely were not doing me any favors, yet their actions encouraged and materially helped me at crucial moments of my career.

Kelli Peduzzi provided superb editorial assistance in helping me reduce the size, streamline the prose, sharpen the argument, and maintain the core of this book. I thank my father for enabling me to employ her services. From Penn State Press, Ann Farkas performed excellent work as the book's copyeditor, as did Cherene Holland and Patty Mitchell in their roles as editors. I benefited greatly from the uncommonly good editorial judgment and personal kindness of the Press's director, Sandy Thatcher. Because of the high quality and innovative character of the Penn State Press's publications and personnel, I am pleased and proud to have it publish *The Platonic Political Art.*

The staff of the Vassar College Library provided many services to me over the years, for which I am forever grateful. I was fortunate to receive Hunter College's Scholar Incentive Award and the one-semester leave it afforded me in the fall of 1992. During it, I cast the basic shape of *The Platonic Political Art.* I also want to thank the Hunter College administration for deciding to grant me a Shuster Award, which defrayed my costs in reproducing and mailing the manuscript version of this book.

All of these individuals and institutions seeded this work. But responsibility for the quality of the harvest, along with the choice of both the ingredients and recipe for the book, is undoubtedly mine. At this point, I can only hope that the book I cooked reflects not merely the work of a pastry-maker (despite its value!) but also that of a chef who produces ever-nourishing food for thought.

My eternal thanks and love go to my friend, wife, and mother of our children, Amanda Thornton. She stayed with me and for me from the beginnings of this book to its publication. Gratitude does not begin to describe what I owe to my daughter and son, Sophia and David, for their wisdom, love, and fountains of youth. Indeed, every member of my intersecting families has sustained me throughout the book's realization.

Plato has been a great teacher for me, but these people have taught me volumes about which Plato knew nothing.

July 2000
Poughkeepsie, New York

INTRODUCTION

We rarely stop to think about the political art. If we do, it may seem like an inspired dream that has become a buried nightmare, one that we dare not recollect. For a moment, however, let us try to imagine its potential.

In its most exemplary form, the political art signifies a capacity to shape well the practice of power in a collectivity. Words are its primary tools; deeds are its direct objects; the common good is its ultimate aim. Exercising the political art transforms discourse into action that would benefit a political community. Ideally, the political discourse would be rational, its display would be virtuous, and the deeds achieved would be just. As such, the political art exhibits the highest possibilities of politics. The skillful practice of the political art by citizens and political leaders would actualize the potential for harmony among reason, ethics, and power, assuring the transformation of words of counsel into deeds of justice.

A democracy formally distributes political responsibilities throughout the citizenry. This makes the good conduct of the political art particularly important for the well-being of a democracy, even if its constitution does not officially require it. Establishing what constitutes the virtuous practice of the political art, therefore, places a critical mirror in front of democracy's self. In other words, it raises questions about the links and gaps between critical reason and democracy.

This book provides a systematic interpretation of the Platonic political art and takes Plato's rendition of it as a series of discursive inquiries about the relation of critical reason to democracy. By reading the Platonic political art against the background of its most relevant contexts, it argues that Plato's

All citations of classical authors refer to Loeb Classical Library editions unless otherwise indicated.

political theory and criticisms of democracy develop primarily out of his criticism of conventional ethics and politics and that, as a result, they can be used to invigorate contemporary political theory and benefit democracy.

This project, however, may appear to be anachronistic, if not badly misguided, on two counts: (1) prevailing conceptions of ethics, reason, and politics, or (2) conventional interpretations of Plato. The inarticulate premises and prejudices that underlie these beliefs pose the greatest challenge to the claims that follow. I shall make them articulate here and then try briefly to dispel them (or at least suspend the reader's belief in them), before I more properly introduce this book.

Contemporary experience makes the conception of a rationally coherent and ethically sound political art hard to fathom. With respect to the *rational* potential of such an art, practical and conceptual factors exist. Practically, the very idea of a political art has no obvious niche amid the highly differentiated division of political discourse and practice in contemporary democracies.[1] The notion of a political art suggests an intellectual competence that transcends mastery of the guideposts of ordinary experience but does not require highly specialized training; its practitioners would easily straddle the boundaries that separate the lives of the ordinary, taxpaying citizen and the paid politician, the ephemeral audience of the media's news and the devoted attention of the political intellectual. Myriad activities make up politics today. Among those who are preoccupied with, if not practitioners of, politics are the following: academic political scientists and theorists; political operatives from the economic sectors, who advise political candidates and public officials; elected politicians and other political officials, charged with the task of doing the people's business; bureaucrats in the public and private sectors; members of the media, who disseminate and frame the issues of public life; political advocates, who amplify the voices of those with specific interests; and finally citizens, whose relation to the political arena is primarily that of spectator.[2] How can the notion of a political art as a whole comprehend these various parts? Moreover, endowing an "art" with the potential of widespread

---

1. The issues posed for political rationality by the contemporary division of political labor have been a continuing concern of John Dunn over the last twenty years. See "Political Obligations and Political Possibilities," chap. 10 of *Political Obligation in Its Historical Context; Rethinking Modern Political Theory; Interpreting Political Responsibility; The History of Political Theory and Other Essays.*

2. See Stephen Esquith, *Intimacy and Spectacle: Liberal Theory as Political Education.*

utility seems positively premodern. "Art" is typically regarded as the province of artists and artisans—neither of whom seem to have any serious role to play in the high-stakes power politics of a hypertechnological world where pushing buttons can instantaneously murder or impoverish millions of human beings.

The major features of contemporary discourse pose serious conceptual obstacles as well. Skepticism dominates today's most prominent intellectual trends—namely, liberalism, pragmatism, and poststructuralism—and the intuitively skeptical dare not believe in the audacious notion of a rational, political art. The world's social contours conspire to support this skepticism. For it often seems that every human activity has a potential, if not actual, political dimension—from the microstructures of personal desire to the global scales of economics and the environment. This makes the distinctive features of "political" discourse and practice particularly hard to define with confidence or clarity.

If the task of identifying a rational and well-practiced political art seems daunting, denoting its *ethical* dimension most often indicates reactionary or utopian—in any case, foolhardy—reveries. For insofar as actual individuals practically wonder about how to make politics rational, we expect them to marginalize concern for ethics and the common good. That's how one man (e.g., Dick Morris, who is hardly unique) can get so well paid by prominent members of the two major, contending political parties in the United States. The political art is taken to consist of nothing more than sophisticated and/or sordid political techniques. Expertise in the currently understood practice of the political art or craft takes ethical considerations to be irrational or irrelevant. That is, "ethics" for "politics" nowadays mostly signifies (1) constraints that regulate, rather than conditions that foster, the skillful practice of politics—a set of technical rules that politicians would not obey if they were not legally forced to; (2) apolitical considerations of character that wonder more about the sexual stains of, rather than the financial chains on, the practical conduct of public officials; (3) an abstract, professional subject for philosophers concerned with apolitical analyses of "the will," "agency," "practical reason," and "desire"; or (4) the rather vapid (and etymologically amoral) idea of "values." In short, political actors rarely regard ethics as a beneficial source of their public service.

Amid the power that fuels and the conflict that marks everyday politics, along with the ignorance, hypocrisy, and disappointment that attend it, it is difficult to seriously assert that politics can seriously promise to be rational, ethical, and beneficial. Contemporary asymmetries between words and deeds, as well as ethics and power, so characterize our experience of politics that we tend to balk at the prospect of investigating what such a political art could or should mean.[3]

Were this practical situation not sufficient to discourage contemporary interest in the political art as a subject of generally beneficial inquiry, its scholarly focus on Plato might seem to be the least likely subject of interest, particularly from or for a democratic perspective. The dominant view of Plato as a political thinker still reflects the scars of the mid- and late twentieth century's political horrors. And indeed, in the public address delivered by Martin Heidegger—the self-proclaimed caretaker of the history of Western philosophy—in May 1933, he seems to have transposed the tripartite class structure of the ideal city in Plato's *Republic* into a background figure for the three types of citizens' normative obligations to the "essence" of German society.[4] It is not surprising, then, that uniting the intellectual currents of liberalism, pragmatism, and poststructuralism is the image of Plato as anti-Christ, ancestor of totalitarianism in its most explicit and subtle forms, symbolizing all that is to be avoided in new and valuable critical discourse.

What can scholarly interpretation of an ancient author (admittedly based on no new "evidence") do to dislodge the hegemony of these beliefs? The whole book provides the full answer to this question. Here, I preview its elements by noting how the philosophical and political problems Plato addressed resemble some of those we face in our efforts to accommodate democracy and justice at the dawn of the twenty-first century. In this vein, the following historical inquiry can open new horizons for us.

The dissonance between words and deeds, ethics and power, to which I alluded above, is not unique to our era. (I'm not even sure we are unusually distressed by it.) These kinds of dissonances disturbed citizens in other times

---

3. Of late, some sparks of interest in this subject have appeared. See, for example, William E. Connolly, "Beyond Good and Evil: The Ethical Sensibility of Michel Foucault," 384 and Arlene Saxonhouse, *Fear of Diversity: The Birth of Political Science in Ancient Greece,* 232.

4. This address followed Heidegger's acceptance of the position of Rector of the University of Freiburg—which was offered to him in April 1933, after his predecessor had been forced to resign by the new Nazi Minister of Culture and Education in Baden. For an English translation of this address, see Martin Heidegger, "The Self-Assertion of the German University," in Gunther Neske and Emil Kettering, eds., *Martin Heidegger and National Socialism: Questions and Answers,* 5–13.

and were particularly well known by Athenians of the fifth and fourth centuries B.C.—when Plato (an Athenian) lived and when the notions of politics, democracy, and political theory were invented.[5]

Starting with the Kleisthenic revolution and continuing through the first half of the fifth century, Athenian citizens forged a democracy that made the practice of politics one of their primary responsibilities.[6] Athenian democracy was a direct democracy, in which adult male citizens bore the burden of deciding whether to send themselves to war. In other words, the proper, skillful practice of politics involved an artful handling of civic affairs, and the Athenians became known as a citizenry that practiced politics extraordinarily well, as an "art" (techne).[7] For Athenians, politics were the bridge that spanned the gap between words and deeds; it functioned as the principal tool for realizing virtue in public life. Having linked their fate to their practice of politics, Athenians came to know its promise and danger. If politics was practiced well, it could promote the well-being of the social order; yet often, it was not and so did not. Athenians knew politics as an instrument of deceitful manipulation even as they also regarded it as the most valuable social practice. Given the rational and ethical volatility of political practice, Athenians were not always or universally sure about what the skillful practice of politics had to involve or who had the capacity to practice it well. Especially in the second half of the fifth and first half of the fourth century, as Athenians managed, lost, and regained parts of their empire, they sought explanations for the slippages in meaning and value between political words and deeds. They questioned whether the dissonance between these was inevitable, whose responsibility it was, and whence it came. They searched for skillful practitioners

5. See M. I. Finley, *Democracy Ancient and Modern*, rev. ed., 13–14; *Politics in the Ancient World*, 51–53, 123–24.

6. For recent scholarship on the origins of democracy, see the recent work of Josiah Ober, *Mass and Elite in Democratic Athens*, 53–103, and Kurt Raaflaub, "The Transformation of Athens in the Fifth Century," in *Democracy, Empire, and the Arts in Fifth-Century Athens*, ed. Deborah Boedeker and Kurt Raaflaub, 15–41. For classic earlier accounts, see Victor Ehrenberg, "The Origins of Democracy," 515–47, and J. A. O. Larsen, "Cleisthenes and the Development of Greek Democracy at Athens," in *Essays in Political Theory: Presented to George H. Sabine*, and Raphael Sealey, "The Origins of *Demokratia*." For a recent debate on the democratic character of the Kleisthenic revolution, see the article by Raaflaub, the response by Ober, and Raaflaub's reply to Ober's response, which appear in the AIA Colloquia and Conference Papers, no. 2, 1997, published as *Democracy 2500? Questions and Challenges*, ed. Ian Morris and Kurt Raaflaub, 11–104.

7. See Thucydides, *History of the Peloponnesian War*, 1.70–71.

of politics and wondered whether politics could be taught to the Athenian citizenry.

It was in this context that the practice of politics became a major focus of Plato's ethical and political thought. His efforts to clarify the problems and prospects of politics led Plato to become the first ancient Greek (to our knowledge) who precisely articulated the notion of "the political art" (*politiken technen* or *politike*), which he defined theoretically as the master art of virtue. At the very least, he was the first to make the political art an object of theoretical scrutiny, and he did so by generating a systematic, critical perspective on ethical and political life that responded to what he took to be the foremost problems and injustices of his time. More than any other political theorist of his era, Plato identified the necessity of the political art for the attainment of justice in the political communities and souls of citizens. This book provides a comprehensive interpretation of Plato's conceptualization of the political art, by focusing on the literary and philosophical connections between words and deeds in his ethical and political dialogues, reading them in large measure as responses to the discursive and practical predicaments of Athenian society and its democracy. In so doing, it suggests a new perspective on debates about the relations of ancient Greek political theory and criticism to politics and democracy.[8]

Plato's experience of the Athenians' defeat in the Peloponnesian War, along with the trial and death of Socrates, formed the core of Plato's ethical and political dilemmas; Athenian political conditions sparked Plato's textual treatment of the political art. But although his arguments are irreducibly historical, they also responded to problems that derived from Greek philosophical traditions. Plato's understanding of the political art operated at the intersection of philosophy and history. It reflected his engagement with what I call "Plato's Socratic Problem."[9] This problem is posed by the apparent incom-

---

8. This is a debate that was first starkly formulated in 1953 by A. H. M. Jones, in his article "Athenian Democracy and Its Critics," which can be found readily in his *Athenian Democracy*, 41–72. It has been revisited a number of times since then, most recently by Cynthia Farrar, *The Origins of Democratic Thinking*, and Josiah Ober, in his more recent book, *Political Dissent in Democratic Athens: Intellectual Critics of Popular Rule*. I shall discuss this debate more fully in Chapters 2, 4, and 6.

9. My first published work on this "problem" is "Plato's Socratic Problem, and Ours." "Plato's Socratic Problem" resembles "the problem of Socrates and Athens," about which Josiah Ober writes in *Political Dissent in Democratic Athens: Intellectual Critics of Popular Rule*. However, Ober's "problem" concerns the relation of political criticism and democracy and does not view democracy as a corollary, if not socially particular, context for the problems of politics. In

patibility between the reason and virtue of the historical Socrates and the conventions of Athenian democracy or, more generally, the conflict between the critical discourse (*logos*) of Socratic virtue and the actual conduct or practice (*ergon*) of the political art.[10] Plato's attempt at resolution took place in many of his dialogues, where he grappled with the issue of how to formulate in words a political art that reduces this dissonance—one that is, at the same time, philosophically valid, ethically virtuous, and practically beneficial.

The issue Plato faced was radically problematic, for if the words of "Socratic virtue" and the deeds of Athenian political life were to unite, if justice were to be realized, the words of virtue could not be entirely Socratic, and the conventional ethics and politics of Athenian democracy could not be relied on automatically to produce justice. Although Plato's attention to this problem did not frame all of his dialogues or all of his philosophy, it did frame its political dimension, and I treat this dimension as crucially important to his philosophical vocation. Learning about how Plato dealt with his Socratic Problem can speak to the aforementioned practical and conceptual obstacles to our coherent formulation of the political art and inform the relation of political theory to democracy today.

Plato can begin to look even more like a reasonable political philosopher if one accepts (at least, for the moment) that none of the responses he provides

---

other words, my rendition of "Plato's Socratic Problem" raises issues of ethics and power that are not reducible to an oppositional, if not antagonistic, relation of critical reason and democracy—that is, to "democracy as a problem." (See Ober, *Political Dissent*, 51.)

I should also say that my phraseology plays off traditional problems of interpretation, namely, "the problem of Socrates," that is, how to identify what makes up the genuinely historical thought of Socrates, when he wrote nothing, and "the problem of Plato," that is, how to identify Plato's thought when he does not directly speak in any of his dialogues. Ober adopts Vlastos's differentiation in Plato's dialogues of what can be ascribed to the historical Socrates and the historical Plato—which I reject for reasons stated and justified in this book and two of my articles, "Socratic Citizenship" and "Plato's Socratic Problem, and Ours."

10. The Greek word *logos,* of course, can mean many things other than "critical discourse" or "initial reason," including the simpler ideas of "words," "speech," or "rational discourse," as opposed to, say, mythical discourse. However, Socratic discourse was distinctive insofar as it criticized conventional understandings, and it is Plato's uptake of the conflict of Socratic discourse with those understandings that concerns me. The fact that *logos* is not sufficiently defined by "critical discourse," even though the best Greek equivalent of "critical discourse" is *logos,* should not be forgotten. There is no Greek equivalent to "critique" or being "critical" in a purely discursive sense, and *logos* often indicates critical rational discourse as the expression of the faculty of "reason." Plato's Socratic Problem certainly addresses problems of ordinary discourse but also goes beyond them, to address more substantive ethical, philosophical, and political issues of "reason."

to his Socratic Problem—no formulation of the political art in any one of his dialogues—is necessarily foundational for the others. Two reasons principally justify this interpretive perspective. First, we cannot precisely isolate a conception of the political art articulated (let alone "held") by the historical Socrates and clearly contrast it with that or those held by Plato. Our evidence for Socrates' conception of a political art comes only from "his" renditions of it in the works of Plato and Xenophon; no determinate boundary clearly separates the philosophies of Socrates and Plato or Socrates and Xenophon from the tainted evidence of Platonic dialogues and Xenophon's writings—most, if not all, of which were composed by these independent thinkers many years, if not decades, after Socrates' death. Moreover, the dialogical form in which Plato presents his philosophy makes suspect the assumption that such a demarcation exists in history or philosophy. Yet this assumption has governed much commendable scholarship on Plato's dialogues since the 1960s.[11]

In short, I regard the philosophical identity of Socrates—at least as we can know it from Plato's dialogues—as radically constituted by Plato's concerns. Not only does historical understanding justify this perspective; it avoids question-begging determinations of "Socratic" or "Socratic-Platonic philosophy" that depend on particular readings of selected dialogues of Plato. Finally, recognizing the gap between the dialogic Socrates and the historical Socrates (or philosophical equivalent) allows a greater appreciation of the dialogue form as a constitutive feature of the Platonic political art, which in turn allows for greater complexity in Plato's political thought. It challenges the reader to interpret the *Apology,* the *Republic,* and the *Laws* as distinct but related attempts to grasp the political dimensions of virtue and the virtuous dimensions of politics.

The second rationale for not identifying any particular dialogue or passage as foundational for conceptualizing the Platonic political art is that no dialogue covers exactly the same aspect of the political art. Each dialogue provides a self-standing critical analysis of a single set of philosophical problems. This suggests that no account of Plato that relies on one or two of his dialogues fully grasps his political thought in general or (therefore) what is

---

11. I say this while acknowledging the scholarly acuity and worthy political motives that apply to Gregory Vlastos's efforts to clarify this division. For his last efforts in this regard, see *Socrates: Ironist and Moral Philosopher.* For my view of the relation between the historical Socrates and the political art, see my "Socratic Citizenship." For a useful account of Vlastos's position and its scholarly lineage, see Daniel W. Graham, "Socrates and Plato."

signified by particular passages, propositions, arguments, narratives, or dramatic flourishes in specific dialogues. As a corollary to this perspective, the issue of Plato's development (the resolution of which typically begs major interpretive questions) does not orient the following interpretations of Plato's views.[12] Reading the dialogues in terms of their distinctive forms, subject matters, and historical background also enables us to identify a family of concerns whose resemblances refute a primarily skeptical, ironic, or deconstructive reading of his ethical and political thought. The interpretive perspective employed here makes possible a determinate evaluation of the Platonic political art, one that reveals the core of Plato's ethical and political thought, if not Plato's philosophy as a whole.

Working within these interpretive guideposts, I make substantive claims about how best to understand the Platonic political art as an art of virtue. With regard to the effect of Plato's context on his philosophical beliefs, I argue (1) that the key starting point for understanding the Platonic political art is its relation to the informally conceptualized but actually practiced political art in the democratic Athens of Plato's time; (2) that Plato crucially conceptualized his versions of the political art as a response to what he took to be the incoherence of that art as a virtuous practice and constituent of justice, in both the Athens of his day and the Greek world more generally; and (3) that Socrates is as much a problem as a hero in Plato's philosophical project.

    With regard to the substantive features of the Platonic political art, I argue that all of its versions involved attempts to resolve justly the tensions between the prevalent Greek couplet of *logos* ("reason," "speech," "word/s," "account," "theory," and/or "discourse) and *ergon* ("deeds," "actions," "function," or "practice/s").[13] As such, the Platonic political art generated criticism of democracy as a form of political power. I also argue, however, that

12. For important articles and collections that support this point of view, see Michael Frede, "Plato's Arguments and the Dialogue Form," in James Klagge and Nicholas Smith, eds., *Methods of Interpreting Plato and His Dialogues: Oxford Studies in Ancient Philosophy, Supplementary Volume* (Oxford: Oxford University Press, 1992); Gerald A. Press, ed., *Plato's Dialogues: New Studies and Interpretations;* J. Gonzales, *The Third Way: New Directions in Platonic Studies;* John M. Cooper, "Introduction," in *Plato: Complete Works,* ed. John M. Cooper, especially xii–xxv. Also see Charles L. Griswold, ed., *Platonic Writings/Platonic Readings.*

13. In Greek discourse, the couplet of *logos-ergon* could indicate opposition or complementarity as it became manifest in various dimensions of ethical and political life. Because of Plato's preoccupation with his Socratic Problem, however, he was mostly concerned with the opposition, which, he believed, too often went unrecognized.

Plato's criticisms are neither essentially nor particularly antidemocratic, because he regarded the political form of democracy primarily as one of many existing arrangements of political power, all of which were unjust because they wrongly ratified prevailing ethical and political "conventions" as exclusive conditions of justice.[14] Although one cannot wholly dissociate criticism of politics from criticism of democracy, because the democratic form of political power radically depends on open political jostling and debate, many mistaken views of Plato's political theory result from the conflation of his criticism of political injustice and domination with criticism of democracy.

This study of the Platonic political art produces new interpretive results. When Platonic dialogues that involve the political art are read as distinct facets of a project concerned with resolving Plato's Socratic Problem, each becomes an individually valuable contribution to a complex, differentiated understanding of the relation of critical discourse to the various aspects of political life. One no longer has to worry about question-begging interpretations about a linear development of Plato's thought, the relations between "Socratic" and "Platonic" thought, the essential propositions of Plato's philosophy or doctrines, or the nature of Platonism. For in this light Plato can become what I believe he intended to be: not a dogmatist advocating a new metaphysics of reason or systematic form of discourse as self-sufficient truth but, rather, a critical interpreter of a multidimensional world of words and deeds. In this perspective, Plato is not a Platonist. As a result, he no longer appears chiefly as the villainous (Nietzsche) or heroic (Whitehead) fountainhead for the Western tradition of philosophical metaphysics but as a critical theorist of ethics and politics.[15] "Platonism" may be implicated in theoretical

14. My rendition of "conventions" requires some comment. In contemporary English, "conventions" can refer to gatherings of the membership of established organizations, or, more simply, generally accepted ways of doing things. Thus, J. L. Austin can refer to linguistic "conventions" as word-usages that have "felicitous" expressions in social life. (See his *How To Do Things with Words.*) Notably, no one Greek word corresponds to the English word "convention." The best approximation is the politically charged word *nomoi,* which refers to written and unwritten laws, as well as socially sanctioned customs, and defines "man-made" things as opposed to phenomena of "nature" (*physis*). The fact that the Greek word *nomoi* more immediately expresses practices and relationships of power than of "conventions" is not insignificant; indeed, it marks the Platonic, if not ancient Greek, recognition of how social practices exhibit forms of power—one that may often be hidden in the English word "convention."

15. For Whitehead's exact words and their context, see his *Process and Reality,* 39–40. Nietzsche's views on Plato are, need it be said, more complicated than my statement suggests. Nevertheless, he frequently condemns Plato via Platonism and identifies it as a precursor of Christianity as a slave morality. See, for example, *The Genealogy of Morals.*

efforts to naturalize patterns of conflict and apodictically stabilize practical hierarchies of power. However, the first theorist to use reason in this way was Aristotle, not Plato. It is Aristotle's metaphysical, depoliticized version of Plato's thought, rather than the evidence of Plato's dialogues, that framed Whitehead's and Nietzsche's visions of Plato as the *arche* for the European philosophical tradition.

Today, the relation of "critical reason" or "discourse" [16] to democracy is typically regarded as unproblematic or antagonistic, and I find both attitudes misleading. Insofar as the relation is regarded as relatively unproblematic, as in the theoretical programs of many "deliberative democrats," [17] it is misleading because it assumes that contemporary political structures linguistically rendered as "constitutional democracies" represent a genuine, modern version of *demokratia*, that is, "rule by the *demos* (a politically empowered class of the many who are not financially well off)," when the one transparently clear phenomenon about contemporary political life—at least in the United States—is the relative powerlessness of what might pass for a current version of the *demos*. Insofar as the relation between critical reason or theory and democracy is rendered antagonistic, it is either resolved in favor of democracy (from the perspectives of Rortian pragmatism or Foucauldian poststructuralism), so as to reveal and affirm the bankruptcy of "theory" as a mode of critical discourse or (from the perspective of neo-Aristotelian theorists of virtue—ranging from Leo Strauss to Alasdair MacIntyre, Michael Sandel, and Martha Nussbaum) is taken to exhibit the inherent limitations of democracy as an ethical and political practice. [18] Typically, Plato is positioned as an ancestral author for *either* the compatibility of critical reason and the elitist rule

16. I distinguish "critical reason" or "critical discourse" from reason or discourse more generally as the expression of self-conscious efforts to call into question the authority of extant discourses and practices. I do not significantly differentiate "critical reason" from "critical discourse." Both were signified by the Greek *logos*, which tended to be associated with "rational," if not always "critical," reason or discourse, principally because "reason" was typically understood to be manifested in "speech." The formal differentiation of "critical reason" from "reason" more generally, to the point that the former became the standard for the latter, is surely a Kantian achievement. For an interesting reinterpretation of the Kantian legacy, see Christine M. Korsgaard, *Creating the Kingdom of Ends*.

17. The theoretical standpoint of "deliberative democracy," which has replaced "participatory democracy" as the rallying cry of the liberal left, has many different versions, including those of Jürgen Habermas, John Rawls, Joshua Cohen, Amy Gutmann, Dennis Thompson, and Cass Sunstein. Some of these are discussed in Chapter 6.

18. For references to the major works of these theorists, see the Bibliography. More specific references to their works are cited in footnotes.

exercised in contemporary constitutional democracies *or* the antagonistic opposition of critical reason and democracy—the forebear of philosophical foundationalism and/or totalitarian politics—twin pillars of antidemocratic forms of theory and practice.

Instead, this study suggests that the basic opposition between theory and democracy in Plato's work is more complex than most interpreters recognize and that the opposition between theory and democracy that contemporary writers either lament or praise is actually not established by Plato. It implies that political and philosophical criticisms of Platonism in contemporary intellectual discourse have a fictional caricature, not Plato's actual philosophy, as their target. To the contrary, Plato is one of the few philosophers in the Western tradition whose critical discourse sustained practical links to democratic life by emphasizing the essentially interdependent relation of *logos* and *ergon*.

Although the Platonic political art was certainly conducive to searing criticisms of democracy, it also reflected aspects of democratic discourse and practice.[19] Moreover, it forged a new kind of discourse of justice that, I argue, could be useful for contemporary democracies. For if (as I believe), the political practices of Athenian democracy during the first half of the fourth century did not constitute a sufficient paradigm for a just society and if the existing non-Platonic forms of ethical and political discourse do not provide adequate tools for understanding justice, then Plato's project of constructing a new understanding of the political art may attract anyone interested in theoretically or practically coordinating justice and democracy. Ultimately, a contemporary employment of the Platonic political art can challenge prevailing views about the relations of theory and democracy or ethics and power in ways that benefit democratic life.

This study begins in Part I, "Settings," by elucidating the contemporary and ancient contexts for my discussion of the Platonic political art. Chapter 1 explains how I interpret Plato's dialogues politically and how my interpretation compares with other, prevailing approaches to our understanding of the Platonic political art. I include a brief overview of the methodology of my approach, which I call "critical historicism." Chapter 2 examines the more

19. For other examples of this "reflection," see S. Sara Monoson, "Frank Speech, Democracy, and Philosophy: Plato's Debt to a Democratic Strategy of Civic Discourse," 172–97, and J. Peter Euben, *Corrupting Youth,* particularly chaps. 8–9.

immediate historical contexts that justify reading Plato's political art as a response to his Socratic Problem. I include parts of the *Apology* and *Crito* in this chapter to fill out my picture of the historical Socrates' contribution to these contexts. Part II, "Interpretations," includes three chapters interpreting the political art in Plato's dialogues. Chapter 3 explains Plato's articulation of his conception of the political art in his aporetic dialogues, as either a direct or indirect concern; it focuses on the *Laches, Charmides, Euthydemus, Protagoras, Meno,* and *Gorgias.* Although I treat them in what may be the chronological order of their composition, the argument does not depend on such a chronology. My principle of coordination follows the differentiation of their topics. In conjunction with the previous discussion of the *Apology* and *Crito,* these dialogues delineate the textual evidence of Plato's Socratic Problem. The second section of Chapter 3, entitled "Liminal Relations of Virtue and the Political Art," sets out the elements of Plato's theorization of this problem via the relation of the political art to particular virtues and virtue more generally, namely in the *Laches, Charmides, Euthydemus,* and *Meno.* The second section of the chapter, entitled "The Critique of Democratic Sophistry," interprets the *Protagoras* and, to a much lesser extent, the *Meno.* Each of these dialogues relates the political art to the democratic practice and teaching of virtue in general. In the last section of this chapter, entitled "Rhetoric and the Political Art," I focus on the *Gorgias* and refer selectively (mostly for comparative purposes) to the *Phaedrus.* Important parts of both dialogues critically analyze the public, discursive dimensions of the political art.

Chapters 4 and 5 interpret Plato's more constructive renderings of the political art, which appear principally in the *Republic, Statesman,* and *Laws.* These depend on his theorization of the relation of the political art to justice, a unique virtue in that its actuality entails the practical realization of all other virtues. Plato constructs this relation in the *Republic.* In Chapter 4, I interpret this relation as "The Constitution of Justice" and identify it as Plato's most thoroughgoing response to his Socratic Problem. The *Republic,* however, does not resolve many questions about the practical realization of a political art that arise in Plato's constitution of justice. Yet Plato does treat the relation of a just political art to the practical development of virtue in theoretically articulated political communities. Such treatments appear in the undeniably late dialogues, *Statesman* and *Laws,* which I interpret in Chapter 5, "The Political Art as Practical Rule." In these dialogues, where the figure of Socrates as a quasi-historical figure has virtually disappeared, Plato articulates two practical conceptions of the political art, in terms of both the art of political leadership and the legal norms of a political society. This chapter assumes previously made points about Plato's view of the political art as points of reference—taking these, rather than Athenian conventions, as the basic framework for the more practical, constructive discourse in these dialogues about virtue, justice, and the political art.

The last part, titled "An Appropriation," includes only one chapter (Chapter 6). "The Platonic Political Art and Postliberal Democracy" justifies a particular way to invest the Platonic political art in critical discourse that would benefit the democracies of our day—which I call postliberal democratic societies. Initially, I indicate how the previously articulated understanding of the Platonic political art can and cannot helpfully inform theoretical discussions about contemporary politics. Then, I spell out some limitations of the prevailing appropriations of Plato in recent political theory and argue how and why Plato could become an asset for citizens critically responding to major issues in contemporary political theory. In this vein, I directly respond to current theories of deliberative democracy, insofar as Plato could be said to be a critic of Athenian deliberative democracy and an advocate of current formulations of deliberative democracy. In the last section of Chapter 6, I consider an updated version of the Platonic political art as an art of critical reason that can be used to address current questions about how to accommodate democracy and education and foster democratic virtue. These days, Platonic questions can yield democratic answers.

Plato's conceptualizations of the political art were spawned by discursive and practical problems that principally appeared in Athenian democracy and were formulated in his dialogues of critical reason. Yet insofar as there remain kindred connections between Athenian and current democracies, Plato's critical discourse and our own, this study of the Platonic political art belongs to the larger study of the problematic relation between critical reason and democracy. Although Plato's issues were not precisely our issues, and his answers cannot and should not be ours, the resonance of Plato's issues and answers with contemporary concerns suggests that his dialogues about the political art may contribute to our critical discourse about politics, virtue, and democracy. At least, that assumption drives the work that follows.

SETTINGS

PART
I

INTERPRETING PLATO POLITICALLY

A. PRACTICAL OBSTACLES: MOVING FROM HERE TO ANTIQUITY

Critical political discourse arises amid geographies of power, even if it is not entirely determined by them. To understand Plato's conception of the political art, we need to account for what differentiates his era and our own. After all, enormous gaps in time, space, and arrangements of human power separate Plato and the Athenian democracy of his time from the technologically advanced capitalist democracies of today.

Five major conditions in ancient Athens pointedly mark the contrasts: (1) The Athenian *polis*, like every ancient society of the Mediterranean, condoned legally unequal statuses for its major social groups. It accepted slavery as a social fact and excluded women from its political life. More than half of the adult inhabitants of Athens lacked the full rights of Athenian citizenship. (But then, less than half of the eligible citizens of the United States vote in presidential elections, and much smaller proportions do so in state and local elections.) (2) Although Athenian citizens sanctioned social customs by practicing religious rituals, religion did not signify circumscribed sets of beliefs or doctrines. For ancient Athenians, monotheism was unknown, and their polytheism was associated with gods of particular city-states. (3) The prominent mode of economic production was precapitalist—artisanal and agricultural, supported by slave labor. Markets were radically local—hardly global—even though some trade occurred between city-states. (4) Oral practices and traditions provided the primary means for sustaining and preserving culture. Many citizens were well educated, but most were illiterate. Persons, not technologies, transmitted information and knowledge between individuals. (5) Their democracy was direct. Ordinary citizens operated the major and minor levers of political power: at the local level, in the *deme* assemblies; in the assembly, council, and courts for the *polis* as a whole. Insofar as specific citizens acted on behalf of the *polis,* their elevated authority resulted mostly from voluntary and/or aleatory procedures—not from electoral representation. Democratic institutions did not rely on election as the legitimate means for enabling citizens to exercise political power directly; indeed, citizens regarded elections as effectively oligarchic.

When it comes to comparing the political practices, ethical norms, or democratic character of ancient and contemporary societies, however, no unbridgeable chasm separates the two.[1] Although the question of which society is more democratic does not have a simple answer, "democracy" could be said to define the political identity of each society—even as each actualized radically imperfect approximations of democratic ideals.[2] The practical obstacles that face a cogent evaluation of Plato's political thought loom large, but qualifying our observations of ancient society by noting them does not make translations of ancient thought into modern contexts impossibly difficult. More imposing conceptual obstacles stem from the prevailing recent interpretive perspectives on Plato and his dialogues.

B. INTERPRETIVE OBSTACLES

I. TEXTUALISM AND CONTEXTUALISM

Over the past twenty years, the issue of how to interpret Plato's dialogues (and, a fortiori, Plato's conception of the political art) has become a major

1. The belief that such a chasm between ancient and modern ethics exists, and the attendant nostalgia for ancient virtue, has been encouraged most recently by Alasdair MacIntyre in *After Virtue.* For a more detailed analysis of that book, see my review in *Telos,* 233–40.

2. Of course, a principal author of the American Constitution of 1787 defended it by praising the way it avoided the ills of "democracy." Ironically, however, the most widely shared idea of democracy today signifies the Madisonian version of a nondemocratic republic.

subject of scholarship and contestation. Starting with E. N. Tigerstedt's book, *Interpreting Plato* (1977), and continuing to the present, scholars have made the second-order question of how to interpret Plato as important as, if not prior to, first-order questions about the substantive meanings of his dialogues.[3] Although newly proposed methods for interpreting Plato elicit substantive consequences for understanding Platonic epistemology, ontology, and ethics, a curious feature of this scholarly activity has been the failure (for the most part) to address either the political significance of the issue or the ways that previous interpretive methodologies have constituted previous interpretations of the substance of Plato's political thought. Scholars have normally framed the issue as whether to interpret Plato's thought according to the canons of analytical philosophy of ethics (a twentieth-century invention) and/or of literary criticism (the tradition for which reaches back to Friedrich Schleiermacher's work of the 1830s).[4]

Plato's political thought still belongs mostly to forbidden terrain. Since World War II, scholars have either taken it seriously and regarded it as authoritarian, if not proto-totalitarian, or have read its radicalism as self-mockery, which then makes Plato's political thought compatible with a stance of aristocratic conservatism in contemporary liberal democracies (or republics).[5] To be sure, there are important exceptions to this inexhaustive classi-

---

3. E. N. Tigerstedt, *Interpreting Plato;* Charles L. Griswold, ed., *Platonic Writings—Platonic Readings;* James Klagge and Nicholas D. Smith, eds., *Methods of Interpreting Plato and His Dialogues: Oxford Studies in Ancient Philosophy, Supplementary Volume, 1992* (Oxford: Clarendon Press, 1992); Gerald A. Press, ed., *Plato's Dialogues: New Studies and Interpretations;* Francisco J. Gonzalez, *The Third Way: New Directions in Platonic Studies.*

4. For applications of the interpretive perspective of analytical philosophy to understanding Plato, see the work of Gregory Vlastos, Terence Irwin, Richard Kraut, Gregory Santas, Julia Annas, and Alexander Nehamas, to name a notable few—especially the recent (and interesting) incarnations of this interpretive perspective, namely those of Nehamas, *The Art of Living: Socratic Reflections from Plato to Foucault,* and idem, *The Virtues of Authenticity: Essays on Plato and Socrates;* and Annas, *Platonic Ethics: Old and New.* For full citations, see the Bibliography. For applications of more literary methods to the understanding of Plato, see Jacques Derrida's 1968 essay on Plato's *Phaedrus,* "Plato's Pharmacy," in *Dissemination;* Harry Berger Jr., "Levels of Discourse in Plato's Dialogues," in Anthony J. Cascardi, ed., *Literature and the Question of Philosophy;* and Martha Nussbaum, *The Fragility of Goodness: Luck and Ethics in Greek Tragedy and Philosophy,* Part II. For Schleiermacher's theory of Platonic interpretation, see his "Introduction," in *Introductions to the Dialogues of Plato,* 1–47.

5. For illustrations of the former perspective, see the interpretations of Platonism and Plato's political thought offered by Martin Heidegger, Karl Popper, Renford Bambrough, Hannah Arendt, Richard Rorty, among others. For examples of the latter perspective, see the work of Leo Strauss, Allan Bloom, and Thomas Pangle. For full citations, see the Bibliography.

fication, but they only prove the rule.[6] The prevailing norms for contemporary scholarship on Plato's political thought indicate that Plato, via his positive conception of the political art, essentially opposes the importance of freedom, equality, and democracy as basic values of political life.

Other interpretive conventions have buttressed these views. Although they agree on little else, many philosophers, political theorists, and historians of varying ideological stripes in the mid- to late twentieth century have agreed on two points: Western metaphysics, as well as systematic and critical political theorizing, chiefly began with Plato; we know Plato by way of Platonism; and Platonism is essentially, incorrigibly, and diametrically opposed to democracy.[7] The prevalence of this interpretive posture has transformed a traditionally antidemocratic belief in the ineradicable opposition between theory and democracy into a mythic premise of the conventional wisdom of democratic thought. It has also depoliticized our understanding of the history of philosophizing and diminished our appreciation of its resources for articulating political possibilities that are both democratic and ethically virtuous. More particularly, it has led to incomplete, if not unsatisfactory, readings of Plato's political thought.

6. Among philosophers, see (prior to recent, revisionist views—for examples of which see Chapter 1, note 10, below) Philip Merlan, "Form and Content in Plato's Philosophy," who identified Plato as neither a "dogmatist" nor a "skeptic." Among classicists and political theorists, see C. J. Rowe, *Plato*, esp. chap. 2.; J. Peter Euben, *The Tragedy of Political Theory: The Road Not Taken,* esp. chap. 8. There is also, of course, a natural law tradition into which Plato's political thought is placed, which has enabled support of a more moderate Plato against Popper. See the pieces by John Wild in Thomas L. Thorson, ed., *Plato: Totalitarian or Democrat?* and more recently by R. W. Hall, *Plato.* However, the guideposts of this tradition clearly emanate from a social strand of Catholicism and support democracy with more pity than praise.

7. For examples, see the writers cited in Chapter 1, note 5, above. This view is perhaps best summarized in the following claim of M. I. Finley (who may be the most disturbing critic of Plato for anyone with democratic sympathies) that Plato is "the most powerful and most radical anti-democratic moralist the world has ever known." See his *The Ancient Greeks,* 140.

I should note that my inclusion of Heidegger and Strauss on this list is somewhat anomalous. Heidegger certainly associates Plato, Platonism, and metaphysics and vigorously condemns the pretensions of both Platonism and metaphysics. For example, see his "Letter on Humanism," in *Basic Writings of Heidegger,* ed. David F. Krell, 193–242, esp. 194, 232. However, his condemnations were not, shall we say, on behalf of democracy. As for Strauss, he embraces rather than criticizes the opposition of theory and democracy in order to justify his own understanding of Platonic metaphysics (actually Platonized Aristotelianism) as the necessary guardian of modern constitutional democracy. The latter succeeds only so long as its political mechanisms and authoritative values ensure that today's *demos* has no directive role in determining the practical course of political life.

The evidence for these interpretive insufficiencies is that the prevailing perspectives on Plato do not adequately take into account the elements out of which he formed his political thought. In particular, they have not made the historically and theoretically dissonant relation of, or gap between, *logos* and *ergon* a primary feature of their readings.[8] They elide the gap that constitutes the Platonic political art and so prevent us from appreciating its defining feature. They have done so in one of two ways—by assuming a systematic dominance of words over deeds or of deeds over words when interpreting that relation. Each marginalizes the problematic significance of the *logos/ergon* relation in both Plato's texts and social practices. The effects of these interpretive schemes—which I categorize as textualism or discursivism (both analytical and deconstructive) and contextualism—have detracted from the historical accuracy and theoretical clarity of our understanding of the political art in general as well as of the Platonic political art.[9]

According to the perspective I call textual discursivism, one views the political art as the application or expression of a philosophical or epistemological perspective or discourse; the fundamental meaning of philosophical ideas depends only marginally on the historical peculiarities of their production.

---

8. This may well seem like a rash, unappreciative statement—because virtually every commentator on Plato interprets the *logos-ergon* relation in Plato's dialogues one way or another. However, I do not think that any has made its problematic status as central to his understanding of politics and political philosophy as the following interpretation does. Two exceptions are worth noting; one emphasizes the more philosophical dimension, while the other makes the historical dimension central to his relation. The first is the recent book by Gerald M. Mara, *Socrates' Discursive Democracy: Logos and Ergon in Platonic Political Philosophy*. However, Mara's interesting book does not take the role of history as seriously as I do in constituting Plato's argument, tends to beg the Socrates-Plato question, and does not respect each dialogue as a separate argument in the way I do. As a result, his book can make points about Plato's political thought that have eluded me, and, I hope, I can make some points about the same that have eluded him. The other is the already mentioned valuable and important book by Josiah Ober, *Political Dissent in Democratic Athens*. Ober makes the *logos-ergon* relation central to his interpretation of six Greek "intellectual critics" by adapting the methodology of Austinian speech-act theory and Gramscian and Foucauldian theories of practical and discursive domination. In so doing, he underplays the philosophical and political significance of the *logos-ergon* relation in Plato's own thought.

9. There are obviously other valuable ways of categorizing the various approaches employed for interpreting Plato. For an important discussion of the variety of possible substantive treatments of Plato, clearly from a previous era, see W. K. C. Guthrie, "Twentieth Century Approaches to Plato," in *Lectures in Memory of Louise Taft Semple, First Series, 1961–1965: University of Cincinnati Classical Studies* (Princeton: Princeton University Press, 1967), 1:229–60. Also see J. B. Skemp, *Plato* (Oxford, 1976), along with E. N. Tigerstedt, *Interpreting Plato*, and Harry Berger Jr., "Levels of Discourse in Plato's Dialogues."

Consequently, ahistorical issues frame the analysis of the ancient Greek political art in general and the Platonic political art in particular (although the categories for understanding them have only recently appeared—such as oppression and human fulfillment, teleology and nihilism, democracy and elitism, or discourse itself). Interest in the politics and history of Athens is minimal, and disagreements between, say, the Sophists and Plato or Plato and Aristotle figure as case studies of current philosophical debates. Thus, around the time of World War II, Karl Popper supported democracy and opposed fascism by favoring Socrates against Plato; Leo Strauss opposed historicism and popular democracy by championing Aristotle and Plato against the Sophists and democrats of ancient Athens; Hannah Arendt fought scientism in political theory and the practices of totalitarianism by praising Pericles and Aristotle while blaming Plato; and most recently Jacques Derrida and Richard Rorty—still arguably reacting to the trauma of World War II—have respectively set deconstruction against logocentrism and pragmatism against analytical philosophy by favoring the Sophists over Plato. Even scholars who have made the study of ancient Greek thought a major focus of their professional careers, ranging in this century from Ernest Barker to Terence Irwin, have absorbed the problems of ancient Greek thinkers into the conceptual language of modern debates—such as that about the primacy of "society" or "the state," in the case of Barker, or the virtues of deontology versus utilitarianism, in the case of Irwin.[10]

A postmodern version of textual discursivism is that of literary deconstruction. It avoids the pitfalls of analytical discursivism by undermining its epistemological self-confidence. It also debunks the confident grasp on "reality" that, as we shall see, most contextualists rely on. Yet it also lacks some of the virtues of each, for it neither provides the justificatory support of the

---

10. Terence Irwin's careful and analytically sophisticated reading of Plato's dialogues represents the most highly developed recent attempt to interpret Plato from a principally analytic and discursive perspective. To be sure, Irwin attends to the Greek intellectual background of Plato's arguments. But his approach emphasizes Plato's "moral" or "ethical" as opposed to his "political" views. This allows Irwin to address more directly "general ethical questions," such as what is morality, what commends it to a "rational man," and "what is the right method in ethics" (Terence Irwin, *Plato's Moral Theory*, 4). These conceptual divisions, however, are themselves problematic for an understanding of a thinker who did not sharply differentiate the ethical and political realms. Their clear-cut separation in Irwin's work reflects divisions of contemporary academic labor and analytical philosophy. They evidence how the compartmentalization of academic disciplines, when reflected in one's interpretive framework, can impede the full appreciation of an author who lived and thought outside them.

former nor attends to the empirical concerns of the latter. By ignoring authorial intention in order to make the most of potential relations harbored in Plato's texts, deconstructionists (such as Jacques Derrida) tend to liquefy the concreteness of the historical situation to which Plato's dialogues responded.[11] In so doing, they presuppose an answer to an issue that Plato's treatment of the political art raised as a question, namely, how we are to understand politically and theoretically the relation of *logos* to *ergon*.

The other important perspective on Plato's political thought is contextualist. Contextualists do not go to the extreme of dismissing Plato's discourse of ethics and politics as nonsense but manifest their suspicion of the authority of philosophical reason by subordinating the meaning of Plato's political thought to the historical forces and political positions of his time. This view, which is typically held by classicists and ancient historians, takes Plato's analysis of the political art to express a class interest, elitist bias, or linguistic convention, and its theoretical character is read in such a way as to prevent any consideration of Plato as seriously responding in his dialogues to the troubles of Athenian democracy or, more generally, of ancient Greek *poleis*. Plato's dialogues become ideological discourses that mask their partisan character by pretending to befriend the community as a whole and to become universal truths. Through this lens, Plato's arguments are rarely seen in terms of a single dialogue's complexity, let alone the combined effect of all of them. In the words of Ellen Wood and Neal Wood, Plato is a "reactionary" and Aristotle a "tactician of conservatism"; M. I. Finley reads the theories of both as marginal, incoherent, ideological failures, whereas Josiah Ober identifies Plato as one among six authors who belong to "an interpretive community" of "political dissent."[12]

---

11. Jacques Derrida's fascinating reading of Plato's *Phaedrus* ignores authorial intention and plays fast and loose with the social context of rhetoric as a kind of political art. This enables him to imagine many possible meanings of that dialogue, but the relation between what Derrida takes those meanings to be and meanings we might reasonably claim to be Plato's becomes, thereby, obscure. Insofar as the coherence of Derrida's reading stems from its claim that Plato is constructing a logocentric discourse that privileges philosophy over literature and democracy, it also fails to recognize the gravity of the historical situation to which Plato's dialogues and Academy responded, as well as the way Plato's attention to rhetoric in the *Phaedrus* exemplifies his more general interest in the relation between words and deeds, the central problematic of the Platonic political art. I take Derrida's interpretation of the *pharmakon* in the *Phaedrus* as an exemplar. The antipathy of deconstructive interpretations to the authority of reason may or may not be accompanied by respect for the weight of history.

12. Ellen Wood and Neal Wood, *Class Ideology and Ancient Political Theory—Socrates, Plato, and Aristotle in Social Context*; Finley, *Politics in the Ancient World*, 124. Josiah Ober

But here the danger arises of contextualizing the thought of a political theorist in a way that fails to appreciate its distinctive meaning and significance. This tends to be the case when the ideas of a theorist are read primarily as instances of ideology or an interpretive community. By privileging a particular configuration of historical contexts in determining the meaning of theoretical texts, this perspective prejudicially rejects any merit to theorists' doubts about their contexts, or contexts more generally, as a sufficient basis for ethical and political justification. It denies the character of certain texts of political theory as, in part, distinctive radical attempts by writers to reorder their contexts of discourse and practice. They do so by articulating issues that inform but also transcend the immediate political context, on behalf of interests that may include but also transcend those of a single class or constitutional order. By underplaying this aspect of theoretical texts, contextualists either question the legitimacy of argumentation itself (which depends on its ability to operate on a different level from deeds and to offer justification for practices on another basis than the mere fact of their existence)[13] or miss the originality of the theorist by viewing him primarily as a member of a circle of critics.

If one is willing to recognize both the historically dependent and transcending (not transcendent) feature of political argument and justification of particularly original political theorists, then one can more easily engage in the crucial activity of translating an author's statement in the past into the languages of contemporary political issues and discourses. Then, one can directly—not covertly—ask the following questions: Does the author's solution to his or her problems help us understand the solution to ours? How do our problems relate to his or hers? Indeed, the work of the first systematic political theorist arises out of acute dissatisfaction with the prevailing discourses and practices of his *polis* as sufficient guideposts for ethical, political, and epistemological justification.[14] Plato's project stems largely from his rad-

---

develops Finley's perspective but makes it more nuanced—particularly in his most recent book—by employing recent work in the critical analysis of linguistic conventions and discourses of domination and hegemony for his methodology and analysis. See his *Mass and Elite in Democratic Athens: Rhetoric, Ideology, and the Power of the People;* idem, *The Athenian Revolution;* and idem, *Political Dissent in Democratic Athens: Intellectual Critics of Popular Rule.*

13. See Michael Frede, "Introduction," in *Essays in Ancient Philosophy*, x–xi and xviii–xix.

14. It is this "context" for Plato's dialogues that Richard Rorty ignores when, as part of his argument for the sufficiency of justification relative to his own artfully designed linguistic context, he dismisses the Platonic theoretical enterprise in favor of sophistry.

ical dissatisfaction with existing social practices as sufficient grounds for understanding virtue for the individual or justice for society.

Because of the prominence of these textualist and contextualist frameworks for interpreting Plato, contemporary readers of his dialogues too often
dismiss his rendition of the political art. They certainly do not take it to provide a cure of sorts for the maladies of the Athenians' souls and society, let
alone read Plato's philosophical claims about the political art as, simultaneously, political diagnoses. Textualists and contextualists have enhanced our
understanding of ancient Greek texts as well as invigorated academic debates.
But when it comes to a thorough understanding of the Platonic political art,
these interpretive perspectives have created significant obstacles to its achievement. Having said this, I must clearly define the political character of Plato's
philosophical work if he is not to be read as a partisan in intra-Athenian political conflicts, a member of an Athenian political sect, a deluded and re-
pressed philosophical tyrant, or primarily as a participant in a coherent discursive community.

2. PLATONISM AND ARISTOTLE

One of the interpretive tenets shared by both textualists and contextualists
is the view of Plato as a Platonist. Indeed, a major part of the problem of the
ascendant interpretations of the substance of Plato's ethical and political
thought, as well as of their analytical, deconstructive, and historicist methodologies for its understanding, derives from the explicit or implicit encapsula-
tion of Plato's political thought in the framework of Platonism. To read Plato
as a Platonist is to hold that Plato presents arguments in his dialogues and
through his characters that postulate an immediately effective reality for true
belief that fully transcends our experience and practical preferences.[15] In other

---

15. The analytical philosopher S. N. Hurley's "Platonism" provides an example of how
Plato's thought is transformed into the disreputable theory of "Platonism." In her book *Natural
Reasons: Personality and Polity,* she refers to Platonism as "a kind of objectivism" wherein conceptions of preference and value are independent of each other (14–15). Now, Hurley's Platonism is not everybody's Platonism, even if it is paradigmatic. Current Platonists—that is, individuals who read Plato as a Platonist—disagree about whether Plato's theory of forms posits forms
as separate (as Hurley suggests) or immanent. But all refer to the immutability of forms relative
to human dialogue and experience. This fosters a quick dismissal of Plato's relevance to contemporary critical inquiry. Hurley concludes her discussion with the following (*Natural Reasons,*
14–15): "Of all the possible objectivist positions available left by the denial of subjectivism,

words, it is to locate in Plato's dialogues the foundation of metaphysics and to read those dialogues as either apolitical or partisanly political applications of this metaphysical foundation. Reading Plato as a Platonist justifies viewing his political thought as a recipe, it seems, for illiberal and antidemocratic thought. It also renders Plato's forms in terms that are most compatible with relatively apolitical and Christian conceptions of Plato in neo-Platonism, from that of Plotinus to its modern interpreters and critics.[16]

As the subsequent reading of Plato's dialogues indicates, one of their animating principles is the belief that preferences and values are distinct but inseparable—which directly contradicts a core belief of Platonism. The interpretation of Plato as a Platonist, however, cannot be easily dismissed. It has a long and noteworthy lineage; it originated with Aristotle. He rendered Plato in terms of Platonism that was, from his standpoint, a notably inadequate metaphysical perspective. Aristotle's limits as a fair reader of Plato have long been recognized, but not adequately acknowledged. His Plato should not immediately be regarded as the authoritative Plato.[17] Moreover, any argument

---

Platonism [is one of the least tempting]. Hardly anyone holds it, there is little point in arguing against it, and there is not very much to say about it . . . in ethics, at least, Platonism is not a live option."

For a version of the "immanent" view, see Kenneth Sayre, *Plato's Literary Garden: How to Read a Platonic Dialogue.* For a more analytical perspective on the contrast between "separatist" and "immanent" understandings of Plato's theory of forms, see the work of Gail Fine, for example, "Separation" and "Immanence." For a discussion of the contrast, see Daniel T. Devereux, "Separation and Immanence in Plato's Theory of Forms." Other contemporary versions of Platonism include Julius Moravcsik, *Plato and Platonism,* and a number of books by T. K. Seung, the most recent of which is *Plato Rediscovered: Human Value and Social Order.*

16. For the establishment of links between Plato or Platonism and Christianity, see, above all, myriad passages in the work of Friedrich Nietzsche (who, however, was unambiguously hostile to Platonism—not so much to Plato). See, for example, Nietzsche's early stated interest in "overturning Platonism," his later condemnation of Christianity as "Platonism for the people" (in his Preface to *Beyond Good and Evil*), and his valuation of Thucydides over Plato (in *The Twilight of the Idols,* "What I Owe to the Ancients," section 2). For a recent interpretation of Nietzsche's complex relationship to both Plato and Platonism, in terms that assess its relevance to contemporary philosophy, see Michael Haar, *Nietzsche and Metaphysics,* trans. and ed. Michael Gendre (Albany: State University of New York Press, 1996 [1993]), especially chaps. 1 and 3. For other linkages of Plato and Christianity, see William Temple, *Plato and Christianity* (London: Macmillan, 1916); A. E. Taylor, *Platonism and Its Influence* (New York: Longman, Green & Co., 1932); Paul Shorey (who typically resisted the lure of Platonism in his own readings of Plato's dialogues) *Platonism: Ancient and Modern* (Berkeley and Los Angeles: University of California Press, 1938); and the work of Gregory Vlastos. On this aspect of Vlastos's version of Plato and Platonism, see my "Plato's Socratic Problem, and Ours."

17. See Harold Cherniss, *Aristotle's Criticism of Plato and the Academy,* vol. 1. For a more recent, sophisticated, and more charitable understanding of Aristotle's reading of Plato, see Gail

for the metaphysical isolation of preferences and values in Plato's thought depends on a belief in the intrinsic validity and practical authority of theoretical knowledge. But this takes Plato to be articulating propositions of theoretical knowledge. Aristotle does this in the *Metaphysics;* Plato does not, anywhere in his dialogues. He had no conception of theoretical knowledge that directly resembles Aristotle's.[18]

Three features of the different philosophical perspectives of Plato and Aristotle call into question the reliability of Aristotle as an interpreter of Plato. First, it was Aristotle, not Plato, who established a discipline of theoretical knowledge that could discursively identify and solve its own problems without regard to their practical relations to the political world. Although Aristotle maintained that all ethical and political inquiry (rightly understood) ultimately issued in ethical and political action and promoted a highly nuanced, non-rule-governed conception of political knowledge (*politike*), he subordinated the general principles and special features of both the political realm and *politike* to a cosmic world of nature whose principles derived from a mode of theoretical inquiry that was ultimately independent of the practical activity of social life. It was Aristotle, not Plato, who "founded" metaphysics and depoliticized *logos.*

Second, in Plato's dialogues, there is no separate category of inquiry called "ethics," or even less, "morality."[19] The term *ethike* was first coined by Aristotle. As we shall see, Plato's "ethical" concerns belonged to, not beside, "political" concerns—that is, to questions of power and community—which arise whenever the operations of power generate unhappy conflict in various

---

Fine, *On Ideas: Aristotle's Criticism of Plato's Theory of Forms.* As one might surmise, I do not agree with Fine's view that the differences between Plato's and Aristotle's philosophies can be reduced to opposed metaphysical intuitions.

18. In the *Statesman,* Plato differentiates "theoretical" and "practical" kinds of *episteme,* or knowledge (259c), but this kind of "theoretical knowledge" would count as "practical knowledge" in the categories of Aristotelian metaphysics; moreover, the significance of this distinction is overrun as the dialogue progresses by the demands attending the definition of *politike.* For Aristotle's authorization of the categories of theoretical, practical, and productive knowledge, see, inter alia, *Metaphysics* 1025b3–28, 1026b4–5.

19. Hurley, *Natural Reasons,* 158. (Similarly and notably, Heidegger criticized Plato for establishing the disciplines of "logic" and "ethics." See Heidegger, "Letter on Humanism" (cited Chapter 1, note 14, above.) The failure to attend adequately to the inherently political dimension of Greek ethics mars the otherwise lucid interpretation of Plato by Terence Irwin, in *Plato's Moral Theory.* This problem is not overcome in his recently expanded and slightly revised edition, *Plato's Ethics.* For the philosophical significance of the distinction between "ethics" and "morality," see Bernard Williams, *Ethics and the Limits of Philosophy.*

communities.[20] To argue, as Aristotle did, for the practical irrelevance of the Platonic notion of the good is simply to ignore the complex efforts Plato made in his dialogues to establish that relevance.[21] Aristotle also believed that ethical inquiry could be heuristically isolated in a different discourse from one that directly addressed questions of power and community in the political world—even though in practice it belonged ultimately under the umbrella of *politike*.[22] Plato did not clearly differentiate between a work on "ethics" (such as the *Nicomachean Ethics*) and "politics" (such as the *Politics*); there were simply dialogues on virtues and the political art and, most centrally, on the matter of the constitution of justice (*Republic*). Ironically, it is Aristotle's metaphysical turn that allows him to criticize Plato's notion of the good as impractical.[23]

Third, it was Aristotle, not Plato, who conceptually differentiated theoretical and practical knowledge and categorized human activities as modes of *techne* or *praxis*.[24] Thus, it was Aristotle, not Plato, who made the unproductive activity of *praxis*, rather than the transformative activity of *techne*, the primary ontological category for signifying rational and ethical political action. In Aristotle's political thought, the practically transformative, productive character of the notion of *techne* is regulated by the intrinsically valuable, unproductive nature of human activity known as *praxis*. In stark contrast, the urgency with which Plato addressed practical questions was theoretically reflected in the centrality of the concept of *techne* to his understanding of vir-

---

20. For an example of this usage of "political," see Sheldon S. Wolin, *Politics and Vision*, particularly chap. 1—despite his reading of Plato as antipolitical in chap. 2. For a less ethical and more ordinary, concrete, pragmatic, and externalist definition of the nature of political questions, note the following words of John Dunn, who defines politics as "the outcomes and consequences of elections; the making of war or peace within or across borders; the public modulation of life chances by taxation, and the provision or denial of health, education, and physical security to women or men or children; or the formation and implementation of public policy over domestic production or international trade," in *International Affairs* 70 (April 1994): 321.

21. See Aristotle, *Nicomachean Ethics* Bk. 1, chap. vi.

22. See his *Nicomachean Ethics* 1.i–iv; vi.i; x.ix; *Politics* iii.xii; iv.i.

23. Derridean criticism of the logocentric bias of metaphysics should make Aristotle's treatises, rather than Plato's dialogues, the chief source of this discursive effect.

24. The failure to understand that Aristotle's differentiation of *techne* and *praxis* was peculiar to his philosophical thought and not to ancient Greek thought more generally gets Habermas's brief history of political thought started on the wrong foot. See his *Theory and Practice*, 42. This misunderstanding has repercussions for Habermas's own theory of deliberative democracy, discussed in Chapter 6.

tuous action. Contrary to the interpretations of Plato promoted by Heidegger and Arendt, typical *technai* did not provide sufficient models in Plato's work for philosophical inquiry or political practice.[25] The notion of a *techne* was used to explore critically the adequacy of various candidates for *arete*, not because it provided a sufficient model for *arete* but because it entailed both rational roots and practical, reliable effects. Moreover, its appearance in the notion of a political art manifested the radical nature of Plato's conception of the requirements of justice in political life, hardly the traits of either totalitarian reason, which denies the constitutive difficulty in relating ideals to actuality, or foundationalism, which, unlike the Platonic political art, radically dissociates truth from action.

Plato surely emphasized oppositions between reality and appearance as well as *logos* and *ergon*, but he never stabilized them. This is because their truth-value involved their capacity to respond to and resolve the persistent, unjust conflicts of extant political life. Plato doubted that such harmony could ever be perfectly, practically realized, and he denied that it could be regularly or permanently achieved. In this sense, his political ambition was moderate and his philosophical authority limited. But, unlike Aristotle, he was convinced that the *failure* to conceptualize such perfection, to entertain the possibility (not the likelihood) of its realization, and to live in accord with that ideal as much as circumstances permitted, implanted the seeds of *stasis* and prevented his fellow Greeks from being as just as they could be. If, as I argue, Plato's dialogues do not present arguments that invalidate dialogue so much as they interrogate the character of the dialogues we readers have, then Plato begins to look less like a doctrinal Platonist and more like a critical, political theorist of a particularly interesting sort.[26]

---

25. For Heidegger, see "Letter on Humanism," 194; for Arendt, see *The Human Condition*.
26. See Philip Merlan, "Form and Content in Plato's Philosophy"; Michael Frede, "Plato and the Dialogue Form," in Klagge and Smith, eds., *Methods of Interpreting Plato and His Dialogues;* Ronald Polansky, "Foundationalism in Plato?" in Tom Rockmore and Beth J. Singer, eds., *Antifoundationalism Old and New,* 41–55; and John M. Cooper, "Introduction," in Plato, *Complete Works,* esp. xii–xxv. This view does not imply that Plato is fundamentally a skeptic, as he appears to Platonists of the New Academy of the third and second centuries B.C., principally Arcesilaus and Carneade. See Julia Annas, "Plato the Sceptic," in Klagge and Smith, eds., *Methods of Interpreting Plato and His Dialogues,* 43–72. Apart from the skeptical Plato appearing primarily as the flip side of neo-Platonism, my concern about these philosophical perspectives on Plato is that Plato, the author of the dialogues, begins to lose his identity, particularly his political identity, and the political meaning of his dialogues begins to be misunderstood or undervalued, if not effaced.

This brief discussion of the potentially distorting effect of Aristotle's philosophy and interpretation of Plato on the uptake of Plato's thought suggests that one ought to take greater care than is usually done in using the phrase "Platonic" with regard to a conception of the political art and call into question any set of propositions indicative of "Platonism." This rejection of Platonism is not meant to obscure or diminish our appreciation of Plato or debunk any claim that a set of specifiable characteristics may justifiably be called Platonic. It should, however, shift the focus on what that involves.

Plato wrote discrete dialogues about distinct but related problems of discourse and practice. A relatively coherent set of impulses informed these writings (and I have hedged no bets in developing a unified argument about the Platonic political art through interpreting many of them). At no point, however, did he affirm a portable doctrine, systematic philosophy, or set of propositions that could be understood or appropriated without also noting the question or problem in the dialogue to which it applied. Although Plato certainly rejected an Isocratean or practical-rhetorical understanding of philosophy and had no special fondness for democracy or any other extant form of political organization, in neither his dialogues, academic vocation, nor political activities did he establish or enforce boundaries for a substantive philosophical ideology or exclusive school of thought. For Plato and his contemporaries, there were Academics and Platonic sympathizers, but there was no such thing as Platonism.[27] That is a later-day notion and reflects subsequent intellectual and political developments.

C. DISCURSIVE HORIZONS: CRITICAL HISTORICISM

There is room and justification for interpreting Plato politically, in a way that differs from conventional interpretations. To justify my alternative approach, I explain, first, what I mean by "interpreting Plato politically;" second, how this involves interpreting Plato without Platonism, and, third, why this approach—an instance of a more general interpretive approach that I call "crit-

---

27. On the un-Platonic efforts by Speusippus, Plato's successor in the Academy, to "pythagoreanize" Plato (which is, in our terms, to Aristotelianize him) and the significance of these efforts for the development of Platonism, see Victorino Tejera, "The Hellenistic Obliteration of Plato's Dialogism," in Gerald A. Press, ed., *Plato's Dialogues: New Studies and Interpretations,* 129–44.

ical historicism"—may improve current readings of the political dimension of Plato's thought.[28]

1. By "interpreting Plato politically," I mean interpreting Plato according to the primary dynamic of ancient Greek politics, namely the interactive, interdependent relation of words and deeds, *logoi* and *erga,* about the ethics and power of *polis* life. The dynamism of this interrelation has been understood to be a feature of Thucydides' thought since, at least, 1957.[29] I believe that the dynamism is not suppressed in Plato, as Parry and other interpreters of Plato via Platonism argue, but rather critically deepened and widened—extended to cover the nature and virtue of political life. In this view, Platonic philosophy is neither antipolitical, as Strauss praises and Arendt criticizes it for being, nor political in a more positivist or pejoratively ideological sense, as Popper, Wood, or Finley argues. Rather, it is political in a critical and theoretical sense, a sense that he innovatively develops and that is not pursued by subsequent Platonists or their Aristotelian critics. I believe that this political dimension of Plato has been hidden from view over the past fifty years because of the legacy of World War II in shaping interpretive perspectives on Plato's political thought.[30]

In order to define this political dimension of Plato's thought, we must answer two questions. (1) What is the political content of Plato's dialogues that would lend itself to the aforementioned political interpretation? (2) How can it be understood independently of an interpretation of his dialogues, so as to ensure that its definition avoids invidious circularity? With regard to the second question, no final solution hovers over the horizon. For there simply is not enough indubitable evidence outside the dialogues to prove any one interpretive hypothesis. But I argue that the existing evidence, such as it is, tends to support my view of both Plato's political identity and the political character of the dialogues. The evidence comes from our best understanding

28. For an illustration of this approach in operation, see my "Contemporary Aristotelianism."

29. See Adam Parry's 1957 doctoral dissertation, "*Logos* and *Ergon* in Thucydides' *History of the Peloponnesian War,*" reprinted in book form as *Logos and Ergon in Thucydides.*

30. Indeed, I argue that pre-war interpreters of Plato—such as Shorey, Barker, Friedlander, Jaeger, Gadamer, Cornford, and Stenzel—tend to get Plato's political thought more nearly right than postwar interpreters—such as Popper, Strauss, Bambrough, Arendt, Guthrie, Vlastos. (For citations, see Bibliography.) With the problematic of World War II no longer constituting the essential aspects of current injustice, we are now in a better position to understand Plato's political thought.

of Plato's biography. (For more on which, see Chapter 2.) Here, the *Seventh Letter* is a valuable source, even for those who doubt its authenticity. It describes Plato as having irreversibly chosen a philosophical vocation for himself after the trial and death of Socrates but also as having chosen it for essentially political reasons. That is, given his view of the probably irredeemable character of conventional politics, the practice of philosophy constituted Plato's chosen path for pursuing justice. The *Seventh Letter* goes on to describe and justify Plato's failed attempts to become politically helpful in Syracuse, in 367 and 361, by endeavoring to educate Dionysius II, its maximal leader.

The *Letter* interestingly establishes stringent conditions for political activism, associates those conditions with ethical and educational goals, and disassociates those goals from prescriptive political programs—other than devotion to philosophy and the constitutional (or political) rule of law—just as Plato distances his own ultimate convictions from their appearance in written form.[31] These features of the *Seventh Letter* neither present a portrait of Plato as a conventionally partisan political activist nor suggest that Plato's Academy was a site for the inculcation and proliferation of political expertise—a "RAND Corporation of Antiquity."[32] To the contrary, they indicate a radical indeterminacy in any Platonic political program beyond its commitment to education in virtue and the constitutional rule of law. (This view of the *Seventh Letter* does not require its Platonic authorship. Nevertheless, it does lean toward a reading of the *Letter* as basically truthful, rather than as an inaccurate apologetic composed by friends of Plato interested in whitewashing his reputation.[33]) To interpret Plato politically involves identifying the political

31. A major critic of the *Seventh Letter*'s Platonic authorship, Ludwig Edelstein, argues that the *Letter* could not be authentic because Plato was simply a philosopher, not a political activist. See Ludwig Edelstein, *Plato's Seventh Letter.*

32. See Trevor Saunders, "'The RAND Corporation of Antiquity'? Plato's Academy and Greek Politics," in *Studies in Honour of T. B. L. Webster*, ed. J. H. Betts, J. T. Hooker, and J. R. Green.

33. The issue of which of these two readings is "right" tends to turn on how one understands Plato's ethical and political dialogues. If one's understanding indicates that Platonic political theory is utopian and/or authoritarian, then the *Seventh Letter* begins to look more like a rhetorical cover-up than a primary source of historical evidence about the life of Plato. But if one understands these dialogues as a series of complex reflections on the relation of critical discourse to ethics and power, which is what I indicate when I suggest that one ought to read Plato's dialogues "politically," then the *Seventh Letter* may be read as plausible evidence of genuinely Platonic views. I read Plato's dialogues that treat the political art in this "political" vein. The relation of the words and views expressed in the *Seventh Letter* to those of Plato is, nonetheless, briefly discussed further in Chapter 2.

content of his dialogues as attempts to resolve conflicts of ethics and power in a political community at the level of critical, theoretical discourse so as to benefit the intelligence and political activity of readers.

2. This "political" viewpoint does not involve reading Plato in terms of a developmental hypothesis, which begins with either a Socratic theory or immature Platonic political theory and ends with either a mature Platonic theory that justifies philosophical authoritarianism as the foundation of virtuous political rule or a deflated political idealism that offers new appreciation of the virtues of procedural democracy.[34] Nor does it involve reading Plato's dialogues as expressions of a unified set of Platonic doctrines. But it also does not mean that Plato's dialogues have to be read as the work of a political refugee or skeptic. Instead, they should be read as a differentiated set of critical inquiries about the prospects of dialogically instantiating justice, originating from distinct perspectives that respond to the politics and philosophies of Plato's day and (potentially) beyond. In Plato's dialogues, these may principally engage the conventional confines of Athenian politics, as illustrated in the *Apology, Crito, Protagoras,* and *Gorgias;* derive from the perspective of purely hypothetical and theoretical starting points, as illustrated in the *Statesman* and the *Laws;* or involve a discourse that moves from the conventions of Athenian politics to the level of theoretical reflection about justice and then back to the life of the individual and the dialogue's readers, as in the *Republic.* In all cases, I render Plato's beliefs in terms of Platonic views of the political art and Platonic instances of the political art itself—keeping in mind that Plato (unlike, for example, monotheistic religions) radically problematized the notion of "belief."

This "political" reading of the dialogues makes sense if one understands Plato's primary motivation in writing the dialogues as an effort to solve the problem of justice in the wake of the Athenians' political turmoil of 411–403; the Athenians' defeat by the Spartans in the Peloponnesian War; the trial and death of Socrates; and the subsequent need to create and defend a mode of critical discourse that could be philosophically viable and politically relevant. (See the discussion of "Plato's Socratic Problem," Chapter 2.) In this view, neither the intellectual life of the Academy nor the meaning of Plato's dia-

---

34. For the most recent application of the developmental approach to Plato's political theory, see George Klosko, *The Development of Plato's Political Theory.* The most notable previous applications of this approach are those of Ernest Barker, *Greek Political Theory: Plato and His Predecessors,* and Werner Jaeger's *Paideia: The Ideals of Greek Culture,* vol. 2: *In Search of the Divine Centre,* and vol. 3: *The Conflict of Cultural Ideals in the Age of Plato.*

logues becomes a site of eristic disputation, politically idle inquiry, or anti-democratic ideology. Rather, each becomes innovative activities that would foster reasonable and ethical conditions for politics in societies where the gap between the conventional exercise of political power and the realization of genuine justice seems immediately unbridgeable.[35]

3. Because the connections and disjunctures between words and deeds mark the principal features of Plato's treatment of the political art as well as politics itself, this study initially presupposes an indeterminate relation of *logos* and *ergon*. Its approach may be called "critical historicism," insofar as its interpretive path occupies terrain between the poles of textual discursivism and historicist contextualism, accepting historical constraints on and conditions of Plato's formulation of his philosophical problem but recognizing the potential of his "solutions" to those problems to apply to more than their own practical origins.[36] It meets many obstacles, because its application will inevitably be regarded from various quarters as insufficiently historical, disrespectful of the standard of historical objectivity, insufficiently philosophical or analytical, or anachronistically beholden to previously deconstructed interpretive categories.[37] But one has to choose one's imperfections, and this

---

35. The approach followed here obviates the categorical isolation of philosophical and historical inquiry, ultimately by problematizing it. In turn, my interest lies primarily in neither the philosophical or historical identity of Plato nor the nature of the idea of the political art about which he wrote. In general, one should not immediately characterize what appears in the dialogues as "what Plato said" about the political art or Plato's concept of the political art. The treatment of the political art in the dialogues is irreducibly Plato's, but it is impossible to isolate neatly in the dialogues a historically determinate entity called the political art from Plato's dialogic conceptualization of it. Following this logic, neither the *logos* of the political art in Plato's dialogues or the Academy nor the *ergon* of Plato's milieu or individual life provides the foundation for this study of the Platonic political art.

36. I actually have not found any employment of this phrase as an interpretive approach. However, the phrase "critical historicism" does appear in an introduction to a set of articles devoted to "The Critical Uses of History." See *Stanford Law Review* 97, 2 (1997). In terms of current writing on the status of knowledge, this approach occupies the ground between Hayden White's deconstructivist statements about the status of history, which retain respect for the durability of the past, and Richard J. Evans's arguments about the existence of a historical reality. For examples of these two viewpoints, see Hayden White, "Historical Emplotment and the Problem of Truth," in Saul Friedlander, ed., *Probing the Limits of Representation: Nazism and the "Final Solution,"* 37ff; idem, "Writing in the Middle Voice," 179–87; and idem, "Response to Arthur Marwick," *Journal of Contemporary History* 30 (1995): 233–46, especially 238–45; and Richard J. Evans, *In Defense of History*.

37. Histories of political theory are notorious for falling short on both fronts. See J. G. A. Pocock, "The History of Political Thought: A Methodological Inquiry," in *Philosophy, Politics, and Society*, 2d series (Oxford: Basil Blackwell, 1964), 183–202; John Dunn, "The Identity of the History of Ideas," in *Political Obligation in Its Historical Context* (cited in Chapter 1, note 1,

approach enables us to address directly the most appropriate questions for illuminating Plato's political thought.[38]

In terms of its intellectual ancestry, "critical historicism" carries debts to the work of John Dewey, R. G. Collingwood, and Michel Foucault. To this extent, it may be called "problematic."[39] That is, "critical historicism" inter-

---

above); and Quentin Skinner's 1969 article, "Meaning and Understanding in the History of Ideas," reprinted in James Tully, ed., *Meaning and Context: Quentin Skinner and His Critics,* 64–97.

38. Moreover, the borderlines between "historical" scholarship and "textual" interpretation have blurred considerably since these disciplinary boundaries originally ossified. For the movement toward history in literary analysis, see the work of Stephen Greenblatt and the so-called new historicism. For recognition of how historical writing and intellectual history engage issues of literary analysis and textual interpretation, see the work of Hayden White and Josiah Ober.

39. Each has recognized how understanding the meaning of texts requires the elucidation of the questions or problems to which they respond—and which originate outside the texts themselves.

John Dewey, whose favorite historical philosopher was probably Plato, succinctly illustrated his view of historical inquiry as "problematic" in a noteworthy passage echoed in the works of both Collingwood and Foucault. "[K]nowledge of the past is the key to understanding the present. History deals with the past, but this past is the history of the present. The true starting point of history is always some present situation with its problems" (*Democracy and Education,* 251). Given his philosophical disposition toward optimistic pragmatism, his belief that philosophy is born of historical conflict is particularly interesting. Thus, "the distinctive office, problems, and subject matter of philosophy grow out of stresses and strains in the community life in which a given form of philosophy arises, and that, accordingly, its specific problems vary with the changes in human life that are always going on and that at times constitute a crisis and a turning point in human history" (*Reconstruction in Philosophy* [Boston: Beacon Press, 1948 (1920)], intro., v–vi).

Over fifty years ago, R. G. Collingwood articulated the importance of systematically linking philosophical and historical inquiry for interpreting the work of political theorists. He argued that to understand the history of philosophy (or political theory), one must clarify the problems to which philosophers of the past sought to provide solutions. For Collingwood, to understand that which is known, one must consider the activity of knowing it. Collingwood proposed the "logic of question and answer," a logic that would apply to the history of philosophical thought. Establishing the correlativity of answers to questions requires historical research, which itself conditions the full understanding of a philosophical statement; the result reduces the gap between historical and philosophical inquiry. See his *Autobiography,* especially chaps. v–vii.

There are limitations to Collingwood's approach, however, and these stem from his view of the relation of the past to the present. He believed rather Whiggishly that our evidence of the past arises entirely from its traces in the present, that historical knowledge reflects the uptake of distant events by more recent ones. As a result, historical knowledge becomes a kind of self-knowledge. Herein lies the difficulty. Although Collingwood recognizes that our interpretation of historical evidence requires that we view it as an answer to a question, he does not worry about the extent to which the solution may be problematic as evidence. His approach to historical interpretation anticipated the hermeneutic philosophy of Hans-Georg Gadamer, who cited his debt to Collingwood as he argued that historical understanding fills out the commonality presupposed by our linguistic traditions and results from a "fusion of horizons" between the

prets the Platonic political art in terms of "problematic" relations between words and deeds, texts and contexts, as well as the cross-cutting relation between author and text. In this perspective, one highlights the dissonant, problematic relation between *logos* and *ergon* (which Plato's political art tries to harmonize), moving back and forth between Plato's dialogues and the historically practical and discursive problems that his conception of the political art would resolve.

Collingwood and Foucault usefully warn us to guard against the theoretical impulse toward historical transcendence. Political theorists who imagine solutions to historical problems tend not to recognize fully their own authoritarian tendencies. Insofar as the work of Dewey, Collingwood, and

---

present and the past. See Hans-Georg Gadamer, *Truth and Method*, 273–74, 337–41. Neither acknowledged the unsettling potential of historical recovery, nor the potential of their own approaches to obscure the distinctive character of other times and ideas as well as their own.

A more thoroughgoing acknowledgment of the problematic character of historical uptake in philosophical inquiry appears in the work of Michel Foucault. Foucault established his own perspective independently of both Collingwood and his followers, but resemblances between aspects of their approaches exist. (The affinity of Collingwood and Foucault has been noted by others, particularly James Tully, in his critical review of the work of Quentin Skinner, who developed Collingwood's insights in an Austinian and Wittgensteinian direction. See his "The Pen Is a Mighty Sword: Quentin Skinner's Analysis of Politics," in James Tully, ed., *Meaning and Context: Quentin Skinner and His Critics*, 7–25, especially 8, 22–25.) For example, Foucault developed his own perspective from a critique of phenomenology, whereas Collingwood took aim at the school of philosophical realism. (The problems are similar, not identical. Derrida has tended to identify the two, by using his critique of Husserl as the basis for his critique of Austin and Searle. See Jacques Derrida, *Limited Inc.*)

Phenomenologists, like philosophical realists, may not have ignored history, but they viewed it from the standpoint of human consciousness as a transcendental agent of history. Foucault held that the *logos* of human agents was not immune to the power and social practices it suffered or sought to control. Theoretical discourse was itself a form of power whose dominating effects had to be exposed. From his perspective, most political theories become forms of rule, positioned in the world of power as one complex of domination among others. For Foucault's critique of phenomenology, see "The Order of Discourse" (inaugural lecture at the Collège de France, given 2 December 1970), in *Untying the Text: A Post-Structuralist Reader*, ed. Robert Young, 51–76; for a good selection of Foucault's writings pertinent to political theory, see *The Foucault Reader*.

Although I disagree with Foucault's rendering of the nature of political theories, his approach reveals the problematic character of historical interpretation. It entails an effort to expose the uncertainties surrounding the "entry" of action into thought. His "critical analysis" of the past "tries to see how the different solutions to a problem have been constructed; but also how these different solutions result from a specific form of problemization." Therefore, problemization should be seen "not as an arrangement of representations but as a work of thought." See "Polemics, Politics, and Problemizations: An Interview with Michel Foucault," in *The Foucault Reader*, 384, 388–90.

Foucault "problematizes" the relation of philosophy and history—noting how relations of power in history essentially constitute philosophical questions and how all historical questions raise issues of philosophical interpretation—it justifies my "political" approach. None of these theorists, however, provides an interpretive model for critical historicism—particularly with respect to its use in interpreting the history of political theory. Major political theorists in the past have framed their arguments as solutions to problems whose nature stemmed significantly from historical issues of theory and practice. It remained crucial to the character of their critical discourse, however, to step beyond the conflicts or gaps featured in the discourses and practices because of their inadequacies. Collingwood and Foucault, in particular, do not adequately account for this essential step taken by political theorists. The arguments of political theorists deserve to be judged according to the ends that guided many of their projects—the importance of attempting in discourse to address and ameliorate the problems of social power and political community, to provide an account, indeed, of the nature of the political art.[40]

Critical historicism subordinates questions of authorial identity to questions about the discursive and practical problems that an author addresses, without ignoring authorial intention.[41] As a result, it may be distinguished from prominently available alternative guideposts.

For example, one may value the weight of what Plato meant solely in terms of what he psychologically intended or linguistically could have meant. This does not result in a solely subjective interpretation if one makes every effort to discover the historical meanings that could have been associated with the terms an author used and the problems he explicitly addressed. Here, Plato's words—but only or primarily Plato's words—indicate the core of what Plato philosophically did. This view (initiated and systematized primarily by Quentin Skinner and J. G. A. Pocock) follows on Wittgenstein's statement that "words are deeds" to argue that the effective actuality of words amounts primarily to their performance in a discursive context.[42] If one has a

40. The most extensive and valuable discussion of the notion of the political art in the history of Western political theory appears in Sheldon Wolin's *Politics and Vision*. Also see his "Political Theory as a Vocation."
41. Concerns about how to understand Plato's authorial identity independently of such contextual considerations guide the inquiry of E. N. Tigerstedt in his *Interpreting Plato*.
42. The most notable presentation of this view with regard to the study of the history of political thought is that of Quentin Skinner, whose methodological essays are conveniently collected in *Meaning and Context: Quentin Skinner and His Critics*, ed. James Tully. For another version of it, see J. G. A. Pocock, "The Concept of a Language and the *métier d'historien:* Some

theory of history and power, those words primarily become effects of those practical structures.

As an alternative to these kinds of contextualism, one may interpret the meaning of what an author does in terms of certain foundational principles about the nature of philosophical argument (Irwin), basic values (Strauss), or unanchored texts of written *logos* (Derrida). These efforts indicate different versions of textualism.

By viewing discourse as a response to problems of both a discursive and a practical character, my approach interprets the meaning of the author's *logos* relative to the power of existing forms of discourse and practice. It differs from the foundationalist perspective, according to which the problems Plato addresses in his dialogues are solutions to universal and timeless problems of philosophy; it admits that an author's own discourse is itself a kind of power and may serve as a constraint on other uses of critical reason. But it also differs from the discourse-centered approach of Skinner by recognizing the transcending, reconstructive aspiration of critical discourse, as well as its deep connections to structures of power that delimit the possibilities of discourse itself. This approach allows one to interpret the meaning of authorial identity in broader terms than an existing discursive code. In so doing, it retains a major role for authorial intention while legitimating the potential use of discourse as an agent of such battered values as justice and truth, which may not be directly addressed in the discussions of the day. At the same time, it suggests that the discourse of theoretical critics of politics and the more ordinary, directly political discourse of citizens and leaders indeed may be related and ought not to be confined within the conventions of professional discourse or the rhetoric of political interest.

The discourse of this kind of interpretive political theory produces no finite set of solutions to problems in the history of political theory. It is as open ended as the history that produces the problems it would help to resolve. Yet, it is designed to illuminate potentially just solutions to actual problems. And by virtue of the constitutive connection of this approach to the interactive political dynamic of *logos* and *ergon* that is so crucial to the legitimacy of democratic social orders, these solutions are not intrinsically antidemocratic. The substantive scholarly tasks for critical historicism as an ap-

---

Considerations on Practice," in Anthony Pagden, ed., *The Languages of Political Theory in Early-Modern Europe* (Cambridge: Cambridge University Press, 1987), 19–38.

proach to understanding the history of political theory divide (for heuristic purposes) into three parts (reflected in the three parts of this book): (1) establishing the practical and discursive conditions that inform the philosophical problematic for speakers and authors—in our case, this means the contemporary and historical "settings" of the Platonic political art; (2) interpreting the texts as responses to problems in discourse and practice; and, finally, (3) critically evaluating their claims as solutions for both the problems of their time and comparable problems in other historical eras. In our case, this "appropriation" involves the task of "de-historicizing" and then "re-historicizing" the Platonic political art. To be sure, the boundaries between these three interpretive activities are porous, but respecting their existence fosters scholarly transparency.[43] Moreover, critical historicism seems most appropriate for understanding the history of that sort of political theory that mimics political deliberation on an abstract plane, contributing to present discourse and practice by critically evaluating philosophical knowledge and political ethics of the past in order to achieve a good (or better) future. In short, it seems most appropriate for interpreting the Platonic political art.

43. What counts as the horizon of one context is itself a difficult issue, but it does not create insuperable difficulties. After all, the alternative is to rely on no historical horizons and color them with a grand theory of history that, by fusing horizons, sharply constrains one's view of the historical possibilities of political freedom or that presupposes a kind of incontestability or objectivity in the history of political theory. One of my differences with Skinner stems from this consideration. Although he recognizes that his historical emphases constitute a form of textual exegesis, he tends not to recognize fully the way his own theoretical and political presuppositions affect how he establishes the coherence of the ideas he is examining, a tendency that stems from his belief in his ability to isolate neatly two levels of rationality in the arguments of his historical subject—the epistemic and the practical—and to hold that his own judgment of the coherence of the former reflects only his own scholarly interests and not other, less objective, dispositions. See "A Reply to My Critics," 239–40 and n. 36, p. 329.

TWO

HISTORICIZING THE PLATONIC POLITICAL ART

Determining the historical way in which Plato constituted the relation between words and deeds in his conception of the political art is especially difficult. For example, he wrote texts in a cultural context that experienced the
creations of new social practices of reading and writing. In addition, the very
nature of his discourse undercut the relevance of the immediate audience it
would address. He wanted his critical discourse and its lessons not only to
supplant inherited meanings, conventional practices, and other forms of discourse, but also to reduce the power and significance of actual political judgments as a sufficient guide for future thought and action.[1] Moreover, the evidence of Plato's words and deeds is uncertain. It derives from biographical
accounts of his life and thought that are noteworthy for their inaccuracy,
autobiographical letters of dubious authenticity that only briefly portray his
actions and beliefs, and a set of written dialogues that surely set forth his considered philosophical and political reflections but in which his voice cannot,
and according to certain passages should not, be directly heard.[2]

---

1. For a classic statement of the liberal alternative to this Platonic view, see Isaiah Berlin,
"Political Judgment," reprinted in the last volume of Berlin's essays published while he was alive,
The Sense of Reality.

2. See Plato, *Phaedrus* 275d–e; *Epistle VII* 341c–d; see the work of the Tübingen school, for
example, H. J. Kramer, *Plato and the Foundation of Metaphysics*, and Kurt Gaiser, *Platons Unge-*

To make sense of the historical character of Plato's work when its meaning as a historical act is called into question seems to require the assignment of weights and values to events whose significance Plato himself problematizes. But even as these interpretive problems seriously vex any historically contextualized account of Plato's thought, particularly his view of the relation between critical reason and democracy, they must be dealt with, however imperfectly, to provide the best possible interpretation of the Platonic political art.[3]

A. THE HISTORICITY OF PLATO'S SOCRATIC PROBLEM

Plato's conceptions of the political art respond critically to a variety of problems concerning power, ethics, and critical discourse in democratic Athens. These problems appear in his dialogues about ethics and politics through the voices of characters who often relate to historical individuals and events. The problems antedate and (to an uncertain extent) stand outside Plato's texts, but the texts themselves attempt to reconstruct and address these problems. As a result, the set of issues that inform Plato's treatment of the political art constitutes a problematic that transcends the conventional boundary between text and context—much as the interpretive approach of the "critical historicism" I presented in Chapter 1 cuts across the dichotomy of textualism and contextualism. (Of course, this suggests that the exteriority of this chapter to the next three chapters is something of a useful fiction, but I hope that readers suspend their disbelief and continue on.)

Outside the dialogues, these problems crystallized in the trial and execu-

---

schriebene Lehre: Studien zur systematischen und geschichtlichen Begründung der Wissenschaften in der platonischen Schule, on which note the evaluation by W. K. C. Guthrie, A History of Greek Philosophy, 4:1–4, 63–64. Also see Leo Strauss, Persecution and the Art of Writing.

3. Moreover, these historically oriented interpretive issues are not merely scholastic. Quentin Skinner, John Dunn, and Judith Shklar—historically minded political theorists—do not hesitate to refer to the importance of reading Plato's Republic for contemporary political understanding—as long as it is read "properly." See Quentin Skinner, "Meaning and Understanding in the History of Ideas," reprinted in James Tully, ed., Meaning and Context: Quentin Skinner and His Critics, 64–67, and idem, "A Reply to My Critics," in Meaning and Context, 262–63; John Dunn, Western Political Theory in the Face of the Future, 110–13; Judith N. Shklar, The Faces of Injustice. Leo Strauss and his followers have made a particular way of interpreting classical texts into the foundation for the correct way of understanding contemporary civilization. See Leo Strauss, The City and Man, preface, and Allan Bloom, The Closing of the American Mind.

tion of Socrates, which probably occurred prior to Plato's composition of any of his dialogues that we have.[4] Inside the dialogues, the problems assume the form of how to reconcile the discourse of Socratic virtue with the actualities of Athenian politics and society. Plato's conception of the political art, therefore, responds to both historical and philosophical problems, which may be conjoined as "Plato's Socratic Problem."[5] By this single formulation, I signify a matrix of problems (as we shall see).[6] But each derives from, even if it is not limited to, Plato's interest in, and reconstruction of, the honorable yet problematic life, death, and memory of Socrates. To explain the historical nature of this problem, I identify various features of Greek political and cultural life and explain how Socrates' life and death would have crystallized these historical dimensions as a philosophical problem.

The term "political art" actually covers a range of Greek terms: a *techne*, or practice, of civic affairs; *politike techne*, the most literal equivalent of the English "political art," "political craft," or "political skill"; and/or *politike*, perhaps a more systematic or scientific conception of the skill or ability to practice the art of politics.[7] By the last decades of the fifth century, the first

4. Friedlander argues that Plato wrote dialogues before Socrates' death. See his *Plato*, 3:456 and n. 9. But see also the remarks by Guthrie in his *History of Greek Philosophy*, 4:54–56.

5. For my initial published elaboration of this problem, see "Plato's Socratic Problem, and Ours."

6. I mention some in the Introduction, note 9, above.

7. The first evidence of the historical presence of a notion of a *techne* of politics comes from the late fifth century, in the Athenian Thucydides' *History of the Peloponnesian War* and a fragment by the Abderan philosopher Democritus. But the evidence is indirect and contested. Thucydides has the Corinthians analogize politics to a *techne*, and he has Pericles ascribe a conceptually uncondensed version of the political art to the (adult, male) Athenian citizenry (Thucydides, *History of the Peloponnesian War* 1.71.3, II.40.2). Democritus cited the practice of the political art (*politiken technen*) as the most esteemed public virtue, but some scholars read the fragment as indicating the art of war (*polemiken technen*) (Democritus, D–K, Fr. B157). The Sophist Protagoras from Abdera may well have employed the notions of a political art and political virtue (*politike arete*) in the last half of the fifth century, but our only evidence of his so doing comes from a Platonic dialogue that was probably written in the late 390s or 380s. Indeed, Plato's fourth-century dialogues provide the preponderance of evidence for the initial literary articulations of "the political art" (either as *politike techne* or *politike*) (Plato, *Protagoras*, 319a, 322b).

In her book *The Origins of Democratic Thinking: The Invention of Politics in Classical Athens*, Cynthia Farrar takes as her principal sources Thucydides, Protagoras, and Democritus. Farrar points out that the conceptual features of each had significant democratic features. However, the claims made in this book outstrip the historical evidence for them. See my reviews of this book in *American Political Science Review* 83 (December 1989): 1362–64; see also Josiah

decades of Plato's life, some sense of a *techne* of politics, or "political art," may have been understood by ordinary Athenians—even if it does not appear in surviving fifth-century texts.

But although ordinary citizens certainly grasped some notion of the political art, the notion itself was extraordinary. The term brought together three interrelated realms of Athenian experience—realms that we often presuppose as philosophically, if not practically, distinct: the area of contest over the exercise of power—let's call it the political realm; the social existence of moral standards—let's call it the ethical realm; and the authoritative display of reason—let's call it the rational realm.[8] For skillful political activity involved the practical, deliberative conduct of public affairs by the citizenry, and its ethical legitimacy was presupposed. Although all politics was not "democratic," it must also be said that politics was irreducibly associated with the vital and widespread political activity of the Athenian *polis*, a relatively egalitarian and participatory democracy that also exercised imperial power.[9] Indeed, the virtuous practice of politics constituted the pivotal normative standard of the Athenian way of life.

Our record of ancient Greek discussions of the political art indicates that the idea signified distinct modes of relating *logoi*—words, discourses, rational arguments—to *erga*—deeds, practices, historical realities—with respect to their effect on the political community as a whole.[10] But how that relation

---

Ober (in a review that dealt with other books as well), "The Athenians and Their Democracy," which now may be found in his *The Athenian Revolution*, 123–39.

8. The Athenians did not sharply differentiate these realms. Only later were they specified as the realms of politics, ethics, and rationality. Such categorical divisions of human experience are mistakenly assumed to be unproblematic, if not universal, in the theories of Jürgen Habermas and Michel Foucault.

9. Hegel characterized the essence of the Greek spirit as a work of art, and the highest practical manifestation of that spirit as the political art of Athenian democracy (G. W. F. Hegel, *The Philosophy of History*, part II, sections I–II, especially 251–62).

For a general interpretation of the political and democratic development of the public uses of *logos* in the fifth century, see G. E. R. Lloyd, *Magic, Reason, and Experience*, chap. 4. On various ways of understanding the rationality of the *polis*, particularly in relation to Durkheimian and Weberian perspectives, see Oswyn Murray, "Cities of Reason," in *The Greek City From Homer to Alexander*, ed. Oswyn Murray and Simon Price, 1–25.

10. This is not to deny that in fifth- and fourth-century Athens, words were themselves deeds, insofar as political practice was initiated by means of political discourse. For recent versions of the truism that words are kinds of deeds, see Ludwig Wittgenstein, *Culture and Value*, ed. G. H. von Wright, 46, 46e; and J. L. Austin, *How To Do Things With Words*, who coined the technical term "speech-act."

was achieved, and exactly what it involved, was ever an open, disputed question. In fact, the relation of the general term for prose discourse, *logos*, to the general term for actualities, *ergon* (which included practices and beliefs), was a crucial issue for ordinary Athenians (probably), Sophists, Thucydides, Isocrates, Plato, and Aristotle—and one that had major political implications. Moreover, the problem assumed an especially significant and general character during the mid- and late fifth century in Athens, when and where politics became democratic in a serious, thoroughgoing way.

In dispute was not the political "fact" of the linkage of *logos* and *ergon* but the nature of its dissonance, for the practice of politics would join categories of understanding and practice that did not easily hang together—categories of discourse and power; ideals and reality; theory and practice; the interests of a part of a community with the interests of the whole. Contention naturally arose over who practiced politics well. Although some denied that the *demos* possessed skill in politics, Thucydides' Pericles understood the practice of politics to be one of the most distinctive virtues of the Athenians' democratic citizenship. Although some believed that political expertise could be developed out of shared experiences in daily life and ordinary politics, political leaders like Cleon (according to Thucydides) believed that it was the province of especially gifted and trained politicians.[11] Plato was the first to make the political art in any of these senses a direct object of critical inquiry or scrutiny. As a result, I think it is fair to say that although Plato was surely not the first to perform the activity of political theorizing—Herodotus, Protagoras, Thucydides, Hippodamus, and possibly Socrates, at least, preceded him in this respect—he was the first critical and systematic political theorist.

Among Plato's reasons for making "the political art" central to his critical enterprise was the fact that, despite the potential of the concept, the practical, ethical, and rational senses of skill or virtue in politics had not been clearly distinguished, related, or understood. In particular, they had not been correlated to the more general issue of the discordant relation of *logos* and *ergon*. Plato's treatment of the political art in his dialogues reconstructs the relation of *logos* and *ergon* in response to the problematic intersections of reason, ethics, and power in Greek political life, and that of his Athenian society

---

11. For evidence of antidemocratic sentiments, see Herodotus, *Persian Wars* III.81–82, and Pseudo-Xenophon's *The Constitution of the Athenians*. For a Periclean eulogy of the Athenians' political virtue and skill, see Thucydides, II.40.2–3. For Cleon's disdain for the judgment of the *demos,* see Thucydides, III.37.

in particular. As used by Plato, the "political art" referred to an art of virtue, a skill informed by knowledge that indicated a disposition in ordinary citizens and, more particularly, statesmen to produce ethical excellence in the political community. But, again, Plato could understand it only by placing it in various dramatic contexts that presupposed different relations of *logos* to *ergon*. In particular, the trial and death of the historical Socrates crystallized the problematic character of the political art.

For Plato, Socrates had obviously lived an honorable life, but it both represented and spawned disturbing tensions between critical discourse about the ethics of virtue (exemplified by the historical Socrates) and the effective political power of democratic Athens (exemplified by Socrates' trial and execution). Although the problems to which Plato's written conception of the political art responds are not reducible to his preoccupation with the historical Socrates, they are essentially constituted by it and always relate to it. At various critical points in Plato's written *corpus*, Plato's Socratic Problem becomes the issue of how to formulate in words a virtuous political art that is, at the same time, practically effective and beneficial.

This problem evidences broader historical issues, but the most direct evidence we have of Plato's Socratic Problem stems from his own dialogues. One cannot, therefore, neatly establish the context for the Platonic political art in terms of a quasi-objective, external historical context in relation to which the meaning of the political art in Plato's dialogues may be discretely connected.[12] In this respect, Plato's Socratic Problem, and his treatments of the political art in relation to it, is both a contextual or historical problem — a problem that arises amid the conflicts among power, ethics, and critical discourse in Athenian democracy — and a textual and philosophical problem —

---

12. Recent interpreters of the nature of historical understanding have noted the difficulty in identifying a bright, shining line dividing historical or contextual and interpretive arguments. See Hayden White, particularly his rejection of the possibility of absolutely differentiating the truth-value of "philosophy of history" and "historical narrative." He notes their difference, instead, in terms of how each construes what counts as a "figure" and its "ground." See his *Tropics of Discourse: Essays in Cultural Criticism,* for example, 114–15, and *The Content of the Form: Narrative Discourse and Historical Representation,* 1–25 and 185–213. I differ from White in emphasizing less than he does the extent to which texts "produce," rather than "identify," meaning — including the meaning of "context." I do so to emphasize the extent to which Plato (at least) is involved in a project of remaking or reconstructing the discursive, if not practical, context. I want to remind the reader of the hardness, as well as the malleability, of the world in which we live. (I don't think White would actually object to this emphasis, although it usually is not his emphasis.)

a problem about meaning that transcends those historical origins (although exactly how is an open question) via the texts of the dialogues.[13]

One can see the interconnections of the historical and philosophical dimensions of Plato's Socratic Problem in the following observations. Although a mere thirty votes (and perhaps more time allowed for the trial) would have led to the exoneration of Socrates, which gives Socrates' conviction and death all the marks of a contingent historical event, the *Seventh Letter* indicates that the trial and death of Socrates marked a critical turning point in Plato's life.[14] In Plato's *Apology,* Socrates is presented as having exhibited an uncompromising devotion to both philosophy and virtue (*arete*). At the same time, he imagined himself to be of great service to Athens. Socrates had believed that acting on behalf of these two purposes—philosophy and virtue, on the one hand, his *polis* on the other—epitomized the virtuous life.[15] In other words, Socrates' mission or vocation had two dimensions: to understand virtue in "words" (*logoi*) and to practice virtue in "deeds" (*erga*).

From Socrates' perspective in Plato's *Apology,* these dimensions complemented and harmonized with each other; his life fulfilled his mission. Moreover, it accorded with the negative dictates of his *daimonion* and his pious regard for oracular wisdom. But he was also convinced that his pursuit did not comport with the discursive practices of the Athenians' central political institutions. An uncompromising pursuit of his vocation required him to stay out of democratic politics. Although Socrates believed that his vocation was

13. Additionally, it is not a problem that can be contained within a particular, existing discourse or civic ideology. For it would seem that such codes of knowledge were themselves called into question by the intellectual work enacted in Plato's dialogues.

The tendency to refer to various kinds of discourse as part of one or another civic ideology has characterized much work done by contemporary historians and classicists on Greek politics, philosophy, and culture. See, for example, the collection of articles published under the title *Athenian Identity and Civic Ideology,* edited by Alan L. Boegehold and Adele C. Scafuro. It is touted as a way of overcoming artificial disciplinary boundaries between history, classics, and philosophy. However, this is often accomplished at the price of intellectual clarity, because the boundaries of such civic ideologies are themselves highly ambiguous. This genre of intellectual history avoids the reductionism of Marxist interpretations of historical ideology, but it falls into one trap Marxists have avoided, ignoring the dynamic relation between critical discourses and social practices.

14. See Plato's *Apology of Socrates* 37a–b, and the *Seventh Letter* 324b–326b. On the evidentiary status of the *Seventh Letter* and the historicity of Plato's *Apology,* see Chapter 2, above.

15. Socrates' religiosity certainly colored his conduct, but apparently it did not independently affect it. Devotion to philosophy, for Socrates, *was* obedience to his god. On the piety of the historical Socrates, see Gregory Vlastos, "Socratic Piety," in his *Socrates: Ironist and Moral Philosopher,* 157–78.

patriotic and political in the broadest sense, the majority of Athenian jurors at his trial found his actions to be impious and subversive. They held that the Athenian collectivity could not tolerate Socratic virtue and wisdom. From their perspective, Socrates' mission proved to be a scourge on their gods, their youth, and their *polis* as a whole. He had "unjustly violated" (*adikei*) their city's sanctioned religious, cultural, ethical, and therefore political, norms and conventions (*nomoi*), the justice of which was presupposed. For them, the "virtue" of Socratic citizenship antagonized the virtues of Athens.[16] The requirements of Socratic philosophy and virtue, on the one hand, and the social practices of the Athenian *polis,* on the other, could not be reconciled. (Even if one argued that Plato reconciled them in the *Crito,* the upshot sanctioned Socrates' execution.)

Indeed, the historical resonance of the trial and death of Socrates echoed increasing discord among critical discourse, ethics, and power. Plato could not have understood Socrates to have fulfilled his life. For Plato, as for the vast majority of his fellow Athenians, a political order must promote the virtue of its citizenry, and the life of virtue had to practically benefit the political world. Now the historical Socrates could have argued that during his life he was doing just that. Although Socrates questioned whether such harmony necessarily arose from the Athenians' current state of affairs, although Socrates' life had reflected tension between the life guided by argument and virtue and the practical life of Athenian citizenship, it still offered the promise of their reconciliation. But Socrates' death broke that tension and snapped the links between critically justified virtues of *logos* and practically validated virtues of *ergon.* Insofar as Plato decided in the wake of Socrates' death to pursue philosophy, that life also could not be intrinsically satisfactory, unless the justice it discovered was ultimately realized in practice. As a result, Plato's relationship to Socrates was itself a political and philosophical problem that related issues of power, ethics, and critical discourse.

If this problem was to be solved, if ethical discourse and political practice were to complement rather than antagonize each other, if justice was to be regularly realized, both the *logos* of Socratic virtue and the *ergon* of Athens would have to be transformed. And yet, as a devoted student of Socrates and a citizen of Athens, what else did Plato have to work with other than the discourse of Socrates and the practices of democratic Athens? The legacy Socrates left for Plato posed a problematic relation between Socratic words

16. See my "Socratic Citizenship."

and Athenian deeds, and its resolution required a transformation of the relation between virtue and conventional politics, a critical definition of the political art. Such questions constituted Plato's Socratic Problem, which then may also be understood as the dilemma of how to bridge a gulf forged by history and preserved in conventional discourse between Socratic virtue and the political art.

The significance of Plato's Socratic Problem must be primarily determined by interpreting Plato's dialogues themselves, but an important part of its meaning can be fairly characterized in historical terms, without presupposing a particular philosophical interpretation of the dialogues. And it ought to be, to help us appreciate how Plato's dialogues concerning ethics and politics critically respond to a world that exists independently of them. For Plato transforms historical questions into the philosophical issues of his ethical and political dialogues.

The following discussion of the historical contexts and conditions of Plato's conceptualization of the political art divides into four sections. In the first, called "the practical context," I briefly set forth the characteristics of Athenian power and ethics in Plato's lifetime as well as of Plato's biography, in relation to both the nature of his vocation and the nature of the Academy. In the second, called "the discursive context," I explain the main genres of discourse and philosophical traditions in relation to which Plato broke new ground with both his dialogues and the Academy. In the third, called "the textual context," I deal with the issues posed by the effect of the chronological order of the composition of the dialogues on their meaning, as well as the issue of how to isolate Plato's voice in his dialogues—because that voice is not directly expressed. In the final section, I address the issue of the relation of Plato's arguments about the political art to the historical Socrates through an interpretation of Plato's *Apology of Socrates* and *Crito*. The end of this section provides a natural link between a discussion of Plato's historical contexts and his conceptualization of the political art in his dialogues.

Identifying and explaining the significance of the historical contexts in which Plato's Socratic Problem crystallized do not provide an exhaustive or innovative account of the many influences on Plato.[17] However, the following attempt to historicize the Platonic political art provides the best framework

---

17. For example, the validity of this argument does not ipso facto reject the Aristotelian claim that the primary influences on Plato's philosophy stemmed from Heraclitus and the Pythagoreans, in addition to Socrates. See *Metaphysics* I.6. See also Diogenes Laertius, III.8.

for understanding the originality and historical logic of his ethical and political thought. In particular, it offers the most economical way of obtaining a complete account of the tools that Plato chose to refashion extant discursive and practical relations among reason, virtue, and politics in his conception of the political art.[18]

B. THE PRACTICAL CONTEXT

Athens and its environs underwent major changes during Plato's lifetime (427–347). We look at this period more synchronically than diachronically, keeping in mind, however, that the thirty years between the Sicilian expedition of 415–413 and the founding of the Academy c. 387–385 would have provided Plato with his major impressions of Athenian, if not Greek, political life.[19] Throughout this portrayal, the point, obviously, is not to attempt to be comprehensive. At the same time, the selection of issues indicates a serious attempt to portray those features of Athenian society that differentiated the world in which Plato came to political maturity from the one in which Socrates made his mark and to pinpoint the problematic aspects of political power and ethics that transcend discourse and that Plato's conception of the political art sought (in part) to reconstruct.[20]

Of most interest are the problems that would have been commonly per-

---

18. I say "contexts" rather than "context," for a singular reference to Plato's world mistakenly implies that that world presented itself as a unity to Plato before he formulated his interpretation of it. The value of articulating an author's "contexts" is argued by Michael Frede, "Introduction: The Study of Ancient Philosophy," in *Essays in Ancient Philosophy*, ix–xxvii.

19. To be sure, the Athens of the 390s, when Plato probably began to write his dialogues (for example, the *Apology* or *Euthyphro*—or whatever they were), importantly differed from the Athens of the late 350s, during which he wrote the *Laws*. Moreover, Plato located the dramatic context of many of his dialogues in the fifth century and some (such as the *Protagoras*) before the outbreak of the Peloponnesian War. But all of them most likely were composed after the death of Socrates (399), whereas after 385–84, Plato was mostly likely preoccupied with his work as head of the Academy, except for his notable trips to Sicily in 367 and 361. These issues involving the chronological order and historicity of the dialogues are discussed later in this chapter.

20. Some of the most revealing work on fifth-century Athenian political thought has been done by Kurt Raaflaub. See, for example, "Democracy, Oligarchy, and the Concept of the 'Free Citizen' in Late Fifth-Century Athens"; idem, "Contemporary Perceptions of Democracy in Fifth-Century Athens"; idem, "Democracy, Power, and Imperialism in Fifth-Century Athens," in J. P. Euben et al., eds., *Athenian Political Thought and the Reconstruction of American Democracy*, 103–46, and his own piece in Deborah Boedeker and Kurt Raaflaub, eds., *Democracy, Empire, and the Arts in Fifth-Century Athens.*

ceived, although differently interpreted, by Plato and his contemporaries. Their identification makes possible distinctions between the relative impact of broader historical currents and narrower Platonic judgments on his conception of the political art. Above all, the practical problems concerned the fragility of internal political unity in the wake of two oligarchic coups and a momentous military defeat, severe conflicts among social groups amid conditions of greater economic scarcity, constitutional reforms, and, perhaps most significantly, the political retrenchment and overall decline of Athenian power. These phenomena diminished the glow of political activity and increased suspicion about its ethical character.

Subsequently and/or simultaneously, discursive problems became evident in widening disagreements about how to respond to the Athenians' new predicament, which involved disagreements about what constituted a virtuous life and what promoted justice.[21] These problems became articulated in increasingly specialized, institutionalized, and professionalized contexts. Neither of these trends—the decline in political power and the increased specialization in public discourse and political institutions—necessarily supports the commonly held (until recently) thesis about general cultural or ethical decline. One clear improvement was the increased (relatively speaking) stability of Athenian political life. Rather, the trends serve to clarify the way in which Athenian history created a political problematic to which Platonic philosophy gave a creative and useful response.

I. POWER AND ETHICS IN PLATO'S ATHENS

A principal cause of the relative decline of Athenian power during Plato's lifetime was the radical reduction of the Athenians' material resources. The ini-

---

21. Plato's views about the nature of the practical issues of his times cannot be trusted; that is, they should not be presumptively regarded as historically accurate or conceptually true. (It should not need to be said that reasonable, historically informed grounds existed for believing that the Athenians' political problems did not stem primarily from the democratic cast of Athens' constitution and that the solution to these problems did not require the contemplation, let alone practice, of philosophical guardianship.) Nevertheless, Plato's analysis of Athenian society deserves serious attention. M .I. Finley has dismissed Plato too quickly as a serious political analyst in his *Politics in the Ancient World* (124–26). I have reviewed this book in *Political Theory* 12 (May 1984): 302–7. On the other hand, some too readily take Plato's accounts of political forms in his dialogues as historical reports. For example, see the interesting recent account of the relation of Platonic theory to democracy in the *Republic* by Arlene Saxonhouse, *Athenian Democracy: Modern Mythmakers and Ancient Theorists*, chap. 5, "Plato and the Problematical Gentleness of Democracy," 87–114.

tial instance of this (relative to Plato's politically cognizant years) was the defeat (in 413) resulting from the Sicilian expedition and the subsequent Spartan occupation of Decelea. The first oligarchic coup took place in 411, and, in 404, the Spartans decisively defeated Athens in the Peloponnesian War—depriving Athens of its allies and initially fostering another oligarchic coup that established the short-lived but brutal regime of The Thirty. After it had reigned for nine months, democratic partisans managed to overthrow this regime and return constitutional democracy to Athens.[22] The reestablished political order lasted until the Macedonian army conquered Athens in 323 B.C. Despite this return to political stability, 403 marked the beginning of a new era of Athenian political life, one that evidenced (1) a sharply diminished capacity to exercise political power and (2) an increased differentiation of political discourse and practice.[23]

Several important postwar trends evidenced the decline in political power. First, with respect to population, the total number of citizens decreased by more than one-fourth and perhaps by as much as one-half between the outbreak of the Peloponnesian War (431), when the male citizenry numbered about 40,000, and the war's end (404). About 18,000 soldiers died in battle, and these losses were disproportionately distributed among social classes. The lower-class thetes suffered twice as many casualties as the middle- and upper-class hoplites, whereas before the war their numbers were equivalent.[24] Moreover, thousands died from war-related diseases, principally the plague.

Second, the Athenians' loss of their empire severely depleted their financial resources. They no longer received the annual income from their tribute-paying allies, which had made up three-fifths of the state's annual revenue. Farming, mining, and commerce were also heavily damaged, and domestic trades suffered as well. In the 390s, an economic depression set in. The value of Athenian private property decreased by over one-third between 428–27 and 378–77.[25]

22. For a discussion of Plato's political activities and sentiments during this time, see this chapter, below.

23. In his *Democracy and Classical Athens,* 147ff, J. K. Davies has good reasons for wanting to consider 413 to 380 as part of a single period, but that de-emphasizes precisely those historical events that provided a benchmark for Plato's turn to political theory.

24. Barry Strauss, *Athens After the Peloponnesian War: Class, Faction, and Policy, 403–386 B.C.,* 5, 70–86.

25. R. Meiggs, *The Athenian Empire,* 257; see Barry Strauss, *Athens After the Peloponnesian War,* 54.

Third, the loss of the war seriously compromised the safety of the Athenian population. Since 412, the Spartans had maintained a garrison in Athens from which they mounted numerous raids on Athenian farmland, in addition to their decimation of the Athenian fleet and destruction of the Long Walls.

Amid the circumstances of economic constraint and military insecurity that followed the loss of the Athenian empire, animosity between rich and poor, and to a lesser extent between the city and the countryside, probably increased.[26] Social antagonism to some extent typified relationships among various segments of the Athenian citizenry during its entire democratic era, but the effects of both the Peloponnesian War and the Corinthian War (395–386) probably sharpened these differences and made them more abrasive.[27] This must have compromised Athens's ability to initiate new political ventures, either internally or externally. Although the Athenians began to revive their imperial hopes by establishing the Second Athenian League in the 370s, it was a shadow of its fifth-century predecessor, and the league was dissolved in 355. Philip had ascended to the Macedonian throne in 359. As Macedonia's fortunes began to rise, Athenian military security declined.

Besides the decline in the Athenians' available material resources, the assembly's judicial power also weakened in the fourth century. After the Social War (357–355), the assembly no longer supervised the conduct of major political trials (eisangeliai). A people's court, manned by citizens drawn by lot, heard and passed judgment on such cases, and around 350 the Areopagus once again became an important force in Athenian politics.[28] To be sure, the assembly itself authorized all of the changes that circumscribed its power, and in this respect these changes did not make Athens less democratic, but this differentiation of the exercise of political power in the wake of war meant that the direct exercise of power by the demos became more structured, segmented, and circumscribed.[29]

---

26. Claude Mosse, *Athens in Decline, 404–86 B.C.*, 12–17. At the same time, Aristophanes is a major source of information about popular sensibilities during this time, and he quite likely exaggerated these cleavages. See Victor Ehrenberg, *The People of Aristophanes: A Sociology of Old Attic Comedy.*

27. Barry Strauss, *Athens After the Peloponnesian War*, 163–67.

28. See Robert W. Wallace, *The Areopagos Council, to 307 B.C.*; P. J. Rhodes, "Athenian Democracy After 403 B.C."; M. H. Hansen, *The Athenian Assembly in the Age of Demosthenes*, 99, 118–20.

29. It would be wrong to say that Athens became less democratic or that "democracy" per se declined in fourth-century Athens. To the contrary, it may well have been strengthened and stabilized as a result of having shed its imperial possessions and established legal reforms. I agree

Further limiting the direct exercise of popular political power in the fourth century were new rules governing the apportionment of revenue, which curtailed the assembly's influence over financial matters. Because the rules were set by law, they were interpreted by magistrates. Also, by the mid-fourth century, an elected official who could be continually reelected managed the new Theoric Fund. This fund included monies to be distributed to citizens for attending the theater and served as a repository for surplus revenue. The fund grew during this period, and as it did, the theoric official became responsible for managing other financial projects of the state, such as the administration of tax collecting, the operation of the dockyards, the building of arsenals and roads, and the making of public contracts—some of which used to be supervised by the council and other magistrates whose appointment was determined by lot. Although these changes may have resulted in greater administrative efficiency, they reduced the direct exercise of power by the *demos*.[30]

Because of the economic and social sources of discontent, the instability of other Greek *poleis,* and the memory of past glory, opportunities for politicians to exploit social tensions abounded. The fluid nature of political organization—rooted in ties of friendship, family, status, and ideology—highlighted this potential even as its variegated character served to prevent any single cleavage from solidifying.[31] The general importance of the competitive or agonistic ideal in Athenian political culture only enhanced the respectability and attraction of antagonistic political discourse about putative foreign or

---

with those who argue that whatever problems the Athenians had in the fourth century did not primarily stem from the democratic character of their constitution. See Finley, *Politics in the Ancient World,* and Ober, *Mass and Elite in Democratic Athens.*

30. S. Perlman, "Political Leadership in Athens in the Fourth Century B.C."; P. J. Rhodes, "Athenian Democracy After 403 B.C.," 312–14.

31. Classical scholars dispute the character of unofficial political groups in Athens. A major issue is the extent to which their makeup was determined by personal or ideological factors. Insofar as a Greek politician was immediately identified with his social background and that background had ideological connotations, this debate cannot be easily resolved. For the individualistic interpretation of Athenian political groups and conflict in the fourth century, see Raphael Sealey, "Callistratos of Aphidna and His Contemporaries"; S. Perlman, "The Politicians in the Athenian Democracy of the Fourth Century B.C." For the ideological interpretation, see Mosse, *Athens in Decline, 404–86 B.C.* For positions in between, see Strauss, *Athens After the Peloponnesian War;* and Ober, *Mass and Elite in Democratic Athens.* For background discussion of these issues, see W. Robert Connor, *The New Politicians of Fifth Century Athens;* G. M. Calhoun, *Athenian Clubs in Politics and Litigation;* Horst Hutter, *Politics and Friendship: The Origins of Classical Notions of Politics in the Theory and Practice of Friendship,* chaps. 1–4.

domestic enemies.[32] The potential for factional conflict and war was palpable, and the troublesome character of political activity stood out, even as its effective scope had shrunk because of military defeats. These practical conditions provided myriad incentives and justifications for imaginative political discourse that radically criticized the status quo for the sake of the overall improvement of Athenian political life.

Paralleling the decline in Athenian political power was the second important development, a steady increase in the institutional and intellectual differentiation of Athenian political life. To a certain extent, prior developments, such as the emergence of Sophists and teachers of rhetoric in the fifth century, fueled these changes, but they gained considerable momentum in the early fourth century. A principal catalyst for this process was the "codification" and inscription of Athenian law, which began in 410 and ended in 403. According to the edict that initiated this process, no law passed before 403–2 would be valid unless it was included in the new inscriptions made in the years 410–403; no uninscribed law was to be enforced; no decree passed by the assembly could override a law; and no prosecution could be brought henceforth for offenses committed before 403–2.

The aim of this effort was in part to rationalize the legal and political systems, which had been so upset by wartime civil strife. Moreover, a grant of amnesty attached to this law for all but the leaders of the Thirty was designed to ensure an amicable field on which virtually all citizens could act politically.[33] This new legal order also contributed to an institutional restructuring of the exercise of political power and granted new political significance and unofficial authority to specialists in the understanding and use of the written word.

The most obvious result of these institutional changes was the segmentation of the political realm. From now on, the assembly would no longer have the power to pass laws (*nomoi*); its authority was restricted to the passage of decrees (*psephismata*). The code established a new procedure for amending the laws of Athens and a new tribunal to authorize the amendments, the Law-Setters (*nomothetas*). Initially, this body was drawn from the same list

---

32. K. J. Dover, *Greek Popular Morality in the Time of Plato and Aristotle*, 229–34; A. W. H. Adkins, *Merit and Responsibility*; Alvin Gouldner, *Enter Plato: Classical Greece and the Origins of Social Theory*, 45–55.

33. See Douglas Macdowell, *The Law in Classical Athens*, 47. Even with the edict calling for arrest of leaders of the Thirty, there was a loophole. See S. C. Todd, *The Shape of Athenian Law*, 113.

as jurors, whereas in the mid-fourth century it was appointed by the assembly.[34] To some extent, this institutional change did not in itself reconstitute the balance of power. After all, membership in the Law-Guardians still derived from a cross-section of the citizenry, and the initiative for all amendments still came from the assembly.[35] Moreover, the stimulus for the new body probably originated from the desire to create legal impediments to the kinds of revolutionary actions undertaken by the Four Hundred in 410 and the Thirty in 404. Nevertheless, its establishment diminished the extent to which the Ecclesia sufficiently manifested the citizenry's general will.[36]

Two other changes in the conduct of politics during the early fourth century exemplified the differentiation of the Athenians' institutional and intellectual life, which surely would have motivated and influenced Plato's conception of the political art. First, political activity performed by leaders and ordinary citizens became specialized. The dual roles of politician and general performed by *strategoi* in the fifth century (for instance, Pericles, Cleon, Nicias, and Alcibiades) gradually devolved on different individuals—politicians in the assembly, known as orators (*rhetores*), and generals in the field (*strategoi*).[37] In addition, Athenian armies, as well as those of other *poleis*, were increasingly manned by mercenaries.[38]

Magnifying this practical differentiation of political roles were new forms of political discourse. In the fifth century, the power of speech-making politicians such as Pericles, Sophists such as Protagoras, rhetoricians such as Gorgias, and, of course, Socrates, attested to the political significance of that supple term, *logos*.[39] Its deployments proliferated at the end of the fifth cen-

---

34. Mogens Herman Hansen, *The Athenian Democracy in the Age of Demosthenes*, 162–65.

35. For the political insignificance of these legal and constitutional changes, see M. I. Finley, *Politics in the Ancient World*, 56, and Josiah Ober, *Mass and Elite in Democratic Athens*, 22–23, 97–98.

36. Macdowell, *The Law in Classical Athens*, 48–49; M. H. Hansen, *The Athenian Assembly in the Age of Demosthenes*, 94–95. But the extent to which this "codification" constrained judicial and political deliberations is in doubt. See S. C. Todd, *The Shape of Athenian Law*, 55–58.

37. Perlman, "The Politicians in the Political Democracy of the Fourth Century B.C.," 347–48; Rhodes, "Athenian Democracy After 403 B.C.," 314–15; Hansen, *The Athenian Assembly in the Age of Demosthenes*, 52–54; see Aristotle, *Politics* v.v., 1305a 7–15.

38. W. Kendrick Pritchett, *The Greek State at War*, part II, 59–116; Perlman, "The Politicians in the Political Democracy of the Fourth Century B.C."; Mosse, *Athens in Decline, 404–86 B.C.*; Hansen, *The Athenian Assembly in the Age of Demosthenes*; Ober, *Mass and Elite in Democratic Athens*.

39. For pre-fifth-century political roles of *logos*, see Jean-Pierre Vernant, *The Origins of Greek Thought*.

tury and the beginning of the fourth. Lysias, a metic with democratic sympathies, most notably developed the craft of writing speeches to be given by others in the assembly or courts; he was known as a "speech writer" (*logographos*).[40] Given the money citizens would have to pay for the work of speech writers, it was as if a new level of political discourse had emerged for the wealthy, who already dominated the ranks of political leaders.[41] Moreover, these speech writers did not have to take responsibility for public arguments. The new legal code had mandated the transcription (from oral consensus to written law) of all politically sanctioned Athenian customs.[42] Understanding the law became then (as now) in part a specialized art of literary interpretation.[43] Virtually every decree passed by the assembly was publicly documented and professionally drawn up. By the 370s, litigants submitted their pleas in written form.[44]

Accompanying the appearance of these new forms of political discourse were tools for perfecting their practice. Handbooks (known as *technai*) for legal and political rhetoric began to proliferate in the late fifth and early fourth century. These "practice and demonstration texts" included "a series of *topoi*," a number of logical arguments about common themes that could be adapted to a variety of oral contexts. They served as a bridge between the virtually readerless society of Socrates and the fourth-century readers of Plato's dialogues.[45]

The increasingly important public role of texts secured a new realm of discourse that lacked roots in the oral tradition and could be subjected to special scrutiny. The "literate revolution" was surely one of the historical condi-

40. A son of Cephalus and brother of Polemarchus, Lysias appears but does not speak in the first book of Plato's *Republic* (328b). As a paradigmatic "speech-writer," he suffers the brunt of Plato's criticism of their discourse in the *Phaedrus*.

41. On the role of the wealthy in the practice of Athenian politics, see J. K. Davies, *Athenian Propertied Families,* and idem, *Wealth and the Power of Wealth in Classical Athens.* However, the power of the wealthy was severely circumscribed by the equality promoted by Athenian laws and protected by democratic ideology. See Ober, *Mass and Elite in Democratic Athens.*

42. On the cultural significance of the reduction of *nomos* to its written form, see Martin Ostwald, *Nomos and the Beginnings of Athenian Democracy,* and idem, *From Popular Sovereignty to the Rule of Law.* On the political insignificance of this development, see Ober, *Mass and Elite in Democratic Athens,* 95–97.

43. Note the (relatively) recent recognition of how the art of interpreting the U.S. Constitution includes many common features with the art of literary interpretation. For example, see the work of James Boyd White, Stanley Fish, and Sanford Levinson. See Bibliography.

44. Rhodes, "Athenian Democracy After 403 B.C.," 308–9, 315.

45. See A. T. Cole, *The Origins of Rhetoric in Ancient Greece,* 71–112.

tions of Plato's theorizing.[46] Each of these developments may have helped to stabilize the Athenian political order in the aftermath of the Peloponnesian War, but they also created new forms of discourse that carried ethically and democratically problematic claims to political expertise.[47]

Public political activity still constituted the highest expression of virtue, but now, with the fragmentation of political activity, the specialization of public discourse, and the dissipation of ideological issues that engaged the Athenians' collective identity, the previous grandeur and luster surrounding the ordinary sense of what politics involved must have diminished. At the same time, the perceived need for their revival was palpable. With the practical means for doing so being obviously ineffective, the seeds of civil strife (*stasis*) still alive, the complexity of political life increasing, and new means of discursive expression more readily available, it is understandable that some turned to oral and written discourse as tools for political rehabilitation. They would have much work to do—work that was called for by the disabilities of conventional politics.

In this context, the practical dimensions of Plato's Socratic Problem may be interpreted as practical problems in the reconstitution of an ethically virtuous political realm, and Plato's conceptualization of the political art becomes more comprehensible as a political as well as theoretical construction. These two major developments in the character of ethics and power in Plato's Athens—the relatively sharp decrease in the wake of the Athenians' military defeat of their political capacity to exercise power, along with the increasingly apparent social conflict between economic classes; and the differentiation and specialization of Athenian political and intellectual discourse—fostered ripe conditions for a creative theorization of a critically articulated, ethical political art that addressed the maladies of Athenian society. The Platonic political

---

46. The term is Eric Havelock's, as is an overemphasis on it. But see his groundbreaking works on the social meaning of the changing technology of communication in ancient Greece: *Preface to Plato* and *The Literate Revolution in Ancient Greece and Its Cultural Consequences*. For a more recent reworking of the Havelock thesis, see Kevin Robb, *Literacy and Paideia in the Ancient Greece*. Other recent treatments of the relation of orality and literacy in this period of Greek life include Rosalind Thomas, *Literacy and Orality in Ancient Greece*, and Ian Worthington, ed., *Voice into Text: Orality and Literacy in Ancient Greece*.

47. Perlman, "Political Leadership in Athens in the Fourth Century B.C."; Mosse, *Athens in Decline, 404–86 B.C.;* Rhodes, "Athenian Democracy After 403 B.C."; G. E. M. de Ste. Croix, *Class Struggle in the Ancient Greek World*, 254; Finley, *Politics in the Ancient World;* Ober, *Mass and Elite in Democratic Athens.*

art thus appears to be less an intellectual aberration, familiar type of political dissent, or splenetic reaction of a disappointed aristocrat deprived of a political career by the limited opportunities of democracy than a radically creative, critical response to disturbing trends in Athenian political life.[48] This is not, however, to diminish the contribution of Plato's personal experience to his vocation.

2. A BIOGRAPHY OF PLATONIC DISCOURSE

a. Plato's Life as a Philosophical-Political Vocation

Plato was born in 427, four years after the outbreak of the Peloponnesian War. According to Diogenes Laertius (who recorded most of what are taken to be "facts" about Plato about six hundred years after they occurred) he was genealogically linked to some of the most prominent political figures in Athenian history.[49] His father, Ariston, supposedly descended from Codrus, the last king of Athens. He died when Plato was three years old. His mother, Perictione, came from a line of Athenians traceable to Solon. Her brother was Critias, leader of the Thirty, and one of her younger cousins was Charmides, who served under the Thirty as part of the Ten who supervised the Piraeus. After Ariston died, she married Pyrilampes, a close friend and supporter of Pericles. Plato's siblings included two older brothers, Adeimantus and Glaucon, and a younger sister, Potone.

Having been raised in a prominent, politically involved family of noble ancestry, it is not surprising that Plato initially desired a political career of his own. That his *polis* was a democracy immediately caused him no concern. But, according to the *Seventh Letter*, Plato's practical experiences changed his political disposition. In the war's aftermath, Plato had observed members of his family, individuals whom he thought had intended to bring salutary reform to their shaken society, commit brutal acts against democrats. Later, he

---

48. For interpreting Plato's practical context in terms of broader sociological and psychological developments, see Alvin Gouldner, *Enter Plato: Classical Greece and the Origins of Social Theory,* and Eli Sagan, *The Honey and the Hemlock: Democracy and Paranoia in Ancient Athens and Modern America.* On the latter, see my review in *Polis* 14, 1 and 2 (1995): 189–97. For viewing Plato's critical discourse primarily as a kind of resistance to the hegemonic power of "democratic ideology" and "democratic knowledge," see Josiah Ober, *Political Dissent in Democratic Athens.*

49. Diogenes Laertius, *Lives of the Eminent Philosophers* III.1–3.

watched the restored democracy indict and condemn to death Socrates, his intellectual mentor and moral exemplar.

The experience of these historical events led him to concentrate his energies in the realm of political thought rather than political action and to make the requirements of philosophy, rather than the arena of politics, the lodestone for his pursuit of justice. In so doing, Plato developed a new intellectual activity, political theory, in which he critically theorized the nature of politics and, in particular, the idea of an ethical, critically justifiable political art.

In the *Seventh Letter,* "Plato" describes the events and attitudes that led him to embark on this vocation. Written seven years before his death (in 356, when Plato was 71), this letter describes how some of Plato's most deeply held philosophical beliefs developed in tandem with his changing political beliefs about the politics of Athenian democracy (and, ultimately, Greek societies more generally) and how he pursued philosophy as the most ethical way of fulfilling his political vocation. The authenticity of this letter has been seriously questioned, but the biographical facts it records about Plato's life are, for the most part, taken to be truthful.[50]

The letter opens (324b) with Plato telling of his early ambitions, so common to young men of well-connected families of his time, to enter "public life." During this period, his political views remained relatively inchoate, but he seemed to share in the disdain (particularly prevalent among the upper classes) for the democratic government that reigned in Athens 411/10–404/3.

---

50. Over the past eighty-five years, numerous studies have discussed the veracity of the *Seventh Letter.* But no new evidence has surfaced to point to a resolution of this question. Although truth is not determined by majorities, the preponderance of scholarly judgment holds that the *Seventh Letter* is either authored by Plato or a reliable representation of Plato's life and basic political and philosophical convictions. Some notable arguments for its utility as a historical document that help us understand Plato's life include the following (listed in chronological order): R. Hackforth, *The Authorship of the Platonic Epistles,* 84; *The Platonic Epistles,* trans., with intro. and notes by J. Harward, 15; K. von Fritz, *Platon in Sizilien und des Problem der Philosophenherrschaft,* esp. chap. 1; *Plato's Epistles,* trans., with critical essays and notes by Glenn R. Morrow, 3–16; W. K. C. Guthrie, *A History of Greek Philosophy,* 5:401, along with his previous, extensive discussion of Plato's biography in *A History of Greek Philosophy,* 4:8–38; a heavily qualified endorsement appears in R. B. Rutherford, *The Art of Plato,* 1–21. Doubts about its genuineness were raised extensively by Ludwig Edelstein, *Plato's Seventh Letter.* His argument, however, relies (in an invidiously circular fashion) on a reading of Plato's dialogues that identifies him as a man of "*theoria*" who could not have been involved in the practical political affairs described in the *Seventh Letter* (65, 167). His arguments have not garnered wide acceptance in the scholarly community. For an initial, thoughtful criticism, see F. Solmsen's review in *Gnomon* 41 (1969): 29–34.

Because very little is known about this period, it is difficult to evaluate the fairness of Plato's views.[51] Given his social position, however, they were not surprising.

Plato placed hope in the Thirty as agents of political reform. We do not know exactly what it was in the person or political attitudes of the Thirty that attracted Plato, but we do know that two of Plato's uncles, Critias and Charmides, were two of its leaders and that, in the *Seventh Letter* (324d), Plato attributed his favorable attitude toward this antidemocratic elite more to the naïveté of his youth than to anything else. In any event, the Thirty quickly disillusioned him, if not by their murderous policies and disregard for the law then because of their attempt to make Socrates an accomplice of an illegal political action (*Seventh Letter* 324e–325a; see also Plato, *Apology* 32b). It is unlikely that he cooperated in any of their antidemocratic activities.

When democratic constitutional government was restored, Plato again sought to take part in political affairs. Indeed, the *Seventh Letter* states that Plato praised the new government for its restraint (325a–b).[52] Given his background, Plato's receptive attitude toward democracy was itself remarkable.[53] But Socrates' trial, conviction, and death sentence altered the nature of his involvement in Athenian political life. For Plato, the Athenians had betrayed Socrates. This betrayal further dampened Plato's political ambition, and up sprang his devotion to philosophy as the road to justice for the individual and the political community. In Plato's words from the *Seventh Letter:*

> The more I reflected upon what was happening, upon what kind of men were active in politics, and upon the state of our laws and customs, and the older I grew, the more I realized how difficult it is to manage a city's affairs rightly. For I saw it was impossible to do anything without friends and loyal followers; and to find such men ready to hand would be a piece of sheer good luck, since our city was no longer guided by the customs and practices of our fathers, while to

51. The only ancient sources are Xenophon's *Hellenica* Bks. I–II.1–2, and Diodorus, XIII.52–54, 66–74, 76–79, 97–103, 105–7. Both accounts emphasize military actions and the enormous role played by Alcibiades in Athenian politics.

52. It can be surmised that he was particularly impressed by its decision to honor debts incurred under the Thirty, to grant amnesty to all but the top officials of the Thirty, and to resist pressure to redistribute property, if only because this government was also praised for these actions in the Aristotelian *Athenaion Politeia* (chap. 40).

53. W. K. C. Guthrie, *A History of Greek Philosophy,* 4:12.

train up new ones was anything but easy. And the corruption of our written laws and customs was proceeding at such amazing speed that whereas at first I had been full of zeal for public life, when I noted these changes and saw how unstable everything was, I became in the end quite dizzy, and though I did not cease to reflect how an improvement could be brought about in our laws and in the whole constitution, yet I refrained from action, waiting for the proper time. At last I came to the conclusion that all existing states are badly governed and the condition of their laws practically incurable, without some miraculous remedy and the assistance of fortune; and I was forced to say, in praise of true philosophy, that from her height alone was it possible to discern what the nature of justice is, either in the state or the individual, and that the ills of the human race would never end until either those who are sincerely and truly lovers of wisdom come into political power, or the rulers of our cities, by the grace of God, learn true philosophy.[54]

This passage does not scorn political action as such; rather, it indicates Plato's increasingly sharp awareness of the obstacles blocking successful and just political action. Plato's belief that a life of virtue could not any longer be founded on the political life of existing societies did not denounce political action as a necessarily less-than-moral form of activity; rather, it required new (philosophical) conditions for its just expression.[55] For Plato, the decision to become personally involved in practical political action always remained an option; whether he chose to become so involved seemed to depend on his view of the conditions of political action—whether his participation would actually help to realize his philosophical and political goals and ideals (*Seventh Letter* 328b–331d).

In other words, the fact that Plato most likely wrote no dialogues before the death of Socrates and took no significant part in Athenian politics after it does not signify the radical separation of politics and philosophy in his life. To the contrary, Plato was a philosophical inquirer before Socrates' death by virtue of being his student. Before and after Socrates' death, he is believed to have fought in the Athenian army, and, once, with the help of Dion, he is said

54. The translation comes from Morrow's *Plato's Epistles*, 217. Similar views were expressed by Socrates in Plato's *Republic* 473d, 487e, 499b–c, 501e; see Chapter 4, below.
55. For a contrary view, see David Grene, *Greek Political Theory*, 78–79.

to have sponsored a *choregus* (dramatic production) for the Athenians.[56] His involvement in Syracusan politics during the 360s, as well as his foundation of the Academy in the 380s and his leadership of it until his death (on which, see below), demonstrates that politics, broadly understood, concerned him through his entire life.[57] Political matters were certainly not behind or in front of every theoretical interest Plato pursued, but the rational and ethical dimensions of political life made up the most continuous and prominent feature of his philosophical career. Whether he chose to engage in practical politics or the activity of theorizing, a single intention informed virtually all of Plato's adult life. Fundamentally, it was the pursuit of justice, which, properly undertaken, required both philosophical and political activity.[58]

That Plato's vocation grew out of dissatisfaction with every political regime of his day makes Plato's political theory more than an attempt at intellectual therapy for disaffected aristocrats and oligarchs (although it has been taken as such). It potentially addressed the political maladies of all Greek societies. Moreover, his establishment of the Academy was essentially political as well as philosophical, for he created a place that would foster a new understanding of contemporary realities by diminishing the intellectual authority of conventional claims about the social world as the primary, if not exclusive, determinant of truth, virtue, and justice.

b. The Academy as a Political Institution

Before Plato acquired it, the *Academus* simply designated an area of land named after a local hero, which was located about a mile northwest of the walls of Athens; it was marked by shady walks and had served as a gymna-

---

56. For a fair-minded review of the biographical details of this part of Plato's life, see Guthrie, *A History of Greek Philosophy*, 4:12–16. Plato is said to have fought in the Athenian army during the Corinthian War of 395–86. See Diogenes Laertius, *Lives* III.8; but see also G. C. Field, *Plato and His Contemporaries*, p. 6, n. 1. The reference to Plato's sponsorship of a *choregus* comes from Diogenes Laertius, III.3 (following Athenagoras).

57. For good, modern accounts of Plato's life, see R. S. Bluck, *Plato's Life and Thought,* and W. K .C. Guthrie, *History of Greek Philosophy*, 4:8–32.

58. See F. M. Cornford, "Introduction," *The Republic of Plato*, xv–xxix. In his 1928 essay "On the Origin and Cycle of the Philosophic Ideal of Life," Werner Jaeger wrote: "The philosophy of Socrates and Plato had a directly political intention." See Werner Jaeger, *Aristotle: Fundamentals of the History of His Development*, app. II, 455. Although my argument may recall Jaeger's views, it differs from them. Besides my unwillingness to accept the evolutionary narrative in which he places these thinkers, his rendition of "political" tends to exclude the philosophical dimension that both Socrates and Plato believed ought to inform it.

sium. Plato purchased the land around 387. Although the exact order of events is difficult to prove, the time at which he began to develop the first institute of what we would call higher education probably occurred after he had begun writing dialogues, after his traumatic first visit to Syracuse (c. 388–387),[59] and before his initial composition of the whole *Republic*.[60]

Plato established the Academy as a community of learning, yet the creation of the Academy was a political act, one that had intellectual and practical dimensions. As such, however, its purposes were neither apolitical nor ideological. But then, how are we to understand the political nature of this act and of the Academy itself? Part of the answer appears by comparing its operations with those of previous modes of higher education. Unlike the kind provided by the Sophists, who never institutionalized their teachings, or Isocrates, who assiduously sought to be relevant to everyday politics, Plato's Academy marked a radical break from other kinds of educational activities. For example, its physical location isolated it from the *agora* and Pnyx, and the presuppositions of Academic discourse maintained a gap between what occurred within its borders and the politics of Athens and other Greek city-states. It was not (and could hardly have been in democratic Athens) a source of propaganda, oligarchic or otherwise. What, then, was its political character?

The conditions of membership in the Academy made it an inherently exclusive and selective institution, but not in a way that established an ideological opposition between it and the Athenian democracy. For example, it did not cost anything to become a member of the Academy, and membership was open to all. Few, if any, intellectual or political criteria blocked students from joining. The young and old, men and women (albeit not many of the latter),

59. The importance of Plato's first visit to Sicily for his political thought as well as his philosophy—that is, for his experience of the Syracusans' cultural and political life as well as his encounter with Pythagoreans—has been underestimated. Until 405 B.C., Syracuse had been the other major democratic *polis* of ancient Greece and had become the largest city in the Greek world. When Plato arrived there in the early 380s, the power of its tyrant Dionysius I, who seized power in 405 and kept it until he died in 367, was secure. Its horrible transition from democracy to tyranny probably provided more of a historical referent for the discussion of the degeneration of democracy in Bk. VIII of the *Republic* than anything occurring in Athens. For two recent overviews of the history of Sicily from 413 to the end of Plato's life and beyond, see the articles by D. M. Lewis and H. D. Westlake in *The Cambridge Ancient History*, 2d ed., 4:120–55 and 693–722. For more on the importance of Sicily for Plato's conception of the political art in relation to democracy, see Chapter 4, below.

60. I say "initial composition," because Diogenes Laertius records statements that the *Republic* "was found several times revised and rewritten" (Diogenes Laertius, III.37).

Athenians and foreigners, became "members."[61] At the same time, the Academy awarded no stipends or fellowships, so that attendance necessitated students' having their own material resources. Membership had its requirements: Students typically ate meals there, although they did not sleep there. In contemplating the Academy's structure, Plato was surely influenced by his meetings with Pythagoreans during his first visit to Sicily, but no rites, rituals, or testimonies of faith characterized Academic life.[62] The Academy was not a sophisticated religious cult (*thiasos*).

At the same time, Academics constituted a group of like-minded individuals who functioned as a community. The Academy provided the kind of friendship Plato thought was essential for—but impossible for him to find in—practical political life.[63] The intellectual activity that characterized Academic life was both communal and abstract. Learning in the Academy transpired by way of disciplined, critical scrutiny—"dialectical analysis," in Plato's language—of a wide range of basic problems about astronomy and mathematics as well as politics and ethics.[64] Dialogues among teachers and students, not lectures by masters to disciples, filled the "curriculum."[65] The ideal education practiced in the Academy may have been limned in the *Seventh Letter* (341c) when "Plato" described the activity of learning the most important things in the following terms: "This knowledge is not something that can be put into words like other sciences (*mathemata*); but after long-continued intercourse (*sýnousia*) between teacher and pupil, in joint pursuit

61. Dionysius mentions the names of two women: Lastheneia of Mantinea and Axiothea of Phlius (Diogenes Laertius, IV.2).

62. J. S. Morrison emphasizes the Pythagorean dimension of Plato's philosophy and, in turn, the Pythagorean character of the Academy, in "The Origins of Plato's Philosopher-Statesman."

63. See *Seventh Letter* 325b–d, and M. Ostwald and John P. Lynch, "The Growth of Schools and the Advance of Knowledge," in *Cambridge Ancient History*, 2d ed., 6:592–633.

64. See Harold Cherniss, *The Riddle of the Early Academy;* C. B. Armstrong, "Plato's Academy," *Proceedings of the Leeds Philosophical and Literary Society* 7 (1953): 94, 98, and, most recently and importantly, M. Ostwald and John P. Lynch, "The Growth of Schools and the Advance of Knowledge."

65. There is a record of Plato having given, perhaps more than once, a lecture entitled "On the Good," but whatever truth there is to it, such instruction clearly occupied a minor part of the Academic "curriculum." For a more enthusiastic evaluation of the role of this lecture, as well as of Plato's "oral doctrines," see the work of the Tübingen school, for instance, K. Gaiser, *Platons ungeschriebene Lehre,* along with his article, "Plato's Enigmatic Lecture, 'On the Good'"; and H. J. Kramer, *Arete bei Platon und Aristoteles: Zum Wesen und zur Geschichte der platonischen Ontologie.*

of the subject, suddenly, like light flashing forth when a fire is kindled, it is born in the soul and straightway nourishes itself."[66]

The distinguishing feature of Academic discourse was its "scientific" character (understood as the systematic pursuit of knowledge), not any mystical experience. Thus, the aim of the Academy was to present *all* assumptions about nature, mathematics, or politics to the bar of dialectical justification. No received wisdom, traditional beliefs, or common interpretations of experience automatically gained critical respect. Because physical perception was unreliable, abstract discursive understanding was the benchmark for intellectual validation. This allegiance to radical criticism underlay the Academy's scientific orientation and differentiated both its educational approach and its understanding of scientific knowledge from more common conceptions. It also justified the distinctive status given to mathematical, particularly geometrical, thinking in the Academy.[67]

Above the walkway into the grounds of the Academy was engraved the saying, *ageometretos medeis eisito* (roughly, "No one who is not geometrical shall enter here"). Why was this so crucial to Plato's educational vision? Geometrical knowledge could not be justified by means of ordinary perception alone.[68] This preference for "geometrical thinking" manifested itself in other fields by a similar commitment to the judgments of critical theory rather than prevailing customs. Thus, "rhetoric" had to be justified by "philosophy," the basic tenets of which could not derive from the style of its ordinary practice or the tastes of its typical audience. As a result of this scientific predilection, the Academy's critical standards were much higher than those of Isocrates and his school, where the discourse of philosophy was supposed to complement the conventional practice of rhetoric.

Despite its adherence to the benefits of scientific education, instruction in the Academy did not have a rigidly doctrinal or programmatic character. By all accounts, Plato himself did not practice an authoritarian style of intellectual leadership. Plato's obvious prominence in the Academy made him

66. *Seventh Letter* 341c. Compare Socrates' characterization of the philosopher-guardian's experience of the good in Plato's *Republic*.

67. See Cherniss, *The Riddle of the Early Academy*, lecture III, "The Academy: Orthodoxy, Heresy, or Philosophical Interpretation," 60–85, especially 65–68. For a good discussion of geometrical inquiry as an agent of critical inquiry rather than metaphysical dogmas, see Paul Shorey, "The Idea of Good in Plato's *Republic*," esp. 218–20.

68. D. H. Fowler, *The Mathematics of Plato's Academy*, 197–202.

"first among equals," but he did not impose doctrinal conformity on its members.[69] For example, Plato welcomed Eudoxus, a renowned proponent of hedonism, to the Academy and chose Speusippus as his successor, a man whose views may have differed radically from Plato on the metaphysical status of "ideas" or "forms."[70]

Other features of the Academy's structure suggest that its education was not programmatic. First, the education was not rule governed. The length of time students spent there varied widely, and as far as we know they did not have to meet any curricular requirements; the Academy itself provided no institutional sanction for successful students in the form of honors or degrees. Second, the scientific character of Platonic dialectic was not hostile to humanistic inquiry. It was no less oriented toward ethics than mathematics, and its critical criteria did not assume the form of axioms or formulae; rather, they were characterized by a thoroughgoing skepticism about experience as an adequate guide to truth. Finally, the scientific nature of Academic inquiry did not strictly prescribe how the education acquired there was to be used or interpreted. Ex-members of the Academy left it to engage in a wide range of activities. Some returned to a relatively quiet life; others continued to pursue mathematical interests; still others became politically involved, either in Athens or abroad. Such diverse practical choices would have been, for Plato, theoretically understandable, for although his intellectual standards may have been monologic, their interpretation was not.

Part of this variety stemmed from the complex, unreproducible character of the educational process itself. The reflections in the *Seventh Letter* on Plato's failure to educate Dionysius II clearly state that any effective transmission of the meaning of a principle required practical judgment on the part of the teacher and a disposition to learn on the part of the student (340b–341b).

In the *Seventh Letter* (341c–d, 344b–c) and Plato's *Phaedrus,* we find complaints about the written word as a sufficient container for the most valued knowledge. The most permanent evidence of a teacher's knowledge, his writing, does not in itself provide a reliable guide to his thought. This makes the application of one's learning to the often unpredictable features of circumstance importantly indeterminate.[71] Plato recognized the role played by

---

69. See John P. Lynch, *Aristotle's School,* 55.
70. On Speusippus and Plato, see Cherniss, *The Riddle of the Early Academy,* 81–85.
71. *Seventh Letter* 341b, 344c.

fortune and luck in affecting the success of any human plan, no matter how "good" or "rational" it might be.[72]

The nonprogrammatic nature of the scientific discourse practiced in the Academy extended into its more practical, political perspective. Whatever formal instruction took place, it would have been used as a *propaideutic* to political judgment, rather than as a foundation for the judgments themselves.[73] As an institution, the Academy seemed to encourage no political view other than a belief in the insufficiency of existing regimes as paradigms of justice and the utility of the knowledge its students acquired for improving extant political orders.[74] The scientific character of Academic education surely contributed to its being less popular than the education received at Isocrates' school, and the critical distance Academics maintained from the daily politics of the courts and assembly made it suspect in the eyes of prominent politicians, but the activities and discourse of the Academy were not, on this account, decidedly oligarchic or inherently antidemocratic. Although the most prominent Athenian politician who we know spent time there was Phocion, an opponent of Demosthenes, Plato and Demosthenes could well have known and respected each other.[75]

At the same time, the Academy surely fostered certain intellectual and political commitments.[76] The dialectical inquiry in which it schooled its stu-

---

72. See *Seventh Letter* 325b–c, 326a, 326e, 327e, 337d, 351c–d. That is why Aristotle's criticism of those who don't recognize the variegated character of political knowledge and its use cannot have as its true object Plato himself. Yet, the belief that Plato failed to appreciate the role of *tyche* in human affairs undergirds Martha Nussbaum's critique of Plato in *The Fragility of Goodness—Luck and Ethics in Greek Tragedy and Philosophy*.

73. See Cherniss, *The Riddle of the Early Academy*, 70–75.

74. Ironically, it therefore may have been the radicalism of Plato's brand of scientific inquiry that made its activities palatable to the democratic *polis* in which they occurred. Because the critical standards of the Academy called into question the legitimacy of *all* existing regimes, the work of the Academy was not particularly, let alone exclusively, opposed to the regime of Athenian democracy. One might say that the lack of any record of members of the Academy leaving it to become active in Athenian politics indicates an implicit endorsement of it, because that might suggest that they required no radical reforms; on the other hand, their avoidance of Athenian politics could signify their belief that Athens was not susceptible to radical reform or that it was too dangerous for ex-Academics to try their hands at it—a conclusion that would have resembled the one Socrates arrived at and that justified his avoidance of the Assembly.

75. Demosthenes, *Third Philippic* 59–62. On the potential acquaintance of Plato and Demosthenes, see Ober, *Mass and Elite in Democratic Athens*, 45–48.

76. For a recent book that argues for the indirectly political nature of Academic training, see Kai Trampedach, *Platon, Die Akademie, und Die Zeitgenossische Politik*. Note its review by

dents included more than the sterile eristics of argumentative games. Academics seriously pursued truth in its various guises. It was the seriousness, not the cleverness, of Academic inquiry that led other philosophical schools to establish positions in relation to it. Similarly, the substantive nature of Academic inquiry would have seriously affected the practical political views of its members in some way. Because the justification for establishing the Academy arose partly because of the perceived inability of existing forms of ethical and political discourse to express justice, its inquiries would have tended to be seriously critical of contemporary political life. In addition, the *Seventh Letter* indicates that Plato held a variety of politically relevant convictions, although none of these entailed a preference for any particular constitutional form. However, these were not essentially antidemocratic.

Above all, Plato believed, first, in moderation as a political virtue and in the harmfulness for any society of the politics of excess. Evidence for this comes from the scorn expressed in the *Seventh Letter* for the extravagant behavior and concomitant corruption of "Sicilian life" (336c–d; see also 326b–c), the friendship between Dion and Plato (which evidently grew, at least in part, because of their shared views about the importance of moderation), and the efforts of ex-members of the Academy to promote this virtue in whatever political situation they affected. Second, he believed that a virtuous political community must adhere to commonly observed values. According to the *Seventh Letter* (336d–337d), such observance must occur on three levels: With respect to the conduct of leaders, it required their restraint by constitutional principles; with respect to the relationships among citizens, it required a devotion to commonality and recognition of equality; with respect to the general state of affairs in which a would-be political reformer intervened, it meant that the *polis* could not be rent by faction (*stasis*). In the *Seventh Letter* (334c–335b, 337c), Plato shows hostility to rule by "strong men" or political factions that flaunt constitutional limitations, and a traditional story about Plato's life states that he refused an invitation by the Arcadians and Thebans to become the legislator for their new colony of Megalopolis because they did not want "to have equality."[77] Finally, the *Seventh Letter*

M. J. Inwood in *Classical Review* 47, 2 (1997): 335–38, who argues that Trampedach may have underestimated Plato's political interests and those of his pupils.

77. The Greek for this phrase is *ison echein*, sometimes translated as "equality of possessions." The story appears in Diogenes Laertius, *Life of Plato* III.23. For an opposing view, see Morrison, "The Origins of Plato's Philosopher-Statesman," 135.

(331c–d, 351c) attests to Plato's opposition to violence as a tool of political reform.

Practical consequences flowed from these political commitments. Plutarch's record of political activities by ex-students of the Academy suggests that it was not uncommon for them to participate in politics after their time at the Academy ended, often contributing to the existing political life of some societies, the reformation of the life of others, and the establishment of constitutions for new societies. They might have advised tyrants to moderate their rule or encouraged their overthrow.[78] In this way, the Academy played a practical political role in Greek life, even that of Athens.[79]

Still, there is no suggestion that the Academy provided instruction in a *techne* of politics to be systematically and practically applied when students left its environs. The diversity of studies pursued there; the absence of a formal, required curriculum; Plato's hostility to Dionysius II's attempt to reduce the learning he acquired from Plato to the form of a *techne* (recorded in the *Seventh Letter* 341b); the varied paths taken by ex-members of the Academy—such evidence indicates that it was neither a training ground for would-be politicians nor the actual referent for the fictional Nocturnal Council of Plato's *Laws*.[80]

Members of the Academy left it as they entered it, with a wide range of political views. Even though the economic requirements for Academic study and its marginal relation to the activity of democratic Athenian politics may have predisposed its members to aristocratic inclinations, the learning they acquired there did not automatically favor elitist regimes. Given the scientific, nonprogrammatic character of Academic instruction and the fact that precise

78. See Plutarch, *Adversus Coloten* 32 (1126c), in Plutarch's *Moralia* 14:305–6; Athenaeus, *Deipnosophistae* 508d–509b; Chroust, "Plato's Academy . . . ," 32–38.

79. Plutarch—albeit hardly an impeccable source—mentions two Athenian generals, Chabrias and Phocion, as having attended the Academy. For a recent expression of the view of the Academy as entirely apolitical, see P. A. Brunt, "Plato's Academy and Politics." Part (not all) of the explanation for these differences involves different views of what "being political" could mean.

80. For the opposite view, see H. Marrou, *A History of Education in Antiquity*, 64–65; Alvin Gouldner, *Enter Plato: Classical Greece and the Origins of Social Theory*, 156–58; and Anton-Hermann Chroust, "Plato's Academy: The First Organized School of Political Science in Antiquity." For supporting views, see Trevor J. Saunders, "'The RAND Corporation of Antiquity'? Plato's Academy and Greek Politics," in *Studies in Honor of T. B. L. Webster*, vol. 1, ed. J. H. Betts, J. T. Hooker, and J. R. Green; and Ostwald and Lynch, "The Growth of Schools and the Advance of Knowledge."

political views on much of the politics and constitutional structure of any particular society could not be deduced from the Academy's scientific discourse, Plato should not be held responsible for the political activities of Academy students. Despite what may have been Plato's earnest entreaties, his belief that political reform must occur nonviolently, if it is to occur at all, did not persuade a close associate like Dion or other members of the Academy to refrain from violence.[81] Although his critical discourse was determinate and developed in a way that Socrates' was not, Plato was no more responsible for the subsequent political conduct of those who set foot in the Academy than was Socrates for the politics or pranks of Alcibiades.

Plato's devotion to the practice of a radically reconceived political art existed before and after the establishment of the Academy, but the creation of this institutional space for the conduct of critical *logos* surely encouraged Plato to explore problems of political theory in greater isolation from the actual problems of contemporary Athenian politics than he otherwise would have. In its tranquil setting, one could conceptualize this art in *logos* without having to figure out exactly how it could become practical in the *ergon* of politics. Plato could attempt to solve his Socratic Problem (at least in part) on a purely theoretical level, in the form of the dialogues. As such, this space is inherently neither antipolitical nor antidemocratic.

C. THE DISCURSIVE CONTEXT

Democratic Athens was a city of words as well as great deeds. Its political discourse in the assembly, council, and courts determined the collective fate of the citizenry; its tragic and comic plays staged discourse that provoked Athe-

---

81. Dion's frustrations with Dionysius II finally led him to mount a violent takeover of the Syracusan state in 357. Some members of the Academy may have contributed to his efforts, despite Plato's opposition. (*Seventh Letter* 331d, 350d–351c.) Not long after, however, Dion himself was assassinated (in 354). The plot may have originated in the political opposition to him of the Athenian Callippus, whom H. D. Westlake refers to as "a close friend [of Dion], who had links with the Academy and had won distinction as a military leader." See his article "Dion and Timoleon," in *The Cambridge Ancient History*, 2d ed., 6:704–5. Plutarch also mentions (*Adv. colot.* 32, 1126c) that two ex-members of the Academy assassinated Cotys, a tyrannical ruler of Thrace. As for the option of nonviolent civil disobedience to a tyrannical ruler, that probably was not a feasible political choice. Even in the twentieth century, that political tactic worked only against regimes that respected, even if they did not perfectly exemplify, democracy.

nians to reflect on their collective identity; its taste for new interpretations of its cultural traditions and ethical norms attracted poets and Sophists from all of Greece. This discursive context surely nourished the discourse of Socrates, who nevertheless found it hostile to philosophical inquiry about virtue. It also nourished the literary work of Plato, who created a new kind of discourse in the form of his philosophical and dramatic dialogues. Yet the discursive context for Plato's dialogues radically differed from that of his mentor in one fundamental way. It had to take into account the fact that Socrates had been found guilty and sentenced to death partly because of his innovative contribution to the Athenians' public discourse about virtue.

Two new genres of discourse emerged in the wake of Socrates' death that influenced the intellectual climate in which Plato made his distinctive mark. One, that of Socratic *logoi,* owed its existence entirely to Socrates' life and death; the other, that of *technai logon,* was significantly indebted to Socrates but also reflected aforementioned trends in the specialization of intellectual discourse.

1. SOCRATIC *Logoi*

Before, during, and for five years after the end of the Peloponnesian War, Socrates of Alopece examined the ethical foundations of the Athenian ethical and political order, but he left no written record of his words and deeds. Given not only the centrality of his words to the questions the Athenians faced in the wake of their military defeat, but also his many well-placed fellow travelers and the controversial character of his conviction, there was understandably great interest in affixing the memory of Socrates after his trial and death. That interest, however, would not have centrally involved a contest over the meaning of who was the real Socrates or what his discourse really signified. Such concern for historical objectivity was alien to both illiterate and literate segments of the Athenian citizenry. Most individuals on whom Socrates' life and death had made significant impressions would have been interested in the present and future, more than the past, remembering Socrates in terms of their own quest to understand the ethics of their society.[82]

Amid these conditions, a form of discourse emerged in the 390s that came

---

82. Even Thucydides constructed his unique brand of objectivity for the purpose of educating readers, particularly future political leaders, about the vagaries of human nature and history. See his *History* 1.22.

to be known as Socratic *logoi*, textually recreated accounts of Socrates' discussions with friends and interlocutors. Some of these justified his condemnation, but more often they sought to highlight his value, to overturn in *logos* what had been executed in *ergon*. Although Plato's dialogues stand out for their literary excellence, philosophical depth, and crucial role in developing a new, critical understanding of the political art (as well as for whatever educational role they played in the Academy), those involving the character of Socrates can properly be read as belonging to this form of discourse.[83]

The images of Socrates found in the written records of his conversations are probably neither fabrications, with no connection to the words or deeds of the historical Socrates, nor reliable records of "the historical Socrates." Any number of purposes—biographical, literary, or philosophical—could inform the composition of these Socratic *logoi*, making their historical status, in Momigliano's felicitous phrase, "a consciously chosen ambiguity."[84] At least, determining the historicity of these *logoi* is radically undecidable. One can say, however, that these authors used the new tools of written prose in important respects for their own ends, and given the life and death of Socrates, along with the practical context of the 390s, these purposes became at least partly political. In other words, these Socratic *logoi* carved out a new form of critical discourse that had potentially political implications.[85]

Prior to Socrates' death, the conceptual object of historical, dramatic, or political texts was always the status of Athens—as a collective ideal, a model (*paradeigma*) that could regulate and guide common fortunes. The Socratic *logoi* were different. They functioned in a smaller, more private domain. They were neither read nor performed in public, and the literate portion of the Athenian citizenry constituted a small fraction of the whole.[86] Their primary concern remained the public realm, yet they existed outside official, public arenas.

Who were the authors of Socratic *logoi*? And what can be said about their particular kind of discourse? For the authors of Socratic *logoi*, a new moral subject and model replaced those of Athens—the *paradeigma* of Socrates. In-

---

83. See Paul Van Der Waerdt, ed., *The Socratic Movement;* Charles H. Kahn, *Plato and the Socratic Dialogue: The Philosophical Use of a Literary Form*, chap. 1.

84. Arnaldo Momigliano, *The Development of Greek Biography*, 46ff; G. C. Field, *Plato and His Contemporaries*, 136–37.

85. See Paul A. Van Der Waerdt, ed., *The Socratic Movement*, and Charles H. Kahn, *Plato and the Socratic Dialogue: The Philosophical Use of a Literary Form.*

86. See F. D. Harvey, "Literacy in the Athenian Democracy," and Chapter 2, n. 37, above.

sofar as his life had been incompatible with the prevailing ways of life sanctioned by the Athenian political order, these *logoi* would possess an inherently critical and politically challenging character (some more obliquely than others). Socratic *logoi* displayed a disjuncture between the practice of virtue and contemporary politics, between the ideal of justice and the constitutional order of Athenian democracy. In so doing, they operated at the margins of political discourse in Athenian public life but also challenged its validity. In this respect, these "Socratics" created a new discourse for themselves relative to the dominant ethics and discourse of democratic Athens without formally constituting a practical, political oppositional force.[87]

No coherent set of political purposes, however, governed the composition of Socratic *logoi*.[88] Indeed, many of their authors—now conventionally known as "Socratics"—had ambiguous, if not marginal, relations to all political orders. One of the more important was Antisthenes (445–360), a young follower and companion of Socrates who was not an Athenian citizen.[89] He founded a school in Athens, known as the Cynosargus, which students had to pay to attend. He taught mainly the sufficiency of virtue (*arete*) for happiness. But according to his conception of virtue, political factors and material goods were irrelevant to its acquisition or possession; it could be obtained only with the study of *logos*, particularly through the lessons he taught and hard work (*ponos*). Another noted "Socratic" was a non-Athenian named Aristippus, born after Socrates and before Plato. In Xenophon's *Memorabilia*, Aristippus proudly stated to Socrates that he defined virtue as freedom (*eleutheria*). For Aristippus, this consisted in not belonging to any political order (*politeia*), which he understood to be primarily a form of constraint, but rather in living the life of a stranger (*xenos*) in every land. The only alternative was the unhappy task of shouldering the burdens of political responsibility as a ruler. Indeed, he showed no interest in pondering the nature of the political art, in part, no doubt, because he felt no personal connection to any political order.[90]

87. For characterizations of "democratic ideology" in fourth-century Athens, see Ober, *Mass and Elite in Democratic Athens,* and idem, *Political Dissent in Democratic Athens.*

88. See Field, *Plato and His Contemporaries,* 158. For references to them as a school, united by an antidemocratic ideology, see Wood and Wood, *Class Ideology and Ancient Political Theory.*

89. For his birth and death dates, see Diodorus 15.76; for further biographical information, see Diogenes Laertius, *Lives* 1.15, 6.1–19. However, the accuracy of these sources must be treated skeptically.

90. Xenophon, *Memorabilia* II.i.7–13, 17. Aristippus discusses ruling in terms of the "royal art" (*basiliken technen*), but only to scorn it. Of much more interest to him were the individual, variegated experiences of pleasure and pain, calculations of which became the focus of the Cyre-

A third Socratic, Euclides, came from Megara. Plato and other followers of Socrates retreated to his *polis* after Socrates' death. He, too, had no significant political interests. Aside from Xenophon and Plato, the only other person known for having written Socratic *logoi* was Aeschines of Sphettus. An Athenian and contemporary of Plato, he spent time in Syracuse at Dionysius's court, probably before Plato, and later wrote speeches for the Athenian law courts (as a *logographos*) in addition to taking on pupils for a fee. But he is not known for having a philosophy—political or otherwise—of his own. Judging from the fragments we have of these dialogues, they resemble Plato's Socratic dialogues only by way of recollecting the conflict between Socrates' active devotion to virtue, which involved abstention from conventional politics, and the ethics of contemporary, prominent Athenian political figures such as Alcibiades.[91]

For our purposes, the most important "Socratic" and author of Socratic *logoi* was Xenophon. Xenophon was born at approximately the same time as Plato, was raised, like him, in an aristocratic family, and was moved, as Plato was, to write about his encounters with Socrates. Xenophon was in Sparta, however, when Socrates was tried and executed. The actual stimulus for writing his *Apology of Socrates* may have come from hearing about or reading the anti-Socratic pamphlet written by Polycrates, which circulated in the late 390s and justified the Athenians' verdict.[92] (In his *Apology*, Xenophon confirmed many of the gross facts about Socrates' defense that appear in Plato's *Apology*, with the major exception that he emphasized Socrates' piety above all his other traits and argued that the major reason for Socrates' lack of success in convincing the jurors of his innocence was a willingness, stemming from his advanced age [seventy], to accept a death sentence.[93]) The other work of Xenophon most relevant to the genre of Socratic *logoi* is his *Hieron*, also written in this period, which discussed the potential virtues and dangers of tyranny and a tyrant's potential for happiness or unhappiness.[94]

Our principal interest in Xenophon, however, does not concern either

---

naics, who adapted this philosophy as a path to happiness (Diogenes Laertius, II.86–97). Of course, the reliability of these sources cannot be uncritically accepted.

91. Diogenes Laertius, II.60–64; see A .E. Taylor, "Aeschines of Sphettus."

92. 2 See Anton-Hermann Chroust, *Socrates—Man and Myth: The Two Socratic Apologies of Xenophon.*

93. Xenophon, *Apology* I.22–23.

94. Leo Strauss takes the work to make "the closest contact between premodern [fundamentally, 'Socratic'] and modern [fundamentally, 'Machiavellian'] political science." See his *On Tyranny*, 24.

the character of his beliefs or the relative veracity of his account of Socrates.[95] Rather, it is how his treatment of the political art can shed light on Plato's distinctive theorization of it. Relative to Plato's conception of the political art in his dialogues, the most striking aspect of Xenophon's Socratic *logoi* is that many similar issues emerge. Four stand out, all of which reflect on aspects of Plato's Socratic Problem.

One is the relation of *logos* to *ergon*. Xenophon's Socrates emphasizes in a conversation with Hippias that he demonstrates his own conception of justice by his deeds (*erga*) if not by his words (*logoi*).[96] Just deeds, for Socrates, here constitute obeying the laws. To illustrate the justice of laws, Xenophon's Socrates mentions the laws of Sparta. The discussion bears a superficial relation to Plato's *Crito,* where Socrates refuses to break out of jail because he believes that would violate the laws of Athens. But there are major differences. In Plato's *Crito,* the laws are *Athenian,* not Spartan, and Plato's Socrates distinguishes between the Athenian unwritten laws and their application by jurors. Xenophon makes no effort to make such a distinction. Still, Xenophon's Socrates illustrates a conflict between Socratic virtue and typical Athenian beliefs; to that extent, his Socratic *logoi* exhibit the Socratic Problem with which Plato grappled.[97]

A second issue is the status of the knowledge Socrates has and uses in his

95. With respect to Xenophon's portrait of Socrates, the boundary line between what is clearly a Socratic and a Xenophonic argument, apart from the features of Socrates about which no one disagrees, cannot be determined. What is clearer is the extent to which the character and sentiment of Xenophon's Socrates resemble those of Xenophon, just as Plato's Socrates significantly reflected his author's perspective on the world. Insofar as the tradition of Greek writers finds greater similarity between Socrates and Plato than between Socrates and Xenophon, I place greater, although far from complete, faith in the Socrates of Plato's aporetic dialogues as a more accurate rendering of the historical Socrates. (For example, Xenophon's Socrates [*Mem.* III.i.] helped those eager to win distinction qualify for their honors, which goes rather directly against the widely held view that Socrates did not encourage the pursuit of public praise.) For Plato's Socrates (in the earlier dialogues) as more historically accurate than Xenophon's, see G. Vlastos, "The Historical Socrates and Athenian Democracy," in *Political Theory* (November 1983): 495–516, and idem, *Times Literary Supplement,* 15–21 December 1989, p. 1393. For Xenophon's Socrates as a more accurate picture of the historical Socrates, see Donald Morrison, "Professor Vlastos' Xenophon."

96. Xenophon, *Mem.* IV.iv.9–18.

97. At some level, however, Xenophon is aware of this distinction. In a conversation Xenophon records between Pericles and Alcibiades, Xenophon does recount an argument that laws enacted by force (*bia*) are not true laws; only those that result from persuasion (*peisas*) are (*Mem.* I.ii.41–48). This passage recalls Socrates' emphasis in Plato's *Crito* on the importance of his ability as an Athenian to try to persuade his jurors as a justification for abiding by their decision against him.

discourse. Describing an encounter of Socrates with Critias, a member of the Thirty who apparently was interested in discrediting Socrates, Xenophon has Socrates deflect a direct association of his form of discourse with a *techne logon*. This art is that which Sophists claim to have and practice. In Xenophon's *Memorabilia*, Socrates does not make any such claim and responds by making fun of it.[98] At the same time, he does not fully characterize the basic features of his own discourse—how it is not a *techne* of the ordinary, particular, practical sort but still demonstrates a kind of skill and insight. The closest he gets is noting the etymological connection between "discussion" and "classification" (both stem from *dialegesthai*), which suggests that one skilled in collective deliberation can become skilled in discussion (*dialektikotatos*) as a kind of dialectic.[99]

Xenophon typically referred to the political art as the "kingly art" (*basilike techne*)—Plato rarely did[100]—which obviously highlights Xenophon's own monarchical sympathies (*Memorabilia* II.1.3–8). This art clearly requires some sort of educational training (*paideia*), along with the virtue of justice, because nature is insufficient (*Memorabilia* IV.1). Xenophon's Socrates humors Athenians such as Euthydemus who think it doesn't require any skill or knowledge and restrains those eager to jump into the political arena without knowledge, such as Glaucon (Plato's brother—which therefore might be a jibe at Plato; *Memorabilia* III.vi.1; IV.ii.2–12).

Correlatively, Xenophon's Socrates scorns the political use of the lot, as well as the ignorance of assemblymen (*Memorabilia* I.ii.9–11; III.vii.1–6). At the same time, Xenophon's Socrates does not hold that acquisition of the political art involves the narrow kind of practical experience that typically accompanies apprenticeship in subordinate and tactical, rather than supervisory and strategic, arts. Instead, it involves knowledge of a general sort that manifests the capacity to control other arts (*Memorabilia* III.iv.2–6). It also involves a kind of virtue that requires a citizen to be just, is the greatest of all arts (*technai*), and makes individuals into good politicians and managers (*politikoi* and *oikonomikoi*; *Memorabilia* IV.ii.11–12). In the *Memorabilia* (IV.iv.1–9), Xenophon's Socrates remarks that there is no one to go to for

---

98. Xenophon, *Mem.* I.ii.31–34.

99. Xenophon, *Mem.* IV.v.12–vi.1. I treat the relation between deliberation and dialectic more systematically in the analysis below of the political art in Plato's dialogues.

100. He does so most significantly in the *Statesman*, but even there it is but one way—not the exclusive way—of defining *politike* or the *politike techne*. See the discussion of the *Statesman* in Chapter 5A, below.

training in the art of justice. Socrates does not teach it, for his wisdom, according to Xenophon's account, derives from unteachable practical wisdom (*phronesis*), not teachable knowledge (*episteme*), and he never promised to make people virtuous (*Memorabilia* I.17; II.1–8). As to Aristippus's belief that the practice of the "kingly" art only constitutes a burden and an obstacle to happiness, Xenophon's Socrates mostly replies with quotations from the poets and stories of the gods (*Memorabilia* II.1.10–34).

These forms of Xenophontic discourse possess their own kind of truth, but they leave the relation between virtue and the political art unexplained. For example, there is the question of the usefulness of virtue. Xenophon the narrator and Xenophon's Socrates have no doubts about its utility. In fact, the usefulness of an activity determines the limits of concern for it exhibited by Xenophon's Socrates. He is not, for example, interested in advanced geometry, astronomy, or the phenomena of the heavens (*Memorabilia* IV.vii.1–6). At the same time, the usefulness of virtue is not reducible to a single set of specifiable activities that it would benefit (*Memorabilia* III.ix.14–x.1ff).

Xenophon's Socratic *logoi* raise many of the issues that pertain to Plato's Socratic Problem, but Xenophon does not critically explore the issues in any depth, and he exhibits little concern about the tension between Socratic virtue and Athenian democracy. Instead, he easily resolves the conflicts he identifies in favor of Socrates over Athenian democracy. For Xenophon, "Socrates" (either the historical Socrates or his self-consciously constructed philosophical image called Socrates) sympathized with those who favored greater power for aristocratic rulers. He suggested that if they had been appropriately empowered in Athens, neither Socrates' death nor Xenophon's exile would have occurred.

The contribution Xenophon provides for our understanding of the discord between a critical discourse of virtue and practical political realities—Plato's Socratic Problem as a historical and philosophical problem—stems primarily from the information he provides about the opinions and activities of Athenian intellectual figures from the standpoint of an Athenian aristocrat whose political activities evidence Spartan and Persian sympathies. Only Plato's Socratic *logoi* frontally engaged the discord between Socratic virtue and democratic Athens.

2. *Technai Logon*

Other forms of *logos* presumed to accommodate virtue and politics without adopting the critical posture assumed by Socratic *logoi*. These systematic efforts to make public discourse ethical, skilled, and successful were known as "arts of words," or *technai logon*. They became central to the discourse of Athenian democracy in the fourth century. These *technai logon* constitute the other element of the discursive context for the Platonic political art.

For all *technai logon,* the common points of reference were the official arenas of power—namely, the deliberative and decision-making bodies of the council, assembly, courts, and (now) *nomothetai*—where politicians, litigants, and ordinary citizens, the descendants of Pericles and Diodotus, had their say. Because the principal guidelines for institutionalized political discourse stemmed from legal constraints and personal beliefs, the discourse of these decision makers, skilled as it may have been, was not associated with a *techne logon.* These *technai* sought some lever for moving and transforming existing public discourse. What differentiated the various *technai logon* were the attitudes toward politics and *logos* each presupposed. Most versions relied on the benchmarks of rationality in existing forms of discourse and presupposed that the constitutional framework of Athens allowed for the accommodation of virtue and politics, justice and democracy. Consequently, most *technai logon* engaged the practical political discourse of the day more directly than did Plato's dialogues.

Two kinds of *technai logon* (other than Plato's) stand out. The first is that of the speech writer. Speech writers wrote speeches delivered by their clients, who probably improvised on a written text for actual oral presentation. The most prominent of these was Lysias, a metic from Syracuse who sympathized with the popular character of Athenian democracy.[101] Because the successful application of Lysias's *techne logon* required a fundamental appeal to the advantage of the audience to whom the speech would be given, Plato could refer to the manner of Lysias's *logoi* as "speeches that would advantage the *demos*" (*demopheleis logoi*).[102] The limitations of Lysias's *techne logon* and *logographoi* more generally as means of accommodating virtue and politics were the ethically and epistemologically untethered character of their prose. They lacked any systematic guide for their use. Plato thought the speeches of *logographoi* lacked the guiding hand of philosophy; in two of his dialogues, he did not allow them to qualify as genuine *technai logon.*[103]

At a second remove from actual politics were the *technai logon* taught in

---

101. See the account of Lysias's life in Dionysius Halicarnassus, and the useful overview by W. R. M. Lamb in his introduction to the Loeb edition of Lysias's speeches.

102. *Phaedrus* 227d.

103. See Plato, *Gorgias* 465a; *Phaedrus* 260c–e.

schools for instruction in public discourse. These schools sought to provide the higher education that citizens needed to become philosophically skilled in dealing with public affairs. The most significant of these in relation to Plato's Academy was the school of Isocrates, which was established within the walls of Athens in c. 392. Isocrates was a politically active Athenian citizen throughout his long lifetime—he was born nine years before Plato and died nine years after him—but, notably unlike Plato, he resided in Thessaly between c. 415–410 to 403, where he studied with Gorgias. He may well have known Socrates and Plato.[104] Between 403 and 393, he wrote speeches for the law courts. Although mostly known in antiquity as a master stylist of public rhetoric, it was Isocrates, much more so than Plato, who effectively straddled the boundaries between politics and intellectual life.[105] His school had no building and did not survive him, but Isocrates' educational ideals outshone those of Plato's Academy in prominence and popularity. For most, Isocratean education embodied Athenian cultural ideals.[106]

No restrictions—except a fee—governed attendance at his school—as was the case for study with the Sophists. But it was designed to offer much more than the technical instruction in oratorical or literary style of his teacher, Gorgias. Its purpose was to supplement the *technai logon* of traditional "schools" of rhetoric with a philosophy of *logos* that would be taught systematically over an extended period of time—years, rather than months. Isocrates distinguished his mode of discourse from that of both Sophists, who tended to rely on handbooks and discursive rules, and the more scientific study of discourse practiced in Plato's Academy. In his view, both were "useless."[107] He believed that there was no *techne* or *episteme* for implanting justice, temperance, or political knowledge in a student. In this way, he could be said to operate in the Socratic tradition. And yet he was convinced that the *techne logon* taught in his school could measurably improve the character of those who went there.

Whatever Plato's personal attitude toward Isocrates, the latter's philoso-

---

104. Plato's Socrates refers to him as a "companion" (*hetairos*) at the end of the *Phaedrus* (278e–279b). Diogenes Laertius (III.8) refers to him as a "friend" (*philos*) of Plato.

105. See H. I. Marrou, *A History of Education in Antiquity*, 79–91. For more recent analyses, see Christopher Eucken, *Isokrates: Seine Positionen in der Auseinandersetzung mit den zeitgenössischen Philosophen*, and Yun Lee Too, *The Rhetoric of Identity in Isocrates: Text, Power, Pedagogy*.

106. See Werner Jaeger's emphasis on Isocrates' role as a teacher of Greek *paideia* in *Paideia*, 46–155.

107. Isocrates, *Against the Sophists* 1–8, 11–13; *Antidosis* 17.

phy of *logos* assumed the form of a relatively popular and systematic educational discourse for accommodating philosophical *logos* and Athenian politics. Indeed, he believed that no natural tension characterized the relation between philosophy and extant political life.

Because of Isocrates' hostility to the utility of specialized philosophical education in general and dialectic in particular, and his acceptance of ordinary *doxa* as the foundations of philosophical inquiry, however, Plato probably disputed his claim to have successfully joined virtue and politics in a *logos* that was both philosophical and useful. What Isocrates believed to be the most thoughtful demonstration of the political utility of philosophy, Plato probably regarded as a failure on both fronts. (See *Euthydemus* 305c–306c and Chapter 3, Section B, below.) A more radical analysis of the grounds of virtuous discourse and the constitution of a political order was (arguably) needed. The systematic *logos* of Isocrates could not provide a solution to Plato's Socratic Problem. Here again, we see that Plato's *technai logon* responded in a historically astute way to a genuine practical and discursive *aporia*.

D. THE TEXTUAL CONTEXT

The problems Plato addressed in his dialogues originated outside the dialogues. It is the dialogues themselves, however, that offer the primary evidence of the Platonic political art. In them, Plato simultaneously inscribed and transformed the significance of external events in pursuing a theory of the political art, an answer to his Socratic Problem. But the dialogues themselves present problems for understanding Plato's thought. Such problems are often called "the problem of Plato," and they generate two other questions: First, how do we understand the relation of the dialogues to one another (which also raises questions about the chronological order of their composition), and, second, how do the dialogues reveal Plato's conception of the political art (which raises the issue of the relation of Platonic argument to that of the historical Socrates)?

1. THE ORDERING OF THE DIALOGUES

Establishing a chronological order of the dialogues creates a particular set of possible or likely conceptual relations among them. It provides a second-order tool for the first-order task of interpreting the manifold topics, narratives, and arguments of Plato's many dialogues. For example, Plato's views on the relation of theory to practice would differ according to whether one believes that he first composed the *Republic* or the *Laws*. Furthermore, by determining the relation between the identity and arguments of Socrates and Plato and correlating this to the chronological order of the dialogues, one can establish a boundary between ideas that stem primarily from the historical Socrates and those that are principally Platonic, along with a conceptual trajectory that relates them.

Because one cannot establish independent criteria for what counts as a historically "Socratic" or "Platonic" argument or claim about the political art in Plato's dialogues, presenting any historical claims becomes delicate and hazardous business. Yet anyone interested in saying something truthful and perceptive about the meaning of Plato's dialogues should not avoid this effort. For if one did, such questions would simply be deferred to questions about the interpretation of any single passage or dialogue; moreover, such avoidance runs the greater risk of relying on inappropriate or inadequately justified assumptions as interpretive starting points.[108] Any reading of a single Platonic dialogue that lacks a conception of how it relates to other dialogues may mistake a marginal or idiosyncratic treatment of the issue as central. One who denies the importance or possibility of establishing some chronological order of the dialogues, or some notion of "centrality," rejects ab initio a whole range of possible interpretations.[109]

Efforts to establish a chronological ordering of Plato's dialogues began in earnest in the mid-nineteenth century, when Platonic scholarship had reached the size of a critical mass and when faith in the objectivity and utility of science encouraged the belief that one could employ scientific tools to investigate the chronological order of their composition. The two principal tools are those of history and stylometry.

Perhaps the best evidence for the dating of the dialogues comes from references in them to historical dates or to one another. For example, the *Menex-*

---

108. This is a particular problem today, when so much scholarship on Plato involves interpretations of single dialogues, many of which run much longer than the dialogue they would illuminate.

109. See Holger Thesleff, *Studies in the Chronology of Plato's Dialogues*, 1ff. Thesleff refers to "the Platonic question" as the question of the chronological order of the dialogues as well as issues concerning their authenticity and interpretation. None of the claims about Plato that follow significantly involves dialogues whose Platonic authorship has been seriously questioned.

enus (see 245e–246a, for example) could not have been written before 387–6, because Socrates has Aspasia refer to historical events of the time of the King's Peace or peace of Antalcidas. At least the main part of the *Symposium* was composed no earlier than 384 because of Aristophanes' reference (193a) to the dispersion of the Arcadians by the Spartans in 385 (see Xenophon, *Hellenica* 5.2.1ff). The *Theaetetus* refers (142a) to an Athenian siege of Corinth that actually occurred in 369 and after which Theaetetus, the name of a main character in the dialogue and an actual Greek mathematician who attended the Academy, contracted dysentery and died. Plato refers in the *Laws* (638b) to the defeat of the Locris, which occurred in c. 356.

With these and other historical markers, scholars have used the criterion of stylometry—the codification of stylistic features of Plato's prose that could be classified only according to verifiable historical references in the texts—to establish broad categorical divisions for the composition of all of Plato's dialogues. Using this method (first done successfully by Lewis Campbell in the mid-1860s), and beginning with the historical anchors of Diogenes Laertius's claim that Plato left the *Laws* unpublished, a number of major scholars agreed about which dialogues were written last, relatively late in Plato's life. By using stylometric tools, they came to agree that (1) the *Phaedrus, Parmenides, Theaetetus, Sophist, Statesman, Philebus, Timias, Critias,* and *Laws* were written after the *Republic;* (2) the *Statesman* was written before the *Laws;* and (3) the *Phaedo* and *Symposium* were written around the time that Plato first completed the *Republic.* The stylometrists also classified virtually all of the shorter dialogues (excepting the *Hippias Major*) as having been composed prior to the *Republic.*[110]

This led to a now commonly accepted chronological division of the dialogues into "early," "middle," and "late" periods.[111] However, absolute con-

110. For a useful summary of these findings, see W. D. Ross, *Plato's Theory of Ideas,* 2, and more recently, Leonard Brandwood, *The Chronology of Plato's Dialogues.* For an extensive, critical comparison of the substantive results of uses of the stylometric approach for establishing the chronological order of the dialogues, see Holger G. Thesleff, *Studies in Platonic Chronology,* especially part 1; for a brief reprise of stylometric findings, see Gregory Vlastos, *Socrates: Ironist and Moral Philosopher,* 46–47 and notes.

111. Such a division was first authoritatively presented and defended by F. M. Cornford, in his article, "Athenian Philosophical Schools." It received significant reinforcement by his successor at Cambridge, W. K. C. Guthrie, in his *History of Greek Philosophy* 4:50.

By relating these relative chronological categories to fixed events in Plato's life, scholars have identified the following dialogues as "early," having been composed prior to Plato's first visit to Sicily in 388–87. I list them in alphabetical order because there is no noncircular way

fidence in these methods and their results is unwarranted. Neither historical references in the dialogues nor stylometry provides incontrovertible evidence for the precise dates of composition. Consider the following: (1) All of
the texts of the existing Platonic dialogues were found long after his death;
(2) Plato could have revised them during his life, as many of the dialogues include anachronisms; (3) the length of some of the dialogues allows the possibility that they were composed over a number of years; (4) as a master stylist,
Plato could have used different styles at will, in the manner of a master com-
poser being able to compose symphonies and string quartets in the same year;
and (5) the historical benchmark for stylometrists, the *Laws*, unpublished by
Plato during his lifetime, may evidence the imprint of its publisher and possible reviser, Philip of Opus.[112] All of these considerations suggest the possibility of some dialogues being composed over periods that cross the boundaries between the "early," "middle," and "late" periods.

These points, among others, have led the most avid recent student of the
problem to warn readers about drawing conclusions about the substantive
development of Plato's thought from claims about the chronology of the dialogues.[113] Total agnosticism about the chronological order of composition of
the dialogues, however, leads one to view that order, for purposes of inter-

---

(including stylometry) of distinguishing the order of composition in these groups. They are *Alcibiades I, Apology, Charmides, Crito, Euthydemus, Euthyphro, Hippias Major,* perhaps the
Gorgias, Hippias Minor, Ion, Laches, Lysis, Protagoras, and *Republic I* (if it was written prior to
the rest of the *Republic*). In these dialogues, the character of Socrates plays a major role, often as
a gadfly, and they (apart from the *Apology* and *Crito*—which hardly constituted "solutions" to
their problems) do not resolve the problem they set out to address. However, Socrates emerges
from them looking like a trustworthy guide to the understanding of virtue and knowledge. Thus,
in addition to the chronological mark of "early," these dialogues are often identified as Plato's
"aporetic" or "Socratic" dialogues. So as not to prejudge their purpose or message, I simply refer to them as Plato's aporetic dialogues.

The stylometrically "middle" dialogues, longer dialogues in which the character of Socrates
and the role of "ideas" or "forms" assume more prominence and authority, are said to have been
written after Plato's first trip to Sicily, in conjunction with the first years of the Academy, and
before Plato's second trip to Sicily in 368–67. They are typically said to include the *Cratylus,*
perhaps the *Gorgias, Menexenus, Meno, Phaedo, Phaedrus, Republic* (at least Books II–X), and
Symposium.

The stylometrically "later" dialogues—the *Parmenides, Theaetetus, Sophist, Statesman,
Philebus, Timias, Critias,* and *Laws*—were supposedly written after Plato's second trip to Sicily.
Argumentatively, some of these are, like the "early" ones, inconclusive, but the topics under consideration are treated more formally and evidence a dialectical method of differentiation appropriate, it is said, for the kind of critical inquiry likely to be occurring in the Academy.

112. See Thesleff, *Studies in the Chronology of the Platonic Dialogues,* 202–3.

113. Thesleff, *Studies in the Chronology of the Platonic Dialogues,* 46.

pretation, either as random or solely in terms of one's interpretation of the meaning of any given dialogue—an entirely self-serving approach. If one believes that Plato's historical context and various events of his life are relevant to understanding the dialogues, the most widely agreed-on conclusions that have been drawn from the evidence of history, at least, cannot be summarily dismissed.[114]

On the basis of historical referents in the dialogues alone, I assume the following with respect to the chronological order in which the dialogues were composed: The *Republic* was composed before the *Statesman;* the *Statesman* was composed before the *Laws;* the *Laws* was one of Plato's last dialogues. Relative to events of Plato's life, one can then locate the dates of composition of these dialogues as follows: the initial composition and completion of the *Republic* (at least its first version—the proto-*Republic* if there was such a thing) around the time of, and probably after, his first trip to Sicily; the time of the composition of the *Statesman* as the 370s or 360s; the period of composition of the *Laws* as the 350s, after Plato's final trip to Sicily.

Other dialogues that are crucial for my study of Plato's discourse about the political art, typically identified as "early" dialogues, probably—but not necessarily—were composed prior to Books II–X of the *Republic.* Although I discuss these dialogues in a particular order and place that discussion before my discussion of the *Republic,* my arguments about them do not depend on their being composed in the order that I discuss them. They conceivably could have been written after the *Republic,* although I consider this unlikely.[115] The narrative order of my discussion of Plato's dialogues resembles what some believe to be the chronological order of their composition. The ones I discuss first are more dramatic, more "Socratic" (in that the character of Socrates plays a large role in them), and more directly reflective of Athenian philosophy and discourse than the ones I discuss subsequently. In my case, however, this order simply indicates the most logical arrangement for an argument about the range of Plato's treatment of the political art. It does not

114. For such a dismissal, see Jacob Howland, "Re-reading Plato: The Problem of Platonic Chronology." Howland's main argument for the irrelevance of considerations of chronology in interpreting Plato's dialogues amounts to the view (stated on p. 195) that "issues of development [and chronology] are irrelevant to the interpretation of a literary cosmos."

115. For an argument that locates the composition of the "early" dialogues after the *Republic,* see Thesleff, *Studies in the Chronology of the Platonic Dialogues,* part II. Efforts to pinpoint the precise chronological relation of the composition of the "early" dialogues inevitably run upon the shoals of *petitio principii.* For a notable recent effort that suffers this fate, see Charles Kahn, "On the Relative Date of the *Gorgias* and *Protagoras.*"

require that one accept particular question-begging claims about the development or substantive alteration of Plato's political thought during his lifetime as a frame for interpreting the political art in Plato's dialogues.

2. THE DIALOGUES AND PLATO'S VOICE

Establishing a loose but meaningful understanding of the chronological order in which Plato composed his dialogues still leaves unanswered major questions about how to affix Plato's voice in his dialogues involving others. This question most obviously arises (1) in relating Platonic thought to that of the historical Socrates and (2) in reference to the corollary issue of the significance of Socrates in Plato's dialogues.

The second issue concerns how we are to use Plato's dialogues to determine his constructive philosophy, given (1) the references in the *Seventh Letter* to his unwritten teachings, along with the comments in both the *Seventh Letter* and the *Phaedrus* about the untrustworthy character of the written word, and (2) the absence in the dialogues of the author's own voice, along with the complications in their philosophical content by the dramatic form of presentation (a form that, according to Socrates in the *Republic,* is not trustworthy).[116]

The relation of Plato's own philosophical voice to that of the character of Socrates in his dialogues initially became an issue of scholarly concern in the first third of this century. Depending on whether one's main interest was Socrates or Plato, the issue was known as "the problem of Socrates" or "the Platonic question."[117] According to a thesis of John Burnet, first published in 1911 and supported by A. J. P. Taylor in 1926, everything uttered by "Socrates" in Plato's dialogues actually represented the beliefs of the historical Socrates.[118] On the other side was Paul Shorey, who argued that everything spoken by the character of Socrates in Plato's dialogues actually represented the philosophical beliefs of Plato. Shorey connected his view of the

116. See *Seventh Letter* 341c–344c; *Phaedrus* 274c–278b; *Republic* 398a–b and 605a–608b, although it must be noted that Plato's dialogues cannot be automatically subsumed under the categories of poetry discussed in the *Republic.*

117. For a recent collection of "solutions" and "answers" to this "problem" or "question," see *Der Historische Sokrates,* ed. A. Patzer.

118. See John Burnet, *Plato's Phaedo,* and A. E. Taylor, *Plato, The Man and His Work.* For a recapitulation and critique of what has become known as the Burnet-Taylor thesis, see W. K. C. Guthrie, *Socrates,* 31ff.

Platonic question to an argument about the philosophical unity of Plato's dialogues.[119]

Between these views are two others. One, a somewhat Aristotelian view, has been taken by Ernest Barker, Werner Jaeger, and to some extent W. K. C. Guthrie, who have found kernels of the beliefs of the historical Socrates in Plato's "early" dialogues, which Plato then developed into new philosophical and political theories that become clear in his "middle" and "later" dialogues. The later, more clearly Platonic views, relate to the views of the historical Socrates as "actuality" to "potentiality."[120] More recently, Gregory Vlastos rejected this Aristotelian perspective by developing rigorous analytical criteria for differentiating the views of the historical Socrates and those of the historical Plato, associating the views of the historical Socrates with those of the dialogic Socrates of Plato's so-called early dialogues, and refusing to see Plato's "mature" views as natural or inevitable developments of the views of the historical and early dialogical Socrates.[121] Vlastos's views have significantly influenced the work of current Plato scholars, such as Terence Irwin, Richard Kraut, Thomas Brickhouse, Nicholas Smith, Hugh Benson, Roslyn Weiss, and other analytical philosophers.[122] Other important solutions to this problem also exist, notably in the work of Leo Strauss and Eric Havelock.[123]

My approach charts a different path.[124] Its principal justification comes from the belief that the different biographies and historical contexts in which Socrates and Plato lived and the different problems each faced prevent one

119. See Paul Shorey, *What Plato Said.*

120. See Ernest Barker, *Greek Political Theory: Plato and His Predecessors,* 112–13; Werner Jaeger, *Paideia: The Ideals of Greek Culture,* vol. II—*The Search for the Divine Centre,* 84–85, 91–97; Guthrie, *Socrates,* 32–35.

121. See G. Vlastos, *Socrates: Ironist and Moral Philosopher,* esp. 45–80.

122. See the contributions to G. Vlastos, *The Philosophy of Socrates;* Terence Irwin, *Plato's Moral Theory: The Early and Middle Dialogues;* Richard Kraut, *Socrates and the State;* Thomas C. Brickhouse and Nicholas D. Smith, *Socrates on Trial;* Hugh H. Benson; ed., *Essays on the Philosophy of Socrates;* Roslyn Weiss, *Socrates Dissatisfied: An Analysis of Plato's Crito.*

123. On Strauss (as well as Popper and Vlastos), see my "Plato's Socratic Problem, and Ours." Havelock summarizes his "solution" to the problem, one that evolved over fifty-five years, in the 1982 "Addendum" and "Postscript" to his 1934 article, "The Evidence for the Teaching of Socrates," reprinted in *Der Historische Sokrates,* ed. Andreas Patzer, 252–58.

124. However, it hardly is unprecedented. For example, see F. M. Cornford's treatment of the relationship of Socrates and Plato in "Athenian Philosophical Schools," 312, and his 1933 lecture "Plato's Commonwealth," which appears in F. M. Cornford, *The Unwritten Philosophy and Other Essays,* 47–67. The failure even to consider the potential ramifications of the issue of the relation between the views of "Socrates" in Plato's dialogues and those of the historical Socrates and Plato radically mars I. F. Stone's popular *The Trial of Socrates.*

from readily comparing the philosophical commitments of each on an analytically smooth plane. Whatever one takes to be the relation of the discourse of Plato's dialogues to the actual views of the historical Socrates and Plato, the philosophies of both need to be read through the lens of their differing historical contexts.

Apart from the significantly different historical and biographical situations of Socrates and Plato, differentiating the views of Socrates and Plato is Socrates' trial and death. Given the political character of Plato's philosophical vocation, this event served as more than a personal tragedy; it would frame his philosophical evaluation of Socrates' words and deeds—indeed all of his ethical and political theorizing. The character of Socrates in Plato's dialogues is not likely to have served in the roles assigned to him by previous commentators, if only because Plato's literary use of "Socrates" would immediately have a different significance than that uttered by the historical Socrates. Plato's Socrates operated in a transformed historical and political context compared with the historical Socrates, and this gap between the historical and dialogic Socrates informed issues in Plato's dialogues that "Socrates" discussed. Certainly, Plato shared certain beliefs with the historical Socrates; it is altogether appropriate to view Plato as part of a "Socratic" tradition. But exactly how Plato belongs to that tradition constitutes a problem with which Plato himself must have been concerned as he wrote dialogues in which "Socrates" played a major role. As a result, Plato's so-called Socratic dialogues cannot be used to locate something called "Socratic philosophizing" or "the philosophy of Socrates."[125]

To view "Socrates" in Plato's dialogues in this light, as a figure whose significance can be understood only in conceptual terms that the historical Socrates could not have fully shared, does not detract from its resonance with the historical Socrates. There would very likely be connections, close or distant, between the views of "Socrates" in any one Platonic dialogue and those of the historical Socrates, similar to those between other characters in Plato's dialogues and their actual, historical counterparts. Just as Plato's dialogues comment (exactly how is yet to be determined) on problems he faced in his own life—involving Athenian politics, foes of Socratic followers, Isocrates, the Academy, Sicily—and do not, for that reason, diminish their connection

---

125. For principal examples, see Vlastos, *Socrates: Ironist and Moral Philosopher*, and the publications mentioned in note 15, above.

to historical reality, so Plato's dialogic Socrates reflects important features of the historical Socrates' words and deeds.[126]

By adopting this approach, the dialogic presence of Socrates in Plato's dialogues itself becomes a critical interpretive problem. What Plato is saying in dialogues involving the dialogic Socrates now must be read somewhat theatrically, against the backdrop of a problematic historical and philosophical relationship between Plato and his principal mentor.[127] Ironically, this approach sabotages prospects for its own unqualified success. For it becomes impossible to establish clearly what counts in the dialogues as either the actual words of the historical Socrates, or the virtual philosophy of the historical Socrates, or a philosophical embryo of Plato's mature theory that was fathered by Socrates, or a problematic reflection of Plato's own views, *in contrast to* what Plato himself believed (independently of the actual or virtual historical Socrates and instrumental to his own particular purposes and problems).[128]

Making the character of Socrates in Plato's dialogues and the ideas he espouses indeterminately associated with the settled philosophical convictions of either the historical Socrates or the historical Plato (as I do) casts a new perspective on the question of the development of Plato's thought. No longer is it essential to differentiate a so-called Socratic phase from a more mature, Platonic phase and then explain the differences between the two as insignificant (Shorey, Strauss), organically or teleologically connected (Barker, Jaeger, Guthrie), or philosophically distinct (Vlastos). The more important task becomes that of (1) understanding each dialogue in terms of both the problems it considers and the treatment, if not solutions, these problems receive and (2) comparing dialogues in terms of the character of these "problems," "treatments," and/or "solutions." If I am right about the roles of the various historical and conceptual dimensions of Plato's Socratic Problem in

126. His reasons for locating many of his dialogues in the past rather than the present may have indicated what he took to be the unity of the period between Periclean Athens and his own time, but other factors could have easily been just as, or more, significant—such as the way this dramatic device produces salutary distance from the actual discursive and practical conflicts of his time, the importance of past events and individuals for the present, or the insight that comes from hindsight.

127. See J. Peter Euben, *The Tragedy of Political Theory.*

128. This approach pours cold water on learned scholarly efforts that make such distinctions, but that may not be so bad, because Plato is unlikely to have been preoccupied with the problems that have informed these efforts or to have observed the distinctions they produce.

constituting the political dimensions of Plato's philosophical vocation, then the dialogues in which *this* problem is involved may be fruitfully read as different kinds of treatments or solutions to that problem. In addition, the resulting interpretations become as little dependent as possible on assumptions about Plato's psychology or intellectual development that have no roots in the dialogues themselves.

During the last thirty years, scholars have raised another set of questions about the interpretation of Platonic dialogues. They reflect general philosophical interest in what constitutes a rational argument or claim, what the value of such an argument or claim is, and what the relation of that argument or claim is to statements not presented in a strictly propositional form. By virtue of the ironic stance taken by the dialogic Socrates and the philosophical leadership of the historical Socrates, in spite of his refusal to assume the role of a teacher of virtue, these concerns pertain to traditional issues of "the problem of Socrates" and "the Platonic question" but proceed on a different level.

These issues lead one to ask whether statements that appear in any one of Plato's dialogues say what they mean in the framework of that dialogue and can be compared to statements in other dialogues, or whether the element of Socratic irony initiates a movement of interpretive regress that makes it virtually impossible to establish any constructive philosophical claims from the discourse of one or more dialogues. This question about the stability and positivity of Plato's philosophy also relates to debates between literary critics and analytical philosophers about the relative importance of the dramatic dialogic frame of each Platonic dialogue in constituting its philosophical meaning, as well as to debates among classical scholars and literary theorists about the relation of Plato's writings to his oral teachings.

In light of the interpretive approach followed here, the issue of whether the dialogues are to be read as literary dramas, with the meaning of philosophical positions mostly limited by the twists given to them by the characters who espouse them, or as discussions of analytical philosophy, with the dialogue form used simply as adornment, becomes moot. The philosophical arguments in the dialogues count for more than their embodiment by characters, because Plato's educational concerns, along with the educational tasks of the Academy, place the highest importance on the content of philosophical debates. The significance of those debates would not be fully appreciated if they were read only as part of a literary genre (helpful as that context might be for understanding those debates). Similarly, the significance of actual history and politics for the characters, scenes, story, and argument of Plato's dialogues suggest that these references are more than artistic window dressing; indeed, they constitute the philosophical problematic that Plato's dialogues would resolve. But how?

The way in which the dramatic elements function in Plato's dialogues is extremely complex. First, Plato's renditions of actual persons and events cannot be relied on as historically accurate; yet they cannot simply be dismissed as evidence of utopian or (pejoratively) ideological thought.[129] They provide serious (if not the most credible) interpretive accounts of Greek history and philosophy. Second, fifth-century personages and settings in the dialogues have to be read against the interpretive screen of possible fourth-century referents. For example, the *Protagoras, Gorgias,* and *Euthydemus,* whose dramatic dates can be put in the 430s or 420s, may be read as commentaries on Isocrates and his school (probably in the 390s or 380s) as well as on the problems of fifth-century discourse and politics. The significance of these "external" historical references essentially constitutes the "internal" philosophical meaning of his dialogues.

The problem of how to understand the relation between Plato's dialogues and his "unwritten doctrines" [*logoi*] is more insoluble but less troubling than the debates about the relative primacy in the dialogues of dramatic play or propositional justification. The importance of Plato's oral teaching has been championed for nearly fifty years by members of the Tübingen School (principally H. J. Kramer and K. Gaiser) and the German expatriate Ludwig Edelstein. Unfortunately, other than terse references to a Platonic lecture or lectures entitled "On the Good," no evidence exists to indicate what those doctrines might be.[130] Any reliance on a view of Plato's oral teaching as a basis for interpreting his written dialogues has to be wholly speculative. On the other hand, the previously cited passages in the *Phaedrus* and *Seventh Letter,* as well as the nearly mystical aura surrounding an encounter with "the Good" in the *Republic,* testify to the importance of not using Plato's dialogues as

129. For the latter, see M. I. Finley, *The Politics of the Ancient World,* 123–28.
130. For the most complete discussion of this lecture, see Konrad Gaiser, "Plato's Enigmatic Lecture 'On the Good'," and the commentary by Thesleff in *Studies in the Chronology of Plato's Dialogues.*

textbook renditions of Plato's beliefs.[131] But that hardly should be taken as scholarly license for constructing interpretations of Platonic dialogues that do not even attempt to correspond to Plato's possible intentions in writing these dialogues. Rather, the references in the *Phaedrus* and *Seventh Letter* to "unwritten *logoi*" indicate Plato's uneasiness about the increasing reliance in his time on written texts and the assumption that intellectual authority somehow resides in them.[132]

One last interpretive issue comprises the argument (favored here) for a "Platonic" reading of the dialogues, that is, a perspective that has a substantive, primary relationship to the authorship of Plato.[133] A properly Platonic reading of Plato's dialogues cannot be settled by analyzing historical evidence or contemporary arguments to the exclusion of one or the other. At the same time, the interpreter must be able to justify meanings claimed to be Platonic but that are not directly linked to Plato's intentions or concerns or that invoke facts and considerations unknown to Plato.

E. THE HISTORICAL SOCRATES
AND THE PLATONIC POLITICAL ART

The *Apology* and, to a much lesser extent, the *Crito* serve as the historical benchmarks of Plato's Socratic Problem in his dialogues.[134] They occupy a

---

131. See *Republic* 506e–507a; however, for a more intellectualized version of what the good involves, see 516b.

132. Jacques Derrida takes this point and runs with it in his reading of Plato's *Phaedrus,* one that, however ingenious, cannot plausibly be related to what Plato was doing in writing that dialogue. See Derrida's essay, "Plato's Pharmacy," in *Dissemination.* For an important critique of Derrida's reading of Plato that is still sympathetic to his deconstructive impulse, see Harry Berger Jr., "Levels of Discourse in Plato's Dialogues." For a more recent reading of Plato that is indebted to both Derrida and Berger, see Jay Farness, *Missing Socrates: Problems of Plato's Writing.*

133. These concerns do not pertain to the cogency of uses of the adjective "Platonic" or "platonic" that do not presume to refer logically or historically to Plato, although part of the motivation of this book is the desire to diminish unwarranted uses of these adjectives and thereby honor the philosophical activity of Plato himself.

134. Except for Plato's *Apology of Socrates*—and even here qualifications must be made— Plato's dialogues must be read primarily as *Plato's* dialogues and nobody else's. The *Crito* may more nearly reflect the thinking of Socrates than any other Platonic dialogue, but only Plato's *Apology* is based on Plato's firsthand experience of Socrates' words. Plato was not present for the

unique position among them, for they stand as Plato's most direct transposition of the trial and tragedy of the historical Socrates into a discursive problem. Even though they do not directly employ the term "political art," they form both a historical and textual launchpad for Plato's effort to articulate a coherent conception of the political art.

The enormous personal significance for Plato of the events described in the *Apology*, its uniquely historical content, and its paradigmatic expression of Plato's Socratic Problem all serve to indicate its special status for understanding Plato's political thought. First, although the *Apology* was not necessarily the first dialogue Plato wrote, the events in it constitute Plato's last, and obviously most vivid, experiential source for his recollection of Socrates. Second, Plato was at Socrates' trial. We have no evidence that Plato witnessed any other of the Socratic dialogues about which Plato wrote. The *Crito* has to be regarded as a much freer reconstruction of the thought of the historical Socrates, insofar as it can be regarded as historically Socratic at all. Finally (as we have noted from the *Seventh Letter*), Socrates' trial and death irreversibly turned Plato away from a practical political vocation. In this regard, it marked the most critical juncture of Plato's life.

Plato's unique perspective certainly filtered and composed Socrates' actual trial in light of his own concerns, but the historicity of Plato's *Apology of Socrates* (in contrast to the *Crito*) is particularly noteworthy; it had to stand up in a public context. Other accounts of Socrates' trial, those by Xenophon and Polycrates in particular, were probably circulating around the time Plato composed and "published" this dialogue. If Plato's account of the trial departed radically from what occurred there, its power to persuade readers of the innocence and virtue of Socrates would be undercut. The *Apology* probably coincides with historical reality to a far greater degree than do any of his

---

private discussion that took place between Socrates and Crito on the day before Socrates' death. However, Xenophon also testifies to an attempt by Socrates' friends to persuade him to escape (*Apology* 23). Crito was one of Socrates' good friends, and inasmuch as he was wealthy and could have bribed Socrates' captors, he could well have been among the plotters. Moreover, Plato most likely knew Crito. This suggests that the conversation between Socrates and the imaginary "Laws of Athens" in Plato's *Crito* probably reflects Plato's good understanding of the basic reasons for Socrates' refusal to escape. But this hardly means that it should be relied on for constructing a historically accurate picture of Socrates' views. For our purposes, therefore, Plato's *Apology of Socrates* provides the basic material for understanding the historical Socrates. See Guthrie, *A History of Greek Philosophy*, 4:93–94.

other dialogues, and Plato's account of the trial in the *Apology* is probably more accurate than competing versions.[135]

The Socrates of Plato's *Apology* surely sheds light on the historical Socrates, but the gap between Plato's transcript of the trial and a reportorial account means that Socrates' discourse in Plato's *Apology* needs to be understood in relation to Plato's dialogues as a whole.[136] In this light, the *Apology* counts as *Plato's* historical point of departure for his own philosophical quests, and especially for his dialogic treatment of Socrates. In particular, Plato's account of Socrates' defense highlights the relations and oppositions

135. The basic historical accuracy of Plato's *Apology of Socrates* is not a matter of major scholarly dispute. The best assessments of its historicity are R. Hackforth, *The Composition of Plato's Apology,* and W. K .C. Guthrie, *A History of Greek Philosophy,* 4:70–80. The former is more skeptical than the latter, as he finds many Platonic elements in the dialogue. But none of Hackforth's judgments of the Platonic aspects of the dialogue (not all of which I accept) undermines the arguments here. Nevertheless, the argument between those who find the Socrates of Plato's *Apology* a fundamentally accurate portrayal of the historical Socrates and those who find the Socrates in it as fictional as the Socrates who appears in other dialogues (some of whose dramatic dates postdate Socrates' death) has no determinate resolution. This debate went on for the whole of the twentieth century. (See the original debate between Burnet and Taylor, on the one hand, and Hackforth, on the other, during the first third of the century.) Recently, there has been a notable effort to establish the historical validity of the *Apology* (see Thomas C. Brickhouse and Nicholas D. Smith, *Socrates on Trial*). I do think, however, that these authors pay insufficient attention to how the *Apology* reflects Plato's artistry and substantive concerns.

Because Plato was present at Socrates' trial and Xenophon was not, his account of the trial in the *Apology of Socrates* is generally considered to be more trustworthy than Xenophon's *Apology of Socrates*. As a general rule, I refer to Xenophon's Socratic *logoi* primarily for either comparison with or supplementation to Plato's account but not for a definitive account of the historical Socrates. Xenophon was a much more partisan figure and conservative ideologue than Plato and more likely to embellish elitist tendencies in Socrates' character and thought. My view conforms to the prevailing consensus among classical scholars. See W. K. C. Guthrie, *Socrates,* 13–28, and Vlastos, "The Historical Socrates and Athenian Democracy." However, Leo Strauss takes Xenophon's account of Socrates to be the authoritative rendition of the historical Socrates. To Strauss, Xenophon is more reliable than Plato because the former was basically a "historian" interested in facts whereas the latter was a philosophical artist more concerned about ideas (see his *Socrates and Aristophanes,* 3–4).

136. Here are just two examples of how impossible it is to isolate neatly those parts of the dialogue that express the real Socrates and those that express Plato's peculiar temperament. Much of the language and concerns of the *Apology* appear as continuing themes throughout Plato's dialogues. Note the literary reinterpretation of the trial of Socrates in the first book of the *Republic,* which portrays a mock arrest of Socrates, from which he frees himself in the dialogue that follows, as opposed to the real arrest and trial, from which he could not escape. In the *Laws* (860–61), a phrase appears, "[N]o one does wrong willingly," which was notoriously associated with the historical Socrates. At the same time, in the *Republic* the dialogic Socrates articulates a theoretical system about which the historical Socrates could not have known, and no "Socrates" of any variety appears in the *Laws*.

of Socratic *logos* and conventional discourse, Socratic virtue and conventional politics, in relation to which Plato formulated his Socratic Problem and conceptualized the political art.[137]

I. THE ATHENIANS' INDICTMENT OF SOCRATES

The focus of Plato's *Apology of Socrates* is Socrates' defense at his trial against an indictment brought against him by three prominent Athenian politicians.[138] It articulates the opposition between Socrates and Athens.[139] Paraphrased by Socrates in the dialogue (24b), it officially read as follows: "This indictment and affidavit is sworn by Meletus, the son of Meletus of Pitthos, against Socrates, the son of Sophroniscus of Alopece. Socrates is guilty of refusing to recognize the gods recognized by the state and of introducing other divinities. He is also guilty of corrupting the youth. The penalty demanded is death."[140]

At first glance, Socrates' indictment might not seem to raise the issue of his (or Plato's) philosophical vocation in relation to Athenian democracy, for his religious beliefs and educational practices appear to be the source of contention. Moreover, it might seem odd that Socrates could be charged with criminal responsibility for the alleged offenses. In modernity, teachers are not held legally responsible for criminal actions of students that the latter justify by the former's teachings. But a closer look at these charges reveals their

137. The informal and formal charges against Socrates, and Socrates' response to them, illustrate the Problem's central aspects. The *Apology* reveals the historical problematic of virtue and the political art that Plato sought to solve in many of his other dialogues—preliminarily in the so-called aporetic dialogues and more positively in the *Republic, Statesman,* and *Laws.* In what follows, I do not try to differentiate between the historical Socrates at his trial and Plato's account. Although I agree that there is a gap between the two, for our purposes that gap can be ignored. In other words, what I take to be words and characteristics of the historical Socrates are probably at least partial functions of Plato's concerns and beliefs.

138. For a valuable recent effort to establish what actually happened at Socrates' trial, see Thomas C. Brickhouse and Nicholas D. Smith, *Socrates on Trial.*

139. Much of what follows derives from my "Socratic Citizenship." A related discussion of "the problem of Socrates and Athens" appears in Josiah Ober's *Political Dissent in Democratic Athens* (within a different interpretive frame).

140. Diogenes Laertius, *Lives of Eminent Philosophers* II.40. See also Xenophon's account in his *Memorabilia* I.1, which is less wordy, less complete, but possibly more accurate. There the indictment mentions "strange" divinities. The account of Socrates' indictment in Plato's *Apology* (24b) is approximate and does not claim to be exact. For the legal status of this kind of indictment, see Douglas M. MacDowell, *The Law in Classical Athens,* 56–58, 64, 200–202, and Todd, *The Shape of Athenian Law,* 99–102, 105–12.

philosophical and political significance, as well as the reason that Socrates might be judged to be responsible for violating Athenian *nomoi*—the sanctioned ethical norms, customs, and laws of Athenian society.

First, note the formulation of the "religious" charge. It refers to the gods "of the state." It indicates the deep connection between religious practices and Athenian *nomoi*.[141] To be sure, because the Athenians had no ecclesiastical hierarchy to contend with, ritual observance of their state-sanctioned religion did not function for them as Christianity and the Catholic Church did, say, for the English in the twelfth century. In Athens, there neither was nor could be any mortal conflict between a king and an archbishop. Yet, the religiosity of the Athenians contributed crucially to their solidarity as a people.[142] Furthermore, laws against impiety and atheism may well have been used to mount charges of treason against political opponents.[143] Earlier in the fifth century, the Athenians may have prosecuted Anaxagoras and Protagoras, two unusual intellectuals, for impiety.[144] At the very least, the conventions of pious behavior lay at the root of the Athenians' shared ethical principles, and ethical principles ultimately had political referents. For these Greeks, the virtues of piety and justice could not be sharply separated.[145]

Second, the charge against Socrates for corrupting the young evoked religious, moral, philosophical, and political connotations. Meletus's charge suggests that Socrates' corrupting influence stemmed at least from his unconventional religious beliefs, but his mode of philosophical conduct and teach-

---

141. On the complex meaning and associations of *nomoi*, see the work of Martin Ostwald, in particular, *Nomos and the Beginnings of the Athenian Democracy*, 20–54, and *From Popular Sovereignty to the Sovereignty of Law*, 89–108.

For a valuable diachronic study of the political character of Athenian religion, see Robert Parker, *Athenian Religion: A History*, esp. chap. 10. For a useful collection of articles on various dimensions of Greek religion, see P. E. Easterling and J. V. Muir, eds., *Greek Religion and Society*. For a comprehensive, traditional account, see Walter Burkert, *Greek Religion*.

142. Blair Campbell provides a useful treatment of the interdependence of religion and Athenian *nomoi* in "Constitutionalism, Rights, and Religion: The Athenian Example."

143. See Macdowell, *The Laws of Classical Athens*, 183–84, 197–201, and Todd, *The Shape of Athenian Law*, 311–12 and notes.

144. See Diogenes Laertius, *Lives* II.12 and IX.52; Plutarch, *Nikias* 23.4; Aristotle, fr. 67 (Rose). However, much doubt has been cast on the truth of this evidence. See K. R. Dover, "The Freedom of the Intellectual in Greek Society," 24ff, and the reference to Todd, *The Shape of Athenian Law*, in the previous note. For good general discussions of Anaxagoras and Protagoras, see W. K. C. Guthrie, *A History of Greek Philosophy*, 2:322–23, on the former, and Guthrie, *Socrates*, 263, on the latter.

145. Euthyphro's legal charges against his father for "murdering" one of their family's slaves was based in his view of the proper conception of piety. (See Plato's *Euthyphro* 4b–e.)

ings were also implied.[146] Moreover, the most significant and obvious examples of Socrates' allegedly corrupting influence were Alcibiades and Critias, political personages of the first order.[147] Finally, at the time of Socrates' trial, a general amnesty was in force, so that the legal dispensation of political grievances would have to appear in an outwardly apolitical form. For the Athenians, corruption became manifest in condemnable political practices, and vice versa. Although it might be hard to pinpoint, the political character of Socrates' indictment on overtly ethical and religious grounds must have been apparent to most Athenians—and certainly to his accusers.

Just as we must alter our conception of the relevant domain for "the political" in order to understand the full meaning of Socrates' "religious" crimes, so too is it important to be clear about what "responsibility" ordinarily signified for Athenians.[148] This requires that we know what would have passed for guilt in the minds of Socrates' accusers and jurors. The Athenians' criteria of guilt were not wholly legal in nature, or at least not legal in our sense. Because their conception of legality included conformity to everything signified by *nomoi*—legislative enactments, their constitutional heritage, and sanctioned social customs—guilt for violating such laws could be much more loosely defined than it is in contemporary Western courtrooms, where the line between political and legal charges is, or at least is supposed to be, firmly drawn.[149] As a result, Socrates' responsibility for his actions should not be assessed simply in terms of a specifiable set of acts by Socrates that materially affected identifiable individuals. One must refer to broader and more politi-

146. For useful recent accounts of the religiosity of the historical Socrates, see Robert Garland, *Introducing the New Gods,* chap. 7, and Parker, *Athenian Religion: A History,* chap. 9. For accounts of Socratic piety in Plato's dialogues, see Gregory Vlastos, *Socrates, Ironist and Moral Philosopher,* chap. 6, and Michael L. Morgan, *Platonic Piety: Philosophy and Ritual in Fourth-Century Athens,* chap. 1.

147. Xenophon, *Memorabilia* 1.2.12–16. On Socrates' relationship to Critias and Alcibiades, see Guthrie, *Socrates,* 298–304, and Vlastos, "The Historical Socrates and Athenian Democracy," 496. It should be recalled that the most notable legal charge and political objection against Alcibiades was that of impiety, for supposedly mutilating the Hermai. See Thucydides, *History of the Peloponnesian War* VI.27–29.

148. If we were to go along with A. W. H. Adkins, the Athenians had no conception of moral responsibility as we understand it. To be sure, they did not if, along with Adkins, we take Kantian moral responsibility as our standard. But insofar as we are not all Kantians now (if "we" ever were), this Kantian definition of responsibility need not constrain us. See A. W. H. Adkins, *Merit and Responsibility,* 2. For a valuable, thorough critique of Adkins's views on Greek morality or ethics, see Bernard Williams, *Shame and Necessity.*

149. See R. E. Allen, *Socrates and Legal Obligation,* 22–32.

cal criteria and evaluate the extent to which the basic beliefs and practices of Socrates' philosophical life violated the fundamental tenets of justice and good citizenship for the Athenian democracy. (A contemporary "legal" analogue for his indictment might be an impeachable offense according to the Constitution of the United States, committed by an ordinary citizen.)

This issue directs us to the charges of his first accusers, accusations that Socrates says are most responsible for prejudicing the jury against him and generating Meletus's indictment, for they refer more directly to Socrates' philosophical vocation. In Plato's *Apology*, Socrates puts them in formal terms: "Socrates is guilty of wrongdoing in that he busies himself studying things in the sky and below the earth; he makes the weaker into the stronger argument, and he teaches the same things to others."[150] As such, he is considered to be a "wise and clever man" or a "philosopher" (*Apology* 18b7, 23d4–5). These charges constitute the substance of Meletus's formal indictment, and Socrates devotes most of his *apologia* to rebutting these claims—principally by giving an account of his life, beliefs, and philosophical vocation.[151]

Rather than paraphrasing Socrates' autobiography in the manner that Plato presents it in the *Apology*, I present it here systematically, drawing mostly on it but on other sources as well to fill out Plato's account.[152] I emphasize two themes pertinent to Plato's conception of the political art: (1) the philosophical aspects of Socrates' vocation—in terms of both how he understood them and how they were understood by ordinary Athenians—and (2) Socrates' political actions and attitudes as an Athenian citizen.

150. *Apology* 19b4–c1; see *Apol.* 18b7–c1, 23d4–8. This translation, as with all others of Plato's *Apology*, is based on the translation of G. M. A. Grube. See Plato, *The Trial and Death of Socrates*. For the Greek, I have relied on the text and commentary of John Burnet, *Plato's Euthyphro, Apology of Socrates, and Crito*.

151. I say "most" because Socrates addresses most of his remarks to the jury and not to Meletus specifically. (See *Apology* 20c–23e, 28b–34b.) Moreover, Socrates' interrogations of Meletus about the impiety charge (26b–28a) and the corruption charge (24d–25b, 25d–26a) are equally applicable to the charges of his "first accusers."

152. This is not the approach followed by Leo Strauss when he discusses Plato's *Apology*. See Leo Strauss, *Studies in Platonic Philosophy*, 38–66. In this piece, Strauss follows his standard interpretive approach, which claims to derive an interpretation from the dialogue itself. In my view, this approach is no more viable than an economic policy governed by devotion to the "free market." Note the extent to which Strauss selectively includes "external" sources, such as Aristophanes and Xenophon, to fill out his own account of "the dialogue itself." Because the interpretive approach followed here seeks to be historically, as well as textually, sound, I try to remain true not only to the dramatic flow of the dialogue but to history as well.

About the early stages of Socrates' philosophizing we know very little. In Plato's *Apology,* Socrates' account of his activities mostly postdates receiving the message from the Delphic Oracle, transmitted by Chaerophon, that stimulated him to begin his questioning of fellow citizens about their knowledge and virtue. Before then, Socrates must have been known as something of a "wise man," for Chaerophon had gone to Delphi to ask the oracle if anyone was wiser than Socrates, to which the Pythian replied that no one was (*Apology* 21a4–7). But we do not know of what that "wisdom" consisted. We have Plato's report in the *Phaedo* (96a–99e) that Socrates in his youth was intrigued but ultimately disillusioned by the teachings of Anaxagoras, who was known for believing in the physical causation of all phenomena and their rule by a substantive "mind" as well as for the view that the sun is stone and the moon earth.[153] But such intellectual curiosity can hardly be the source of Socrates' reputation for Chaerophon.

We also do not know whether Socrates received the oracle's message before or after Aristophanes wrote the *Clouds* (first presented in 423), which was apparently an important cause of Socrates' long-standing unpopularity among the Athenians.[154] So what we are mostly left with is Socrates' account of his conduct after he began his "service to the god" that was stimulated by Chaerophon's message from the oracle.[155] The nature of that conduct may be called "philosophical," for Socrates loved pursuing wisdom, but its character needs to be clarified, especially in the midst of other contemporary claimants to the title of "wise man," such as other Sophists.

Socrates was hardly the first Athenian "wise man." Solon, founder of the constitutional framework in which Athenian democracy developed and poet of the Athenian mind, belonged to a famous group of Greek "sages" (*sophoi*) who lived at the end of the seventh century B.C.[156] However, Solon was one of

---

153. *Apology* 26d4–5. On Anaxagoras, see his fragments in Diels-Krantz (B11–14) and Diogenes Laertius, *Lives of the Eminent Philosophers* II.8.

154. In the play, Aristophanes depicts a character by the name of Socrates who holds Anaxagorean beliefs and runs a comical "Thinkery" (*Phrontisterion*). See Aristophanes, *Clouds,* abridged ed., ed., with intro. and commentary by K. J. Dover (London: Oxford University Press, 1970), line 94. This and other translations of the *Clouds* are drawn from those of Alan H. Somerstein, which appear in Aristophanes, *Lysistrata, The Acharnians, The Clouds,* trans. with an intro. by Alan H. Somerstein (Penguin, 1973).

155. In Plato's *Apology,* Socrates frequently refers to this "service" in describing his philosophical vocation (22a, 23c, 29d, 30a, 33c, 37e).

156. See W. K. C. Guthrie, *The Sophists,* 27–29.

a kind; he did not generate a tradition of politically engaged and philosophically minded Athenians. During the sixth century B.C., philosophical thought evolved along lines drawn by more speculative natural philosophers. Although their categories of understanding resonated with political forms of thought and many of them made sundry remarks about ethics and law, philosophers from Anaximander to Heraclitus did not concentrate their inquiring gaze on the nature and well-being of citizenship and the *polis*.[157] It was not until Kleisthenes restructured the Athenian *politeia* and the Athenians consolidated democracy during the first half of the fifth century that philosophical inquiry again became political.[158]

The chief practitioners of such "political" philosophy by the mid-fifth century were Anaxagoras, in his position as adviser to Pericles, and Protagoras of Abdera, also an adviser to Pericles as well as a prominent Sophist. Sophists came from Ionia and Italy to Athens to teach a variety of forms of knowledge as skills (*technai*) for a fee. The teaching specialty of Protagoras— who was probably the most prominent, perhaps the most respected, and certainly the wealthiest Sophist—involved a *techne* of teaching young men a *techne* for becoming good citizens and acquiring *arete*, as understood in the Athenian *nomoi*. Apparently, Anaxagoras had no similar educational goals. Yet both of these intellectuals came into conflict with Athenian political norms. Given the Athenians' history of suspicion toward such politically involved thinkers, it should not have been surprising that Socrates, who was associated with Anaxagoras and the Sophists in the *Clouds,* also tested the limits of Athenian toleration.

But Socrates did not place himself in the same category as previous philosophical victims. In his speech to the Athenian jury recorded in Plato's *Apology,* Socrates made clear how his philosophical vocation differed from that of both Anaxagoras and the Sophists. One could say that Socrates' trouble with ordinary Athenians stemmed from their inability to distinguish what he was doing from what they were doing, but that does not answer the question of why Socrates might have been associated with them or what was actually dis-

---

157. These remarks should not diminish the impact of the insightful work by Gregory Vlastos and Jean-Pierre Vernant on the political character of "pre-Socratic" thought. See Vlastos's "Equality and Justice in Early Greek Cosmology," and Vernant's *The Origins of Greek Thought,* esp. 119–29, and idem, *Myth and Thought Among the Greeks,* 190–211.

158. See Vernant, *Myth and Thought Among the Greeks,* 212–34, and G. E. R. Lloyd, *Magic, Reason, and Experience,* 240–67.

turbing in Socrates' relation to the established norms of Athenian democracy. It is necessary to examine the form and substance of the Socratic *elenchus*, in order to evaluate whether the Athenians' association of Socrates with Anaxagoras or the Sophists was reasonable and why that would work in Athens to condemn Socrates' quest for wisdom and virtue.

2. THE PHILOSOPHY AND POLITICS OF THE SOCRATIC *Elenchus*

To orient our analysis of Socrates' method of *elenchus*, we may begin with a rough definition of it. A suitable one appears in Richard Robinson's classic, if imperfect, book on the logic of Plato's early dialogues: "'Elenchus' in the wider sense means examining a person with regard to a statement he has made, by putting to him questions calling for further statements, in the hope that they will determine the meaning and truth-value of his first statement. Most often the truth-value expected is falsehood; and so 'elenchus' in the narrower sense is a form of cross-examination or refutation."[159] Vlastos has called the Socratic *elenchus* "a method of investigation" whose merit is assumed rather than proved.[160]

Much has been written about the Socratic *elenchus*.[161] Yet most of it has not confined itself to the analysis of Plato's *Apology* but rather has sought to develop a model of it from Plato's early dialogues, the so-called Socratic dialogues. Because our interpretive rules foreclose this mode of analysis—it inextricably conflates the historical Socrates with arguments that form central parts of major Platonic dialogues—we mostly restrict the basis for our understanding of Socrates' *elenchus* to the material offered by Plato's *Apology*. Fortunately, this does not unduly constrict our basis, for there, as in other Socratic dialogues, Socrates demonstrates his mastery of a verbal art or skill. As

---

159. Richard Robinson, *Plato's Earlier Dialectic*, 7.

160. Gregory Vlastos, "The Socratic *Elenchus*," 27–28. Compare Vlastos's definition of *elenchus* (30–31) with Robinson's. It assumes the integrity of Socrates' analysis throughout Plato's early dialogues, as if Socrates' method does not—I think it does—change the terms of the debate in Socrates' favor as he uses it.

161. In addition to the good work by Robinson and Vlastos, see the comments by Norman Gulley, *The Philosophy of Socrates*, 37–62, and Trevor J. Saunders, in his introduction to Plato, *Early Socratic Dialogues*, 29–32. Recent discussions of the Socratic *elenchus*, along with a valuable bibliography, appear in Hugh H. Benson, ed., *Essays on the Philosophy of Socrates*.

a result, although the characteristics of Socrates' discursive method differentiate it from conventional *technai* and "Socrates" did not see his own critical approach to discursive understanding as a *techne,* I paradoxically refer to the Socratic method of *elenchus* in what follows as a *techne.*[162]

The display of this *techne* indicates why Socrates' intellectual sting would hurt democratic Athenians. Because Socrates did not teach any doctrine, did not possess, as other Sophists claimed they did, a *techne* of wisdom, the meaning of his *techne* surfaces only negatively, namely through his use of the notion of *techne* as a critical device and a model for knowledge and virtue. In the Athenian culture of the classical age, *techne* served primarily as a descriptive term that covered systematic, practical activities which were informed by implicit or explicit norms that could be passed on by teaching. They could be undertaken manually, such as in carpentry, or mentally, such as in geometry, grammar, or rhetoric. They could have artistic, or worldly, or distinctively human aims, because poetry, navigation, and medicine were all considered to be *technai.*[163] Some could be reduced to instructional handbooks, which were also known as *technai.*[164] *Technai* occupied *particular* domains of knowledge and experience.[165]

Although the notion of a *techne* may well have represented a kind of practical intelligence that symbolized the peculiar talents of Athenians, it did not serve as a *general* criterion for social knowledge or virtue, at least not in its form as a specialized, practical expertise. Even Protagoras, who was known for teaching a *techne* of *arete*—possibly the *politike techne* for citizens and statesmen—relied for his standard of knowledge on that which was implicit

162. The Socrates of Plato's *Apology* denies that he has any *techne* of *arete* to teach (20a–c), whereas Xenophon identifies a distinctive "art of words," or *technai logon,* with central features of the Socratic *elenchus.* See Xenophon, *Memorabilia* I.ii.31, 34.

163. *Odyssey* XLII.382–86, XIX.135; Hippocrates, *On Ancient Medicine* and *De Arte;* Plato, *Hippias Major* 285c–e.

164. See George A. Kennedy, *The Art of Persuasion in Greece,* 54–62, and W. K. C. Guthrie, *A History of Greek Philosophy,* 3:44–45.

165. For general accounts of the practical meaning of a *techne* in the fifth century, see F. Heinimann, "Eine vorplatonische Theorie der *Techne*"; O'Brien, *Socratic Paradoxes and the Greek Mind,* 53–54, 57; Guthrie, *A History of Greek Philosophy,* 3:115, n. 3; E. R. Dodds, *The Ancient Concept of Progress,* 11. The most complete account of the pre-Platonic meaning of *techne* appears in David Roochnik's *Of Art and Wisdom: Plato's Understanding of Techne,* 17–88. For a thorough account of the various conceptions of *techne* in ancient Greek thought in terms of their relation to claims to knowledge, see James Allen, "Failure and Expertise in the Ancient Conception of Art," in Tamara Horowitz and Allen I. Janis, eds., *Scientific Failure,* 81–108.

in Athenian *nomoi*.[166] Ultimately he was a high-minded apologist for the conventions of Athenian society. He never offered a means for their critical evaluation, as Socrates sought to do.[167] By contrast, in carrying out his philosophical vocation, Socrates used the notion of a *techne* as a critical standard for evaluating the wisdom and virtue of his fellow citizens. The paradoxical nature of Socratic citizenship can be seen in how his use of it forged genuinely new advances in critical social reasoning but also—and this was not an entirely necessary byproduct—served to undermine the ethical and political norms of Athenian democracy. On the one hand, the criteria of knowledge assumed by the *techne* of his *elenchus* suggest that its skillful exercise is a necessary condition for the knowledge, wisdom, and virtue that constitute the public values of the Athenian *polis*. On the other, this unique *techne* is practiced only by Socrates. Moreover, Socrates' practice of it prevents him from fully participating in the public life of the *polis* and expresses an opposition between the pursuit of virtue according to Socrates and according to the ethics of Athenian democracy.

In Plato's *Apology of Socrates*, Socrates' *elenchus* appears in two modes—indirectly, when Socrates recounts his past practice of it, and directly, when he interrogates Meletus. In his intellectual autobiography, Socrates describes how he questioned first Athenian politicians, and then poets, the writers of tragedies and dithyrambs, and craftsmen about their knowledge of wisdom and virtue. As a result of his investigations, Socrates came to believe that neither the politicians, poets, nor dramatists possessed anything at all like knowledge. The craftsmen, by contrast, knew something, namely, how to practice their own trade. However, when it came to knowing anything out-

---

166. If one took Plato's *Crito* as a reliable account of actual Socratic views, which I do not, one might say that Socrates' obedience to "the laws of Athens" in that dialogue indicates a similar respect for *nomoi*. However, Socrates, unlike Protagoras, did not rely on these *nomoi* as a standard for critical evaluation; rather, he referred to them as a basic consideration in a more comprehensive justification of his refusal to break out of jail and flee from Athens.

167. This view does not comport with the view of Protagoras as a philosopher of natural law, which is articulated in the otherwise illuminating book by Dirk Loenen, *Protagoras and the Greek Community*. His interpretation cannot be derived from Plato's *Protagoras* and *Theaetetus*, the most extensive accounts we have of Protagoras's views, and certainly not from the fragments of his writings that remain—one of which (D–K, Fr. 1) sets forth the core teaching of humanistic relativism and another of which (Diels-Kranz, Fr. 3) announces his theological agnosticism. For more on the historical Protagoras and Plato's *Protagoras*, see Chapter 3, Section C, below.

side their sphere of expertise, their ignorance matched that of the others. What had Socrates found to be lacking in the claims of these persons to knowledge and virtue? The answer to this question partially comes into view during Socrates' direct questioning of Meletus, which deals both with the charge of corrupting the young (24d–26a) and with the charge of impiety (26b–28a).

Socrates deals with the issue of corruption in two stages. In the first, he relies on a fundamental tenet of Socratic and Platonic thought, the model of knowledge of a *techne* for knowledge of all kinds. Knowledge of a *techne* for Athenians tended to be specialized, available to a few rather than to citizens generally (or "the many"). The major exception to the rule was the *techne* of politics or political virtue—a skill that the Athenians as a whole reputedly possessed.[168] In his interchange with Meletus, Socrates elicited this ordinary view, for Meletus answered Socrates' question about who taught the Athenians *arete* by citing the laws, the assembly, the courts, the council, and public opinion (24e–25a). This democratic view roughly conforms to that put forth by Protagoras in Plato's dialogue by the same name.[169] Indeed, a distinguishing mark of Athenian democracy was the sense that the citizenry, through their public institutions and *nomoi,* taught themselves and one another the arts of social ethics and politics. Socrates scornfully rejected this view by suggesting that no exception to the model of a specialized *techne* for the knowledge of virtue existed. Just as "one" or "a few" know and "the many" do not when it comes to, for instance, horse training—only the horse-trainers know the art—so, too, when it comes to educating the young "the few" are the ones who know how to educate and improve them (25b). Therefore, by implication, "the many," instead of Socrates, become the prime suspects for corrupting the young—a highly antagonistic argument in this highly democratic context.

Socrates now shifted tack in order to discuss the charge of corrupting the young. Socrates believed that the charge could hold up only if it could be shown that Socrates intended to corrupt the young. Although this assumption stands somewhat at odds with the Athenian tendency to care more about results than intentions when it comes to assigning moral blame, Meletus did not object to it because he believed that Socrates "deliberately" or "willingly"

---

168. Thucydides, *History of the Peloponnesian War* 1.70–71, II.42.
169. Plato, *Protagoras* 322d–323a, 326c–328c.

corrupted the young (25d).[170] Socrates disputed this charge simply by asserting the innocence of his intentions. Here his argument is not very "elenchic."

Socrates' defense against the impiety charge is slightly more elenchic because he tried to show that the charge was self-contradictory.[171] Meletus admitted that Socrates believed in divine activities. Socrates then defined these beliefs as tantamount to a belief in the activities of divinities, who are either gods or children of gods. Meletus accepted this definitional and conceptual equivalence, even though he had charged Socrates with not believing in gods. What Socrates has done resembles what occurs in many of the so-called Socratic dialogues of Plato. After establishing a common ground of agreement with his interlocutors, Socrates develops a quasi-deductive argument that leads to a contradiction with another belief that his interlocutor had held.

On what does the logic of Socrates' arguments depend? Socrates' *techne* possesses critical standards that give his *elenchus* conceptual power. But the extent to which this *techne* possesses power in discourse is culturally and politically problematic, for it assumes the capacity of Socrates' discursive art to reflect or grasp Athenian reality. The power of this *techne* cannot be obvious or very potent because it counters the intellectual norms—the conceptual reality or civic ideology—that constitutes the ethical and political views of the individuals he interrogates. But the extent to which Socrates' *techne* does have any power suggests that Socrates has a claim to understanding the nature of things that other Athenians do not have. Insofar as his subjects saw themselves as upholding conventional social, intellectual, and ethical norms and acknowledged the power of Socrates' *techne,* they could easily have seen Socrates as a threat to their *nomoi,* their ethical and political world as a whole.

The practical political corollaries to Socrates' philosophizing appear in his account of his involvement in the workings of Athenian democracy. They are just as troubling as the philosophical practice of the *elenchus,* because Socrates' practical devotion to it prevents him from fully participating in the public life of the *polis* and generates an opposition between the pursuit of virtue according to Socrates or according to the ethics of Athenian democracy.

In Socrates' political autobiography, the outward signs of his public life were unremarkable, as far as we can tell, for his first sixty years. Insofar as his father was a craftsman, Socrates' earlier years would have been spent acquir-

---

170. See A. W. H. Adkins, *Merit and Responsibility.*
171. See Gulley, *The Philosophy of Socrates,* 38–39.

ing his father's skills and absorbing Athenian culture. When the Peloponnesian War broke out, he served in the Athenian army and fought bravely at Delium, in 424, when he was 45.[172] But this normality only barely disguised Socrates' unique, marginal status in the Athenian *polis:* He was in it but not of it. Socrates described this marginality in Plato's *Apology* by recounting the history of his engagement in the public life of the Athenian democracy.

The most obvious evidence of this was his present appearance before the Athenian court. In this institutionalized public setting, Socrates said that he was a stranger (17d). Even though he was being very much prosecuted as a citizen, Socrates portrayed himself as an outsider, and he made this clear in describing his attitude toward the court. Although he had not been chosen (by lot) in the past to serve on the court, it seems that Socrates would not have wanted to serve if he had been, for he disliked the court's procedure. To him, the time for argument was foreshortened—especially in contrast to the more private realm of conversation with which he was comfortable—and its guidelines for a successful argument discouraged simple, truthful speech (*Apology* 17a–18a, 18c–19a). More evident of his anomalous political attitudes, however, was his deliberate decision to avoid the other voluntarily constituted Athenian political body—the assembly. He believed that active participation in the assembly contradicted the pursuit of virtue and that outspoken fidelity to his beliefs in its arena would jeopardize his life (31a–32a).

As proof of this, he cited two events that occurred relatively late in his life. In 406, during the years of the restored democracy, Socrates served on the council, as a result of his tribe's having been selected by lot to preside in it. His first memorable political encounter occurred at this time, when he refused to go along with the council's decision to present ten Athenian generals for trial in the assembly (as a result of their not having rescued the Athenian survivors of the battle of Arginusae, the last Athenian victory of the war). The second arose after the tyrannical, antidemocratic Thirty had come to power. They asked him, and he answered by refusing, to arrest Leon of Salamis for execution. These events demonstrated how difficult it was for a publicly involved Socrates to conform easily to extant political practices. But it is important to keep in mind that both occurred long after Socrates had decided to stay away from the assembly. In addition, each was an unusual and infamous act by the existing authorities, some of whom saw themselves as enemies of traditional

172. Plato, *Laches* 181b, 188e–189b, and *Symposium* 221a.

Athenian *nomoi*. These events reinforced—but did not precipitate—his antipathy toward Athenian politics.[173]

Socrates had carved out a unique political position for himself. By bucking the majority on the council and refusing to submit to the dictates of the Thirty, Socrates upheld a standard of justice and public action that did not automatically support the authority of institutionalized power. He exemplified this standard in deeds. At the same time, he never suggested that the assembly or the courts were socially dispensable or that they ought to be reformed in a more oligarchic direction. And his documented associations with political figures do not place him in an oligarchic camp.[174] This is why the charge that Socrates was a clever right-wing conservative is far-fetched.[175] But because he did not clearly articulate his own standard of justice (to the extent that he had one) in words, the relation of his public posture to Athenian *nomoi* was not publicly clear.

What Socrates was clear about was his antagonism toward many public practices, institutions, and values. Socrates challenged the Athenians' institution of political deliberation as the best means to good public action by the Athenian citizenry. He believed that private deliberation was better at reaching the truths of virtue and generating beneficial political action. And yet full citizenship in Athens—almost by definition—included active participation in the public life of the city, and standard attributions of *arete* referred to individual excellence in this realm.[176] Surely, many adult male Athenian citizens

173. Hackforth, *The Composition of Plato's* Apology, 117–28, makes the interesting argument that Socrates' dislike of the political arena, as voiced in Plato's *Apology,* more nearly reflects Plato's, rather than Socrates', revulsion, because of the parallels among *Apology* 31c–32d, *Republic* 496b–d, and *Seventh Letter* 324b–326b. Hackforth is right to point out that Plato's antidemocratic sentiments were stronger than those of Socrates and may have affected his treatment of Socrates' political attitudes in the *Apology;* however, Socrates was probably in some political hot water before 406, if only because of his reputation as reflected and/or promoted by Aristophanes.

174. See Vlastos, "The Historical Socrates and Athenian Democracy," 511–12.

175. The most interesting recent attempt to anathematize Socrates on such grounds is Ellen Meiksins Wood and Neal Wood, *Class Ideology and Ancient Political Theory,* chap. 3 passim. This view reappears in the context of their critique of Vlastos's more democratic Socrates, "Socrates and Democracy: A Reply to Gregory Vlastos." A misguided rendition of Socrates as an oligarchic sympathizer appears in I. F. Stone, *The Trial of Socrates.*

176. See the funeral oration by Pericles in Thucydides, *History of the Peloponnesian War* II.40; Democritus, fr. 157 (D–K, 7th ed.); *Anonymous Iamblichi* fr. 3 (D–K). See A. T. Cole, "The *Anonymous Iamblichi* and His Place in Greek Political Theory," particularly 143; A. W. H. Adkins, *Merit and Responsibility,* 206–8 and chaps. x–xii passim.

had only a minimal interest in public affairs. But the interdependence of their lives with the fate of their *polis* as determined by the assembly and courts typically ensured more than token involvement by most citizens in public business.[177] And public esteem naturally focused on those citizens who performed that business particularly well. In Pericles' eulogy of Athens as recorded by Thucydides, citizens who did not participate in the public affairs of the *polis* were considered useless, a very damning ascription.[178] Socrates' conception of virtuous and just behavior therefore directly contravened the standard ethical ranking of behavior by the Athenians.

But even so, these attitudes were not in and of themselves sufficient to incite major conflict between Socrates' vocation and the Athenians' standards of justice. This arose only with Socrates' obedience to his *daimon* and his unique pursuit of wisdom in the company of his fellow citizens. After having avidly studied the mechanisms of nature according to the teachings of Anaxagoras, Socrates found this pursuit to lead nowhere, so he abandoned it (at what age is unclear) for an interest in more ethical matters.[179] Socrates' turn toward "human affairs" constituted, for Aristotle and Hellenistic authors in particular, a pivotal turning point in the history of philosophy.[180] The message from the Delphic Oracle—that no one was wiser than Socrates—could have only hastened this transformation of Socrates' intellectual concerns.[181] Because Socrates knew that he was not wise, he felt impelled to seek out the true meaning of the oracle's statement by asking those who were reputed to be wise about the nature of their wisdom. (Why this was the most appropriate reaction to receiving the oracle's message is not clear. Socrates might well have sorted out the nature of his knowledge and understanding without questioning public figures in the *agora*. But it seems that his knowledge was so negative that it could guide him only if he discussed with reputable others the nature of their knowledge and understanding.[182])

177. See M. I. Finley, *Politics in the Ancient World*, 70–84.

178. Thucydides, II.40.2.

179. Plato, *Phaedo* 98a, d–e.

180. Guthrie, *Socrates*, 97–99. However, if one was less hostile to the Sophists, it might seem that this turning was initiated as much or more by the older Sophist, Protagoras of Abdera.

181. The actual role played by the oracle in motivating Socrates' mission is subject to some dispute. See Hackforth, *The Composition of Plato's* Apology, 88–95.

182. See Hackforth, *The Composition of Plato's* Apology, 89–92, and Guthrie, *Socrates*, 85–89, for reasonable interpretations of Socrates' reaction to the Delphic Oracle. For insightful observations about the oddity of Socrates' reaction, see Ober, *Political Dissent in Democratic Athens*, 173, n. 33.

Subsequently, the nature of his wisdom, "human wisdom, perhaps," became clear. In relation to others, who seemed to be possessed by false conceits of wisdom, he found himself to be wiser, "to this small extent, that I do not think I know what I do not know" (*Apology* 21d). Such "wisdom" required interpretation for its practical application, because Socrates' *daimon,* which intervened when he was about to do something wrong, was never a source of positive guidance (40aff, 41d). Thus the practice of Socratic wisdom manifested itself in the reasoning of the Socratic *elenchus* as an authoritative, albeit negative, *techne.*[183] And indeed it was the exercise of this reason as a *techne* through the years that most alienated the Athenian public and, in Socrates' view, principally contributed to his ultimate indictment.

As I have discussed, the root of the fissure that erupted between Socrates and democratic Athens was the problematic character of Socratic citizenship. But in disliking Socrates, the Athenians felt more than discomfort caused by criticism. In addition to providing a haunting critical conscience of the *polis,* serving as a gadfly who aroused citizens from intellectual complacency, Socrates affirmed certain values. In so doing, Socrates' verbal ambling signified more than stinging questions. It suggested, albeit incompletely, an alternative way of life to the prevailing modes of thought and action in democratic Athens.

By combining his use of *techne* as a tool of conceptual critique with his belief in both the superiority of personal dialogue as the foundation of public truth and the sanctity and interdependence of virtue, justice, and the soul, Socrates promoted cultural anomalies. The incompleteness of his posture stemmed from Socrates' inability or unwillingness to offer a coherent political theory that addressed the activities of ordinary citizenship and statesmanship and could replace the prevailing conceptual and political norms, whose limitations he had so trenchantly exposed.[184] (Were Socrates' political views less incomplete, the character of his citizenship could well have been less open to the harsh interpretation given to it by the Athenian democracy, but this is speculation.) Nevertheless, Socratic citizenship possessed a coherence all its own, one that Socrates summarized in his *apologia* before the Athenian court.

183. Xenophon, *Apology* 12. Compare Xenophon's *Memorabilia* 4.8.6, and Plato, *Alcibiades I* 124c.

184. This is why Richard Kraut's frequent references to a Socratic "political theory" are vastly overstated. See Kraut, *Socrates and the State,* 1–3, 24. My view receives support in Vlastos, "The Historical Socrates and Athenian Democracy," 508–9, and his review of Kraut's book in the *Times Literary Supplement,* 24 August 1984.

3. THE ART OF SOCRATIC CITIZENSHIP

In his speech to the Athenian jury, Socrates not only described and exhibited his *elenchus*. He presented his primary and long-held beliefs about the central values of human life. They constituted the core of Socrates' teaching, the core that remained after he finished his negative critiques, and the essence of his affirmative views of citizenship. They made up the image of Socrates by which he wished to be remembered. For analytical purposes, these beliefs may be somewhat artificially divided into three domains: philosophical, ethical, and political. We have interpreted them in our account of the Socratic *elenchus,* but they have yet to be fit into a whole. Summarized, they include a *philosophical* belief in the critical authority of an art of discourse (a *techne* of *logon*), as exercised in interpersonal dialogue, over and above conventional opinion, particularly as it is expressed in the public domain, as the basis for knowledge and virtue; an *ethical* belief in the supreme importance of the soul and its care over the body and its pleasures; and a *political* belief that demonstrated affection and respect for the Athenian *polis* while it questioned crucial conceptual principles and institutional pillars of its democratic structure. Together, these beliefs constitute the art of Socratic citizenship.

The first step in understanding this art is to note its nature as a *techne* of social practice, and not as a type of politics, philosophy, or theory. This is to emphasize its unique form, namely as exemplar. In not wanting to transpose his art into writing, Socrates surely sought to prevent it from being reduced to fixed rules or formulae for thought or action. Consequently, he defined his art orally and contextually, amid dialogic interaction with his fellow citizens. In contrast to the arts of the other Sophists, which were often encoded in written handbooks, Socrates prevented both the ossification of his teachings and their learned misreadings and misappropriations by professional literary critics. However, Socrates, by this method, did not refuse to give form to his example. He controlled the fluidity of his argument by clear discursive guidelines and linked it to certain beliefs, all of which made plausible Xenophon's association of Socrates' name with a distinctive *techne logon.* Socrates used this *techne* in unpatterned practical engagements.[185]

185. It obviously was a *techne* of an unusual sort. Unlike other *technai,* whose products were determinately governed by specifiable norms, Socrates' *techne* did not aim to be productive in the ordinary sense. That is why he could plausibly deny being a teacher. His *techne* produced no predictable products, and its use-value could not be readily translated into any socially recognizable currency. This is also why Xenophon's portrayal of Socrates as a counselor of practi-

It might seem that what Socrates had developed was a new epistemology, but that view would subordinate Socrates' *elenchic* practice to a theoretical approach, and Socrates most decidedly did not possess a "theory" of knowledge. Nor did he exercise his *elenchus* to advance a "theory."[186] It distorts Socrates' art to reduce its essence to a conceptual technique, a form of ethical instrumentalism, wherein knowledge is a *techne,* understood as an instrument or tool that produces virtue.[187] By its very nature, Socrates' art served the purpose of elevating the power and authority of ideas and critical intelligence as bases for human activity. Correlatively, it promoted the value of immaterial reality—the things of the soul, which constitute the *telos* of *arete* for Socrates

cal advice must be misleading; it cannot be reconciled with Socrates' view that he did not impart discrete teachings (*Apology* 19d–20c). (See Xenophon's Socratic writings, especially the *Memorabilia* and *Oeconomicus.*) For these reasons, it may seem inappropriate to categorize Socrates' *elenchus* as a *techne* at all. But the *elenchus* possessed a clear form and achieved a clear purpose. It was designed to demonstrate a new kind of critical intelligence about what counts as knowledge and virtue and the way to go about acquiring them, even if itself could not produce knowledge or virtue.

186. The point here is more than semantic. It can be illustrated by what Plato's *Apology* tells us about Socrates' use of "ideas." In that dialogue, Socrates finds no occasion to employ the words *eidos, idea,* or *paradeigma,* the Greek words that are typically translated as "form," "idea," and "model." Of course, the occasion of the trial may not have called for the use of those words, because the subject was more Socrates' vocation and his beliefs about virtue than his criteria of knowledge. But even in the *Euthyphro,* a dialogue that Plato probably wrote very early in his literary life, which involves the use of such terms, *idea* and *eidos* are used to add power and authority primarily to Socrates' definitions and *elenchus* rather than to any second-order beliefs or methods that establish first-order truths (*Euthyphro* 5d, 6d–e). Aristotle would agree. See his *Metaphysics* 987b1–3, 1087b15–32. This view receives support from professional critics of the *Euthyphro,* who nonetheless persist in attributing to such views the quality of a "theory." For a good example, see R. E. Allen, *Plato's 'Euthyphro' and the Earlier Theory of Forms.* It is not supported by those who hold to expansive views of what counts as Socratic. Both Terence Irwin and Richard Kraut draw on all of Plato's earlier dialogues, up to and including the *Gorgias,* for their characterization of Socratic views. Because each tries to find a philosophically consistent "Socratic" position articulated in those dialogues, it is not surprising that both assign to Socrates a particular "moral theory" or "political theory." See Irwin, *Plato's Moral Theory,* and Kraut, *Socrates and the State.*

One of the fine aspects of Versenyi's book on Socrates, *Socratic Humanism,* is how the author interprets Socrates mostly according to the thematic contours provided by Socrates as a socially engaged dialectician rather than according to those of twentieth-century philosophy. (This is true despite the Christian existentialism that colors the author's overall approach to understanding Socrates.)

187. Irwin, *Plato's Moral Theory,* 6–7, 71–75. To ignore the social, oral, and interactive character of Socrates' philosophical vocation and the beliefs he holds for the sake of logical parsimony eases the way for a contemporary analytical discussion of Socratic thought at the expense of its uniquely historical and Socratic aspects. "Socrates" becomes a modern, philosophical fiction.

(*Apology* 31b)—over material reality—the things of the body, for the authority of reason depended on its power to control the desires of the body (*Apology* 36b). The exercise of any *techne* involved the control of the producer over the material on which he worked for the sake of creating a good product. With respect to *logoi*, the exercise of the Socratic *techne* meant the control of reason over the determination of meaning. With respect to the human person, it meant the control of the mind or soul over the body.

Socrates' political niche signified skepticism of, if not antagonism to, the major political institutions and the behavior of the people who direct them, yet loyalty to the city.[188] This distinction could hold on the margin, in terms of his opposition to the illegal actions of the council and the tyrannical actions of the Thirty. But insofar as it derives from Socrates' hostility to the political power of the *demos* and skepticism about its virtue, the political coherence of this creed as that of a loyal Athenian citizen becomes difficult to maintain. Socrates' belief that it is never just to disobey a superior, whether god or man, is not problematic if "god" and "man" agree. Socrates believes they do, which is why service to his god entails for him service to his city and why he believes that if jurors judge according to the law, he will be found innocent (35c). But what if "god" and "man" conflict, as his pursuit of philosophy conflicted with the majority's interpretation of the laws of Athens? What if "staying at one's post" requires continued obedience to unjust commanders, as would have been the case if Socrates had followed the orders of the Thirty, or indicates stubbornness rather than courage? To be justified, these practices require argumentative support. But his disdain for the many and the institutionalized political practices of Athens suggests that in actuality Socrates and most Athenians importantly disagreed. There is a gap between Socratic *logoi* and Athens, between Socratic virtue or moral practice and Athenian—perhaps any—practical politics. To some extent, Socrates recognized this already; it explains his refusal to participate in the city's public life, while still obeying its laws. But the question then becomes What is the relation of these laws to the public institutions of the city, when he views those who pass the laws and run the city with such disdain?

The *Apology* frames these questions posed by Socrates' trial and punishment, but it does not answer them. The *Crito* may constitute Plato's first effort to

---

188. It is a position that Plato assigns to him in the *Crito,* by arguing his belief in the justice of the "laws" of Athens, if not the individuals who act in their name.

do so. In addition, the *Crito* provides a crucial source for the only other teaching that is widely attributed to the historical Socrates—the belief that, in order to protect the purity and well-being of the soul, one ought never to do wrong.[189] In the *Crito*, Plato has Socrates say that he has held this belief for a very long time. And Socrates demands that it serve as the basis for any constructive deliberations between Crito and himself over the issue of whether Socrates could justifiably break out of jail and flee from Athens. The argument of the dialogue offers Plato's literary extrapolation of what might have justified this refusal, what it was about Socratic virtue that would entail devotion to the Athenian laws, institutional procedures, and decisions that resulted in his execution. It provides discursive means for reconciling in *logos* Socratic virtue and the Athenian political order.

The constructive argument of the dialogue depends on the acceptance of the belief that Socrates affirms in his discussion with Crito (49d): "[N]either to do wrong or to return a wrong (*antadikein*) is ever right, not even to injure in return for an injury received." For the purpose of understanding the art of Socratic citizenship, this belief is, perhaps, the most significant, because it constitutes a Socratic first principle of social relationships, one that is incompatible with conventional political relationships. It may serve as a critical ideal for interpersonal relationships, but it cannot be reconciled with the requirements of Athenian (or any other) political life. One need not agree with Weber that the essence of a state consists in its monopoly of the legitimate use of violence, or with Mao that political power comes out of the barrel of a gun, to recognize that maintaining the security of a political community may require the official use of injurious force.

It is not clear that Socrates recognized this belief as being so radically antipolitical. For one, by agreeing to conform to the procedures of his trial and execution, Socrates recognizes (at least) the procedural justice of Athenian law. For another, he fought in the Athenian army (although this may be discounted because of the typical Athenian belief that a different code of ethics applies to dealings with outsiders). And in the *Apology* he expresses much care and concern for the Athenian *polis*, to the point of saying that his vocation constitutes a profound "service" to the *polis* and that, unlike many citi-

189. Socrates does not expressly articulate this principle in Plato's *Apology*, but it is clearly consistent with his unwillingness to participate in the debates of the assembly or to tolerate the indictment of the ten generals or to arrest Leon of Salamis, as well as his statements that neither Meletus nor Anytus can harm him and his only concern is to prevent the jury from wrongdoing (*Apology* 30c–d).

zens, he cares less for "the things of the *polis*" than he does for "the *polis* itself" (*Apology* 30a, 30e, 36c).

This is not the voice of a Platonic idealist speaking about the *polis* as it is constituted in an individual's soul (for example, *Republic* 591a, 592a–b), for Socrates' life history testifies to his affection for the basic laws and customs of Athens. But although Socrates in Plato's *Apology of Socrates* argues that his life as a citizen exemplified virtue, that virtue, were it imitated by his fellow citizens, would undermine their skills as ordinary political participants or leading citizens and statesmen—which, according to Thucydides' Pericles, were the trademarks of Athenian greatness.[190]

At the outset of a discussion that will reconcile Socrates to his death at the hands of the Athenian political order, he begins with a proposition that places him outside the boundaries of conventional discourse. The first principles of philosophical deliberation that would guide Socratic virtue contravene those of practical political deliberation in Athens. The challenge Plato's Socrates then meets is to explain why he should ally himself with an Athenian political order that has rejected him, having begun with philosophical propositions to which virtually no Athenian agreed—that is, why suffering an unjust verdict is the necessary means of avoiding doing an injustice himself. Here begins Plato's effort to construct the dynamic that constituted his Socratic Problem.

The arguments of "the laws" of Athens are designed to meet this challenge. These laws constitute the city to which Socrates is loyal, and they provide arguments that justify his loyalty. Their arguments fall into two basic parts.[191] First, the city stands in relation to its citizens who have been born and raised there as parents do to children. The *polis* appears as the guardian of its citizens. It imparts to the citizens a natural sense of obligation, which they tacitly accept once they choose to live in the city. This obligation is limited by a second condition. The citizen is entitled to challenge the laws and "persuade" them (actually "try to persuade").[192] But if one is not successful, then the obligation to obey the laws remains (51e–52b).

A question then arises. What if the law requires one to do an injustice? In

---

190. Thucydides, II.40.2.

191. Kraut's *Socrates and the State* provides an illuminating and exhaustive analysis of these arguments.

192. See Kraut, *Socrates and the State*, and Vlastos's review in the *Times Literary Supplement*, 24 August 1984.

the *Apology,* Socrates said he would refuse to give up philosophy, even if that would prevent a death sentence, because it constituted his expression of virtue. In the *Crito,* Plato, arguing for Socrates in absentia, has tried to eliminate this paradox by establishing an ideal standard of law and political order over and above its practical determination by human agents. But as of yet there is no basis for suggesting that the standards of such an ideal political order would either countenance Socratic virtue or decisively rebut Meletus's indictment.

For Plato, this creates a severe philosophical problem. How does one relate the hypothetical "laws of Athens" to the actuality of an Athenian court that put Socrates to death? On the discursive level of the *Crito,* Plato has harmonized Socrates and Athens, making Socrates patriotic and legitimizing Athenian political institutions and decisions. But this harmony cannot provide a political model for ethical action, for the "politics" of "the laws" have not been sufficiently articulated. There was no simple way of ascertaining from the laws themselves what counts as their proper application, for the Athenian court ordinarily determined what "the laws" practically meant. Given Socrates' respect for "those who know," could there be "experts" who possess a *techne* in interpreting these laws and politics more generally, and if so, should one be obligated to obey them? If there were, this would justify authoritarian decision making, particularly when here, as in the *Apology,* there is no initial effort to differentiate the criteria for knowledge that applies to specialized matters for which identifiable experts exist and more general, political matters. But neither the *Apology* nor *Crito* indicates that such political knowledge of virtue or such experts exist.

So then what practices are we to infer as legitimate from the standpoint of Socratic virtue? To some extent, the question is mis-posed, for the central meaning of Socratic virtue denies necessary legitimacy to any social action. But then what were the Athenians of Plato's time—or what are we—to make of the political bearing of Socratic virtue, especially given Socrates' own assertion this his virtue and wisdom benefit the *polis* and its citizens?

Socrates had not found a way to reconcile the exercise of his virtue with the social beliefs and practices that were needed to maintain the Athenian *polis* or, perhaps, any society. His virtue would be corrupted, its discursive expression would be silenced, and his life would be endangered if Socrates sought to make his virtue into a political art. Therefore, Socratic virtue was incomplete as a model for virtuous action by Athenian citizens. This lack could not be easily remedied. No minor reform of Socratic virtue or Athenian society could harmonize the two. Both the meaning of Socratic virtue and the practice of the political art would have to change if their presupposed mutual entailment was to be socially and intellectually affirmed. In this way, the incoherence of Socratic virtue, as well as its tragic conflict with Athenian democracy, produced for Plato his Socratic Problem.

What, then, are we to conclude about the relation of Socratic ethics and virtue to the Athenian political order, of Socratic citizenship to the political art? My own answer to these questions must be presented alongside ones offered by others who have considered the political dimension of Socrates' ethics and the relation of his *logos* to the political practices of Athenian democracy. Interpretations range from views of Socrates' speech as being rather disingenuous because his morality is so consistently antidemocratic as to make him a genuine political threat to the city, to views of Socrates as a good democrat who lost his life because of unfavorable idiosyncratic circumstances.[193] In be-

---

193. The antidemocratic view comes through most clearly and forthrightly in the argument of Neal Wood and Ellen Wood in *Class Ideology and Ancient Political Theory*. For the Woods, Athenian democracy, despite its dependence on tribute from subordinate allies, exclusion of women from the political realm, endorsement of slavery, and reliance on noncitizen residents for much of its economic activity, was a fundamentally rational society. Its democratic politics not only promoted egalitarian values and encouraged diversity and toleration among the citizenry; they fostered a good society. In their view, Socrates' association with individuals closely tied to oligarchic and aristocratic interests makes his criticism of Athenian institutions on ethical grounds politically antidemocratic. Their evidence, however, does not come primarily from the *Apology*. For their account of Socrates' politics, the Woods rely heavily on Xenophon's portrayal of Socrates. But if one doubts whether the recollections of Xenophon are historically authoritative and believes that the Socrates of the dialogues of Plato blends historical information about Socrates with Plato's philosophical purposes, then these historical records cannot provide straightforward guides to the historical Socrates, and the authority of their evidence disintegrates. (The Woods' view has received more recent support from I. F. Stone in his *The Trial of Socrates*. But Stone makes no effort to differentiate which views of the character Socrates in Plato's dialogues may be plausibly related to those of the historical Socrates and those that cannot be.) To support their view of an antidemocratic Socrates, they cite passages spoken by the character Socrates in virtually any and all of Plato's dialogues.

J. Peter Euben paints a democratic picture of the historical Socrates and uses primarily Plato's *Apology* and *Crito* for his colors. He emphasizes Socrates' devotion to the Athenian *polis* (to the end, he never left it, except to fight in its army) and his belief that his vocation of criticism constituted a service to its way of life—in a way that placed him within a high democratic tradition of Athens that includes Solon and Pericles. This view, however, fails to give adequate weight to Socrates' hostility to democratic politics and his antimajoritarian impulses. Although Socrates conversed with anyone who would respond to him, his disdain for the many, his fundamental belief that most citizens lacked virtue, at least in political gatherings, and his rejection of the Peri-

tween are those who find Socrates seriously at odds with Athenian democracy, but not so much as to warrant his conviction and execution.[194]

---

clean ideal of citizen involvement in political deliberation seriously compromised whatever democratic sympathies he had. In Plato's *Crito,* much less historically reliable than the *Apology,* he elaborated his devotion to the laws of Athens by praising the free speech and open forums of Athenian democracy. But although Socrates in the *Apology* never argues for a nondemocratic political order, "Socrates'" devotion to those laws does not entail endorsement of democratic procedures, apart from free and frank speech, for constituting them. See J. P. Euben, "The Philosophy and Politics of Plato's *Crito,*" and, on Plato's *Apology,* idem, *The Tragedy of Political Theory,* chap. 7. For an interesting treatment of the significance of "free and frank speech" (*parrhesia*) in Athenian discourse, see Michel Foucault, *Discourse and Truth: The Problematization of Parrhesia.*

194. This more moderate picture of Socrates appears in the work of Gregory Vlastos, Richard Kraut, and Terence Irwin. It acknowledges his hostility to democratic politics but nevertheless identifies him as an Athenian ethical hero. This view depends on the isolation of Socrates' ethical ideals from his political practice. According to Vlastos, the picture of Socrates in Plato's *Apology* can be filled in by reference to other "early" dialogues of Plato. In these, particularly the *Euthydemus,* Socrates puts forth a definition of the "royal art" that functions as a kind of political art, but it has an exclusively "moral" dimension. It is not designed to be a guide for practical politics, about which Socrates has no systematic views, and cannot be used to suggest that Socrates held flatly antidemocratic beliefs, even though no democracy admits "royal rule." Apart from relying on a complex, sophisticated philosophical dialogue such as the *Euthydemus,* which lacks credibility as evidence for the views Plato held of Socrates at the time of the latter's trial and death, the presumption here is that Socrates' ethical beliefs have no immediately practical political corollaries. Although this view has many plausible defenders, especially by scholars working in a liberal tradition that seeks to protect the individual from the burdens of citizenship and the constraints of political order, it does not seem to be the view of Socrates. Neither he nor any other of his contemporaries had any point of reference for their views about ethical relations other than the laws and traditions of the *polis.* In this sense, all ethical views had a political dimension. Socrates' *daimonion,* for example, never told Socrates what ideals he ought to hold but rather what actions he should avoid. And in the *Apology* (and more obviously, the *Crito*), by defending himself and proudly recalling his actions as a steadfast Athenian soldier, Socrates demonstrated allegiance to the legal form of Athenian political procedures. Clearly he believed that his ethical principles entitled him to live freely in the Athenian political order. But just as clearly, a majority of the jurors did not. One can now argue that the minority in the jury was right, but for Plato, that view could not be sufficient. It could not provide adequate philosophical justification of Socrates' ethical principles, because although they might be true in *logos,* they were not true in *ergon,* at least in terms of the practices of the established Athenian political order.

Richard Kraut's view offers a variation of Vlastos's view. In his detailed, well-argued study, he too finds a lack of continuity between Socrates' ethical principles and his politics. But that does not stem from the view that they had no political dimension. Kraut holds that Socrates indeed believed in the existence of moral expertise, and consequently in "moral authoritarianism" (Kraut, *Socrates and the State*). But Socrates is disinclined to use this view as a first principle for political practice, because he doesn't believe that, practically speaking, such moral expertise or virtue can be taught. Barring such practical means, the best possible political order, according to

The political orientation of Socrates is indeterminate, and therefore, to some extent, problematic.[195] For the evidence of Plato's *Apology* and *Crito*

Kraut's portrayal of the historical Socrates, is democratic. Kraut's concern is to establish consistency between the *Apology* and the *Crito*, that is, between Socrates' insistence in the *Apology* that he would not stop practicing philosophy, in spite of the urging of the court, to save his life, and the argument in the *Crito* that his allegiance to the laws of Athens prevents him from escaping from prison. His central focus is the *Crito*, in which he looks for and finds "a consistent [Socratic] theory of justified disobedience" (p. 24)—consistent with the "theory of political loyalty" put forward by the "Laws of Athens"—when he refuses to escape from jail on the grounds that he would be "doing a great injustice" (pp. 3–4). Yet Kraut takes for his evidentiary basis all of Plato's early dialogues, up to and including Book 1 of the *Republic*, as evidence of the views of the historical Socrates (pp. 3–4, n. 1). Kraut assigns to the historical Socrates a belief in the existence of moral expertise based on the craft analogy, despite the fact that in the *Apology* and *Crito* the references to the craft analogy do not imply that Socrates himself possesses a *techne* of *arete* rooted in *episteme*, that, were it mastered, would justify an authoritarian political order led by experts. Nor does he admit the possibility that the inability to teach an art constitutes a reason for suggesting that such an art does not exist, at least for Socrates. The result is that the only significant theoretical difference separating the political views of Socrates and those of Plato concerns the teachability of virtue. Lacking a belief in the theory or practice of philosopher-guardianship, Socrates endorses a democratic political order that protects dissent as the best possible society.

Kraut's view received a strong endorsement from Terence Irwin, whose earlier book on Plato's early and middle dialogues established methodological procedures that Kraut employs in his own book. (See Kraut, *Socrates and the State*, and Irwin, *Plato's Moral Theory*.) Irwin differs from Kraut, but not in that Socrates was a theoretical opponent to democracy, only in that his opposition was not tempered by a belief in the unteachability of virtue. Therefore, Irwin draws an even closer connection between the political beliefs of Socrates and Plato, even as he sharply distinguishes their "moral" views. (Irwin's argument on this score is discussed below.) But for Irwin, this does not make either Socrates or Plato practical opponents of democracy. In his view, Socrates and Plato, albeit theoretical opponents of democracy, find democratic decision procedures to be the best practical means for actualizing the advice of moral experts.

All of these books, however, are marred by their interpretive understanding of the historical Socrates. Kraut and Irwin tend to set aside the issue of who is the author of the theory they have found. Vlastos confronts the issue in chap. 2 of *Socrates: Ironist and Moral Philosopher*, but the opposition between "Socrates 1" and "Socrates 2" is too clear and self-serving to be plausible without more external evidence. For each of these interpreters, the conceptual terms of the theory assigned to the historical Socrates unproblematically derive from the dialogues of Plato. None harbors any concern that Plato may be adopting the historical character of Socrates for his own purposes, or that the *aporiai* of the early dialogues actually signify what they explicitly suggest—namely the existence of problems rather than the affirmation of philosophical propositions concerning the existence of a morally justified art for constituting the political order. But the only way to argue my case is to provide (as I try to do below) a more plausible interpretation of the evidence of the other early dialogues of Plato with respect to the understanding of the relation of virtue and the political art.

195. This is why the assertion by Socrates in Plato's *Gorgias*—that he alone, rather than more noted statesmen such as Themistocles, Pericles, Cimon, or Ephialtes, was the true practitioner of

yields no views about the proper organization of political institutions. Moreover, although he respected their existence and seemed to recognize their necessity, his world of virtue seems to lack politics as we know it. That is the chief reason that there is no evidentiary basis for viewing Socrates as an advocate of oligarchic conservatism.[196] But Socrates incontrovertibly *was* a major Athenian political figure.[197] Resolving this apparent paradox requires acknowledging the asymmetry of the relation between Socrates' art of citizenship and the political form of the Athenian democracy, along with the subtle links and gaps between Socrates' devotion to the Athenian political realm and his commitment to democracy.

Much as one may like Socrates' critique of conventionalism and intellectual and ethical integrity, it is painfully clear that his "defense" in Plato's *Apology* failed to reconcile Socrates and Athens. Socratic citizenship produced an unresolvable tension between Socratic reason and Athenian democracy. But it did not argue for an ineradicable opposition between political reasoning and democracy. This is because in spite of the major political consequences and ramifications of Socrates' art of citizenship, it was not an art of citizenship that fully addressed the problems of exercising political power. Plato met the challenge left by Socrates' life and death by conceptualizing the political art in terms of ethics and power on many levels in diverse dialogical contexts.

---

the *politike techne*—indicates the views of a fictive, Platonic Socrates rather than the historical Socrates. The historical and theoretical meaning of the passage (*Gorgias* 521d) can be understood best in terms of the development of the concept of the political art in Plato's dialogues. See Chapter 3, Section D, below.

196. The only way to associate a conception of the political art with the historical Socrates is to accept the Socratic *logoi* recorded by Xenophon in his *Memorabilia* as historically accurate—a highly implausible claim. By doing so, a decidedly oligarchic Socrates emerges, one whose views are very compatible with Xenophon's.

Vlastos identifies the Socratic challenge to Athenian democracy as "moral" and not "political" because Socrates' "knowledge" is "exclusively moral" rather than "political" ("The Historical Socrates and Athenian Democracy," 506–9). I do not accept Vlastos's clear-cut differentiation of "moral" and "political" views, for reasons that by now should be apparent. Moreover, his "moral" Socrates is drawn from a reading of the Socrates of many Platonic dialogues, including the relatively late *Euthydemus*.

INTERPRETATIONS

PART
II

THE POLITICAL ART IN APORETIC DIALOGUES, OR PLATO'S SOCRATIC PROBLEM AMID ATHENIAN CONVENTIONS

The historical Socrates had searched for virtue amid the ethical and political practices and discourse of Athenian life. In doing so, he believed that his conduct consistently related *logos* and *ergon.* With Socrates' trial and death, however, the gap between the effects of Socrates' life and the political application of Athenian laws must have seemed to Plato to have become unbridgeable. Plato disagreed with the Athenians' conviction of Socrates, but he had to comprehend its significance and aftermath. This raised an issue: How could one value the words and deeds of Socrates' life when the practical embodiment of the *polis,* the apparent source and final court of virtue and justice, could not tolerate it? For Plato to solve his Socratic Problem, he had to redefine the conflict between Socrates and Athens.

In the aporetic dialogues, Plato's relationship to Socrates became itself a political and philosophical problem about the discordant relation between critical discourse about virtue and political practice. For there to be any solution to this problem, both the *logos* of Socratic virtue and the *ergon* of Athens had to be transformed. If any future reconciliation of the two was to occur, Plato became convinced that the meaning of virtue could not be wholly Socratic and the politics of a just society could not be conventionally Athenian.

The problematic character of the historical Socrates functions as a subtext in virtually all of the aporetic dialogues.[1] Rather than offering a series of authentic recollections of the historical Socrates' own words or equivalent philosophical arguments,[2] the Socrates of these dialogues presents a "paradigm" being subjected to critical scrutiny.[3] In the aporetic dialogues, Plato transposed into *logos* the historical figure of Socratic virtue, with Socrates' character in them defining *arete* in *logos*. The *aporiai* ("difficulties" or "blockages") in them reflect unresolved issues regarding the legacy of Socratic citizenship, particularly as an art of virtue that coherently related *logos* and *ergon*. The aim of these dialogues, therefore, involved exploration of the intersection and conflict of Socratic *logos* and virtue, on the one hand, and the *ergon* of conventional Athenian beliefs and practices, on the other.[4] The dialogic Socrates presents an exemplary paradigm of virtue, but given Socrates'

1. For example, the teaching of virtue is the overt subject of the *Laches, Euthydemus, Protagoras,* and *Meno,* but their subtext is the relation of these discussions to the historical Socrates—in relation to the Athenians and Sophists—as teachers of virtue. The meaning of virtue *simpliciter,* or its exemplars of piety, courage, wisdom, and moderation, constituted the overt subjects of the *Euthyphro, Laches, Euthydemus,* and *Charmides,* but in their background is the question of how the words and deeds of the historical Socrates exemplified these virtues and virtue itself.

2. The latter position is the one taken by Gregory Vlastos and presented most fully in his last book, *Socrates: Ironist and Moral Philosopher;* he staked out this position, however, over twenty years earlier. It is generally followed by many of his students, some of whose names and works are Terence Irwin, *Plato's Moral Theory;* Richard Kraut, *Socrates and the State;* Hugh Benson, ed., *Essays in the Philosophy of Socrates.* For a more detailed discussion of Vlastos's perspective in relation to the concerns of this study, see my "Plato's Socratic Problem, and Ours," especially 379–82.

3. One might further specify the dialogic Socrates as follows. In the *Apology* (23b), a relatively historical Socrates reports that the oracle believed him to be a "paradigm," or exemplar, of *arete.* In the *Euthyphro* (6d–e), Plato uses the notion of a "paradigm" to refer to an *eidos,* which is typically translated as "form" or "idea." In the *Laches* (187a), Plato uses *paradeigmos* to signify an exemplar that serves as proof or evidence of the existence of a skill. For discussions of the meaning of Plato's use of *paradeigma* in relation to the metaphysical status of his theory of forms, see William J. Prior, "The Concept of *Paradeigma* in Plato's Theory of Forms," and Richard Patterson, *Image and Reality in Plato's Metaphysics.*

4. It is a conflict that his dialogues would only partially overcome. In emphasizing the limited solubility of this conflict, I differ from Hans-Georg Gadamer, who, throughout his long philosophical career, presupposed their reconciliation in Plato's dialogues. See "Plato and the Poets" and "Plato's Educational State," which appear in Hans-Georg Gadamer, *Dialogue and Dialectic—Eight Hermeneutical Studies on Plato,* trans., with an intro. by P. Christopher Smith, 39–72 and 73–92, along with an 1989 interview, "Gadamer on Gadamer," printed in *Gadamer and Hermeneutics,* ed., with an intro. by Hugh J. Silverman, 13–19.

fate, as recounted in Plato's *Apology* (and discussed in Chapter 2), this paradigm was radically insufficient. This insufficiency provides the background for Plato's efforts to define virtue in relation to the political art in his aporetic dialogues, which reflect conventional conceptions of Athenian ethical and political life.

In some of these dialogues, Plato offered solutions to his Socratic Problem—as the *politike techne* in the *Euthydemus,* the art of measurement in the *Protagoras,* and the *politike techne* of Socrates in the *Gorgias.* But each of these "solutions" was either rebutted or unsustained, as in the first two, or unjustified, as in the last. Through the creation of *aporiai* in all of the dialogues discussed below, however, Plato began to construct potential meanings of virtue as an ethically grounded political art, one that probably could be fully realized only in critical discourse, but still could be a useful guide in practical life.

After explaining the primary conceptual tools Plato used to define his Socratic Problem—*techne, episteme,* and *arete*—I sketch its analytical outlines by indicating briefly the relevance of the *Laches, Charmides, Euthydemus,* and *Meno* for understanding the Platonic political art. These dialogues both illustrate Plato's use of these tools to bridge the gap between virtue and the political art and exemplify the unique interaction of history and theory displayed in the form and content of Plato's dialogues. Then I offer more extensive interpretations of the *Protagoras* and *Gorgias,* dialogues in which Plato more systematically and thoroughly explores possible relations between a critical discourse of virtue and political practice.

A. CONCEPTUAL TOOLS

Some of the conceptual tools Plato employed in his attempt to solve his Socratic Problem must have been learned from his contacts with the historical Socrates. Among the most important of these was the Socratic *elenchus,* a discursive method of producing self-contradictions. However, the meaning of Plato's use of this and other tools about which he might have learned from the historical Socrates would have been different because of the different context in which he employed them. Surely Socrates' trial and death would have altered the significance of those tools and their use, but these transformative events only constituted part of the different historical and intellectual context in which Plato lived. There also were changes in the atmospherics of power and ethics, critical discourse, and Plato's life. (See Chapter 2.) Most apparent, however, was the different Platonic medium for their expression—the written, in contrast to the spoken, word. Plato's fame derives from his written, rather than his spoken, dialogues. Although this literary medium had its limitations, it also allowed for a more fully sustained and developed intellectual project.

When grappling in written dialogues with his Socratic Problem, Plato discursively employed social practices and conceptual schemes that offered stable counterpoints to the negativity that resulted from the "Socratic" *elenchus*.[5] They tended to signify relatively objective, reliable, and beneficial activities. Foremost among them were modes of thought and action associated with the practice known as a *techne* (art, craft, or skill) and the knowledge that typically informed it, namely *episteme* (stable, systematic knowledge).[6] Such a practice and its skillful, knowledgeable exercise could be exercised by an individual (like Socrates?) or a group (like the Athenians?).[7]

Plato used these conceptual tools as conditions, benchmarks, and analogues for his discussions of the *logos* and *ergon* of *arete*. At the same time, however, he never understood them to be wholly paradigmatic for virtue itself.[8] There are both analogies and disanalogies of *episteme* and *techne* to *arete*, and they illustrate potential links and discontinuities between these terms. Exploring these relations preoccupied Plato in the aporetic dialogues.

5. In the *Euthyphro* (11b–d, 15b), Plato's Socrates referred to the slipperiness of Euthyphro's unjustified statements as comparable to the runaway statues of Daedalus and worried that his own arguments and skill might be mistaken for them. See *Meno* 97d–98b.

6. Insofar as virtue and the political art were taken to be possessions of all Athenians, Plato's use of *techne* in his dialogues was simultaneously symbolic of, and a threat to, the prevailing beliefs and practices of Athenian democracy. But those references are indirect in the dialogues, for there it is overtly used as a tool of conceptual clarification. Neal Wood and Ellen Wood disregard the significance of this overt use when they interpret Plato's use of the notion of *techne* in his dialogues as an illegitimate appropriation and manipulation of democratic Athenian discourse. See their *Class Ideology and Ancient Political Theory*, 128–133.

7. According to the Corinthians' speech in Thucydides' *History* (1.70–71), the Athenians collectively possessed the *techne* of politics. The special sphere mastered by the *techne* was the set of complexities and uncertainties involving the exercise of collective power. Its product would be the benefit of the political community as a whole. *Technai* could refer to collective talents, but typically they referred to the skills of individuals.

8. The failure to understand the functionally imperfect fit between *episteme* and *techne*, on the one hand, and human virtue, on the other, characterizes Terence Irwin's analysis of Plato's early and middle dialogues. See his *Plato's Moral Theory*.

Understanding them is essential for obtaining a firm grasp of the Platonic political art. Before interpreting Plato's use of these tools in some his aporetic dialogues, their conventional meanings—which Plato was both relying on and transforming—need to be set forth.

1. *Techne* AND *Episteme*

Technai represented a determinate relation between a particular set of ideas and practices; they identify activities that systematically linked *logos* and *ergon*. Insofar as the concept involved "the systematic application of intelligence to any field of human activity," *technai* provided useful reference points for reliable and successful forms of practical activity.[9] In particular, Hippocratics used the notion of a *techne* to identify the benefits and limitations of their practice of medicine; it represented the best knowledge available for producing health for the human body, as virtue identified the best conditions and practices for the human being as a whole.[10] At the same time, however, practicing a *techne* did not automatically yield beneficial or ethically virtuous results (as notably illustrated by Aeschylus's *Prometheus* and Sophocles'

9. The limpid quotation comes from E. R. Dodd's "The Ancient Concept of Progress," in his *The Ancient Concept of Progress, and Other Essays on Greek Literature and Belief*, 11. Martha Nussbaum has usefully summarized scholarship on the analytical dimensions of *techne* in her *The Fragility of Goodness: Luck and Ethics in Greek Tragedy and Philosophy*, 442, n. 2, and 443–44, n. 10.

Gregory Nagy's exegesis of the etymology of *techne*, which links it to both mental and manual activities, for instance, poetry and carpentry, and to these activities insofar as they are "fitting" or "harmonious," supports my focus on *techne* as a critical concept in Platonic thought, if not ancient Greek thought more generally. For *techne* stands for the appropriate linkage of *logos* and *ergon* in the entire range of social activities. This would make a very attractive term for Plato, who sought both to understand and reconstruct all forms of social activity. See Gregory Nagy, *The Best of the Achaeans: Concepts of the Hero in Archaic Greek Poetry*, 297–300.

The Greek concept of *techne* has become something of a political football in recent academic discourse. A generation ago, it signified a technique for domination of the other and contrasted with the seemingly kinder, gentler, and more egalitarian Greek idea of *praxis;* more recently (and most directly as a result of the historical research of Michel Foucault), it has come to signify a practice for the liberation of the self.

10. For use of the notion of *techne* in Hippocratic writings, see, above all, "On the Art" and "On Ancient Medicine." On the theoretical dimensions of the ancient Greek practice and conception of medicine, see W. H. S. Jones, *Philosophy and Medicine in Ancient Greece;* Owsei Temkin and C. Lilian Temkin, eds., *Ancient Medicine: Selected Papers of Ludwig Edelstein;* and the more recent, lucid overview by Michael Frede, "Philosophy and Medicine in Antiquity." Michel Foucault offers an interesting interpretation of ancient Greek dietary regimens as *technai* in *The Use of Pleasure—The History of Sexuality*, 2:95–139.

Antigone). Nevertheless, *technai* possessed extraordinary, and generally positive, symbolic value for the Athenians, if not the Greeks more generally.[11] The linkage of some recognized ability to know, express, and teach one's *techne* with having the practical skill itself suggests why *techne* might be a useful analogue for looking at virtue. *Arete* required the harmonious concordance of word and deed, which *technai* demonstrated. As a practice and concept used for critical evaluation, however, the notion of a *techne* had not been significantly developed before Plato.[12]

Down through the fifth century, we find close correlations of *episteme* and *techne*. But although an *episteme* sometimes involved a practical skill, *techne* always did; whereas *episteme* always involved a relatively complex mental skill, *techne* only sometimes did. Although both *episteme* and *techne* implicitly refer to activities that connect thought (if not "rationality") and action, *technai* evidenced a broader consensus backing their social practice. Plato's Socrates suggested in the *Euthyphro* (7c–d), however, that ethical ideas such as good and bad, beautiful and ugly, just and unjust could not be reduced to a simple *techne* or *episteme*. The standards of the latter brooked no serious dispute whereas those of the former constantly did.

---

11. In relationship to Solon, see G. Vlastos, "Solonian Justice." In relation to tragic discourse, see Aeschylus, *Prometheus Bound* (particularly lines 441–506), and Sophocles, *Antigone,* lines 332–69. In relationship to Thucydides, see Lowell Edmunds, *Chance and Intelligence in Thucydides.* In terms of the Athenians as a people, see M. M. Austin and P. Vidal-Naquet, *Economic and Social Analysis of Ancient Greece: An Introduction,* 5–6, 107. Moreover, the ancient Greek reverence for craftsmanship, if not the craftsman, is legendary and is reflected in both Greek myths of Athena and Hephaestus (as well as Prometheus and Pandora) as patron deities of the arts and more ordinary interests in the aesthetics of sculpture, painting, and music. For scholarly illustrations of these points, see Alison Burford, *Craftsmen in Greek and Roman Society,* 96ff; J. J. Pollitt, *Art and Experience in Classical Greece,* and idem, *The Ancient View of Greek Art,* 92–93; Martin Robertson, *A History of Greek Art;* Warren D. Anderson, *Ethos and Education in Greek Music: The Evidence of Poetry and Philosophy,* and idem, *Music and Musicians in Ancient Greece.* J. J. Pollitt provides a useful compendium of ancient sources on various aspects of Greek art in his *The Art of Ancient Greece: Sources and Documents.* That the belief in the political significance of the art of music was not unique to Plato is no more clearly shown than in the surviving fragments of the mid-fifth-century sophist of music, Damon of Athens, particularly fr. 10 (D–K, 5th ed.): "Musical modes are nowhere altered without (changes in) the most important laws of the state" (trans. K. Freeman). Plato refers to Damon in both the *Laches* (180c, 197d, 200aff) and *Republic* (400bff, 424c). Plato used all these traditions by invoking *techne* as a critical tool. This becomes most obvious in the *Republic, Statesman,* and *Laws* (see Chapters 4 and 5, below).

12. This is not to say, however, that *techne* played no interesting roles in pre-Platonic written prose. For a good, recent discussion of such usages, see David Roochnik, *Of Art and Wisdom: Plato's Understanding of Techne,* 17–88.

The issue in the aporetic dialogues was not the ordinary meaning or value of *episteme* and *techne* but, rather, their transferability to, or presence in, domains of life where they were not easy to discern and where claims to their relevance were novel—that is, with respect to the meaning of virtue, its practice, and the existence of a capacity to teach it. In this way, both *techne* and *episteme* provided useful conceptual tools for critically exploring the rational and ethical dimensions of political practice—in other words, the relation between virtue and the political art.[13]

2. *Arete*

Ancient Greek virtue, *arete,* denoted a habitual capacity to achieve success in the performance of a specific practice or set of practices. It could refer to specific actions of an individual or animal as well as to the character of an individual or animal "as a whole." The agent's exhibition of an *arete* fulfilled skillfully an esteemed function of the animal or person. But when *arete* referred to human beings, it also connoted excellence and superiority. Insofar as it denoted achievement, it connoted success, and insofar as it denoted success, it connoted a social and intellectual judgment of merit and ethical or moral worth. Thus, the possession of *arete* was extraordinary, and its possessor shone forth amid his, her (although this was unusual in a society that gave women no opportunities to excel in public), or its (because *arete* could refer to the character and actions of an animal) peers.[14] Even though the achievements of *arete* were supposed to warrant praise, they could conflict with other social and political requirements.[15]

13. For a useful consideration of the interconnections between *episteme* and *techne* in Plato's aporetic dialogues, see John Gould, *The Development of Plato's Ethics,* 7–10.

14. See K. J. Dover, *Greek Popular Morality in the Time of Plato and Aristotle,* 61.

15. This understanding of the social meaning of *arete* in ancient Greece differs from that of A. W. H. Adkins, who viewed conflicts involving it as between "competitive" and "cooperative" or "quiet" values. See his *Merit and Responsibility,* 6–7. (This opposition may be seen as a mutation of the conflict between shame-culture and guilt-culture in ancient Greece articulated by his teacher, E. R. Dodds, who conceptualized this conflict in *The Greeks and the Irrational.*) It is inappropriate for me to deal extensively with the problems of Adkins's categories here. Suffice it to say for the moment that "competitive" virtues, such as those of Achilles and Agamemnon in Homer's *Iliad,* always received some sort of communal, and therefore cooperative, endorsement, whereas "cooperative" virtues, such as those of Plato's Socrates, exhibited a competitive character. Different conceptions of virtue, and the conflict between them, should be seen less as a conflict between ethical postures, one of which becomes more prominent in time, and more as evidence of political competition in Greek political communities about which interpretation of

The performative character of *arete* allowed it to be critically examined in terms of the practical benefits and reliability of *technai*. Insofar as *arete* was understood to be a kind of excellence or goodness that was exhibited in identifiable actions and modes of behavior, the expert performance of a *techne* could offer the occasion for the expression of *arete*. But that activity had to be practiced in a way that was compatible with all of the standards of *arete*, and this was not necessarily the case. Thus, in Plato's *Laches* (181c, etc.), courage was initially defined in terms of the *episteme* of horse riding, insofar as fighting in battle on a horse was traditionally understood to exhibit virtue in action. But in the dialogue, *episteme* was not sufficient to define courage, and no specifiable set of practices could adequately define it. In Plato's *Euthyphro* (12e–13e), even the benign and helpful practice known as "caring" (*therepeuein*) could not be an adequate exemplar of *arete*. Plato's dialogic Socrates often employed the criteria of *epistemai* and *technai* as starting points in his effort to define one of the virtues, or virtue itself, but they were never sufficient.

Plato also used other criteria for identifying *arete;* they stemmed from the different facets of human activity that *arete* represented. These different activities and the different values they embodied may be distinguished as first-order and second-order. The more general, second-order value referred to an excellence of the agent that transcended the immediate practicality and value of particular first-order actions. Implicitly, second-order activities controlled the effect of first-order activities on the individual agent's or social entity's character "as a whole," understood as that for the sake of which individuals performed particular activities.[16] Plato suggested that such a whole-

---

virtue ought to prevail. One of the most misleading aspects of Alasdair MacIntyre's *After Virtue,* which relies on Adkins for its understanding of the history of Greek ethics, is to suggest that "the Greeks" operated in a more harmonious ethical tradition than "we" do. For a useful, recent critique of Adkins's version of the history of Greek ethics, based on exposing its un-Greek (Christian) progressivist and Kantian presuppositions, see Bernard Williams, *Shame and Necessity,* 4–8, 41, 61, 75–81, 98–101, and accompanying notes.

16. *Lysis* 218d–220d; *Laches* 185d–e; see *Gorgias* 468b. Aristotle would later refer to this aspect of an agent's "wholeness" as its *telos,* but in order to avoid anachronism, I avoid the use of the Aristotelian term for interpreting Plato. R. K. Sprague employs the categories of *first-order* and *second-order* to differentiate kinds of *technai* in Plato's dialogues, but she neglects to point out the constitutive relation of second-order arts to Plato's concern for the self and the political community as "wholes." See her *Plato's Philosopher-King.* In *Plato's Moral Theory,* Irwin analytically reduces all *technai* in (what he calls) Plato's early dialogues to first-order practices and their products to first-order values. For a standard, modern use of the distinction between first-order and second-order, see Harry Frankfurt, "Freedom of the Will and the Concept of the Per-

ness or constitutive purpose naturally belonged to various species and that virtue could refer to individuals or communities as "wholes," but defining that wholeness vexed Plato throughout the aporetic dialogues.[17]

Even if Plato had trouble determining the actual features of the virtue that harmonized words and deeds, such harmony was surely his aim. An *ergon* gained legitimacy by the words that would describe it, and *logos* was understood to be empty and useless if it had no practical exemplar. These conventions (which remained effective, at least, from Homer to Aristotle) automatically associated the political realm with an ethic or idea of virtue.

B. LIMINAL RELATIONS OF VIRTUE AND THE POLITICAL ART: *Laches, Charmides, Euthydemus,* AND *Meno*

Plato may well have written these dialogues over the course of a decade (or more). In particular, some major interpreters of Plato categorize the *Euthydemus* and *Meno* as products of his "middle," as opposed to his "early" period (in which the other two dialogues would have been written).[18] But this dispute need not distract us. At issue are the points made in each dialogue and their relation to the Platonic political art. Altogether they perform a useful function for our project, laying bare the conceptual *aporiai* that characterize Plato's effort to relate virtue and the political art in the terms of Athenian ethical and political conventions.[19]

---

son," reprinted in Harry Frankfurt, *The Importance of What We Care About—Philosophical Essays*, 11–25. For Frankfurt, there is no assumption that any second-order belief or desire ultimately grounds any first-order belief or desire, serving as a contextual whole for the first-order part.

17. *Apology* 20a–b; *Hippias Major* 283e–284b.

18. For two prominent examples, see F. M. Cornford's overview of Plato in his "Athenian Philosophical Schools," in J. B. Bury, S. A. Cook, and F. E. Adcock, eds., *Cambridge Ancient History*, 6:302–51, and G. Vlastos's categorization of the chronological order of Plato's dialogues in *Socrates, Ironist and Moral Philosopher*, 46–47, in which the *Laches* and *Charmides* belong to Plato's early installments of his first group of dialogues and the *Euthydemus* belongs to the "transitional" (slightly later, more theoretically developed) dialogues of this first group. For useful brief commentaries on these dialogues, see W. K. C. Guthrie, *A History of Greek Philosophy*, 4:124–34 (on the *Laches*), 155–74 (on the *Charmides*), and 266–83 (on the *Euthydemus*).

19. My grouping together of these three dialogues derives from the argument developed here, but it is worth noting that, long ago, Ernest Barker linked them as well. See his *Greek Political Theory: Plato and His Predecessors*, 143–47. Werner Jaeger linked the *Laches, Charmides,* and *Euthyphro* as various discussions of "the problem of *arete*" as "courage, self-control, and

1. *Laches*

The dramatic date of the dialogue is between 424 and 418 (when Laches was killed at the battle of Mantinea). The dialogue opens with Lysimachus (son of Aristides the Just, who had been ostracized) and Melisias (son of Thucydides, the oligarchic Athenian general and opponent of Pericles) posing to Nicias (a major Athenian general from 427–413, highly regarded by Thucydides the historian) the issue of how they might use discourse (*logos*) to teach courage (*andreia*, which calls up images of both bravery and manliness) to *their* sons, as they do not have the experience in battle or in their own lives that would demonstrate to their sons what the virtue of courage practically entails. Moreover, they complain about not having been taught courage by their fathers, who had no time for such private, familial concerns, occupied as they were with public affairs (179b, 180b, 197a). Nicias joins their discussion and suggests that Laches will also be interested. They want to enlist Socrates as well, for he is known for not only his fine words but also his courageous actions on the battlefield at Delium—in contrast to Laches' shamefully admitted readiness to retreat (not unlike most of the other Athenians who fought there, 181a–b).[20] Among Socrates' interlocutors, there is a disjuncture between *logos* and *ergon* with respect to their capacity for the teaching of courage, and Lysimachus and Melisias want to learn from Socrates a kind of knowledge (*episteme*) that can serve as a *techne* for fathers teaching sons the virtue of courage (181d–185e).[21] Despite having written the dialogue in the 390s or later, at least a decade after the Athenians' final defeat by the Spartans, Plato constitutes the argument of the dialogue at least partly in response to these historical and political events.

So Lysimachus and Melisias—undistinguished but still relatively

---

piety." As such they serve as "the material [of the] foundations [of the *Republic*]." See his *Paideia: The Ideals of Greek Culture*, 2:93–95.

20. Socrates' unusual bravery at this battle is further attested to in Plato, *Apology* 28d–e, and *Symposium* 221a. In the latter dialogue, it is the character of Alcibiades who praises Socrates' performance in battle in contrast to Laches'. Later on in Alcibiades' speech (which generally praises Socrates), he notes that Socrates has slighted him, among others such as Charmides and Euthydemus (222a–b).

21. See Michael J. O'Brien, "The Unity of the *Laches*," in *Yale Classical Studies* 18, ed. Lawrence Richardson Jr. This article usefully points out many aspects of the relation between *logos* and *ergon* in this dialogue, but not always appropriately. In particular, he takes Socrates as an unproblematic exemplar of their harmonious relation (p. 147).

wealthy and potentially prominent citizens—ask, Is it a matter of teaching a particular first-order practice like fighting in armor? Nicias claims (181e–182d) that courage may be induced by acquiring the skill (*episteme*) of horse riding. Laches disagrees, claiming that courage does not depend on the possession of this or any sort of first-order practical knowledge (*episteme*). Socrates is asked to resolve the disagreement.

Because first-order practices such as fighting in battle, riding horses, or enduring adversity do not guarantee courage, Socrates argues that they need to be regulated by a prior disposition and larger purpose, namely education in virtue and care for one's soul (185e, 187e–188c). But an examination of virtue itself goes beyond the concerns of the interlocutors and the temporal constraint of their discussion, so the focus returns to that aspect of virtue most pertinent to the evaluation of the merits of the arts of battle and riding for the cultivation of virtue: courage.

Laches offers two inadequate definitions of courage: the practice of "staying at one's post, not running away in battle" (see *Apology* 28e) and the capacity or power (*dynamis*) of "endurance of the soul" (190e, 192c). But all of the first-order practices that might exemplify these dispositions also fail to illustrate virtue. Again there is a discordance between *logos* and *ergon* (193e), one that results in a dialogical blockage (194c).

Nicias then argues that courage possesses characteristics of the virtue of wisdom (*sophia*) and practical knowledge (*episteme*). In this way, he identifies the need to join first-order practical knowledge with second-order ethical knowledge and proceeds to define the subject matter of knowledge in a way that entirely differs from the *episteme* of ordinary craftsmen: It is the knowledge of hopes and fears (194e–195a). Initially, Laches responds by pointing out that craftsmen who possess *episteme* normally lack such knowledge and are not courageous (195a–c).

In a remark that intimates Plato's reference to the ideal unity of philosophy and political power in the *Republic*, Socrates suggests that Nicias was on the right track with his definition, and that it would be very good indeed if a man in charge of great public affairs, a man who would be courageous, also had practical wisdom (*phronesis*) (197e). But Socrates notes that the knowledge (*episteme*) is not restricted to the future and so could not be the equivalent of Nicias's future-oriented knowledge (198d–199a).[22] After Socrates has

---

22. In so doing, Socrates implicitly criticizes Nicias, who relied on prophecy for his decision making in Sicily.

teased out the logical limits of Nicias's conception of courage as a kind of *episteme* of hopes and fears, it appears that a man who had the *episteme* of courage would also have all the other virtues. As a result, it seems that they have begun to define virtue as a whole, rather than in terms of one of the cardinal virtues and the direct object of concern—courage.

Some take this ending to imply a Socratic belief (that is, a belief of the historical Socrates, the Platonic Socrates of the "early" dialogues, or both) in the unity of the virtues.[23] But this proposition has not been positively argued in the dialogue. What has been set forth is the need for a *logos* of teaching virtue, particularly the virtue of courage with a specifiable subject matter that can be transmitted as a *techne* to young men. But as the dialogue identifies only first-order knowledge and skills as examples of what might constitute such a *techne* of *arete*, they have found themselves in another *aporia* (200e).

2. *Charmides*

The interlocutors in the *Charmides* also search for a definition of virtuous activity. But here the focus is not courage, but self-control (*sophrosyne*). Socrates' principal interlocutors are Critias and Charmides. To recall, the former was a leader of the Thirty and cousin of Plato's mother; the latter was the brother of Plato's mother and a nephew and ward of Critias, and he served under Critias as a magistrate during the Thirty's nine-month reign in Athens. Notably, both were killed during the restoration of democracy in 403; Socrates was executed in 399, and Plato probably wrote the dialogue in the 390s or early 380s. Also present is Chaerophon, the democratic partisan and follower of Socrates who found out from the Delphic Oracle that "no one is wiser than Socrates" (Plato, *Apology* 21a).

The dramatic date of the dialogue is c. 432, because Socrates has just returned from Potidaea, where he fought to help put down its revolt from Athens.[24] This makes the date of the dialogue's composition at least forty years after its dramatic date. The fates of the characters in the dialogue invest its discussion of *sophrosyne* with enormous historical and political signifi-

---

23. See, for example, the article by Gregory Vlastos, "The Unity of the Virtues in the *Protagoras*" (with "Appendix: The Argument in *Laches* 197eff"), reprinted in Gregory Vlastos, *Platonic Studies*, 221–69.

24. See Plato, *Symposium* 219e.

cance. They also indicate the dialogue's relevance to Plato's effort to conceptualize the principal elements of virtuous political conduct in terms of the problematic relation of *logos* to *ergon*.[25]

The dialogue opens with Socrates inquiring about the new crop of young men in Athens. Were any noteworthy for their wisdom or beauty or both (153e)? Critias mentions Charmides, comparing his dazzling physical beauty to the dazzling discourse and soul of Socrates.[26] Critias then calls him in, on the pretense that Socrates might know the "remedy" (*pharmakon*) for his headache (155c–d). Socrates plays along, suggesting that he knows a "charm" of *logos* to go along with a material remedy, but then speaks frankly and asserts the view of a Thracian doctor that one cannot cure the part without curing the whole or heal the body without healing the soul (155c–156e). This doctor also held that self-control entails the condition of a healthy soul, which could not be acquired by means of wealth, good birth, or physical beauty (157b).

Socrates elicits from Charmides three different definitions of *sophrosyne:* "quietness," "modesty," and "doing one's own." The first two definitions describe specific actions or modes of behavior. Despite their ability to denote second-order character traits, Charmides cannot differentiate a meaning for these concepts from practices that at times do not exhibit virtue. Plato's Socrates exposes incoherence in relatively short order (159b–161a). Because they are first-order practices or states of mind, they fail the test of defining *sophrosyne* as a second-order character trait that clearly directs first-order practices toward the well-being of the individual as a whole.

The third proposed definition is the more abstract (and ultimately psychological) notion of "doing one's own" (*to ta heautou prattein,* 160b).[27] In the *Charmides,* the phrase potentially suggests a connection of a particular first-order practice to a second-order ethics-based political art. However,

25. Contra Adkins, *Merit and Responsibility,* and Irwin, *Plato's Moral Theory,* respectively.

26. In her brief commentary on Plato's *Charmides,* Helen North remarked that Socrates in this dialogue "demonstrates the true nature of *sophrosyne* more memorably—for most readers— through his *ethos* [that is, his composure relative to that of his interlocutors] than his dialectic." See her *Sophrosyne: Self-Knowledge and Self-Restraint in Greek Literature,* 154. I do not recognize her contrast between ethics and dialectic as particularly Platonic.

27. This phrase serves as a fulcrum for Socrates' conception of justice in Plato's *Republic,* wherein the virtue of *sophrosyne* uniquely belongs to all members of the ideal *politeia.* See Chapter 4, Section B, below.

Socrates points out that this definition is confusing, insofar as "doing one's own" means not "doing other people's business" (*polypragmosune*) or not meddling. The only productive activities seem to involve such dealings with others, but as such they signify a disreputable activity (161d–e). To illustrate this absurdity, Socrates describes a *polis* in which no one did work that was useful to another (161e–162a), asking Charmides whether he thinks that "a city would be well-managed by a law commanding each man to weave and wash his own cloak, make his own shoes and oil flask and scraper, and perform everything else by this same principle of keeping his hands off of other people's things and 'making' and 'doing' his own?"[28]

This notion of "good management" indeed suggests a first-order practice that also involves a second-order activity. As such, it meets the necessary criteria for an "art of virtue." Socrates attempts to advance the argument further by noting that what craftsmen do is a kind of "making" (162e), that such activity is "temperate" (that is, self-controlled, 163a), and that "making" and "doing" may be the same thing (163b). Critias disagrees with the way Socrates has conflated typical first-order crafts with virtue. He calls on the authority of Hesiod to differentiate "making" from both "doing" and "working." Socrates does so, which enables Critias to differentiate the practice of *sophrosyne* from ordinary craftsmanship (163b–c). But Socrates aborts that development by trying to identify examples of self-control. Medicine could be one, but it is a first-order *techne* in which the practitioner has no control over whether his action results in benefit or harm (163e–164c). As such, "doing" (*praxis*) is not necessarily good.[29] Critias then tries a new definition of self-control, suggesting that it means "to know oneself" (164d–165b, which recalls the Delphic Oracle's admonition, "know thyself"). Socrates again looks for examples and mentions those of "sciences" (*epistemai*). Because first-order *epistemai* are not reflexive, Socrates' reference to them bodes ill for Critias's definition.

28. The translation of this and the subsequent lengthy quotation from the *Charmides* are those of R. K. Sprague and appear in *Laches and Charmides*, trans., with an intro. and notes by Rosamond Kent Sprague (Indianapolis: Hackett, 1992).

29. Ibid., 161–63. Plato does mention a distinction noted by Prodicus between *praxis* and *poiesis*. *Praxis* supposedly involves the production or making (*poiesis*) of good things. But Plato's Socrates does not make much of it, either here or in the *Euthydemus* (284b–c). For Plato the problem does not seem to be one of linguistic or conceptual differentiation (as it is for Aristotle). To him, there simply is no action yet defined as a *praxis* or *poiesis* that necessarily entails good or virtuous activity. And yet it is precisely that activity that the practice of *sophrosyne* is supposed to exhibit.

Critias tries to get out of the trap by distinguishing theoretical from practical *epistemai*, but each of these also has the nonreflexive characteristic. Because all sciences are sciences of something outside themselves, there is no prospect of finding an *episteme* that satisfies Critias's definition.

Yet Critias now distinguishes a new meaning for *sophrosyne*, as a science that is both of itself and other sciences (166e). As such, it is a kind of second-order *episteme* and approximates what Socrates seems to require. However, the discussion falls into an *aporia* (169c). The stumbling block is the identification of a clear content for the kind of second-order *episteme* that *sophrosyne* seems to be. One has to be able to identify a clear *use* of such knowledge and show it *works*. The failure to do so can be tragic. The obscurity surrounding what was the substantive nature of virtue as sought by the historical Socrates, in part produced by his elenchic method of identifying it, gave his accusers leeway to define that content in the worst possible way.[30]

Socrates is seeking a form of knowledge that is both comprehensible in *logos* and useful in *ergon*, because one without the other cannot constitute the virtue of *sophrosyne* or, for that matter, virtue in general. The dialogue at length reaches a point where a theoretically possible connection exists between *logos* and *ergon*, between virtue and the political art. In answering the question of what benefit stems from having temperance, Socrates envisions a *polis* governed by *sophrosyne*. He suggests that it involves a faculty of discernment or judgment that would assure that the activities in the *polis* are performed well. With the virtue of *sophrosyne*, citizens of this *polis* would be able to distinguish those who knew from those who did not know how to perform *technai* well, and the right people would perform the right tasks (171d–172e, 173b):

> Everything would be done according to science: neither would anyone who says he is a pilot (but is not) deceive us, nor would any doctor or general or anyone else pretending to know what he does not know escape our notice. This being the situation, wouldn't we

---

30. There is a conspicuous absence in the text at this point (170b–c). After referring to the arts of medicine and politics in the same terms and stating that medicine involves the knowledge of health and the political art involves the knowledge of justice, Socrates says that one knows health not through wisdom or temperance but does not say that one can know justice without wisdom or temperance. The failure to continue the parallel here is understandable, because neither Socrates nor Plato would promote that statement as a propositional argument.

have greater bodily health than we do now, and safety when we are in danger at sea or in battle, and wouldn't we have dishes and all our clothes and shoes and things skillfully made for us, and many other things as well, because we would be employing true craftsmen?

This political image of coordination between virtue and crafts again intimates their coordination in the *kallipolis* of Plato's *Republic*. The political representation of *sophrosyne* in the *Charmides,* however, is not embodied in a radically restructured society; nor is it embodied in a specific craft or institutionalized practice. It simply would be a general art that all members of the *polis* possessed. To this extent, such an art resembles the putative art of the Athenian citizenry hailed by Thucydides' Pericles and described by Protagoras in Plato's *Protagoras* (see Chapter 3, Section C, below). Yet it differs from them in lacking a specific political substance; it only signifies the competent practice of sundry crafts.[31] Socrates' fantastic vision reveals an important, albeit unmet (and, in the dialogue, unspecified), need and desire. The possession and competent practice of *sophrosyne* require the additional, complementary, and virtuous practice of the political art.

The unanswered concern about the knowledge that would generate knowledge of utility leads Socrates to search for an *episteme* of advantage, or good use, which then is defined as the science of good and evil (174b; see also Plato's *Protagoras* 351b–357b and Section C, below). But here, too, another *aporia* is reached. All the available practical examples for such an *episteme* involve craftsmen whose *techne* is insufficient for the display or production of *sophrosyne*. This suggests that *sophrosyne* cannot provide a knowledge of advantage or utility, but everyone in the dialogue finds this view absurd. The dialogue ends disappointingly, for knowledge of good and evil, like that knowledge of other kinds of knowledge and oneself, turns out to be the empty set (174–75).

3. *Euthydemus*

In contrast to the fifth-century dramatic locations of the *Laches* and *Charmides,* the *Euthydemus* dramatically (and anachronistically) seems to occur in

---

31. Thucydides, *History of the Peloponnesian War* ii.40; Plato, *Protagoras* (322a–324c).

the fourth century.[32] Despite this consequential difference (discussed below), the subject of this dialogue belongs to the set of concerns that animated those "fifth-century" discussions, and the *Euthydemus* resonates with both the *Laches* and *Charmides,* in two principal ways.

First, like them, its subject is the nature of the proper *logos* for teaching virtue and what a *techne* for teaching *arete* would discursively involve. But its subject is more abstract, being focused on the practice of discourse itself. It is not, as was the case in the *Laches,* the practical meaning of the virtue of courage or, as in the *Charmides,* the theoretical and practical meaning of the virtue of *sophrosyne.* Here, the focus is less the meaning of a substantive virtue than the proper discourse *about* virtue, which is exemplified not through actual fighting in deeds but through the capacity to fight with words (271c–272a).

Second, like the interlocutors of the *Laches* and *Charmides,* those of the *Euthydemus* seek out an art that has both first-order and second-order characteristics. They try to identify knowledge that combines "both how to make something and how to use what is made" (289b). The substantive focus is the *logoi* of the Sophists themselves, whether they teach virtue and guarantee the virtuous use of their words (277e). This dialogue additionally offers critical reflections on the characters of its participants, including that of Socrates as both a historical and dialogic figure. Whereas the *Laches* made the courage of the interlocutors themselves as much an issue as their discourse about it, and the *Charmides* called into question the interlocutors' possession of *sophrosyne,* the *Euthydemus* raises the issue of whether the Sophists and Socrates possess the virtue of wisdom and can provide a useful discourse that both has the character of a systematic art and inclines their students to philosophy and the practice of virtue. It addresses the question of whether their art harmonizes *logos* and *ergon.*

In the *Euthydemus,* Socrates has four principal interlocutors. The primary ones are two Sophists, Euthydemus and Dionysodorus. They come from Thurii, the *polis* whose founding in the 440s was promoted by Pericles and whose constitution was drawn up by the Sophist Protagoras. The others include Ctesippus and Clinias, grandson of Alcibiades. Most of the dialogue is recollected by Socrates for the benefit of Crito (see *Crito*), who is particu-

---

32. In *A History of Greek Philosophy,* 4:267, Guthrie dramatically locates the *Euthydemus* in the fifth century, in virtue of its reference to Alcibiades as being present (who died in 404). However, the reference is to the grandson of "the famous Alcibiades" (275a).

larly concerned about how he might teach virtue to his sons. At the close of the dialogue, Crito recalls for the benefit of Socrates a conversation he had with an anonymous individual who overheard Socrates' discourse with the Sophists. This character is probably a dramatization of Plato's philosophical rival, Isocrates,[33] and these dramatic features directly connect the dialogue to Plato's own concerns about Isocrates' conception of "philosophy" relative to the kind of philosophy and discourse he had begun to institutionalize in the Academy.

Socrates opens the discussion by making a rough sketch of what the practice of wisdom and virtue might be (278d–e), initially focusing on the conception and practice of "doing well." He implicitly accepts the common belief that the excellence of virtue must be practical, which suggests that *eu prattein* represents a corollary to *sophrosyne* as characterized in the *Charmides*. The question becomes, What would guarantee the acquisition of the traditionally accepted components of *eu prattein*—namely, the conventionally praised traits of health, good looks, wealth, power, honor, good birth, temperance, uprightness, bravery, knowledge, and good fortune (279a–c)?

Socrates suggests that *sophia* naturally guarantees a beneficial outcome of an action; an action informed by *sophia* should bring good fortune. Wisdom is initially defined as a kind of knowledge or science (*episteme*) that guides and straightens out action (*praxis*) (281a–b). Just as Nicias did in the *Laches*, Socrates here slides between *episteme* and *sophia* as well as *phronesis*, as similar forms of second-order practical reason that, when exercised in conjunction with first-order activities, reliably generate good, practical results. This slide enables the discussion to turn toward the question of what characterizes the *episteme* of *sophia* and how it can be taught. It simultaneously puts on the table the competence of the Sophists, who claim the possession of, and the ability to impart, such *episteme*.

The discussion soon takes a familiar turn. As in the *Charmides*, where there was trouble in identifying an *episteme* that provided knowledge of other *epistemai* and knowledge of itself, there is trouble here in identifying a *techne* that not only is productive but also entails knowledge of how to use properly that which is made. There seems to be a need for two arts rather than one (289b). The speech-making art does have two components—making speeches and giving or using them—but it does not produce happiness (289c–d).

33. See W. H. Thompson, *The Phaedrus of Plato*, app. 2, "On the Philosophy of Isocrates, and His Relation to the Socratic Schools," 170–83.

In their initial efforts to identify the appropriate *techne*, Socrates and Clinias focus on second-order arts that use other arts. Examples include the "art" of dialecticians, who "use" the art of speech makers, and the "art" of politicians, who "use" the art of generals (290c–d). Their search ultimately leads them to look for the royal or political art (291b–c). In the dialogue, Socrates recounts to Crito the part of the discussion he had with the Sophists (291c–d): "To this art the generals and the other craftsmen gave over their own trades, as being the only art knowing how to use them. Thus it seemed clear to us that this was the art we sought and the cause of doing right in the state, exactly as the version of Aeschylus describes it, sitting alone at the helm of the state, steering all and ruling all, and making all useful." Insofar as the Sophists at the beginning of the *Euthydemus* were deemed to be "know-it-alls" (271e), skilled in many arts (272a), this political art evokes their own art and points to the political character of what they do. Moreover, it indicates how the discussion in which they were engaged had a larger political dimension, for this political art in Athens was understood not as a royal art but as the democratic art of Athenian citizenship.

Plato quickly undercuts this identification of the political art as the end of their search in two ways. First, the political art they have identified is rendered as a typical first-order productive activity, similar to the arts of medicine or agriculture. Its aims involve producing a citizenry that is rich, free, and lacking faction. But these "products," the "works of politics," may be put to evil use (291c–292b); therefore, it cannot "make other people good" as it is supposed to or impart every kind of beneficial knowledge (292d–e). Apparently, another kind of *episteme* or *techne* is needed to make people virtuous. But this political art has another limitation. It must have a substantive domain, but because that domain is occupied by first-order practices, it seems that the practical knowledge involved in the political art as a second-order art of virtue is, like the second-order knowledge of *sophrosyne* in the *Charmides*, the empty set. It is unclear how this art could make one wise or virtuous.

This rejection of the *politike techne* and the "works of politics" as illustrative of the art and work of virtue constitutes an epistemological and practical reduction of the political art and the political sphere to its first-order dimensions; it recalls Socrates' reduction of the virtue of *sophia* to first-order practices in the *Laches*. Athenians were not as sanguine in the fourth century as they were in the fifth about the possibility of virtuous politics or the likelihood that such politics would bring about practical success. It is not surprising, therefore, that in Plato's *Euthydemus,* a dialogue written in the fourth century about fourth-century intellectual discourse, the works of politics possessed neither the substance of virtue nor the epistemological form that would make the acquisition of the political art the road toward becoming virtuous, that is, "faring well" (*eu prattein*).

This exasperation with the political art ends the dialogue's consideration of the substance of *arete* as *eu prattein*, but the need for a link between them has been clearly raised. At the same time, the end of the dialogue seems to illustrate how fruitless is the search for a *techne* that is virtuous in both *logos* and *ergon*. Crito is disappointed, and Plato's Socratic Problem remains unresolved. But the reader is led to believe that its solution, were there to be one, would be an art that constituted virtue and associated philosophy and politics.

4. *Meno*

The *Meno* is rarely read as a dialogue about ethics, let alone politics. For the most part, interpreters focus on the epistemological puzzle of "Meno's Paradox"—that it is impossible to learn anything new or, in Guthrie's words, "One can never find out anything new: either one knows it already, in which case there is no need to find it out, or else one does not, and in that case there is no means of recognizing it when found."[34] Issues concern the particular relevance of this paradox to Socrates' effort to teach a slave boy a geometrical principle as well as its more general relevance to the question with which the dialogue opens—Meno's question to Socrates about whether virtue is teachable, whether it comes by practice or training, or whether it simply comes naturally to its possessors (70a). Insofar as ethics is discussed, its epistemological dimension takes center stage. Other standard points of interest for interpreters are Socrates' use of the hypothetical method as a way out of Meno's Paradox (86eff); the dialogue's distinction between "true belief" (or "true opinion") and "knowledge" (97b–99a); and Socrates' invocation of a theory that knowledge comes via recollection (*anamnesis*), which counts as a kind of answer to Meno's Paradox and serves to explain the slave's acquisition of geometrical knowledge.[35]

34. Plato, *Protagoras and Meno*, trans. and ed. W. K. C. Guthrie (Penguin, 1956), 104; *Meno* 80d–e.

35. For an excellent discussion of the ethical and epistemological dimensions of the *Meno*, as well as a good account of previous scholarship on the subject, see Alexander Nehamas, "Meno's Paradox and Socrates as a Teacher," in *Oxford Studies in Ancient Philosophy, vol. 3, 1985*, ed. Julia Annas, 1–30. However, Nehamas ignores the political dimension of the dialogue,

A naive encounter with the dialogue, however, suggests not only that these apolitical emphases leave out many crucial political elements of the dialogue but that the dialogue directly concerns the Platonic political art. First, when Socrates turns the tables on Meno and begins to ask him about the nature of virtue, it becomes clear that his interest in its nature and teachability essentially involves its political character (71eff, 91a). Indeed, the subject of "virtue" is implicitly (when not explicitly) understood to be "political virtue." Second, Socrates tests various accounts of such virtue by analogizing their teachability to that of *technai* while noting that teaching virtue cannot be precisely analogous to teaching in ordinary *technai* (90b–91d); Gorgias and Protagoras are mentioned as possible teachers of virtue (71c, 73c, 95c; 91eff), and the political nature of their arts stands front and center when Plato discusses their "arts" in separate dialogues (see Chapter 3, Sections B and C, below). Third, Socrates' other interlocutor (besides Meno) is Anytus (91c–95a)—one of the men who indicted the historical Socrates for his "crimes" against the state—who is horrified by the very idea of Sophists as teachers of virtue and by Socrates' doubts about the capacity of the Athenians' greatest politicians to know or teach virtue. Fourth, Socrates' theory of recollection functionally correlates with the politically "noble lie" of the myth of the metals in the *Republic* (on which see Chapter 4, Section B, below). Finally, the dialogue ends in *aporia* because of Socrates' and Meno's inability to identify anyone—particularly any politicians, including Themistocles and Pericles (93e–94e)—able to teach virtue (99c–100b; see also *Ion* 540e–542b, and *Gorgias* 517c).

The crux of the *Meno*, like the crucial points of the *Laches, Charmides,* and *Euthydemus,* consists of the inability of Plato's Socrates to find a coher-

---

and his conception of Socrates and Socratic virtue—whether that of the historical Socrates or Plato's Socrates in the aporetic dialogues—is so negative, individualistic, and Nietzschean as to encourage one to agree with the historical Socrates' accusers and deny Socrates' virtue as an Athenian citizen. See his "Socratic Intellectualism," in *Proceedings of the Boston Area Colloquium on Ancient Philosophy,* 2:275–316, and "What Did Socrates Teach and to Whom Did He Teach It?" Each of these accounts now appears in a newly published collection of Nehamas's articles on ancient Greek ethics, *The Virtues of Authenticity.*

Other exemplary but apolitical accounts of the *Meno* include *Plato's Meno,* ed. with intro. and commentary by R. S. Bluck (Cambridge: Cambridge University Press, 1961), and Irwin's *Plato's Moral Theory.* The dialogue is barely mentioned in the most recent comprehensive account of Plato's political thought, namely, George Klosko's *The Development of Plato's Political Theory.* In the 1920s, Paul Friedlander wrote a provocative and politically sensitive account of the *Meno.* See his *Plato: The Dialogues, II,* 273–97.

ent *logos* of virtue that has an evident practical—which is to say political—
function. Given the confidence of the historical Socrates' jurors that they
knew *he* corrupted his fellow citizens, this dialogue belongs among those
dialogues that constitute Plato's indictment of the Athenian accusers and jurors who convicted his hero. But Plato did not write this or any dialogue out
of resentment or spite or to settle a grudge, but to explore a philosophical
problem. In the cases of his ethical and political aporetic dialogues, this philosophical problem is also political and may well be called Plato's Socratic Problem. It is also an essentially democratic problem, relevant to questions about
democratic education and the nature of democracy-friendly political leadership. For how does one conceptualize, let alone practice, the form and/or
content of ethical education and political leadership for a democratic society—that is, a society that presupposes a natural, basic equivalence in the
moral status and ethical judgment of every citizen?

We now turn to those dialogues in which Plato's Socratic Problem is
manifested directly as a conflict between a *logos* of Socratic virtue and the extant intellectual, ethical, and political discourse and practices of virtue. We examine these in detail because they directly address this conflict as a problem
for the Platonic political art.

C. APORETIC TREATMENTS OF THE POLITICAL ART

Plato's *Protagoras* and *Gorgias* probe the dimensions of his Socratic Problem much further than the *Laches, Charmides,* and *Euthydemus,* and *Meno,*
because they present for sustained investigation direct links between virtue and the political art.[36] In the *Protagoras,* the vehicle is Plato's treatment

36. The relative order of composition of all of these dialogues, apart from their probably
having been completed before the *Republic* was completed, is uncertain but not crucial to our
concerns. Nothing in my discussion of the *Protagoras* or *Gorgias* depends on the relative chronological relation of *their* dates of composition. It is impossible to identify confidently and precisely the year or years in which either the *Protagoras* or *Gorgias* was composed. The standard
view suggests that Plato wrote the *Protagoras* before he wrote the *Gorgias.* See Guthrie, *A History of Greek Philosophy,* 4:213–14. More recently, scholars have argued that the *Gorgias* was
written first. See Holger Thesleff, *Studies in Platonic Chronology,* 118ff, and Charles Kahn, "On
the Relative Date of the *Gorgias* and the *Protagoras,*" in *Oxford Studies in Ancient Philosophy,*
ed. J. Annas, 6:69–102. However, the evidence offered by each of these interpretations depends
on a constructed reading of Plato's dialogues. With respect to these two dialogues, different readings generate different orders.

of Protagoras, who had claimed to be able to reconcile critical discourse and the Athenians' democratic understanding of virtue as a political art; in the *Gorgias*, the topic is rhetoric in Athenian democracy, and the characters range from Gorgias, one of the first teachers of rhetoric, to Callicles, a probably imaginary politician who seeks to use rhetoric to increase his power and influence over the *demos*. These dialogues provide historical and political commentaries as well as philosophical explorations. By dramatically engaging "Socrates" with other major historical figures who themselves articulated versions of the political art, they offer extraordinarily rich material for understanding how Plato articulated his conception of the political art in relation to conceptions of ethics, the practice of politics, and the nature of critical discourse that (he believed) prevailed in Athenian democracy itself.

Neither dialogue provides a settled reconciliation of virtue and the political art. However, they provide Plato's most thorough treatment of the relation between virtue and the political art outside the *Republic, Statesman,* and *Laws*—dialogues that do present relatively settled versions of their reconciliation. As such, the *Protagoras* and *Gorgias* offer the best evidence available of Plato's understanding of the political and theoretical problems to which the more expository dialogues provided partial solutions.[37] In particular, they reveal Plato's understanding of the ethical and critical limitations of prevailing forms of public discourse about virtue and politics in the Athenian democracy; they indicate how acceptance of social conventions limits philosophical inquiry; and they justify Plato's simultaneous turn to ideal theory and rejection of conventional practice as guides for understanding an ethically virtuous political art.

---

37. It is impossible to identify the precise years in which either the *Protagoras* or *Gorgias* was composed. All that is essential for my argument is that they were composed after the Athenians' defeat in the Peloponnesian War and after the trial and death of Socrates. It is conceivable that they were composed after Plato wrote his first complete version of the *Republic;* however, it strikes me as unlikely that Plato wrote dialogues that take as their points of departure the ethical beliefs and political practices of historical Athens after he had decided (in the *Republic*) that for justice and virtue to be understood they had to be theorized independently of Athenian conventions. They most certainly were composed before the *Statesman* and *Laws.* (For more on the general subject of the ordering of the dialogues, see Chapter 2, Section D, above.)

I refer to the expository dialogues as providing "partial" solutions to the problems identified in the aporetic dialogues because the former do not replace or necessarily supersede the intellectual work of the latter.

I. PLATO AND DEMOCRATIC SOPHISTRY:
VIRTUE AND THE POLITICAL ART IN THE *Protagoras*

Plato's *Protagoras* concerns the meaning of the political art and virtue as subjects that can be discursively taught to the general (paying) public.[38] Insofar as sophistry was the most prominent medium for formal education in these subjects during the Athenian democracy of Plato's time, the *Protagoras* offers a critical evaluation of the practice of democratic sophistry, an art of critical discourse whose teachers would foster in their students an art that accommodated virtue, politics, and democracy.

The full meaning of the dialogue emerges from considering its arguments in terms of their exponents, the characters of the dialogue. They are Hippocrates, the would-be student of Protagoras; highly political, powerful, and dangerous Athenian citizens such as Alcibiades and Critias; a company of notable Sophists, including Hippias and Prodicus; Protagoras, the most famous Sophist of all, who was known for his links to Pericles; and Socrates. Together, these characters represent a wide range of experience in the Athenian political realm, one that is of a different order from, but is nonetheless comparable to, degrees of philosophical distance between practice and theory. In the *Protagoras*, Plato weaves the historical and dialogic identities of these characters together, creating a text of historical and theoretical critique.

The relations of the conversational exchanges in the dialogue to both their dramatic and historical settings are crucial for understanding their significance. Because its dramatic date is approximately the late 430s—before Plato was born and prior to the outbreak of the Peloponnesian War—Plato's composition of the dialogue thirty to fifty years later provides him with the opportunity to reflect critically on the educational and ethical climate of Athens before it experienced the war and its disastrous consequences.[39] It

38. As such, it may be fruitfully compared and contrasted to the *Meno*, in which the subject of whether virtue can be taught is addressed in relation to a private, teacher-pupil relationship. Because the significance of the *Meno* for Plato's conception of the political art per se is either indirect or marginal, we discussed it only briefly, in Section B4, above. It is also referred to subsequently whenever portions of it relate to the subjects of the *Protagoras* and the Platonic political art more generally.

39. The commonly agreed-on dramatic date of the dialogue is 433 or earlier. See W. K. C. Guthrie, *A History of Greek Philosophy*, 4:214–15. John Walsh has more recently pointed out

raises issues about the roles of its prominent ideas, institutions, and individuals (via their modes of discursive expression) in subsequent Athenian troubles—such as their defeat by the Spartans, the internal strife of Athenian politics, and of course the Popular Court's judgment against Socrates. This invests the philosophy and drama of the dialogue with political meaning. For one might say that Plato reconceptualizes democratic sophistry at its best (in the person of Protagoras), when Athenian democracy was (at least from Plato's fourth-century perspective) most powerful and unified, against the background of its later defeat, division, and political weakening.[40] To interpret the dialogue more narrowly—via a primarily internal analysis of the dialogue's drama or certain concepts in it (such as *akrasia* or hedonism) or a mostly external analysis of the text as a dramatic conflict between warring class interests—ignores the complex interaction between history and theory that the dialogue represents; the result reduces or distorts our appreciation of what the dialogue has to offer.[41]

The critical significance of the *Protagoras* for understanding Plato's thought in general and his conception of the relation between virtue and the political art in particular calls for an interpretation that accounts for its multiple dimensions.[42] In what follows, I try to identify the appropriate balance among history, textual argument, and political theory as elements of the dialogue's meaning—first by establishing the historical aspects of the dialogue and then by interpreting its dramatic and philosophical renditions of the political art, virtue, and how they could be taught.

---

that aspects of the dialogue place its dramatic date in the 420s. See his "The Dramatic Dates of Plato's *Protagoras* and the Lessons of *Arete.*" However, Thomas Cole has pointed out that the date has to be before 429, the year that Pericles died, because Pericles' two sons, who predeceased him, are nonspeaking characters in the dialogue.

40. For an evaluation of Athenian power during the Periclean era, see Thucydides, III.65.5. Insofar as Walsh is right in arguing that some aspects of the *Protagoras* must reflect Athens in the late 420s, this division and weakening are already underway as the *dramatic* dialogue is taking place—which only serves to heighten the poignancy of Plato's critique of Protagoras.

41. For an influential "internal" analytical interpretation, see T. Irwin's *Plato's Moral Theory,* 102–14. For an "external" interpretation, see Ellen and Neal Wood, *Class Ideology and Ancient Political Theory,* 128–37.

42. The analytical divisions that follow are necessarily artificial. For example, the historical dimension of this dialogue (and that of others) does not operate as a set of unalloyed facts to be evaluated by Platonic theorizing. It is impossible to get fully "behind" the dialogue to a firm, factual foundation. However, one cannot ignore the way in which the dialogue operates against a historical background that transcends it in some ways.

a. The Historicity of the *Protagoras*

The historicity of the *Protagoras* does not involve its historical plausibility; it derives from Plato's dramatic and philosophical engagement of actual—now re-presented and reinterpreted—historical figures.[43] For Plato, Protagoras was particularly important. Of all the Sophists and rhetoricians in Plato's dialogues, Protagoras receives the most attention and greatest respect. More specifically, his intellectual relation to democracy and his specific views about both the possibility of a democratic education in virtue and the political, if not personal, relativity of virtue directly relate to Plato's theoretical concerns. One ancient author declared that almost all of the ideas in Plato's *Republic* appeared originally in Protagoras's *Antilogoi*.[44] Although this statement is surely false if taken literally, the character of Protagoras offers the most important historical benchmark (besides Socrates) for Plato's conceptualization of virtue and the political art as well as his understanding of the relation of critical reason to democracy. Protagoras's fame stemmed from his activity for over forty years as a Sophist, which made him very wealthy.[45] In Plato's *Meno* (91e), Socrates remarks to Anytus that Protagoras was highly regarded throughout his long career.[46] His fame and fortune in Athens made him a

---

43. Although the relatively historical Socrates of Plato's *Apology* does not mention that he had any experience in questioning Sophists about their profession or understanding of virtue—for the purposes of his defense, he noted only his interest in the claims of politicians, poets, dramatists, and craftsmen (all citizens, in contrast to the mostly foreign-born Sophists)—Socrates might have questioned Protagoras during his life, for Protagoras would have been a prime candidate for the Socratic *elenchus*. The question of whether the historical Socrates actually challenged Protagoras, however, cannot be definitively resolved. The historicity of the exchange must be evaluated from the perspective of its author, who wrote about this encounter two generations after it might have occurred. That is why I believe its historical actuality is best understood in terms of Plato's conceptual framework and interest in solving his Socratic Problem. For the view that Protagoras's discourse in Plato's *Protagoras* and *Theaetetus* represents straightforward accounts of the thought of the historical Protagoras, see Guthrie, *A History of Greek Philosophy*, 4:265–66.

44. Diogenes Laertius, III.37.

45. For Protagoras's probable wealth, see Plato, *Theaetetus* 161d; *Hippias Major* 282d; *Meno* 92d. Also see Diogenes Laertius, ix.52.

46. This discounts the story of his expulsion, which appears in the biographical tradition. There it is asserted that the Athenians at one time burned his books and prosecuted him for impiety—if so, probably under the decree of Diopeithes. See Diogenes Laertius, ix. 52, 54. For a complete listing and interpretation of the fragments about the prosecution of Protagoras as well as other intellectuals in Athens, see K. J. Dover, "The Freedom of the Intellectual in Greek Society."

model for any other Greek intellectual—to be imitated, revised, or rejected. In his own way, his intellectual position in Athens was as pivotal as that of Socrates, insofar as he may have been a student of Anaxagoras, was a counselor of Pericles, undoubtedly knew his fellow Abderan, Democritus, and had Isocrates and Prodicus as pupils.[47]

Unfortunately, we have very little evidence of Protagoras's beliefs that can be verified independently of Plato's dialogues. Diogenes Laertius (not the most reliable source) mentions titles of books he wrote, which covered matters of ethics, politics, mathematics, wrestling (see Plato, *Sophist* 232dff), the origins of society, the art of eristics, theology, and a book on opposing arguments (*Antilogoi*). But we lack extended excerpts from them. Among the existing fragments is the following well-known precept that Plato makes the subject of inquiry in the *Theaetetus* (152aff): "Man is the measure of all things, of things that are that they are, and of things that are not that they are not."[48] Two other fragments should inform our understanding of Protagoras in Plato's *Protagoras*. One is a statement about the gods. It suggests that the religious dimension of Protagoras's "Great Speech" in the dialogue should not be emphasized: "Concerning the gods I cannot know either that they exist or that they do not exist, or what form they might have, for there is much to prevent one's knowing: the obscurity of the subject and the shortness of

---

Dover interprets them in a way that makes fifth-century Athenians much more tolerant than the biographical tradition suggests.

The decree of Diopeithes made it a crime to deny the gods of the city and/or to offer instruction about astronomy. Plutarch, *Peric.* 32.2; Diogenes Laertius, IX.52. The decree may have been passed with Anaxagoras in mind—because his views about such matters were more fully developed—and was probably used against him. But Anaxagoras was a teacher of Pericles, and Protagoras counseled Pericles. The decree seemed to have been a vehicle for combating Pericles' influence. See G. B. Kerferd, *The Sophistic Movement*, 21–22. Ironically (given the opposition between Protagoras and Socrates in the *Protagoras*), it may have ensnared Socrates as well, in that it provided legal grounds for popular suspicion of Socrates. (Plato, *Apology* 19b.) Protagoras may have been convicted under this decree and forced to leave Athens, but later he was allowed to return, possibly to advise a budding, would-be successor to Pericles named Alcibiades. See Morrison, "The Origins of Plato's Philosopher-Statesman," 14–16. On the evidence for this decree and its application, see Todd, *The Shape of Athenian Law*, 308, n. 22, and 312, n. 27.

47. See Sprague, *The Older Sophists*, 6–7. Philostratus claimed that Protagoras was a disciple of Democritus, but Democritus's life span appears to have postdated Protagoras's, which makes this relationship highly unlikely.

48. The full quotation comes from Diogenes Laertius, ix.51; Plato leaves out the qualifying phrase.

man's life."[49] The other statements directly reflect the educational ethic Protagoras articulates in Plato's *Protagoras:* "Teaching requires natural endowment and practice," and "They must learn starting young."[50]

The Sophists who became prominent in fifth-century Athens were the first professional intellectuals.[51] In Plato's *Protagoras* (316d–317a), Protagoras identifies his vocation, his *techne*, by linking it to the poetry of Homer and Hesiod, the prophecy of mystery religions, as well as to the teaching of athletics and music, which makes it a traditional, centuries-old activity. But he also states that these practices were conducted in disguise. Whether or not this is true (and it probably isn't), Protagoras was the first to practice sophistry in the open, and it is indeed the case that not before the middle of the fifth century did individuals make a living teaching intellectual subjects. Most of those who initially did, namely those of Protagoras's generation, were not Athenians but rather individuals from other Greek *poleis* who came to Athens to profitably practice their craft, notably Protagoras, Prodicus of Ceos, Hippias of Elis, Gorgias of Leontini, and Thrasymachus of Chalcedon.[52] Their subjects were wide-ranging, including lessons in mathematics, poetic interpretation, music, geography, grammar, etymology, gymnastics, and virtue. Given the absence of any higher education in fifth-century Athens, these subjects were the constituents of discursive schooling appropriate for an intellectually cultivated (indeed, sophisticated) Athenian citizen. By having Protagoras position himself as the heir of this discursive tradition, Plato and the Platonic

---

49. D–K, Fr. 4. Translation by R. K. Sprague in *The Older Sophists*, ed. Rosamond Kent Sprague, 20. However, this fragment does indicate why Protagoras may have become an object of popular suspicion in Athens.

50. Diels-Kranz, Fr. 3. Translation R. K. Sprague, *The Older Sophists*, 20. However, the character of the source of this fragment suggests that it may have been derived from Plato's *Protagoras*, depriving it of independent significance. A worthy recent effort to forge a coherent Protagorean philosophy out of the fragments is Edward Schiappa, *Protagoras and Logos*, 89–153.

51. Relatively complete and recent monographs on the Sophists in English include W. K. C. Guthrie, *The Sophists*; G. B. Kerferd, *The Sophistic Movement*; Jacqueline de Romilly, *The Great Sophists of Periclean Athens*. Useful collections of articles on the Sophists include C. J. Classen, ed., *Sophistik* (Darmstadt, 1976), and G. B. Kerferd, ed., *The Sophists and Their Legacy* (Wiesbaden, 1981).

52. A notable exception is Damon of Athens, a teacher of music. In Plato's *Apology* (20b), Socrates refers to Evanus of Paros as a Sophist who earned money by claiming to teach a *techne* of *arete*. He also mentions Gorgias, Prodicus, and Hippias as prominent Sophists. Interestingly, he does not mention Protagoras, the most famous of them all—perhaps because he had probably been dead for twenty years.

Socrates take on not only Protagoras but the entire tradition to which he belongs—up to and including fourth-century Sophists.[53]

b. The Dramaturgy and Philosophy of the *Protagoras*

i. The Dramatic Frame

The dramatic frame of the dialogue anticipates in miniature two of the problematic relationships discussed in the rest of it. The first concerns the relationship of Protagoras and Protagoras's art to Socrates and Socrates' art. Plato presents Socrates as a kind of teacher of Alcibiades. The historicity of this relationship would have resonated with the immediate readers of the dialogue. Because of Alcibiades' notorious behavior, the relationship may have sullied the historical Socrates' reputation. Yet in the dialogue, Socrates says that *he* also listened to Alcibiades. This functions as a Socratic *apologia*, insofar as it suggests that Socrates did not deliberately shape Alcibiades' intellect or influence his ethical behavior in any determinate way. Plato has dramatically portrayed Socrates in such a way as to counter the public reputation of the historical Socrates as a corrupting influence on Athenian youth. And yet, by linking Socrates and Alcibiades in the dialogue, Plato asks the reader to reflect critically on the political and ethical meaning of Socratic education.

The second problematic relation involves the relative compatibility of the "arts" or modes of discourse of Protagoras and Socrates to the principles and practices of Athenian democracy. In the course of the dialogue, Plato creates two distinct portraits of Socrates and Protagoras and raises the question of whether the form and substance of their modes of understanding and teaching virtue corrupt or improve democratic citizenship. Because the Athenians' virtuous practice of citizenship ethically justified their democratic system of government, Plato is addressing not only the educational meaning of Protagoras's and Socrates' "arts" but also the ethical and intellectual coherence of

---

53. As much as or more than the actual beliefs of the historical Protagoras (although Plato probably tried to be true to them), the discourse of Protagoras in Plato's *Protagoras* represents the character of fourth-century neo-Sophistic justifications of an education in democratic civic virtue. (Despite my use of "neo-Sophistic" to define a category of discourse, the evidence we have prevents us from clearly differentiating fifth-century and early fourth-century sophistry.)

On Plato's interest in demarcating his mode of philosophical inquiry from "sophistry," which he redefined to his rhetorical advantage, see A. Nehamas, "Eristic, Antilogic, Sophistic, Dialectic: Plato's Demarcation of Philosophy from Sophistry," in *The Virtues of Authenticity*. For the categorical opposition of "philosophy" and "sophistry" as a Platonic theoretical invention, see Cole, *The Origins of Rhetoric in Ancient Greece*, 99.

Athens's democratic principles and practices—one version of which led to the conviction and execution of Socrates.

The dialogue opens with an unnamed friend of Socrates approaching him and asking him from whence he has come. The friend surmises correctly that Socrates has just come from a visit with Alcibiades and presumes that Socrates has been chasing him. Socrates replies that he has been with Alcibiades but lost interest in him during his discussion with Protagoras of Abdera, a Sophist who, Socrates says (ironically, given *Apology* 21a), is "the wisest of all living men" (309d). Socrates' friend is intrigued and asks Socrates to tell him about the conversation he had with Protagoras, and Socrates agrees.

Socrates says that the conversation between Protagoras and himself occurred because of a request from another Athenian youth, Hippocrates (namesake of the reputed father of Greek medicine), to help him become a student of Protagoras. Unlike the historical Socrates, who did not claim to be a teacher of a specifiable body of knowledge or set of practices that constituted virtue, the historical Protagoras was noted for knowing how to teach a practical art of virtue.[54] The passage resonates with the life of the historical Socrates and his trial, insofar as Socrates apparently took pains in his trial (*Apology* 20d, 21d) to differentiate his vocation and discourse from that of Sophists such as Evenus of Paros, who charged a large fee to students who came to him to learn the *techne* of *arete*.[55]

After hearing of Hippocrates' eagerness, Socrates urges him to reflect on

54. *Protagoras* 311b, d; compare *Apology* 20b. Actually, there is no record of the historical Protagoras's having actually referred to his teaching or knowledge as a *techne*, independently, that is, of Plato's dialogues. Inasmuch as Protagoras's words in this dialogue are really Plato's, despite whatever historical grounding they have, we cannot therefore be certain that the historical Protagoras referred to his calling as a *techne*. This term simply could serve Plato's desire to interpret the character of Protagoras's discourse as an art. After all, throughout the early dialogues, Plato has displayed an interest in analyzing various forms of discourse in terms of arts (*technai*). But it was common knowledge that Sophists used *technai* (handbooks) for teaching and that many were known for teaching their subjects as *technai*, albeit in a non-Platonic sense. (See A. Thomas Cole, *The Origins of Rhetoric in Ancient Greece*.) So I think it is fair to infer that the historical Protagoras understood himself to be teaching a *techne* and that he viewed his own profession as a Sophist to be a *techne*; however, his conception of a, or his, *techne* was not Platonic. This is important for our interest in linking Plato's *logos* to historical *ergon*, especially because Protagoras's reference to "his" professional discourse as a *techne* provides the central issue for his ensuing discussion in the dialogue with Plato's Socrates.

55. The comparison is substantiated later in the *Protagoras* (322e–323a), when Protagoras refers to the subject matter of his *techne* as human virtue or political virtue.

precisely what it is that he hopes to obtain from Protagoras. But Hippocrates does not believe that the teaching of Protagoras's art, or what he wants from learning it, parallels the craftsman-apprentice relationship, so that Hippocrates ashamedly blushes when Socrates asks him whether he wants to *become* a Sophist like Protagoras. This is not surprising, because Protagoras's craft was not highly regarded as a vocation by fifth-century Athenian citizens. Well-to-do and politically ambitious Athenians were not craftsmen and would not welcome being seen as devoting their education to the acquisition of a trade. Moreover, its practitioners were not citizens, and it was practiced apart from the conventional political realm. Hippocrates wants an education (*paideia*), not a trade, one that "befits a freeman" and enables him both to become a dashing political speaker and to achieve prominence in Athenian public life—although his private life appears to be disarrayed, in that his slave has just run away.

Socrates first asks Hippocrates what Sophists do and what knowledge they impart. Hippocrates says that they "make one wise" and teach wise things.[56] But, Socrates then asks, what kinds of "wise things?" Over what branch of knowledge do they lay claim to expertise? (310e, 312d, 313e). Socrates has begun to press Hippocrates to define the knowledge he seeks in terms of *episteme*. The indeterminacy of its content bothers Socrates. Because the power of such knowledge is potentially so deep, it possesses significant and potentially dangerous ethical consequences. One is unable to deliberate about its use after one has received it, and yet Hippocrates is eager to learn what Protagoras has to offer without having deliberated about its value (313a–b).

To put this issue more formally, an art of virtue, a second-order art that involves ethical regulation, is being treated like a first-order art, which does not. To emphasize the danger for Hippocrates of a Sophistic education, Socrates employs the metaphor of shopping. A customer interested in purchasing items sold in a retail store, say food or drink, may consult an expert about their suitability for eating or drinking before ingesting them. But one who buys Protagoras's teaching directly ingests it, and it quickly becomes part of oneself. There is no opportunity for seeking advice or a "second opinion" (314a).

Protagorean knowledge possesses its own standards of evaluation, yet its

---

56. See *Charmides* 162eff, and Section B, above.

self-validating character prevents an independent critical evaluation of its worth—the kind of task that Hippocrates is asking *Socrates* to perform, to advise him about Protagoras's advice about how to succeed in Athens. Thus, Socrates goes on to say, one should have as much or more confidence in the skill of a Protagorean teacher who claims to impart knowledge of virtue as a patient does in a physician who would improve the health of his body. Indeed, if the effects of Protagoras's art were reliable and sound, he would be a physician of the soul (313e). Thus, by "going" to Protagoras, Hippocrates would be submitting his soul to Protagoras's care (*therapeuein*) about matters of good and evil (312c, 313e).[57] Plato's Socrates has therefore evoked the memory of the historical Socrates, who urged those with whom he spoke to care for their souls, as well as the historical Hippocrates, who cared for human bodies (311b). Plato has likened the Sophists' education to a (bogus) verbal cure for the soul, comparable to a physical cure for the body.[58]

In this series of exchanges with Hippocrates, Socrates has generated concern about the significance and problematic character of Protagoras's art of virtue on four closely linked levels: 1) the epistemological—its content as knowledge; (2) the practical—its identity as a craft; (3) the ethical—its effect on one's soul; and (4) the political—its public consequences. The rest of the dialogue navigates among these levels.

Now Hippocrates and Socrates proceed to the house where Protagoras is staying, the house of a wealthy Athenian named Callias. They find there not only Protagoras but other notable Sophists, namely Hippias and Prodicus; dangerous political men, including Alcibiades, Critias, and Charmides; political moderates, such as the sons of Pericles; and citizens from other city-states.[59] Socrates' questioning begins. Socrates' initial request of Protagoras is for him to decide the place and forum for explaining his art to Hippocrates. Should it be in private or in the company of others? Protagoras responds by recounting the ancestry of his art. He proudly proclaims that sophistry is an ancient *techne*, but one that was previously disguised by its practitioners, who veiled their art in other activities such as poetry, gymnastics, or music.

---

57. Which makes one wonder about what Plato's view would be of the millions of "therapeutic" interactions that occur throughout the West.

58. Which he does in other dialogues, such as *Charmides, Gorgias, Phaedrus, Republic, Statesman,* and *Laws.*

59. For an interesting interpretation of the different characteristics of these circles of association, see Paul Friedländer, "Protagoras," in his *Plato,* 2:5–10.

Now it no longer needs concealment; he can affirm openly his identity as a Sophist. Yet he seems to enjoy most displaying his skill in private and so asks to have the discussion inside Callias's house, amid Callias's visitors (316c–317c).

Socrates proceeds to try to understand the nature of this art that would complement the natural ability of Hippocrates, a young, ambitious Athenian citizen. Protagoras believes he can teach the distinctive skill Hippocrates desires. In fact, he claims that his students acquire the education he provides in the manner of a *techne*—systematically and cumulatively (318a). Protagoras claims his students will learn "Good judgment about one's own affairs, enabling one to manage best one's own household and the affairs of the city, so that one will be able to be most powerful in the city with one's acting and speaking" (318e–319a).

Plato's Socrates then translates Protagoras's vocation into a different conceptual language—probably not that of the historical Protagoras (as argued below). He characterizes Protagoras's self-representation as a claim to teach the political art (*technen politiken*) and make men good citizens. This skill in judgment, this virtue, this political art, is what all Athenians supposedly possess—at least to some degree.

Socrates suggests reasons for believing that this art cannot be taught, for it does not seem to be either taught or communicated man to man (319b). To dispute the possibility of this art, he initially points out the apparent anomaly of Protagoras's art amid the prevailing understandings and practices of Athenian democracy. First, the Athenians typically obtain "advice" in the assembly from "experts" (*demiourgoi*) in particular, practical first-order arts—such as construction or shipbuilding—because they have knowledge about the matter at hand that assemblymen generally do not possess. Yet, because the assemblymen's judgment is final, the expertise of the *demiourgoi*—the knowledge of their craft—contributes to but does not directly determine the assembly's decision about the matter at hand.[60] Second, Socrates notes the difficulty that virtuous citizens have in teaching their virtue to their sons

---

60. Of course, the assembly may simply follow the advice of the *demiourgos* providing counsel, but because that advice is supposed to be more technical than political the assembly validates it with a distinct deliberative act.

This passage offers an important historical analogue to Plato's view that first-order *technai* and *epistemai* are necessary but not sufficient for understanding virtue and the political art. See Chapter 3, Section B, above.

(319e–320c).[61] By citing these two examples as evidence that contradicts Protagoras's claim to teach the political art as an art of virtue, Socrates has established a problematic relationship between Protagoras and the norms and practices of Athenian democracy, one that Plato elaborates in the rest of the dialogue.

ii. Protagorean Sophistry and Athenian Democracy

In order to respond to Socrates, Protagoras now launches into an extraordinary two-part speech—what has come to be known as "the Great Speech" of Protagoras, despite its uniquely Platonic features—which seeks to allay Socrates' doubts about his art.[62] He tries to justify his understanding of the nature of the *politike techne,* as well as his ability to teach it.

In the first part, Protagoras tells a story (*mythos*) that indicates basic presuppositions of Athenian democracy. It justifies the existence of virtue and the political art as "natural" possessions of all Athenian citizens that nevertheless can be improved by teaching. It describes how human beings came to possess the *politike techne,* what its relation is to other *technai* and to human nature in general, and how the democratic, egalitarian, deliberative practices of the Athenian assembly confirm, rather than disprove, the existence of his art. In the second part, he supports these mythical and phenomenal descriptions with a rational account (*logos*) of actual Athenian social, political, and educational practices. He explains why his art is teachable and how it complements and improves the conventional *paideia* performed by Athenian parents educating their children. Both parts of the speech justify the possession and practice of virtue and the political art by all Athenian citizens, demonstrate its efficacy in both private and public matters, and provide a role for Protagoras in perfecting its practical use. Protagoras can associate his knowl-

---

61. This is a problem Plato treats in the *Laches,* and it is made historically poignant here in virtue of the presence of Pericles' sons.

62. See the Jowett-Ostwald translation of the *Protagoras,* ed. Gregory Vlastos (Indianapolis: Bobbs-Merrill, 1956). The relation of this speech to the ideas and intellectual style of the historical Protagoras recalls the interpretive puzzle discussed in Part I, above. On the one hand, the carefully constructed scheme of concepts in the speech evidences the order, intellect, and artistry of Plato. The issues of the dialogue and the mode of their consideration fit with a pattern of analysis and argument that Plato has used in roughly similar ways throughout his aporetic dialogues. On the other hand, the image of Protagoras that Plato depicts fits the other evidence of the teachings of the historical Protagoras, evidence that derives from other fragmentary written records of his thought.

edge with the inherent cultural virtue and conventional practices of Athenian society while also maintaining that he has a special skill for educating Athenian citizens in the *politike techne* or *arete* (a virtual equivalent for the political art in the dialogue, whose equivalence is not explicitly discussed).

Stories exalting the Athenian collectivity were publicly spoken in the fifth century, suggesting that something like the *mythos* of Protagoras's speech could well have been presented by the historical Protagoras (although they may have more nearly resembled tales of individual heroism than allegory).[63] The fragmentary *testimonia* of the historical Protagoras also find support in the Great Speech.[64] These aspects of the Great Speech endow it with historical seriousness. However, the conceptual language in which its basic features appear reflects Plato's concerns. As indicated previously, Protagoras may not have conceptualized his own discursive practice as a *techne* and probably never analytically articulated the idea of a *politike techne*. More important, the way the dialogical Protagoras justifies his role must have been crafted by Plato to lead him ineluctably to the corners in which Socrates boxes him.[65] However, the confirmation of the stylistic presentation and content of the Great Speech by non-Platonic sources, the testimony of Protagoras's own writing, and records of Protagoras's political alliances suggest that the weaving of *mythos* and *logos* in Protagoras's speech offers an excellent source for Plato's understanding of both the historical Protagoras and the

---

63. See A. T. Cole, *Democritus and the Sources of Greek Anthropology.* But Cole is skeptical about the historical connections of the discourse of Plato's dialogue and fifth-century discourse, and he would probably emphasize the qualifications of my claim more than the historical truth of the claim itself.

64. See Edward Schiappa, *Protagoras and Logos.*

65. Historical records suggest that Protagoras was both a declaimer and a debater. But for Plato, his specialty was that of a "platform man" who is better at spelling out the intricate unity of his own thought in lectures than engaging in verbal dialectic with others. Not surprisingly, then, Plato has Protagoras in this dialogue "win" the argument with Socrates whenever he states his views synthetically and lengthily and "lose" the argument when he must conform to Socrates' mode of elenchic exchange.

This use of "Protagoras" more closely resembles Plato's use of "Protagoras" in the *Theaetetus;* it reflects an independently Platonic use of the historical Protagoras, which makes the positions taken by "Protagoras" in Plato's dialogues unreliable as sources for the thinking of the historical Protagoras. Nevertheless, because more of what Protagoras has to say in the *Protagoras,* relative to the *Theaetetus,* is presented in the form of a declamation rather than in response to a Socratic *elenchus,* the *Protagoras* is a much more reliable source for the views of the historical Protagoras than is the *Theaeteus,* where Protagoras's elaboration of the meaning of his famous "man the measure" fragment directly results from the interrogation of Plato's Socrates.

basic principles and practices of democratic political thought in late fifth- and early fourth-century Athens.[66]

a) The Political Art as Protagorean *Mythos*
The mythical portion opens with Protagoras recounting how the gods allotted various capacities or powers to animate species for their self-preservation. With technical skills, human beings were able to develop the particular practical skills of language, tilling the soil, and making houses, clothes, shoes, and bedding. Collectively, these skilled capacities were instances of the craftsman's art (*demiourgike techne*, 322b). Protagoras also classified these arts as outgrowths of the intelligence that supports life (321d). (I regard these *technai* as particular practical first-order arts, on the order of Plato's references to typical *technai* in other aporetic dialogues.)

Protagoras describes these human arts as the basic powers or skills that humans needed to survive, much in the manner that animals use their own special natural attributes and powers to survive, for they are almost as basic to human nature as needles are to the porcupine—almost, but not quite. For the myth makes clear that these *technai* were in some sense acquisitions that came to human beings over time by means of their efforts, making these "natural" powers of human beings of a different order from the natural powers of nonrational animals. So far, the story covers ground that is familiar to fifth-century myths of human progress.[67]

In the next part, however, Protagoras's *mythos* charts an innovative course. He says that these *technai* proved to be insufficient for assuring the survival of the human race. To preserve itself, humankind needed the capacity and art to act together as a collectivity. Humanity (which seems to have

66. And yet, because the *Protagoras* itself is so clearly the handiwork of Plato, it does not testify to the historical presence of this mode of thought among fifth-century democrats and should not be taken to provide historical evidence of democratic theory in mid-fifth-century Athens. This tendency appears in Eric Havelock's interesting book, *The Liberal Temper of Greek Politics,* and more recently Cynthia Farrar's book, *The Origins of Democratic Thinking.* During the fifth century, democrats were activists and partisans of their constitutional order and unlikely to stand back from it and offer theoretical defenses of it—particularly when it was not challenged. Thucydides' account of Pericles' funeral oration offers a much sounder basis for the conceptual environment of the late fifth century than Protagoras's Great Speech in Plato's *Protagoras,* even as many of the ideas in the speech and those of Thucydides' Pericles remain consistent (as one would expect, given the close political ties between Pericles and Protagoras).

67. See E. A. Havelock, *The Liberal Temper in Greek Politics,* chaps. iii, v, vi, and A. T. Cole, *Democritus and the Sources of Greek Anthropology.*

particularly Athenian traits) recognized this need and began to come together in cities so as to gain the necessary strength to fight off the wild beasts. However, people were frustrated by their lack of the *politike techne,* also identified in the myth as "political intelligence," of which the art of warfare was a necessary but insufficient part (321d, 322b). The inability to ward off hostile beasts stemmed from the inability of human beings to cooperate with one another in a productive, collectively helpful manner.[68] Possessing these first-order arts was *politically* insufficient. As a result, the human race began to destroy itself and scatter once again.

At this point in the story, Protagoras describes how Zeus, fearing the annihilation of humanity, sent Hermes to bring "reverence and justice" (*aidos te kai diken*) to mankind, "to be the ordering principles of cities and the unifying bonds of friendship" (322c).[69] These were not distributed as were the skills that made up the original practical arts of survival. The latter were allotted in such a way that certain individuals would be experts and others would be virtually incompetent. By means of interactive exchange amid a social division of labor, the products of each art could be used by individuals who did not produce them. However, "reverence and justice" in this story are together known as the *politike techne;* they constitute a second-order *techne* for the individual and collectivity as wholes. In contrast to the manner in which the particular practical skills were distributed by the patron god Prometheus, Zeus bestowed the *politike techne* in such a manner that everyone could share in it (322d). As such, it constitutes a democratic rendering of the second-order art of virtue, the kind of art that Plato is unable to specify with confidence in other aporetic dialogues.

Protagoras does not claim that every democratic citizen automatically practiced this art, although every human being seemed to be capable of possessing it.[70] In fact, the only entity that seemed to possess and practice it al-

---

68. In light of Adkins's division of *aretai* into the competitive and cooperative sorts (*Merit and Responsibility: A Study in Moral Values,* 6–7), the *politike techne* appears anomalous, for it enables man both to fight and to cooperate. Perhaps Adkins's categories, rather than the evidence they would help us understand, are anomalous.

69. It is difficult to define *aidos* precisely. Dodds called it "respect for public opinion" in *The Greeks and the Irrational,* 18. Snell said that it indicates "the feeling of shame" (and) "[t]he reaction which the holy excites in a man," and "the consideration extended to one's equals." See *The Discovery of the Mind,* 167. For a sympathetic account of the Greek sense of shame, deliberately posed in contrast to Dodds's account, see Bernard Williams, *Shame and Necessity,* particularly chap. 4.

70. See G. B. Kerferd, "Protagoras' Doctrine of Justice and Virtue."

ways was the upright citizenry of a functioning, relatively democratic political community.[71] Consequently, the political community had to be protected against those individuals who did not practice the *politike techne*. In the story, this resulted in Zeus's condemning to death those who did not demonstrate the traits of reverence and justice that belong to practitioners of the political art, as if they were a sickness that could destroy the body politic (322d).[72] In this myth of democracy, the constitution of a democratic political community establishes boundaries around itself—with one set defending it against external enemies and the other defending it against internal enemies.

Having told this *mythos*, Protagoras proceeds to account for the conventional practices of the Athenian assembly in a way that also explains and justifies Protagoras's own *techne*. In the assembly, various citizens might possess an expertise, a particular *techne*, which gives them special authority in the provision of certain kinds of information to the assembly. This coincides with the uneven distribution of specialized talents portrayed in the *mythos*. Similarly, there is equal respect given (not equal value assigned) to the opinion and judgment of each citizen in deliberations involving *politike arete* (322e–324a). This sort of deliberation seems to signify deliberations about issues concerning the city as a whole rather than about specialized issues. In addition, it seems that the purpose of *politike arete* is to inform the practice of the *politike techne*.[73]

The practice of this art *and* virtue does not come automatically; nonetheless, anyone in the assembly who claimed that he did not have a sense of justice is regarded as mad, just as Zeus would have killed anyone who does not exercise "reverence and justice." Because each citizen in fact may believe that another is voluntarily acting unjustly, Plato's Protagoras admits that Athenians believe in the actual possession of the *politike techne* as a matter of po-

---

71. I say "relatively" democratic because Protagoras does not specify a precise distribution of political power in his community; nor does he specify the actual means of decision making. However, it does not seem that Protagoras clearly developed a theoretical standpoint that was independent of Athenian democracy, and the thrust of the myth justifies the sovereign, deliberative capacities of the *demos* that Socrates mentioned in the dialogue's beginning when describing the workings of the Athenian assembly.

72. For an interesting, somewhat speculative account of this *mythos* in relation to other ancient Greek myths about technological progress, see Jean-Pierre Vernant, "Prometheus and the Technological Function," in his *Myth and Thought Among the Greeks,* 237–47.

73. Their complementarity is relevant to Plato's larger theoretical project. For in the *Republic,* the need for a harmonious relation between *aretai* and *technai* determines the much less democratic class structure of *kallipolis.* See Chapter 4, Section B, below.

litical trust. They think and act *as if* all possessed it, because to think or act otherwise would challenge the integrity of the assembly's deliberations, the judgments of the law courts, the very foundations of the Athenians' democratic political order.[74]

b) The Political Art as Protagorean *Logos*

Having shown how the *politike techne* came to be and currently exists, Plato's *Protagoras* now presents those social practices and factors of Athenian life that call for Protagoras's special skill in teaching the *politike techne*. In so doing, Protagoras tries to answer Socrates' other doubt about Protagoras's *techne* in teaching the *politike techne*—namely, whether it is teachable, given the trouble that people reputedly have in teaching it to their sons, and therefore whether Protagoras is rightly regarded as a teacher of virtue.

At the same time, Protagoras continues to elaborate his views of the nature of the *politike techne*, which he begins to refer to as *arete*. These practices, which constitute the *politike techne*, also serve to educate citizens in *arete*. The practices Protagoras cites reflect ordinary Athenian practice. They further link Protagoras's views to conventional Athenian beliefs and establish the basis for justifying a role for himself as the educator of Athenian citizens such as Hippocrates.

In Protagoras's *logos*, he refers to the prevailing social institutions of Athens as constituents of *arete*. They include the penal system, as well as the tributaries of *paideia*—the family, schools, poets, gymnastics—all of which implicitly express the *nomoi* of the *polis*. With respect to the institution of punishment, Protagoras notes how Athenians regard with pity those individuals who either lack a valuable trait that normally comes by nature or possess a regrettable trait that they have acquired by chance, but pitilessly chastise those who lack qualities that come by exercise and training. Among these is the *arete* of the good citizen (323d–324a). Much like the presumption in the assembly that all citizens speak out of a desire to bring about justice and that their collective contribution brings about the best possible result, punishment

---

74. Speakers in the assembly could be prosecuted for having proposed an "illegal" decree; speakers in the assembly or council could be "impeached" (via *eisangelia*); jurymen had to swear an oath of fidelity to the laws and decrees of the Athenian people before exercising their judicial capacity. See Todd, *The Shape of Athenian Law*, 54, 113–15. The Athenians also punished speakers in the assembly who had been found to have been bribed by foreigners to speak as they did or, more vaguely, to have "wronged" the Athenian people. See Macdowell, *The Law in Classical Athens*, 180–81.

is based on the presumption that *arete* can be developed by training and that punishment provides this training. Otherwise, according to Protagoras, there would be no rationale for the penal system as a social institution that benefits the *polis*.

He views Athenian *nomoi* as educative practices that produce determinate results. They guide citizens, just as a teacher who gives a child a writing style to copy does, so that he can learn how to write and so that the teacher has an objective standard to justify correcting mistakes when the student makes them (325e–326d). This argument complements the *mythos* if one interprets Zeus's bestowal of *aidos* and *dike* as "the teaching which all people receive in the community."[75] By suggesting that the natural endowment of human beings requires training in order to realize its full potential, Plato's Protagoras has prevented a possible disjuncture between natural and acquired talents and in so doing democratically justifies his own position as a teacher who develops and perfects talents that citizens already are supposed to possess.

Protagoras believes that most individuals are educated quite well by these institutions, to such an extent that even were an Athenian citizen to be wicked, the inevitably positive effect of living under Athenian *nomoi* would make him a better man than anyone not educated amid the conditions of the civic community (327d). He also believes that the exercise of justice and virtue, the practice of the *politike techne* by the citizenry as a whole, educates the individual citizen in *arete*. Plato has Protagoras articulate a quintessential element of virtually any democratic political ethic: "[A]ll men are teachers of virtue, each one according to his own ability" (327a–b, 327e).

By making this point, Protagoras draws attention to his own role in providing citizens with the *politike techne* and *arete*. In his description of the Athenian custom of punishment, Protagoras said that unremediable criminals also ought to be killed or exiled (325b, 326d; see also 322d). One must have virtue and the political art to some minimal degree in order to be among men. But beyond that there is a wide range of individuals who possess various degrees of *arete*. It is here that Protagoras's *techne* comes into play. Protagoras believes that he can significantly augment the beneficial effects of the *nomoi* and the mutual self-education of the collectivity without in the least subverting the fundamental principles that guide these practices.

75. Kerferd, "Protagoras' Doctrine of Justice and Virtue," 44. See also Meletus's belief in Plato's *Apology* (24d–25a) that an education in virtue naturally results from the operation of Athenian political institutions, as well as Chapter 2, Section E, above.

The historical Protagoras occupied an ambiguous social niche in Athenian society. In Protagoras's and Plato's Athens, the positions of professional educators were only beginning to become secure, and political leaders had no official status that differentiated them from other citizens (throughout Protagoras's life and the first half of Plato's life). In Protagoras's speech, the different but often conflated roles of educational expert and layman, political leader and ordinary citizen, as well as the coincidence of the mere existence of Athenian institutions and their educational value, conceptually replicate these practical ambiguities. The effect of these conceptual ambiguities, however, casts doubt on Protagoras's capacity and skill as a teacher in democratic Athens who would make men into good citizens and ordinary citizens into prominent public figures.

Protagoras's justification of his role in Plato's *Protagoras* asserts more than it argues for solutions to difficult theoretical and political problems. First, for Protagoras to say that any human being could be improved by learning from him suggests that there are irreducible deficiencies in the way that the *demos* normally exercises the *politike techne.* Although he does not seek special authority and could not, given his legal status as a foreigner, he seems to regard his ethical and political judgment as superior to that of the *demos,* unless its judgment has been tutored by his (328b).

Second, throughout his *logos,* Protagoras's description of the Athenians' sense of justice, his belief in the successful and beneficial nature of the Athenian penal system, his praise for the harmonious nature of the *nomoi* and their effect on the young, and his conviction of his own positive contribution to the political community assume what he has to prove. He identifies no basis for affirming their merit other than their existence.

Third, Plato's Protagoras supports both conventional democratic practices and the superiority of an elite.[76] This is not entirely contradictory, because any democratic society must accommodate some combination of equalities and inequalities. Yet Protagoras is particularly vulnerable on this point. His conceptual language and principles ascribe virtue and competence to the political activities of ordinary democratic citizens, and yet he favors the

---

76. A. W. H. Adkins makes what I take to be an unfounded jump from identifying this ambiguity to charging Protagoras with having created a "smokescreen." See his "*Arete, Techne,* Democracy, and Sophists: *Protagoras* 316b–328d," 11. Adkins argues that Protagoras's speech is designed so that he partially deceives everyone in order to antagonize no one fully, but it may be read less presumptively as a rationalization of an inherently ambiguous intellectual and political position.

wealthy not only by charging a sizable fee for his services but also by uncritically referring to them as the group most "capable" of taking advantage of his craft (326c).[77]

As formulated by Plato in the Great Speech, Protagoras's claim to know how to teach the *politike techne* and *arete* articulates many features of what could be an interesting and provocative theory of democratic education. But Plato presents these features as conceptually vague and politically unreliable, a not altogether false claim about their particular fifth- and early fourth-century Athenian embodiments. Protagoras claims that he is able to make his students "better," so as to become "fine and good" citizens (318a, 328b; see also 326b). But his *techne* of teaching *arete* and the *politike techne* possesses no standards that give it integrity as a critical instrument in the service of justice.[78] Perhaps these sources of incoherence in Protagoras's thought are exclusively of Plato's making, but the three problems of Protagorean thought I have mentioned most likely represent both the historical Protagoras and Plato's Protagoras. They depend on much more than the basic attributes of Protagoras's social and intellectual status; they are the potential problems of anyone who would claim to be a democratic sophist.

These concerns are basic to the line of questioning in the remainder of the dialogue, where Plato's Socrates criticizes Protagoras's inability to identify, among other things, more secure ethical or critical foundations for his conception of *arete* than the extant *nomoi* and conventional practices and values of Athens. But Plato has his own points to prove as well, which shed as much light on Plato's concerns as they do on Protagoras. From Socrates' criticisms in the dialogue, it becomes clear that Hippocrates could never confidently rely on Protagoras for ethical instruction or political education. The norms that Protagoras has adopted for his art claim to furnish knowledge of "how to succeed," but they offer no guidelines for how to put success to work for good purposes. In Platonic terms, there is no clear "knowledge of use." The Sophist's art provides no systematic guidance for determining the good for the political community or oneself, even as it confidently presumes to have offered sufficient intellectual means for doing just that. As was the case with other aporetic dialogues, there is no successful candidate for a second-order art of virtue.

---

77. Indeed, he offers a money-back guarantee to his student/s if he/they are not satisfied by their Protagorean education (328b).

78. Irwin, *Plato's Moral Theory*, 221. See Paul Friedlander, *Plato*, 2:18.

Yet, as in other aporetic dialogues, Plato still seems to believe in the conceptual possibility of such an art, an art of virtue and politics, and so he has Socrates question Protagoras more closely. Significantly, Socrates must reconstitute the rules of discourse between himself and Protagoras in order to proceed more effectively. This becomes apparent after his first attempt to explore the views of Protagoras, in particular those of his conception of the relations between the virtues.

iii. Protagorean Sophistry, Socratic *Elenchus*, and the Art of Measurement
a) The First *Aporia:* Undermining Protagoras

After recovering from Protagoras's speech, Socrates collects himself and begins to ask Protagoras questions about the *arete* he is supposed to impart. He would have Protagoras formalize the conceptual relations among the virtues he is supposed to teach: "Tell me exactly whether virtue is one whole, of which justice and self-control and piety are parts; or whether all these are names for one and the same thing. . . . [A]re they parts . . . in the same sense in which mouth, nose, and eyes, and ears, are the parts of a face; or are they like the parts of gold, which differ from the whole and from one another only in being larger or smaller?" (329c–d).[79] With this question, Socrates has already shifted the terms of discussion away from Protagorean conceptual territory. By focusing only on the search for a formal definition of virtue, he pays no direct attention to the political and cultural judgments reflected in Protagoras's understanding of *arete* and the *politike techne.* But in so doing, he also exposes the critical ambiguities of Protagorean thought. The first exchange between Protagoras and Socrates displays the philosophical distance between them.

Protagoras's response to Socrates indicates that he does not think about human qualities in terms of a single essence called virtue. To him, there are simply kinds of virtues. The basis on which Protagoras conceptualizes wisdom or justice or piety is the taken-for-granted array of social practices and values that do not experientially exhibit systematic relations among themselves except for their co-presence in an ongoing political community. Protagoras associates the standards for his own *techne* with these vaguely defined, complex conventions. Indeed, the only source for their unity or coherence seems to lie in their empirical association with the unity and coherence of the Athenian *polis.* In the dialogue, Protagoras can provide no criti-

---

79. The Jowett-Ostwald translation.

cally justified understanding of the relation among the virtues or virtue as a whole. One might argue that no such understanding is possible that does not transpose some implicit assumption into a critical theory of virtue.[80] But there is no reason to doubt the legitimacy of Socrates' question or to search for an answer in this dialogue, with respect to either the historical or dialogic Protagoras. It seems that neither *could* provide an answer. In other words (and for different reasons), the historical Protagoras could not have had, and the dialogical Protagoras does not have, a critical conception of virtue apart from "their" endorsements of the conventional beliefs and practices of the Athenians' democratic society.

Protagoras's argumentative difficulties extend to his conversational style. Protagoras rarely makes a statement that describes one of his own beliefs; he maintains a distance between himself and any opinion he holds.[81] Protagoras is unprepared for the rigor and seriousness of the Socratic *elenchus,* in which the interlocutor must always "say what he believes."[82] Plato's Socrates draws attention to the instability of Protagoras's beliefs as well as his ambivalent relationship to the *demos* whose values he both champions and teaches (331c, 333c). Plato's Socrates goes on to link these Protagorean problems with those of democratic political rhetoric, for he simultaneously criticizes the style of Protagorean discourse and associates it with the speech of Pericles (329a). He criticizes Protagoras for talking as if he were making a public address before a large audience while he proceeds in the mode of a private conversation with a friend. In order to avoid having Protagoras and himself talk past each other, Socrates concludes that new rules of discourse must be constituted so that a constructive dialogue can ensue. But unlike the *Crito,* where Plato's Socrates was able to obtain Crito's assent to the basic belief that "no one does wrong willingly" as a basis for deliberation, Plato's Socrates here doubts whether a common ground for the interlocutors can be found (335c–336b).

The discussion has reached an impasse. "Protagoras" has difficulty critically conceptualizing *arete* in a more systematic way, and "Socrates" has difficulty identifying a single Protagorean proposition with which he can argue.

---

80. This point is integral to empiricist (Popperian), poststructuralist (Foucauldian), and pragmatist (Rortian) critiques of critical theories about *society* as a whole. See Chapter 6, below.

81. I say "rarely" rather than "never" because Protagoras seems to affirm directly the irrationality of purely retributive justice. I thank Thomas Cole for this point.

82. On the Socratic *elenchus,* see Gregory Vlastos, "The Socratic *Elenchus,*" in *Oxford Studies in Ancient Philosophy,* and subsequent discussions, listed in *Early Socratic Dialogues,* ed. Trevor J. Saunders, 30, n. 2. See also Chapter 2, Section C, above.

Many in the private audience listening to this dispute now join together in an attempt to keep the discussion going. They contend over the proper way to hold a productive intellectual discussion. As readers, we witness a political exchange over a philosophical dispute, that is, a conflict between irreducible and opposed positions about a proposition. It is a dispute that cannot be resolved in a way that satisfies everyone and yet must be resolved in some fashion for the philosophical conversation to proceed. This dispute about methods has a direct effect on the content of the argument between Protagoras and Socrates about whether and how *arete* and the *politike techne* can be taught.

The best-known figures in attendance contribute their own ideas about how to proceed. Callias, the Sophists' Athenian host, seeks to avoid the issue and prefers to allow each party to do as he likes, the result of which favors Protagorean eloquence. The competitive Alcibiades, historically a student of Socrates as well as the Athenians' powerful and feared enfant terrible, views the dispute as a contest for intellectual preeminence and wants the discussion to proceed according to Socrates' more confrontational style of question-and-answer rather than Protagoras's diffuse rhetorical style.[83] The notorious Critias then steps in and argues for the sake of the discussion rather than for the victory of either participant. Prodicus follows by noting the difference between "wrangling" (*erizein*) for the praise of an audience, which occurs between contestants, and "genuine conversation" (*he sunousia*), which occurs between friends.[84] He believes the latter ought to characterize the discussion between Protagoras and Socrates for reasons approved by virtually everyone present:

> In this way you, who are the speakers, will be most likely to win esteem and not praise only, among we who are your audience. For esteem is a sincere conviction of the hearer's souls, but praise is often an insincere, verbal expression of men uttering falsehoods contrary to their conviction. And thus we, who are the hearers, will be gratified and not pleased, for gratification is of the mind when receiving wisdom and knowledge, but pleasure is of the body when eating or experiencing some other bodily delight. (337b–c)

83. Apparently, this is the assistance Alcibiades gave to Socrates, which Socrates referred to at the beginning of the dialogue (309b).

84. "Eristics" was a form of discussion for which Sophists were famous. See Aristotle, *Sophistic Elenchus* 183b36. *Sunousia* was a hallmark of the Academy. See above, Chapter 2, Section C.

The Sophist Hippias now suggests means for ordering the discussion so as to comport with Prodicus's words. Hippias offers a plan by which Socrates and Protagoras will proceed in the manner most natural to them but, in the case of a dispute, will abide by limitations imposed by the rule of an "outside" chairman or arbitrator (*epistates*).[85] (This suggestion accords with the historical Hippias's belief that *nomos* and *physis* are wholly distinct entities, and that *nomoi* normally constrain rather than enhance *physis*.[86]) This person would decide when either took advantage of the other and exceeded his proper "measure" (338b).

Hippias's plan reflects a major bone of contention between Protagoras and Socrates. It presumes that by a mere agreement a community can establish positions of authority and endow its members with a power that immediately commands respect and obedience, regardless of the agreement's correspondence to what is appropriate. But Protagoras does not hold to this extremely conventional viewpoint. Socrates does not either; he declares that it is improper to choose such a referee for an argument; no legitimate referee knows anything about that which he is regulating:[87]

> To choose an umpire of discourse (*logon*) would be unseemly, for if the person chosen was inferior, then the inferior or worse ought not to preside over the better; or if he was equal, neither would that be well, for he who is our equal will do as we do, and what will be the use of choosing him? And if you say, "Let us have a better, then," to that I answer that, as a matter of fact, you cannot have anyone who is wiser than Protagoras. And if you choose another who is not really better, and who you only say is better, to put another over him as though he were an inferior person would be an unworthy reflection on him—not that, as far as I am concerned, any reflection is of much consequence to me. (338b–c)

Without assigning any independent value to the counsel provided by members of the audience (as a democrat might), Socrates suggests an alterna-

---

85. We may hear echoes of the Athenian assembly and council, where an *epistates* presided over debates. Also note the use of *epistates* as a "supervisor" of sons or animals in the *Apology* 20a–b.

86. On Hippias, see Plato, *Hippias Major* and *Hippias Minor*.

87. This view contrasts with contemporary justifications of refereeing, which claim that the referee is competent as long as she or he is knowledgeable about the "game" being refereed and "disinterested" in the outcome of the contest.

tive. Protagoras, rather than Socrates, will be assigned to ask the initial questions. When Protagoras finishes, Socrates can then ask questions and Protagoras will answer. If any listener believes that either participant is ruining the discussion, he is to ask that person to change his ways. In this new order, "it will not be necessary for any one person to become the chairman; all of you will act collectively as chairmen" (338e).

The subsequent agreement of the assembled individuals marks a unique moment in this dialogue and Plato's dialogues more generally. Socrates has obtained the support of this elite audience for his mode of rational discussion. Equally important, he has ascribed to them the authority and competence to judge. They are endowed with an equivalent of the *politike techne* that Protagoras had ascribed to the assembled citizenry of democratic Athens. But *this* skill is more strictly defined than that of Athenian assemblymen, just as the audience is more select. It further becomes clear that the formal neutrality of Socrates' "equal opportunity" procedural solution favors his own discursive style and ethical commitments. Moreover, as soon as the discussion begins, the imputed authority, power, competence, and judgment of the assembled audience become virtually irrelevant, a literary anticipation of the diminished intelligence and virtue that will be assigned to ordinary citizens at the end of the dialogue.

The reconstituted discussion between Protagoras and Socrates begins with Protagoras's selection of poetic interpretation as the test case for discussing his *techne* (338e–347a). His questions and answers do not exhibit a Socratic form; instead, they provide a vehicle for the demonstration of Protagoras's interpretive artistry rather than for the display of his knowledge of poetry. Socrates then challenges Protagoras's claim to *episteme* in his *techne* by offering his own interpretation of the poem, one that he presents with the rhetorical flair of a Protagoras and that resonates with the issues at stake in the dialogue.[88] Hippias chimes in and offers another interpretation of the

---

88. I can identify six distinct resonances. First, whether, and if so, how, one can be good or noble plays off Protagoras's claim to be able to make men "better" or "fine and good." Second, Socrates' use of Prodicus to challenge the conventional meanings on which Protagoras relies and his own dubious references to local dialects as sources for assessing poetic meaning point to the trouble of using poetic interpretation as a *techne* based on *episteme*. Third, Socrates' emphasis on the way in which the personal conflict between Simonides and Pittacus affects the intention of the poem evokes reflections on how Athenian politics influences the content of what Sophists teach. Fourth, interpreting goodness and badness according to the degree to which they are available to individuals by nature or by practice recalls Protagoras's comments in his Great Speech as well as Protagorean testimonia (for instance, Diels-Kranz, Fr. 4). Fifth, Socrates' interpretation

poem, which only provides more evidence for how poetic interpretation offers no basis for proving and/or persuading another of one's skill or knowledge. Indeed, now Socrates shuns this line of discussion, calling it entertainment, fit more for drinking parties than for logical discourse. The dialogue has reached another impasse.

The sorry outcome of following a path that Protagoras initially selected shames Protagoras to the point of not wanting to continue, but the rules of discussion that Socrates had suggested earlier now come into play, as the other listeners entreat Protagoras to stay. Socrates joins them and ironically shows his esteem for Protagoras by stating that dialogue with the best men is the best way of reaching the truth and that his discussion with Protagoras offers the best opportunity for taking that course.

b) The Second *Aporia*—Overcoming Protagoras

Thus far in the dialogue, Plato has identified the problems that arise from allowing *nomoi* to define the political art or virtue. Now he mounts a major attack on Protagoras. He puts Socrates clearly in charge of the form and content of the discussion by having him employ his elenchic method. Plato's Socrates takes up the earlier aborted discussion of the relation among the virtues and the particular example of courage. He asks Protagoras whether they are related like parts of gold or like parts of a face, each with its own separate power. In response, Protagoras reiterates his belief that they cannot be reduced to a single form, even as they resemble one another, and refers to the virtue of courage, which he and others find most unlike the rest of the virtues (349d).

Socrates' first move is familiar. He gets Protagoras to agree that all who are courageous are confident or daring, thus reducing an ethical value to a nonethical behavioral characteristic. He then argues that to be confident without simply being foolish is to have knowledge about the situation that calls for the daring deed. Finally, he points out that confidence in *technai*, such as diving and horsemanship, stems from *episteme* about the art.

If the skill in courage is generated in the same way as skills in other *tech-*

---

of Simonides wins his backing for his own maxim that no one does wrong willingly. Sixth, Socrates' evaluation of how Simonides criticizes Pittacus for the manner in which he assigns praise and blame suggests how Socrates might criticize Protagoras himself, for Socrates ends his interpretation of the poem (347a) by mimicking Simonides in an imaginary dialogue between Simonides and Pittacus. See Leonard Woodbury, "Simonides on *Arete*," and Dorothea Frede, "The Impossibility of Perfection: Socrates' Criticism of Simonides' Poem in the *Protagoras*."

nai, then Socrates will have proved Protagoras wrong, and if courage depends on *episteme,* it will be virtually identical to *sophia.* (As in the *Laches,* firm distinctions among the virtues almost disappear.) But Protagoras has never held to that view and does not do so here.[89] For him, confidence in *these* skills may be a product of art, knowledge, or ability, but courage is not: "Confidence may be given to men by art, and also, like ability, by madness and rage, but courage comes to them from the nature and good nurture of the soul" (351a–b). Despite the somewhat murky relations between *techne, arete,* and *dynamis* in Protagoras's response, he is being consistent.[90]

The examples of particular, practical *technai* proved inadequate to the task of refuting Protagoras. In the next part of the discussion, Socrates tries to identify another analogue for expertise in living well; he directly confronts Protagoras about the true source of the virtuous life. Here, Socrates asserts, the basis for one's expertise is not an uncritically defined knowledge of what the situation requires, but knowledge of pleasure. "Pleasure" is defined as the common "good" of human action.

Protagoras becomes uncomfortable with the new line of questioning, especially when Socrates argues that there is no logical basis for automatically placing those things that are good and noble on a higher scale than those that are conventionally viewed as pleasurable. For without those distinctions, Protagoras can no longer claim to be a cultivator of the people's virtue. The distinction Protagoras seeks to preserve here resembles a distinction he made earlier in the dialogue—that he knew of good things that were not immediately pleasurable or beneficial to men (333e). Consequently, he tries to refine Socrates' initial identification of pleasure and goodness in the following way: "There are some pleasant things that are not good, and . . . some painful things that are not evil, and some that are, and . . . some that are neither good nor evil" (351d). This position preserves some distance between Protagoras's beliefs and the more popular view Socrates has just put forth, which would call any human action good if it achieved pleasure.[91]

---

89. Whether the unity of the virtues is a cardinal "Socratic" belief is, I believe, a moot point, because of the instrumentality of "Socratic" beliefs in Plato's dialogues to Plato's wider theoretical concerns. Nevertheless, there have been illuminating discussions of this Socratic-Platonic problem by those not as impressed as I am by the Platonic influence on Socratic argument in Plato's dialogues. See Gregory Vlastos, "The Unity of the Virtues in the *Protagoras.*"

90. Compare Vlastos and Irwin on the logic of Socrates' argument. My interpretation does not reveal a contradiction with the views of Socrates in the *Laches.* See Chapter 3, Section B, above.

91. This move recalls J. S. Mill's effort to develop qualitative distinctions in the utilitarianism of Bentham and his father. However, Socrates' hypothetical association here of pleasure and

Socrates identifies another way in which Protagoras's position entangles him with "the many." According to Socrates, they hold the opinion that "knowledge" is not "powerful, lordly, commanding" enough to direct or rule a man's actions; rather, it is readily overcome by anger, pleasure, pain, love, or fear—like a "slave . . . dragged about by these other things" (352b–c).

In the earlier discussion about courage, Protagoras suggested that it was not a product of knowledge or art; other factors influenced its development. So Socrates asks Protagoras whether he shares this view of the many (352c). Protagoras responds firmly and aligns himself with what he takes to be Socrates' view by praising *sophia* and *episteme* and scorning the views of the many as thoughtless, much as he did earlier in the dialogue, when he said that "the many" have no minds of their own and only parrot the ideas of their leaders—and as he did not in the Great Speech (353a; see also 317a).

Plato's Socrates now tries to knock the straddling Protagoras off his fence. First, he takes Protagoras at his word and asks him to join him in interrogating "the many" as a hypothetical interlocutor (recalling Socrates' hypothetical dialogue with "the Laws" in Plato's *Crito*), whose views about the relative power of pleasure and knowledge Protagoras has just shunned. Perhaps the two of them can convince "the many" that their opinions are in error and that they should change their minds. Thus, Protagoras has allied himself with Socrates in regard to both the form of his questioning and the content of his views. But Socrates has become like Protagoras, too (or rather more like the historical Socrates), in that he is now trying to educate the citizenry in virtue, a position he had called practically ungrounded at the opening of the dialogue, in order to provoke Protagoras into clarifying his art and knowledge. The opinion of "the many" that Socrates and Protagoras now challenge is the belief that an individual "can be overcome by pleasure" (353c).

---

goodness as evidence of Socratic hedonism illustrates the interpretive dangers of being insensitive to the dramatic character of the dialogue. This proposition appears in part as a means of trapping Protagoras and in part as an initial step toward the later formulation of the art of measurement, which does not ultimately receive Socrates' endorsement in this dialogue. Moreover, there is the question of whether any proposition offered in these dialogues should be viewed as evidence of any settled belief of Plato, let alone his Socrates or the historical Socrates. Nevertheless, Terence Irwin has made a sophisticated argument for this part of the *Protagoras* as the basis for Socratic hedonism (see *Plato's Moral Theory*, 102–14). In the *Gorgias* and other probably "later" dialogues such as the *Republic, Phaedrus,* and *Laws,* Plato clearly holds that no pleasurable experience is good if it does not also bring about some measure of harmony to the soul. See *Gorgias* 464d–465a, 467e–468a, 495d–e, 497a; *Phaedrus* 68a; *Republic* 505b, 588c–591e; *Laws,* 662dff, 667d–668a.

Socrates' interrogation of "the many" begins with him characterizing the results of the competent performance of particular practical *technai* such as gymnastics, warfare, and medicine as painful but good. Their goodness derives from their instrumental value in achieving what are deemed to be the purposes of each *techne,* namely physical prowess, victory in warfare, or health. These beneficial results are pleasurable, even if the means for obtaining them are not.

Now Socrates makes a multifaceted argument: Given the presupposed value of competently practicing these *technai* for achieving the good life, as well as Socrates' view that the results of these *technai* define their value, it appears that "good living" entails excellence and success in a *techne* of the knowledgeable pursuit of pleasure. Because instrumental activities, just like the products for the sake of which they are performed, possess various measurable quantities of pleasure and pain, one ought to be able to calculate what is the best or most pleasurable thing to do according to a single scale. A "bad" result comes from a failure in calculation or in not knowing how to calculate or measure properly (356b–c).

Socrates and Protagoras agree that no one would choose evil or painful results willingly. Because the phrase "being overcome by pleasure" indicates an unwanted outcome for the individual, when one "is overcome," the causal agent is not pleasure. Instead, Plato's Socrates calls it "the power of appearances." He suggests that a new art might enable one to make the necessary calculations and measurements for living a good life and calls this "the art of measurement." It would have the power to "invalidate the power of appearance and, showing the truth, would teach the soul to find lasting rest in the truth, and would thus save our life."[92] The introduction of this art marks a

---

92. *Protagoras* 356d–e. Despite the resemblance of the art of measurement to the utilitarian calculus (something that J. S. Mill and modern commentators have recognized), this art is different in kind. For the art of measurement does not merely involve calculations of subjective sensation, no matter how long the run. Here, pleasure is what objectively brings well-being to the individual in "reality," rather than appearance, a distinction that utilitarian calculations of pleasure typically do not observe. Similarly, this art of measurement must be distinguished from modern understandings of rational calculation, because the moral integrity of a "natural" self is not presupposed. Nevertheless, in terms of the relations of this art to the political community, the art of measurement resembles modern notions of rational calculation and conceptions of the authority of theory in certain respects, ones that illuminate Plato's developing conception of the real nature of virtue and the political art. This becomes clear in the final portion of the dialogue. For "utilitarian" readings of this art, see J. S. Mill, *Utilitarianism,* chap. 1, par. 1, and Robert W. Hall, *Plato and the Individual,* 69–82, where he refers to Plato's use of *techne* in the early dialogues as utilitarian. Of course Mill was a great lover of Plato and devoted careful attention to the many

crucial moment in the dialogue, for such an art fulfills the two criteria of embodying both knowledge and virtue; and functionally, it seems to be able to replace the "political art" or "art of virtue" that Protagoras claimed to be able to teach. Immediately, however, "political" problems arise.

"The many" are stupefied by how Socrates and Protagoras have undermined their conventional beliefs and seemingly replaced them with "truer" beliefs. They are stung by having discovered themselves to be ignorant about matters they presumably understood. Socrates and Protagoras now summarize how "ignorance" is the obstacle that prevents people from living a good life and also keeps them from understanding the nature of their beliefs, thus linking virtue and knowledge (357d–e). Protagoras, as well as the other Sophists present, agrees with Socrates about the nature of this new art that provides knowledge about how to live a pleasurable and good life. For he seems to have justified a specialized art in virtue. Plato's Socrates flatters them by suggesting that they might be "physicians of ignorance," thereby rationalizing their profession in a democratic society.

Protagoras can now happily join Socrates as he criticizes the *demos* for being foolish when they do not send their sons to Sophists because, given the fact that *arete*, or "good living," depends on *episteme*, it by definition can be taught. It is the "ignorance" of "the many" that makes them "worse off in public and private life" (357e). Perhaps it is up to the Sophists to help them out. But the Sophists should not be too pleased, for Socrates has completely undermined the basis for a Protagorean version of the art of measurement, namely his standard of cultivated conventional human judgment and art of teaching virtue as the *politike techne* articulated in the Great Speech. Socrates has redefined the constituents of virtue so that the distinctive features of Protagoras's art have no firmer epistemological status than the opinions of the many, whom he disdains. The Sophist's ambiguous relationship to Athenian democracy—supporting its constitutive principles while distancing himself from the untutored virtue of its ordinary citizens—has been turned against him.[93]

The next part of the dialogue makes clear that Protagoras's art of virtue cannot meet the necessary requirements of the newly defined *techne* and that

---

dimensions of the *Protagoras*. See John Stuart Mill, *Essays on Philosophy and the Classics*, ed. J. M. Robson (Toronto: University of Toronto Press, 1978), 39–61.

93. The manner in which Socrates plays with Protagoras's relationship to "the many" is nicely described by Friedlander in his *Plato*, 2:21–29.

the Socratic art of measurement and the Protagorean *techne* of *arete* are epistemologically and politically incompatible. First, by having defined the possession of *episteme* as the necessary and sufficient condition for "good living"
or virtue, Plato's Socrates has shown that the distinctive status of courage in
contrast to wisdom now disappears. Courage merely represents the skill of
episteme in weighing the pleasures and pains, goods and evils, which concern
the question of what is and is not to be feared. The virtues seem to exhibit a
unity that Protagoras had vigorously denied at the outset of the discussion.
Second, in Protagoras's Great Speech it was the *politike techne* that saved the
life of the human community. Its knowledge only partially resembled the
knowledge of particular practical *technai*. Like them, it was a skill that could
be improved by teaching; yet it was distributed and acquired differently, and
every citizen could practice it as a matter of course. Yet in this part of the dialogue such *technai* serve as direct analogues for Socrates' conception of the
art of measurement. The common cultural and political aspects of Protagoras's conception of virtue and the political art have no distinctive role to play
in Socrates' newly formulated art. Practicing it involves reducing all social
phenomena, experience, actions, and their consequences to quantities of pleasure. All distinctions that could lead one to treat future goods or pleasures on
a different scale than present ones, assign special value to historical events or
collective traditions, or attribute a unique status to shared citizenship or the
political community cannot be translated without reduction into such a calculus.[94] The unique weight of historical, cultural, political, and natural factors
that contributed to the development of the Protagorean *political techne* in
general, and to the virtue of courage in particular, disappears in this new art
of measurement.

The epistemological and political discontinuities between the Protagorean and Socratic positions need to be understood together, for Socrates'
new epistemological criteria justify political transformation. First, the epistemological standards of the art of measurement recognize no distinctive character in political, as opposed to personal, deliberation. The rational standpoint of the Athenian citizen participating in public affairs was not supposed
to be primarily that of personal benefit, although it was self-interest, broadly

94. This view is obviously not shared by utilitarians or their economistic advocates, "rational choice" theorists. But I cannot go into my judgment of the political dimensions of this perspective here. For a useful critique of rational choice theory that nevertheless accepts (at least for
the purposes of argument) some of their assumptions, see Donald Green and Ian Shapiro, *The
Pathologies of Rational Choice* (New Haven: Yale University Press, 1994).

understood.[95] A citizen's personal experience of pleasure in the long or short run was not supposed to contribute significantly to his political judgment, for the end that informed all issues involving the whole political community had at best an obscure relation to pleasure. For example, as far as Pericles was concerned, it involved the ability of the citizenry to preserve its community as a public-spirited democracy, and, as far as "Protagoras" was concerned, citizens benefited one another by their public pursuit of *arete*. But from the standpoint of the art of measurement, collectively exercising the *politike techne* as a deliberative art no longer has any special value.

Second, insofar as this art was not generally practiced, the political deliberations of the Athenian assembly could not exemplify the art of measurement; instead, they would display incompetence. Indeed, if most people live their lives in ignorance, it would be foolhardy to believe in their deliberative measurements of the constituents of virtue and the good life. The epistemological redefinition of the art of virtue—its formalization as a particular practical *techne*—transforms the basis of political authority. It no longer stems from a historically rooted collectivity engaged in political deliberation but from a relatively ahistorical and disembodied art of measurement. According to its standards, the political power of an unskilled citizenry should be ruled by practitioners of the new art, for "the many" are typically lost in ignorance and deceived by appearances.

To be sure, the Protagorean and Socratic arts of virtue share important features. Both are *technai,* can be taught, and theoretically can be practiced by everyone. The aims of good form and grace of Protagorean virtue reappear in the aims of good measurement. Both are consequentialist.[96] But the truths of the latter are no longer legitimately constituted by the political practices of Athenian democracy. Implicit in Socrates' critique of Protagoras is a critique of Athenian *nomoi* as the major guides for an art of virtue. The guideposts of the political art no longer stem from the experience of Athenian public life, as they had for Pericles, Thucydides, and Protagoras. Instead, they derive from the systematic unity provided by the canons of *episteme*.

Yet Socrates' affirmation of the art of measurement does not mark the di-

---

95. On the calculable benefits of Athenian democracy for its citizens, see M. I. Finley, *Politics in the Ancient World.*

96. Therefore, it simply is misleading to suggest that a relatively noninstrumental Protagorean *techne* has been replaced by an instrumental Platonic *techne* (see Irwin, *Plato's Moral Theory,* 109–10). Michael Gagarin emphasizes (in my view, overemphasizes) the similarities between Protagoras and Socrates (see his "The Purpose of Plato's *Protagoras*").

alogue's conclusion. Clearly, Plato is uncomfortable with the disjuncture between the different arts of virtue articulated by Protagoras and Socrates. He ends the dialogue by noting that the preceding argument has turned on Socrates himself, as well as Protagoras, insofar as he initially held the position that *arete* could not be taught and now seems to be saying that it can be. Of course, when he presented his initial position Socrates may not have been conveying his own views but simply current ones. Nevertheless, Plato's Socrates closes by distancing himself and Protagoras from the preceding discussion, subjecting the two men to the authority of "argument." *Logos* now assumes a voice of its own (similar to "the laws of Athens" in the *Crito*) and says (361b–c):

> Socrates and Protagoras, you are strange beings; there are you, Socrates, who were saying earlier that virtue cannot be taught, contradicting yourself now by your attempt to prove that all things are knowledge, including moderation and courage, which tends to show that virtue can certainly be taught; for if virtue were other than knowledge, as Protagoras attempted to prove, then clearly virtue cannot be taught; but if virtue is entirely knowledge, as you are seeking to show, Socrates, then I cannot but suppose that virtue is capable of being taught. Protagoras, on the other hand, who then hypothesized that it could be taught, is now eager to prove it to be anything rather than knowledge; and if this be true, it must be quite incapable of being taught.

The center cannot hold. We are given hints of what may replace it, namely a philosophy of virtue based less on the conventional practices and values of Athens than on the claims of *episteme*. But we are not given any insight into how an art of virtue or political art, based on *episteme*, would connect to a political community. Indeed, Socrates' art of measurement, designed to be the instrument of "good living," has generated a relationship to "the many" that is at least as unclear as that of the Protagorean political art to its "artist" and "subjects" or "objects." Still to be determined is a *techne* of reason for ruling the body, directing it to choose activities that ultimately generate the most pleasure, and for ruling the soul, because such pleasures become instrumental for the virtuous life.

The radical political and philosophical dimensions of Plato's Socratic Problem have now become clear. By separating Protagoras from the *demos,* democracy becomes ruled by an ignorant and ethically wayward majority, and Protagoras loses the practical sanction for his intellectual authority. Both conventional political practice and critical political discourse, ordinary democratic citizenship and conventional political leadership, have lost their ethical legitimacy. The only truly critical discourse about virtue and politics will have to be unconventional. Because the conventions to be criticized were democratic, Plato's unconventional critical reason cannot be. And by conflating democratic ethics with Protagorean sophistry and then revealing the critical limitations of unprincipled sophistry, Plato's *Protagoras* also undermines an ethical justification of Athenian democracy. It shows how Plato's development of a political theory that was radically critical of democracy was both historically and theoretically understandable, if not altogether necessary. The price of solving Plato's Socratic Problem, of articulating a truly virtuous political art, was high. For there seemed to be no available position between Protagoras's conventional defense of democratic ethics and what would become Plato's critically coherent but theoretically antidemocratic reformulations of a virtuous political art.

2. RHETORIC AND THE POLITICAL ART: PLATO'S *Gorgias*

We have seen Plato provide searching critiques of the conventional practices of Athenian politics, ethics, and higher education. Although he has undercut the legitimacy of these conventional forms of discourse and practice, he has not indicated what would replace them. Our reading of the *Protagoras* suggests that Plato does not endorse "the art of measurement" as an adequate substitute for Protagoras's art; yet Plato's use of it performs critical work in the dialogue (which suggests that its use is not entirely ironic).[97] We still have no clue about what a political art rooted in virtue and justifiable in critical discourse would look like. Plato's *Gorgias,* however, does offer clues and, in so doing, breaks new theoretical and political ground. By critically examining rhetoric, an "art of discourse," amid the ethical and political conventions of Athenian democracy, the dialogue offers a glimpse of Plato's solution to his Socratic Problem. The *Gorgias* also belongs among Plato's primary treatments of the political art. Although the overt subjects of the dialogue are

---

97. In this respect, my position differs from that of Irwin, *Plato's Moral Theory,* in the first case, and Roochnik, *Of Art and Wisdom: Plato's Understanding of Techne,* in the second.

the nature of rhetoric and its contribution to happiness, Plato links these to the political art as smoothly as he linked the political art to virtue in the *Protagoras*.

In accord with my interpretive approach, I first establish the historical context and dramatic frame for the issues and personages of the dialogue. Doing so highlights the dialogue's centrality to Plato's understanding of the political art, particularly insofar as it relates the *logos* of critical reason to the *ergon* of (Athenian) democracy.[98] The interpretation of the dialogue then falls into two parts. The first concerns the various ways that rhetoric is defined in *logos*. The second concerns the power of rhetoric or the effect of rhetoric in *ergon*.

a. Historical and Dramatic Contexts

The practice of rhetoric was not a "people's art." In Pericles' vision of Athenian political life in his funeral oration recorded by Thucydides, most citizens actively participated in the public affairs of the *polis*. But among these, not all were active political speakers. Even in the Athenians' relatively small democracy, the principle and practice of rotation in office could not be directly transferred to rotation on the podium. Certain citizens would be particularly prominent, and a primary tool for achieving their prominence was skill in public speaking.

Although a *rhetor* simply referred to a public speaker and thus potentially to any citizen speaking in an official political forum, skill in rhetoric was typically associated with especially prominent and powerful citizens, such as *strategoi*, who occupied the only elective office in this direct democracy during the fifth century (when they functioned as both military generals and political leaders, unlike the fourth century, when these responsibilities devolved on different individuals who acted in much different practical contexts). Themistocles, Miltiades, Pericles, Nicias, Cleon, and Alcibiades—the first four of whom make up the pantheon of widely acclaimed Athenian political leaders to whom Socrates refers in the *Gorgias*—were known as both *rhetores* and *strategoi*.[99]

---

98. In his analysis of political rhetoric in classical Athens, Harvey Yunis emphasizes the political irrelevance of Plato's various arguments in the *Gorgias*. See his *Taming Democracy: Political Rhetoric in Classical Athens*, chaps. 6–7.

99. In the fourth century, the division of political labor advanced and differentiated the tasks of generalship and public speaking, but even as a "rhetorician" and "general" were no longer one

Because rhetoric featured the discursive practice of the political art, it possessed political and theoretical features that distinguished it from the political art taken as a whole. Although the practice of rhetoric was integral to the political life of Athenian democracy, the practice of rhetoric was not wholly coterminous with the practice of *arete*. In this respect, Plato's discussion of rhetoric in the *Gorgias* treats a different aspect of the political art from that discussed in the *Protagoras*.

Unlike the acquisition of Protagoras's art, learning Gorgias's art did not make a citizen good. Its scope concerned the formal character of words, arguments, and speeches. As such, it was used in order to persuade the judgment of citizens, to inform what they would determine to be a virtuous instance of the exercise of the political art. Thus, the *Gorgias* particularly concerns the critical and ethical underpinnings of political leadership—not citizenship in general. The discussion of rhetoric in the *Gorgias* entails a discussion of which *logos* of leadership, that of a politician or philosopher, most contributes to the understanding and practice of virtue and justice. In this respect, Plato wrote about a choice that he himself had felt forced to make.

Given these historical, political, and theoretical references in the *Gorgias*, Plato's examination of rhetoric in it raises questions about five topics: (1) the principles and practices of Athenian democracy; (2) the skill and virtue of its political leaders, past and present; (3) the discourse of its new educators; (4) the significance of the historical Socrates; and (5) Plato's own vocational choices. These historical associations of rhetoric filter into the *Gorgias* and constitute its political and theoretical significance.

Exactly how these references do so is not immediately evident, especially because neither the dramatic nor the compositional dates of the dialogue can be precisely fixed. (Nor would there be a one-to-one correspondence for a writer of Plato's skill.) Yet this much is clear. The dialogue dramatically depicts Athens during the Peloponnesian War, after Pericles had died but before the Sicilian expedition. It was a time when the rhetoric of Cleon, Nicias, and Alcibiades was shaping the decisions of the Athenians about crucial matters concerning the conduct of the war and the well-being of the Athenian

---

and the same, both were understood to belong to the political leadership of the *polis*. See Hansen, *The Athenian Assembly in the Age of Demosthenes,* and R. K. Sinclair, *Democracy and Participation in Athens,* 136–41.

people.[100] What some identify as the precise dramatic date of the dialogue, 427, coincides with the year of both Plato's birth and the Mytilenian debate (which Thucydides highlighted as an example—one wonders how representatively—of rhetoric in the assembly). The date at which Plato composed the dialogue is more difficult to establish, although many scholars have sought to do so.[101] Most likely, it was c. 390–380, hence thirty to forty years after the dramatic date of the dialogue.

Because of the gap of nearly two generations between the dialogue's dramatic and compositional dates, along with the enormous political and intellectual developments that bridge this gap and affect Plato's life, it is unwise to read the dialogue as a literary reenactment of a dialogue that actually occurred. The historicity of the dialogue needs to be interpreted through the historical and theoretical problematic that animated Plato when he wrote the dialogue; yet the words and deeds of the characters of the *Gorgias* clearly resonate with their historical namesakes. In particular, Gorgias apparently visited Athens in 427 and during that time may well have had conversations with Socrates and prominent Athenian politicians. Consequently, the historical weight of the dialogue cannot be ignored in determining the theoretical significance of the text.

Gorgias's "art" of rhetoric constitutes the explicit subject of the dialogue, and to that extent he is its primary character. The historical Gorgias who informed Plato's literary and philosophical portrayal was born in 490 in Leontini, a small *polis* in Sicily. His life extended into the fourth century; by its end,

---

100. See E. R. Dodds, *Plato: Gorgias*, 17–18.

101. By using stylometric analysis or applying general interpretive principles about the character of the Platonic corpus, most scholars have located the *Gorgias* at the tail end of Plato's so-called early period—after most of what I have called the aporetic dialogues but before the *Republic*. (See Chapter 2, above.) More recently, Charles Kahn has identified it as one of Plato's first dialogues. See his "On the Relative Dating of the *Protagoras* and *Gorgias*." But because its epistemology reflects conceptual categories that become prominent only in undeniably later dialogues—for example, epistemological dualism, the method of division, the use of a myth that resembles the *Republic*'s myth of Er—I doubt Kahn's dating. See Dodds, *Plato: Gorgias*, 4–5, 20–27. For my purposes, it is sufficient to identify the dialogue's date in a way that makes Plato's treatment of the issues in it most salient and significant in relation to comparable issues in other dialogues. Insofar as the endorsement of the philosophical life in the *Gorgias* would be less interesting to someone who had not yet read (or written) the *Republic*, it makes sense to interpret the *Gorgias* as a dialogue whose composition preceded the time in which the *Republic* was initially composed and the Academy was established, both of which probably occurred in the 380s. See also Barker, *Greek Political Theory*, 155, n. 1.

Gorgias's professional practice of rhetoric had brought him great fame and wealth.[102] During the earlier part of his life, he may have studied with Empedocles.[103] At any rate, he may have been familiar enough with the forms of critical discourse current in Western Greece to compose a sustained critique of Parmenidean ontology.[104]

We do not know the extent to which this critique evidenced Gorgias's personal convictions or intellectual sensibility — as David Roochnik has commented, it could be an "exercise" or a "joke."[105] But the piece is important because it argues that *logoi* must be treated in a domain separate from physical substances and that external reality does not directly participate in *logoi*. At the same time, in a fragment of this critique, he defines *logoi* as media that constitute our grasp of the external world. Thus:

> *Logos* is not substance and existing things. Therefore, we do not reveal existing things to our neighbors, but *logos* which is something other than substances. . . . *Logos* arises from external things impinging upon us, that is, from perceptible things. From encounters with a flavor, *logos* is expressed by us about that quality, and from encounters with a color, an expression of color. But if that is the case, *logos* is not evocation of the external, but the external becomes the revealer of *logos*.[106]

Gorgias's fame derived primarily from his later life, when he traveled among many Greek *poleis*, teaching and employing his art of rhetoric. As part of this art, he wrote model speeches. He also participated in politics. During his Athenian visit, he served as ambassador from Leontini to speak before the Athenian assembly on behalf of the Leontinians. He managed to convince the Athenians to aid them in their war against the Syracusans, a decision that foreshadowed the Athenians' subsequent disastrous Sicilian expedition.[107]

---

102. A statue of him may have been erected in his honor in Olympia after he died; however, some ancient sources claim that *he* had the statue erected. See Philostratus, *Lives of the Sophists* 1.9.2; Pausanias VI.17.7ff.

103. Diogenes Laertius, VIII.58–59. Plato apparently believed this, in that he associated Gorgias with Empedoclean theories of color as effluence in the *Meno* 76c.

104. Our record of this critique is the account by Sextus, *Against the Schoolmasters* VII.65. Admittedly, this source is not reliable, but I think it's better than no source.

105. The source of this comment is personal correspondence.

106. Diels-Kranz, B3.84–85; compare B1, B2.

107. Diodorus Siculus XII.53.1.

The historical Gorgias's actual professional contributions have ambiguous theoretical and political implications. To be sure, he was a great intellectual innovator whose art seemed to complement the democratization of Athenian public discourse. Gorgias's *technai logon* could be seen as relatively innocent practices that could enhance the power and influence of citizens who might not have "naturally" gained confidence or knowledge from their families about speaking in public. The lack of theoretical constraints on their practical use made them available to all potential speakers, and this contributed to the apparently democratic character of Gorgias's art.

Gorgian rhetoric had a dark side, however, and this is what attracted Plato's attention in the *Gorgias*. There was a quasi-independent power in Gorgias's *technai logon*, whose dangerous aspects the historical Gorgias himself recognized in writing about the power of *logos* in his encomium to Helen. In that text, Helen is not blameworthy if it was *logos* that "persuaded her and deceived her heart," because

> Speech (*logos*) is a powerful lord, which by means of the finest and most invisible body effects the divinest works: it can stop fear and banish grief and create joy and nurture pity. . . . The effect of speech upon the condition of the soul is comparable to the power of drugs over the nature of bodies. For just as different drugs dispel different secretions from the body, and some bring an end to disease and others to life, so also in the case of speeches, some distress, others delight, some cause fear, others make the hearers bold, and some drug and bewitch the soul with a kind of evil persuasion.[108]

In one sense, this last possibility counts as the most probable outcome, for *logos* as a persuasive force unavoidably functions as a power of deception: "All who have and do persuade people of things do so by molding a false argument" (*Helen* 11).

In addition, the basis in most people for their "judgment" of *logoi* is "opinion" (*doxa*), and its connections to "reality" are insecure. Gorgias's text acknowledges that a public speech, including this very one that he composed, may be dangerously powerful, for it may be "written with art (*techne*) but not spoken with truth . . . [it] bends a great crowd (*ochlos*) and persuades" (*Helen* 13; see also *In Defense of Palamedes* 33). Gorgias refers to his rhetoric as a

---

108. *Helen* 8, 14.

"drug" (*pharmakon*); although this drug is not poison, its magical bewitching powers as a *techne* suggest the danger of its indiscriminate use. The danger is especially real because most people are not "doctors" trained in its proper use. The psychotropic character of rhetoric becomes a critical issue in both the *Gorgias,* where Socrates refers to rhetoricians as quacks who are more persuasive than legitimate doctors, and in the *Phaedrus,* where the pharmacological and erotic nature of *technai logon* renders them potential cures as well as dangers, sources of soulful harmony or madness.[109]

The historical Gorgias may have acknowledged the existence of the danger, but he does not seem to have been terribly worried about the adaptation, or uptake, of his *technai.* At the end of his encomium to Helen, he refers to his writing as a "diversion"—perhaps because Gorgias himself had not systematically conceived of his *techne* in theoretical terms that would reveal its ambiguous relation to ethical practice, democratic or otherwise.[110]

Plato wrote the *Gorgias* to grapple with the promise and danger of such an art of rhetoric. The debate between "Socrates" and "Gorgias" is less a debate between Plato and the historical Gorgias or an example of a timeless encounter between "philosophy" and "rhetoric" than it is a critical review of the political application of Gorgian rhetoric in late fifth- and early fourth-century Athens. The text of the *Gorgias* supports this view, for the problematic absence of ethical tethers in Gorgias's *techne* appears in Plato's pointed emphasis of this absence to the discomfort of Gorgias (459cff), in Polus's defense of Gorgias's art against Socrates' criticism, and in the subsequent anti-Socratic intervention by Callicles.[111]

Besides Gorgias, the two other major interlocutors with Socrates are Polus and Callicles. Polus was actually a Sicilian student of Gorgias who was young enough to be the son of either Gorgias or Socrates. Although not a cre-

109. *Gorgias* 456bff; *Phaedrus* 268a–270c, 244a–257b; see also 230d, 242e. Jacques Derrida generates support for his deconstructive approach to the interpretation of texts in his 1968 reading of *logos* as *pharmakos* in Plato's *Phaedrus.* See "Plato's Pharmacy," in *Dissemination,* 61–171. For a classicist's more careful rendering of related themes, see G. R. F. Ferrari, *Listening to the Cicadas: A Study of Plato's Phaedrus.*

110. The nontheoretical dimension of Gorgias's *technai* is argued by Cole against Kennedy and Segal. On Gorgias's ethical agnosticism, see Guido Caliagero, "Gorgias and the Socratic Principle: *Nemo Sua Sponte Peccat,*" in C. J. Classen, ed., *Sophistik,* 408–42.

111. Notably, Plato does not ridicule Gorgias directly in this dialogue or in other dialogues where he is mentioned. See *Apology* 19e; *Meno* 70a–b, 76aff, 95c; *Symposium* 194e–197e; *Phaedrus* 238d, 261b, 267a; *Philebus* 58a.

ative intellectual or powerful political figure in his own right, he was a teacher of rhetoric and may have composed a *techne logon* that the historical Socrates read.[112] In Plato's dialogue, he attempts to provide a more theoretically sophisticated defense of Gorgias's art than Gorgias himself did, but becomes tangled in his own (Platonically induced?) lack of critical understanding of the ethics of conventional morality. Callicles is more significant than Polus and, in one respect, more so than Gorgias. Gorgias provides the intellectual subject for the dialogue, but because Callicles is the first as well as the last interlocutor of Socrates, he (along with Socrates) frames the issue of the dialogue's interpretation and application. Intriguingly, we have no information outside the *Gorgias* about Callicles.[113] In the *Gorgias*, he signifies a politician who makes use of rhetoric for his own purposes. He recognizes Polus's confusion about the relation of rhetoric to conventional ethics but is more interested in condemning Socrates' seeming other-worldliness and affirming anticonventional and political rather than philosophical uses of rhetoric. He exemplifies Plato's belief about the potential political employment of Gorgian rhetoric.[114] The bullying character of Callicles must reflect Plato's concern about the rendering of Gorgias's "art of discourse" in the context of Athenian democratic politics. In the framework of Plato's treatment of rhetoric as an example of the problematic relation of *logos* and *ergon*, Callicles' discourse operates as a radical alternative and challenge to that of Socrates.

The only other character in the dialogue is Chaerephon, a sympathetic follower of Socrates and loyal supporter of Athenian democracy (who also appears briefly in the *Apology* and *Republic*).[115] He is unwilling to assume responsibility for any particular argument about rhetoric; in this respect, he may reflect the interested but dubious attitude of most Athenians toward rhetoric as an "art of discourse."

In the dialogue, the dramatic action is not as complex as that of the

---

112. *Gorgias* 461a, 462b. See Dodds, *Plato: Gorgias*, 11–12.

113. The historicity of other Socratic interlocutors in Plato's dialogues and the detail Plato uses to describe him may but need not suggest that he was a historical as well as fictional character. See Dodds, *Plato: Gorgias*, 12.

114. In his commentary on the *Gorgias* (15), Dodds overstates the responsibility of Gorgias for Callicles when he says that in the dialogue, "Gorgias' teaching is the seed of which the Calliclean way of life is the poisonous fruit."

115. Plato cites him as the person who asked the Delphic Oracle whether anyone was wiser than Socrates. See Plato, *Apology* 20e–21a; Xenophon, *Memorabilia* 1.2.48; see also *Charmides* 153b.

Protagoras, and yet the specific exchanges in it must be read with due regard for their dramatic context, for each part of the dialogue depends on the one that precedes it. Overall, the linear progress of the *Gorgias* indicates an ever-deepening consideration of rhetoric as a *techne logon* in a Platonic sense—that is, as a second-order master art whose exercise affects one's understanding of the good of the *polis* and the good of one's soul.[116]

b. *Techne* and the *Logos* of Rhetoric

Although the most striking and memorable parts of the *Gorgias* result from the exchanges between Callicles and Socrates, some of the most important ones for our purposes occur during the dialogue's early sections, where Plato's Socrates implicates the philosophical, political, and ethical dimensions of rhetoric by relating it to the concept and practice of *techne.* These passages express Plato's most complex effort to determine what can count as a *techne* of *logos,* a skill to which the rhetoricians, Sophists, and even the historical Socrates (in a contrary sense) might have laid claim. In these passages, he delegitimizes entire realms of discourse by categorizing certain types as inherently false or misleading. He makes the philosophical articulation in discourse of the meaning of *techne* to the standard for authorizing its ethical and political value.

As suggested by our discussion of Plato's contexts in Chapter 2, this differentiation of *logos* reflects in part the increasing diversity of forms of discursive expression in Athens. Plato's argument in the *Gorgias,* however, establishes an epistemological hierarchy among kinds of *logos* that radically challenges the political and ethical *ergon* of Athens, where the democratic constitution was supposed to guarantee the best possible or virtuous enactment of public critical reason. Gorgias's medium is words and arguments, which are available to anyone who knows how to use the Greek language; yet by teaching rhetoric as a skill, Gorgias claims that one's public discourse can be improved by the acquisition of certain special techniques. (This parallels the function of the *techne* of *arete,* the *politike techne* taught by Protagoras in Plato's *Protagoras,* as a skill of both the many and the few.)

The dialogue opens with Callicles referring to speech as a method of warfare, discourse as an instrument of (violent) deeds. Socrates' initial line of questioning raises the basic issue of the responsibility of words for deeds. As

---

116. This is a rather common pattern in Platonic dialogues, but is most closely paralleled in Book I of the *Republic.*

was the case in the *Protagoras,* where "Socrates" asked "Protagoras" about the identity of his art, "Socrates" now asks "Gorgias" about the identity of his: What constitutes the nature of what he does and who he is? Why does he benefit those who learn it, such that his teaching warrants payment of a fee by students?

Socrates opens this questioning of Gorgias about the nature of his skill in rhetoric by trying to identify the province, scope, or subject matter over which his *techne* provides expertise, the special arena over which he claims a mastery that others do not possess (448c; 449a, c; 451a). Socrates' analytical method immediately poses problems for Gorgias, for it isolates form from content in a way that is unfamiliar to Gorgias, for whom the nature of his art becomes manifest only in its skillful application to specific contexts. Having isolated the form of rhetoric from its contextual application, Socrates has made it vulnerable to his own style of ethical and philosophical critique.

Gorgias initially defines the field of rhetoric as words and thoughts, and the art of rhetoric as enabling its possessor to speak and think well with words (450b–c). This definition proves inadequate, because an art must have a product. Plato's Socrates has begun by viewing the rhetorician as a crafts-man engaged in productive activity. This product need not be tangible, for there are other recognized arts, such as geometry and calculation, which also accomplish their purposes solely through the medium of words. The art, however, must produce more than "good speaking"; it must have a speci-fiable *use.*

Plato's Socrates induces Gorgias to say that in the manner of doctors pro-ducing health and gymnastic instructors producing beautiful physiques, the product of rhetoric is quintessentially public: "It brings freedom to man-kind in general and to each man dominion over others in his own country" (452d–e). In the words of Plato's Gorgias, it involves the ability or power (*dynamis*)[117] "To persuade by words and argument the jury-men in the Jury-Court, the counselors in the Council, the assemblymen in the Assembly, and in any other political gathering where citizens would reason together. And ... with this power you will hold the doctor as your slave, the trainer as your slave, and this money-maker here will turn out to make money for someone else, not for himself, but for you with the power to speak and persuade the masses (*ta plethe*)" (452e). This art of persuasion, therefore, would provide the means for exercising enormous political power in Athens, where oral ar-

117. On *dynamis,* see 456c, 460a.

gument in public forums was the most proximate influence on, and often precipitating cause of, political decisions.

This last characterization continues to create problems for rhetoric as a *techne*. Gorgias has characterized rhetoric as an ethically and politically neutral first-order art. It signifies an activity guided by a specific kind of knowledge concerning a specific practical arena with a specific product and benefit. Insofar as its end or product is "to produce persuasion in the soul of the hearer," it resembles standard teachable arts, which "persuade" no less than rhetoric. At this level, rhetoric appears as a particular practical first-order *techne* that lacks an ethical dimension.

Socrates initially treats it on this level (454b). He notes that rhetoric may be used to persuade people into believing things that are incorrect or evil. In a passage that recalls Socrates' description in the *Protagoras* of the operation of the Athenian assembly, which served to point out that the skills of assemblymen seemed independent of a Protagorean *techne* of *arete* that could be taught, Plato's Socrates points out the apparent political uselessness of the art of rhetoric by mentioning the greater usefulness of all other first-order *technai* and their skilled practitioners (*demiourgoi*) when it comes to political deliberation:

> Whenever there is a gathering in the city to choose doctors or shipwrights or any other professional group (*demiourgikou ethnous*), surely the rhetorician will not then give his advice, for it is obvious that in each such choice it is the real expert (*technikotaton*) who must be selected. And when it is a question about the building of walls or equipment of harbors or dockyards, we consult, not the rhetoricians, but the master builders, and again when we need advice about a choice of generals or some tactical formation against the enemy or the occupation of positions, military experts will advise, not rhetoricians. (455b–c)

Gorgias disputes this judgment, however, by claiming that his art has the power to subject all other faculties and claims to knowledge by craftsmen under its control, when they are made before a crowd (456bff). It is the skill that Athenian political leaders such as Themistocles and Pericles used in persuading citizens to embark on major new courses of action, such as building the Athenians' dockyards and walls (455d–e). Consequently, the art of rhetoric involves essentially the art of democratic political leadership and democratic statesmanship. In a democratic political community, such an art indeed has power, or at least influence, and Gorgias acknowledges this (456d–457c).

Insofar as the state of persuasion created by rhetoricians is the last determinant of political action and rhetoric's particular power appears in mass gatherings where skills of persuasion can be more effective than the knowledge and skill of experts, rhetoric, not the expressed virtue of the citizenry, constitutes the sovereign art in the *polis*. The few rhetoricians, rather than the many citizens, hold the real reins of political power (456b–c).

Although rhetoric as an "art of discourse" is supposedly only a means for enhancing the practice of virtue and the political art, it has become its constitutive determinant. Thus, what a rhetorician really knows how to do is to manipulate power like a commodity. Indeed, brute force is the tool of the rhetorical "craftsman," and its benefits derive from its power to enable its user to manipulate power. As a result, the political power of the rhetorician is undependable and dangerous, especially if it becomes an end in itself, for then it can feed an insatiable, unlimited desire to expand the realm of power under one's control. Socrates can rightfully make two charges against Gorgias and his art: its lack of ethical and political control over, or responsibility for, the ultimate use of this art, and its ignorance of the matters about which it claims to have knowledge.

The problems Plato's Socrates finds with Gorgias's art resemble those "he" found in the discourses of other Sophists who claimed to teach a *techne* of *arete*. In the *Gorgias,* however, Plato outlines a substitute art by securing a conceptual basis of ethical and political judgment for a second-order art of virtue that has no direct links to either the first-order ordinary experiences, perceptions, and desires of conventional Athenian life *or* the conventional second-order norms that typically regulate and direct them along the path of justice. With this result, Plato has accomplished an important political, as well as conceptual, reduction. Just as the *demos* was deprived of any ethical compass in the *Protagoras* when "Socrates" described it as dominated by an untutored desire for pleasure, so in the *Gorgias* the intellect of the many has been reduced to the emotional state of a crowd. In addition, Plato's critique of the art of rhetoric used by politicians undermines the authority of all extant political elites. Plato has delegitimized the potential authority and virtue of both the *demos* and the politicians who presume to lead them on their behalf.

Plato's Socrates develops some of these epistemological and political beliefs in his exchange with Gorgias and some in his exchange with Polus. First, he draws a distinction between knowledge (*episteme*) and belief (*pistis*). Thus, he indicates a dualistic epistemology that was not evident in other aporetic dialogues we have discussed.[118] Both are products of persuasion. But the latter is not necessarily true, whereas the former invariably is (454c–e, 458e). In addition, knowledge as *episteme* involves instruction, which includes but goes beyond persuasion. The difference is between persuasion that merely changes the listener's beliefs or convictions and one that actually instructs or teaches an individual about a kind of knowledge. This distinction undercuts Gorgias's hope that his rhetoric helps to produce reliable and ethically acceptable results. Understood only as an art of persuasion, the rhetorician's skill becomes the art of persuasion via ignorance (rather than knowledge) about matters of great concern. As such, it is an art of deceit (459c–e).

In the *Gorgias,* the relevant criterion for the successful practice of Gorgias's art is the assembled *demos,* which Plato signifies as a "crowd." Unlike the assembled *demos* in Protagoras's Great Speech, it deliberates and decides without the *politike techne,* without *euboulia.* Given this state of affairs, the rhetorician's ignorance about matters pertaining to a *techne* does not affect his ability to persuade a crowd about how to view these matters. Socrates therefore concludes, and gains Gorgias's enthusiastic assent for the statement, that the peculiar "skill" and success of the rhetorician derive from his ability to persuade the ignorant, a comment that evidences Plato's doubt about the allegiance of Gorgias to the *demos.*[119] This enthusiasm quickly turns to embarrassment. The rhetorician's unique ability to control other crafts, to function as a *politike techne,* depends on his ignorance of everything about which he claims to be an expert. As far as Socrates is concerned, this means that his "art" is merely a contrivance, which makes the rhetorician the antithesis of a true expert in practicing a *techne* (459b–c).

Plato's Socrates now turns to the ethical and political level, initially drawing on assumptions that inform many Platonic dialogues. He asserts that "a man who has learned anything becomes in each case such as his knowledge makes him" (460b). In other words, the knowledge of the practice of a *techne* essentially constitutes the identity of the craftsman: One who learns the art of music becomes a musician; one who learns just acts becomes just. Socrates

---

118. However, this distinction parallels the distinction between "knowledge" and "opinion" or "true opinion" in the *Meno* (97aff).

119. See 459a–b, 463a; see *Phaedrus* 260c–d.

then draws on another conventional Athenian belief—that orators must speak the truth and that all citizens are regarded as just lest they be mad (460c–d).[120] If the art of rhetoric is to teach about matters of right and wrong, justice and injustice, a good rhetorician is right about what he teaches and, in order to guarantee his good judgment, should himself be just.

Plato's Socrates now couples this conventional view with a tenet traditionally ascribed to the historical Socrates—that no one does wrong or commits unjust acts willingly. Because the just never deliberately act unjustly, this seems to suggest that the rhetorician is incapable of making a wrong use of rhetoric and is unwilling to do wrong, whereas Gorgias, in an effort to distance himself from disreputable students of the skill he teaches, had said that the proper practice of his art does not depend on its practitioner's being just—which leaves him blameless for the use to which his *techne* is put, not responsible for whether his *techne* is used justly or unjustly (460a–461a).

It is Socrates' combination of conventional beliefs and his own analytical definition of them that completes the exasperation of Gorgias. Polus comes to the defense of Gorgias, and in his discussion with Socrates, the claim Socrates advanced with Gorgias about the epistemological and ethical requirement of an art such as rhetoric receives more extensive theoretical support. The essential precondition for this support is that Socrates no longer build his own claims from intuitions he shares with his interlocutors but from claims he independently asserts to be true. Socratic discourse in Plato's dialogue, rather than Socrates' interlocutors, becomes the subject of the *elenchus*.[121] This context indicates a new kind of argument. It rejects the intellectual and ethical integrity of conventional norms and the capacity for critical judgment among ordinary citizens; it possesses no obvious links to the conventional beliefs of his interlocutors or society and no necessary links to the beliefs of the historical Socrates as found, for instance, in Plato's *Apology*.

In what follows in the dialogue, Plato uses the *techne* analogy as an analytical and critical tool, rather than as a prescriptive model, for the development of a new perspective on both ethics and politics. The *techne* analogy should not be read simply or primarily as Plato's theorizing and rejecting a

120. See *Apology* 17a–c, *Protagoras* 323a–b.
121. Kahn has an interesting discussion of the role of the *elenchus* in the *Gorgias*. See his "Drama and Dialectic in Plato's Gorgias." As I mentioned above (Chapter 3), I view the *elenchus* in relation to Athenian public discourse, not, as does Gregory Vlastos, in relation to epistemology, acontextually understood.

moral theory such as utilitarianism or instrumentalism, or in terms of a focus on an ethical matter (such as *sophrosyne*) to the exclusion of politics or justice.[122] Rather, it marks an essential stage in the articulation of a theory of justice whose first principles do not depend on conventional ethical and political norms. Plato's use of it makes possible a new critical understanding of the discourse of rhetoric and the political art.

Plato's Socrates lays the first step along this theoretical path by making a categorical claim about the nature of rhetoric. To him, it is no *techne* at all, but rather a kind of *empeiria* (462c). Socrates is playing off Polus's previous reference to *empeiria*—alternatively translated as "experience," "routine," or "knack"—as the foundation for the knowledge of a *techne* of rhetoric:[123] "There are many arts . . . among mankind experimentally devised by experience, for experience guides our life along the path of art, inexperience along the path of chance. And in each of these different arts different men partake in different ways, the best men (*hoi aristoi*) following the best arts" (448c). Polus's conception of the relation between "art" and "experience" seems to exemplify the self-confidence that informed Athenian social understandings in the mid-fifth century, as well as those of Protagoras.[124] Polus upholds this view with the following qualification. Knowledge and mastery of such an "art" of "experience" will not be acquired by the many, only by the few who possess the "best" human powers and arts—given the context, presumably those who have been trained in rhetoric.

Plato's Socrates refers disdainfully to *empeiria*. He denies its usefulness for the acquisition of knowledge and skill and thereby radically rejects the intrinsic merit of society's conventional practices. Socrates also draws on Gorgias's association of rhetoric with the *politike techne* to show that there is an

---

122. See R. W. Hall, "*Techne* and Morality in the *Gorgias*," in J. P. Anton and G. L. Kustas, eds., *Essays in Ancient Greek Philosophy*, 202–18; T. Irwin, *Plato's Moral Theory;* N. P. White, "Rational Prudence in Plato's *Gorgias*," in Dominic J. O'Meara, ed., *Platonic Investigations*, 139–62.

123. The significance of this contrast is obscured by most English translations (such as Woodhead, Hamilton, Irwin), which render *empeiria* here as "routine" or "knack," but earlier in the dialogue, when spoken by Polus, as "experience."

124. Thucydides noted the compatibility of "art" and "experience" when he described the presence and absence of various skills in the practical conduct of the Athenians and Spartans. Protagoras also believed that *empeiria* contributed to *techne*, in that one's experience of Athenian *nomoi* fostered the acquisition of *arete* and the *politike techne*, as well as the development of a sense of justice. The historical Socrates must have held this view to an important extent as well, insofar as his unwillingness to quarrel with the laws of Athens indicated that they provided the necessary (not sufficient) conditions for his conceptions of virtue and justice.

art of rhetoric and a political art, but that they cannot be gained from one's "experience" of Athenian democracy. Indeed, whereas all that is left of the subject matter of Gorgias's *techne* is flattering contact with the people, the identity of a proper *techne* consists in its being immune to being affected by any contact with them. The *demiourgos* of rhetoric must look to the standards of his own art to be a true practitioner of it. The standards of the public are irrelevant, even when the subject matter is political. In this way, the criteria governing the proper practice of a *techne* now provide an independent basis for analyzing and evaluating practical thought and action, one whose practical connection to the conventions of Athenian democracy has been theoretically severed.

For Plato's Socrates, the true nature of Gorgias's art is "flattery" (463b, 502d). As a "routine and knack" (*empeiria kai tribe*), its aim is the production of pleasure and the gratification of desire. In the *Gorgias,* as opposed to the *Protagoras,* this clearly has nothing directly to do with the production of anything good (462c, 465a). Because all *technai* must be useful and beneficial, producing some good, and by itself pleasure is no good—its goodness depends on its use—Plato's Socrates has shown that, properly speaking, rhetoric cannot be a *techne* at all.[125]

In a seminal passage that displays the abstract criteria of Platonic *techne* and reason, Socrates indicates that the inability of rhetoric to produce anything good is tantamount to lacking reason. Accompanying the categorical opposition between *techne* and *empeiria* is a new definition of *techne* itself that roots its possession in the comprehension of its relevant *logos.* Rhetoric, Socrates says, "[i]s not an art but a routine because it has no rational principle (*logon*) by which it applies the things it applies, to explain what they are by nature, and consequently is unable to point to their cause. And I refuse the name of art (*techne*) to anything (*pragma*) irrational (*alogon*)" (465a).[126] This statement situates the knowledge of a *techne* on an abstract rational plane that appears nowhere in other aporetic dialogues but is presupposed in Book 1 of the *Republic.*[127] Having reduced rhetoric to *empeiria* and the standards of *empeiria* to those of rhetoric (not really standards at all), Plato is claiming that one can no longer rely on *empeiria* for knowledge about reality. Conse-

---

125. *Gorgias* 462b, 463a–b, 480a–c. Similar critiques of pseudo-*technai,* although not buttressed by the subsequent articulation of a rational standard for *technai,* appear in the *Ion* 532cff, and *Phaedrus* 260e, 262c, 270b.

126. See *Phaedrus* 270b. Translation based on Irwin.

127. *Republic* 342c. See Dodds's note on 465a, 228–29.

quently, the politics of "experience" become a field of illusion, and the realm of political action dominated by the Gorgian art of rhetoric also becomes a field of illusions (*eidola*); it can no longer be regarded as the fundamental domain in which real power is exercised.[128] For this dialogical Socrates, only philosophy determines what is "natural," and only philosophy can produce good for one's city and one's soul; only it knows what is "best" for them.

If rhetoric is merely an illusory reflection of a genuine art, Plato now has the obligation to define the nature of the genuine art. Socrates introduces a method of division in order to avoid the excesses of *makrologia*, the rhetorician's long-winded style of argument.[129] This new method, which becomes more prevalent in later dialogues (including the *Phaedrus* and *Statesman*), is "the language of geometers."[130] It is a formal method, the proper use of which does not rely on knowledge of "experience." He states affirmatively that rhetoric is a semblance of a part of *politike*, a single term that Plato uses to refer to the political art as a master art of the soul.[131] It is an art of the soul and becomes manifest in the arts of (1) legislation and (2) justice, which correspond to the arts of the body, (3) gymnastics, and (4) medicine.

For Socrates, there is a corresponding practice that tries to impersonate each of these four arts. Such so-called arts are really forms of flattery. Rhetoric is a flattering semblance (*eidolon*) of justice; sophistic is a flattering semblance of legislation. Correspondingly, beautification is a flattering semblance of gymnastics, and cookery of medicine (463a–465b).[132] Notably,

---

128. See 463a–c, 464b–465e. Michael Oakeshott condemns this condemnation of "experience" as the constitutive foundation of the political art in an essay that serves as a keystone of both his critique of "rationalism" and his affirmative theory of political conservatism. But he notably differentiates Platonic critical reason from the "rationalism" of modern science that derives from Bacon. See his "Rationalism in Politics," in *Rationalism in Politics and Other Essays*, 1–36.

129. *Gorgias* 449bff. Plato's Socrates also opposed this form of address when used by Protagoras in the *Protagoras* 329a–b, 334ff.

130. *Gorgias* 465b–c. See *Phaedrus* 265cff. On the significance of mathematics for Plato, see D. H. Fowler, *The Mathematics of Plato's Academy*. Also see Vlastos's discussion in "Elenchus and Mathematics."

131. *Gorgias* 463e. The differences in meaning, if any, between *politike techne* and *politike* in the *Gorgias* stem more centrally from the context of their use than any intrinsic difference. *Politike* appears in a context of the formal differentiation of arts; *politike techne* appears where Socrates distinguishes what he is doing from that of ordinary politicians. It is not surprising, then, that *politike* is the term of art in Plato's formal discussion of political leadership in the *Statesman*. See Chapter 5, Section A, below.

132. For commentary on these analogies, see Dodds, *Plato: Gorgias*, 226–27, and Guthrie, *History of Greek Philosophy*, 4:287–88, 299–300. I take Dodds's comments to be particularly apt. He points out that this analogical construction anticipates the method of *diairesis* that is used more extensively in the *Sophist* and *Statesman*. On the *Statesman*, see below, Chapter 5, Section A.

"justice" (*dikaiosyne*) here is a subdivision of the political art (*politike*, 464b).[133]

A striking feature of this *techne* is its substantive domain. Socrates states that it concerns the soul and not the body. Critics have referred to this relation as evidence of Platonic immaturity or confusion or indicative of the essentially ethical, nonpolitical character of the Socratic conception of the political art.[134] However, given Plato's frequent efforts in the aporetic dialogues to arrive at a positive conception of a second-order art of virtue that would enable him to resolve his Socratic Problem, this interpretation seems inadequate. Insofar as this *techne* appears in the dialogue alongside a theoretical rejection of ordinary experience as a guide to *techne*, justice, and the good of one's soul, it seems to evidence less a confusion or differentiation of "Socratic" and "Platonic" beliefs than to signal the intellectual emergence of a new ethical and political vision, one that rejoins ethics and politics at the level of Platonic theory. Such a conception of the political art could be said to reflect the efforts of both the historical Socrates and Plato to shift the ultimate context for evaluating political success from the acquisition of wealth and strength to the care of the soul.[135]

Socrates' confident affirmation of the existence of *politike* as an art of virtue that produces good for the soul and the political community as a whole does not appear in the other aporetic dialogues that involve the political art. Here, it indicates Plato's capacity for radically new theoretical claims based on a new power and authority granted to judgments based on the criteria of his *techne* of *logos,* claims that are made possible by having broken the link between his interpretation of the social world and extant received understandings of it (even as he drew from them). *Techne* has become a model for a form of critical and ethical reason that would directly inform practice.[136]

133. In the *Republic,* that relation is reversed, although the discussion of justice as a virtue (*arete*) flows from a discussion of the *techne* of justice, which itself flows from a discussion of the political art of ruling.

134. On Plato's rendering of *politike* in the *Gorgias* as immature, see Dodds, 227, and R. K. Sprague, *Plato's Philosopher-King: A Study of the Theoretical Background,* 22–28. For its ethical, nonpolitical character, see Vlastos, "The Historical Socrates and Athenian Democracy."

135. In the *Gorgias,* it is Socrates' insistence that the value of rhetoric be measured in terms of the good of one's soul that directs the subsequent exchange between himself and Polus and Callicles over the power of Gorgian rhetoric and Athenian rhetoricians or political leaders. This move is paralleled in the *Phaedrus* (270d–271a, 276e–277a), where the only legitimate *techne logon* is one that is used with an understanding of the soul of its subjects.

136. This theorization of *techne* should not be interpreted, following David Roochnik, as an illustration of an Aristotelian division between theoretical and practical reason, to which Plato

Plato's innovation lies in the new strictures that have been placed on what counts as knowledge and his ethical but nonsubjective focus on the soul as the basis for any art of rhetoric or political art. Concomitant with these is a more explicitly negative judgment of the virtue and competence of ordinary citizens. In the dialogues, these features have appeared as responses to the lack of clear standards in the practices of Protagoras and Gorgias for the proper performance of their arts, which clearly affect the soul.

Plato's new theoretical criteria for the practice of a *techne* empower reason as a relatively independent critical faculty for guiding the performance of a *techne*. As such, the *techne* endows rational human practices with integrity and relative autonomy. Plato's aims may be compatible with the Athenians' democracy as the constitution that fosters autonomy for the sovereign citizens of a political community, paralleling the desired condition of autonomy based on reason for the individual. But he does not follow this route. Instead, he hints at a new relation of rhetoric and the political art to the collectivity. The key to understanding this new relation appears in Plato's characterization in the *Gorgias* of the nature of power itself.

c. The Power and Practice of Rhetoric

Plato's attention now turns to the examination of the power and practice of rhetoric. His interlocutors are Polus and Callicles, each of whom offers different practical interpretations of rhetoric, with Polus's being the more moderate. Insofar as both see themselves as students of Gorgias and yet profess contrasting ethical and political views, they attest to the moral indeterminacy of rhetoric as understood and taught by Gorgias.

i. Polus and the Conventional Power of Rhetoric

Socrates' concern is the actual effect of rhetoric on its practitioners. Polus doubts both Socrates' rejection of the existing practice of rhetoric as a *techne* and his denial of its power. After all, rhetoricians clearly exercise power in the political realm (466a). Socrates' response is crucial. He shifts the domain for the evaluation of power from the public context of collective judgment to the private context of individual choice. In a statement just as unprecedented as

---

did not subscribe. See David Roochnik, "Socrates' Use of the *Techne*-Analogy." Werner Jaeger's classic discussion of *techne* in the *Gorgias* is better on this score, although he, too, reduces conceptions of "theory" to their Aristotelian incarnation. See his *Paideia: The Ideals of Greek Culture*, 2:129–30.

his earlier stipulation of the inability of *empeiria* to contribute to the development of *techne*, Socrates claims that "power" (*dynamis*), as the capacity to achieve something, not only involves the ability to achieve something but also requires the ability to achieve something good (466b). Despite the wide-reaching implication of this claim, Socrates gains Polus's assent to this definition as if it were a commonplace assumption, just as he had gained Gorgias's assent earlier for the statement that a person who has learned something "becomes in each case such as his knowledge makes him."

Taken together, these definitions imply that the personal power involved in an individual's activities is determined by how they affect the good of the agent's soul. This proposition is important in "depriving" rhetoricians of their "power," because someone who does not know what he is doing or what his action is "good for" is not likely to accomplish in his act what he wishes to accomplish except by virtue of nature or chance, which are not subject to control by human agency. Because Socrates has previously shown that the activity of rhetoricians is based on ignorance rather than knowledge and concerns semblances rather than reality, it becomes clear that, properly speaking, rhetoricians have no power. Plato has taken a major step in developing the supposedly Socratic maxim that "no one does wrong willingly" in a radical political direction—probably one that the historical Socrates had not taken. By asserting the power of *logos* to determine the power of *ergon*, Plato's Socrates has virtually claimed that no one who does wrong has any practical power. He proceeds to argue that rhetoricians have no power because they do not do what they will.

Socrates justifies this claim by transposing to the ethical-political domain the arguments he had used for his new definition of a *techne* and linking them to his previous statements concerning the "logical" criteria for *technai* that would benefit the soul. The logic he employs for doing so does not stray from conventional patterns of Greek thought, for there was no "logical" reason for not treating *arete* in terms of *techne* (because an activity guided by good intentions that did not produce good results generally did not express *arete*). Plato breaks new ground here, however. In other aporetic dialogues, the usefulness of the *techne* analogy regarding first-order practical activity ultimately broke down when second-order activities, ethical and political matters involving virtue, were at stake. The connection was maintained either incoherently, by Socrates' interlocutors, or impractically, by Socrates himself. Plato could not sustain theoretical arguments for a second-order art of virtue, because they depended on assumptions that were constituted by the conventional realm of practical experience, a realm that was ethically compromised but still the only available context in these dialogues for the articulation and evaluation of a concept of virtue.

In the *Gorgias*, Plato removes these impediments. Ordinary conceptions of the "goodness" of practical activity, whose moral context extended only as far as might be allowed by conventional judgments of benefit or advantage, are made to depend on evaluations of the good of one's soul that do not need to take conventional judgments into account. Plato has demarcated a domain of ethical and political evaluation that clearly showed the insufficiency of typical first-order arts as models of virtue.

Plato's Socrates now develops his argument further by drawing on the maxim "No one does wrong willingly" (468d; see also *Crito* 49a, *Protagoras* 358c). Plato begins by affirming the ordinary belief that whenever a person "wills" an action, he intends to do something. He has an end or purpose in mind, "that for the sake of which he acts." This definition of human action affects conceptions about the nature of power in the political world. Because one's power depends on having knowledge guide one's actions and because having knowledge is synonymous with knowing how to do good or to benefit oneself, one's power depends on knowing the good. And given that the possession of knowledge directly affects one's being, having power requires one to be good. This means that the knowledge of the nature of a good action is to be ascertained independently of the judgment of the action's agent. Plato presupposes that the determination of the good use of the product of a *techne* has nothing inherently to do with the individual who is deliberating about and judging the usefulness of the action in which he is engaged. The only real power comes from knowledge. Tyrants who do what they please without regard for the "goodness" of the consequences of their actions do not know what they are doing; in Plato's terms, therefore, the tyrant is powerless.

Polus cries out that no one would believe Socrates' views about the nature of power; he "speaks absurdities." Polus raises two new issues concerning whether or not the power of Socrates' *techne* of rational action truly benefits the agent. First, would it not be preferable to use power for evil, even as a tyrant, if the alternative is to suffer from having such power used against oneself? Are there not times and instances, illustrated by the life of the tyrant Archelaus, in which one benefits from evil or wrong, such that one would do well by doing wrong willingly? Socrates answers that he would be happier choosing to suffer than to do wrong (469c). He employs views that appeared in Plato's *Crito*—that it is better to do just rather than unjust (or "wrong") actions—but now justifies them as being more advantageous to the individual; they generate greater happiness. Second, Polus claims that it would be better to escape rather than endure punishment for doing wrong. Socrates replies by saying that the doer of evil is happier if he receives punishment from gods and men for his actions than if he escapes it (472e, 476a, 476c).[137]

As far as Polus is concerned, Socrates continues to speak absurdities. But in the following exchange, Socrates finds irreducible contradictions in Polus's position, which stem from his adherence to the restrictions of conventional criteria for determining right and wrong (whereas Socrates' own criteria have no such restrictions).[138] Socrates mounts his critique by inducing Polus to agree that shamefulness and harm or evil can be evaluated according to a single measure—*to kalon*—whose criteria are the greatest amount of "pleasure and the good" and the smallest amount of "pain and evil." Socrates exploits the ambiguous equivalence of pleasure and the good, pain and evil. If one action is more shameful than another, it is so because of an excess of pain or evil. Given that doing injustice (*adikein*) is more shameful than suffering it (*adikeisthai*), and given that Polus would not allow those who commit injustice to experience more pain than the victims who suffer it, those who commit injustice must experience more evil than those who suffer injustice. So Polus cannot be right that it is worse to suffer injustice than to inflict it.

Polus resists this form of argumentation, but Socrates asks him to submit to it as a patient should to the treatment of his doctor. The *logos* has assumed a new power to rule those to whom it applies when used by those who are skilled in it. The rest of the dialogue is designed to prove the supremacy of this "art" of *logos*—supposedly objective but obviously artistically rendered by Plato—over the power of the conventional "art" of rhetoric.[139]

In refuting Polus's second objection, Socrates also relies on conventional assumptions to argue that it is better to suffer punishment than escape it. Here

---

137. Again, a reader of the *Apology* and *Crito* hears resonances with those dialogues. But again, here there is a distinction with a difference because the historical Socrates apparently justified his own punishment, even though he had done nothing wrong. There is no conceptual space offered for that position here, primarily because no set of conventional practices possesses the necessary virtue to be authoritative.

138. At this point in the dialogue (470e), Socrates identifies the criteria for happiness as "education" and "justice," a harbinger of the *Republic*, where substantive connections between education and justice, on the one hand, and happiness, on the other, are elaborately explained.

139. Plato allows for a "good" art of rhetoric in the *Phaedrus* (277b–c) and *Statesman* (304c–d); however, it is differently defined in each and subordinated to the art of dialectic (*Phaedrus*) or philosophy (*Statesman*). See Chapter 5, below.

the assumptions are that those who suffer legal punishment are disciplined justly and all just things are fine (*to kalon*) insofar as they are just (476a–b). Socrates is thus able to argue that (1) everyone wants *to kalon*, because it is pleasurable and beneficial; (2) a shameful action is such because of its great pain; (3) injustice is the most shameful of actions; (4) punishment rids one of injustice and thus pain; (5) he who suffers punishment is benefited; and (6) it is finer to experience more justice, even if it entails disciplinary punishment.

Socrates is able to obtain Polus's agreement to the claim that injustice is a greater evil than poverty or disease, and that it is an evil of the soul. Therefore, the *techne* that eliminates this greatest of evils is the *techne* of justice.[140] Because the man who escapes punishment continues to harbor evil within himself, he is worse off for not having been punished (477b–478d). Insofar as the happiest man experiences no evil, the next happiest is he who has been delivered from it. According to these criteria for a reliable, practical, and beneficial *techne* for the good of the individual, a *techne* of rhetoric is useful only if it encourages those who are evil to submit to punishment that rids them of their evil, or, if one believes that it is better to do injustice, to make sure that those who commit it escape punishment for their evil deeds. Again, Polus finds Socrates' arguments absurd, but he cannot refute their logic.

Now Callicles intervenes. He believes that Socrates must be joking, because, he says: "If you are serious and what you say is true, then surely the life of us mortals must be turned upside down and apparently we are everywhere doing the opposite of what we should" (481b–c). Of course, this is precisely what Socrates is arguing. With Callicles as his interlocutor, the radical implications of his beliefs become clear.

ii. Callicles and the Natural Power of Rhetoric

Callicles assigns no merit to conventional beliefs and gives no weight to the opinions of the many. He argues only for what he believes. Because of this, he is a perfect foil for Socrates to test his own beliefs. Moreover, Callicles requires consistency from Socrates. For Callicles' intervention was motivated by more than emotional exasperation. He rightly pointed out that Socrates himself had been ambiguous in his exchanges with Polus. In Callicles' words, if Polus assumed the basis of convention (*nomos*), Socrates would question

---

140. This particular notion of an "art" of justice anticipates (or recollects) Socrates' reference to the "art" of justice in Book 1 of the *Republic.*

him on the basis of nature (*physis*), and if he followed nature, Socrates would follow convention.[141] He accuses Socrates of exploiting Polus's *logos* to suit his own.

Unlike Protagoras, who believed that *nomos* and *physis* harmonized in a democratic *polis*, Callicles asserts an inherent tension and opposition between *nomos* and *physis*, with the former constraining the more fundamental and necessary vitality of the latter.[142] It is in Socrates' argument with Callicles that Plato partially resolves the ambiguity of his Socratic Problem. For that problem had stemmed from Socrates' own ambiguity about his links to the customs of Athens and the opinions of its citizens, the virtue and justice of its laws. These are now subjected to the rigors of argument, which grant them no natural value or authority.

With Callicles, Plato's Socrates in the *Gorgias* confronts one who believes he knows the means for the proper and successful defense of Socrates and has a theory of justice that could justify a critique of Athenian *nomoi*. But Callicles' rationale for such a critique is much different from the historical Socrates' or Plato's Socrates'. It stems from a conception of a "law of nature," "natural justice," and the justice of "the better and the stronger" (488b). As far as Callicles is concerned, these qualities are just as independent of the judgment of the many as those of Socrates' conception of justice based on the model of a *techne*. Better yet, Callicles believes them to be much more helpful than the philosopher's art in protecting one against the abuses of the many (486b–c); he charges that Socrates' "art" is powerless in terms of the power of the world, even though, as a *techne*, it is to have power and to produce something useful and beneficial.[143]

An unbridgeable gap has appeared, which exemplifies the gap between virtue and the political art that constitutes Plato's Socratic Problem. The gap lies between an argument on behalf of a seemingly powerful but unjust *techne* of *logos* and one on behalf of a seemingly powerless but just one. Thus, to meet Callicles' challenge, Socrates must endow his *techne* with new power, transforming it, at least theoretically, into an authoritative political art. The development of the final portion of the *Gorgias* provides just such a structural foundation for a positive, reconstituted notion of the political art.

141. *Gorgias* 483a. This appeared most clearly in Socrates' use of the ambiguous standard of "the pleasurable and the good," which enabled him to alter his standpoint from that of an individual whose views might conflict with those of the many to one that had to harmonize with it.

142. See Antiphon, Diels-Kranz 44.

143. *Gorgias* 510a; see also *Republic* I, 348d, and Bk. VI, 488aff.

Socrates refers to the example of craftsmen as knowledgeable producers of objects and then asks, In what are "the better and more powerful" better and more powerful? As did Gorgias and Polus, Callicles responds by referring to a second-order craft, that is, a *techne* that enables one to use or control other *technai*. His reply recalls Gorgias's earlier definitions of rhetoric as a superordinate art of "the whole" that could deal with any political issue. Those who perform this craft are not typical craftsmen such as cobblers or cooks, but are "wise (*phronimoi*) in affairs of the state and the best methods of administering it, and not only wise but courageous, being competent to accomplish their intentions and not flagging through weakness of soul" (491a–b). Callicles' political art is antidemocratic insofar as it does not involve the skill in political deliberation, which, according to Thucydides' Pericles and Plato's Protagoras, is possessed and practiced by virtually all Athenian citizens. Rather, it involves "ruling over and having more than their subjects" (490a).

Socrates transfers his line of questioning to this second-order political and rhetorical *techne* of Callicles and asks, What is the sphere of action for these individuals? What is the substantive content of this surplus power owed to "the better"? Callicles does not know what Socrates wants in addition to what Callicles has already said. Nor is that readily evident to the reader, for Socrates takes a new tack and directs the focus of his analysis of Calliclean rhetoric and politics to the soul and the self.

There is no formal, logical, necessary connection between Socrates' questioning in terms of *techne* and his new focus on the soul. Nevertheless, this is clearly the direction in which Plato thinks the argument must go. Socrates asks whether the capacity to rule others must be grounded in an individual's ability to rule himself, which is equivalent to having the virtue of moderation (*sophrosyne*).[144] This move is very important, for Callicles' response, in which he describes the personal aspect of his political art as expertise in the gratification of pleasures, returns him to the camp of Gorgias and Polus. This ground will prove shaky for Callicles, especially because the principal difference between him and them lies in the fact that Callicles' skill is possessed by

---

144. This is evident because, first, Socrates does refer favorably to contemporary, conventional characterizations of *sophrosyne*. In so doing, he creates links to ordinary understandings that are rare in the *Gorgias*. Such links will be cut more thoroughly in the *Republic*. Second, in proving the validity of such a *techne* in the *Republic*, Plato's Socrates initially will refer to the well-being of the political community as a whole, and thus by extension (for him) of the individual.

the few and not the many and so has its own internal criteria of success. Callicles responds as follows: "Anyone who is to live aright should suffer his appetites (*epithumias*) to grow to the greatest extent and not check them, and through courage and intelligence (*phronesis*) should be competent to minister to them at their greatest and to satisfy every appetite with what it craves. But this, I imagine, is impossible for the many" (491e–492a).

However, Socrates argues that it is no easier to find a standard of personal pleasure which, if followed, leads to a satisfactory life than it is to find one for a practice that caters to the pleasures of the crowd. Socrates' search for a standard in this context may seem like the commission of the metaphysical fallacy, in which he tries to endow a socially constructed norm with a transcendental status. But such criticism misses the political significance of Socrates' assertion of the need for "standards," namely, concern about the reduction of *logos* to a mere instrument of coercive power or personal desire.[145]

Plato's Socrates bolsters this point by making claims about the nature of a healthy soul and its need for order and harmony. The formal qualities that conventionally pertain to a good product of a *techne* and count as the formal end or purpose of an activity informed by *techne* now apply to the soul and provide substantive criteria for determining its well-being. Socrates asserts that the need for order and harmony is not satisfied by the active pursuit of pleasure (which nonetheless constitutes a part of the life of the soul). As if to signify the appearance of a new dimension of thought, he introduces these criteria not by another *logos* but by telling a story, which he actually calls a *mythologos* (493a):

> I once heard one of our wise men say that we are actually now dead, and that our body is a tomb, and that that part of the soul in which dwell the desires (*epithumiai*) is of a nature to be swayed and to shift to and fro. And so some clever fellow, a Sicilian perhaps or Italian, writing in allegory, by a slight perversion of language named this part of the soul a jar, because it can be swayed and easily persuaded, and the foolish he called the uninitiated, and that part of the soul in foolish people where the desires reside—the uncontrolled and non-

---

145. This concern has parallels in the *Meno* (97aff), where Socrates seeks a more stable basis for practical reason than "true opinion" or "correct opinion"; in the *Phaedrus* (272d–273c), Socrates evidences a similar dissatisfaction with the absence of other criteria for the rhetorician's *techne logon* than "probability" as determined by a "crowd." In these dialogues, however, the political significance of Socrates' concern is obscured (more so in the *Phaedrus* than the *Meno*).

retentive part—he likened to a leaky jar, because it can never be filled. And in opposition to you, Callicles, he shows that those in Hades—the unseen world he means—these uninitiated must be the most unhappy, for they will carry water to pour into a perforated jar in a similarly perforated sieve. And by the sieve, my informant told me, he means the soul, and the soul of the foolish he compared to a sieve, because it is perforated and through lack of belief and forgetfulness unable to hold anything. (493a–c)

Socrates pursues this analogy against Callicles' preferred form of a happy and just life and evokes from Callicles the objection that Socrates is "absurd," like a "demagogue," and should be "ashamed" by this kind of talk (494d; see also 482c). But Socrates will not be waylaid. His story provides standards of harmony and order for the soul, which conform to the criteria for a good *techne* he had articulated earlier. The new standard of critical *logos* that would regulate the pursuit of pleasure and harmonize the soul provides an ethical basis for self-control and self-rule.

Such a story is not enough; there has to be an argument as well. Socrates therefore sets out standards of a second-order notion of the good. It will provide a standard of good and bad pleasures and an authoritative rationale for a *techne* of the soul whose aim is not the pursuit of pleasure. He recalls his discussion with Polus in which he identified good action as the ultimate end of any productive activity, any *real* art, so as to conclude that "the good is the end of all actions and that everything else should be done for its sake, not the good for the sake of everything else" (499e).

Socrates has allied the criteria of *techne* with those for evaluating good action. In Plato's *Protagoras*, Socrates had proffered a similar art, the art of measurement. Its foundations were insecure, however, because it conflated the pleasurable and the good. In the *Gorgias,* where Plato's Socrates rejects any dependence of his critical discourse on the opinions, wishes, or pleasures of the many or the *nomoi* of Athens as bases for establishing a *techne* of anything, he differentiates pleasure and goodness, rooting all ethical and political calculations concerning what is good for the individual, his soul, and the political community as a whole in a *techne* of goodness alone.[146]

---

146. *Gorgias* 495a–497a, 499b–e. A compatible distinction is made in the *Phaedrus* 239c. A more dialectical discussion of "pleasure" and "goodness" as standards of action appears in the *Philebus*, where the political relevance of this distinction is not discussed. Socrates' use of the

The *Gorgias* does not, therefore, represent the rejection of an earlier Socratic or Platonic "hedonism."[147] The art of measurement in the *Protagoras* reflected an incipient explanation of a second-order art of virtue. For it to be more developed, the ties of such an art to conventional opinions, desires, views, and laws had to end. Plato cut such ties in the *Gorgias.* He developed the theoretical foundation for an art of virtue by, first, justifying the logic and coherence of a *techne* of *logos* independently of *empeiria* and, then, using that model as a basis for a *techne* of *arete,* with the context for evaluating the benefits of such an *arete* altering from the social judgments of the Athenian citizenry to the judgment of the good of one's soul according to Socrates' philosophical *techne* of *logos.* Thus Callicles and Socrates agree on the need of what amounts to an art of measurement to produce a good life, one that the many cannot have. But they differ on what that art is.

Plato now secures a new context for evaluating the success of this art, moving it from the public to the private realm, from the collectivity to the individual, so that a *techne* of happiness does not depend for its success on exercising power in the public realm (where rhetoricians excel) but on a Socratic life of philosophy. Callicles' acquiescence to this argument is actually irrelevant, for the testing ground for the theoretical coherence of Socrates' argument has already become the soul.

Socrates' interest in securing a *techne* for the good of the soul does not ignore the requirement that any *techne* must have practical benefits. His new theory of a *techne* of *logos* for the good of the soul is inherently practical and therefore inherently political. Plato maintains the conventional Athenian belief that community and social rationality reflect each other, that goodness in the soul is realized by the practices of social life. However, he dramatically shifts their referents. As a result, Socrates' inward turn in his argument with Callicles provides the basis not only for Socrates' response to Callicles' claim about the power of politicians but also for his radical criticism of renowned Athenian political leaders.

In his last attempt to answer Socrates' logic by reference to the world he knows, Callicles argues for two kinds of rhetoricians—on the one hand,

---

example of courage in the *Gorgias* to make his point, parallel to the use of the example of courage to illuminate the relation between *episteme* and *arete* in the *Protagoras,* seems to buttress the argument that the *Gorgias* represents a theoretical if not chronological step ahead of the *Protagoras.*

147. See Irwin, *Plato's Moral Theory,* and idem, *Plato's Ethics.*

political leaders who really flatter the many, are rather servants than statesmen, supposedly the politicians of the day, and, on the other, the famous political leaders of Athenian history: Themistocles, Miltiades, and particularly
Pericles (503a–d). But Plato's Socrates argues that not even the latter knew
the genuine political art. His rejection of the great Athenian political leaders
makes sense in terms of the philosophical categories he has established.[148] For
they seemingly did not improve the souls of citizens, despite their many other
accomplishments.

Plato's Socrates has established a philosophical basis for a political art
that the historical Socrates lacked. Its foundation consists in the articulation
of a second-order *techne* of *arete* that can be expressed and evaluated. Virtue
and justice need no longer be judged in terms of the *nomoi* of Athens, the actions of its great leaders, or the judgments of its citizens, but in light of the actions of the soul (503d–504a). The new political art will be based on a *logos*
and an *eidos* and will treat the potential disorder of desires, disciplining them
into a harmoniously ordered whole and providing the new foundation for
what counts as lawful (504d). These claims, states Socrates, are secured by
logoi of steel and adamant. But such *logoi* are not rooted in the beliefs or
practices of citizens but in the abstract beauty of pure truths and geometrical equality (508a). They cannot be perfected by acting in accord with conventional ethical and political norms, as Pericles, Meletus, Protagoras, and
Polus imagined they could be. But if they are rejected in exchange for the life
of a Calliclean rhetorician, one's "surplus of power" will dissipate as water
through a sieve, in an endless pursuit of an elusive and illusory satisfaction. A
new impasse has been reached, out of which Plato's Socrates now leads Callicles, and the reader.

iii. Power and the Socratic Political Art

Socrates argues that the *techne* of a statesman and rhetorician who would
be guided by the wishes of the people rather than the *eidos* of philosophical
logos is not a reliable or beneficial *techne* for the good of one's soul or the political community as a whole. In previous dialogues, the practical requirements of a good *techne* had been used to show the uselessness of philosophi-

---

148. Some have explained this as an emotional reaction on Plato's part to certain events in
his life, thus requiring a particular compositional date for the dialogue. For a good example of
why such arguments are rather weak, see Brian Calvert, "The Politicians of Athens in the *Gorgias* and *Meno*."

cally grounded second-order arts of virtue. But now, with the substantive practical ground of the good of one's soul as support, they become central to practical criticism in the political domain, the public dimension of the life of one's soul.

This introduction of the epistemological and substantive criteria of *techne* into the political domain makes possible the wholesale rejection of the practice of politics that was so integral to the power and glory of Athenian democracy. Socrates asks Callicles what is the proper standard for becoming active in public life and making citizens as good as possible (515b–c). Socrates states that if the great Athenian statesmen made the citizens better, they would steadily make the souls of the citizenry more orderly and harmonious (517c). Yet no Athenian statesman has been able to do this. Themistocles and Cimon ultimately fell out of favor as each was ostracized, and Miltiades and Pericles were publicly and officially condemned. Either these statesmen were not good at what they did and so were justly chastised by the citizens, or the citizenry was wrong, which meant that the statesmen's art was ineffective.

Plato's use of the *techne* analogy to evaluate the activity of political leadership has been roundly and often rightly condemned.[149] In the *Gorgias*, the analogy leads Socrates to refer to statesmen as animal trainers and therefore to citizens as animals (516aff). He supposes that any slippage in politics between plan and result, *logos* and *ergon*, reflects the inadequacy of the *techne*. Taken literally, this makes no sense, for it endows the politician with potentially total control over the well-being of his citizenry; it is as unreasonable as judging a doctor to be a poor practitioner of medicine because some of her patients died. But we ought not take the analogy literally. To some extent, it seems that Socrates attributes no legitimacy or natural virtue to the individual freedom or collective wishes of ordinary citizens. But let us remember the most salient context for the Platonic Socrates in the *Gorgias*, namely, the life of the historical Socrates. The alternative to this critical standard for good practice is allowing the meaning of virtue in political action to be sufficiently determined by the citizens themselves, in which case the jury's verdict against Socrates could be justified. By having "Socrates" raise the issue of whether Callicles' rhetorical political art, if practiced according to the standards of

---

149. For example, Renford Bambrough, "Plato's Political Analogies," in *Philosophy, Politics, and Society*, ed. P. Laslett, 98–115; Hannah Arendt, *The Human Condition*. However, Bambrough's article also has serious faults, which I point out in my discussion of Plato's *Republic* in Chapter 4.

Athenian statesmen, might endanger him, Plato reintroduces the issues underlying Socrates' trial (519a–b).

Socrates is exploiting the ambiguous standards of the rhetorical art; because no critical standard exists for justifying *nomoi* as constraints on the pursuit of pleasure, a determination of rhetoric's successful practice may depend simply on pleasing its subject. In the *Gorgias*, Plato implies, if not asserts, that criteria for an art of rhetoric exist but have not been met in practice. The aporetic dialogues suggest that no art or statesman, rhetorician, or Sophist exists whose practice manifests or constitutes second-order arts of virtue, varieties of the political art. (In Plato's hands, a radical argument for unconventional critical discourse in politics is linked with unargued assumptions about the inadequate judgment of the majority of ordinary citizens.[150])

The historical Socrates was apparently accused of practicing a *techne* of his own. In Plato's *Apology*, Socrates was virtually charged with possessing a corrupting second-order *techne* of *arete*. He disclaimed having any such art, let alone a corrupting one, although he believed that he did provide "therapy" for the souls of his interlocutors and for his city. In Plato's *Gorgias*, "Socrates" believes that his *techne* of *logos* provides the kind of therapy that makes him a legitimate practitioner of the political art, the art for the good of the soul and the political community as a whole.[151] "I think I am one of a few Athenians—not to say the only one—who undertake the real political art (*politike techne*) and practice politics (*prattein ta politika*)—the only one among people now. I don't aim at gratification with each of the speeches (*logous*) I make, but aim at the best, not the pleasantest" (521d). So in response to Callicles' charge that Socrates would be defenseless in court, Socrates can say, with the categories of his discussion with Polus in the background, that were he to be tried, it would be "like that of a doctor prosecuted by a cook before a jury of children" (521e).

The political art thus cannot be practiced and developed in the political deliberations of assembled Athenian citizens. Rather, it must emerge from carefully controlled training in common in the art of Platonic knowledge about good living (527d). Philosophical training must precede, even as it con-

---

150. For a compatible view from a different interpretive perspective, see C. Kahn, "Drama and Dialectic in Plato's *Gorgias*," 117.

151. In this passage, Socrates does not *say* that he knows the political art, but according to the previous statements in the dialogue, practicing the art requires him to know it, at least insofar as having a *logos* of it makes its possession and competent practice possible.

stitutes, the art of politics. In Plato's *Gorgias,* Socrates believes that if one develops a critical perspective from this training one can then enter the political realm. Presumably political activity could be practiced as a genuine *techne;* the practices of political and conversational deliberation that had been perverted by rhetoricians and their art could be transformed.

We do not yet know what a society shaped by such an art would look like. The *Gorgias* has told us, however, what the tools for its construction will be, in that it represents a thoroughgoing critique of the ethics and politics of Athenian society thus far. It reflects, to a point, Plato's answer to his Socratic Problem.

d. Rhetoric, the Political Art, and Democracy

This dialogue clears the ground for a more complete critical account of justice itself. The *Gorgias* suggests why the connections of Plato's critical discourse to extant ethical and political conventions may be contingent rather than necessary; it also affirms the value of a new Platonic critical discourse and educational practice. It provides a new complementarity of *logos* and *ergon,* one that opposes their complementarity in the conventions of Athenian democracy and one whose truth and validity derive from a constitutional order that is articulated in rational discourse (*logos*) but unrealized in actual practice (*ergon*).

Viewed in this light, Plato's treatment of rhetoric and the political art in the *Gorgias* suggests a more complicated relation of Plato's critical reason to Athenian democracy than is typically thought. In the past twenty years, there has been a resurgence of intellectual sympathy for "rhetoric" as opposed to "philosophy" or "theory." It has been stimulated by the view that Gorgian rhetoric is more "democratic" than Plato's critical discourse. The earliest version of this view was Grote's nineteenth-century defense of the Sophists against the conservative appropriation of Plato.[152] It received major new supporters during and after World War II, with the dissemination of Popper's indictment of Plato as a proto-totalitarian and Havelock's reconstruction of Greek Sophists and rhetors as protoliberals.[153] But this formal contrast is simplistic and misleading, for it runs together many lines of argument that Plato

---

152. George Grote, *Plato and the Other Companions of Socrates.* Note W. M. Calder and S. T. Trzaskoma, eds., *George Grote Reconsidered.*
    153. Karl Popper, *The Open Society and Its Enemies—Vol. 1: The Spell of Plato;* Eric Havelock, *The Liberal Temper in Greek Politics.*

employs in criticizing Gorgian rhetoric, lines that do not necessarily belong together.

Plato's critique of rhetoric neither directly nor necessarily constituted a radical critique of democracy. Although the current practice of rhetoric as a *techne* endowed its practitioners, a subset of the *demos*, with rational authority and persuasive power, it was not practically defined or limited by criteria that would prevent it from being employed as an instrument of ignorant or unjust political agents. Moreover, Plato's concerns about rhetoric as a *techne* do not lead him to reject rhetoric, writing, or any *techne logon* entirely but rather to establish new grounds for them.[154] His grounds establish the superiority of dialectical philosophy to politics. But it is not to "eliminate" politics itself or the *polis* as a deliberative society as much as to obtain an ethical tether for the political art, one that had been frayed by the experiences of recent Athenian history.[155] At the end of the *Gorgias,* Plato does not so much reject democracy or eliminate politics as argue that both need nourishment from critical philosophical discourse if they are not to destroy the possibility of actualizing their rational ethical potential.[156]

Insofar as Plato's critical *logos* denaturalizes all conventional forms of power, and insofar as its critical focus in the *Gorgias* is more politically directed to those who exercise power over others, it is potentially useful to democratic partisans objecting to political authorities who uncritically justify their political influence over ordinary citizens in the name of democracy. Plato's empowerment of the art of critical *logos* in the *Gorgias* as a political art develops a new tool for democrats as much as for democracy's critics, if the former would justify their practices on the basis of what ought to be rather

---

154. A similar view is elaborated in the *Phaedrus*, where Plato's Socrates argues for the need for an ethical, oral understanding of written, potentially narcotic arts of discourse (including, I suppose, Plato's own writings). In trusting Thamus over Theuth, he recalls the relation that Protagoras articulated in Plato's *Protagoras* between general civic virtue/the political art (that comes from Zeus) and the particular practical arts that Prometheus gave to man; he implicitly argues for a new, more philosophical Zeus to make up for the limits of Prometheus's gifts.

155. For a recent statement of this position, see C. Farrar, "Ancient Greek Political Theory as a Response to Democracy," in J. Dunn, ed., *Democracy: The Unfinished Journey, 508 BC–1993 AD,* 17–39.

156. For a more robust view of the potential for democratic education lodged within the *Gorgias,* see J. Peter Euben, "Democracy and Political Theory: A Reading of Plato's *Gorgias,*" in J. Peter Euben et al., eds., *Athenian Political Thought and the Reconstruction of American Democracy,* 198–226.

than what is. Overall, it (albeit unintentionally) provides a tentative justification of theoretical discourse for democrats. Such critical discourse is not simply "philosophical" rather than "political," because Plato develops the philosophical dimension of *logos* as a political response to practical, as well as conceptual, problems. In this dialogue, Plato's critical reason constitutes a new dimension of political discourse. It has been named philosophy, but its ethical and political tasks remain to be defined.

FOUR

THE CONSTITUTION OF JUSTICE

The Political Art in Plato's *Republic*

The *Republic* provides a theory of the political art as the constitution of justice. It relates pivotally to the aporetic dialogues, for it provides a theoretical resolution of the tension between virtue and the political art. In relation to Plato's later dialogues, it serves as a conceptual background for a theory of the political art as the art of political leadership (*Statesman*) and as hypothetical laws for a second-best city (*Laws*).[1] For this study of the Platonic political art, therefore, the *Republic* occupies center stage.[2] No other Platonic dialogue

1. See Chapter 5, below.
2. Debates persist about the precise relation of the *Republic* as either a historical or philosophical text to Plato's other dialogues. When was it composed relative to the other dialogues? When was it "published" or circulated in manuscript form? Does it mark a development in Plato's thought, one that disputes his previously held views and one that is modified by "later" dialogues? Or does it possess the status of a master text, like the *Leviathan* for Hobbes, which should guide our understanding of the possibly "early" or undeniably "late" dialogues? These important questions cannot have definitive answers, despite the fact that efforts to provide them have served as points of departure for interpretations of what is "Platonic." Examples: the unitary view (Shorey, Kahn); the developmental/organic view (Barker, Jaeger, Klosko); the trichotomous view (Vlastos—the philosophy of the "early," "Socratic" dialogues; the philosophy of the "middle" dialogues, including the *Republic*; the philosopher of the "later" dialogues [for our purposes, the *Statesman* and *Laws*]). For relatively recent arguments for the opposition between the theories of *Republic* and *Laws*, see Vlastos, "The Theory of Social Justice in Plato's *Republic*," in Helen North, ed., *Interpretations of Plato*; and articles by Christopher Bobonich (see Bibliography); for arguments affirming the compatibility of the political theories

deals more extensively or intensively than the *Republic* with the relation of the political art to the art and virtue of justice. No other dialogue presents as starkly the radical opposition between the good practice of critical reason and the typical conduct of political and democratic life.

In the aporetic dialogues, Plato had searched for a better philosophical, ethical, and political significance for virtue. He looked for one that would not conform to the ordinary Athenian or typically Sophistic interpretation of what virtue meant but would speak to other interpretations, in that it constituted a second-order art of virtue, a master art whose function entailed caring for and benefiting the political community as a whole. Plato's aporetic dialogues strived to secure coherent accounts of relevant ethical and political realms for such a virtue. And, indeed, they cleared the ground on which a proper knowledge and practice of virtue could be established. Yet, as long as the arguments for a second-order *techne* of *arete* assumed the form of social practices whose value had been discredited at the level of *logos* or *ergon* and the ultimate means for evaluating such arguments were provided by the prevailing beliefs, practices, and institutional norms of Athens, there could be no sustainable solution to Plato's Socratic Problem. These efforts to solve his Socratic Problem provide keystones for the construction of the *Republic,* but their foundations are insufficient for a theoretical constitution of justice. Book I and the first part of Book II (through 367e) of the *Republic* summarize these limitations in terms of a new problem, the problem of justice, a problem that Plato does not critically or directly address in any of his other dialogues.

Plato mentions "justice" (*dikaiosyne*) in other dialogues, but he does not focus on it. In the dialogues that do not expressly analyze the political art (particularly those not clearly written after the *Republic,* such as the *Protagoras* and *Gorgias*), "justice" belongs to the standard list of virtues (courage, wisdom, moderation, and, at times, piety), while it also is associated with virtue as a whole.[3] However, its precise relation to the practical world is left unplumbed, for in these dialogues Plato has not critically or comprehensively analyzed the ethical character of practical life.

---

of the *Republic* and *Laws,* see Saunders, "Introduction to Plato, *Laws,*" and G. R. Morrow, *Plato's Cretan City.*

3. *Laches* 198a, 199d; *Meno* 73ff, 78dff; *Alcibiades I* 134c; *Phaedo* 69d–e; *Symposium* 196c; *Phaedrus* 247d; *Parmenides* 131a (also *Protagoras* 361b). Notably, in the passages from *Alcibiades I, Phaedrus, Symposium,* and *Meno,* "justice" is most often associated with "temperance," each of which is, in Adkins's terms of art, a "quieter virtue." Also see *Gorgias* 492b–c, 504d–e, 519d.

In the *Crito*, for example, justice stands opposed to the practical judgment of the majority, to the judgment of actual citizens, but it conforms to what is lawful, and what is lawful is ideally projected as "the laws of Athens," whose substantive effects in Athenian political life depend on the practical judgments of citizens. There is no analysis of how or why a gap has appeared between the justice of Athenian "laws" and the judgments of Athenian citizens—the gap that became unbridgeable for Plato with the Athenians' condemnation of Socrates as an impious corrupter of Athenian young men. In the *Hippias Minor* (375d–376c), the meaning of justice does not stabilize because the knowledge/power that informs it can produce both good and bad.

In the aporetic dialogues that directly consider the political art, justice is either (1) identical to the political art, (2) a condition for the virtuous practice of the political art, or (3) a product of the possession of the political art.[4] The idea of justice is never able to stand on its own. The defense by Plato's Protagoras of the coherence and virtue of the political art of Athenian citizens does not hold up under the critical scrutiny of Plato's Socrates. "Protagoras" could not clarify how his ethic of the political art related to an ethic of leadership in contrast to an ethic of citizenship or how it might provide critical guidance for citizens themselves without uncritically endorsing whatever they personally wanted or politically claimed.[5] In the *Gorgias*, the power associated with the *logos* of justice, understood via the political art that Plato's Socrates asserts he possesses, has no practical domain for its exercise. So the relation of justice to the political art or the other virtues is unclear, for its possible agents—the citizenry as a whole, the laws and constitution of Athens, a particular ethic of leadership, or the critical discourse of Sophists—do not clearly express it.

The distinctive contribution of the *Republic* to the Platonic corpus involves harmonizing virtue and the political art in the *logos* of justice as a proper "constitution," or *politeia* (apparently Plato's title for the dialogue[6]),

---

4. Re (i) *Protagoras* 322b–d, 329c; re (ii) *Protagoras* 323a–b, 327b; *Gorgias* 519a; re (iii) *Gorgias* 464b–c, 527e.

5. See Chapter 3, Section C2, above.

6. Actually, we do not know if Plato gave the *Republic* its title, but it was known as *Politeia* by Aristotle (*Politics* 1261a6). By the time of Diogenes Laertius, it had acquired a subtitle, "On the Just, Political" (Diogenes Laertius, III.60). I have decided to translate *politeia* as "constitution," although no single English word is satisfactory. This inadequacy is made obvious by the way that English translators typically translate *politeia* as "republic" when assigning a title to the book but as "constitution" or "polity" when the word appears in the dialogue itself. Plausible translations of *politeia* in Greek literature are, in addition to the above, "citizenship" or "the po-

particularly the constitution of the soul (*psyche*) and state or political community (*polis*). To understand the dialogue, one must identify the relation of the political art to the constitution of justice in the soul and the state. In this vein, the *Republic* provides the necessary context for the ultimate realization of Plato's conception of the political art.

Besides its theoretical significance for seeing Plato's arguments in his dialogues as parts of a coherent whole, the *Republic* bears a unique relation to Plato's life. No other dialogue so clearly signifies Plato's understanding of his own theoretical vocation.[7] In this respect, the *Republic* transcribes his philosophical vocation as an agency of justice. It indirectly justifies his "profession" as a political art in opposition to the more conventional practice of the political art and reconstructs that art as a philosophically informed practice of political education. In this regard, the "constitution of justice" to which I refer involves not only the "constitutions" in the text but also the intentionally active, constituting quality of the whole text of the *Republic* in relation to Plato's life and that of the reader, in Plato's day and our own.[8]

As for the date of Plato's composition of the *Republic,* the evidence does not allow us to pinpoint precisely the year in which it was begun or completed. The current consensus is that it was composed—or, at least, initially finished—after Plato's first visit to Sicily, in 387, after the establishment of the Academy (c. 385) and before his second visit to Sicily, in 367—most likely in the 370s.[9] Yet parts of it may well have been composed in the mid- to late 390s.[10] Diogenes Laertius (III.37) reports claims of others that Plato revised

---

litical." I believe that "constitution" is preferable to "republic," because the latter fuses the notion of "the public" with its governmental structure; it obscures the relation between the two, which appears in the Greek etymological connection of *politeia* and *polis*. The first section of this chapter identifies the relation of Plato's rendering of *politeia* to that of his predecessors and immediate successors.

7. *Seventh Letter* 325e–326b.

8. Plato's self-consciousness about the effects of writing on the reader suggests that he was aware of this dimension of the *Republic*'s "constitution."

9. See Guthrie, *A History of Greek Philosophy*, 4:437.

10. We cannot pinpoint an exclusive date of composition or publication for the *Republic*, and it may even have undergone substantial revisions. Holger Thesleff has argued that there may well have been an early or "proto-*Republic*" that included only the outlines of *kallipolis* and that many of the literary and philosophical discussions were added on later. See his *Studies in Platonic Chronology*. Although one cannot prove this claim, it is worth keeping in mind the following two bits of evidence: (1) Aristophanes' *Ecclesiazusae*, produced in 393 or 392, includes gross formulations of important features of Plato's *kallipolis*; and (2) in the *Seventh Letter* (326a–b), Plato states that he became convinced of the need for the coalescence of philosophy and political power as the key to the realization of justice *after* the death of Socrates and his subsequent conviction

the beginning of the *Republic* several times and was fiddling with it at the end of his life. Besides suggesting a desire to achieve literary perfection, this comment, if true, indicates that the *Republic* had commanding importance for Plato throughout his life. It still must for anyone who would identify a single passage of the Platonic corpus as "Platonic."[11]

Four dimensions of the political art stand out in the *Republic* and are addressed in this chapter. The first is how Plato's text operates as a historically new and distinctive critical discourse, both confronting his particular historical context and trying to transcend its limitations. The second identifies how the new *logos* of justice in the *Republic* is a unique kind of political *techne* and so belongs to Plato's lifelong preoccupation with the relation of virtue to the political art. Third, the relation of Plato's theoretical conception of justice to democracy is explored. The last articulates the intended effect (*ergon*) of the *Republic*'s critical discourse (*logos*) of justice as an ethical, philosophically informed political art, illustrating how it operates in a distinctively educational and political way.[12] The result offers an interpretation of the *Republic* that redeems its political and theoretical character even as it does not accept many elements of its theory of justice.

A. THE *Republic* AS ORIGINAL POLITICAL THEORY

Prior to Plato's *Republic*, there had been critical accounts of politics, leaders, and social forms by Homer, Hesiod, Solon, lyric poets, dramatists, and his-

---

about the wholesale corruption of all existing states but *before* his first visit to Sicily in 387. (On the relation between the *Republic* and Aristophanes' play, see the discussion by S. Halliwell in *Plato: Republic*, 5:224–25.) In short, Plato may have composed, mentally and/or in writing, major parts of the *Republic* in the 390s. In addition, others have argued for the independent composition of Book 1 relative to the rest of the *Republic*, a view that does not currently have favor. As a result, the relation of the *Republic* to other Platonic dialogues depends more on the perspective of the interpreter than on any independent evidence that might constrain that perspective. With respect to our discussion, all that needs asserting is the unique contribution of the *Republic* to the discussion of questions involving the political art.

11. Besides the caution that needs to be exercised in relying on the statements of a writer who wrote perhaps six hundred years after Plato died, the passage to which I refer cites Aristoxenus's claim that most of the *Republic* could be found in Protagoras's *Controversies* (*Antilogikoi*).

12. The argument of this interpretation of the political art in the *Republic* does not directly follow the dialogue's narrative structure, but it respects the effect of that structure on the meaning and significance of the dialogue as a whole.

torians. There had been logical analyses of various social discourses by Sophists and teachers of rhetoric, from Protagoras and Corax to Antiphon and Socrates. There had been philosophical discussions of abstract ideas for hundreds of years and, more particularly, general formulations of constitutional forms by Herodotus, the ethics and politics of existing political systems by Thucydides (and perhaps by Protagoras), and utopian political orders by Hippodamus. Plato's *Republic* was the first text, however, to provide an account of both "justice" and "constitution" in relation to a unified, critically articulated theoretical standpoint.

Relative to what preceded it, Plato's *Republic* was unique in the way it theorized justice, by dynamically linking *logos* and *ergon* and providing both an ethical critique of political power and a political conception of ethics. It constituted distinctive links between politics, ethics, and critical reason. Plato's *Republic*, therefore, also stands as the first systematic and critical account of the interdependent relation of ethics and power in a collectivity. It may be regarded as offering the first comprehensive political theory in the Western world. In my view, the principal respect in which it breaks new theoretical ground is the way in which Plato weaves together critical considerations of ethics and power as a theoretical constitution of justice.[13]

---

13. Most studies of the *Republic* fail to identify the relation of its discursive form and political content or, in other words, the historically specific character of Plato's use of *logos* and his conception of the political. The problem has been especially evident since World War II, for the experience and significance of that war made any theoretical endorsement of substantive political value appear as a threat to both rational criticism and democratic freedom. In this respect, interpretations of the *Republic* have corresponded to interpretations of Plato's political theory more generally.

The unprecedented destruction of the war contributed to a search for precedents in every historical period. Most important for our purposes is the way it contributed to anachronistic views about the overall purpose of the *Republic* that devalued its critically useful conception of the political. For if the *Republic* was simply a practically political dialogue, then its affirmation of lying, censorship, and elitist rule becomes its most salient feature, and Plato's discourse becomes theoretically doctrinaire. The most famous exposition of this interpretive angle is Karl Popper's 1940s interpretation of Plato as a proto-totalitarian whose theoretical perspective is essentially antidemocratic. Less extreme, but kindred and more current views appear in liberal, neo-Marxist, deconstructivist, and pragmatic criticisms of "Platonism." See Karl Popper, *The Open Society and Its Enemies, Vol 1: The Spell of Plato*. For paradigmatic liberal, neo-Marxist, deconstructivist, and pragmatic readings, see, respectively, Gregory Vlastos, "Slavery in Plato's Thought," reprinted in *Platonic Studies*, 147–63; Ellen Wood and Neal Wood, *Class Ideology and Ancient Political Theory: Socrates, Plato, and Aristotle in Social Context*; Jacques Derrida, "Plato's Pharmacy," in *Dissemination*; and Richard Rorty, *Philosophy and the Mirror of Nature*. My remarks in Chapter 1, above, pertain here.

The only alternative approach, whose attraction comes from its capacity to salvage some philosophical value from the *Republic*, became reading it apolitically, minimizing the role of pol-

I. UNIQUE THEMATIC CONTEXTS: "JUSTICE" AND "CONSTITUTION"

The discussion of Plato's historical contexts in Chapter 2 specifies the practical and discursive lacunae filled by Plato's critical conceptualization of the political art. In this section, I particularize that context with respect to the major thematic concerns of the *Republic*. At first glance, the fifth-century Greek terms for "justice" and "constitution" describe contrasting sets of phenomena: The former has more clearly "ethical" implications, indicating standards of judgment about social practice, whereas the latter's references are more clearly "political," insofar as they indicate a practical order of power. However, the range of each overlaps with that of the other. One could not

---

itics and history as constituents of its meaning, and emphasizing its concern with ethics or philosophy rather than politics. Leo Strauss and his followers, on the one hand, and analytical philosophers, on the other, have followed this approach. A recent, extreme example of this in the analytical tradition of interpretation is the new Oxford translation of the *Republic*, in which the Greek word *dikaiosyne*, which has usually been translated as "justice," appears as "morality." Plato, *Republic*, trans. Robin Waterfield (Oxford: Oxford University Press, 1993), "Introduction," xi–lxii, especially xii, xiv–xix: "a great deal of the book is simply absurd if read as serious political philosophy" (p. xviii). This approach follows a path charted by Hoerber, *The Theme of Plato's* Republic; Murphy, *The Interpretation of Plato's* Republic; Cross and Woozley, *Plato's* Republic; Guthrie, *A History of Greek Philosophy*, 5; Irwin, *Plato's Moral Theory*; White, *A Companion to Plato's* Republic; Annas, *An Introduction to Plato's* Republic; Klosko, *The Development of Plato's Political Theory;* and Reeve, *Philosopher-Kings*. For a useful counter to the Waterfield translation and line of interpretation, see Plato *The Republic*, ed. G. R. F. Ferrari and trans. by Tom Griffith.

Historians, including interpreters of the history of philosophy, often conspire in this attitude, because they view Plato's political analyses in the *Republic* as either irrelevant to the political questions of his time or flatly antidemocratic. The most notable historian in this vein is M. I. Finley, *Politics in the Ancient World*, 123–26. A more recent example is the otherwise illuminating interpretation of ancient Greek life by Paul Cartledge in *The Ancient Greeks*, which ignores Plato's *Republic* in his discussion of literary accounts of *politeia*. As for historians of philosophy, there is the traditional approach reflected in W. K. C. Guthrie's "ethical" reading of the *Republic* in his *A History of Greek Philosophy*, 4:434, 449, 561, and so on.

The result of the dominant influence of these interpretive perspectives is the impairment of our understanding of the distinctive character of Plato's critical efforts. Our understanding is partly obscured by viewing Plato through an interpretive perspective that presupposes a bifurcation between theoretical and practical knowledge—an Aristotelian division that Plato did not accept. See Hannah Arendt, *The Human Condition;* Leo Strauss, *The City and Man;* Alasdair MacIntyre, *After Virtue: A Study in Moral Theory*, and idem, *Whose Justice? Whose Rationality?* For the significance of this distinction between Plato and Aristotle, see W. Jaeger, "On the Origin and Cycle of the Philosophic Ideal of Life," in *Aristotle: Fundamentals of the History of His Development*, 2n ed., trans. and ed. Richard Robinson, 426–61. Guthrie did appreciate *this* difference between them. (See Guthrie, *A History of Greek Philosophy*, 4:436.) With respect to previous interpretive approaches to (not necessarily substantive claims about) the *Republic*, the

analyze the ethics of justice without making judgments about the collective exercise of power. One could not judge the conduct of power without determining a meaning for justice. Each implicates the other. The originality of the *Republic* as political theory stems from Plato's distinctive argument that an understanding of "justice" necessitates a reconstruction of conventional meanings of "constitution," and an understanding of "constitution" requires a reconstruction of conventional meanings of "justice." In other words, the constitution of justice in the *Republic* resolves at the level of critical discourse the problematic tension of virtue and the political art.

For both Plato and his predecessors, "justice" is the capstone of ethics or morality.[14] It upholds an ideal standard for the social expression of individual behavior. "Justice" does not simply express the official practice of punishment. Nor is it limited, as in contemporary liberal theory, to, for example, "fairness," that is, how to accommodate independent values.[15] Rather, it denotes an ethical ideal that concerns the fundamentals of morality in the practical arrangements of human community. The practical location for expressing the morality of "justice" is political life, broadly understood as the appropriate and inappropriate exercise of power by the citizens of a *polis*.[16]

---

ones that most closely resemble the one followed here are those of pre-war interpreters: R. L. Nettleship, *Lectures on the Republic of Plato;* Paul Shorey, "Introduction," in Plato, *The Republic;* and Hans-Georg Gadamer, "Plato and the Poets," and idem, "Plato's Educational State," in *Dialogue and Dialectic.* The most troublesome aspect of Gadamer's Plato is the fuzziness of his interpretation of the practical implications of Plato's conception of the political. One may speculate that this results from the compromised political status of Martin Heidegger, his teacher, who had given an inaugural lecture in 1933 for a post to which he had been appointed by the Nazis; the lecture managed to link the philosophy of the *Republic* to the educational potential of the German state. Gadamer subsequently further obscured the political dimension of Plato's discourse by joining its redemptive features to Aristotle's. See *Truth and Method* and *The Idea of the Good in Platonic-Aristotelian Philosophy.*

The gaps left by these interpretive approaches become clear if this dialogue is read, instead, as a critical response to the philosophies *and* politics of his time. If we do, then the critical and political features of Plato's *logos* of justice can assume their proper shape.

14. For a discussion of the intellectual baggage that accompanies these terms in contemporary philosophical discourse, see Bernard Williams, *Ethics and the Limits of Philosophy.*

15. Communitarian criticisms of the "limits of justice" typically focus on the liberal conception of justice. See Michael J. Sandel, *Liberalism and the Limits of Justice.*

16. As a particular structure of collective power, the *polis* does not directly refer to the behavior of individuals, but the distinctive character of its power depends on the character of its citizens. As M. I. Finley once put it, the *polis* was a "[w]hole . . . bound together not merely by economics or by force, but also psychologically, by a feeling among the members of the community of a unity fostered by common cult and tradition (both mythical and historical) . . . it was people acting in concert." See M. I. Finley, *The Ancient Greeks: An Introduction to Their Life and Thought,* 19, 41; see also Hannah Arendt, *The Human Condition,* 198.

Plato's critical discourse links the appropriate ethics for handling the exigencies of power with the nature of the appropriate practical framework for nurturing ethical excellence, forming a uniquely political conception of justice.[17]

With respect to the context for Plato's new conceptualization of the political realm in relation to justice, it is important to note that a distinct "political realm" did not always exist and was not always subjected to criteria of "justice."[18] To be sure, if "political" activity refers to discourse and practical action involving the exercise of power in a collectivity, it certainly existed prior to the fifth century, but the first usages of justice only vaguely or metaphorically referred to a *polis* as a site of conflict and community.[19] Just as the appearance of "political art" in the historical record marked subtle changes in social discourse and practice, the articulation of *dikaiosyne* and *politeia* in the fifth century marks a new development.

This appearance of both "justice" and a "constitutional" political realm accompanies a series of epochal political events of the fifth century. The century opens during the democratization of Athenian political authority that was initiated by Kleisthenes' reforms. This process was soon legitimized by the involvement of the *demos* in the Athenians' contributions to Greek victories over the Persians and later consolidated in the reforms of Ephialtes.[20] This period's best example of a discourse of justice is probably the monumental *Oresteia* of Aeschylus, produced in 458. As was the case with Solonian justice, justice in the *Oresteia* responds to *stasis,* fomented by aristocratic resistance to democracy, and locates the arena for establishing justice in the

17. In this respect, "justice" does not primarily signify, as A. W. H. Adkins claimed, a "cooperative" virtue as opposed to other, more traditional, "competitive" virtues; rather, it operates as a critical, ethical precondition for the practical sustenance of individual and political life. See A. W. H. Adkins, *Merit and Responsibility.* For a more complete discussion of the limitations of Adkins's interpretive framework for understanding conceptions of justice in ancient Greek literature, see note 47 in this chapter, below.

18. Conceptions of the political realm varied in ancient Greek thought, and it is often confusing or misleading to presume that a single "Greek" conception existed. This tendency to reduce the differences to a conceptual unity appears in the work of theorists and historians alike. Perhaps the most prominent theoretical work that displays this tendency is Hannah Arendt's *The Human Condition;* the most prominent historical work is Christian Meier's *Die Entstehung des Politischen bei dem Griechen,* translated as *The Greek Discovery of Politics,* esp. 13–25.

19. To be sure, the order of power in the *polis* as an order of justice concerned Homer, Hesiod, and Solon. Solon's writings in particular provide the most relevant conceptual background for the subject of justice in the *Republic,* although the words *politeia* and *dikaiosyne* were not used for another two hundred years.

20. For an interesting account of the effect of military victory on political thought, see J. Peter Euben, "The Battle of Salamis and the Origins of Political Theory."

public political realm, now more democratic and deliberative than before.[21] The term *dikaiosyne* probably appeared first in Herodotus's *Histories* (although perhaps in a couplet of the sixth-century poet Theognis as well).[22] There it appears five times and refers to the character of individuals (I.96.2; II.151.1; VI.86.2–4; VII.164) or a people (VII.52.1), signifying a particular kind of virtuous behavior. In Thucydides' *History*, it appears only once (III.63. 3–4) and designates a general disposition to return to another that which is his due. Among the Sophists, Thrasymachus (D–K, B8) refers to it as a virtue and the greatest blessing of mankind. Damon (D–K, B4) mentions it as a virtue comparable to "courage" and "moderation" that may appear in a boy's singing and playing the lyre. Antiphon (D–K, B44) states that it depicts conduct that would harmonize with both "law" and "nature," even though they often conflict. This emphasis on character as an element of justice does not distinguish the use of *dikaiosyne* from earlier references to *dike* or *dikaios*, for *dike* always operated as a relational term that accommodated ethics and political power. The identification of "justice" as one of the virtues, however, is relatively new. Unlike *dike*, *dikaiosyne* is a virtue. It clearly characterizes the behavior of individuals, whether singly or as part of a collectivity.

Initially, *politeia* simply defined the organized reflection of the activities of citizens.[23] Herodotus (IX.34.1) provides the first written reference to *politeia*, when he contrasts a Spartan citizen's claim to his "citizenship" (*politeian*) in contrast to another's claim to a "kingship" (*basileian*). The activities of monarchs with respect to their own people did not literally belong to a "political" realm. Similarly in 403, Lysias defined *politeia* as the substantive realm for the exercise of political power by ordinary citizens, a realm that the

---

21. See the *Eumenides* (977–79), in which the Furies, who were once bent on promoting *stasis* to defend the position of Clytaemnestra (310–11), agree to the resolution of their battle with Orestes and Apollo offered by Athena. On the concept of justice in the *Oresteia*, see J. P. Euben, "Justice in the *Oresteia*," in *The Tragedy of Political Theory*, 67–95. Although he does not specifically point to the centrality of *stasis* as the antipode to the distinctive features of Aeschylean justice (81–82), he does so in a general statement that accompanies his chapter on Thucydides' account of *stasis* in Corcyra. "*Stasis* destroys the common will and life and as such is the obverse of justice" (167).

22. See E. A. Havelock, "*Dikaiosune*: An Essay in Greek Intellectual History," and his later *The Greek Concept of Justice*.

23. In the Aristotelian *Athenaion Politeia*, the author/s discuss eleven different *politeiai* of the Athenians, five of which antedate the fifth century. However, this work was composed in the 320s. But the previous discussion should make clear that I do not intend to put too much emphasis on developments in the Greek vocabulary as direct and timely indicators of developments in Greek life.

Thirty had destroyed and the democrats had reestablished.[24] A *politeia* existed only when citizens shared in the exercise of political power. In this respect, *politeia* signified the schematic practical form of the *polis* as a public deliberative community. Its substance may be generally referred to as the political realm, which included a domain of expressive *and* instrumental activity involving the exercise of collective power.[25] In ancient Greece, this realm was officially reserved for adult male citizens and provided the context for the practice of a "political art."

Unlike *polis, politeia* clearly identifies a political structure that is distinguishable in some respects from the citizens who participate in it. However, "constitution" had a far more extensive meaning than we typically give it today. Although it referred empirically to the procedures governing the exercise of political power, it included not only the laws that delimit the structure of government or even the sum total of social regulations. Its meaning extended to the character of the collective life of citizens. *Politeia* signified the citizenry's common soul, as well as the soul of the state (a meaning that Isocrates gave to it in the 350s and 340s[26]). In Thucydides' account of Pericles' funeral oration, a city's "constitution" expressed, as much as it regulated, the way of life of its citizens (11.36.4). Other facets of *polis*-life, such as its economic condition, the occupations of its citizens, metics, and slaves, its religious functions, remained distinct—for no Greek *politeia* was totalitarian—but the *politeia* established the social value of each of these practices.

The powers sanctioned by the ancient *politeia,* particularly in Athens, essentially constituted the freedom of citizens. This notion sharply contrasts to modern liberal conceptions of both "freedom" and "constitution." They typically associate freedom with the exercise of rights, which supposedly takes place in protected spheres, outside the official realm of power authorized by the constitutional order,[27] whereas the substantive meaning of the ancient

---

24. Lysias, XXXIV.1, 3.

25. Meier (expressive, *Die Entstehung der Politischen bei dem Griechen*) and Finley (instrumental, *Politics in the Ancient World*); see also Hansen, *The Athenian Democracy in the Age of Demosthenes.*

26. Isocrates, VII.14.1; XII.138.

27. On the integral relations among freedom, power, and *politeia*, see M. I. Finley, *The Ancient Greeks,* 41; Meier, *The Greek Discovery of Politics,* 169–70; and Kurt Raaflaub, "Democracy, Power, and Imperialism in Fifth-Century Athens," in Euben et al., eds., *Athenian Political Thought and the Reconstruction of Democracy,* 103–46. Finley seems to have modified his earlier perspective to accommodate a more Weberian, utilitarian, and instrumentalist view of all politics *and,* perhaps, to differentiate his own perspective from Meier's. See *Politics in the Ancient*

Greek political realm did not clearly transcend the practical activities of its citizens. Moreover, "constitutional" or "political" activity had a fundamentally "public" character that was contrasted to the "private" lives of citizens; the political realm depended economically on individuals who were officially excluded from it (slaves, metics, and women). This makes any view of the ancient Greek political realm as "autonomous" misleading. To be sure, by the end of the fifth century, the political realm had achieved a sufficiently distinct status to become the subject of critical discourse and the particular expression of one's political identity. It had not, however, become so clearly isolated from other forms of social life that its description did not also involve them. Only much later, after Plato (first?) wrote the *Republic*, would *politeia* refer to the character of institutional practices in contrast to the public character of a citizenry.[28]

This expansive noninstitutional notion of *politeia* must be kept in mind, not only in reflecting on Pericles' reference in Thucydides' *History* to the Athenian *politeia* as a "democracy" but also in appreciating the scope of *politeia* in Plato's *Republic* and, of course, of the *Republic* as a whole. For there was a special, historical connection between "democracy" and the first meanings of "constitution." In contrast to citizenship that was radically restricted in Sparta relative to Athens, Athenian democracy provided the conditions for the full exercise of *politeia*.[29] Anachronistically employing Aristotelian categories, one might say that, initially, democracy and *politeia* had the same disposition; only their "being" was different. "Democracy" signified the wide-

---

World, and my review in *Political Theory* (May 1984). For paradigmatic examples of modern, liberal conceptions of this relation, see Benjamin Constant, "On the Freedom of the Ancients and Moderns," in his *Political Writings;* and Isaiah Berlin, "Two Concepts of Liberty," in *Four Essays on Liberty* (both of which are discussed in Chapter 6, below).

28. See Christian Meier, *The Greek Discovery of Politics,* 172, and Mogens Herman Hansen, *The Athenian Democracy in the Age of Demosthenes,* 67, with references to Isocrates (*Areopagiticus* 14, and Aristotle (*Politics* IV.11, 1295a35–41). This initial meaning of *politeia*—much more than its definition by Isocrates or Aristotle—starkly contrasts with modern associations of constitutional authority with the sovereignty of state. For example, Hobbes refers to sovereignty as "the Artificiall Soul" of the Commonwealth (Leviathan), whose establishment as an overarching coercive presence in the lives of citizens was necessary to prevent the anarchy that would result from their following the dictates of their own souls. See Thomas Hobbes, *Leviathan,* intro.

29. Aristotle noted this in the *Politics* III.i (1275b5–7). But there he is referring to a definition of the citizen. For him, a *politeia* is simply "an arrangement of the inhabitants of a state." Because all the inhabitants of the state are not citizens, Aristotle differentiates "constitution" from "citizenship." For good synoptic discussions of the Spartan political order, see A. H. M. Jones, *Sparta;* W. G. Forrest, *A History of Sparta: 950–192 B.C.;* Paul Cartledge, *Sparta and Lakonia: A Regional History* and *Agesilaos and the Crisis of Sparta.*

spread and interested exercise of political power, whereas "constitution" designated the community in which that occurred.[30] At the end of the fifth century, however, major alterations and additions to the meaning of *politeia* appeared, mostly as the result of political events. They would have affected
Plato's use of the term. I have in mind the political turmoil of 411–403, the resulting codification of Athenian law and establishment of a board of *nomothetai* to safeguard the constitution, and, of course, the trial and death of
Socrates. (Here one may note that the bulk of scholarly tradition places the
dramatic date of the *Republic* between 421 and 411, the most convulsive period for the constitution of Athens in its history.[31])

The new constitutional order of 403 (that lasted more or less intact and
effective for the next eighty years) differentiated basic "laws" and "decrees"
(*psephismata*) that might subsequently be passed in the assembly.[32] More important for the interpretation of the *Republic,* the notion of an "ancestral constitution" (*patrios politeia*) became important in the fourth century. It often
signified "Solonian democracy" and was used by Isocrates, among others, to
criticize the performance of the existing democratic *politeia* of Athens.[33] In
other words, there was a semantic context in early fourth-century Athens for
a notion of *politeia* that was critical of, yet related to, the Athenian democracy.

The *politeia* denoted in "the ancestral constitution" fused three ideas:
(1) "constitution" as a general political form that authorizes particular methods of exercising power, such as monarchy, oligarchy, or democracy; (2) "constitution" as the expression of the fundamental, shared principles of Athenian
democracy; and (3) "constitution" as an ethical structure for everyday politics, the political expression of justice.[34] The idea of the ancestral constitution

---

30. The comparable distinction appears in Aristotle's *Nicomachean Ethics* (VI.viii, 1141b23–
24) where he states that *politike* and *phronesis* have the same "disposition" (*hexis*); it is the
"essence" (*einai*) of each that differs. This is not to say, as did Victor Ehrenberg, that democracy
was the *telos* of the *polis* (see his *The Greek State,* 43). His interpretive claim presupposes a philosophical commitment to teleology in history, which I do not embrace. But I do believe that the
widespread exercise of political power in a political community promotes its health and well-
being—indeed, justice itself—more than any other constitutional scheme.

31. For 421, see A. E. Taylor, *Plato, The Man and His Work,* 264; for 411, see Boeckh, *Kleine
Schriften,* 4:437ff, esp. 448, cited in Paul Shorey's introduction to his translation of the *Republic,* viii.

32. Mogens Herman Hansen, *The Athenian Democracy in the Age of Demosthenes,* 162–65.

33. See Isocrates, *Areopagitica* 7.16ff, *Panathenaicus* 12.144ff, *Antidosis* 15.232ff, and Mogens Herman Hansen, "Solonian Democracy in Fourth-Century Athens."

34. To be sure, the notion of "the ancestral constitution" served variously as a tool of political unity, a rhetorical cover for partisan ends, and a code for "the return of the father," sometimes
all at once. As a tool of political unity, see M. I. Finley, "The Ancestral Constitution"; as rhetor-

did not clearly differentiate constitutional principles from democratic principles or "the sovereignty of law" from "popular sovereignty."[35] In this way, it reflected the fact that the only critical standards for differentiating the meaning of justice in Athenian democracy from the direct product of popular will were reducible to informal constraints on the discursive interaction of rhetors and the *demos*.[36] Institutional checks in the fifth century had been ostracism and the *graphe paranomon;* in the fourth century, they included the latter plus the board of *nomothetai,* which was chosen by lot. The *nomothetai* surely filtered the judgment of the *demos,* but because it made up a rough cross-section of the citizenry; the new board did not institutionally establish a level of authority that was higher than the people themselves.

Important as these institutional procedures were for Athenian democracy, they could not be sufficient to ensure that the practice of *politeia* was just. As negative checks, they would be sufficient only if the critical discourse that informed them and led to their practical results was likely to become just in the process. Insofar as the prevailing practices were not automatically just, rhetors might seek their own advantage more than that of the political community as a whole. Because the institutional procedures did not remedy deficiencies in the judgment of rhetors or the *demos,* one might seek a theory of a *politeia* in *logos* that could provide critical assistance to the *politeia* in *ergon.* It is not, therefore, unreasonable to interpret Plato's *Republic* as not only an ethical discussion of the virtue of justice but also a contribution to the political discourse of fourth-century Athenians who sought to make their constitution just, even if the *Republic* was not geared toward the popular political arena or the realm of legislation. In this respect, the *Republic* is properly

---

ical cover, see Alexanders Fuks, *The Ancestral Constitution;* as a code for "the return of the father," see Barry Strauss, *Fathers and Sons.*

35. Contra Martin Ostwald, *From Popular Sovereignty to the Sovereignty of Law: Law, Society, and Politics in Fifth-Century Athens.* To be sure, the laws codified in 403 instituted new limits on the power of the assembly by requiring that decrees believed to affect the basic laws be submitted to a specially constituted board of legal guardians or law makers (*nomothetai*) for approval. But although membership on the board was more restricted than was the right to vote in the assembly, these restrictions were not significantly antidemocratic: *nomothetai* had to be over thirty years of age; they were elected, but by the Council of 500 (chosen by lot) and the deme assemblies; no property qualifications applied. Moreover, in lieu of the slightly reduced prominence of the assembly, popular courts—whose membership was also drawn by lot—assumed more importance and became the scenes of pivotal conflicts in fourth-century politics. See Josiah Ober, *Mass and Elite in Democratic Athens.*

36. Ober's work emphasizes the former; Hansen's, the latter. See Josiah Ober, *Mass and Elite in Democratic Athens,* and Mogens Herman Hansen, *The Athenian Democracy.*

read in relation to the search not only for a definition of virtue but also for a practical, political context for its "constitution."

Historians have tended to isolate Plato's theoretical discourse from practical Athenian discourse; however, the *Republic* in part indicates Plato's contribution to that discussion.[37] Plato offers a distinctive theoretical meditation on the nature of *politeia*—what we might call "the political"—in terms of a constitution of justice. Such a notion does not directly relate to the partisan conflicts that presuppose the terms of debate set by practical politics and the social order, because Plato finds them problematic. Nevertheless, the resolution of those conflicts on credible ethical and critical grounds appears to be one of Plato's basic concerns.

The differentiation between Plato's ideal constitution of justice in the *Republic* and existing arrangements for the exercise of power is not so much a formal distinction about conceptual meaning as it is a philosophical, political, and ethical judgment about the relative justice of current constitutional regimes. That judgment is framed in a theory of the constitution of justice, which contrasts critically to the political order of Athens and all other extant *poleis*. Such a theory was not present in the *Crito* (54b), when Plato's Socrates distinguished between the Athenian *nomoi* that citizens ought to follow and practical interpretations of them that do not accord with their basically virtuous character.[38] It is what Plato produces in the *Republic* against a practical and discursive background that leaves a place for—even if it may not seek—its ultimate realization.

2. TEXTUAL CONTEXTS

A brief look at two texts written in the last quarter of the fifth century, in the wake of the disruptive effects of the Peloponnesian War, enable us to see more clearly the conceptual background to the major terms of art in the *Republic* and, consequently, the originality of the argument of the *Republic* as a constitution of justice. Each articulates a kind of democratic ethics and associates

---

37. In "The Ancestral Constitution" (50–52), M. I. Finley holds that Plato's political theory bears no relation to discussion or debates about the ancestral constitution. A practical, as well as interpretive, divide between Platonic and ordinary discourse is implied in Kenneth Dover's *Greek Popular Morality in the Time of Plato and Aristotle*.

38. In this dialogue, Plato also does not differentiate between "laws" and "decrees," although their official differentiation in 403 was presumably known to Socrates in 399 and to Plato whenever he composed the dialogue.

justice with the democratic *politeia* of Athens. They are Thucydides' account of Pericles' funeral oration of 431 and "The Old Oligarch's" description of "the Athenian Constitution."[39] The first text is less of an argument than a rhetorical device: It identifies Athenian democracy with political virtue, as a defense against the prospect of *stasis* at home engendered by the stress of war. Thucydides' Pericles discusses the "constitution and way of life that made us great." For him, it is entirely an Athenian creation, owing nothing to imitations of other forms of citizenship; moreover, it constitutes a "model" or pattern" (*paradeigma*) for other societies.[40] In this eulogy to the Athenian *politeia*, the virtue of the city articulated in *logos* served as a critical ideal to guide the *ergon* of practical life, now being tested by a Spartan invasion. It obliquely endorses what the Syracusan Athenagoras says more directly later in Thucydides' *History* (VI.39): The political equality affirmed by democracy constitutes justice, and the principal agents of power in a democratic society—the *demos* and its leaders—act on behalf of the political community as a whole.[41] Pericles asserted that the Athenians' deliberative conduct of democratic politics displayed virtuous care for the political community as a whole, whereas the society's regard for law, political equality, individual virtue, personal freedom, and a participatory public life served as a *paradeigma* for Greece as a whole.

These democratic notions of justice marked a particular kind of relation between ethics and power. But this articulation of a democratic ethic has limited value as a critical discourse of justice. Pericles' association of justice with the actions of democratic citizens, even at their best, revealed pride bordering on arrogance. It suggested that the practice of Athenian democracy matched its idealization, even as the need driving the speech—to bolster the depressed

---

39. Otanes' speech in Herodotus's *Persian Wars* (3.80) also deserves mention. It justifies democracy over monarchy, because its procedural check on the abuse of power prevents the typical problems of monarchical rule, and praises its validation of *isonomia*, "equality before the law." But the discussion is so short that it mostly signifies rather than explains an ethic of democratic justice. On the notion of *isonomia*, see Gregory Vlastos, "*Isonomia Politike*," in Gregory Vlastos, *Platonic Studies*, 164–203.

40. Thucydides II.36.4, II.37.1.

41. I say obliquely, because a direct endorsement of the virtue of the *demos* in the funeral oration would sound partisan; moreover, as a political leader from an aristocratic background, Pericles naturally distances himself from the *demos*, even as he would be their voice. This does not make Pericles or his funeral oration secretly antidemocratic. Thucydides' reference to Pericles' uniquely authoritative power in democratic Athens (II.65.8) does not suggest that he opposed the interests of the *demos* or sought to reduce their influence in political life.

collective spirit of the citizens—undermined the unqualified truth of the *paradeigma* as a description of actual life.

In Pericles' speech, the potential harm of such pride does not appear in the *paradeigma* itself but at its margins, with his exaltation of the ethics of military sacrifice over that of individual behavior and off-handed reinforcement of the political subordination of women. One must make allowance for the restricted context of the speech, and, relatively speaking, Pericles may not have been militaristic or sexist. However, the way in which the *logos* idealized the present left no space for critically asserting a gap between the present and the realization of justice, except in the mode of having citizens trust their leader.[42]

In the funeral oration, the Athenians themselves, at least their best selves, exemplified the practice of justice; Pericles had reconciled the democratic principles of freedom and equality with the practice and ideal of *arete*. In the hands of Pericles/Thucydides, a *logos* of Athenian political life *becomes* an idea of justice. This transposition of a practice of power into an unqualified ethical ideal ignored the fissures and conflicts that characterized its actual existence. Given the occasion of the funeral oration, this is understandable and perhaps justifiable.[43] But Pericles' idealized unity of *logos* and *ergon* obscured a critical understanding of how that society may or may not be just. To be sure, by providing *logoi* in history that inform future *erga*, Thucydides' *His-*

---

42. The other text that deals with critical standards for justice in a general political context in Thucydides' *History*—"the Melian dialogue"—supports this claim. The text is purely a Thucydidean construction, but it reflects the ethics of power that informs Athenian politics—at least when it comes to the treatment of outsiders. As they try to persuade the Melians to surrender and take what they can get, the Athenians justify their dictatorial terms by referring to their superior, dominant power: "[Y]ou know as well as we do that, in human discourse, justice depends on the equality that comes from necessity and that in fact the stronger do what they have the power to do and the weak accept what they have to accept" (v.89). In the Mytilenian debate (iii.44.4), Diodotus refers to Cleon's policy of revenge against the Mytilenian people as more consistent with a strict understanding of "justice," but he states that this notion of justice applies to justice in a courtroom rather than an assembly, a political rather than a legal context. However, this qualification—although resulting in a more lenient policy—does not establish a more ethical ground for public policy than what is "useful" to the Athenians, that is, the self-interest of the Athenians as a political power intent on achieving superiority over their rivals (even if Diodorus manifested a greater respect for human life than did Cleon, certainly an ethical value of some sort).

43. At times, this seems to be the message of the important discussion of the genre of the funeral oration in Athens by Nicole Loraux, *The Invention of Athens: The Funeral Oration in the Classical City*.

tory critically stands outside Pericles' rhetoric and reveals much of the gap between Pericles' idealized picture of a perfectly just Athenian constitution and the realities of Athenian life. But Thucydides' "history" of the relation between *logos* and *ergon* could not help Plato solve his Socratic Problem.[44] For in Thucydides' book, justice is readily overwhelmed by an excessive desire to rule—a desire that contributed to the outbreak of the war and the ultimate defeat of the Athenians.

Our second text does not eulogize democracy; it harbors oligarchic criticisms of it. But it, no more than Thucydides' account of Pericles' funeral oration, could not be said to provide (ironically) a critical ethic for democracy, a theory of justice for democratic Athens. Near the beginning of his *logos* (1.2), the Old Oligarch asserts that because of its "power," its contribution to the material well-being and security of the city, the *demos* who rules in this *polis* is "just." In one sense, he was of course right. The Athenians' democratic *politeia* may have offered the best political structure possible in ancient Greece for preventing *stasis* and realizing justice for the political community as a whole. However, the Old Oligarch's ethic of justice simply identifies an ethics of class interest with the democratic ethic of justice. The *demos* is clearly a segment of the community, not an agent of justice in the community as whole, and it rules in its own interest (1.14–15). Moreover, he refers to the *demos* as "the worst sort," in contrast to "the better sort," who possesses *arete* and *does* safeguard the political community as a whole (1.3–5, II.19). And, unlike Pericles, he says that this means that the *demos* does not tend to recognize the merit of the wealthier, more "useful" classes (1.3–9, II.3, 19).

For the Old Oligarch, the accommodation of democracy and virtue in Thucydides' account of Pericles' funeral oration was a rhetorical distortion of what he regarded as political reality. And yet he also affirms the greater freedom in democracies over oligarchies, praises the political responsibility of the *demos,* recognizes the relative absence of corruption in the courts, and admits that the way of life of the democratic *politeia* of the Athenians works and works well (II.19–20, III.1, 3). Yet, the Old Oligarch does not offer a critical

---

44. The best account of the relation between words and deeds, discourse and action in Thucydides' *History* remains Adam Parry, *Logos and Ergon in Thucydides.* Parry believes that their relation was more complementary and equal, although marked by tension, in Thucydides than in Plato; he argues that this tension disappears in Plato. To the extent that Plato does not believe his *logos* can inform Athenian politics in the way Thucydides believed his *logos* could, the tension disappears, but that tension is central to Plato's conception of the ethical and political dimension of *his* logos.

discourse of justice that would justify or limit the exercise of power by the *demos* for the political community as a whole—*except* by promoting greater power for the "better sort" relative to the *demos*. How this could occur is notably unspecified.[45]

Conventional ethical justifications of Athenian democracy did not generate a critical discourse of justice. To be sure, there was a democratic notion of responsibility, which was consistent with the power of the Athenian *polis*, its citizens, and the principles that guided its constitutional order. It involved freedom and equality and included important ethical or moral ideals, such as the value of political equality among the citizens, an ethic of political participation, and a moral code that protected the dignity of each citizen.[46] It is simply anachronistic to say that the ancient Greeks had no conception of "moral responsibility."[47] However, the ethical discourse associated with Athenian de-

45. See Ober, *Political Dissent in Democratic Athens*.

46. For the notion of "dignity" as a guiding ethical norm in Athenian courts, see Josiah Ober and Catherine Vanderpool, "Athenian Democracy"; Josiah Ober and Catherine Vanderpool, "What Democracy Meant." In a sense, this ethical code provides the critical discourse of justice that theorists such as Plato and Aristotle ignore. However, although it belongs to and reflects the values of democratic Athens, it refers to a legal defense of individuals, not a political defense of a constitutional order. Moreover, its critical foundations lie only with the individuals who affirm it. Institutionally, that may be the best foundation for any political ethic; however, it depends on the virtue of those individuals themselves. In an ethical and political context where such individuals do not provide good reasons for trusting their inherent virtue, such discourse will be insufficient as a discourse of justice.

47. To say that the Athenian democracy lacked any notion of "moral responsibility," as A. W. H. Adkins has done in his influential book *Merit and Responsibility*, ultimately implies that "moral responsibility" cannot be used to justify a particular order of power, that "moral responsibility" cannot be "political." As argued in Chapter 2, this application of Kantian standards to the interpretation of ancient Greek discourse misses the uniquely political dimension of Greek ethics. (For examples of the influence of Adkins's argument, see Alasdair MacIntyre's *After Virtue*, and M. I. Finley's *Politics in the Ancient World*.) Adkins holds that no Greek writings about ethics express coherent thought about "moral responsibility," the model for which is provided by Immanuel Kant. This is because their discourse about *arete* from Homer to Aristotle essentially concerned the practical, political effects of individual behavior.

In Adkins's scheme, this discourse is simply amoral discourse about skills and abilities. Such discourse was able to provide a coherent ethical system at one time in Greek life—in the Homeric period, where such behavior was denoted by competitive virtues and limited by respect for the gods. But afterward, subsequent ethical writings reflected only incoherent (albeit interesting) attempts to accommodate the changing character of society to their fundamentally Homeric ethical vocabulary. Once the religious sanction lost its power and the abilities of aristocrats became less central to the preservation of society, the quieter virtues of "justice" became more prominent. But such ethical values were still justified as skills or abilities. Although they now were skills of deliberating about justice in political community rather than those of war making, they

mocracy did not provide clear critical standards for its application besides the rationalization of its inherent goodness.[48] One is entitled to dismiss the discursive and practical tensions between democracy and justice that led Plato in the *Republic* to differentiate a *politeia* in *logos* from the *politeia* in *ergon* of Athenian democracy only if one accepts its idealized account in the Periclean

---

still could not coherently provide an ethic of "moral responsibility." Adkins's narrative is revealing because he ignores Greek writings about justice that deal explicitly with problems of *political* responsibility. Notably, Adkins barely discusses Solon in his treatment of the various dimensions of *arete*. Because he slights the political dimensions of *arete* involved in Solonian justice, he does not acknowledge its potential for resolving *stasis*. Similarly, when he argues for the persistence of "Homeric," "competitive" conceptions of *arete* in the fifth century, he cites a passage from Herodotus's debate on political orders (III.82.3), in which *arete* is deemed to foment *stasis*, but ignores the specifically oligarchic character of that *arete* (192, n. 15). Finally, he doesn't acknowledge the ethics of the *Oresteia* and Pericles' funeral oration in Thucydides' *History* as democratic responses to problematic relations of ethics and power in political communities. For him, Aeschylus's trilogy simply revisits Homeric themes about pollution, and the ethics of the *Eumenides* simply indicates an argument for political advantage. This enables Adkins to agree with Plato and to reduce fifth-century democratic ethics to an ethics of domination. Plato's and Aristotle's philosophies make improvements on Greek ethical discourse—Plato's by elevating respect for the justice of *logos,* Aristotle's by linking that *logos* to regard for community (*koinonia*). But each is irredeemably limited by its association of ethics with the justice of political community, and for Adkins this has nothing to do with "moral responsibility." For Adkins, "moral responsibility" involves the instrumentalization of political life. But the effect of this philosophical move is the evisceration of ethical justifications for "political responsibility." The dissociation of ethics from power in the discourse of "moral responsibility" has not clearly led to more humane effects in society. Perhaps the progress Adkins associates explicitly with Kant and implicitly with Christianity has mixed blessings. For other criticisms of Adkins and the position Adkins represents, see Bernard Williams, *Shame and Necessity,* and an unpublished lecture, "The End of Moral Responsibility."

48. As far as M. I. Finley is concerned, this is not terribly problematic. He agrees that Athenian democrats did not provide a critical ethic for their politics other than the justification of their own constitutional order, which unabashedly approved of the domination of cities beyond their borders and of the domination, via political exclusion, of slaves and women within. He then admits the compatibility of the doctrine of Thrasymachus with the ethical foundations of Athenian democracy. Now, Thrasymachean ethics is not the doctrinal equivalent of Athenian democratic ethics, insofar as the latter included an ethic of political quality, mutual respect, and reverence for both law and freedom. There was no coherent and systematic critical discourse that formulated an ethics of democracy distinguishable from either an ethic of power as domination (the Old Oligarch, Thrasymachus) or an ethic of rationalization (Pericles' funeral oration). See M. I. Finley, *Democracy Ancient and Modern,* 79, 88, 91, 103–5ff (see also p. 48, where Finley notes the Old Oligarch's justification of democracy in terms of its "immorality").

Finley rejects Platonic theorizing about politics as either irrelevant or ideological and harmful to democracy, but his comments about the discourse of Athenian democracy inadvertently justify the critical value of Plato's project. Finley acknowledges the importance of Plato's ethical

funeral oration or its reductively realistic account in the Old Oligarch's "Constitution of the Athenians."[49]

This argument suggests a different twist on the forty-five-plus-year-old discussion of the relation of democracy and democratic argument to political theory in ancient Athens. The first entrant in this contest, who has set the conceptual framework for every contribution since, is A. H. M. Jones. In his article "Athenian Democracy and Its Critics," Jones argued that the reason for the absence of prodemocratic arguments in ancient Greece was primarily the practical ascendance of democracy itself.[50] This interpretation makes the discursive arenas of political theory and democracy seemingly dichotomous byproducts of historical developments in the Athenian *polis*. It also suggests that the conceptual advances in political theory cannot be associated with the practices of democracy, insofar as political theory was designed in opposition to them. This argument bears the marks of its time (the 1950s), insofar as Jones projects a view of Athenian democracy as a society of middle-class proto-bourgeois citizens. Moreover, it fails to identify the abundance of surviving texts that in fact reveal important elements of a democratic ideology. Both of these deficiencies have been roundly and rightly criticized.[51] More troubling, however, is its tendency to naturalize an opposition, if not antagonism, between political theory and democratic discourse, such that if political theory is to be democratic, it must trim its sails, linking its foundational principles to the pragmatic operating practices of a conventional democratic order. (In contemporary theoretical argument, the most notable champion of this position is Richard Rorty.)

---

concerns at other points in this text (30, 46–47), particularly with respect to education and the value of a political community's overcoming *stasis*. But for Finley, the substantive value of Plato's comments reflects only concerns expressed by other Greek writers and thinkers, such as Aeschylus and Protagoras.

49. Yet there is an important tension between "constitution" and "democracy" when the form of a constitution is invested with power. On this, see Sheldon Wolin, "Norm and Form: The Constitutionalizing of Democracy," in Euben et al., eds., *Athenian Political Thought and the Reconstruction of American Democracy*, 29–58.

50. This article, first published in 1953, appeared as one of a collection of articles under the title, *Athenian Democracy*.

51. See Josiah Ober and Catherine Vanderpool, "Athenian Democracy," 30–32. Cynthia Farrar's attempt to counter Jones by finding democratic political theory in the works of "elite" writers—such as Protagoras, Thucydides, and Democritus—is less successful, especially as historical reconstruction, although it is useful as a vehicle for innovative democratic theorizing today.

The argument developed here, however, rejects Jones's dichotomy. It does not do so by finding political theory in democratic rhetoric (Ober) or the work of elite writers who never make specific arguments on behalf of democracy (Farrar). Rather, it suggests that critical and systematic political theory—of the sort, say, that Plato offers in the *Republic*—does not develop so much in opposition to democracy per se as to the injustices that (seemingly) suffuse not only democratic Athens but every existing political order. In other words, the theoretical, critical, and ethical articulation of "the political" is subtly and irreducibly linked to, as well as separable from, democratic practice. Plato originated a new kind of political discourse and did so in part by rejecting democratic Athens as an adequate incarnation of justice. Moreover, his capacity to do so (as I argued above, in discussing the origins of the political art as a coherently articulated conception) was made possible by the democratization of political life. But that does not establish a historical opposition between political theory and democracy. To the contrary, it opens up intellectual pathways for various alliances between political theory and democracy, depending on the historical context and strategies of their agents. The following reading of Plato's *Republic*, and its location in a comprehensive reading of the Platonic political art, supports this argument.

Plato's conception of the political art in the *Republic* must be understood in terms of a theory of the constitution of justice, a theory of the political that is neither amoral, nor pejoratively ideological, nor inherently antidemocratic, but rather a uniquely philosophical political art that can be a critical asset for any attempt to understand and promote the potential for harmony between a critical ethics and the power of politics, between the *ergon* of democracy and the *logos* of justice. This is not to suggest that Plato's political theory directly or indirectly enhances that potential, only that any attempt to do so could be well served by understanding Plato's articulation of the constitution of justice. Let us now, then, undertake that venture.

B. *Techne* AND JUSTICE

In the *Republic*, as in the previously discussed aporetic dialogues, the notion of *techne* itself is not the focus of Plato's attention; nevertheless, here as before it performs a crucial function in enabling Plato to discuss the subject of his focus. There it was central to the articulation of his Socratic Problem; here it plays a pivotal role in Plato's articulation of its problematic solution in the constitution of justice. Throughout the *Republic,* the notion of a *techne* provides critical assistance for Plato's project of creating a new constitution of justice that links ethics and power.[52] It demonstrates a complementary relation of *logos* and *ergon,* providing practical conditions for the articulation of justice as a virtue and rational conditions for the constitution of power.

The significance of *techne* for understanding justice in the *Republic* changes as the dialogue progresses, reflecting the different contexts of its employment. In Book I, it serves as a model of knowledgeable, productive activity that still corresponds to the discursive and practical conventions of Athenian society. In Books II–X, it belongs to models of political and psychological order that can be used to evaluate and guide the lives of individuals and the political community as a whole toward justice, an activity that is complicated by the gap between the standards of genuinely critical discourse and the actualities of dominant practical conventions. Plato's continuing use of the notion of *techne* to produce a constitution of justice indicates his belief in the continuing possibility of a dynamic link between theoretical *logos* and practical *ergon* in human/political affairs.

52. This argument counters prominent readings of Plato's theory of justice in the *Republic,* which argue that its innovative character stems from Plato's "abandonment" of the craft analogy that he used in Book I and other aporetic dialogues. For examples of the "abandonment" argument, see John Gould, *The Development of Plato's Ethics,* chap. II; Robert W. Hall, *Plato and the Individual;* Terence Irwin, *Plato's Moral Theory;* C. D. C. Reeve, *Philosopher-Kings;* and others. This chapter and the previous ones show how this claim reflects a reductive understanding of the notion of a *techne* and a sorely incomplete understanding of Plato's use of it in his dialogues. Plato does not accept the Aristotelian differentiation of practical activity (*praxis*) from productive activity (*poiesis*) or the categorical isolation of theoretical and practical knowledge, for these distinctions effectively subordinate the dynamic practice and theory of *techne* to naturalized and static modes of critical discourse and social practice. Such *technai* are simply two-way powers, practices whose social effects are essentially technical and amoral. For the Aristotelian characterization of *technai* as two-way powers, see *Metaphysics* IX.2, 1046b1ff. Notably, Aristotle links this characterization to his theory of potentiality and actuality, which in turn derives from a conception of nature that has roots in convention—a conception of nature that Plato does not share. The interpretation of Plato's use of the *techne* analogy through such an Aristotelian perspective—simply as a technical, two-way power—has been an important factor contributing to modern misreadings of Plato's political theory as totalitarian or authoritarian, such as those of Popper, Arendt, and Bambrough. For criticisms of their arguments from a more strictly philosophical perspective (sometimes still informed by an Aristotelian bias), see Richard P. Parry, "The Craft of Justice," and, especially, J. E. Tiles, "*Techne* and Moral Expertise," in F. J. Pelletier and J. King-Farlow, eds., *New Essays on Plato.*

We discuss three places in the *Republic* where Plato prominently uses the notion of *techne*. The first is Book I, where Plato's Socrates subjects prevalent understandings of the meaning and power of justice offered by Cephalus, Polemarchus, and Thrasymachus to critical analysis by means of the tool of *techne*. The second is in the subsequent three books, where he responds to Glaucon's and Adeimantus's reformulations of Thrasymachus's attack on the desirability of a just life by constituting a theory of justice in the soul and the state that involves each part of both doing its own work (*ergon*), realizing its own power or capacity (*dynamis*), and exercising its appropriate art (*techne*) in a way that produces virtue (*arete*) and justice (*dikaiosyne*). Finally, in Books VI and VII, Plato's Socrates provides a rationale for these constitutions by sanctioning the *techne* of dialectic whose object is the good with the authoritative agency of philosopher-guardians, whose incomparable vocation combines the *technai* of dialectical understanding and political reform. These three employments of *techne* illuminate Plato's understanding of the rational and virtuous character of the political art as the constitution of justice as well as its relation to the ethics and politics of democracy and education. (See Sections C and D of this chapter.)

I. *Techne* AND THE PRACTICES OF JUSTICE

The distinctive features of Book I of the *Republic* form integral components of a dialogue about the political art as the constitution of justice. They evidence a literary and theoretical reprise of a Platonic interpretation of the major factors contributing to the trial and death of Socrates: the state's failure to understand the meaning of justice and therefore to appreciate the virtue of Socrates' life.[53] The uniqueness of the *Republic*'s introductory passages consists of the parameters they establish for the constitution of justice. They

---

53. The first book of the *Republic* differs markedly from the subsequent books by virtue of the complexity of its drama and elenchic exchanges. In the view of various commentators, these characteristics indicate an earlier date of composition than the rest of the *Republic* and/or a different philosophical perspective than the one articulated in the dialogue's subsequent books. One cannot disprove these commentators. The names and arguments of these commentators are usefully summarized in a recent article by Charles Kahn that criticizes them (and that does not require one to accept his larger interpretation of Plato), "Proleptic Composition in the *Republic*, or Why Book I Was Never a Separate Dialogue."

indicate how existing definitions of justice could be used to condemn the historical Socrates and eliminate any ethical justification of the Athenian political order. Plato uses the character of Socrates for dramatic effect to show how these definitions lead to a disjuncture between genuine virtue, which appears to be impractical, and practical power, which appears to be immoral, as well as between the good of the individual and the good of the *polis*. The problem that the constitution of justice would solve also derives from greedy, overreaching, limitless desire (*pleonexia*), a deformation of the moderation of *arete* and a prime factor in fomenting harmful factional conflict (*stasis*).[54] Whereas *pleonexia* disrupts the *politeia* of the soul (*psyche*), *stasis* sabotages the *politeia* of the state (*polis*).[55] These conflicts can be ameliorated only by a new constitution of justice.[56]

Plato's employment of the notion of *techne* to articulate the constitution of justice reveals the problematics it engages. Socrates first mentions the notion of a *techne* in his discussion with Polemarchus, in which the model of a craft is used to determine what counts as appropriate action toward others

54. For the relation of *pleonexia* and genuine justice as opposites, see Socrates' discussion with Thrasymachus in Book I (349b–350d, 351d) and with Glaucon and Adeimantus in Book II (359c, 362b), about the problematic nature and origins of justice. In both Book I (351d, 352a) and Book IV (440b–444b), "justice" remedies the problems of divisive conflict among individuals or within one's soul, which accompany the expression of *pleonexia* or the less severe but related trait of "meddlesomeness" (*polupragmosune,* 433b, 434b, 444b).

55. As various commentators have noted, *stasis* is an unusual term. Literally, it signifies only "standing." Insofar as citizens need to take stands in their *polis* if the politics of their society is to be democratic, it seems that nothing is problematic about it. However, the distinctive significance of *stasis* in Greek thought is political activity that resists accommodation of the differences between contending parties and makes the practice of political community impossible. For Thucydides, *stasis* in Corcyra marked the antinomy of political community, and the presence of *stasis* in Athens was a—if not the—principal factor leading to its defeat in the Peloponnesian War (III. 69–85, II.65.12). In formulating a concept of justice that responded to *stasis,* Plato confronted the central problem of Greek political life. One may argue about the extent to which he located responsibility for it in the proper quarters—Athenian democracy was the least *stasis*-prone polis in ancient Greece—but the problem itself was all too real. On the meaning of *stasis* in Greek writings, see Dirk Loenen, *Stasis;* M. I. Finley, "Athenian Demagogues," in *Democracy Ancient and Modern,* 44ff; N. Loraux, "Reflections of the Greek City on Unity and Division," in Molho et al., eds., *City States in Classical Antiquity and Medieval Italy,* 33–51.

56. For Aristotle, *stasis* is not an ethical phenomenon; it is principally a contingent problem of politics that vitiates the preeminence of his natural order. Recently, political theorists have emphasized Aristotle's appreciation of conflict. But his philosophy of natural harmony precludes *stasis* from becoming a primary concern, whereas Plato's theory of justice is incomprehensible apart from his analysis of *stasis*.

and thereby to identify what a *techne* of justice might be (332c–d).[57] In response to Socrates' introduction of the model of a *techne*, Polemarchus defines "justice" as "doing well" or "producing good" with regard to one's friends and doing badly or producing harm toward one's enemies (332d). His definition of the *techne* of justice is frequently taken to indicate the nature of politics, for example, by twentieth-century political theorists, Platonic commentators, and classical historians.[58]

For Plato, such activity would not be just unless it was grounded in an understanding of what constitutes a friend or enemy of justice. So Plato's Socrates proceeds to unpack Polemarchus's definition. He uses the model of a *techne* to identify its practical sphere of operation as well as the advantages and disadvantages it produces. The subsequent important exchange generates two determinate results. First, Polemarchus cannot identify a sphere of action that possesses identifiable and reliable social value. Polemarchus recognizes that just action is not directly comparable to practical productive activities, such as agriculture or the art of the cobbler (333a–c). "Justice" concerns "associations" that would *regulate* those actions (333a).[59] This kind of activity— which initially involves "money matters" and then "guarding" (*phulattein*, 333d)—has no sphere of usefulness as a regulator of action; its sphere appears to be inaction. Second, it seems that insofar as it could be a practical productive activity, it could be *used* for at least two ends, one of which may be bad. Thus one who is able or skillful (*deinos*) at fighting could attack or defend; one who is skillful in affecting physical health could produce disease as well as remedy it; and one who is a "good guard" of a military campaign would know how to steal secrets and plans from an enemy as well as to protect one's

---

57. I follow the practice of Grube and Irwin in translating *techne* in the *Republic* as "craft," with the following qualifications. *Techne* also referred to the human ability to perform a craft. Indeed, possessing a craft meant having a corollary capacity or power (*dynamis*). (See *Republic* 346a1–b1.) When it connotes an individual's capacity, "skill" might be a better translation. And insofar as the practice of a *techne* often required the extensive exercise of individual judgment, it might also be properly translated as "art." I may slide between these translations for *techne*, but their denotation of *techne* is always noted.

58. Carl Schmitt, *The Concept of the Political*, 26ff; Wayne Leys, "Was Plato Non-Political," in Vlastos, ed., *Plato: A Collection of Critical Essays*, vol. 2, 168; and Christian Meier, *The Greek Discovery of Politics*, 15ff.

59. It is worth recalling what Paul Shorey said in his note to this passage in his translation of the *Republic:* "Justice (the political art) must be something as definite as the special arts, yet of universal scope. This twofold requirement no definition of a virtue in the minor dialogues is ever able to satisfy. It is met only by the theory worked out in the *Republic.*" He also cites his 1903 study, *The Unity of Plato's Thought*, 14.

own. In sum, it seems that one who is skillful at "justice as guarding" could be a skillful thief as well (332d–334b). This impasse recalls those of the aporetic dialogues. But it reflects not only the critical use of *techne* to expose the ethical indeterminacy of conventional practical activities; it points to the need for a theory of a political art grounded in a constitution of justice.

Socrates does not mention *techne* in this particular exchange with Polemarchus and instead refers to a typically Homeric and specifically Odyssean disposition to use cleverness (that is, *deinos*) strategically as the only constraint on Polemarchus's definition of justice as a *techne*. Puzzled but unfazed, Polemarchus sticks to his substantive definition of justice as benefiting one's friends and harming one's enemies.

Socrates then embarks on a new tack, differentiating types of action according to whether they are rooted in belief or knowledge, appearance or reality. Polemarchus believes that his statement would have to hold in both respects. This allows Socrates to introduce a set of qualifiers for Polemarchus's definitions of "good" (*agathos*) and "bad" or "evil" (*kakos*), so that it now becomes "benefiting friends who are good and harming enemies who are bad." In so doing, Socrates introduces critical discursive standards for determining the justice of actions and potentially a new practical domain for their institution. These criteria do not presuppose a theory of the transcendental foundations of reality; nor do they abandon the linkage of *techne* to an ethic of justice because of a "fallacy" in the use of *techne* for such argumentation.[60] They simply indicate the importance of justifying the value we assign to our actions as extensively as we can. For Plato's Socrates, the "use value" of an action cannot be adequately assessed by focusing solely on the immediate outcome/s of particular actions.[61] The entire range of consequences for an action must be considered, particularly insofar as they affect the constitution of the soul.

Socrates takes advantage of the change in Polemarchus's definition. For now, both Polemarchus and Socrates agree that the *ergon* of human beings is to achieve their *arete*, which is justice. Insofar as harming anyone or anything detracts from or damages their *arete*, making them less "good," harming human beings makes them more unjust than they otherwise would be. Therefore, it cannot be just to harm anyone, whether enemies or friends (335b–e).

---

60. The first criticism appears frequently in the work of antifoundationalist critics of Plato, from Popper to Rorty. For the second criticism, which appears frequently in the work of analytic critics of Plato, see Guthrie, *A History of Greek Philosophy*, 4:440.

61. This point was well made by H. W. B. Joseph, *Ancient and Modern Philosophy*, 1–14.

Not only is the definition of justice offered by Polemarchus and derived from Simonides refuted, but the beliefs of the historical Socrates, who believed that it was never just to harm or injure any fellow citizens, are implicitly affirmed.[62]

By not only rejecting a definition of ethical and political life (which is rooted in traditional beliefs as well as the normal political practices of Athens) but also affirming the views of the historical Socrates, Plato reestablishes his Socratic Problem at the heart of the *Republic.* For he has constructed a gap between the *logos* and *ergon* of virtue by invoking the conflict between the historical Socrates and the conventional meanings and practices of virtue in Athens.

At this point, Thrasymachus breaks into the dialogue and raises the discussion of justice to a new level of sophistication, abstraction, and distance from conventional beliefs about justice. He verbally attacks Socrates for the so-called wisdom of his elenchic approach, in which Socrates' own beliefs are never the topic of critical analysis, and demands that *he* present *his own* beliefs for examination. To continue the implicit analogy of Book 1 to Socrates' trial, one might say that Polemarchus arrests Socrates whereas Thrasymachus presents the indictment. Although Socrates seems to accept Thrasymachus's point, he refuses Thrasymachus's demand and deftly resumes his characteristic discourse, managing to get Thrasymachus to subject his own beliefs about the meaning of justice to *elenchus* (336b–338b).[63]

According to Thrasymachus, "the just" or "justice" is "the advantage of the stronger" (338c2). On Socrates' prodding, he expands on this so that it

---

62. In Plato's *Apology of Socrates,* probably the most empirically and historically rooted of any Platonic dialogue, Socrates simply states that the just man cannot be harmed. In Plato's *Crito* and *Gorgias*—more obviously Platonic constructions—a dialogic Socrates argues this point positively. Insofar as the entire defense of Socrates' own justice in Plato's *Apology of Socrates* is based on his conviction that he has never harmed, wronged, or corrupted anyone willingly, and that it is unjust to do so, it is hard to imagine the historical Socrates believing that it is just to harm or injure any fellow citizen. Socrates' views about the treatment of noncitizens (and perhaps that includes lesser Athenian citizens, such as women and slaves, although this cannot be proved) is less clear—especially if one takes killing someone in war as harming or injuring them, because Socrates fought bravely for Athens and presumably killed its military enemies. (See Chapters 2, Section E and 3, Section C, above.)

63. On the character of the Socratic *elenchus* in Plato's dialogues, see Richard Robinson, *Plato's Earlier Dialectic,* and, more recently, the article by Gregory Vlastos, "The Socratic Elenchus," in *Oxford Studies in Ancient Philosophy,* vol. 1, ed. Julia Annas, and the numerous articles *it* has spawned. (See also Chapter 2, Section E2, above.)

means as well "the advantage of the established government or ruler" (339a 1–2), whether the form of rule is tyrannical, democratic, or aristocratic (338d 7–8).[64] This definition is more abstract and systematic than Polemarchus's, for it concerns not only types of activities in a society but the political order of that society itself. However, it does not simply exemplify institutional arguments for justice.[65] Thrasymachus is no synecdoche for the theory of Athenian democracy, although he may encapsulate its sophistic justification.[66] For Thrasymachus reduces institutions to their instrumental value for the exercise of power as rule or domination (*arche*).

Socrates now exploits an ambiguity with Thrasymachus's definition (which parallels the one he pointed out in the initial definition of Polemarchus), namely the possibility that what one takes to be the just, stronger, and advantageous is not really the case, that appearance does not coincide with reality. For if it did, rulers might give orders that are bad for themselves. Cleitophon suggests that Thrasymachus's definition applies only to what rulers believe to be the case, but Thrasymachus rejects this interpretation, saying, "Do you think that I would call stronger a man who is in error at the time he errs?" (340c).[67] To support his point, *he* (not Socrates) introduces the model of craftsmanship and a definition of it that diverges from ordinary discourse:

> If your argument (*logos*) is precise (*akribe*), no craftsman (*demiourgos*) ever errs (*hamartanei*). It is when the knowledge (*episteme*) of his craft leaves him that he errs, and at that time he is not a craftsman. No craftsman, wise man (*sophos*), or ruler (*archon*) errs when he is a ruler in the precise sense. However, everyone will say that the physician or ruler is in error. To speak with precision, the ruler, in so far

64. Compare *Laws;* see Chapter 5B, below.

65. In chap. 1 of his book *Philosopher-Kings*, Reeve distinguishes the definitions of justice offered by Polemarchus and Thrasymachus as those that describe "actions" and "institutions," respectively. This distinction is interesting and useful, but it does not fully capture what Plato is doing in Book 1 of the *Republic*. For he is not only establishing a new kind of philosophy; he is providing a searching critique of the ethics of Athens as the politics of power.

66. Adkins, *Merit and Responsibility,* 235ff.

67. Some interpreters find Cleitophon's weaker reading of Thrasymachus's initial definition to be attractive and wonder why Thrasymachus didn't adopt it. But for the Greeks in general and Plato in particular, claims about justice would not amount to much if they relied only on belief that was admitted to be loosely connected to knowledge about the world. The lack of any concern that justice be connected to knowledge is peculiarly modern.

as he is a ruler, unerringly decrees what is best for himself and this the subject must do. The just then is, as I said at first, to do (*poiein*) what is to the advantage of the stronger. (340e–341a)[68]

This new, "precise" level of discourse about craftsmanship enables Socrates to introduce the model of *techne* and begins Plato's theoretical construction of a concept of justice.[69] In paraphrasing Thrasymachus (and anticipating the ship-of-state discussion in Book VI), Socrates states that a ship's captain has that title because of his *techne* and authority or rule over (*arche*) his sailors. An argument now ensues over the implications of *techne* as a standard of evaluation for the meaning of justice.

Plato's Socrates begins by offering a genealogy of crafts that also produces a "precise," unconventional definition for them, but Socrates' definition differs from Thrasymachus's. Crafts were developed, Socrates says, to produce an "advantage" that essentially involves the perfection of their subject matter (341e). Socrates claims, unlike Thrasymachus, that the welfare of the practitioner of a *techne* is not relevant to its character as a craft. When it is practiced well, however (which is to say perfectly), it produces excellence (*arete*) in its object of concern (341e–342b). In functional terms, therefore, *techne* automatically evidences a technical sort of *arete* in its user, which suggests that the *techne* of justice necessarily possesses a certain kind of ethical value. This stipulation enables Socrates to turn the tables on Thrasymachus, for insofar as the object of concern for the craft of political rule is the citizenry, as distinct from the rulers, Thrasymachus's definition of justice as the advantage of the stronger who rule must be incorrect. At the same time, a gap is opened between the "good" produced by a *techne* and the "good" of its agent (see 346e).

Thrasymachus exploits this gap. He scornfully rejects the substance of this *logos*, turns Socrates' model of a *techne* on its head, and develops a new argument. He associates the *techne* of justice as the advantage of the stronger with "another's good" (343c) and supplements this claim with an endorsement of injustice as the major constituent of happiness, turning on its head

---

68. All major translated passages from the *Republic* are based on the Paul Shorey translation, which may be found in the Loeb Classical Library version of Plato's *Republic*, and in *The Collected Dialogues of Plato*, ed. Edith Hamilton and Huntington Cairns.

69. Nettleship notes that a concern for "precision" launches Plato's discussion of the good at 504b (in contrast to 414a) as the justification of justice. See his *Lectures*, 214.

the original claim presented by Cephalus, and accepted by Polemarchus and Socrates, of the essential interconnection between justice and happiness.

To support his claim, Thrasymachus reiterates his conception of crafts-manship (as a practical activity that the practitioner of a craft undertakes pri-marily to benefit himself) by characterizing the activity of shepherding. Ac-cording to Thrasymachus, shepherds fatten sheep for their own benefit, not for that of the sheep. In other words, rulers act as shepherds who regularly exploit their citizen-sheep as much as possible. Citizens practice justice as a *techne* in the Socratic sense but produce advantage for their rulers, not them-selves. Given the disadvantage of being just, one would want to be unjust if one wanted to be happy, and injustice in these circumstances would involve taking advantage of or exploiting (*pleonektein*) fellow citizens. This rendition of justice assures the existence of conflict between rulers and ruled, as well as between the individual and society. The perfection of *this* activity, notably not described by Thrasymachus as a *techne,* is accomplished by a tyrant (who might masquerade as a shepherd). One who is not willing to do wrong is not happy but "most wretched" (344a). Plato's Socrates is not persuaded: "I do not believe that injustice is more profitable than justice, not even if one gives it full scope and does not put obstacles in its way" (345a).

To begin his defense, Socrates again refers to the precise meaning of *techne,* which Thrasymachus has selectively interpreted. For Socrates, ac-cording to the precise meaning of *techne,* a true shepherd would care for his sheep. He also introduces a new term, power not as domination but as "capacity" (*dynamis*), as that which differentiates the practice of crafts (346a1–3). Doing so enables Plato's Socrates to isolate the benefits of ruling from its exercise as a craft. The craft of wage earning, not ruling, will be that which benefits the ruler. This explains why Socrates believes, in opposition to Thrasymachus, that no one rules willingly. Rulers rule only for the money they receive, because the craft of ruling benefits only its subjects and not the rulers themselves (346e). Because the best men act not merely for the sake of money or honor, they must be compelled to rule, and they do it, finally, not out of a love of ruling but out of fear of what will happen to themselves and their fellow citizens if they do not rule.

Socrates' account of the *techne* of justice as a craft of ruling explains why it will not produce injustice in society but does not explain why its perfor-mance, like that of any *arete,* will benefit its agent. In this conceptual vacuum may appear a domain of power that involves neither a consideration of prac-tical benefits nor the practice of domination. Plato has made room for a theory of just agency.[70] But much theoretical work needs to be done. For a gap still exists that may harbor conflict between what is good for the individual and for society as a whole.

Despite this lacuna, Plato's Socrates appears to be satisfied with his treatment of this issue. He now turns to Thrasymachus's more daunting claim that the life of the unjust man is more profitable than that of the just man (347e) (which Glaucon also disputes). As in the previous discussion, Thrasymachus is tripped up by accepting some of Socrates' definitions, which in this case derive from common meanings. Here, justice is discussed not in terms of *technai* but as a "virtue" (*arete*). The focus is not justice as a practice that produces particular goods or benefits (*agatha*, 348a) but as a disposition that leads to particular kinds of activities. Notably, by switching the discussion of justice from its character as a *techne* to its nature as an *arete* without abandoning the craft analogy, Socrates lands his most disabling blow on Thrasymachus.

Thrasymachus begins his response by unconventionally associating the traits of "good judgment" (*euboulia*)—which includes practical intelligence (*phronesis*) and wisdom (*sophia*)—with injustice but accepting the identification of justice as virtue and injustice as vice (348c–e).[71] The subsequent argument leads to a significant victory for Socrates. It enables him to show the unprofitability of injustice, that it does not bring benefits to its practitioner.

Socrates conducts the argument by relying on conventional connotations of *techne* and *arete*. According to Socrates' rendering of them, insofar as a just man's action does conform to the models of *techne* and *arete*, it possesses inherent—one might say natural—standards and limits.[72] Adherence to these standards by a just man motivates him to try to outdo, or get the better of (*pleon echein*), the unjust man but not the better of another just man, whereas an unjust man, because he seeks to get the better of his fellow citizens without adhering to such limits, tries to outdo the just and the unjust (349b–c). The performance of a craftsman is informed by knowledge (*episteme*) (349e) and conforms to a proper measure, and those who do well achieve excellence

---

70. This aspect of Plato's argument is emphasized in Julia Annas, *An Introduction to Plato's Republic*.

71. Notably, Plato does not here differentiate *phronesis* and *sophia*—as Aristotle later did— as markers of practical versus theoretical wisdom.

72. However, one cannot find such limits through available modes of either reasoning or perceptual observation—as one is inclined to think is possible from an Aristotelian perspective on the character of (natural) reason.

(*arete*). The standards of *techne* and *arete* informed by *episteme*, therefore, ensure the presence of propriety and goodness in anyone's skillful and knowledgeable practical activity and the absence of an unlimited desire to have more than or exceed what is due to another (*pleonexia*). The unjust man who is motivated by unlimited desire now appears to be ignorant and to lack the positive qualities that Thrasymachus had associated with him. Plato's Socrates has conformed a surplus of desire to the measure of justice.

Thrasymachus very reluctantly agrees with this argument. He has almost been reduced to the condition of Polemarchus. Socrates proceeds to argue that because justice *is* wisdom and virtue, a just *polis* must be stronger than an unjust one. Thrasymachus acknowledges that this is Socrates' claim, but he affirms that an unjust *polis* is stronger than a just one. To refute this claim, Socrates simply continues his previous line of reasoning. Because unjust activity harms everyone inasmuch as it tries to get the better of the just and unjust, it generates strife and confusion (*stasiazein*) internally and externally, sabotaging or making impossible any collective action by a political community or personal action by an individual (351d–352a). As a political and personal strategy, injustice assures not power and strength but powerlessness and weakness. There cannot be power without justice (351b–352a).

Socrates completes this preliminary defense of justice as a constituent of happiness by turning his attention to the benefits that supposedly accrue to the individual life of the unjust man. Here Socrates analyzes the ordinary connotations of "function" (*ergon*) and "virtue" (*arete*) with respect to the "soul" (*psyche*), the seat of happiness. As Socrates pointed out earlier in the dialogue, types of activities, whether they are social activities such as pruning or physical activities such as seeing, are performed by instruments or agents (such as pruning-knives or eyes) that actualize their function by performing it well—in which case they exhibit *arete*. They must have the capacity for that virtue in order to actualize it, and eyes or ears, say, that do not perform their function well lack their own virtue. Having said this, Socrates now states (352e–353c) that there is a function of the soul that itself achieves a good life (*eu zen*). It involves "caring for things (*epimeleisthai*), ruling (*archein*), and deliberating (*bouleuesthai*)," highly political activities (353d).

There also is an *arete* of the soul, which enables the soul to fulfill its function. In accord with Socrates' previous point that the soul of an unjust man would make him incapable of achieving anything, the *arete* of the soul must be justice (352a, 353e). Plato associated the *ergon* and *arete* of the soul with the *politike techne* in the *Protagoras* and *Meno*. Here, the soul is characterized in political terms but independently of the conventional practice of political activities. The just man will live well and be happy; injustice cannot be more profitable than justice. Justice is the particular virtue that realizes the virtue of the individual as a human being.[73]

So goes Socrates' initial refutation of Thrasymachus's argument, but neither he nor Socrates is satisfied with the *logos*. Socrates points out that in his elenchic defeat of Thrasymachus's argument about whether injustice was either vice and ignorance or wisdom and virtue, whether it was more profitable than justice, he did not define the nature of justice. Socrates laments: "For when I do not know what justice is, I shall hardly know whether it is a kind of virtue or not, or whether the just man is just and happy" (354c1–3). Indeed, although Socrates has been able to refute Thrasymachus at the level of *logos,* Thrasymachus remains emotionally unconvinced, for the practical authority and personal benefit of Socratic definition, as was the case with his earlier definition of *techne,* have not been shown (in Book 1). Socrates' elenchic approach enables him to make the most abstract arguments in the dialogue, but the domain of practical reference for proving its contribution to happiness is disturbingly opaque. The crisis created by the inability to harmonize virtue and the political art persists.

2. THE *Logos* OF JUSTICE AS CONSTITUTIONS OF STATE AND SOUL

The unsatisfactory and seemingly unproductive conclusion of Book 1 results from factors that typically caused the *aporiai* of earlier dialogues. Socrates cannot develop positive, lasting arguments for the meaning and practical value of justice. What is required is a second-order *techne* of *arete*, which itself requires a theory of the political art operating in a good and just *politeia.* For such a theory not to be confounded by the problems that beset conventional conceptions of the other virtues and Socrates' incomplete critique of them; the links to ordinary beliefs, practices, customs, and laws must no longer count as sufficient criteria for evaluating the meaning or value of an ar-

---

73. For a useful discussion of the roots of Plato's argument in ordinary Greek understandings of "function," "virtue," and "soul," see Nettleship, *Lectures,* 42–43, 222–26.

gument. For Plato, the only possible theory of justice is a radical theory of justice in an ideal *politeia*.[74]

This problem produces a sense of paralysis or *aporia* in Glaucon and Adeimantus (358c, 368d), who proceed to impress further on Socrates the seriousness of Thrasymachus's challenge to the mutual implication of justice and happiness. Thrasymachus had argued that justice produces good only for another, not for oneself, and in so doing actually presented the views of most citizens (358a), but he did not offer the best defense. Glaucon articulates a metaphorical *ergon* of injustice (358e–362c), and Adeimantus presents a *logos* that justifies it (362d–367e).

Plato has them employ his own philosophical categories to comment on the unjust politics of the day. For each story emphasizes the distortion of "reality" through the manipulation of "appearances" by the unjust power of individuals and the inadequate *logoi* of justice provided by poets and religion. Thus do society's *erga* and *logoi* ultimately reward the greed of unlimited desire, which we know inevitably produces *stasis*. To respond to the challenge posed by Glaucon and Adeimantus, Socrates must articulate a constitution of justice. Because conventional practical contexts always seem to justify immoral or unjust behavior, Plato's Socrates must produce a *logos* of justice that indeed has practical value for the individual but whose value can be justified only without relying on the estimations of value that typically prevail in society. This is justice "in itself."

Such a notion of justice must be beneficial, but its benefits are atypical, for they must directly affect the power or capacity of one's soul (357c, 358b, 366e, 367b). To arrive at a notion of justice that both exemplifies virtue and promotes happiness, Socrates cannot simply provide an alternative *logos* for the value of justice as a *techne;* for the value of using such a *techne* is practically determined by the powers and politics of conventional society—powers and politics that themselves devalue justice.[75] He needs a *theory* of justice

74. See Rolf Sartorious, "Fallacy and Political Radicalism in Plato's *Republic*" (although I do not entirely agree with his specification of what Plato understands by "political"). Julia Annas does not take sufficient account of the political dimension of the problem of justice in the *Republic* and the way that it relates to Plato's conceptualization of its solution in order to emphasize its "moral" dimension—an insufficiency that she admits, in "Plato and Common Morality," esp. 449, n. 32.

75. Notably, it is for the sake of articulating the disjuncture between power and justice that Glaucon describes the origins of society on the social contract model. "Justice," in this context,

that *constitutes* the domain of practical value for the political art, for justice as a *techne* that enhances the capacity and power of one's soul. The *logos* of justice in the *Republic* would harmonize the good for oneself and the good for one's society.

Because the "proof" of the value of such a theory is the state of the *psyche*, this political theory is rooted in "psychology." At the same time, this psychology is constituted by the *polis*, critically understood. Plato's *logos* presupposes the need for an account of the good condition or order of one's self or soul, an account of happiness. Plato understands the structure of this order as a "constitution." Because the components of this constitutional order involve one's relationship to others as well as to oneself, and only justice guarantees the goodness of this order, an account of happiness requires a theory of the constitution of justice, understood in both "psychological" and "political" terms.[76]

The guarantees of Plato's solution come from the theory of the good as expressed in the harmonious "constitutions" of soul and state; this theory provides the structure that assures the goodness of political and personal deliberations about how to promote happiness. The *Republic* covers conceptual terrain that closely resembles that of earlier dialogues, where various kinds of human virtues were explored. Here, however, not just *a* virtue is explored but human virtue as a whole, and not only does Plato survey various kinds of arguments for the nature of practical value, as he did in the earlier dialogues, but the nature and value of *logos* itself.

That task cannot be proved by relying on the craft analogy alone, for its measures of success are either practical and insufficient, such as the good products of carpentry, or theoretical but disengaged from the context of social practices and evaluations of justice, as in the definitions of the meaning of craftsmanship and the functions and virtue of the soul (which Socrates used to silence Thrasymachus). It is misleading to suggest, however, that the new argument for the meaning of justice "abandons" the craft analogy altogether.

---

is a compromise of self-interest. It remains as such in liberal political philosophy. The loss in the value of "justice" is compensated for by the gain in the value of "freedom."

76. For a compatible view of the dynamic interrelation of soul and state in the *Republic*, which however places more emphasis on the psychological dimension, see Jonathan Lear, "Inside and Outside the *Republic*." For a more recent version of his views on the meaning of Plato's dialogues and their contemporary utility, see Jonathan Lear, *Open-Minded*.

That suggests that the notion of a *techne* becomes marginalized in Plato's theory of justice and that a sharp divide differentiates the philosophy of the so-called Socratic dialogues and the *Republic*. Insofar as *techne* is no longer employed as a standard of knowledgeable practice to disprove the arguments of interlocutors in subsequent books of the *Republic*, it is not because of *its* failures as a positive standard for Platonic theory; rather, it indicates the need for *supplementary* conditions and arguments to provide a genuine solution to Plato's Socratic Problem.

These appear when Socrates launches his analysis of justice that is good "in and of itself" for the soul by means of the "large letters" of a *polis* (368d–369a). He does so not because of any strict "analogy" between soul and state. Plato neither uses the word nor suggests that each requires an independent portrayal.[77] Later in the dialogue, he suggests that one may move back and forth between "psychological" and "political" contexts in order to grasp fully and clearly the meaning of justice (434d–435a).[78] He simply states that there would be "more justice" in the *polis*. That facilitates comparisons to the "idea" of justice in the soul and makes the entire investigation easier to comprehend (368d–369a). The narrative priority of the discussion of the *polis* to the discussion of the *psyche* reinforces my argument that the Platonic theory of justice involves a dialectical response to problems generated by a crisis in the ethics and politics of the Athenian *polis*, even as the Platonically just soul becomes the new practical ground for realizing Plato's solution to his Socratic Problem.

Plato's Socrates proceeds to describe the origins of the *polis*; in so doing, he narrates a story about justice. (It is the first of four in the *Republic*—the others being the allegory of the metals, the parable of the ship, and the myth of Er.) Here, as elsewhere in the Platonic dialogues, analysis proceeds genealogically, as an attempt to resolve problems that appear in practical or discursive time. The distinctive character of this story appears by comparing it

---

77. On the general use of "analogy" in ancient Greek thought, see G. E. R. Lloyd, *Polarity and Analogy*; for its philosophical significance in the *Republic*, see Richard Robinson, *Plato's Earlier Dialectic*, 204–18. For an exhaustive exploration of the analogy that emphasizes the instrumental role of the discussion of the *polis* for understanding the *psyche*, see Torseten J. Andersson, *Polis and Psyche—A Motif in Plato's Republic*.

78. This extraordinarily rich interplay of contexts for dialectical reflection is sterilized for analytic, liberal reasons in John Rawls's notion of reflective equilibrium, which involves the interplay of "theory" and "intuition." See *A Theory of Justice*.

with the mythic explanation provided by Protagoras in Plato's *Protagoras* for the presence in virtually all Athenian citizens of the political art. In order for the narrative in the *Republic* to facilitate a *logos* of justice, the *polis* must look radically different from the political community in which the ordinary Athenian citizen was understood to be virtuous and just. For against the background of Book I and Plato's Socratic Problem more generally, that community harbored injustice more than justice, *pleonexia* and *stasis* more than moderation and harmony.

To recall, in the Protagorean story mankind acquired skills from Prometheus that enabled it to provide for its basic material needs. As a way of both satisfying them and defending themselves against external threats, individuals and groups joined together to form a political community. But that community could not survive without its members acquiring the *politike techne*, in the form of "reverence and justice," from Zeus. Socrates' story in the *Republic* includes no divine interventions; the *polis* initially takes shape as a result of individuals realizing that each is not sufficient to provide for his own material needs. Providing for such individual satisfactions depends on collective cooperation, and a nascent city emerges as a network for the exchange of goods produced by the activity of individual farmers and craftsmen.[79] The health of the city amounts to each person's performing one *techne*,

---

79. The result is not so much an economic division of labor as a differentiated collection of skills, although the relation between the two is worth pondering. Plato's theoretical division of *technai* does not directly foreshadow the modern notion of division of labor. Other ancient Greeks, notably Xenophon, had conceptualized the origins of society in terms of the division of *technai*, and for both Plato and Xenophon the purpose of the cooperation that makes their division cohere is not, according to Austin and Vidal-Naquet, "an increase in production per se but . . . an improvement of the quality of the goods produced through greater specialization" (see their *Economic and Social History of Ancient Greece: An Introduction*, 15, 173, as well as Xenophon, *Cyropaedia* VIII.ii.5–6). Furthermore, Plato would not consider that merely the structured use of labor marked the possession of a *techne*. How much this contrasts to the modern understanding of the division appears by considering Adam Smith, who believed that the social expression of individuals' interests and needs in a division of labor, restrained only by the discipline of the market, constituted the foundation of a just society. Smith held that a force characteristic of human nature and inherent in the market system of economic exchange—self-interest—could provide the basic network for a just society. The productive activity of a "market economy" could generate the basic constitution for a harmonious society. Although the market provided the basic system of justice, a judicial system was necessary, government was needed to promote the general welfare in those marginal instances when the market could not, and the market was useless as an engine of basic public education. Still, insofar as Smith recognized a political art, it was understood as the art of the statesman, and his interference in determining the pursuit of individuals' needs in the economic system would typically harm the public good. See

his proper *ergon,* well (369d–370c). As the range of productive activities in the city becomes more complex, three new kinds of individuals become necessary for the "associations" of citizens: shopkeepers, merchants, and wage earners (371a–e). Their functions facilitate the exchange among citizens of goods produced in the *polis* and the exchange between citizens and foreigners of goods produced in the *polis* and those produced abroad. Plato has thus sanctioned a kind of economic reciprocity among citizens and between citizens and foreigners as a necessary condition of justice.[80] (Nothing in this economic state of affairs precludes its operation in a democratic political order— as long as most of its citizens do not assume major political responsibilities.) In what follows in the dialogue, however, even this society cannot maintain its peaceful "division of labor"—an indication that the character of justice is not essentially antidemocratic.

Socrates allows that the state they have described is, in a sense, fully grown and complete. But he wonders where justice and injustice can be found in it. Adeimantus states that "justice" could possibly be found in some need that the citizens have for one another. Socrates states that there is something to what Adeimantus has said. But Socrates proceeds to increase the material standard of living of the city, egged on by Glaucon, who refers to the now lavishly endowed city as "a city of pigs." Indeed, there seem to be no limits on the activities and goods that may satisfy the citizens' needs. Socrates refers to what he has been describing as a "true" and "healthy" city, adjectives that probably refer to the city's historicity and material well-being. Yet he goes on to enhance the material standard of living even further. Why? The "luxurious city" that Socrates has begun to describe may help them grasp the emergence of justice and injustice in *poleis* (372d–373a).

Plato's Socrates states that nothing hinders this new step in the discussion. Indeed, nothing in the healthy city would prevent the developments that Socrates subsequently describes. The "healthy city" was designed to satisfy material—not any particularly political, let alone democratic—needs. These can be met through the system of exchange; but nothing in the city was de-

---

his *The Wealth of Nations,* iv.ii.9–10, v.b.16, vi.c.88. For Plato, as we shall see, the forces of the market are notable for their inability to generate a system of justice.

80. See George Grote, *Plato and Other Companions of Socrates,* vol. iv, chap. 36, esp. 110–12. Grote goes on to argue that Plato contradicts himself when he later associates the institution of justice with the activity of a ruling class. Plato may be wrong in his sanctioning of philosophical authority, but that aspect of his theory is designed to supplement, not oppose, these practical foundations of justice.

signed to limit those needs. There was nothing to guide the uses of the city's productive activities. Socrates had wondered where justice and injustice could be found in such a city, and Adeimantus had replied that he could not conceive where, unless it was in some "need" that citizens had for one another. However, the only practical activities in that city devoted to the relationships between citizens were those of shopkeepers, merchants, and wage-laborers, all of whom benefit from the absence of limits on the material exchanges or associations among individuals. Thus in practice, as well as in Socrates' *logos,* there was nothing to stop this city from becoming inflamed, greedy, or imperialistic, and eventually stumbling into war (373e). Although Socrates has referred favorably to this city, its order is idyllic and unreal. Its harmony presupposes no threat of conflict, and the city lacks any mechanisms by which it could deal with problems that arose. There are no leaders in this city and no sense that citizens themselves are capable of protecting themselves and their community. It is useless for the argument Socrates needs to make for Glaucon and Adeimantus, which must relate to a conflict-filled environment where injustice appears more attractive than justice. In this sense, then, there was no meaningful justice in the healthy city, because there was no need for it, and there certainly is none in the luxurious city, which operates without limits. Without the practice of justice, Socrates' ideal-typical *polis* easily becomes faction-ridden and driven by greedy desire—just like Thrasymachus's unjust man, as inadequate to the task of self-preservation as the community of citizens in Protagoras's Great Speech, who possessed particular practical *technai* but as of yet had no *politike techne.*

The lack of the political art in Protagoras's Great Speech in the *Protagoras* prevented the political community from fending off wild beasts and led its members to act unjustly toward one another; the lack of justice in Socrates' city in the *Republic* leads to war with foreigners, for which it is unprepared.[81] To save either city, learning the art of warfare becomes necessary. But in both stories this art is subordinated to the political art. Notably, in neither city

---

81. Later in the dialogue, Plato's Socrates redefines "foreign" as that which is not Greek. He insists on the vigilant defense of the "Greek" *polis* against barbarians and so emphasizes the divide between "insider" and "outsider"—even as he encircles this divide around a larger community than was typically done in Plato's time. Contemporary critics of the politics of identity who defend the politics of difference often evade the question of whether some positive role for collective identity is not only necessary but desirable for human well-being and as a condition for overcoming widespread injustice. This limitation of their argument stems in part from their inability to define or conceive of contemporary political community in any other terms than the contemporary nation-state. Of course, this debility is not easy to overcome.

does this new art prevent war; rather, it prevents the civil strife that destroys political unity and sabotages any effort to defend oneself in war.[82]

Plato's Socrates in the *Republic,* like Plato's Protagoras in the *Protagoras,* identifies the need for a *techne* that differs from all other particular practical *technai* by virtue of its direct concern for the welfare and virtue of the city as a whole. But whereas the distinctiveness of this political art in the Protagorean city involved its possession and practice by virtually all citizens, in the city of the *Republic* the political art is lodged in the unique class of guardians, ultimately philosopher-guardians, whose *techne* exclusively concerns understanding justice and maintaining it in the *polis.* The practice of the political art in *kallipolis* thereby embodies the principle of "one man, one art" as a condition for the practical realization of justice as "doing one's own." But the need for this principle and practice arises in the dialogue from the *stasis* that results from *pleonexia*—a general social malady—rather than from uniquely democratic disorders.

The critical difficulties of the Protagorean political art involved how the whole citizenry could actually possess this specialized art and how it was critically distinguishable from the mere will of a potentially ignorant majority. The philosophical quandaries in the *Republic* about the *politeiai* of a just *polis* and *psyche* invariably concern two issues: (1) how to integrate the differences that result from the distinctive natures of every "one" in the *polis* so as to achieve not only unity but justice, and (2) how to make sure the new leaders are not tyrants.

Plato's philosophical project fundamentally concerns the rationality and ethics of leadership for both the political community and the self. Plato was certainly too hard on Athenian democracy and its ordinary citizens; their resources for dealing with their own conflicts were superior to those of any other *polis* or citizenry of the day. Moreover, the politically problematic character of Plato's ideal city has already become apparent, insofar as he lodges the sources of his solution entirely in a ruling class. Yet, insofar as questions about the ethics of leadership and political rule were not sufficiently answered by the actuality of Athenian history and that history evidenced harmful *stasis* of both an ethical and political kind, Plato's questions ought to be asked by partisans of democracy in general as well as by those of Athenian democracy in particular; they inevitably will be by democracy's opponents.

---

82. Hence, war is not politics by other means (Clausewitz); nor is politics war by other means (Foucault). For Plato, if politics is simply another manifestation of war or war a manifestation of politics, the *polis* is on the road to self-destruction or defeat.

In locating the origins of the war that comes to plague the once healthy city, Plato points to desires that lead individuals to produce and enjoy beyond their proper measure, desires that appear as natural outgrowths of the activities of the major portion of the Athenian citizenry (the craftsmen and farmers, 374a). Without virtuous souls to regulate their activities, they and their cities will not be just. Platonic justice would regulate their surplus of desire so as to maintain "for each, his own."

When Plato defines justice more precisely in the *polis* and *psyche,* it again appears as the activity by which the perpetual potential for conflict and disorder in each becomes harmonized in new constitutional orders. "Justice" neither eliminates differences among citizens nor stigmatizes the satisfaction of desire; rather, it accommodates the diversity of individual pursuits in a way that simultaneously prevents psychological or political *stasis* and promotes the happiness of each individual and the political community as a whole. The complementary "wholeness" of *psyche* and *polis,* soul and state, constitutes the condition for the elimination in each of *stasis,* and such "wholeness" *is* justice, in either the *psyche* or *polis.*

Socrates expects that difficulties will arise, however, in convincing the citizenry—including the first guardians—to accept the "one man, one art" stipulation, as well as his new tripartite class structure. In response, he invokes a "noble lie"—the myth of the metals—which posits simultaneously a common origin of all citizens and a justification of their social differentiation (414c–415c; see also 376efff, 382a–383b, 389b–d). It may be read as a political version of his "theory" of recollection in the *Meno.*

This story about citizens having been born from one earth-mother yet possessing different "metals" is, indeed, a "lie" (*pseudos*) not merely a fiction (actually, it is not entirely one or the other), but its consequences are not as pernicious as, at first, they might seem.[83] For the initial "natural" differentiation becomes validated only by the relative capacity of citizens to develop and display their inborn potential for virtue. (As a political myth that accommodates diversity and unity, it may be no more—indeed, perhaps less—insidious than the American "noble lie" of "equality of opportunity."[84] For its pur-

---

83. For evidence of the ambiguity, see 376eff, 382a–383b, 389b–d. Part of our difficulty in understanding what Plato is up to here is our belief in the existence of "facts." I am not sure that Plato had that belief; in any event, he certainly did not believe in that which is curiously denoted today as a "true fact."

84. For an excellent discussion of this issue, particularly in relation to (and against) Straussian interpretations of this myth—particularly that of Allan Bloom in *The Closing of the Ameri-*

pose is to assure the satisfaction of every citizen and the practical realization of his or her potential, whereas the American "dream" of "equal opportunity" assures an end-state of winners and losers to a competitive race whose fairness it uncritically sanctions.)

The definition of justice presented so far still remains incomplete. Although Plato's Socrates may have established the class structure of the *polis* and identified it as "good" (427e), the presence of virtue among these classes is not yet clear. There may be a new structure of *technai*, but we do not know how and why these *technai* will produce justice for the political community as a whole. Plato's Socrates states that they still need to find "where justice and injustice" reside in the city (427d). Hence, the discussion proceeds to focus on virtues in the *polis* (428d–434d) and *psyche* (435b–444a). Socrates trades on the belief in the necessary similarity of their individual parts, overall structure, and attitudes toward collective well-being (434d–435b, 462a–e). In the *polis,* the virtues function in the citizenry to ensure that its particular practical activities effectively constitute the political community as a whole, that productive work is put to "good use," and that the three "classes" work together, as well as separately, thereby assuring that each does its own in the fullest possible sense, avoiding the "meddlesomeness" that effects *stasis* and producing harmony and justice in the political community as a whole. The result integrates the externality and productivity of the practical activity of *technai* with the regulative, performative, but also more internal standards of *aretai.* In the individual, the right ordering of the soul's three elements reduces their potential to produce the harmfulness of *stasis* and produces an internal sense of togetherness and integrity (440b, 440e, 442d, 444a–b, 470d–e).

As Socrates says later in the *Republic,* the idea that one who is by nature a cobbler or carpenter ought to do nothing else if he is to do what is appropriate for himself turns out to have been an "image" (*eidolon*) of justice (443c; see also 423d, 432d–433a). For "justice"

> Does not lie in man's external actions, but in the way he acts within himself, really concerned with himself and his inner parts. He does not allow each part of himself to perform the work of another, or the sections of his soul to meddle with one another. He orders what are

---

can Mind—see Edward Andrew, "Equality of Opportunity as the Noble Lie." Andrew points out the potentially (albeit not necessarily) democratic message of this myth. To this extent, he confirms my argument about the radically democratic potential of certain aspects of the Platonic political art.

in the true sense of his word his own affairs well; he is master of himself, puts things in order, is his own friend, harmonizes the three parts like the limiting notes of a musical scale, the high, the low, and the middle, and any others there may be between. He binds them all together, and himself from a plurality becomes a unity. (444d–e, Grube translation)[85]

This image contrasts not only with the actuality of democratic Athens but with any society in which citizens individually or collectively lack *arete* and incompetently perform their *technai*.[86] It also sketches the basic practical di-

---

85. The next two sentences describe the character of this inner harmony and anticipate the discussion of the just man in Book IX (591c–592a), on which see Chapter 4, Section D, below.

86. It also interestingly contrasts with Marx's vision of the just society in *The German Ideology,* where the division of labor is not moralized but abolished:

> In communist society, where nobody has one exclusive sphere of activity, but each can become accomplished in any branch he wishes, society regulates the general production and thus makes it possible for me to do one thing today and another tomorrow: to hunt in the morning, rear cattle in the afternoon, criticize after dinner, just as I have a mind (*Lust*), without ever becoming hunter, fisherman, shepherd, or critic. (Karl Marx and Friedrich Engels, *Collected Works* [New York: International Publishers, 1975], 5:47)

Beyond the obvious issue between Plato and Marx—whether the proper division of labor and trades is a human ideal or the sign of human oppression—is another. Although Plato would approve of the deinstitutionalized character of Marx's ideal of "social regulation," he would be skeptical that human needs could be fully and properly satisfied, even if each gave to the community "according to his ability" and received from the community "according to his needs." To Plato, this could happen only if one's "mind" (*Lust*), which informs this "giving" and agrees to the "receiving," is also informed by another ability, the *arete* of justice performed as a *politike techne.* For Plato (as well as Socrates, Protagoras, and Pericles, for that matter), the political art does not emerge naturally from the performance of nonpolitical *technai,* no matter the social conditions in which they are exercised, and it is not a natural byproduct of allowing each person to develop his or her talents. It has its own unique identity, and it is essential for preserving a society as a justly constituted community. Thus the shoemaker in Marx's *Critique of Hegel's "Philosophy of Right"* would need this ability in order to be truly "representative" of the species, performing his "definite social activity" that "fulfills a social need." (See Karl Marx, *Critique of Hegel's "Philosophy of Right"* [Cambridge: Cambridge University Press, 1970], 119–20.) The proletariat, as described in *The German Ideology* (86–89), would need it more desperately, even with its correct historical position. Because its full revolutionary potential was secured by preventing its engagement in the political order of the day, all of its humanity and individuality, political or otherwise, had yet to be developed. For Plato, there is no possibility of transcending the necessary links among virtue, the political art, and justice. In this and other respects, I want to resist the Popperian association of Plato and Marx, despite my affection for each's complex understanding of social injustice.

mensions of Plato's radical reconstruction of the Athenian constitution so that it harmonizes virtue and the political art.

Plato now has Socrates discuss the cardinal virtues and their relation to his *politeia* in *logos*. There are four of them, each of which is present to some degree in every individual and the political community as a whole. The first two discussed—"wisdom" or "critical reason" and "courage"—belong primarily to the guardians, with "wisdom" only fully possessed and practiced by the philosophical guardians.[87] The second two—"moderation" and "justice"—are distributed throughout the body politic. Although the *kallipolis* is typically regarded as having a tripartite structure (and ought to be for analytical purposes), its political structure is binary, with the principal divide between rulers and ruled (442b; see also 444d).

"Wisdom" (which certainly includes what has been called here "critical reason") constitutes the ethic of leadership; it provides the intellectual guidance that coordinates the practical activities in the *polis* into a well-functioning "whole" (428b–429a). It is primarily possessed by those guardians who have the most fervent desire for wisdom and the good of the political community "as a whole" and who have the most highly developed capacity for deliberation (*to bouleutikon*).[88] Plato differentiates such guardians from the lower class of guardians—who now are regarded as administrators, defenders, or auxiliaries (*epikouroi*) who take orders from these more philosophical guardians. "Courage" enforces the determinations of critical reason (429a–430c).[89] Although the philosophical guardians certainly possess courage, they need the auxiliaries, who are particularly notable for their pos-

---

87. It is important to say "primarily" here, because not to do so suggests that the craftsmen and farmers lack "reason" entirely. That clearly is not the case. They are citizens who lead productive lives and are relied on to pay for and legitimate the political authority of the guardians. In this sense, they may be viewed as having about as much reason as the reason that Lockean individuals naturally receive from God and possess in the state of nature. What the farmers and craftsmen lack is the particular, highly developed form of reason called *phronesis*. And although these ordinary citizens may not be expected to possess and exercise the "courage" of the guardians, they, too, demonstrate that courage insofar as they remain loyal adherents to a just *polis*.

88. *Republic* 428a–429a, 439d. Plato interchanges *sophia* and *phronesis* as terms of art for this virtue. See, for instance, 433b.

89. This differentiation of the virtues of "wisdom" and "courage" contrasts with a portion of the *Protagoras*, where Socrates temporarily argues for their identity. Although many have used this difference as a fulcrum for differentiating "Socratic" from "Platonic" thought, it can just as readily—and less speculatively—be explained in terms of the presence in the *Republic* of a theory of justice that provides a justificatory framework for the proper practice of the political art.

session of this virtue as well as for the strength of the "spirited" part of their souls (*to thumoeides*).

The latter two virtues consolidate the political community. "Moderation" (*sophrosyne*) ensures agreement among the various components of the *polis* (430d–433a). It contributes to the harmony, beauty, and order of the whole, because it signifies the habit of knowing what is "one's own"; it thereby particularly reinforces the principle of "one man, one *techne*." Unlike "wisdom" and "courage," virtues of the ruling class, "moderation" is shared by the body politic, making possible concord (*homonoia*) between superior and inferior classes, the rulers and the ruled (432a).[90] One must keep in mind here that what is idealized is a harmony or agreement among different groups, not strict (let alone coerced) unanimity.

Precisely what motivates the lowest (or bronze) class in the ideal *polis* to act with moderation is not entirely clear, particularly because Plato does not grant this class much in the way of "reason" or "courage" to guide and restrain the most developed part of the souls of the bronze and the largest part of everyone's soul, the appetitive part (*to epithumetikon*), which does not naturally exhibit either. (See 431a–c, 439d, 440e–441a, 442a; indeed, *stasis* is the more "natural" condition.) To some extent, moderation comes from the "outside," from the ruling philosophers and their auxiliaries, but each citizen who is ruled has a portion of the wisdom and courage of the rulers. For Plato, the relationship of rulers to ruled is unequal but educative; he does not envision it as coercive or oppressive (although it certainly would become such if impostors assumed the offices of political leadership).[91] The "moderation" and deference of the lowest classes are made possible and justified by the (limited) reason, courage, and justice in their souls.[92]

90. This "moderate" or "temperate" community resembles the one praised in the *Charmides* (Chapter 3, Section B, above). However, in the *Charmides,* all was well ordered because each craftsman had perfect knowledge of his craft, and there was no evidence of either the political art or justice. In the *Republic,* the "moderation" in the ideal *polis* stems from each person's practicing the *techne* that is appropriate for him or her, but its sustenance requires the critical affirmation of justice by a distinct class of philosopher-guardians. Notably, the community in the *Charmides* could not be argumentatively sustained.

91. Indeed, that is why they are not "rulers" in the precise sense but "guardians" (414b). The change in language may seem Orwellian, but Plato is trying to make a conceptual point. Although Plato does not deny that rulers in less than ideal conditions have to use force, the first methods of choice would be persuasion and the rule of law. On Plato's opposition to the use of violence as a practical means of political change, see *Seventh Letter* 351c, and the *Statesman* 276e, 296a–297b. For more on these passages, see Chapter 5, Section A, below.

92. As Bernard Williams noted, this aspect of Plato's soul-state analogy lies behind the oppressive character of Platonic justice. See "The Analogy of City and Soul in Plato's *Republic,*" in

The last virtue is "justice." Its nature as a virtue is unique. On the one hand, it sits beside the other virtues, one among four; on the other, it coordinates the other three virtues in order to facilitate the constitution of justice "as a whole" more generally. (This explains how "justice" as a particular virtue can also be regarded as a "residue" in a comprehensive *logos* of justice; 433c; see also 427e–428a.) This Platonic justice builds on the notion of "one man, one *techne*," which Socrates refers to as an "adumbration," "type," and "original principle" of justice (443b–c). It also regulates the other three virtues in conjunction with the principle of "one man, one art" and "doing one's own" in a way that effects the critical authority of reason in making the polis "good" (433b–c). It is "[a] power that made it possible for [the other virtues] to grow up in the body politic and which when they have sprung up preserves them as long as it is present" (433b). Justice, therefore, has a dual character. It not only reflects the principle of "for each, his own" but also harmoniously regulates the perpetual potential for *stasis* that lies in each individual and among members of the political community, regulation that is necessary for the practical realization of this principle. Insofar as the communities produced in the *psyche* and *polis* require active, one might well say "political," effort in overcoming conflict and constituting them as wholes, justice functions as a quintessentially "political" art.

As an art, Platonic justice makes no sense unless agents can promote its realization, and in the *Republic* the primary agents are philosophers. The justificatory standard of justice is "the idea of the good" (which has not yet

---

E. N. Lee et al., eds., *Exegesis and Argument: Studies in Greek Philosophy Presented to Gregory Vlastos*, 196–206. Williams is certainly right, insofar as Plato naturalizes the unequal capacities of citizens to be fully just and prevents the principle of rotation in office from ever including members of the "working classes." But one should keep in mind that Plato finds no evidence of this natural hierarchy in the extant *poleis* and that the lowest class of citizens in the ideal state possesses a rational capacity—albeit not equal to that of the philosopher-guardians—to understand justice. (See *Republic* 518b–c; *Phaedrus* 249b.) Moreover, Plato would have Socrates' *logos* of justice respond to Adeimantus's ideal that each person become his own guardian (367a). Plato is hypothesizing an ideal of agreement between rulers and ruled (a relationship that only anarchies completely lack), where the initiatives of the rulers are especially informed by reason and ethics. Therefore, rational agreement between rulers and ruled—that is, mutual understanding that reflects the consent of the parties—in Plato's just city is possible—at least to the extent that we can say that such agreement exists today between legislators (whom no one would mistake for philosopher-guardians) and voters who invest them with power and legitimacy. The gap between rulers and ruled in *kallipolis* diminishes in the *Statesman* and *Laws*, but this does not necessarily represent a significant departure in Plato's thinking about justice. See Chapter 5, below. On the significance of this gap for the relation of Platonic justice to democracy, see Chapter 4, Section C, below.

been explained). Only by possessing the *dynamis* and practicing the *techne* of dialectic, a practice of philosophers, can this idea be grasped. This complementarity of *logos* and *ergon* justifies philosophical activity as an appropriate and just response to *stasis* in *psyche* and *polis;* it harmonizes differences without eliminating them (443d–e).[93] With Socrates' specification of the political authority of philosophical guardians in an ideal city, he has completed the *logos* of justice as a virtue (443b–444e).

Plato has thus identified the political art as an art of critical leadership possessed and practiced by philosophers who rule over the general citizenry. The practice of politics as the continuing constitution of the political community as a whole has been redefined and divided into active and passive dimensions, with the leadership class practicing its active, directive character and a class of ordinary citizens limited to the relatively passive activity of paying for and consenting to the practical authority of the leadership class.

To be sure, this alteration of the distribution of virtue and political art is, relative to the "Protagorean" and conventional Athenian distribution, antidemocratic, for it categorically reduces the political authority of ordinary citizens. One must keep in mind, though, that what Plato is doing is providing critical and ethical standards of leadership that did not appear in the Protagorean myth or in the Athens he knew. Indeed, insofar as the Platonic authorization of leadership responded to *stasis,* it may be usefully compared to either the Lockean justification of a parliamentary state as a response to the breakdown of the state of nature into a state of war, a justification that is currently readily accepted as a justification of contemporary "democracy," or to the American Federalists' justification of the transfer of political authority from the states to a national capital in order to institute a new Constitution. The major difference between Plato's "solution" and these liberal solutions is that the latter presuppose that justice will result from institutional procedures, whereas Plato (like Rousseau) would identify the ethical utility of these procedures as injustices that have been legitimated by conventions.

---

93. The tendency to associate harmonizing tendencies with repressive ones is not Platonic; rather, it attends to the construction of theories of "identity," the origins of which are post-Platonic. This harmful tendency does not indicate how Plato or Aristotle used the words *harmonia* or *xumphonia* to characterize either music or politics. For a fascinating essay on ancient ideas of "the harmony of the spheres" (which happens to support my view), see Bonnie MacLachlan, "The Harmony of the Spheres: *Dulcis Sonus,*" in *Harmonia Mundi—Musica e filosofia nell'antichita/Music and Philosophy in the Ancient World,* ed. Robert W. Wallace and Bonnie MacLachlan, 7–19.

3. THE AGENCY OF JUSTICE

For Plato's Socrates in the *Republic,* a theory of justice that harmonizes *technai* and *aretai* depends on a notion of critical reason that is not reducible to the practical judgments of either the subjectivity of individuals or the objectivity of a state. In the ideal city of Plato's *Republic,* this reason can be authoritatively practiced only by a special class of citizens. This is the class of philosopher-guardians, made up of women as much as men, who do not function as members of "nuclear" families but as a group responsible for the harmonization of the *polis* with the *psyche* of every one of its members.

Platonic justice does not immediately privilege any particular group of individuals, certainly no traditionally constituted one, as the sovereign authorities for determining the practical nature of justice. Indeed, the principal significance of Plato's notion of "justice" as a "form" prevents its subordination to either the will of a group or the dictates of an ideological program of practical change.[94] As a result, Plato's exaltation of the authority of philosophy does not immediately signify aristocratic ideology (let alone fascism). And in fact, the economic structure of *kallipolis* in the *Republic* tolerates much less economic inequality—and certainly less antagonism—between "rich" and "poor" than was the case in democratic Athens. Plato's Socrates regards extreme differences in wealth among the citizenry as one of the principal causes of *stasis* (421d–422a).[95] Nevertheless, assigning a politically authoritative role to philosophers is surely disturbing, and Plato's Socrates recognizes that this proposal will arouse more intense scorn and disbelief than any other dimension of his theory of justice—more than the equality of men and women, the deconstruction of monogamy, or the collective rearing of children among the guardians. The disdain of Callicles in the *Gorgias* and

---

94. In this light, it is worth recalling that the word "ideology"—although a composite of two Greek words, *eidos* and *logos,* is an invention of the politics of the historical period that followed on the French Revolution. The two best recent discussions of ideology wisely avoid referring to Plato. See Raymond Geuss, *The Idea of a Critical Theory,* and Terry Eagleton, *Ideology.*

95. This suggests that a Platonic political program today could well befriend those on the left, rather than the right, side of the political spectrum. See Chapter 6, below. For a thorough discussion of Plato's attitude toward "the social question" of economic inequality in ancient Greece, in both the *Republic* and the *Laws* (dialogues that he takes to be complementary), see Alexander Fuks, *Social Conflict in Ancient Greece,* 80–171. As for the economic differences among citizens of *kallipolis,* they may be understood in terms of the general principles Rousseau laid down in *The Social Contract* (in particular, see Bk. I, chap. 9, note, and Bk. II, chap. 11, note).

Thrasymachus in the *Republic* (as well as Meletus in both Plato's *Apology* and, probably, historical actuality) for the political practicality of philosophy shows Plato's awareness of the widespread and thoroughgoing ridicule such an assertion faces.[96] Even partisans of the historical Socrates might well find the suggestion bizarre, because their hero pointedly stayed away from the major official political arenas, one of which ultimately authorized his execution, and never questioned the legitimacy of Athenian laws.

In Plato's *Republic,* Socrates refers to his assertion of the complementarity of philosophy and political power as an idea that contradicts ordinary belief and may be viewed as a "paradox" (473c, 473e). By no means, however, is the paradox unparalleled. The institution of philosophical guardianship simply constitutes one of the three "waves" of paradox, all of which need special attention in order to justify the "possibility" of Platonic justice and to convince Polemarchus, Adeimantus, Glaucon, and Thrasymachus (449b–450a; see also 456c, 458b) of its intrinsic value. And yet its explanation elicits the most radical discussion in the dialogue about the relation of critical discourse to the power of practice, of *logos* to *ergon* (471c–473b).

Relative to the other "waves," the argument for philosophical guardianship as the primary agency of justice also produces the most anxiety for democrats—more than his arguments for the equality of women and men as potentially virtuous human beings or for the abolition of the nuclear family among the guardians. To be sure, his argument for equality between male and female guardians, on the basis that sexual difference is insignificant when it comes to practicing the art and achieving the virtue of philosophical guardianship (451c–457b), is not as thoroughgoing as it might be. It does, however, justify a radical equalization of the extant sexual relationships in the Athenian democracy. To this extent, it should give no serious pause to democrats. His argument against the "nuclear" family (457c–461e), because of its being an

---

96. Time has not diminished the prevalence or intensity of such disdain. Among the *Republic*'s readers, the political role of the philosophers in Socrates' ideal city has been the lightning rod for criticism of the Platonic project in general and the Platonic political art in particular—especially when Communist and Nazi political parties referred to themselves as apostles of political reason while instituting totalitarian states and various philosophical parties asserted the authority of scientific logic, noetic reasoning, or linguistic analysis as the primary basis for rationally evaluating human affairs. But the frequently heard disdain for philosopher-guardians often comes from those who pay little or no attention to the precise characterization of their function. Given Plato's apparent awareness of many of the arguments that have subsequently been lodged against the cogency of philosophical-guardianship, the nature of its identity deserves careful consideration before issuing yet another judgment of it.

agent of *stasis* (459e) and an impediment to political community, is also not per se antidemocratic.[97] The most direct challenge to the Athenian democratic ethic derives from his authorization of philosophers as political rulers.

Like every other idea Socrates promotes in the *Republic*, the idea of philosopher-guardians responds to a need, which itself needs definition. So far in the *Republic*, Plato's Socrates has cited the need for justice as a response to *stasis* and a condition for the establishment of political community and psychic harmony (most recently, 470d–471a). He notes here that the coalescence of philosophy and political power is simply the "smallest" change in the conduct of society that would generate justice (473b). In this respect, philosophical guardians are means, albeit "constitutive means," to the achievement of justice.[98] He has not yet explained in detail, however, why philosophers must be its agents. He proceeds to do so in three stages.

First, he characterizes the "nature" of philosophical guardians, attempt-

---

97. Of course, on another level, both of these are profoundly inegalitarian, antidemocratic, and misogynist, insofar as they regard childbearing and sexual equality more generally as merely instrumental to and not constitutive of the promotion of justice. But nuclear families may or may not be assets to democracy. All depends on the relationships among members of such families and between such families and the larger society—that is what being "for" or "against" the nuclear family practically entails.

Plato's arguments on women and the family notably produced considerable qualms among Straussians. See Allan Bloom's argument that Plato's argument for sexual equality is comedic, in "Interpretive Essay," in *Plato's Republic*, trans., with an interpretive essay, by Allan Bloom. More recently, see Arlene Saxonhouse, "The Philosopher and the Female in the Political Thought of Plato," who gives the Straussian argument a feminist twist.

The literature on this argument in Plato's *Republic*, and Plato's attitude toward women in general, has become vast in the wake of the feminist movement. Those who believe that Plato's argument for sexual equality within the guardian class is radically limited as an argument for the basic equality of women and men take it to be either an instrumental argument about the means for achieving community or inextricably linked to Plato's unproblematic inscriptions of conventional, derogatory views of women in the *Republic* and other dialogues (particularly the *Laws*). The former critics tend to be utilitarians who see Plato as one of them, for example, Julia Annas, "Plato's *Republic* and Feminism." The latter are generally suspicious of critical reason as a gender-neutral category. See Mary Lefkowitz, "Only the Best Girls Get to," 484, 497. More sympathetic views of Plato's argument, which find him breaking important critical ground in the effort to justify and achieve equality between the sexes, include Susan M. Okin, "Philosopher Queens and Private Wives: Plato on Women and the Family," and Gregory Vlastos, "Was Plato a Feminist?" 276, 288–89. An interesting collection of articles about Plato on women (including those by Saxonhouse and the exchange between Vlastos and Lefkowitz), along with a good bibliography of discussions of this issue, may be found in Nancy Tuana, ed., *Feminist Interpretations of Plato*.

98. On the difference between means that are constitutive in contrast to means that are merely instrumental, see John Cooper, *Reason and Human Good*.

ing to show how and why the conventionally separated natures of philosophers and politicians could be combined in the nature of one person and one *techne* (485a). Doing so is crucial for any response to Thrasymachus, who believed that a philosophical understanding of justice makes one suffer from the exercise of political power. In accord with previous discussions of "nature" by Socrates in the *Republic,* the "nature" of philosophical guardians accords with the "idea" of philosophical guardianship.[99] Philosophers are to "imitate" the "pattern" (*paradeigma*) of the "ideas" of beauty, justice, and goodness that they have imagined in critical discourse (484c–d, 500b–c).[100]

Such imitation involves the practice of a *techne,* insofar as *technai* produce the harmony and orderliness evidenced by these ideas.[101] Because the idea of philosopher-guardianship would achieve justice in the political community, the "nature" of philosopher-guardian constitutes an array of features that make possible that achievement. Philosophical guardians attach themselves to the good of "the whole" (474c–d, 486a)—to that which is essential and eternal rather than particular and temporary (486b)—so as to love "wis-

99. Which is why Plato is much less easily used to invoke "nature" as a limit on political reform than, say, Aristotle. Although Aristotle's notion of "nature" indeed conforms to an "idea," that idea is rooted in "convention" in ways that Plato cannot countenance. See my "Contemporary Aristotelianism." Straussians, who interpret Plato as if he anticipated Aristotle, like to see "nature" as a limit on political reform and so interpret each of Plato's most radical reforms (for the Athenians)—the equality of male and female guardians, the abolition of the nuclear family for the guardians, and the coalescence of philosophy and political power—as "against nature." Thus, Plato provokes them only to demonstrate their foolishness.

100. No traces of an Aristotelian conception of nature appear here, where "nature" has to be hypothesized rather than discovered. For Platonic "ideas" as *paradeigmata* and *paradeigmata* as "patterns" rather than "exemplars," see William J. Prior, *The Unity and Development of Plato's Metaphysics,* 17–20.

101. For the practice of a *techne* exhibiting these qualities, see Plato's *Gorgias* 503a–504a, 506d–e, and *Laws* 903e, in addition to the *Republic* 401a. Of course, Plato honored the formal qualities of the practice of a *techne* rather than the actual individuals who typically performed them in Athens. This isolation of the *logos* and *ergon* of *technai* reflects both Plato's critical philosophy and his aristocratic disdain for the work of ordinary craftsmen, a view that was prevalent in democratic Athens, even though its political constitution gave craftsmen more power and authority than they had anywhere else in the ancient world. Neal Wood and Ellen Wood rightly note that Plato has in some ways expropriated a practice—the practice of a *techne*—that was politically connected to a democratic form of life for antidemocratic purposes. Unfortunately, they pay insufficient attention to the way in which this expropriation was also integrally connected to a kind of critical, political reason that is also necessary for the sustenance of democratic life.

Other interpreters deny the character of philosophical-guardianship as a *techne* and so do not view the "nature" of philosophical-guardians as conforming to the traits of a *techne.* Their denial stems from either a reduction of the many dimensions of *techne* in Plato's thought (Irwin) or a resistance to Plato's insistence on an ideal, political connection between *logos* and *ergon* (Gadamer).

dom," "truth," and the pleasures of the soul in preference to those of the body (485c–e). They have good memories, are quick to learn, do not lust after wealth, exhibit moderation and courage (490b–d, 491b), and combine temperaments that often seem contradictory, such as quickness and gentility, activism and orderliness, as well as those of conventional soldiers and (some, rare) philosophers (485e–487a, 491b, 503c–e, 525b). Their education would cultivate these characteristics.

Still, Plato's Socrates has not yet convinced Thrasymachus; one might say that he has not yet fully responded to the Thrasymachean critique. A second stage of exposition is required. Here, Plato's Socrates does not simply affirm propositional elements of the character of philosopher-guardians; instead, he invokes an "image" (*eikona*)—that of the ship of state—to counter the prejudice against joining philosophy and political authority (487c). It is the first in a series of "images" (the sun, line, and cave come later) that Socrates employs as tools for explaining this conjunction.

The need for this "image" is understandable. He has identified the most productive and useful members of the *polis* as those whose *techne* has been considered to be the least productive and most useless in generating happiness or justice for the individual or the state. The "image" represents the philosopher as a navigator ignored by a gullible ship-owner and despised by greedy and incompetent sailors who would guide a ship in an unruly sea. Socrates follows this with an explanation of the causes of the philosopher's "bad image." He says that it should be useful for teaching those who are surprised that philosophers are not honored and persuading them that it would be more surprising if they were (489a). This "image" is often cited as evidence of the incoherence, as well as the antipolitical and antidemocratic character, of the Platonic political art.

Because of the importance of this "image" or parable, a word-picture that would imitate truth and goodness (488a), I here reproduce it in its entirety. Socrates begins:

> "Conceive this sort of thing happening either on many ships or on one: Picture a shipmaster in height and strength surpassing all others on the ship, but who is slightly deaf and of similarly impaired vision, and whose knowledge of navigation is on a par with his sight and bearing. Conceive the sailors to be wrangling (*stasiazontas*) with one another for control of the helm, each claiming that he deserves to steer though he has never learned the art (*technen*) and cannot point out his teacher or any time when he studied it. And what is more,

they affirm that it cannot be taught at all, but they are ready to make mincemeat of anyone who says that it can be taught, and meanwhile they are always clustered about the shipmaster importuning him and sticking at nothing to induce him to turn over the helm to them. And sometimes, if they fail and others get his ear, they put the others to death or cast them out from the ship, and then, after binding and stupefying the worthy shipmaster with mandragora or intoxication or otherwise, they take command (*archein*) of the ship, consume its stores, and, drinking and feasting, make such a voyage of it as is to be expected from such, and as if that were not enough, they praise and celebrate as a navigator, a pilot, a master of shipcraft the man who is most cunning to lend a hand in forcing or persuading the shipmaster to let them, while the man who lacks this [art] they censure as useless. They have no suspicion that the true pilot must give his attention to the time of the year, the seasons, the sky, the winds, the stars, and all that pertains to his art (*techne*) if he is to be a true ruler of a ship, and that he does not believe that there is any [art or science] of seizing the helm with or without the consent of others, or any possibility of mastering this alleged art and the practice of it at the same time with the science of navigation. With such goings-on aboard ship, do you not think that the true pilot would in very deed be called a star-gazer, an idle babbler, a useless fellow, by the sailors in ships managed after this fashion?" "Quite so," said Adeimantus. "You can learn from what I have said, I presume, and do not need to see the parable (*eikona*) explicated, showing that what we have described resembles the relation of the *polis* to the true philosophers." "It is indeed," he said. . . . "But you will make no mistake in likening our present political rulers to the sort of sailors we were just describing, and those whom these call useless and star-gazers to be the true pilots." (488a–489a, 489c)

The chief elements of the image Plato's Socrates emphasizes are that (1) it "proves" why philosophy is currently viewed by the many as useless, and (2) it demonstrates how dreadful a situation this is, because the depicted situation of ship-master, sailors, and pilot is tantamount to sick patients seeking help for their maladies not from knowledgeable physicians but from self-interested quacks. For the image to be coherent, one must agree with Plato's Socrates that contemporary politics is as desperate as he describes, and that there is a political equivalent of the art of navigation that could save Athenians from probable disaster. Socrates does not justify his characterization of the ship-owner, sailors, and navigator as an accurate representation of contemporary Athenians or a specifically democratic society (although both are probably implied), except insofar as the *stasis* on the ship indicates or reflects the *stasis* of Athenian political life. Yet the most important referent for the story Plato's Socrates presents of the plight of the philosopher in contemporary Athenian society may be the fate of the historical Socrates.

Plato has tried to persuade his readers and Socrates' interlocutors that an art of politics exists that is not a function of pursuing power and yet can promote the well-being of individuals and their community. It is the art of philosophical guardianship, a practical projection on the level of *logos* of the art of political theory. In other words, one cannot dismiss the imagery by asserting that "politics is not like navigation or medicine" (not as specialized, not as determinate in its knowledge of what is the good practice of these arts) without dismissing the cogency of Plato's enterprise, in the *Republic* and other dialogues, of trying to identify a critically justifiable art of virtue that genuinely promotes justice and happiness or the possibility and practicality of ethical political thought. (Yet this has been done in the prevailing interpretation of the political significance of this passage.[102])

---

102. See Renford Bambrough's "Plato's Political Analogies," most readily available in *Plato: A Collection of Critical Essays*, ed. Gregory Vlastos, 2:187–205, first published in Peter Laslett's collection of essays (which began with Laslett's eulogizing the death of political theory), *Philosophy, Politics, and Society*, and his article, "Plato's Modern Friends and Enemies," first published in *Philosophy*, and later in R. Bambrough, ed., *Plato, Popper, and Politics.*

Unlike Irwin, *Plato's Moral Theory*, Bambrough believed that Plato conceived of moral and political knowledge as a craft or *techne*. To Bambrough, who (like Irwin) views any Platonic *techne* as a technique, the problem is "logical." A "political art" for Bambrough is a "prescriptive art," and there can be no such thing as a prescriptive art, "for the inescapable logical reason that anything which can be properly called a *techne* will be by its very nature instrumental, and the decision about the purpose for which it is used will lie outside its own scope." (See "Plato's Political Analogies," 201–2, and "Plato's Modern Friends and Enemies," 106.) Plato's "error" stems from his ignorance of the "logical" (and notably Popperian) distinction between facts and values. It is a problem of "overassimilating questions about ends to questions about means, of demanding that there should be neutral and definitive answers to deliberative questions as well as to questions of logic and questions of fact" ("Plato's Political Analogies," 202).

This mistaken reduction of *techne,* and the idea of a political art more generally, to a technique constitutes Bambrough's interpretation of the quoted Platonic parable of the ship of state. In his interpretation of it, Bambrough says that Plato fails to distinguish "between knowledge and skill or [obviously following Ryle] between knowing that and knowing how," or "the science of theory and ability to apply the science in practice" ("Plato's Political Analogies, 194). But, again, the failure is Bambrough's. First, we know that, as a *techne,* the art of the philosopher-guardian is ideally one of "theory" *and* "practice." It involves knowledge *and* an ability to make

The second stage of the justification of philosophers as rulers involves Socrates glossing this image in order to explain why philosophy is useless to the many (489e–503b). Notably he does not lay the principal blame for this state of affairs on the "nature" of the many. (Because many of his arguments are crucial to understanding the relation of Platonic justice to democracy, we postpone much of the consideration of this stage of justification to the next section of this chapter.) At the same time, as Socrates describes the condition of the true philosopher in contemporary society, a man hampered and threatened by a hostile environment who nevertheless could improve it if given the chance, he manages to make a friend of Thrasymachus (496b–498d). To the satisfaction of Thrasymachus, he has explained the discord between genuine philosophy and contemporary politics while maintaining both the ultimate tension and complementarity of the two. The tension comes from the experience of radical constraints on the freedom and authority of critical thought that stem from the practice of politics, whereas the complementarity results from the claim that without the conjunction of philosophy and politics neither the philosopher nor society will completely flourish (499b–d, 500d).

In the third stage of Socrates' validation of philosophical guardians as agents of justice, he justifies the rational and ethical authority of philosophical guardianship as a *techne,* namely its capacity to grasp and interpret the idea of the good. It is this capacity that makes possible the beautification of society, which Socrates describes as the *techne* of imitating a divine "pattern"

---

use of this knowledge practically, which reflects attributes common to *all* Greek *technai.* Second, Bambrough's conceptual lenses lead him to change the content of Plato's parable to fit his interpretation. He understands the art of navigation, the equivalent of the "political art" in the parable, to be about obtaining the most efficient means to a given end. He compares the navigator—Plato's philosopher who ought to lead the state—to "a navigator who is not content to accept the fares of his passengers or the fee of his master, and then to conduct them where they might wish to go, but who insists on going beyond his professional scope by prescribing the course by which the route can best be travelled and the destination most suitably reached" ("Plato's Political Analogies," 195). But the ship of the parable has no "passengers." The boat is not "for hire," as it would be in today's market economy. But reading the parable this way legitimates Bambrough's view of *techne* as technique and his criticism of Plato for treating the "technical" art of navigation (about scientifically validated facts) as if it were a "prescriptive art" (about indeterminate, deliberative values). When Plato employs the art of navigation in other dialogues to illuminate the nature of the political art, he describes the art as a practice performed for the good of everyone on the ship, providing safety and well-being for those on board. And in these other dialogic contexts, this art "of the whole" clearly is to provide not only life but the good life. (See *Statesman* 296e–297a, and *Laws* 945c, 961d–e, along with Chapter 5, below.) The antidemocratic (in contrast to the antipolitical) aspects of the parable, as interpreted by Bambrough and myself, are addressed in Section C of this chapter, below.

(*paradeigma*) with paint that mixes ideals with the practical pursuits of social life to create a constitutional scheme of the best possible human characters (501a–c; see also 529d–530a).

In articulating the notion of the good, Socrates, as he did in explaining the disrepute of philosophers, invokes images in order to explain it. They are the images of the sun, line, and cave (508a–521b).[103] Each serves to invert the perceptual ordering of phenomena that had isolated genuine philosophy and political power. In this respect, they, like the parable of the ship of state, perform an educational function in relating Platonic *logos* to the experiences of his readers and Socrates' interlocutors. We discuss that function more directly in the final section of this chapter. Insofar as they characterize the activity of philosophical guardians as agents of justice, their significance consists primarily in their contribution to understanding the basis for that activity as a *techne,* namely the idea of the good.

Each image helps to explain particular dimensions of that idea: The "sun" illuminates the character of the idea of the good as the foundation of justice. The "line" illustrates dialectic as the ultimate activity that must be practiced before the good can be grasped. The "cave" emphasizes the unique educational difficulties of philosophical guardianship, namely the tension its practitioners experience in combining the conventionally separated arts of philosophy and politics, the tension between the freedom of practicing dialectic and the compulsion of service to the political community that follows. These may not be explanations, but they certainly frame our understanding of Plato's full response to Thrasymachus. (And little in the *Republic* reduces without loss to propositional forms.)

Plato's Socrates introduces his exposition of the good with considerable trepidation. It serves as the subject of the greatest, most difficult studies necessary for the complete acquisition of the skill of philosophical guardianship and the perfection of the constitution of justice its practitioners would secure (506a–b). It is "something greater than justice and the other virtues," which have been only schematically defined; it is the perfect "measure [of such things] ... by reference to which just things and all the rest become useful and beneficial" (504a–505a).

---

103. There have been hundreds of scholarly discussions of these Platonic images. For fair-minded, nontechnical accounts, see Guthrie, *A History of Greek Philosophy,* 4:506–17, and Julia Annas, *Introduction to Plato's Republic,* chap 10, especially 242–58. For a listing of literature on the subject until the late 1960s, along with an idiosyncratic discussion, see the introduction by D. A. Rees to James Adam, ed., *The Republic of Plato,* 1:xxxi–xliii.

Moreover, the many hold that "pleasure" is the measure of all things, a virtual equivalent of "the good," whereas their opponents who value critical reason (*phronesis*) become vague in defining the good as *its* ultimate object. More than "justice" and the other virtues, the "good" requires precise critical justification (505b–d). Yet Socrates refuses to describe exactly what the good is; instead he chooses to describe its offspring in the form of an "image," defining it formally only in terms of previously mentioned justifications of the importance of single "ideas" and "notions of being" as preconditions for the knowledge of the multiplicity and diversity of experience (506d–507b). Plato does not provide here any explanation, justification, or "foundation" of "Platonism"—just as he never presents the forms as part of a "theory."

The best "image" of the good is the sun, which Socrates describes as "the author and cause" of light. It links the power of sight and visibility, making "our vision see best and visible things to be seen" (507e–508a, 509b). It is "analogous" to the good, for "as the good is in the intelligible region to reason (*nous*) and the objects of reason, so is this in the visible world to vision and the objects of vision" (508b–c). But it is the good, not the sun, from which knowledge and truth derive their "being" and the knower derives his or her power to know the truth—even as the capacity of "the good" transcends being (which is not to say that "the good" is ontologically independent or transcendent). The good remains "finer" than the sun to the extent that it cannot be "seen" (508e–509b). In this regard, it primarily expresses Plato's belief in the need for a *logos* beyond power as a condition of power becoming just.

The most distinctive character of the good in relation to justice appears in its indirect characterization as the sun. For in the realm of the visible, there is no *techne* for seeing the sun. Any systematic concentration on its appearance produces blindness. Knowing the good has similar properties, in that there is no *techne* that directly apprehends its nature. One must be satisfied with a *techne* of comprehending its offspring. Thus although Plato's Socrates asserts the importance of the good transcending justice, that "transcendental" foundation can never be systematically occupied. In the *Republic*, Plato's "foundation" of the good offers philosophical guardians no place to rest.[104] In this respect, it is unclear how a metaphysics of the good is relevant for un-

---

104. Of course, he may have provided such a foundation elsewhere, for example, in his "Lecture on the Good" that reputedly concerned higher mathematics; however, I find such speculations unproductive. The most prominent school of thought for these speculations has been led by H.-J. Kramer. See his "Die grundsatzlichen Fragen der Indirekten Platonüberlieferung."

derstanding Platonic justice.[105] For there can be no "proof" of the good in theoretical, "invisible" discourse, even as there also can be none in the realm of practical, "visible" action.

The closest approximation of a *techne* of the good is provided by the *techne* of dialectic. Plato facilitates its exposition by invoking the "image" of the line. Introduced as a further aid to the exposition of the good, the "image" of the line offers an epistemological complement to its ontological representation as the sun (509d–511e). Its major division separates the realms of the "intelligible" and "visible." "Images" make up the substance of the visible realm (and one such image is the line itself); the visible realm includes actual entities, such as animals and plants, as well as their reflections (*phantasmata*) in water and other surfaces. The intelligible realm includes both the practice of hypothetical understanding that works down from assumed first principles (*archai*), such as geometry, and the power (*dynamis*) of dialectic, which begins from such assumptions and uses only "ideas," not "images," to transcend them and grasp the ultimate first principle, namely the "idea" or "form" of the good (510e–511e; see also 507b, 532a–b, 534b). Only dialectic systematically provides a "way" (*methodos*) that makes possible the determination of ideas, "what each thing is in itself" (533b). It produces liberation from the shackles of the realm of the visible, enabling one to see the "phantasms of god" and "the shadows of being" through its grasp of the good (532a–c).

The power (*dynamis*) of dialectic constitutes an "art," but it is unlike all other arts. Like the others, it can be learned and productively used. But unlike "the visible arts," its focus is neither opinions and desires nor generation and decay. Its practice propels one past phenomenal limitations, past the orderly composition provided by the arts of music and gymnastics that philosopher-guardians had learned earlier, past the "assumptions" (*hupothesei*) of lower-level "arts of the invisible" such as geometry. It enables one to give a precise account of the reality or being of each thing, in virtue of its apprehension of the good. This "art of dialectic" enables philosophical guardians "to ask and answer questions in the most scientific manner" and serves as the "coping stone" of their studies (533a–534e). Without it, they cannot be agents of justice capable of constituting a political community as a whole. Indeed, the *techne* of dialectic is the ultimate intellectual achievement of philosopher-guardianship as an "art of the whole." The "whole" exemplified

---

105. A useful, recent discussion of the strictly philosophical dimension of this issue in Plato is Ronald Polansky, "Foundationalism in Plato?" in Tom Rockmore and Beth J. Singer, eds., *Antifoundationalism Old and New*, 41–55.

by the good is constituted by the art of dialectic, whose practice constitutes "wholes" from parts. Dialecticians "gather the studies which they disconnectedly pursued as children in their former education into a comprehensive survey of their affinities with one another and with the nature of things" (537c). Such an art ultimately aims at the good because of the links between Plato's views about knowledge, nature, and the ethics of states and souls and his theory of justice.

As a "method," dialectic is intrinsically valuable and beneficial; its principles are not separable from its practice. As a result, the art of dialectic cannot be reduced to a technical activity bound by objective rules.[106] Moreover, the rule-free character of dialectic is complemented by the ideas or forms that constitute its object of concern. The "patterns" of the forms provide no blueprint and immediately constitute no identifiable structure. Relative to the activities of individuals practicing the art of dialectic, the forms may be objective, but their principal features are understandable only by a person who is "good at" this art.

Like the critical standards of the art of dialectic, the meaning of "the good" itself is not reducible to rules. Although the standards operate as critical ideals, they are goals that can never be fully realized in the practices of thought or action—even though they guide every kind of practice that fosters goodness.[107] A form, and particularly the form or idea of the good, stands as a constant goal of the dialectical philosopher and goad of the philosophical statesman. In this sense, belief in the forms more nearly requires an act of faith than a passive reliance on foundations. For some, this silence intimates Plato's ultimate religiosity, if not mysticism. But although it might suggest that belief in Platonic justice requires faith, that method offers no place in which such faith might find refuge. (Surely, this is one of the main reasons for the inability of Plato's work to generate large political or religious followings—without major supplements.)

It is essential to understand how, then, the art of dialectic provides norms for the proper political rule of the philosopher-guardians. The key is appre-

---

106. As Richard Robinson said, in contrasting dialectic with Cartesian method, "Plato's belief that dialectic would achieve certainty must not lead us into supposing that he held that dialectic could be exhausted by a set of rules and acquired by memorizing them. The sure and certain may be mechanical to us; but it was not to him. Dialectic was not a substitute for thinking but a way of thinking. . . . Dialectic is a skill to be acquired much more than it is a body of propositions to be learnt." See Richard Robinson, *Plato's Earlier Dialectic*, 73–74 (see also 62–63).

107. For a description of this kind of idealism, see Nettleship, *Lectures*, 220–21.

ciating the positivity of these critical standards, which may be understood as
the transposition of the ideal characteristics of *techne* itself. Harmony, order,
unity, beauty, proportionality, and measure have become substantive principles, the bases for eliminating *stasis* in the souls of individuals and the practical life of political communities. Understanding these "principles" through
the art of dialectic provides the theoretical wherewithal for practicing a political art that would care for the souls of all citizens and the good of the political community as a whole. Only understanding souls and the state via the unfettered practice of dialectical thought assures the just constitution of political
power. Dialectic perfects deliberation that accommodates the *logos* of virtue
with the *ergon* of politics.

The reconciliation of virtue and the political art in the discussion of
philosophical guardians as agents of justice most vividly appears in the "image" (515a) of the cave. Presented as a means of explaining the absence of education in the idea of the good (514a), it invokes the previous imagery of the
line and the sun. The cave may be said to complement the images of the sun
and the line, embedding each in an ethic of education. It also contrasts the
truth and freedom of dialectical philosophy with the falsity and constraints of
ordinary practical life. The result emphasizes the difficulty of integrating philosophy and politics in a single *techne,* of solving Plato's Socratic Problem.
"Socrates" describes the image of the cave, whose prisoners are "like us," as
follows:

> Picture men dwelling in a sort of subterranean cavern with a long en-
> trance open to the light on its entire width. Conceive them as having
> their legs and necks fettered from childhood, so that they remain in
> the same spot, able to look forward only, and prevented by the fet-
> ters from turning their heads. Picture further the light from a fire
> burning higher up and at a distance behind them, and between the
> fire and the prisoners and above them a road along which a low wall
> has been built, as the exhibitors of puppet-shows have partitions be-
> fore the men themselves, above which they show the puppets. . . . See
> also, then, men carrying past the wall implements of all kinds that
> rise above the wall, and human images and shapes of animals as well,
> wrought in stone and wood and every material, some of these bear-
> ers presumably speaking and others silent. . . . If then they were able
> to talk to one another, do you not think that they would suppose that
> in naming the things that they saw they were naming the passing ob-
> jects? . . . And if their prison had an echo from the wall opposite

them, when one of the passers-by uttered a sound, do you think that they would suppose anything else than the passing shadow to be the speaker? . . . Then in every way such prisoners would deem the truth to be nothing else than the shadows of artificial objects. (514a–515c)

This image belongs to a narrative, a narrative that would constitute justice as happiness. Its point is to show how the agents of such justice and happiness liberate themselves from the intellectual deception, physical constraint, and ethical emptiness of life in the cave. The means for such liberation are the temporarily painful but ultimately enjoyable process of education. It is a process seemingly unfulfilled by the historical Socrates, whose liberation, to the extent that he experienced it, was isolated and incomplete.

The cave in the *Republic* takes one beyond the experience of the Socratic *elenchus*. In describing the educational journey of a "prisoner" of the cave who breaks from his bonds, turns away from the images projected on the cave wall, and begins his or her movement toward experiencing the light of the sun, Plato's Socrates characterizes the initial experience as that of befuddlement or *aporia*. One has been disabused of false beliefs but has not yet acquired true ones, which recalls how many felt who were stung by the Socratic *elenchus*. In the *Republic,* this unfettered prisoner has not yet left the cave and acclimatized his vision to the life and light outside the cave, in the sun, but he or she will. It requires further education, in order to habituate him- or herself to the previously unknown and inexperienced light and life. *This* experience of habituation will bring him happiness (515e–516c).

His journey is not complete. For the complement of this liberation, ultimately achieved by acquiring the art of dialectic, is not an end in itself, any more than full sight can be utilized by staring at the sun. Having understood that and how his previous life constituted imprisonment, the free man or woman must go back down into the cave and do his best to liberate the other prisoners (516e, 519d, 520c). Insofar as he or she does so, the rehabilitated prisoner educates them, performing an art of education that cultivates the capacity of sight, of critical reason (*phronesis*) itself, which the "students" (like the rehabilitated prisoner) already possess. As a synecdoche for the philosophical guardians as a class, he turns their bodies and souls around, which enables them to experience the difference between natural sunlight and fabricated imagery (518c–e). Recalling the experience of the historical Socrates, this time his trial and death, Plato's Socrates notes the danger of such education: "And if it were possible to lay hands on and to kill the man who tried to release them and lead them up, would they not kill him?" (517a). In the *Republic*, however, the educator is not killed; to the contrary, his activity as educator fulfills his vocation.[108]

Understanding the *logos* of the good completes the constitution of justice and makes up the final component of the *techne* of philosophical guardians, a single *techne* that comprehends two ways of life (520c). We must, however, somehow understand the experience of such education as "compulsion" belonging to a demonstration of the affinity between justice and happiness.[109] Plato's Socrates offers no new logical demonstration. What he does provide is a reiteration and development of his previous assertion (421b–c) that the happiness of the guardians stems from their *techne*, which is realized by attending not solely to their particular situation but to the manner in which it effects the good of the whole society and self. Plato's Socrates reminds Glaucon:

> The law is not concerned with the special happiness of any class in the state, but is trying to produce this condition in the city as a whole, harmonizing and adapting the citizens to one another by persuasion and compulsion, and requiring them to impart to one another any benefit which they are severally able to bestow upon the community, and that it itself creates such men in the *polis*, not that it may allow each to take whatever course he wills, but with a view to using them for the binding together of the *polis*. . . . Observe, then, Glaucon . . . that we shall not be wronging (*adikesomen*), either, the philosophers who arise among us, but that we can justify our action when we constrain them to take charge of and care for the other citizens and be their guardians. (519e–520a)

108. The radical ambiguity of Plato's Socrates' description of the philosopher's return must be noted. After all, it does represent the actual process of "Platonic" education. The silence on this point is not altogether unusual, however. Just think of Plato's silence regarding the actual political activities of philosopher-guardians while they undergo their fifteen-year apprenticeship, as well as their five years of authoritative political rule. To what extent does it require constantly innovative and reformative practices, especially given his pessimism about the capacity of any ideal society to maintain its constitution for long? This ambiguity reflects the more general ambiguity in Plato's thought about the prospects of both education and political reform—each of which requires the other.

109. Nicholas White, "The Rulers' Choice." See the response by Richard Kraut, "The Defense of Justice in Plato's *Republic*," in R. Kraut, ed., *The Cambridge Companion to Plato*, 311–37.

For Plato, the happiness of any one person is not solely determined by himself alone; therefore "self-interest" is not adequate for understanding its achievement.[110]

For Plato's Socrates, and I daresay Plato himself, happiness depends on the relation of one's life-activity to one's nature, as well as the ability or power of that nature to flourish in society. Explaining the significance of these rela-

---

110. By emphasizing the independence of the rationality of self-interest and asking how Plato's argument about the imperative of just action, including the philosopher's return to the cave, can appeal to such rationality, Platonic commentators miss the fact that Plato's principal concern in the *Republic* is to justify rejection of *that* kind of rationality as the appropriate form of rationality to guide the constitution of the *psyche* and *polis*.

In the literature of analytic interpreters of Plato, this concern about the justifiability of Platonic justice for the ordinary calculations of individual self-interest represents a continuation of the discussion initiated by Foster in the 1930s and recharged by David Sachs in the 1960s. Analytic philosophers have been preoccupied with whether Plato actually "proved" that happiness requires belief in and practice of justice "in itself." Debate has hovered around David Sachs's 1963 resurrection of a 1937 argument by M. B. Foster that Plato had not proved it. Foster believed that Plato had made a "mistake" and had not justified justice "in itself" but only "for its consequences." Sachs argued that this mistake relied on a "fallacy," the effect of which was to render Plato's conclusions in the *Republic* "irrelevant" as a response to the problem set by Thrasymachus, Glaucon, and Adeimantus. See David Sachs, "A Fallacy in Plato's *Republic*"; M. B. Foster, "A Mistake of Plato's in the *Republic*." The debate was shaped by disciplinary preoccupations with the merits of utilitarianism versus Anglo-American neo-Kantianism. As these preoccupations have persisted among analytic philosophers, so has this interpretive framework for understanding Plato's theory of justice. See, for example, Vlastos, ed., *Plato: A Collection of Critical Essays*, vol. 2; Irwin, *Plato's Moral Theory;* as well as the articles I have cited by Williams, Lear, and Kraut. More recently, the neutrality and validity of claims about analytic logic in the human sciences have been subjected to critical attack, from both within the tradition of Anglo-American philosophy, for instance, by Richard Rorty, and from without, by French deconstructionists and poststructuralists. But these also fault Platonic theory, not because it is *not* "logical" but because it *is* (or claims to be). Analytic liberal political theorists, such as Karl Popper and Renford Bambrough, as well their Continental critics, such as Hannah Arendt, have argued that Plato made a category mistake by conceptualizing an ethical art of political rule as a *techne*. The effect, they argue, is to make Plato's theory either antiliberal or antipolitical—and hence antidemocratic. To the extent that the criticisms are parochial, they need not concern us; but because they so radically affect how Plato is read, we need to address them in order to allow a more contextually based reading of Plato's theory of justice to be understood. The specifically antipolitical and antidemocratic dimensions of this argument will be addressed in Chapter 4C, below.

A good summary of this analytic discussion appears in Julia Annas, "Plato and Common Morality," and idem, *An Introduction to Plato's Republic*, 266–71. A valuable, more recent account of this problem in the analytic tradition is Richard Kraut, "The Defense of Justice in Plato's *Republic*," in Richard Kraut, ed., *The Cambridge Companion to Plato*, 311–37. Although Kraut begins to broaden the discussion, the practical contexts he enlists are, curiously, outside—indeed, important negations of—the ethics of political community, the fractured character of which gave rise to the problem of justice in the *Republic*. In this literature, I find John Cooper's article to be the most persuasive. See "The Psychology of Justice in Plato."

tions has occupied Socrates as he has tried to respond to Thrasymachus, the arch-defender of the rationality of self-interest, on the plane of *logos*. An individual whose capacities enable her to grasp the *logos* of the good that justifies justice must also act so as to realize the *ergon* and *arete* of justice that *logos* explains.

Such action does not provide the personal happiness that accompanies the practice of dialectic, perhaps, but it possesses a distinct value and imperative of its own. For Plato, grasping truth and the good is the highest and finest *experience*, but realizing justice is the greater and more difficult *achievement*. The pairs of philosophy and politics, happiness and justice, *logos* and *ergon*, do not reduce to a single form and exhibit a certain tension. But they must belong to a single art, if either element of the pair would flourish (520c–521b). In this sense, they complement each other.[111] A precondition of each flourishing, of the elimination of *stasis, is* the unwillingness of those who rule to exercise political power, their experience of this activity as a compulsory necessity. Where this unwillingness in Book 1 allowed Thrasymachus to argue for the attractiveness of a life of injustice, here it belongs to that argument's refutation.

The fact that this art includes such a tension does not for that reason prevent it from it being a *techne*.[112] This art cannot be easily, straightforwardly,

---

111. Commentators who assert the incompatibility, rather than the productive tension, between each member of these pairs, misconstrue a central dimension of the *Republic* and perpetuate an interpretation of Plato that is less true to Plato than it is to Aristotle. The principal source of this argument in political theory is that of Leo Strauss and his followers. For Strauss, the philosophically informed political art does not involve the practical complement of philosophical activity but the "popular treatment of philosophy," a kind of benevolent condescension toward the irreducibly ignorant "many." See Strauss, *What Is Political Philosophy,* 10, 39–40, 80–82, 90–93, and *The City and Man,* chap. 11. For Allan Bloom, Strauss's student, the arts of philosophy and politics are to be separated because Plato treats the conjunction of philosophy and politics ironically. The ideal political order cannot exist in reality, only in speech. Consequently, for Bloom, any attempt to allow philosophical truths to shape political action contradicts, rather than exemplifies, Plato's teaching. Bloom reads the ideal state as a "utopia" designed "to point up the dangers of utopianism." Furthermore, because the good state cannot actually exist, "Socrates' political science" in the *Republic* "is meant to show the superiority of the private life." See his "Interpretive Essay" in his translation and commentary, *The Republic of Plato,* especially 387, 391–92, 410, 415. For a third-generation version of this argument, see Arlene Saxonhouse, *Fear of Diversity,* 132–57. For a useful, detailed critique of Strauss on just this point—the denial of the art of philosophical guardianship as a single art—see M. F. Burnyeat, "Sphinx Without a Secret," 30–36.

112. This tension of *logos* and *ergon* and its implications for Plato's constitution of justice in the *Republic* are more fully and directly addressed in Chapter 4, Section D, below.

"technically" practiced, because of the irreducible ontological gap between *logos* and *ergon*, in *both* the worlds of justice and injustice. However, only it can bridge the more ethically and politically threatening gap that Thrasymachus exposed. Only the interdependence of philosophy and politics can make the political art virtuous; and such virtue is fully realized only in the *logos* and *ergon* of justice. Consequently, the *Republic*, more than any other dialogue, provides the linchpin of Plato's conception of the genuine political art.[113]

The claim by Plato's Socrates of the interdependence of justice and happiness, philosophy and politics, critical *logos* and practical *ergon* is central to Plato's understanding of the educational enterprise, both the one in which the dialogical Socrates is embarked in the *Republic* and the one in which Plato is embarked in and outside the Academy. Such interdependence does not immediately produce hostility to democracy, for democracies would also nurture the mutuality of these pairs insofar as they would provide harmonious lives for their citizens according to a constitution of justice. Yet in this dialogue, Plato's Socrates evidences considerable hostility to democracy. The time has come for us to explore directly its nature and sources.

C. PLATONIC JUSTICE AND DEMOCRACY

In a world where the rulers of nearly every established political order claim to be democratic, where the most radical internal critics of those regimes mount their criticism in the name of democracy, and where the foes of either are deemed foes of democracy, understanding the relation of Plato's conception of justice to democracy becomes the most emotionally charged topic for any interpretation of the *Republic*. Current interpretations of Plato regard this relation as essentially antagonistic, with Plato's political theory characterized as the ancestor of antiliberal and antidemocratic discourses and practices. These claims may derive from plausible interpretations of Plato's texts; however, their persuasive power draws heavily on the effects and specters of the hot and cold wars between the liberal capitalist democracies of the West

---

113. As opposed to, for example, the *Statesman*, as is argued by R. K. Sprague, *Plato's Philosopher-Kings: A Study of the Theoretical Background.*

and the forces of fascism and communism, which dominated world politics from the 1930s to the 1980s. In the most original and striking version of this interpretive posture (by Karl Popper in the early 1940s), Plato's political thought is proto-totalitarian. In its postwar, more abstract formulations (by Leo Strauss, Renford Bambrough, Hannah Arendt, and Richard Rorty, among others), Plato's metaphysics is essentially antidemocratic.[114]

Apart from the effect of contemporary political concerns on historical understanding, the origins of these misleading interpretive postures lie in how interpreters identify the content of Plato's views about democracy. They tend to argue that Plato generally identifies the power of the *demos,* and democratic politics more generally, as the primary source of hostility to a philosophical political art and the primary cause of injustice; they justify this view by conflating Plato's attitude toward democracy in general with both criticism of the politics of crowds and his discussion of the democratic *politeia* and *psyche* in Book VIII. I do not believe that Plato harbored democratic sympathies. Yet I do believe that these interpretations of Plato's political theory, especially evident in their readings of the *Republic,* misconstrue this dialogue's principal critical focus and constructive interest. In the *Republic,* Plato rejects the necessary connection between any existing political order—which includes the democratic ruling ethic—and the definition of justice.[115] The good of any actual *demos* cannot be identical to the good of the political community as a whole, which is a version of Plato's view that politics cannot be as good as philosophy—even as each requires the other to reach its full potential—and that the good of *ergon* can never match the good of *logos.* This does not mean, however, that the theory of justice in the *Republic* either idealizes the *polis* as an antidemocratic order or negates the *polis* as a historical reality.[116] Rather, it establishes an ethic of power for the individual and the

114. More recently, writers on Plato who wish to redeem his philosophical value do so by marginalizing the role of his comments on democracy for his theory of justice. Annas believes Plato's treatment of democracy marks a philosophical "confusion." See *An Introduction to Plato's Republic,* 299–303. There have been interpreters who have taken Plato's views about democracy seriously, such as Ernest Barker and Werner Jaeger, but these early twentieth-century writers are no longer read seriously by Plato scholars; moreover, each did so primarily by taking for their point of departure Plato's discussion of the democratic *politeia* and *psyche* of Book VIII.

115. In this respect, he is critically addressing the ambiguous meaning of *demos* as either a particular class in the *polis* or the *politeia* of the *polis* as a whole in action. See Gregory Vlastos, "*Isonomia Politike,*" in Vlastos, *Platonic Studies,* 172–73, n. 37.

116. In *Class Ideology and Ancient Political Theory,* Ellen Wood and Neal Wood argue that the ideas of Socrates, Plato, and Aristotle amount to the negation of the ideal of the *polis* and de-

polis that does not presuppose the justice of any existing rulers or forms of political rule. Platonic justice does not operate directly as a criticism of the *politeia* of democracy in the state or soul; it functions primarily as a critique of the ethic of power as domination. In this respect, Platonic justice, indeed, stands in opposition to democracy. The opposition, however, is neither direct nor wholly antagonistic. Rather, it is critical, indicative of Plato's effort to construct a critical ethics of politics and politics of ethics that would genuinely conciliate justice and power.

In my discussion of the relation of Platonic justice to democracy in the *Republic*, I argue why and how the aforementioned readings of Plato's political theory as essentially antidemocratic stances are faulty. I do so by identifying, first, the critique of democracy in the *Republic* that appears amid the construction of the idea of justice in Books II–VII and, then, the meaning of the critique of democracy in Book VIII in light of the previously articulated criteria of justice and injustice. Plato's criticisms of democracy in the *Republic* ought to be read as particular and secondary expressions of his larger critique of the roots of injustice.

I. THE GENERAL OPPOSITION OF PLATONIC JUSTICE TO DEMOCRACY

Plato mentions democracy only twice before his discussion of it as a constitutional form of states and souls in Book VIII. The first occasion is his presentation of Thrasymachus's argument (338cff) that the just is the advantage of the stronger. It is an argument made by Thrasymachus in exasperation, as Socrates had nominally rebutted more conventional definitions of justice that derived from the general notion "To each what is owed him" (331e) and the Simonidean notion "To each what is appropriate for him" (332c). Thrasymachus's definition possesses the greatest coherence, and he glosses this statement to Socrates by referring to the power of the ruling authorities in any society to define the meaning of justice:

> Don't you know that some cities are governed tyrannically, others democratically, others aristocratically? . . . And is not this the thing that dominates each, the ruling class? And each form of rule enacts

the laws with a view to its own advantage, a democracy democratic laws, a tyranny tyrannical laws, and the others likewise, and by so legislating they proclaim that the just for their subjects is that which is for their—the rulers'—advantage and the man who deviates from this law they chastise as a lawbreaker and wrongdoer. This, then, my good sir, is what I understand to be the just in all cities, the advantage of the established government. (338d–339a)

In arguing against Thrasymachus, then, Socrates is not directly arguing against democracy; rather, he is arguing against the capacity of ruling authorities who dominate their subjects to usurp the definition of justice for their selfish purposes.

The only other reference to democracy prior to Book VIII reinforces this significance. In what some regard as an Orwellian flourish, Plato's Socrates emphasizes (463a–b) that a society where genuine justice exists does not have ordinary rulers—who are called "despots" or, in democracies, "rulers," that is, authorities who dominate or regulate—instead, they have individuals who are regarded not only as "fellow citizens" (which is the case in ordinary cities as well) but also as "saviors and helpers" and "fellow guardians." Other cities (including democracies, one must presume) regard their subjects as "slaves," but the ideal just society regards them as "payers of their [the guardians'] wages and supporters." In *kallipolis,* the relation of coercion that typifies relationships between rulers and ruled has disappeared. In this city, the *stasis* that generally requires such coercion has also disappeared, for there exists a symphonic familial unity, a "community" of pleasures and pains (463c–465b).[117] The essential point, again, is that Plato's idea of justice articulates primarily an ethics for the exercise of power in which *stasis* and domination do not exist. In that sense, Plato's Socrates does not construct his idea of justice in direct opposition to democracy. Platonic justice primarily opposes democracy insofar as it, like other conventional political orders, evidences *stasis* and domination.

To be sure, in the midst of Plato's argument for philosopher-guardians, antidemocratic elements appear. As pointed out in the previous section, the

---

117. The use of imagery from the family is metaphoric, given the departure from conventional familial relationships that marks the relationship among citizens in this city. Given the tormented character of family relationships that marked Plato's time, let alone our own, Plato is again hypothesizing the best possible features of this form of community, features that Socrates also drew on in explaining his loyalty to Athens in Plato's *Apology.*

political ethic of democratic Athens (as articulated in Pericles' funeral oration in Thucydides' *History of the Peloponnesian War* and the Great Speech of Protagoras in Plato's *Protagoras*)[118] makes justice both a constituent and product of the political art, the practice of which is available to all citizens. For (Plato's) Protagoras and (Thucydides') Pericles, this "democratic political art" (no such phrase ever appeared in Greek) was unique among all the arts because it was possessed and practiced by the citizenry in general rather than by a specially trained class of experts. The citizens interpreted and applied the advice of specialists and experts.

Not intellectually or politically subordinated to expertise or experts, the citizenry used both for its own purposes as it engaged in political deliberation. In this way, the citizenry's political art dominated the authority of the other arts when it came to determining the collectivity's political well-being. Its virtue was entailed by the free exercise of political authority through the deliberative practice of democratic citizenship. For Plato, that authority was problematic because it had no critical limits. An art of democratic citizenship, as Plato knew it, could not be relied on to ensure virtue and justice in the political community as a whole, and Sophists who presumed to improve on it had no clear critical standards of their own. The power of the *demos* and the *logos* of the Sophists could be all too easily manipulated by an unscrupulous few, whose ultimate aim was to benefit themselves—most likely at the expense of an exploitable gullible *demos* along with the political community as a whole. Thus, whereas the political art of Protagoras's democratic citizens (importantly supplemented by the wisdom of Protagorean sophistry) was best practiced when all citizens exercised it freely and equally, regardless of the order of their souls, the ideal Platonic political art was practiced best when those with properly ordered souls trained in dialectic could authoritatively deliberate about political affairs and decide how to resolve the conflicts that inevitably characterize political life. The presumptuousness of this claim is as shocking and unconvincing now as it was then, but one must keep in mind its catalyst: the desire for justice, a kind of justice that would accept no injustice as necessary to the natural order of social life. Rather than being essentially antidemocratic, such a desire is necessary in the majority of citizens if their democracy would reach for justice. On this, not only "Pericles" and "Protagoras" but also Plato and, for example, Rousseau would agree.[119]

118. Notably, in neither case was the author of the ethic its actual expositor, which indicates the absence of democratic theory in ancient Greece.

119. See Jean-Jacques Rousseau, *The Social Contract*.

Given Plato's views of the apparently natural limitations of most human beings, he is not interested in enabling the citizenry as a whole to acquire and practice the political art. The citizenry simply deserves education that enables it to appreciate and judge rightly the leadership of the philosopher-guardians. *Harmonia* in the *polis* results from each class holding true beliefs, even as no class can have full knowledge of the good. The bare form of the virtue and art whose exercise achieves the good of the political community as a whole in Plato's ideal city often duplicates the form of the political art that (in Athenian democracy) was vouchsafed to the citizenry as a whole. The difference consists in the fact that the form's content is not generated by the political participation or authoritative deliberation of ordinary citizens.[120]

Dialectic (available to only a few in *kallipolis*) must condition and control political deliberation (typically practiced by the many in Athenian democracy) if Platonic justice would be achieved. Although Plato's Socrates believes that the human nature of the many makes them open to education (499d–500e, 518b–c), he does not believe in the possibility of cultivating a dialectically grounded practice of the political art in the democratic citizenry as a whole (590d–591a).

The issue of the relation between radically critical political theory and democracy in the *Republic* thus arises in the form of the opposition between philosophical dialectic and democratic deliberation.[121] The relation is wholly oppositional if democratic deliberation exercised in collective public fora is taken to be sufficient for the discourse and practice of justice. For as we have noted earlier, Plato objected to the ethical and rational sufficiency of the form of speaking that took place in the Athenian assembly and courts. In Plato's *Apology of Socrates* (17a–18a), Socrates recounted his intolerance for the assembly and emphasized the anomalous character of his "judicial" discourse. In the *Protagoras*, Plato's Socrates insisted that Protagoras change his oratorical style as a precondition for mutual dialogue. In the *Gorgias*, Plato's Socrates argued that the successful practice of the typical art of rhetoric displayed ignorance about the topic on which rhetoricians claimed to have knowledge. By specifying the art of dialectic as the proper form of reasoning about fun-

---

120. This antidemocratic feature of Plato's thought needs to be noted, although this antagonism to effective, authoritative political participation by ordinary citizens is, perhaps, no greater than is the case today.

121. Plato's ideas about the relation of philosophically and politically adequate deliberation to democracy bear on contemporary discussions of the discursive and practical standard of "deliberative democracy." The contemporary relevance of Plato's political theory (via the Platonic political art) to these discussions is addressed in Chapter 6, below.

damental human political concerns, Plato's Socrates in the *Republic* has stiffened the criteria for true discourse about justice by restricting both the domain in which it could occur and the persons who could practice it. In a conversation unstructured by Plato's criteria, an argument could go astray, but by following the art of dialectic one would not make mistakes. And yet, stating this does not make it so. Although conventional practices and the immediate judgments of political majorities may not provide sufficient criteria for a political art that constitutes justice in the political community as a whole, what theoretical justification or practical basis does dialectic have for genuinely constituting justice (rather than some philosopher's aberrant fantasy)? Let us look more extensively, then, at the nature of dialectic.

In the *Republic* and other "late" dialogues, Plato calls dialectic "the power of conversing," the "art" or "method" of discussion, which enables its possessor "to ask and answer questions" most "scientifically."[122] When Plato's Socrates describes the art of dialectic as the capacity and art of conversation, of asking and answering questions properly, of dividing according to "real forms," he is doing more than engaging in fanciful etymology.[123] He is illustrating the ties to, as well as the differences between, the art of dialectic and the political deliberation of democratic citizens. Plato hardly abjures deliberation; rather, he believes that it demands the greatest precision if one's soul and state would fully benefit from its practice (504b–e).

The demands of such precision, however, drive a wedge between democratic deliberation and philosophical dialectic. A democratic deliberative skill involves the ability *both* to understand how the given sentiments expressed and political problems experienced by the political community as a whole condition the possibilities of proper collective action *and* to respond actively to such exigencies. As described by Protagoras in Plato's *Protagoras*, having this art encouraged the *demos* to listen to "experts," *demiourgoi* in practicing *technai* whose relevant knowledge of the matter at hand could inform the citizenry, but to reserve the ultimate power of judgment for itself. The "ground" of such political decisions was the community's shared experiences and the sensibility of each citizen. Such a "ground" did not *determine* the community's conception of the good of the whole. That was established through the deliberative process itself; nevertheless, there was no need to filter the ground

122. *Republic* 511b, 534d; *Cratylus* 390c, 398d–e; *Phaedo* 90b; *Sophist* 227a.
123. *Republic* 454a, 532d–e, 533a, 534d, 537d–e, 539c; see also *Philebus* 57e, 58d–e; *Phaedrus* 269b, 277b–c; *Statesman* 286d–287a; *Sophist* 253d; *Cratylus* 390c.

soil through some external authority or higher law. Democratic deliberation linked thought and action in ways that were deemed sufficient for the skillful and virtuous practice of the political art.[124] In this sense, the practice of the democratic political art was good in itself and for its consequences—and thus fulfilled one criterion for just activity that Socrates agreed to in the *Republic.*

Yet two differences between this democratic deliberation and Platonic dialectic stand out. First, the art learned by the philosopher-guardians was immediately developed outside the realms of both ordinary social experience and practical politics. For the knowledge that informed their art and the ideal of harmony that guided its practice initially demanded physical and reflective escape from the contradictory phenomena of ordinary experience.[125] Only *after* the deliberations of the philosopher-guardians are no longer determined by the contours of conventional ethics and experience, only after they have experienced the good through dialectic, can they become actively engaged in the practice of politics—learning about the character of their society and then governing it. Philosophers will try to fashion a *politeia* for the *polis* and for the *psyche* of its members after the transcendent image of the good, because that provides the *paradeigma* for what a harmoniously constituted state and soul might be.

Ideally, there would be practically nothing external to the philosopher-guardians themselves that would constrain their aesthetic impulse to shape society in their image of justice. They would be able, as it were, to paint on a blank canvas, for only then would the full imprint of the good appear clearly (500d–501a). And Plato's Socrates notes that the scheme of *kallipolis* would be most easily realized if those over ten years old were rusticated (541a), making the guardians the sole "parental" authority for those over ten—not a par-

124. So stated Pericles in his funeral oration, when he referred to the Athenians' practice of political deliberation in the following way: "We decide public matters ourselves or at least consider them deeply and rightly, in the belief that it is not discourse that is a hindrance to action but rather not to be instructed by discourse before the time for action comes" (II.40.2). My translation of this passage depends on Charles Foster Smith's for the Loeb edition of Thucydides (London: William Heinemann, 1928), which I regard as far more literal than and superior to those offered by Warner in the Penguin translation and by Crawley in the Modern Library translation.

125. This model for the acquisition of an art of virtue appeared in more primitive forms in the *Protagoras,* as the art of measurement, and in the *Gorgias,* as the philosophical way of life Plato's Socrates said had to be followed before politics could be practiced rightly. Each model was deemed necessary because of Plato's political diagnosis and philosophical conviction that *empeiria* no longer provided a sufficient ground for a virtuous art of politics (which had been taken to be true in democratic Athens). For Socrates in the *Republic* (539e), "knowledge" derived from *empeiria* had to be controlled by a philosophically trained *techne.*

ticularly comforting thought but one that certainly cuts to the chase. Of course, in more realistic and "imperfect" environs, where political orders are not amenable to—indeed, may be hostile to—the practice of this art, the best that would-be philosopher-guardians can hope for is to make sure that their practical lives do not corrupt the constitutional order of their souls (592a). That may or may not involve them in the democratic practice of political deliberation.

Second, the philosopher-guardian does not experience his practical political activity as pleasurable in the least. Although neither "Pericles" nor "Protagoras" referred to the activity of politics as pleasurable or enjoyable, neither did they refer to politics as a constraint or imposed obligation. For them politics did, after all, provide the ultimate means for the expression of virtue in the individual and political community.[126] Political life was the highest form of life. Yet for philosopher-guardians, the political art can be practiced properly only if one does not enjoy the process, and one would (if one could) spend one's time doing dialectic rather than attending to the requirements of political harmony. Of course, one can't. Although practicing politics does not make a philosopher palpably happy, a life in which he cannot practice politics would be worse. "Taking shelter from the storm" is a limited achievement for a Platonic philosopher (496d–97a). Making philosophy political enables philosophers to realize their true natures, for then they can perform the practical as well as theoretical aspects of the *techne* and *ergon* appropriate to them.

Plato has transformed the ideal of democratic deliberation into philosophical dialectic by instituting stricter, more objective, and less worldly conditions for the virtuous, skillful practice of political deliberation. At the same time, he has shifted the ground for testing its value and competent performance away from the practical political arena, to the soul. This move reflects Plato's political and philosophical belief that the world of politics has become so corrupted that it is impossible to be both virtuous and successful while conventionally practicing the political art.

The distance between philosophical dialectic and democratic deliberation necessarily creates tension between them. That tension becomes antagonistic, however, only if philosophy would undermine, rather than supplement, the deliberative process of democracy or if democracy jeopardizes and disparages the political contributions of philosophy. In condemning Socrates, democ-

---

126. I say "means," because the "end" was in one sense death in war for the individual and political security and well-being for the community.

racy assaulted philosophy. In Plato's theoretical response, philosophy significantly depoliticizes the *demos* in order to establish the authority of its political *techne.*

But is this depoliticization entirely and directly antidemocratic? I do not think so, particularly with regard to how this case is put by Renford Bambrough, who ruled out the compatibility of any political art with democracy. This point becomes clearer if we return to the parable of the ship of state, which appears in Book VI—that is, in that part of the *Republic* where Plato conflates the injustices of political life and democracy. By assuming the relevance of an art of navigation for the political art, Plato assumes that there is no ultimate contest or conflict about the proper ends of sailing, the best destination, or the best resolution of a particular political conflict and, more positively, that political consensus is ultimately a practical possibility. At the same time, such a consensus is theoretically presupposed and does not depend on the collective interaction and deliberation of the citizenry. Indeed, the citizenry in the parable has no knowledge of how to use the power that derives from its ownership to achieve good means and ends for its ship. But, again, this demotion of the *demos* belongs to Plato's attempt to establish authority for philosophical dialectic in producing useful political knowledge against the practical claims of dominant political powers. In this respect, it is an argument for the existence of a skillful practice of an ethic for using power and the potential practical power of such an ethic—in *any* political society, not just democracies.

Modern critics cite Plato's view that very few can possess this skill as part of an argument that denies the existence of such a skill. For Bambrough, it is Plato's belief that such a skill exists, rather than his belief in who does or can possess it or what constitutes it, that makes his political theory antidemocratic: "Ethical and political disagreements [in general] are disagreements between customers [that is, passengers], and ethical and political skill, in the only sense in which the phrase can be properly used, is incapable of composing such disagreements."[127]

Such a skill seems to require the attributes of a logarithm, but that is hardly what Plato has in mind, for the identity of dialectic entails the capacity to transcend the formulaic. And yet Bambrough is surely right to doubt the apparent belief of Plato's Socrates that the proper locus for sovereign authority over the course of the ship is the knowledge of the genuinely skilled

127. Bambrough, "Plato's Political Analogies," 201.

navigator. For him, by contrast, the locus for sovereign authority in a political community ought to lie with the passenger, customer, or consumer.

But problems exist with Bambrough's formulation as well. To see consumers as the locus of sovereignty means that the individuals who are charged with the responsibility of guiding the destiny of the political community make choices without having to consider the good of the political community as a whole. For Bambrough—and for advocates of the paramount importance of poststructuralism for political ethics—that is fine, because there can be no systematic way; there is no common good. But what are the consequences of this position? Just as the Platonic navigator does not have to respond to anyone who does not have expert knowledge of the art of navigation, Bambrough's passenger-consumer-citizen does not have to take into account the welfare of any of his or her passengers-consumers-citizens.

Whereas Popper charges Plato with being totalitarian, because his "technique" of political reason makes citizens into mere instruments, Bambrough (not poststructuralists) reduces the political community to a merely instrumental tool of individuals. As a result, politicians become technicians, for, as "managers" of the political community, their duty is that of expertly devising the most efficient means to the ends of the citizens they serve. In this vein, however, there is no more need for politicians to consider the political judgments of citizens than in Plato's parable. There would be no need for citizens to elect their leaders, because the professional class of political technicians could easily calculate what was best for the citizen-consumers. Bambrough's expert is an expert in political means, whereas the navigator is an expert in political means and ends. At least in Plato's case, however, the parable is only that. That is, it functions as a means for establishing the legitimacy of a political art not dependent on raw contests for power. Plato never asserts that political wizards can issue political solutions without dialectical engagement with the individuals and issues that constitute the problematic conflict. Moreover, the consensus he presupposes—although more problematic than he probably believed—is couched in myriad qualifications.

It is important to recall that Greek writers did not presuppose an inherent antagonism between belief in any *techne* of politics and the ethics of democratic practice. We know from Thucydides that the possession and practice of a *techne* of politics by the Athenians distinguished the character of their public life and contributed to their strategic superiority over the Spartans (1.70–71). We also know from the Protagoras of Plato's *Protagoras,* if not the historical Protagoras (as well as, perhaps, Democritus), that political *techne* designated the highest virtue and badge of honor of Athenian democracy. But

Thucydides was primarily characterizing the so-far successful exercise of Athenian political power; he was not suggesting that such a *techne* of politics was just, at least not in any critical ethical sense. Furthermore, Plato exposed the dubious ethical and rational coherence of a Protagorean political art. Given the failures of these attempts to theorize an ethical *techne* of politics on democratic terms, and the fact that the virtuous practice of the Athenians' democratic politics was not regarded as the province of a special class or form of knowledge but rather a quasi-natural product of its enactment, Plato's criticisms of democracy do not so much indicate hostility to democracy per se as they do a rejection of the sufficiency of conventional political and democratic ethics as criteria for the production of a perfectly just society.

2. DEMOCRACY AS A FORM OF INJUSTICE

Plato's discussion of democracy as a "form" or "idea" in Book VIII (544a–d) is just one of his many comments that make up his theorizing about democracy. It is not "paradigmatic" for his theorizing and ought not to be read as Plato's equivalent to Aristotle's discussions of the constitution/s of democracy in Books IV–V of the *Politics*. Rather, it belongs to a dialogical excursion into the (still "undisciplined") study of the relation of empirical social phenomena to formal standards of rational argument.[128] Because it is merely an excursion, an instrumental device for persuading the interlocutors of Plato's Socrates of the meaning and value of the constitution of justice, it must not be interpreted as direct evidence of Plato's views about the actual practice of ancient (or Athenian) democracy. Instead, Plato's discussion of democracy in Book VIII ought to be placed in the light of the *logos* of justice that he had just finished articulating at the end of Book VII.

Plato himself urges us to do this. In Book VIII, Socrates states that describing the worst regimes will enable him and his interlocutors to determine whether they should agree with Thrasymachus and practice injustice or pursue justice instead (545a–b). Plato's Socrates' conceptualization of justice and

---

128. That innovation was the product of Aristotle's genius, not Plato's, and appears in the former's systematic study of *politike* in the *Nicomachean Ethics, Politics,* and parts of the *Rhetoric.* On the character of Aristotelian political science and its contemporary interpretation, see my "Contemporary Aristotelianism." With the secularization of social science in the nineteenth century, the relations of political theory and practice became subdivided into the social science disciplines of political science, sociology, economics, anthropology, and psychology—resistance to which was sustained only by unconventional, pathbreaking thinkers, such as Marx, Mill, Weber, Freud, and Foucault.

its justification in the idea of the good provide the critical point of departure for his inquiry in Book VIII and part of Book IX of the *Republic* into unjust regimes and the souls that enforce them (continuing a discussion that was promised at the end of Book IV [445c–e] but that was sidetracked by the need to show how to master or withstand "the three waves").

The fulfillment by the end of Book VII of the goal of Plato's Socrates to articulate a theory of justice enables him to cast "democracy" in a new light. No longer is it enmeshed in the array of beliefs and practices that belong to the world's constellation of injustice, which impedes the philosophical understanding of justice and the good. The point of reference for understanding democracy in Book VIII is no longer primarily the world of phenomena but the purified *logos* of justice that would authorize order and harmony in the world.

Socrates asserts that they would get nowhere in their inquiries into the forms of injustice if they catalogued all the varieties of existing regimes (544c–d).[129] As a result, certain forms are chosen, on the (unargued) assumption that the multifarious character of the world of existing (that is, unjust) states and souls can be explained in reference to the four *eide* of political and psychological injustice. The democracy of Book VIII neither constitutes a theoretical equivalent of the historical actuality of Athenian (or Syracusan) democracy nor evidences the essence of Plato's view of the merits of that society, any more than the portrayal of the degeneration from the best to the worst states and souls reflects a Platonic synopsis of the past or future of Greek history.[130] Rather, it is a distillation of the phenomena of Greek history and politics into *eide* that facilitate the effort of Plato's Socrates to explain the nature of justice and its constituent relation to happiness.[131] In this respect, their most kindred conceptual figure is that of Weber's ideal-types.

Despite these qualifications, the comments of Plato's Socrates on democracy in Book VIII contribute importantly to an understanding of the relation

129. For a different, more practical basis for the categorization of regimes, see Machiavelli, *The Prince*, chaps. I–IV.

130. How could it? The point of "historical" departure never existed in history. Even the particular description of degeneration from one form to another does not refer to a specific political context, let alone one that is integrally related to the "previous" regime (549c).

131. For interpretations of the meaning of "democracy" in Book VIII as illustrative of Plato's essential views about democracy—even, perhaps, Athenian democracy—see (most recently) Arlene W. Saxonhouse, "Democracy, Equality, and Eide: A Radical View of Book 8 of Plato's *Republic.*" See also a chapter of her recent book, *Athenian Democracy: Modern Mythmakers and Ancient Theorists,* entitled "Plato and the Gentleness of Democracy," 87–114. Less recent but kindred views include those of Murphy, Guthrie, White, Annas, Hall, Klosko, and Reeve.

of Platonic justice to democracy. For they amount to a complex account of democracy as a constitutional form that prizes equality and freedom as sufficient substitutes for virtue and justice as guiding principles for its psychological and political order. Moreover, although the foundation for the treatment of democracy in Book VIII differs significantly from its more indirect treatment in the first seven books of the *Republic*, one major element links the two analyses. The catalyst for Plato's formation of the idea of justice in Books II–VII lay in the subordination of an ethic of justice to an ethic of power, as presented by Thrasymachus, Glaucon, and Adeimantus. For Plato's Socrates in these books of the *Republic*, the need for an ethic of justice arose from the conditions of *stasis* that attended its absence. As Plato's Socrates proceeds in Book VIII to describe the form of unjust souls and states, he also presents them as products or results of *stasis*. The characterization of existing states as exhibiting various forms of injustice or (what is virtually a Platonic equivalent) forms of *stasis* displays the "nonacademic" character of Plato's typological analyses. To Plato, political phenomena (what today might be called "political realities") do not present a collection of discrete, amoral, anodyne bits of sensation, information, data, or difference. Rather, they are various constellations of conflict, which Plato's theory of justice was designed to help overcome (even though they could only be overcome completely in *logos*, not *ergon*).

To understand the significance of Plato's treatment of democracy as a form of injustice, it must be situated in the broader account of Plato's Socrates of a process of degeneration that extends from the best form (*aristokrateia* and the psychological education of philosopher-guardians) and proceeds to a characterization of the worst (tyranny and the soul of the tyrannical man).

First, the process of degeneration originates in the natural limitations of the philosopher-guardians. They are unable to regulate perfectly the process of human sexual reproduction—indeed, sexuality in general. As a result, various philosopher-guardians mate out of season, producing children whose natural dispositions do not evince a complete devotion to justice. Socrates' observation not only indicates a partially genetic or genealogical account of injustice; it reveals Plato's awareness of how fragile are the forms of justice in souls and states and how natural tendencies in human life resist their authority and foster injustice.[132]

This does not indicate a belief in the "natural" predominance of "evil"

---

132. Contra the view of Plato put forth by Martha Nussbaum in *The Fragility of Goodness: Luck and Ethics in Ancient Greek Thought*.

over "good" or "injustice" over "justice." Nor does it display a visceral hatred of desires of the flesh or the materiality of the world. To recall, nature in the ideal sense is just and good. Rather, it evidences the conflicts and gaps between *logos* and *ergon* that appear *within* Plato's conception of the ultimately ethical and political composition of the phenomenal world (545d–546d). For although the *logos* and *techne* of the philosopher-guardians may be perfect, other aspects of their natures are not. As a result, Plato recognizes how philosopher-guardians in practice could be responsible for creating the seeds of dissension, disharmony, and disunity in the souls and state that they had unified and made harmonious (546d–547d).

Second, Plato's Socrates notably locates the effective cause of dissension in neither nature nor the *demos* but rather in the ruling class (545c–d; see also 421a–b, 426d). The very ones who can save the state may also be responsible for its destruction. The responsibility of the ruling class for political vice (as well as political virtue) characterizes Plato's descriptions of each unjust regime, as well as his explanation of the degeneration from one to the next. Moreover, the major flaws producing degeneration in the ruling class of each polity possess a similar characteristic (which downplays democracy as the principal source of injustice). The clearest sign of a tendency toward injustice is the tendency to prize the value of wealth or money and the power these can bring.

In a timocratic state, the desire for such wealth and power stems from the dominance of the spirited element of the soul over the rational or deliberative component, whereas in the oligarchic and democratic state, it stems from the intensity and power of the appetitive element, but even in the timocratic man the subordination of "reasons" to the spirited element results from the pull of the appetitive element (550a–b).[133] Given this analytical framework, desires for wealth and power that produce the seeds of injustice are most directly institutionalized in the oligarchic state, based as it is on a property qualification that guarantees political office for the rich and excludes it for the poor (550c).[134] The text makes clear how all of the evils that bedevil each of the un-

---

133. This point serves to enforce the importance of a binary, as well as tripartite, division in both the soul and state. In the soul, a single, basic division separates the rational and nonrational components; in the state, one separates rulers and the ruled. See Chapter 4, Section B, above.

134. An informal property qualification for office now exists in the United States, for none but the wealthy have the financial security to conduct a political campaign without mortgaging their electoral destiny to entrenched, moneyed interests. Only multi-multimillionaires (such as Ross Perot and Steve Forbes) can credibly claim to wage an "independent" political campaign,

just regimes are paradigmatically present in the constitution of the oligarchic state and the soul of the oligarchic man.

In addition to their subordination of the value of virtue to the self-interested acquisition of wealth and power, oligarchies notably (1) come to power by means of fear and terror (551b); (2) manage to do so by fooling the *demos* into believing that their regime will serve the interests of the many (550d–e, 551e, 554b); (3) disregard the value of skills, and merit more generally, as criteria for determining one's contribution to society and status in the state (551c–552b); (4) institutionalize antagonistic divisions in the city, particularly the one between rich and poor (551d)—which for Plato signifies the essential constituent of *stasis* (see Book IV, 422e–423a); (5) foster the illusion of the competence of existing leaders in the political art (552b); (6) resist the restrictions of laws that require the practice of virtue (556a); and generally diminish the presence of *sophrosyne* in the political community as a whole (555c). In his initial discussion in Book VIII of the four unjust regimes, Plato's Socrates points out that oligarchy—not democracy—is "full of many evils" (544c). Only tyranny is more dramatically condemned.

After acknowledging the litany of evils Plato links to oligarchies, one may still rightfully point out that "oligarchy" stands closer to the perfectly virtuous and just soul and state than does democracy. Yet if one looks for what, in oligarchies, maintains their superior status in Plato's narrative of degeneration, it is difficult to identify. All that Plato's Socrates grants oligarchies is the residual intuitions of oligarchs about what ought to be authoritative in the soul and state, along with a certain stinginess about spending money that indicates some respect for limits (554c–d, 555d). Neither point argues for the inherent superiority of oligarchy to democracy.

Not only does Plato's Socrates heap his greatest scorn on the constitutive features of oligarchy; the democratic constitution of the soul and state is the only order apart from the perfectly just soul and state whose distinctive characteristics receive his praise. Timocracy and oligarchy possess diminishing quantities of the virtue that ordered the just state and soul. Although democracy possesses even less of *that* virtue, it possesses *other* attributes that Plato's Socrates approves, which suggest Plato's awareness of his own debt to Athenian democracy.

---

and, of course, for these political entrepreneurs such "independence" rarely favors the interests of the many—rhetorical posturing notwithstanding.

Three positive remarks about democracy stand out. The first one made by Plato's Socrates is the (partly ironic) observation that a democratically constituted *polis* provides the most fertile ground for philosophical inquiry because it includes the greatest number of examples of constitutional forms for both state and soul (557c–d, 561e). Insofar as skill in dialectic develops from intellectually stimulating contrasts, this feature of democracy actually nourishes dialectic (as John Stuart Mill later argued). Connected to this aspect of democracy is a second, which harkens back to Pericles' funeral oration in Thucydides' *History of the Peloponnesian War*. Plato's Socrates states that the character of democracy effects a sympathetic tolerance toward different ways of life, even if these violate conventional proprieties (558a–b).[135] He phrases this ethic in a more negative light when he assigns a propositional equivalent to it: "[E]quality to equals and unequals alike" (558c). Third, democracy cherishes freedom—and so does Plato's Socrates, as long as it is a freedom that constitutes justice (562b–563d). For Plato, then, it seems that the problems of democracy do not reside in its diversity, its ethic of sympathetic toleration and equal respect, or its high regard for freedom.[136] Rather, they stem from the *excessive* power of these in the constitutional order of the state and souls of its citizens.

This "excessive power" and its relation to the constitution of injustice is not simply an "excess of democracy," for the essential components of democracy mentioned above are not inherently problematic. In this respect, Plato does not anticipate the animus of contemporary neoconservatives toward democracy.[137] Rather, it results from the absence in democracy itself of any natural direction toward virtue or inherent respect for the law. (Of course, no actual society that reasonably could be called democratic lacks all regard for virtue or the law; otherwise, it would have no legal order or ethical priorities.)

135. I translate *suggnome* in this way because the word suggests a warm, embracing attitude toward diverse points of view, an attitude not suggested in the much colder, English "tolerance," which indicates that one puts up with, rather than embraces, difference. Notably, there is no Greek equivalent of the English "tolerance," despite efforts by many of Plato's English translators to have us think otherwise.

136. One might find this association of Plato with an ethic of diversity overly charitable, given that the good that ultimately governs a just society has only one form. But one must keep in mind that the good is more a theoretical than a practical entity, and the practical presence of diversity does no more to vitiate the practical realization of the good than the existence of diverse kinds of trees does to vitiate the form of the tree. The issue for Plato is how may diversity effectively contribute to the formation of just souls and states.

137. For a classic statement, see Samuel Huntington, "The United States," in *The Crisis of Democracy: Report on the Governability of Democracies to the Trilateral Commission*.

But this only emphasizes the ideal-typical character of Plato's rendition of democracy here. For Plato, the practice of democracy, like the *eros* of desire, is not inherently good. As a result, democratic states and souls harbor the need for criteria—the practical equivalents of which would be leadership and education—that would channel their energies in virtuous directions. With respect to the discursive values of that society, they need the help of philosophical criticism (in the political Platonic sense); with respect to the practical direction of that society's power, they need enlightened politicians. But neither of these requires the transformation of democratic institutions in an essentially antidemocratic direction.

When democracies become corrupt, the process begins with impostors assuming the offices of philosophical and political leadership and unjustly arrogating power and authority to themselves, fooling or misleading the *demos*. The fluidity, indeterminacy, and openness of democracies make them susceptible to perversions of its "decent" (somewhere short of virtuous) attributes. That is why democracies need critical philosophy, along with virtuous citizens and politicians, if their constitutions would thrive. Democracies need the critical perspective of philosopher-guardians if they would realize their full potential for justice. By virtue of its emphasis on the absence of and need for good leadership at the personal and political levels, this criticism of democracy, indeed, seems elitist. But it is not as antidemocratic as it appears, for Plato's criteria for genuine philosophy and political leadership cannot be met by society moving toward oligarchy, timocracy, or tyranny, and he can visualize no practical method for achieving a transition from *any* unjust society to a just one. Moreover, the other unjust societies institutionally limit the potential effects of philosophical education and virtuous leadership, whereas democracy offers the greatest opportunities (albeit the greatest likelihood of frustrations as well) for education in what is philosophically and politically good. To that extent, democracy possesses the greatest potential for the accommodation of power and virtue, even as it refuses to institutionalize a governing conception of virtue (558c, 560bff), offering instead a menu of virtues, from which each citizen has an equal opportunity to select his own repertoire (which provides a countervision to the proper selection process articulated in the subsequent myth of Er).[138]

138. Indeed, one of the greater oddities of this description of the (unjust) ideal type of democracy is the absence of any description of how a democracy functions at all. According to the description of the behavior of democratic citizens by Plato's Socrates—they do "whatever they like" (557b)—no one respects the law. But without such respect, no constitutional order can sur-

Still, we know that, for Plato at least, Athenian democracy has not actu-alized that potential. To the contrary, he probably believed that it destroyed the possibility of accommodating political power and the ethic of virtue through its excessive pursuit of empire, resulting defeat in the Peloponnesian War, and legal but unjust condemnation and execution of Socrates. When Plato's Socrates reviews the character of the democratic constitution of soul and state in Book VIII, he notes the insufficient complexity of practically ef-fective ethical judgments. At this point, he introduces a philosophical distinc-tion by differentiating necessary and unnecessary desires (558d). Such judg-ments obviously limit an ethic of freedom understood as "do as you like," but that ethic is not sufficient to sustain any political community or sane soul, let alone democratic ones.

Despite these positive aspects of the portrayal of the democratic consti-tution of state and soul offered by Plato's Socrates, one cannot disregard his view of it as the third worst of the four unjust constitutions and as one that provides fertile soil for tyranny. Insofar as the constitution of tyranny and the tyrannical man creates the worst *stasis* of all, to such a degree that neither soul nor state actually has a constitution, the democratic toleration of freedom and affirmation of equal regard for persons as principles for guiding social rela-tionships may seem to bear the greatest responsibility for political instability and *stasis,* the worst possible social conditions. Indeed, that has been the crit-icism of democracy from its appearance in fifth-century Greece to the seven-teenth and eighteenth centuries, when it reentered Western political discourse and was excoriated by Hobbes and the American Federalists as each sought to authorize new forms of state power.[139]

Yet if we view Athenian democracy in a more appropriate historical frame, it turns out to be the most, not least, stable form of governance in the ancient Greek world. Moreover, the political order Plato labels democracy in Book VIII is unlike any contemporary political order that calls itself demo-cratic. Major features of Plato's democratic constitution and that of Athens it-self, such as the institutional absence of any provisions or guidelines for se-

---

vive. The absence of any characterization of a "good" democracy may indicate the perils it might hold; it might require the kind of concrete characterization of an actually existing society that Plato has no interest in undertaking. Moreover, the result might uncomfortably resemble many features of Plato's democratic Athens.

139. For a good, recent review of the antidemocratic appropriation of democratic Athens, see Jennifer Roberts, *Athens on Trial: The Antidemocratic Tradition in Western Thought.*

lecting political leaders (although there was a social elite from which most political leaders emerged), the actual involvement in politics of a widespread
cross-section of the *demos,* and the narrow parameters of time and space that
framed the political deliberations and decisions of the Athenians do not characterize any extant democracy.[140]

Indeed, the proportion of relatively sovereign agents of political power to
ordinary citizens is probably lower in today's democracies than in the oligarchies of Plato's time (which is not, however, to say that current "democracies" are "really" oligarchies). Even for Plato, the cause for the degeneration
of the democratically constituted soul and state into tyranny stems less from
their specifically democratic character than from the eventual domination by
those elements in the soul and state that had instituted the constitutional form
of oligarchy (552b–d, 564b–d)—elements that overwhelm the imputed instability of democracy. Plato's Socrates highlights oligarchic tendencies in democracy as the primary agents of its misfortunes.

For Plato, life in a democracy does not perfectly respect boundaries
that legitimately separate distinctive social roles and functions; such respect
requires supplementation by some order of virtue and law. These lacks are
minor, however, compared with the overwhelming tendency of tyranny
to obliterate them. It disregards the differences between what is conscious
and unconscious, sane and insane, child and parent, human being and god
(571a–574a). At the same time, the arbitrary domination of an irrational, ob-
sessively driven tyrant hoards all political power and dictates the tolerable
limits of psychological and political activity. The tyrannical state and man
function as the nihilistic opposites of the ideal state and nearly angelic souls
of philosopher-guardians (576c–577a).[141]

---

140. Recent historical work has taken pains to point out that many Athenian citizens did
not avidly participate in politics. See L. B. Carter, *The Quiet Athenian.* Granted. But the proportion of the population that performed significant political duties during their lives and directly wielded the levers of power by judging what laws, policies, or judicial decisions ought to
be was far greater in Athens than in today's democracies—undoubtedly, if one looked at the citizen population proper, but also if one included the many slaves, metics, and women in the population of Athens. See R. K. Sinclair, *Democracy and Participation in Athens.* On the practical
constraints affecting the conduct of political decision-making in Athens, see M. I. Finley, "Athenian Demagogues," reprinted in *Democracy Ancient and Modern—Revised Edition,* 38–75.

141. One qualification is in order here. The tyrannical soul and state are not mirror-oppo-
sites of the ideal state and soul of the philosopher-guardian. Tyrants are not dominated or led by
"evil"; they respect nothing higher than themselves. And their "selves" amount to nothing more
than desires. By contrast, the best soul and state are not led by agents but by "reason" and "the

Moreover, Plato's views of the nature of the *demos* are not particularly prejudicial. Insofar as injustice does appear in democracies, it does not result from the nature of the *demos* or the inherent hostility of democracies to philosophy. According to Plato's Socrates, the *demos* does not have a highly developed capacity for critical reason, but its nature is not perverse, and perversity is what incites injustice. Its primary limitations appear in mass meetings, where the gravity of emotion controls the direction of argument and a few individuals find personal advantage in exploiting the intellectual vulnerability of the many. For Plato, the problems of democracy stem from its susceptibility to perverse leadership more than from its actual constitutional character. The injustice manifested in democracies results from the insufficiency of their institutions as an order ruled by virtue and the political art and their susceptibility to influence from impostors who disguise themselves as champions of the people.

Finally, Plato does believe that the many are educable to the point of being rational supporters of the rule of philosopher-guardians. After all, they employ the philosopher-guardians, even as these employees exercise political authority over their employers. They possess a sufficient capacity of critical reason to recognize the good that is taught to them and to practice *sophrosyne* in their lives (499d–500e, 518c). In the discussions by Plato's Socrates of both the general sources of injustice and the particular sources in a democratic constitution, the primary problem of "the many" involves their lack of sophistication and susceptibility to manipulation by individuals who not only are more interested than they in acquiring and wielding power but who would take advantage of them for their own purposes.

To be sure, for Plato's Socrates, democracy provides tyranny with its necessary conditions. No class structure prevents certain types of individuals from becoming leaders. No psychological structure assures the repression of certain desires. Yet, democracies do not institutionalize injustice, and it is not their specifically democratic character that produces tyranny. If a particularly tyrannical individual manages to gain influence in a thriving democratic society, he would be removed, for he would not be able to acquire constitutional protection and legitimization. Plato acknowledges this possibility insofar as a democracy's disrespect for laws occurs only when it has begun to degenerate

---

good." The tyrant may have power but cannot have authority, because his force stems from the intensity and wildness of his brute agency, whereas the power of the philosopher-guardians has impersonal and immaterial sources. It is power legitimated by authority that stems from their rational capacity to imitate the good.

into tyranny (563d). A democracy unable to sustain its democratic character is susceptible to takeover by tyrants, and that is the kind of democracy Plato emphasizes in Book VIII, namely, a democracy where the *demos* does not care for the responsibilities of politics (565a) and has no sense of how to understand or practice a virtuous political art.

Because Plato's Socrates stipulates that no order or restraint exists in the practices of the individual or the city as a whole, democratic politics can reduce to factional, oligarchy-like, quarrels between rich and poor, which finally give rise to the abolition of democratically controlled political power by a tyrant (561d–e). Echoing Thucydides' account of the Corcyran revolution, Plato describes this condition as one in which "[k]nowledge, right principles, true thoughts are not at their post, and the place lies open to the assault of false and presumptuous notions" (560b; see also Thucydides, *History* III.80–84).

Even so, for Plato's Socrates, tyrants are not "men of the people." Tyrants, like oligarchs, gain power through their capacity to manipulate and mislead the *demos* by means of discursive and practical acts of deception (567a–568a, 568d–569c, 575c–d; see also 550c–e). The effects are horrendous. Tyrants destroy the freedom and friendship among democratic citizens, which provide the most nourishing soil for philosophy (among unjust regimes) and replace them with enslavement and mutual hostility. Tyrants despise the fluidity of democratic arrangements of politics and souls and so replace them with the stark antithesis of the just soul and state.

Although the constitutional democracies of state and soul in Book VIII of the *Republic* are not simulacra of the Athenian state or its citizens' souls, this text nevertheless sharply criticizes the adequacy of Athenian political arrangements as guarantors of justice. For the Athenians put faith in the political participation and judgment of the *demos*. The decisions of the Athenian citizens were presumed to be just as long as they had previously deliberated formally about the matter together—in the assembly, council, and courts. Determinations were left to the will of the majority. But unless the choices of the *demos* always hit the mark of the good, democratic institutions and the power effected by majority rule would not be sufficient guarantors of justice.

Did not Athenians already recognize this? Is not human frailty a regular preoccupation of Greek poetry and Athenian tragedy and comedy? If so, what did Athenian democrats actually have to fear from Plato's *Republic*? To the extent that democrats might accept Plato's designation of the three parts of the soul and state, they would honor the freedom and dignity of the *demos* in the state and the desiring component in the soul to a greater extent than

Plato. But for them no less than for Plato would the practical basis for the allotment of political power or the anarchic expression of desire be sufficient as a critical guide for the determination of justice. Yet, besides religion and the law, there was no technical or substantive guide offered in democratic Athens for such determinations, other than the effective pronouncements of political leaders, the voting citizenry, the solicitations of rhetoricians, the rationalizations of Protagorean sophistry, or the entertainment of poets.[142] For Plato, these should not be regarded as sufficient for the constitution of an ethic of justice. That means that something was awry in the *polis* of Athens that no Athenian was currently prepared to acknowledge. Conventional democrats would regard this as a threat, but democrats courageous enough to admit their own imperfections would not.

Here one must keep in mind that Plato's interest in justice in the *Republic* arises as a radically critical response to the difficulty of justifying "justice" as a practice whose value outweighed "injustice." The primary justifications being offered, in Plato's day, were those generated by conventional concerns for reputation, cynical calculations of self-interest, loyal support for the established political order, and the desire for domination. In contrast, Plato's Socrates affirms the political authority of philosopher-guardians. However, Plato's Socrates speaks theoretically. Insofar as that class did not exist in practice, and could not unless there was a fortuitous coincidence of philosophical skill and political power, the effect of the critical affirmation of the art of philosopher-guardianship in *logos* is not so much to condemn democracy as to concretize the first theoretical analysis of the rational and ethical character of political leadership that is not determined by the authority of tradition, convention, or individual or group self-interest.

If democratic alternatives were not critically sufficient to satisfy Plato's desire for a constitution of justice that was discursively adequate "in itself," the

---

142. In *Mass and Elite in Democratic Athens,* Josiah Ober has argued that rhetoricians were more agents than manipulators of the *demos.* The conceptions of justice they employed are rightfully called democratic, but it is radically unclear whether their conceptions of justice provided sufficient ethical or rational criteria of leadership that would benefit the *demos* and Athenian democracy as a whole. This is not to say that as rhetoricians they were bad but rather that they were only rhetoricians, that is, political leaders bent on achieving immediate success in law courts, assemblies, and the military battlefield. Democracies need more kinds of critical discourses than those provided by rhetoricians if their ethical and political deliberations are to produce the greatest possible justice.

question remains of how Plato's theory of justice could be useful for democracy. Plato was writing in a society than had not yet developed either a monotheistic ethic of equal dignity for all human beings or a complex political division of labor.[143] His political world was that of direct democracy in a precapitalist society. Yet he was skeptical of those arrangements that had privileged rule by various elites and rejected all existing oligarchic arrangements that promoted the authority of an elite unskilled in virtue. Amid the political order of democratic Athens, which Plato never sought to overthrow, the primary significance of Plato's theory of justice in relation to democracy is less the elimination of democracy than its investment with critical standards of political judgment that would enable it to reduce the gap between its practical power and the ethic of justice.

Indeed, Plato, like democrats, valued individual and political freedoms (395c, 547c, 560e–561a). He simply believed that their exercise was insufficient as a guarantor of justice. Critical reason was needed to achieve that end. This was so for philosophers as well as for ordinary citizens. Thus Plato's Socrates would not only criticize the democratic value of "do as you please" for the *demos* but would limit the freedom and desires of philosopher-guardians, by requiring them not to devote themselves exclusively to dialectic but to perform the responsibilities of political office. Philosopher-guardians do not seek out political activity, but neither do they experience it entirely as an externally imposed duty; it belongs to the art that defined their identity as a whole. Without that service, philosophers would succumb to the temptation of excess as much as ordinary citizens. In the case of philosophers, they would become either drunk with the pleasures of contemplation to the point where they forgot about the care of the world or so cynical about politics and contemplation that they devoted their intellectual energies to the tyrannical accumulation of wealth and power.

Plato's Socrates in the *Republic* did not fairly recognize the contributions of political freedom and equality to the goodness and justice of Athenian

---

143. A textually careful critique of Platonic justice as not respecting basic liberal values appears in Gregory Vlastos, "The Theory of Social Justice in the *Polis* in Plato's *Republic*," in Helen North, ed., *Interpretations of Plato*, 1–40. Unfortunately, this and other similar criticisms of Plato's ethical limitations often ignore how the establishment of liberal values as a social norm was the flip side of the authorization of the power of the modern state (and, later, a capitalist economy) in delimiting the practical content of that freedom and equality.

democracy. In addition, Plato was unreasonably hopeful about the possibility of finding or educating a person or class that could exercise his conception of critical reason. But this does not create an inherent contradiction between democracy and Platonic justice. The extent of their opposition depends on the extent to which the problems that generate the discord and disease of a political community are understood to be either socially produced and politically remediable by the *demos* or products of necessary conditions of human nature that are immune to any conscious effort at political transformation by citizens themselves. The issue concerns the prospects of political education. In this light, the *Republic* directly addresses the political significance of the tension underlying the argument of itself as a text, the problematic efficacy of critical discourse as an agent of justice, the political tensions between *logos* and *ergon*.

D. *Logos* AND *Ergon*

I. GAPS AND BRIDGES

Because of the singular importance of the relation between *logos* and *ergon* for Plato's overall philosophical project, the task of isolating it for critical scrutiny in an interpretation of the *Republic* poses serious problems involving the relation of part to whole. Yet this relation is manifestly crucial for understanding both the dialogue and the Platonic political art more generally. In general, the political art constitutes justice by translating critical discourse into practice, actions, or deeds that would benefit every citizen and the political community as a whole. In the *Republic*, its virtuous practice secures the conditions under which (inter alia) each member of the community has "the power of doing one's own" (433d; see also 433e–434a).

But Plato's argument about justice in the *Republic* consists not only of a first-order discussion of the nature of justice but also a second-order discussion about how we should interpret the first-order discussion. When the character of Socrates urges his interlocutors at various points in the *Republic* to pay attention to the relation of *their* dialogue to understanding "his" theory of justice, Plato urges us (as his readers) to reflect on the second-order issue of the dialogue's philosophy of interpretation. Moreover, insofar as the reader's activity of interpretation translates *logos* into the *ergon* of his own psychological or political life, the *logos-ergon* relation in the *Republic* literarily expresses the educational relation of his dialogue about justice to the life of the dialogue's reader.

The second-order discussion of the theme of *logos-ergon* in relation to first-order views of justice appears in four places in the *Republic.* In each case, comments about the relation of *logos-ergon* precede—and thereby, to some extent, frame—a subsequent discussion of justice. These are (1) in Books II–III, as Socrates lays out the program of early education for all citizens (but especially the guardians) of *kallipolis;* (2) in the middle of Book V, where Socrates pinpoints the problematic relation of *kallipolis* to political possibility and forecasts the problematic character of his argument for philosophers as the only possible just rulers; (3) at the end of Book IX, where Socrates interprets the implications of his ideal *politeia* and *logos* of justice for an ordinary citizen who believes in the ideal of justice but lives in an unjust city; and (4) Book X as a whole, where Plato provides a more theoretically comprehensive treatment of the phenomenon of "imitation" or (more appropriately here) "representation" than he had done in Books II–III and does so in terms of the *logos-ergon* relation. In Book X, Socrates relates his discussion of representation to psychological, ethical, and political reform—indeed, to education and the nature of reality more generally—and glosses his justification of the positive relation of justice to happiness with a myth about the afterlife that coheres with his prior philosophical arguments.[144]

We focus on the four aforementioned parts of the dialogue that directly address the problematic relation of *logos* to *ergon*, attending particularly to the adequacy of "imitation" (*mimesis*) as a model for the art of (political) education—for imitation may be seen as one way of incorporating *logos* into *ergon*.[145] In this sense, we see how education (*paideia*) for Plato involves the

---

144. For complementary readings of the integral relation of Book X to the rest of the *Republic,* see Catherine Osborne, "The Repudiation of Representation in Plato's *Republic* and Its Repercussions," especially 53–55, and S. Halliwell's "Introduction" to *Plato: Republic 10.*

145. Plato's discussion of *mimesis* has been one of the more controversial topics for interpreters of the *Republic.* This is not surprising, for Plato's comments on it include the justification of censorship, the political use of myths that directly conflict with factual reality, the activity of political reform as painting on a blank canvas, and the expulsion of mimetic poets from his ideal city. Plato's hostility to *mimesis* has been so great that some scholars have read Platonic justice as hostile to any kind of artistic *mimesis,* and others have regarded his critique of mimetic poetry in Book X as philosophically "gratuitous and clumsy . . . impossible to reconcile with [his critique of poetry in] Book III," part of a book that, with respect to "the main argument" of the *Republic,* is an "excrescence." (For a reading of Plato as hostile to *mimesis* in general, see Eric Havelock, *Preface to Plato,* 34–35, n. 37. For these dismissive comments about Book X, see Annas, *An In-*

use of various discourses and practices as parts of an art that genuinely cultivates virtue in citizens. By viewing education in this perspective, Plato criticizes poets and Sophists in the *Republic* as faulty educators of virtue and the
political art.[146] For Plato, bad poets form the complement to bad politicians;
each distorts a dimension of the political art. Whereas the latter pervert the
proper relation between *logos* and *ergon* at the level of political practice, the
former do so in the realm of education, which cultivates the psychic ground
in which the institutions of power take hold. The ancient quarrel between
philosophy and poetry to which Socrates refers in Book x (607b) complements the opposition between philosophy and conventional power that was
previously discussed in the *Republic* and to which the *Republic* as a whole is
a response.[147]

    The four junctures at which Plato raises the issue of the relation of *logos*
to *ergon* directly involve critiques of prevailing forms of *mimesis* as constituents of political education. Each of these sections of the *Republic* also recognizes the obstacles to establishing justice and perfecting the political art.
Altogether, they amount to a reprise of his Socratic Problem, the conflict between virtue and the conventional political art. In particular, they belong to
his substantive concern about uncritically accepting the utterances of poets

---

troduction to Plato's Republic, 335–36.) But if the *Republic* is read as an innovative, critical discourse on the ethics of political power, one that would reconstruct the bases of political education, then Plato's treatment of *mimesis* throughout the dialogue appears to be not only philosophically coherent but central to the project of the *Republic* as a whole.

    The argument for the coherence of Book x with Book III was first made clearly by J. Tate,
in "'Imitation' in Plato's *Republic,*" and idem, "Plato and 'Imitation.'" It has been picked up and
developed in the light of recent scholarship by S. Halliwell, *Plato: Republic X;* G. Ferrari, "Plato
and Poetry," in George A. Kennedy, ed., *The Cambridge History of Literary Criticism,* 1:92–
148; Elisabeth Asmis, "Plato on Poetic Creativity," in R. Kraut, ed., *The Cambridge Companion
to Plato,* 338–64; and Christopher Janaway, *Images of Excellence: Plato's Critique of the Arts.*

    146. By treating them in this light, Plato reflects commonly held beliefs of his time, and this
historical context informs the discursive argument of the dialogues. See H. I. Marrou, *A History
of Education in Antiquity;* Eric Havelock, *A Preface to Plato;* Kevin Robb, *Literacy and Paideia
in Ancient Greece.*

    147. To recall, according to Pericles in Thucydides' *History,* the Athenians of the mid-fifth
century did not "imitate" others; they made use of their *politeia* in a way that became a "model"
and "education" for all Greece. They also did not need an unreliable Homer to sing their praises,
for their own deeds were sufficient memorials to their way of life. See Thucydides, *History*
II.37.I, II.41.I, II.41.4. On the relation of *logos* to *ergon* in Thucydides, see Adam Parry, *Logos
and Ergon in Thucydides.*

and politicians, as well as written texts, as signs of truth, virtue, or justice.[148] These "junctures" also are self-referential, for they relate to Plato's own philosophical activity as a just political art, whose *logos* would produce harmony rather than discord in the souls of those affected by it. They should be understood, therefore, as parts of Plato's own philosophical drama about the difficulties of an education in justice, a kind of "apology" *for himself* as an educator and practitioner of the political art.

The relation of *logos* to *ergon* in the *Republic* most clearly emerges, therefore, as the issue of education as an inherently and distinctively political issue and activity. This education is not political in any conventional sense. For the power of its *logos* depends on the rejection of any accommodation to institutional or personal rule that is not rooted in both the *logos* of virtue (that guides the just soul) and the rejection of the discourse of power as domination (that characterizes political conventions). Addressing the issue involves a philosophical reconstruction of justice in terms of a new order of power, the ideal *politeia* of soul and state. Ultimately, Plato's treatment of the relation between *logos* and *ergon* in the *Republic* clarifies the uniquely political character of the *Republic* as a constitution of justice—namely, as a critical art of political education.[149]

After the Athenians' defeat in the Peloponnesian War and their trial and execution of Socrates, the Athenian *politeia* could no longer be a *paradeigma* for Plato, and the best evidence of that was his view of the conceptions of justice that prevailed in it, neatly presented in Book 1 of the *Republic* by

148. For example, in Plato's *Apology*, where he favorably reports Socrates' questioning of the authoritative status of poets and politicians; in Plato's *Ion*, where Socrates undermines the authority of rhapsodes; in Plato's *Protagoras*, where Socrates criticizes the authority of the sophist Protagoras as a teacher of the political art and interpreter of poetry; in Plato's *Phaedrus*, where Socrates cautions one's direct acceptance of the authority of written texts, and in the *Seventh Letter*, where "Plato" asserts the insufficiency of his writings as full representations of his teachings.

149. By reading the *Republic* as a dialogue about education, I am, of course, not breaking new ground. In *Emile*, Rousseau notably referred to the *Republic* as "the finest treatise on [public] education ever written" (London: Dent, 1974, 8). But this passing comment glides over the character of this education, and it has too often been read to justify a depoliticized reading of the text. (For example, see Havelock, *Preface to Plato*, 3–19, especially 18, n. 37. Interestingly, Havelock follows Cornford in taking Book 1 of the *Republic*, where the political context for education most graphically appears, as separable from the rest of the dialogue.) The educational character of the political dimension of the *Republic* was first noted by German scholars in the 1920s, particularly Friedlander, Jaeger, and Gadamer, and has been more recently by J. Peter Euben.

Cephalus, Polemarchus, and Thrasymachus. Plato's new constitution of justice in *logos* in the *Republic* provides a new *paradeigma* for education, one that is neither conventionally Athenian nor entirely Socratic (although it would remain true to what is redemptive in the historical realities of both). However, the very coherence of Plato's *logos* of justice involves a new gap and potential tension between the new *paradeigma*—the *logos* of justice in an ideal *politeia*—and the *ergon* of everyday life. Each section of the *Republic* in which the *logos-ergon* frames a subsequent discussion reveals this new gap even as it establishes bridges over old ones.

2. THE EDUCATION OF *Mimesis*

In Book I, Plato's Socrates had been only provisionally successful in establishing a *logos* of justice over and against the *ergon* of conventional definitions. He had defined justice in terms of what he said it did rather than what it was, and analytical definitions of just activity in *logos* carried little authority as long as its significance was framed in existing conventions or patterns of political understanding—the prevailing ethical and political constitutions. Platonic justice needs legitimization, in both theoretical and practical terms, as a discourse that makes sense for the constitution of a happy life. Plato's Socrates recognizes this, insofar as the establishment of the *politeia* of justice in Books II–VII of the *Republic* involves the reformation of existing educational institutions for the soul and state.

In the previous sections of this chapter, we have noted how the character of genuine justice in the *Republic* appears in response to the deformations of social life caused by the pursuit of excess in personal wealth and political power. In Socrates' previous genealogy of a "city of justice," there was a relatively healthy stage in which mimetic artists had not yet appeared; the appearance of mimetic artists in the city parallels or marks (even if one cannot conclude that they particularly caused) the appearance of "excess." Socrates' initial efforts to construct a regime of justice in Books II–III involve reducing the new fever that has beset this city of excess. His first steps along the way implement an educational process that cultivates those formal characteristics of grace and rhythm that mark the good practice of ordinary, practical *technai* (see 401c–402b). This educational art (or process) makes sure that the elementary arts of psychic and physical development, *mousike* and *gymnastic*, dispose the characters of citizens toward virtue and justice by providing appropriate "models" (*tupoi*) and "images" (*eikona*).[150] The new education would provide imitative models that, unlike the models of gods and heroes promoted in Homeric discourse and mimetic poetry more generally, are free from falsehood and vice.[151]

For Plato, Homeric discourse imitates the gods in ways that do not produce health; it offers models of alterity and vice more than constancy and virtue and so distorts the nature of God and gods. It amounts to genuine falsehood (382a), which "is hated not only by gods but by men" (382c). Plato's Socrates analogizes the activity of Homeric poets to that of a charlatan craftsman who harms those who rely on his *techne* for authoritatively connecting *logos* and *ergon;* politically they function as the sailors who mislead the ship of state (389c–d; see also 488aff). This condition justifies the guardians' use of falsehoods in words and censorship more generally. They operate as a kind of medicine (*pharmakon,* 382d, 389b) to remedy the condition of the souls that are sick from imitating these falsehoods, which sustain ideals and social conditions that promote injustice.[152]

Plato's Socrates justifies these reforms not by referring to metaphysical givens but by invoking indisputable values, teasing out their practical requirements, and then comparing this standard with (his description of) cultural conventions (which would not be widely accepted). Here, education— *mousike,* to be precise—is an instrument; it operates as a process of "imitation," whereby one uses images of virtue to foster its actualization among the

---

150. *Republic* 373b, 377a, 378e, 399e–400e, 402d. Here, the Athenian discursive context again appears as the background of Plato's innovative discourse but only as the vehicle on which Plato could reform educational practices.

151. Evidence for this characterization of Socrates' initial discussion of the "musical" content of education (*paideia*) begins in the middle of Book II and continues into Book III (376e–403c). Particularly relevant passages are 377b–c, 377e, 379a, 380c, 382a–383b, 389b–d, 402a–d.

152. The practice of censorship is horrific to us, because it is associated with censors who are typically ignorant, self-serving, and fearful. But the censorship Plato believes to be necessary does not close down critical inquiry or foster obedience to existing authorities; rather, it operates at the elementary stages of education as the basis for developing critical thought. Moreover, the educational content with which he is concerned cannot be compared with contemporary literature for it expressed the *religious* discourse of ethical value, that is, the ultimate discursive bases for a *logos* of virtue. We teach Homer in secular college courses, not as the template of knowledge for youth. In this respect, these passages of the *Republic* manifest an ancient version of parental dissatisfaction with educational media for offering sources of imitation that fail to develop the bodies and minds of children to their full potential.

young.[153] If the imitative process does not engender health, that is, virtue, in the soul, then educational cures become necessary.

When Socrates turns to the procedural forms of education in Book III, he introduces further regulations. He is particularly upset about the mimetic form of discourse—here defined more narrowly than before—in contrast to narrative discourse. It conceals the relation of the poet, who functions socially as an authority, to the epistemological and ethical value of the discourse being presented (392d–393c). Mimetic discourse anarchically proliferates models for ethical and political education and induces (or seduces) citizens to indiscriminately make one or more of them models for themselves. Ultimately, Plato's Socrates wants "unmixed imitators" of the proper likenesses of virtue (397d; more generally, see also 392d–403c). This criticism reiterates in the *Republic*'s general context of political and psychological reformation criticisms made in other Platonic dialogues about Sophists, rhetoricians, and poets who claim to practice *technai* but whose discourse incoherently relates to what they effectively accomplish.[154]

Motivating the narrative of the next four and one-half books of the *Republic* is the need to make sure that the guardians themselves will imitate virtue as they perform their political art. The myth of the metals, a verbal noble falsehood (414c), is a constitutive means to this end. The myth provides an imitative model that will enable everyone to practice the *techne* most appropriate to his or her nature in the most virtuous way, assuring the well-being of each individual and the political community as a whole. It is one among many other material and intellectual conditions, which are designed to guard against the excessive behavior that produces the *stasis* of injustice.[155] As ideal educational guides for all citizens, these conditions enable the guardians to be "craftsmen of civic freedom" whose *techne* cultivates both psychic and political *arete*, the harmonious unity that characterizes the just constitutions of souls and states (395c, 402b–c). Even guardians need to presuppose the truth of the noble lie during their early education. Throughout the early stages of

---

153. The "forms" (*eide*) of virtue have not yet been introduced as part of the educational process. See 402c.

154. On the matter of poets as practitioners of *technai*, see Christopher Janaway, "Arts and Crafts in Plato and Collingwood," and his *Images of Excellence*. This point also highlights Plato's antagonism toward tragedy, an art form that was particularly associated with Athenian democracy. He develops his criticism of tragedy much further in Book x.

155. For the harmonious unity of justice, see 420c–424b, 433a–b. For references to excessive behavior and its links to injustice, see I.344a, 349a–350a; II.359c, 362b, 365d; VIII.586a–c.

the education of the guardians, Socrates' discourse is primarily instrumental, paving the way for the establishment of Plato's idea/l of justice.[156] In this way, Plato initially establishes a hypothetical model of justice, which he then (partially) justifies.

The second Platonic reference to the relation of *logos* to *ergon* directly addresses the problematic character of the issue of actualizing these discursive ideals. Just before his argument in Book v for the political authority of philosophy and philosophers, Socrates directly considers the question of whether the practicability of his ideal state affects the coherence of his *logos* about it (472b–473a). Here, too, his answer points out a gap in the relation between the critical discourse of justice as an idea/l and political practice.

The textual context for my remarks is Glaucon's interruption of Socrates' account of the legislation that would govern the rule of the philosopher-guardians. The continuation of Socrates' narrative sketch of the ideal, just *politeia* cannot go on without a further specification of the possibility of its *logos* being practically achieved (471b–c, 472b). Glaucon's demand takes Socrates aback. A proper response to it, he says, requires the sympathetic tolerance or forbearance (*sungnome*) of his interlocutors, because it literally entails a "paradox" (472a; see also 473c). Plato's Socrates notes that this difficulty is inherent in their inquiry into the nature of justice and injustice.

In a crucial exchange, Socrates asks Glaucon:

> "If we do discover what justice is, are we to demand that the just man shall differ from it in no respect, but shall conform in every way to what it really is? Or will it suffice us if he approximates it as nearly as possible and partakes of it more than others?" "That will content us," [Glaucon] said. "A pattern [*paradeigma*], then, was what we wanted when we were inquiring into what justice itself is and asking what would be the character of the perfectly just man, supposing him to exist; and likewise, in regard to injustice and the completely unjust man. We wished to fix our eyes on them, so that whatever we discerned in them of happiness or the reverse would necessarily apply to ourselves in the sense that whosoever is likest them will have the

---

156. I deliberately combine idea and ideal, because, for Plato, ideas are understood rationally, and such rationality inherently possesses both an ethical and a critical relation to the current world (where injustice reigns).

allotment or fate most like to theirs. Our purpose was not to demonstrate the possibility of these ideas coming into being." "In that," he
said, "you speak truly." "Do you think, then, that he would be any
the less a good painter, who, after painting a pattern [*paradeigma*] of
the really [ideally] beautiful man and omitting no touch required for
the perfection of the picture, should not be able to prove that it is actually possible for such a man to exist?" "Not I, by Zeus," he said.
"Then were not we, as we say, trying to create in words (*logo*) the
pattern of a good *polis*?" "Certainly." (472b–e)

Plato's Socrates has now authorized his own special version of artistic *mimesis*.[157] Ironically, it partly resembles the forms of *mimesis* that he has rejected.
Like pseudo-*technai*, its foundations are immaterial and its reliability as a
genuine *techne* is not practically verifiable. But unlike them, its *paradeigma*
evidences the character of virtue, so that its imitation cultivates rather than
corrupts the possibility of virtue in actual life.[158] More significantly, the activity of Platonic imitation cannot be justified in terms that Plato himself has
used to justify a practice as a *techne*. For evidence of expertise in the practice
of a *techne* comes from its *ergon*. With the *techne* of Platonic imitation, however, no particular practical deeds are required, only the practical effort to
produce them in ethical and political discourse. Plato acknowledges practical
limits on the realization of his ideal, but this diminishes neither its power nor
authority; to the contrary, the gap constitutes the distinctive authority of Platonic *logos*.

As Socrates states to Glaucon:

"Do you think, then, that our words are any the less well spoken if
we find ourselves unable to prove that it is possible for a *polis* to be
governed in accordance with our words?" "Of course not," he said.
"That, then," said I, "is the truth of the matter. But if, to please you,
we must do our best to show how most probably and in what respect
these things would be most nearly realized, again, without a view to
such a demonstration, grant me the same point." "What?" "Is it possible for anything to be realized in deed as it is spoken in word, or is
it the nature of things that action should partake of truth less than
speech, even if some deny it? Do you admit it or not?" "I do," he

---

157. For other examples, see 396c–398b and 501a–c. The latter passage is discussed below.
158. The compatibility of this activity with the arguments of Book x, where Socrates rejects
poetic *mimesis* altogether, is discussed below.

said, "Then don't insist," said I, "that I must exhibit as realized in deed what we expounded in words. But if we can discover how a *polis* might be governed most nearly answering to our description, you must say that we have discovered that possibility of realization which you demanded. Will you not be content if you get this? I for my part would." "And I too," he said. (472e–473a)

This is how Plato maintains a connection between *logos* and *ergon*, understood as theoretical knowledge and practical life.[159] The connection is not embodied in the discourse itself, taken as a metaphysical foundation; nor can the discourse provide a blueprint for either political or personal life; on the other hand, the discourse is not merely utopian. Instead, that connection exists in one's inevitably problematic *effort* both to identify genuine justice discursively and philosophically and to exemplify it practically and politically.[160]

Plato's Socrates takes pains to emphasize how radically different this activity is from conventional understandings of how to be just. For example, its performance is not primarily signified by the activity of helping friends and harming enemies; to the contrary, it is marked by the persuasion of education, not the coercion of violence. It consists of an art but not one of authoritarian imposition. The essentially noncoercive aspect of the educational relation of Platonic *logos* to *ergon* becomes clear in two subsequent passages. One portrays the more practical and political and the other the more intellectual and personal side of this persuasive activity.

The first occurs in Book VI, after Socrates has explained why true philosophers possess authority as rulers despite being scorned in conventional deliberations about who should rule. He proceeds to characterize more precisely than he has before the nature of such philosophers and the form in which they would rule if they had the power. In so doing, he employs the lan-

159. Aristotle severs this gap because he cannot find any clear practical referent for what the good requires. (See *Nicomachean Ethics* 1.6, and the separation of theoretical and practical knowledge in the *Metaphysics* 1025b1–26, 1026b4–5; see also *Nicomachean Ethics* 1106b8–18, and *Politics* 1288b21–22.) But Aristotle can make this argument because he has ignored or denied the critical problem that informs Plato's solution, namely the *stasis* generated by the gap between virtue and the political art.

160. Those who find in Platonic justice a fundamentally metaphysical argument with authoritarian or totalitarian political significance (from Karl Popper to Richard Rorty) tend to reduce to insignificance Plato's problematization of the relation between *logos* and *ergon*. Interpretively, this amounts to the view that when Plato says that the quickest way to establish his ideal city in a nonideal setting is the rustication of those over ten years of age (540d–541a), he either demonstrates his philosophical affinity with the Khmer Rouge (Popper) or manifests his literary art (Rorty).

guage of imitation. A philosopher-guardian "[f]ixes his gaze upon eternal things of the mind,[161] and seeing that they neither wrong nor are wronged by one another, but all abide in harmonic order as reason (*logon*) bids, he will endeavour to *imitate* [italics added] them and, as far as may be, to fashion himself in their likeness and assimilate himself to them" (500c). Having done so, she or he uses this divine *paradeigma* as the ideal point of reference for his or her work as a "true musician" (402c; see also 591c–d) or craftsman who paints moderation, justice, and all forms of civic virtue in "the figure of the constitution" (500d–e).

The best work requires a "blank canvas," but this does not imply the philosopher-guardian's ignorance or coercion of citizens. To the contrary, this philosophical-political artist attends to the human nature with which he works, and the radical demand for a "clean slate" simply reflects a radically critical judgment of how humanity deserves to become as close to divinity as it can. The effect of this activity engenders political consensus; it convinces the many, at least those who are moderate, of the justice of the philosopher's political art (501b–e).[162]

The second passage describes the encounter between the virtuous practitioner of the political art, who has seen the good and those who have not. Socrates describes it as the *techne* of education, and, again, the engagement is not coercive. It depends on the ruler's recognition of the inherent capacity for learning of the ruled. Such a *techne* does not operate like ordinary *technai* that might try to insert vision entirely from the outside. Rather, it is an art of turning the soul. The teacher-practitioner who interpretively applies the *logos* of this *techne* assumes that his or her student-material possesses vision but does not rightly employ it (518b–d). To be sure, this is an argument about leader-

161. These things or "beings" are typically understood to be "the forms," but their onto-logical status—at this juncture, in any event—is unclear.

162. Note Thucydides' account of Pericles' funeral oration, where he praises the aesthetic judgment of the Athenians as part and parcel of their excellent citizenship. This passage from Thucydides is cited with admiration by Hannah Arendt in her essay on culture, even though she also criticizes in this essay and in *The Human Condition* the conceptualization of politics as a *techne*, which she also attributes to Plato. For Arendt, Collingwood, and others, *techne* has an inherently instrumental quality, which differentiates it from aesthetic activity, whose uniqueness stems from its noninstrumental character. This distinction reflects the modern differentiation of arts and crafts, the distinctions and borders between which Plato does not observe.

The harshest critics of Plato, such as Popper, find in this image traces of the fascist impulse to politicize the aesthetic or aestheticize the political. But this interpretation presupposes the modern (that is, Kantian) isolation of the realms of politics and art, the political and the aesthetic, a distinction that neither Plato nor Greeks more generally recognized.

ship as well as education, and the leadership is inherently political. However, its distinctive quality does not involve increased power for leaders but rather the educational dimension of their political rule, a dimension that derives from Plato's supposition that conventional politics plays with illusions of justice, just as puppeteers might manipulate puppets on the stage of a cave (514aff).

Socrates now directly confronts the obstacles that prevent an educational closure of this gap between leaders and led, those who have seen the light and those who still remain in the dark, and suggests means for their removal. His measures involve paradoxical formulations that are extremely difficult to accept. In the *Republic,* however, they are familiar. At the moment of transition between *logos* and *ergon* or the translation of *logos* into *ergon,* Plato's Socrates most frequently introduces his most famously shocking proposals. These are the censorship of all literature in society (for the sake of cultivating healthy powers of imagination in the citizenry—an action reviewed and reevaluated in Book x), the myth of the metals (on behalf of the appropriate social and political division of labor), the necessary coincidence of philosophy and political power, the regulation of procreation among the citizenry as a whole (but particularly strictly among the guardians), the expulsion of children over ten from the city (in order to expedite the process of political transformation of conditions of injustice to those of justice), the political supervision of the work of poets and playwrights by philosopher-guardians (in order to eliminate the potential of mimetic artists to foster injustice). Each of these demonstrates how serious and imposing are the obstacles to the practical realization of truth and justice. Their consistency with the general Platonic project of articulating a discourse of justice that reveals the mutual interdependence of justice and happiness emphasizes the difficulties facing its perfect completion.

The vehicles suggested by Plato's Socrates in the *Republic* for crossing the gap between *logos* and *ergon* constitute what critics of Plato take to be the incriminating evidence against him. If these changes are necessary to make Platonic justice practical, so the argument goes, then the theory itself must be radically flawed. The complaints of the critics are well-founded insofar as history contains far too many stories of human suffering caused by those who believe that they themselves are agents of justice and refuse to compromise while advancing their cause. But Plato's *Republic* is not responsible for these stories. Plato's portrayals of changes in practice need to be taken seriously for the ends they signify, but he does not offer them as proposals for public policy. Rather, they function as critical signs of the distance between Plato's critical discourse of justice and (what he takes to be) the typical habits of extant societies. Platonic justice indeed provides a theoretical architecture for polit-ical education, but it is one without blueprints.

When Plato directly focuses on the educational journey from the world of injustice to the understanding of justice, his Socrates notes that it will not transform the souls of travelers who do not go willingly. The education by which one learns the difference between sunlight and shadowy reflections cannot be summarily imposed. In the *Seventh Letter,* "Plato" abjured the use of violence as a political tactic and verified this belief with events from his own life. In the *Republic,* the philosopher-guardians are the only rulers who do not come to power through force and fear—which is why they are not liter-ally called "rulers" (463a–464a). These points do not deny Plato's efforts to affirm the objectivity of the good or the degree to which the imitation of the conceptions of truth, goodness, and justice offered by his Socrates constrain conventional freedom and desire. They assert the need for persuasion, rather than violence, as the necessary (if not sufficient) condition for making sure both that the most rewarding kinds of freedom and desire reign and that power enacts justice.[163]

That Plato's word-picture of a comprehensive and genuinely educational dis-course constitutes the core of Plato's philosophy of politics is confirmed at the end of Book IX, with his last major series of comments on the proper con-nection of *logos* and *ergon.* Having characterized the constitutional order of unjust states and souls, Socrates summarizes his argument for why a life of justice has intrinsic benefits and why it constitutes happiness. The subsequent argument, like his previous bridges between the ideals of discursive *logos* and the actualities of practical *ergon,* is presented self-critically.[164]

---

163. The discussion here pertains to the consideration of Platonic justice. In the *Statesman* and *Laws,* Plato justifies the use of coercive force, but the context for those remarks must be con-sidered. As a result, I do not comment on them extensively until the next chapter. All that needs to be said here is that his justifications for force in them is not significantly different from those that justify the police and army today. Plato is neither pacifist nor anarchist.

164. Briefly put, it involves (1) a recapitulation of the assertion that internal harmony and order, as opposed to disharmony and *stasis,* accompany the justly constituted state and soul (580b–c, see also 586e); (2) an argument that the philosopher of justice, rather than the man of injustice, is better at evaluating what counts as a beneficial experience or way of life because of his greater experience of the variety of pleasures the world has to offer (580d–583a); and (3) an account of the nature of pleasure that ultimately links the fullest experience of it to a life of jus-tice (586e–587a). These passages evidence good reasons for J. S. Mill's so admiring Plato. Recall Mill's citation in *Utilitarianism* of the philosophical inquirer as the individual who is both most experienced with and most enamored by the highest human pleasures.

Plato's Socrates offers an account of how a just man would order his life in an unjust world. He asserts that the just man can be best understood (once again) by an "image." When it comes to human beings actually living their lives, their nature as individuals amounts only to a shell. What counts is not their essence as individuals but the relationship among the components of an individual's inner self.[165] These parts, previously identified as the rational, spirited, and appetitive parts of the soul, appear in the images of a man, lion, and beast (588b–589c). Insofar as every human being possesses these three parts of the soul and every human being has this "manly" part in him (or her—*anthropon* is not exclusively male), this imagery suggests every person has the capacity to live a justly ordered life. At the same time, however, Plato asserts that manual workers are typically unable to order their souls properly; they require guidance from an external agent, namely philosophers, to assure the goodness and justice of their lives (590c–d). Socrates analogizes the purpose of such rule to that of a parent over a child (590e). This passage is the most blatantly paternalistic in the *Republic*. It has been used as major evidence for viewing the relation of Platonic reason to ordinary citizens as that of master to slave and Platonic justice as "a radical denial of democracy," essentially opposed to government based on the consent of the governed.[166] To be sure, it evidences Plato's prejudices about the natural psychological limitations of individuals whose lives involve hard, manual, subservient labor. The most distinctive part of Socrates' argument here, however, is not its paternalistic component. For Plato's Socrates bemoans the hierarchical relationship that exists between ruler and ruled, and he points out its presence in Thrasymachus's explanation of justice as rule by the stronger (590d). As long as justice is a meaningful critical concept for ordering the lives of individuals and states, and unless anarchy produces justice (such that individuals "naturally" or self-sufficiently know how to constrain their behavior for the good of themselves and their society), there will have to be limitations on individual autonomy. That hierarchies will characterize the exercise of political power and limit the autonomy of individuals (and that of some more than others) is neither controversial nor what distinguishes this Platonic passage. Its signifi-

165. Such relations are themselves critically shaped by the external environment. This passage does not controvert other parts of the *Republic* that affirm the critical role of social conditions in shaping the characters of individuals.

166. See Gregory Vlastos, "Slavery in Plato's Thought," reprinted in his *Platonic Studies*, particularly 147–53, and Bernard Williams, "The Analogy of City and Soul in Plato's *Republic*," in *Exegesis and Argument*, ed. E. N. Lee et al.

cance lies primarily in pointing out the unique character of Platonic rule, which seeks the greatest possible reduction of the experience of domination and the establishment of the ideal *politeia* in the soul of everyone in order to achieve freedom and justice (590d–591a). Autonomy and freedom that accord with justice constitute Plato's conception of justice itself.

The more important issue raised by asserting a leadership role for Platonic *logos* is whether philosophy and philosophers can be helpful agents in achieving justice for workers. Ultimately, it leads to the question of what can be the practical efficacy of (the discourse of) Platonic justice in an unjust society. In the individual, Platonic justice is achieved when the "man" controls the lion and beast in himself. But, Glaucon asks, how does the reality of his internal justice relate to a world ungoverned by that constitution? This circumstance was initially noted in Book VI (497a), when Plato pictured the philosopher as seeking shelter from the storm of lawlessness that pervades existing societies. That comment, however, sheds no light on the relation of the *logos* of justice in the individual to his activity as a just agent in an unjust society. Glaucon's question in Book IX requires that Socrates say more, for it highlights the gap between *logos* and *ergon,* virtue and the political art, ethics and power, posing once again Plato's Socratic Problem.

Socrates answers him in the following way. The activities acquiring wealth, power, or bodily health and fitness do not produce happiness. This is not to say that they are inherently harmful, only that the just man or "true musician" (see 402c) ultimately pursues only those activities that contribute to the harmonious ordering of the parts of his soul. For Socrates, this theoretical criterion practically means the following:

> "He will not let himself be dazzled by the enjoyments of the multitude and pile up limitless amounts of wealth, having unlimited, bad results [as do the few]." "No, I think not," he [Glaucon] said. "He will rather," I said, "keep his eyes fixed on the constitution within himself, and guarding it, lest he disturb anything there either by excess or deficiency or wealth, will so govern himself and add to or detract from his wealth on this principle, so far as may be." "Precisely so," he said. "And in the matter of honors and office, too, he will keep his eyes fixed on this guiding principle: He will gladly take part in and enjoy those which he thinks will make him a better man, but in public and private life he will shun those that may overthrow his established habit within." "Then, if that is his chief concern," he said, "he will not want to practice politics." "Yes, by the dog," said I, "in

his own *polis* he certainly will, yet perhaps not in his fatherland, except if some providential good fortune befell it." "I understand," he said, " you mean the *polis* whose establishment we have described, which exists in our rational discourse (*logois*); for I think that it can be found nowhere on earth." "Well," I said, "perhaps there is a pattern [*paradeigma*] of it laid up in heaven for him who wishes to see it, and thus seeing to establish that pattern within himself. But it makes no difference whether it exists now or ever will come into being. The politics of this city only will be his and of none other." "That seems likely," he said. (591d–592a)

For Plato, the good life is a political life. In order to justify one's unqualified participation in it, however, the constitutional order must be perfectly just. But no one lives in such an order, so how are we, as individuals living in unjust orders of one kind or another, to interpret the practical significance of this statement? On the one hand, this argument certainly does not promote political activism as an intrinsic good, certainly not as a strictly or inherently democratic argument would. To the contrary, Plato's emphasis on moderation or self-control (*sophrosyne*) might seem to devalue the kind of courageous risk-taking that strongly affirmative and oppositional political activity requires. On the other hand, Platonically just individuals are philosophers who perform just deeds. This suggests that an agent of Platonic justice cannot be virtuous or just while supporting an unjust regime. In other words, living in an unjust society—as everyone does—does not relieve citizens of responsibility for acting as justly as they can. Consequently, political passivity cannot be a favored norm; indeed, that would regularly undermine the connection and coherence of word and deed required by the perfectly practiced political art in a just, constitutionally well-ordered society.

Plato provides no direct answer to the question of how one should participate in a moderately unjust regime or society. Nor does he sketch a road to political reform, travel on which would systematically improve a moderately unjust regime. Still, although acting in a Platonically just manner does not necessarily involve political activism as it is conventionally understood (although that may at times promote Platonic justice), it does require active philosophical interpretation of the meaning of justice and good faith efforts to actualize its requirements. For Socrates' discourse in the *Republic* notes how a political environment can make it more difficult for just individuals to survive. The precise degree to which such a life would be (conventionally) political and the particular character of its (Platonically appropriate) political involvement depend on the degree and character of injustice in the world around one and on the prospects for political education. In other words, how Platonically just persons relate to the politics of their countries differs, depending on whether the country resembles Nazi Germany or the Federal Republic of Germany, Stalin's Soviet Union or Putin's Russia, South Africa with or without apartheid, the United States in 1856, 1968, or 2000 (as well as, for example, whether one is black or white, male or female, Christian, Muslim, or Jew, rich or poor, homosexual or heterosexual), the democratic *polis* of Athens or the republican regime of the United States.

At the minimum, however, this passage does make clear that a Platonically just individual can be neither tyrannically despotic nor violent. Moreover, his or her politicalness involves (1) radically critical judgment about the gap between the *logos* of justice and the array of factors impeding the harmonious constitution of his soul and state, and (2) a way of life that would reduce the size of that gap without corrupting him. It is a philosophical life engaged in political education. As such, it radically differed from the kinds of politics and education that prevailed in fourth-century Athens but not to the point of involving immediate or necessary practical opposition to—or support of—its democratic constitution. The question always to be asked in determining how to live justly involves how to make one's own society more virtuous—a question that involves not merely the nature of one's individual character but the constitutional order of ethics and power in society. Certainly, establishing the Academy (at least, in Plato's view) would serve this end. And yet, given Plato's decision to advise Dionysius II (and "his" version of it in the *Seventh Letter*), doing so did not completely fulfill Plato's own—that is, the philosopher's—political responsibilities to his vocation.

Having completed his account of how different the politics of Platonic justice or *kallipolis* are from the politics of his day, as well as his account of their relation to his conceptions of the forms and the good, Plato turns once again, in Book x, to the subject of education. Book x neatly completes Socrates' narrative response to Thrasymachus, Glaucon, and Adeimantus.[167] Socrates has

---

167. A partial list of especially useful accounts of Book x of Plato's *Republic* in relation to Platonic philosophy includes those of Ferrari, Halliwell, Janaway, and Osborne (mentioned previously), along with those of Charles Griswold, "The Ideas and the Criticism of Poetry in Plato's *Republic*, Book x," and Alexander Nehamas, "Plato on Imitation and Poetry in *Republic* 10," in *Plato on Beauty, Wisdom, and the Arts,* ed. J. Moravcsik and P. Temko, 47–78.

just finished discussing how to order one's soul amid the uncertainties, injustices, grief, and misfortunes of everyday life. Typically, tragic poets and other "imitators" dominate the commentary on such circumstances in existing (that is, unjust) states. In Book x, Plato indicates more clearly than in Books ii–iii how radically different *his* kind of education was from conventional forms. Its two parts make up the final installments of Plato's account of the relation between the *logos* of justice and the *ergon* of daily life. Each justifies the value of Socrates' discourse of justice in relation to current ethical and religious discourses that educate the souls of citizens.

These parts are (1) the critical evaluation of the place of imitative poetry in the just state and (2) the elaboration of a myth that substantiates the rewards of justice, not in this life but in the life to come.[168] These two parts would answer the questions of (1) what is the place of imitative poetry in a constitution of justice? and (2) if imitative poetry was allowed, how could it be just? Ultimately, they address the issue of how readers of the *Republic* could understandably use the text for an education in justice.

To answer the first question, one must understand how Socrates' treatment of imitative poetry in Book x relates to the previous discussion of *mimesis* in Books ii–iii. When he was reforming *mousike* in Book iii, he was reconstructing its character for the sake of fostering justice in the ideal *politeia;* in Book x, he appends his discussion to an analytical discussion of imitative or representational art as an instance of the more general relation of the forms (whose nature had not been explained in Book iii) to productive activity or, more roughly (and in our terms), of *logos* and *ergon.* Yet the statement made about the role of the poets does not radically differ from the previous discussion. For Plato's general interest in each instance stems from the pivotal role of poets in educating the perceptions of citizens. He subjects their discourse to radical critique because they fail to make good on the promise of their discourse to usefully connect *logos* and *ergon*—which means, in the context of the *Republic,* the capacity to cultivate justice in the souls of citizens. He regards imitative poetry as an imitation of an imitation, a third step removed from reality (like the chained individuals who see only shadows in the cave) and ultimately argues for its expulsion from the just city (in its present form). Extant societies produce hostility to the Platonic ideal, and imitative poets enable that hostility to take root.

---

168. These two parts of Book x are nicely presented in Halliwell's introduction to *Plato: Republic* x.

Such poets produce the discursive complement to the more directly harmful conduct of political leaders. Just as the latter feign competence in the skill of practicing the political art (493a–b), the former feign competence in understanding what is good and bad, the critical roots for conceptualizing what is just and unjust.[169] Both tend to fool the many, and poets are capable of corrupting even the best of citizens (602b, 605c). Like the political rhetoricians whom Plato excoriates in the *Gorgias* for presuming to have knowledge of all practical matters while they actually understand none, poets presume to understand the entire range of human experience relevant to ethics and politics without carefully employing their rational faculty.[170] The quarrel between philosophy and poetry ultimately involves conflict about the meaning of justice (606d, 607b). This quarrel may not be as ancient as Plato's Socrates claims it to be—insofar as it is more a function of Plato's interpretive categories than the Greek literary tradition—but, as we have seen, it certainly was a serious and important conflict in Plato's time. Moreover, it involved Plato's views about the value of democracy.

Plato's preoccupation with "poets" and "poetry" might seem strange today; in particular, it might seem that he is expressing hostility to what we understand (and rightfully cherish) as free speech. The power Plato ascribes to poets is not, however, signified today by the work of poets or the critical opposition to established powers generally associated with free speech. For in Plato's time, the "poets" *made up* the establishment; today, they most certainly do not. Contemporary equivalents are, rather, advertisers, the increasingly monopolized mass media, and the vast, ever-growing, entertainment industry—all of which function as authoritative exponents of ethics and popular culture.[171] Socrates justifies his reprise of a subject that had been previ-

---

169. Recall that Socrates in Plato's *Apology* (18a–c, 19a–c) believed that it was his bad reputation, generated in large measure because of Aristophanes' play, that was most responsible for the popular resentment of him that made possible his indictment.

170. The best that Plato said about them in his aporetic dialogues, and he did so ironically in the *Ion* (541d–542a), was that the poet's presumptive *techne* of knowledge about virtue ultimately derived from a divine lot (*theia moira*). For a more complex Platonic view of poetry, see his *Phaedrus*, and, for a commentary on which, see G. R. F. Ferrari, *Listening to the Cicadas—A Study of Plato's Phaedrus*.

171. Again, I argue that this Platonic criticism of unjust cultural hegemony tends to complement those currently offered on the left, rather than the right, side of the political spectrum. (See Chapter 6, below.) For an interesting application of the philosophical theory of Plato's arguments in Book x to contemporary concerns about the mass media, see Alexander Nehamas, "Plato and the Mass Media." I demur from Nehamas's arguments mostly in terms of his eager-

ously addressed by saying that now, having distinguished the three parts of the soul, the rationale for expelling imitative poets from the just city is more clearly apparent (607b). Without an antidote (*pharmakon,* 595b) to counter its effects, imitative poetry harms the soul. In explaining this, Socrates makes use not only of the intervening portrayal of the soul but of his characterization of the knowledge that informs its most rational part, the knowledge of ideas as forms. He introduces two new tripartite philosophical schematics.

In the first, he articulates "degrees of reality," and *mimesis* appears as a deformed variety of the human poetic crafts of "making" or "producing." They include the "production" of both things and words and are potentially beneficial. Although Socrates introduces the notion of "making" or "producing" by referring to the activity of a (bronze-blooded) carpenter (597b), it was the (gold-blooded) philosopher who previously was said to use the idea of the good as a *paradeigma* for his productive craft (*techne*) of ruling (540a). A carpenter may produce a useful piece of furniture; however, he does not directly produce the "truth" or "reality" of, for example, a couch. Instead, he produces a practical instance of the ideal divinely created "idea" or "form" of a couch.[172] Socrates emphasizes that his *techne* is one step removed from the ultimate form of making, which Socrates here associates with the *techne* of God.[173] Still, the utilitarian value of the carpenter's craft is undeniable.

The mimetic art, however, remains disconnected from the "truth" and "justice" of "reality." In fact, it is two steps—or "thrice-removed"—from "reality," because it imitates or represents apparent objects without grasping how either those objects or what they "make" relate to "reality" as a whole

---

ness to apply Platonic arguments *directly* to contemporary debates (for instance, 220–22, 227–30) and his failure to recognize the value of most television as routinized, mindless, titillating entertainment.

172. See *Republic* 596b, 597b. Agreeing with Shorey, I do not see a significant difference between the intrinsic meaning of these two terms for Plato. (For example, compare *Republic* 508e and 510d in relation to the "idea" or "form" of the good.) It is more important to pay attention to how Plato uses them. Here, "ideas" count as "forms." See Shorey's Loeb translation of the *Republic,* 2: xxv–xxxvii, 104, note a, and 110, note a.

173. *Republic* 596c–e; see also 379c. Also see the *Timaeus,* where Plato's Socrates refers to "God" as a *demiourgos,* a producer who produces all good things that really exist, the furniture of a human world. I refer to the god's products as "furniture" because they include not only what we would call natural phenomena, such as the plants of earth and the stars of heaven, but also the basic tools of human life, such as shoes and beds. This limited, obviously precapitalist, view of the basic range of appropriate human tools was not confined to Plato; Aristotle held it as well, as evidenced by his conception of a natural form of *chrematistike* in *Politics* i.8–10.

(598b–c).[174] Imitative poets simply hold up a "mirror" to the world, reflecting one perspective on actual objects while potentially fooling their audience into believing that they are perceiving the phenomenon itself, in the manner of a trompe l'oeil (596e).[175] They possess the same feature that Plato's Socrates criticized in those aporetic dialogues that undermined the intellectual authority of poets, Sophists, and politically empowered democratic citizens, namely, that they claim to know many things but actually have no expertise in knowing any of them, which makes their actions products of ignorance (598c–d; see also 478eff, 557d, 561e–562a).[176] Insofar as philosophers also do not have the experience or expertise of practical craftsmen such as carpenters, one may wonder how they can be immune from this criticism. The answer of Plato's Socrates is that their expertise in dialectic (532b–533c) enables them to grasp how the various parts of reality relate to its nature as a whole. But insofar as the *Republic* and its "academic" discussion would provide an education in justice, these passages raise the issue of the legitimacy of Plato's own *techne* and mark a new battleground for the ancient quarrel between philosophy and poetry (607b).

One who is not convinced of the value of the *logos* of dialectic might be attracted by the *logos* of mimetic poets, even though they produce only "phantasms" (599a–d, 601b). To provide proof of the value of philosophy over poetry, Plato reinserts the discussion of mimetic poetry into his discourse about justice and employs a standard of judgment that appeared in other aporetic dialogues. If mimetic poets were genuine *demiourgoi*, their discourse would produce practical examples of their knowledge; their discourse about *arete* would produce fine deeds (599b).

---

174. Note that Plato's Socrates here presupposes an external world of phenomena as the basis of the poet's legitimacy as an artist or craftsman. As mentioned before, for Plato and ancient Greeks more generally, there is no sharp differentiation between an "art" and "craft," especially in the modern sense that the former may operate relatively subjectively and the latter more objectively. In the Greek language, there is no equivalent for "creation" or "invention." The closest equivalent is *gignomai*, "to come into being," whose Indo-European etymological root is GEN, from which comes the Greek word for family or clan, *genos*.

175. Ironically, Richard Rorty's critique of philosophical discourse in *Philosophy and the Mirror of Nature* never acknowledges Plato's criticism of the "mirror" image or metaphor.

176. See, especially, the *Ion, Protagoras, Gorgias,* along with, of course, the *Apology of Socrates.* In the *Laws* (700e–701a), the Athenian Stranger criticizes the Athenian *politeia* for having encouraged citizens to act like "theatre-goers," which resulted in their democracy becoming a "theatocracy." See Chapter 5, Section B, below. For a modern critique of enchantment by means of spectacles on behalf of democracy, see Stephen Esquith, *Intimacy and Spectacle.*

For Plato's Socrates, the standard of comparison for judging Homer's expertise is not other poets but lawgivers, practitioners of the political art. Thereby, he reconnects the (never entirely disconnected) political and aesthetic realms. As in the *Gorgias,* Plato employs extremely demanding criteria for the justifiable determination of success in the practice of this art. Homer dealt with its practical elements, such as wars, generalship, the government of cities, and the education of men—subjects surely relevant to the political art—and their *techne* should be judged by its political effects. Strictly speaking, however, his discourse was not virtuous. Given the gap between Homer's supposedly truthful and virtuous *logos* and the *ergon* of his interpreters and their audiences, he falls far short of the claim that the authority of his *logos* implies.

To support this point, Plato's Socrates hypothetically asks Homer: "What city credits you with having been a good legislator and having benefited them?" Then he asks Glaucon whether any war in Homer's time was better fought by his command or counsel or, short of that, whether he had founded a new way of life, like the Pythagoreans, or a new constitution, like Solon (599e–600b).[177] Because the answer to both of these questions is no, the imitative poetry of Homer has even less substance than the activity of Sophists, whose numerous followers attest to the capacity of their *techne* to connect *logos* and *ergon* to some extent (600c–d). Homeric poets use colorful phrases and rhythmic sounds to adorn the subjects of their art, but they communicate only the "appearance" and nothing of the genuine being of which they speak (601a–b; see also 596c). These questions express Plato's continuing concern with his Socratic Problem: How can the *logos* of virtue serve in *ergon* as an effective political art?

At this point in the dialogue, Plato introduces a second tripartite schematic for explaining the knowledge that informs human activity. Socrates says that human activity may be grouped under three separate *technai* (601d), "using, making, and imitating." The best judge of proficient human activity is the user of tools, not their maker. The latter has only trust or true belief in the excellence of what he or she makes (601e–602a). Imitators do not even have that. But they continue to imitate, not knowing whether their representations are bad or useful, while conforming their words to the desires of the many

---

177. For another instance of this linkage between poets and lawgivers, see the critique of writing in Plato's *Phaedrus* (258b, 278b–c).

and the ignorant, that is, the uneducated (602b); as a result, their *logos* operates two steps away—thrice removed—from truth (599d, 602c).

This scornful judgment of the knowledge of the many reflects Plato's immersion in, as well as his criticism of, the democratic ethics of his time. For as was attested by Pericles and Protagoras, ordinary democratic citizens already have the basic *techne* of knowing how to judge or make use of the expertise presented to them for deliberative consideration in the assembly and courts, even if they do not have the *technai* of either particular kinds of practical knowledge or the more general knowledge needed for crafting public policies. The judgment also more directly reflects Plato's critique of those who would educate the judgment of citizens. When Socrates says that the knowledge of using depends on the knowledge of measuring and weighing experience so as to know how to live a life of virtue (602d), he echoes the critique of Protagoras in the *Protagoras*. There, Plato's Socrates reduced "Protagoras's" supposedly educational discourse about virtue and the political art to pandering to mass ignorance, because Protagoras did not know how to explain or, perhaps, how to use the political art or virtue that he presumed to be able to teach. In Book x, Plato's Socrates criticizes mimetic poetry for inflaming the least rational part of our souls; it compounds the effect of injustice by exciting the *stasis* that human beings inevitably experience (602c–603d). Mistaking the *eidola* of justice for justice itself, it establishes a "bad constitution" in the souls of its listeners. Given democracy's lack of institutionalized norms for regulating ethical life and abundance of model lives for imitation, mimetic poetry tends both to flourish in democracy's midst and to endanger its existence.

Socrates suggests that because the conception of justice fostered by mimetic poets typically fails to help one deal with the misfortunes that beset human life, poetic activity requires critical supervision in a justly ordered society. Although Socrates initially authorizes the expulsion of poets, he ultimately allows them back in, under the condition that their imitations facilitate the imitation of justice (607a–d). Indeed, Plato can no more ban poetry from his city than he can ban shadows and reflections from the natural world. Moreover, just as such shadows and reflections can acclimatize the eyes of inhabitants of the cave to the point that they ultimately can view the light of the sun, so too can the work of "imitators" provide an education in justice. Plato spreads such images and reflections throughout the *Republic* as he tries to show how justice and happiness implicate each other. What is most important, says Plato's Socrates, is that poets not be taken too seriously (607e–

608b). In other words, poets are to become secondary educators for the city, not the primary educators that they currently were.[178]

Replacing poetry as the superior educational *logos* in the *polis* would be the *logos* of Platonic dialogue. A dialectical treatment of justice evidences the necessary skill in making use of or judging the ultimate value of the artifacts of the world. It is the only discourse that properly imitates the form of justice.[179] It resembles the *logos* of Sophists, poets, rhetoricians, and democratic citizens to the extent that it does not produce anything practical, as a flute maker does, but, unlike them, the virtue of its *logos* depends on valuing the sufficiency of neither the images of poetry nor the power of domination as the relevant *ergon* for estimating success. Genuine (that is, Platonic) critical discourse provides the medicine that everyone needs so as not to be deluded by the misfortunes of ordinary life into instituting regimes of injustice. As the superordinate *techne* of the whole soul and political community as a whole, it ultimately consists of the knowledge of how to "use" the other arts of making and imitating.

The "patients" for whom this *logos* of justice would be most useful are not merely subordinate classes of ordinary citizens forced to slavishly follow expert rules; rather, all human beings are regarded as patients in need of the medicine of philosophy. In this light, the unique *techne* of Platonic discourse works effectively to harmonize the *logos* and *ergon* of justice: (1) Its *ergon* cures the ills of injustice that beset both states and souls; (2) ipso facto, its *logos* criticizes the authority of democratic citizenship as a sufficient agent for constituting justice in the *polis*. But, again, the force of *this* claim is not essentially antidemocratic, because the injustice of democracy simply manifests the harmful tendency of all existing *politeiai* to identify justice with the interest of the stronger.

3. THE MYTH OF ER AND DEMOCRACY

The closing portions of the dialogue remind readers of the ultimate court of judgment for the value of this discourse, that of the individual reader. The

---

178. This point confirms Havelock's argument that Plato's critique of Homer was primarily a critique of the existing educational establishment without accepting his theory of historical development that frames it. See his *Preface to Plato*.

179. As Ferrari has pointed out, Plato condemns "imitativeness," not "imitation." See "Plato and Poetry," 142. For a different view, which seems to criticize Plato for not appreciating art for art's sake, see Alexander Nehamas, "Plato and the Mass Media," 215, 232, n. 14.

recontextualization of the *logos* of justice in relation to the happiness of individuals reminds the reader that the *logos* of the *Republic* is primarily designed for the sake of its readers, all of whom live in unjust societies. It also prepares them for the conclusion of the *Republic,* which has a demotic, if not democratic, twist.

The *Republic* closes with a myth that justifies its *logos* of justice for the lives of ordinary human beings, not in terms of its intrinsic effect in this life, but in terms of the rewards that come after this life ends. Appearing here rather than at the beginning or middle of this dialogue about justice, the myth of Er (614a–621d) does not constitute the core of Socrates' (or Plato's) treatment of justice, but it nonetheless occupies a crucial place in the dialogue. Plato's Socrates tells it only with the permission of Glaucon and Adeimantus, who had initially compelled Socrates to justify the value of justice without regard to rewards or punishment, which feature centrally in the myth. Rather than belonging to the formal argument about justice, the myth of Er functions as a poetic *mythos* about the rewards of justice, which complements and supplements the previous, more philosophic *logos.* It also suggests that Plato believed in the significance of mythic poetry as well as formal philosophy for the constitution of justice in the souls of his readers.

The myth is prefaced by an argument for the immortality of the soul that emphasizes the primacy of personal responsibility for the happiness of one's life (608c–613e). In the myth itself (621bff), one's power to choose the actual shape of one's life is sharply limited by the allotment one is given by forces beyond one's own control. But within those constraints, there is scope for individual choice, and that freedom to choose a life of virtue is equally provided to all human beings (617e–618d). In this way, the myth illustrates how Platonic justice honors both freedom and equality; it shows the potential value of Plato's critical reason for democracies that honor justice as well as freedom and equality. As in Pericles' funeral oration, the obstacles to a just life in the myth notably come not from impoverishment or the lack of consummate intellectual power; they do not stem from basic features of the lives of members of the *demos.* Instead, the most horrendous choices that result in the greatest punishment in the afterlife come from conditions of plenty and power, the material preconditions of greed and arrogance. Again, the sins of oligarchy figure more prominently than those of democracy in Plato's characterization of injustice.

What is needed above all is the vigilance of critical reason that refuses to be fooled by wealth and practical power as signs of genuine justice, as well as a firm belief that the happiness promised by their appeal is more illusory than real (619a–b): "A man must take with him to Hades an adamantine belief in this, that even there he may be undazzled by riches and similar trumpery, and may not slip into tyrannies and similar doings and so work many evils past cure and suffer still greater himself but may know how always to choose in such things the life of the mean and shun excess in either direction, both in this world so far as is possible and in all the life to come; for this is the greatest happiness for man." This critical reason provides the basic skill for choosing among the *paradeigmata* of lives (618a) that are offered to souls in the afterlife, for it tells one that the value of a way of life does not come from material worth but from its use for a life of justice. In this respect, the critical discourse of Platonic justice has prepared the way for believing that this myth illustrates the best way to justice and happiness.

The myth itself, however (let alone the *Republic*), provides no solace to its readers. There is no theodicy in Plato's political philosophy.[180] Practicing the philosophical skill that is promoted in *kallipolis* or the myth, or reading the *Republic* as a whole, remains insufficient for achieving justice or happiness. For the value of each arises from the extent to which the practitioners or users of Platonic justice respond appropriately to their experiences of injustice. Left adumbrated but undeveloped, therefore, in both the myth of Er and the *Republic* as a whole, is a way or method for envisioning the particular horizon of possibility for justice in one's life. Plato recognizes that after individuals are allotted a genetic nature, parents, and a birthplace, they (and we) retain an opportunity for shaping their (and our) souls and state to accord with justice.

His comments about precisely how this ought to be done, however, are highly indeterminate. Apart from a miraculous coincidence of philosophy and political power, the direction of the road from injustice to justice remains uncharted. Plato's *techne* of justice provides no answers for would-be technicians of the common good. The path of learning that one must go down to acquire the political art that would constitute justice cannot be found ready at hand in an off-the-shelf *techne* for handling the unjust circumstances that beset ordinary ethical and political life.

The practical indeterminacy of the "lessons" of the myth of Er, however, does not reflect theoretical skepticism. Rather, it signifies a critical discourse of political ethics or ethical politics that inquires into both the possibilities of,

180. For a complementary view, see Halliwell's "Introduction" to *Plato: Republic X*, 21–23.

and the obstacles to, the accommodation of power and justice. As such, it is critical of but not inherently antagonistic to democracy. Insofar as democracy partakes of injustice, the *logos* of justice clearly opposes democracy, but Plato does not specify the proper extent of the democratic component in political life relative to other practical possibilities.

In terms of Plato's intent and Plato's time, the arguments of the *Republic* that link democracy and injustice have the effect of devaluing democracy in two important respects. First, the *Republic* evidences Plato's belief that the power of democracy was so great in the constitutions organized by it that it diminished the potential scope for the exercise of critical reason in political life. Established democratic institutions rewarded the skills of rhetoric and tended to value poetry over philosophy. By and large, practitioners of democratic politics did not see any need for a Platonic education. There was competition and isolation, rather than cooperation and interaction, between democratic politicians and Platonic philosophers.[181] As a result, the *Republic* does not suggest that practitioners of the *logos* of Platonic justice could improve the deliberations of Athenian democracy. Although the opportunities for practicing the *logos* of Platonic justice were greater in the Athenian democracy than anywhere else, he did not see how that *logos* could directly be a just agent of political *ergon* amid the conventional discourse of Athenian democracy. (This radically critical judgment of democracy stemmed in part from its remarkable success. Despite Plato's perception of *stasis* in the world of politics, the Athenian constitution in the fourth century was practically stable. Athenians had experimented briefly with alternatives to democracy, and these had failed miserably. They were not about to experiment with any more. This "practical reality" justified Plato's calculation that only a miraculous coincidence of philosophy and political power would enable his *logos* of justice to become more practically effective than it currently was.)

There was, however, a second, more deeply antidemocratic effect of the *logos* of Platonic justice as expressed in the myth of Er. Although Plato's disaffection with democracy was not greater than it was with any other political

---

181. Although we cannot dismiss the possibility that Demosthenes either visited the Academy or conversed with Plato, they surely did not develop a relationship comparable to Protagoras and Pericles. On the ideology of Demosthenes and fourth-century rhetoricians more generally, see Josiah Ober, *Mass and Elite in Democratic Athens*. Of course there was Isocrates and his school, which stood somewhere between the extremes of Platonic philosophy and conventional politics. But as far as Plato was concerned, this school was skillful at neither philosophy nor politics. See *Euthydemus* 306a–c and Chapter 3, above.

regime, the immediate effect of the *Republic* was to delegitimize the ethic of Athenian democracy. In the dialogue, the philosopher of justice "took shelter from the storm" and refused to participate in the politics of its *politeia* because of the indissoluble linkage between its constitution and injustice. When the philosopher's mythic exemplar, modest Odysseus in the myth of Er, chooses the lot of a peaceful private life, he does not exemplify an ethic of democratic citizenship or contribute to democratic well-being. Because Athenian democracy required an ethic of participation to legitimate its actions as just, the immediate effect of this Platonic discourse was antidemocratic. Plato's reconnection of *logos* and *ergon* that solved his Socratic Problem was indeed conservative, insofar as it tended to counsel withdrawal from, rather than reform of, the relatively activist project of Athenian democracy. In relation to the constitution of Athenian democracy, the constitution of Platonic justice accepted a narrower range of human activities that might accommodate power and justice in the soul and the state. In the *Republic,* the discourse of Platonic justice as the art of political education was presumptively for the few, not the many. Potentially, however, it could be read, and learned from, by all.

FIVE

THE POLITICAL ART AS PRACTICAL RULE

The *Republic* left unexplored any systematic discussion of the way in which the *logos* of justice and its ideal *politeiai* of soul and state could be practiced— that is, any discussion of the political art as the ongoing exercise of practical rule in the political domain. The *Statesman* and *Laws* undertake this discussion. These dialogues offer Plato's most extended analyses of the political art as an art of producing virtue that enforces practical political rule. The *Statesman* focuses directly on the meaning of the political art as a personal art of leadership. The *Laws* institutionalizes that art in a system of laws for a non-ideal, unreal, best practicable (or second-best) society. Each answers different questions and responds to different problems from those in other dialogues. In this vein, they break new ground.

At the same time, both the *Statesman* and *Laws* were written after the *Republic* and presuppose a conception of justice as the ultimate authorization of practical rule. The probable period in which Plato wrote the *Statesman* is 367–362; sometime later, probably after his visit to Sicily in 361, Plato began to compose the *Laws*, which remained unfinished (and "unpublished") at the time of his death in 347.[1]

---

1. For example, W. K. C. Guthrie, *A History of Greek Philosophy*, 5:163, 321–23.

No consensus has formed about how this "lateness" constitutes the meaning of these dialogues or how they relate to the *Republic* or Plato's political theory more generally. At one extreme are unitarians, who view these dialogues as wholly compatible with the philosophy expressed in Plato's other dialogues; at the other are developmentalists, who view them as crucial evidence for Plato's gradual "abandonment" of the political ideals of the *Republic* for the rule of law and a greater appreciation of the rational capacities of ordinary citizens.[2] (Political pessimism may well have particularly marked Plato's later years. That would be understandable, given his disheartening experiences of trying to educate Dionysius II, help Dion, and, more generally, better the political condition of Sicilians. But his pessimism need not have been much greater than before, because Plato's Socrates in the *Republic* admits the improbability of *kallipolis*'s ever being realized and both the *Statesman* and *Laws* include favorable references to its ideal standards.[3]) Another strand of criticism reads them an independent works, two of many dialogues Plato wrote.[4]

Insofar as the parties in this dispute have had adherents for nearly one hundred years, it is unlikely that the dispute can be resolved without the discovery of new primary evidence. The advantage of the perspective I have used throughout my discussion of the Platonic political art is that it does not depend on answers to begged interpretive questions. From the perspective of Plato's ongoing interest in resolving his Socratic Problem, these "late" treatments of the political art enhance, modify, and qualify "the Platonic political art," but they do not obviously contradict or negate previous renditions of it.

---

2. See Martin Ostwald, *Plato's Statesman*, "Introduction," xiv–xxvii; see also Guthrie, Klosko. For the most persuasive recent defense of a developmental view of Plato's political thought, emphasizing his greater appreciation of the rationality and virtue of ordinary citizens, see Christopher Bobonich, "Persuasion, Compulsion, and Freedom in Plato's *Laws*"; idem, "Akrasia and Agency in Plato's *Laws* and *Republic*"; idem, "The Virtues of Ordinary People in Plato's *Statesman*," in Christopher J. Rowe, ed., *Reading the Statesman, Proceedings of the III Symposium Platonicum*, 313–29.

3. *Statesman* 293c, 297c; *Laws* 739c–e.

4. For an example of those who work along this strand, see Christopher Gill, "Rethinking Constitutionalism in *Statesman* 291–303," in *Reading the Statesman*, 292–305, and his article, "Afterword: Dialectic and the Dialogue Form in Late Plato," in Gill and McCabe, eds., *Form and Argument in Late Plato*, 283–311, esp. 310—although he vitiates this in two places, by claiming that an "objectivist-participant" epistemology informs all of Plato's late dialogues (284–85), and by maintaining a belief in some doctrinal or philosophical contrast between the Plato of the early and the Plato of the late dialogues (which I would qualify by attending to the different political, as well as literary and philosophical, contexts of the arguments).

To be sure, they presuppose an "answer" to the question of the meaning and significance of justice—that is, the *Republic*—but that dialogue does not operate as a hidden first principle from which the two later dialogues could be deduced.[5] Overall, these dialogues may be fruitfully read as further evidence of Plato's unique understanding of the political realm as a complex set of relations between critical reason, ethics, and power.[6]

With regard to the context of their composition, however, it bears repeating that Plato wrote them almost coterminously with his most extensive (albeit, indirect) involvement in practical politics since the death of Socrates. The best evidence we have for Plato's practical activities are the *Seventh* and *Eighth Letters,* the only two letters bearing his name that are widely regarded as genuinely his and/or historically accurate.[7] The *Seventh Letter* offers insight into the sources and character of Plato's relation to practical politics— Sicilian politics in particular—during the period in which he composed the *Statesman* and *Laws.*

The letter was probably written c. 354–353, after Plato wrote the *Statesman* and before or during the time in which he wrote the *Laws.*[8] It is addressed to the friends and followers of Dion, although its public nature indicates that it was also written with a broader, Athenian audience in mind (for example, 330c, 333a–334b). Its purpose is to justify Plato's refusal to help Dion's party revenge the assassination of their leader. Given his acceptance of two previous invitations from Dion, to better Sicily's political affairs by educating its leader, Dionysius II, the letter necessarily has the tone of an "Apo-

---

5. This point was well made by Sinclair, *A History of Greek Political Thought,* 173.

6. Although I am fascinated by the (relatively) recent attention given by philosophers to the relevance of the dialogue form to the argument of the late dialogues, I find most of the discussions overly disconnected from the substantive issues raised in the dialogues—particularly the ethical and political ones—and their connection to similar issues addressed in other dialogues. An excellent collection of articles on the late Plato is *Form and Argument in Late Plato,* ed. Christopher Gill and Mary Margaret McCabe. The depoliticizing tendency in this approach appears in Christopher Gill's "Afterword" to this collection, where he claims (307–8) that the dialectic of the late dialogues can be practiced with less regard for the ethical or political character or convictions of its practitioners than Plato held to be the case in the Socratic or aporetic dialogues. Interestingly, he simply sets aside a possible objection to this point that stems from the claims made by Christopher Bobonich about the *Laws* in "Reading the *Laws*" (which also appears in *Form and Argument,* 249–82, and which he acknowledges on 294 and n. 32).

7. See Chapter 2, above. The most ingenious opponents of the authenticity of these letters are Ryle and Edelstein. See Gilbert Ryle, *Plato's Progress,* 55–101, and Ludwig Edelstein, *Plato's Seventh Letter.*

8. Morrow, *Plato's Epistles,* 45.

logia Platonica," a defense of his politically restricted philosophic life as head of the Academy, a life that he has chosen to continue leading instead of coming to the Sicilians' aid (352a). Its tone is notable in light of his belief in the necessity of connecting his philosophical ideas to political practice, which had earlier justified his teaching of both Dion and Dionysius II (327a, 328c; see also 323e–324a).[9] In explaining his rationale, the Platonic *Seventh Letter* provides an extensive explanation of criteria for justifiably linking his philosophical *logoi* to political *erga*.

First, Plato tends to respond favorably to requests for the political use of his philosophy in situations that call for more than strategic political advice or piecemeal political reform. He is particularly interested in the amelioration of *stasis,* which threatens the viability of a political community as a whole (329b, 336e). Given our previous discussion of the *Republic,* this is not surprising. Second, Plato places conditions on the citizens with whom he would work or the students he would teach, just as a doctor can practice his *techne* successfully only if his patient understands and respects him (*Laws* 720). The students must be intelligent, willing to listen to reason and to accept his authority, and inclined to practice the virtues (330c–331c, 340b–341a, 343–344b; see also 344dff). Third, he would not have his *logoi* incite or promote the use of violent force, for it foments *stasis* (336e–337b). Indeed, Plato counterposes the authority of critical reason and the power of force (331b–d, 350d, 351c). These passages, although highly selective, do endorse the view that Plato's politics are theoretically radical, not practically revolutionary. Fourth, Plato values the stability of *nomoi* in practice, albeit not in theory, a view in line with his opposition to *stasis* and violence.

Fifth, the *Seventh Letter* illustrates Plato's view of particular, extant political regimes as types of injustice. Thus, both oligarchy and democracy come in for criticism (326d, 330d–e; see also 325c–326a), but Plato specifically praises Athenian democracy insofar as it acted moderately on regaining power from the tyrannical Thirty (*Seventh Letter* 324d, 325b). At the same time, the *Seventh Letter*'s description of Plato's involvement in Sicilian affairs during Sicily's rule by tyrants indicates that he was willing to work with tyrants, as long as they would begin to act like constitutional monarchs.[10]

---

9. See Morrow, *Plato's Epistles,* 220ff, esp. n. 17.

10. *Seventh Letter* 326d, 332a–b, 334c–d, 336e, 337b; *Eighth Letter* 354a, 356c–d. One philosophical point that Plato could have used to justify his work with tyrants and to complement his theory of justice in the *Republic* would be the following: Just as philosophers, free from the constraints of daily life and conventions, have the greatest opportunity to grasp the good, so

Sixth, the author of the *Seventh Letter* takes pains to emphasize that his *logos* should not be regarded as a *techne logon,* that is, as a set of rules that can be directly embodied in writing (341b–d, 342e–343a, 344c; see also *Phaedrus* 274c–275e, 276e–278c). Rather, its interpretive application always requires the exercise of independent judgment. Plato's genuine "students" cannot be dutiful followers; if they were, they would have forsaken the critical aspect of *logos.*

Although these six criteria for relating *logos* to *ergon* may not have been expressed in exactly the same form in the *Republic,* nothing in them contradicts what we have found to be the favored beliefs and arguments in the *Republic.* At the same time, each of them has corollaries in the *Statesman* and *Laws.* Plato's experiences in Sicily must have intensified Plato's interest in the problems facing the practice of a philosophically informed, ethical politics in imperfect, unjust societies. As such these dialogues may well be motivated by experience as much as by any preconceived *logos* that he is abandoning or applying.

A. POLITICAL LEADERSHIP: ON PLATO'S *Statesman*

The *Statesman* was probably composed in the mid-360s, certainly after the *Republic* and seemingly soon after the *Theaetetus* and *Sophist.*[11] The dramatic date of the dialogue is 399, just before Socrates faces Meletus's indictment against him.[12] Participating in the dialogues of the *Statesman* are the mathematicians Theodorus of Cyrene, supposedly a teacher of Plato, and

---

do individual leaders have the greatest capacity to institute justice for a *politeia.* The misguided nature of this Platonic prejudice is discussed in Chapter 6, below.

11. The dialogue opens with Socrates expressing his debt to Theodorus for having introduced him to Theaetetus and the Eleatic Stranger. Theodorus responds by stating that he will be indebted thrice as much once they have defined the "statesman" and "philosopher" as well as the "sophist" (257a). For the chronological date of the composition of the *Statesman,* in its own right and in relation to other Platonic dialogues, see J. B. Skemp, "Introduction" to *Plato's Statesman,* 13–17; Guthrie, *A History of Greek Philosophy,* 5:321–33; M. Ostwald, "Editor's Introduction," *Plato's Statesman,* vii–xi.

12. The direct connection between the *Theaetetus* and *Statesman* asserted at the opening of the *Statesman* (257a–c) allows us to pinpoint the *Statesman*'s dramatic date. See *Sophist* 216a; *Theaetetus* 210d. Further references to Socrates' trial and death appear in the dialogue, particularly at 299b–c. On this connection, see Mitchell H. Miller Jr., *The Philosopher in Plato's Statesman,* 1–3, 96–101. This connection is noted but unfortunately dismissed (because of reliance on overly narrow interpretive criteria for what counts as a "point") by Julia Annas in her new edition of the *Statesman:* Plato, *Statesman,* ed. Julia Annas and Robin Waterfield, 66, n. 64.

Theaetetus; Socrates, very briefly; Younger Socrates, a friend and fellow student of Theaetetus at the Academy who may well have been asked to draft a code of laws for an Athenian colony; and, principally, the "Stranger" from Elea in Sicily, who moves the narrative forward. I read the Stranger's statements in generally the same vein as those of the other predominant interlocutors in Plato's dialogues—namely, as those that, relative to those of the other interlocutors, most closely approximate Plato's views but are not identical to Plato's views (to the extent that Plato "holds views"). The distance between the "views" of the Stranger and those of Plato is a function of the effect of their dramatic location on the reader's interpretation of those views.[13]

As is typical of the course of many Platonic dialogues, the path of argument followed in the *Statesman* includes some rough transitions. Moreover, it involves questions about the proper discursive method for identifying, as well as determining the substantive content of, "the political art." Early in the dialogue, the Stranger states that a crucial aim of their efforts to identify the nature of *politike* is to make them good philosophers.[14] The method employed

13. See Ostwald's "Introduction" to Plato, *Statesman*, xxvii–xxviii. The Sicilian *polis* of Elea was the home of many Pythagoreans and Parmenideans. The Parmenidean and Pythagorean connection for the dialogue's principal voice may lead one to doubt the credibility of his statements (or, much less likely, to believe that Plato has adopted the views of Parmenides), but this connection perhaps more nearly amounts to Plato's literary touch, in which he conforms the characters to the nature of the discourse—which, in the case of the *Statesman*, involves the employment of a formal, analytic method for a relatively abstract discussion of *politike*. There is no specific worldly or practical context to which this discussion of the political art obviously refers. But this does not mean that the primary context for reading the *Statesman* ought to be that of the *Theaetetus* and *Sophist*, to which it is dramatically linked—legitimate as that is—*rather than* to his discussion of the political art in other dialogues. Moreover, arguments about the *Statesman* need not be qualified by anxiety about the unwritten Platonic dialogue about "the philosopher"—promised when he pledged to discuss "the sophist" and "the statesman" as well (*Sophist* 216c–218d). After all, there can be no one dialogue by Plato about "the philosopher," insofar as Plato is a philosopher and, as a philosopher, has written all of his dialogues.

There is much scholarly disagreement about the relation of the Stranger's discourse to Plato's voice. For examples of their virtual identity, see Guthrie, *A History of Greek Philosophy*, 5:164–96; T. J. Saunders, "Plato's Later Political Thought," in R. Kraut, ed., *The Cambridge Companion to Plato*, 464–92. For examples of their dialectical opposition, see Mitchell J. Miller Jr., *The Philosopher in Plato's Statesman*, and, more implausibly, H. R. Scodel, *Diairesis and Myth in Plato's Statesman*. My view is much nearer to those of Guthrie and Saunders, although, as I say in the text, I do not want to read the Stranger's words as directly indicative of Plato's beliefs; they need to be read against the dramatic exchanges of the dialogue as a whole. Indeed, this viewpoint is essential to the relevance of Plato's Socratic Problem to "the Platonic political art."

14. *Statesman* 285c–286b. C. J. Rowe emphasizes the nature of the *Statesman* as a philosophical exercise without disputing the significance of its content. See Plato, *Statesman*, ed. with a trans., intro., and commentary by C. J. Rowe, 3.

is that of "division" (*diairesis*)—the division of a concept into its component parts—which Plato also used in the *Sophist* (most likely written just before the *Statesman*). Its extensive use in the first part of the dialogue may reflect an approach followed in the Academy.[15] The Stranger deliberately abandons this method later in the dialogue, however, in order to aid their efforts to identify the meaning of *politike*. He generates this new effort by introducing a myth. Yet the Stranger employs the method of division once again in the dialogue's final section. This alternation of the dialogical and methodological frameworks for pinpointing the definition of *politike* should no more distract the reader from focusing on the "real meaning" of the political art than do comparable sections and statements in various aporetic dialogues, where conventional practices and ideas in the hands of "Socrates'" interlocutors resist philosophical analysis.[16] At the same time, the use of the method of *diairesis* in the *Statesman* presents a distinctive starting point for Plato's investigations.[17]

In the *Statesman*, where "Socrates" plays a notably insignificant role, there is no dramatic resistance to Plato's philosophical inquiries. The obstacles facing a successful definition of *politike* are internally generated by the activity of dialectical philosophizing itself, rather than by the discursive or practical conventions of daily life.[18] As such, they are more easily overcome than the conventional and practical obstacles of the aporetic dialogues, with the result that the *Statesman*'s interlocutors successfully conclude their philosophical search for a definition of *politike*. This "success," however, does not mark the perfection of Plato's reflections about the political art.[19] Rather, it displays Plato's efforts to define the political art against the background of the *Republic*, which had already (albeit problematically) answered philosophically prior questions about the relation of justice to the political art.

We interpret this dialogue by moving from the initial abstract definition of *politike* to the increasingly vivid and concrete descriptions of its operation.

15. See M. Ostwald and John P. Lynch, "The Growth of Schools and the Advance of Knowledge," in *The Cambridge Ancient History*, 6:592–633, particularly 602–10.

16. This is what Ryle argues, that it has purely disputational interest, and not very great interest at that. See his *Plato's Progress*, notably 285–86.

17. For a valuable analysis of the complementarity of the method of *diairesis* and the politics of the second part of the dialogue, see Melissa Lane, *Method and Politics in Plato's Statesman*.

18. However, the ultimately relevant practical context for the definition of *politike* in the *Statesman* is "the world of Zeus," which manifests obstacles or resistance to the skillful and virtuous practice of *politike*. On *this* context, see Section A2, below.

19. See Rosamond Kent Sprague, *Plato's Philosopher-King: A Study of the Theoretical Background*.

Thus, we move from discussing *politike* as a theoretical art, to *politike* as it must operate in a world of conflict, to the rational status of such an art in an imperfect world—as a "paradigm" illustrated by the comparable arts of medicine and navigation and as an art of measurement—to its status in relation to various constitutional orders, and, finally, to its relation to democracy as an art of weaving.

1. *Politike* AS THE THEORETICAL ART OF THE STATESMAN

After selecting the "statesman"—not the "philosopher" or "the Sophist"—as the subject of discussion, Plato uses analogies from the "arts" to define the particular nature or "expertise" of the political art of the "statesman" (*politikos*).[20] The ease with which Plato employs this analytical tack recalls the extent to which he took for granted the relevance of the analogy for his purposes. Not only did he identify all systematically and successfully performed activities informed by knowledge as *technai;* he also presupposed that one could sufficiently define the activity of a professional craftsman by describing the craft and the knowledge that informed its practice.[21] To define a *po-*

20. C. J. Rowe prefers to view *politike* as an "expertise" rather than "art," "craft," or "skill." See his edition of Plato's *Statesman, Plato: Statesman,* 1–4, especially p. 2, n. 6, and p. 178, re 258d5.

There is no single English word that happily translates *politikos* in this dialogue. And it is rendered differently by the various translators of the dialogue. Those I have consulted are Harold N. Fowler, in the 1925 Loeb edition of the *Statesman;* J. B. Skemp, in his 1952 Routledge edition of the *Statesman,* esp. 18–20; Ostwald/Skemp, in the 1992 Hackett edition of the *Statesman;* R. Waterfield, in the 1995 Cambridge edition of the *Statesman;* and C. J. Rowe, in the 1995 edition of the *Statesman.* I have drawn on all of these for my translations of Plato's text.

Other Greek words were typically used to refer to "politicians," such as *rhetoroi kai strategoi, politeuomenoi,* and *symbouloi.* See M. H. Hansen, "The Athenian 'Politicians,' 403–322 B.C." And unlike other Platonic dialogues in which the term carries negative connotations (with the activity of *politikoi* being associated with sophistry and established political leadership, indicating an art of domination), it here possesses dignity. See *Apology* 21c; *Meno* 99d, see also 95a; *Gorgias* 473e, 513b, 519c, 527d; *Republic* 489c. However, Plato had noted a potentially virtuous identity for the *politikos* in the *Republic* at 426d (*te aletheiai politikoi*), which suggests an analogy with the notion of "true rhetoric" in the *Phaedrus* (276a–277a) in contrast to the "art" of rhetoric criticized in the *Gorgias.* But whereas "statesman" may be a better translation than "politician" for *politikos,* it is not quite right either, insofar as it designates an individual of a wholly different order from that of a "politician"; moreover, no one today understands "statesman" as a "true politician."

21. Literally, *politikos* designates a man professionally concerned with the public business of the *polis,* and Plato was notably the first writer of record to use the word *politikos* in this sense, for it had been previously used only as an adjective.

litikos, one need only explain *politike.* That *politikos* does denote a "professional," that is, a specialized craftsman or *demiourgos,* justifies the first of three distinctive perspectives employed by Plato for explaining *politike* in the *Statesman*—(1) a *techne* or *episteme* that is (2) revealed by means of a model or paradigm (*paradeigma*), and (3) demonstrated in the actualized capacity for skillful measurement. The array of arts—or "sciences" (*epistemai*)—among which *politike* must be isolated includes "theoretical" as well as "practical" activities. Plato has the Eleatic Stranger initially locate *politike* under the category of "theoretical" rather than "practical" arts, that is, as a kind of *gnostike.* This enables him to say that one can possess *politike* without actually practicing politics (259b; see also 292c, e). This notion of "theoretical" is not, however, Aristotelian, for it does not preclude activities such as *politike* from having worldly effects.[22] Indeed, what is typically translated as "theoretical" is *gnostike,* which, unlike *theoria,* has particular, rather than general, objects of its knowledge.[23] Moreover, not only is *politike* productive; it is the architectonic activity for *all* practical, productive arts.

Plato demonstrates the practical importance of this "theoretical" art when the Eleatic Stranger spells out criteria for the analytical method of "division" that he begins to employ for the definition of *politike.* It notably differs from the elenchic method, in that it does not take another person's views or claims as its point of departure.[24] Rather, it begins from the realm of discourse, not the world of practice and opinion. Despite its relatively impractical discursive standpoint, Plato insists that one must use the method of division (or "diairetic method") carefully, always making sure that the dis-

22. For Aristotle (*Nicomachean Ethics* 1.2), *politike* is also architectonic, but it falls under the category of "practical" rather than "theoretical" or "productive" knowledge (*episteme*). (See Aristotle, *Metaphysics* 1.2, 982a5–983a23; II 993b19–30. For Aristotle, "doing"—*praxis*—was "higher" than "making"—*poiesis*—and the latter designates the effective activity of the intellectual virtue of *techne.* See his *Nicomachean Ethics* 1.1 and VI.4; see also *Politics* 1.4.) Insofar as "theoretical" activity was "higher" than "practical" activity for both Plato and Aristotle (as well as being higher than "productive" activity for Aristotle), Plato's categorization of *politike* as a "theoretical" activity in the *Statesman* affirms that it occupies a higher position in Plato's hierarchy of human activities relative to Aristotle's. It does not necessarily indicate Plato's "confusion" about the epistemological identity of *politike,* which Aristotle simply clears up. (See Lobkowicz, Annas.) Rather, it evidences Plato's distinctive understanding of the practical efficacy of theoretical knowledge.

23. See Hans Jonas, *The Gnostic Religion: The Message of the Alien God and the Beginnings of Christianity,* 35.

24. On the elenchic method, see R. Robinson, *Plato's Earlier Dialectic,* part I, and G. Vlastos, "The Socratic *Elenchus.*"

tinctions it generates pertain to "real" distinctions that are practically meaningful but not based on "opinion" (262b, 286d). For example, the Stranger identifies a division of the class of human beings into two—Greeks and barbarians—as a mistaken application of the method, because the category of "barbarian" is too general to helpfully describe the varieties of people in the world who are not Greek (262d). There must be a correlation, even if there is a disjuncture, between categories of critical discourse and (what Plato takes to be) natural divisions in the world—especially, it seems, when it comes to defining the political art.

The next part of the dialogue, until the invocation of the myth of Cronus, applies this method. The Stranger proceeds to locate the subject matter of *politike* among various categories of animal life and ultimately defines it as the art of shepherding hornless, noninterbreeding bipeds (267a–c). The Stranger notes that this definition is itself too broad, for it doesn't differentiate the peculiar characteristic of *politike* in relation to other arts of "herd-tendance" that also fall under this category, namely merchants, farmers, teachers of gymnastics, and doctors. Anticipating the myth, the Stranger notes that these groups may challenge the distinctive authority of the *politikos* over his "flock." In other words, the Stranger has himself misused the diairetic method. It is uncertain whether this is because of a lack of skill or a flaw in the method. Some commentators have decided the latter, which enables them to minimize or disregard the positive claims of this part of the dialogue in assessing its ultimate meaning and significance.[25] That reading is too simple, however. For the myth that follows, designed to correct the error displayed in the previous use of the method, primarily challenges it by altering the context in which the method is employed, from that of discursive harmony to that of potential conflict between ideas and reality (267e–268c). *This* is the context for the practice of *politike* and so must delimit its discursive categorization.[26] We shall identify this new context before explaining the use of "paradigm"

25. For the most recent example of this, see Stanley Rosen, *Plato's Statesman: The Web of Politics*, particularly chap. 2.

26. Plato may simply be doing what is necessary to assure that his method is rightly used and not (at least immediately) abandoned. But the issues raised by the use of the diairetic method reappear later, in the discussion of how a *paradeigma* can aid the art of teaching (as opposed to the art of learning or discovery) and how the notion of a measure provides two types of criteria for evaluating the rightness or justice of a practice.

If this is the case, Plato's treatment of the method of division complements the overall view being argued here that the substantive claims in the *Statesman* do not necessarily conflict with those of the *Republic* or *Laws*, because of the different political and philosophical character of the problems each dialogue addresses.

and "measure" as further conceptual devices for elaborating the definition of *politike*.

2. THE WORLD OF ZEUS AS THE CONTEXT FOR *Politike*

The Eleatic Stranger refers to the myth he is about to tell as a playful diversion (268d), but it does not operate as a childish tale in the dialogue; it fundamentally alters the critical framework for determining the nature of *politike*— from that in which harmony is possible and practicable to that in which conflict is inevitable. Moreover, its contrast between two worlds, the worlds of Cronus and Zeus, presages the analytical division between two types of measurement. In the myth, the age of Cronus depicts an age of perfection, where human beings are peaceably guided by demigods (*daimones*). It no longer exists, however; now we live in the world of Zeus, in which human beings naturally resist following the "right" way to live and, in so doing, establish their autonomy. Similarly, the art of measurement needs to be understood with regard to both an absolute measure that determines what is "right" in the perfect world of *logos* and also excess and deficiency in a world of imperfection.

The initial difficulties experienced by the Eleatic Stranger in defining *politike* can be seen as reflecting the absence of an epistemological context for the definition of the political art as an art of practical rule. The myth aids in the (re)definition of this context. Relative to the political art as an art of virtue in the *Protagoras*, the political art (*politike*) in the *Statesman* is clearly an art of statesmanship, not an art of citizenship. In other words, it is an art of ruling, rather than an art of ruling and being ruled in turn. Relative to the political art as the art that constitutes virtue and justice in the *Republic*, the political art (or art of political science) in the *Statesman* is an art that is exercised in a realm of conflict and imperfection rather than harmony and perfection.

Notably, the Eleatic Stranger's depiction of the age of Cronus as one where no *politeiai* and no *technai* existed, where rule was exercised as "caring" (*epimeleia*) by divinities for human beings, just as shepherds manage sheep, suggests that in the world of Zeus there is no way to perform an art of practical political rule that produces perfect harmony, a place without *stasis*. This suggestion, however, does not undermine the merits or significance of Platonic justice as expressed in the *kallipolis* of the *Republic*, for the political art of *that polis* directly effected justice. Whereas the *Statesman* provides no definition of justice and, in the language of the *Statesman*, no definition of the absolute standard of the art of measurement, the absence of such articulated standards in it no more serves to deny the dialogue's significance for understanding the political art than does the independent leadership of an effectively good statesman, who is not fully able to provide theoretical justifications for his actions, deny the significance of his or her actions for understanding the good practice of the political art. What has changed is Plato's focus and interests, so that the search for *paradeigmata* in the *Statesman* now points to the world of practical examples rather than the world of forms, and thus "weaving" rather than "painting," to define the political art as an art of justice.

By having the Eleatic Stranger articulate the myth and the world of Zeus, Plato has (provisionally) accepted a particular relation of *politike* to the realms of both perfection and imperfection as the appropriate context for defining the political art. The relevance of both realms to the definition of the political art in the *Statesman* enables one to understand how it can be defined in the dialogue as an art that mediates conflict and requires the consent of the people, an art whose practitioners must be much closer to or friendlier with their subjects than shepherds are to sheep, and an art that epistemologically depends on an absolute measure, so that it can be practiced independently of the consent of the people (291e, 292b–c, 293b–e). Belief in the independence of the theoretical definition of the political art from the practical consent of the people simply indicates the relevance of the worlds of both Cronus and Zeus to the actual practice of the political art. The "normal" resistance to the just exercise of the political art previously referred to in the *Statesman* is now understandable (and, willy nilly, inevitable), just as Socrates in Plato's *Republic* recognized a perpetual and irreducible tension between *logos* and *ergon* as a condition for the articulation of his theory of justice.[27]

3. *Politike* BETWEEN *Logos* AND *Ergon*

a. *Paradeigmata*

After an initial set of divisions and the myth of Cronus, which locates the participants of the dialogue in an age of imperfection, the Eleatic Stranger states that the *logos* of their discussion is too much like "a portrait which is as yet

---

27. On the relevance of the myth of Cronus and Zeus to the problematic of *logos-ergon*, see Pierre Vidal-Naquet, "Plato's Myth of the *Statesman*: The Ambiguities of the Golden Age and History," and Melissa Lane, *Method and Politics in Plato's Statesman*.

an outline sketch and does not represent the original (*pharmakon*) clearly because it still has to be painted in colors properly balanced with one another."[28] Then he asserts (in the vein of *Republic* 472e–473b) that *logos* (particularly with regard to ethical assertions) more closely indicates reality than physical phenomena and identifies the tool that can help communicate the *logos* of *politike* (or help one acquire its scientific understanding) as *paradeigma* (277d), a significant term of art throughout the Platonic dialogues.[29]

As tools of instruction, *paradeigmata* perform differently from the method of division. They refer to known phenomena that stimulate better understandings of things that one can, but currently does not, know. *Paradeigmata* may provide one with a "true belief or opinion" (see *Meno* 97aff) rather than "knowledge" of something (277c–278c). But their use can do so only if one does not start from a "false belief" (278d–e).[30] This makes investigation into the nature of *politike*, of course, extremely difficult, because there *are no* true practitioners of it and no extant, just constitutions whose ethical and political norms would be likely to promote one. But such an investigation may be successful, if one uses *paragdeigmata* appropriately. Thus, the Eleatic Stranger:

> [Would we] not at all be in the wrong in having first attempted to see the nature of models [*paradeigmata*] as a whole in their turn in the specific case of a further small model, with the intention then of bringing, in order to apply it to the case [*eidos*] of the king [that is, the statesman], which is of the greatest importance, something of the same sort from smaller things somewhere, in an attempt once more through the use of a model to skillfully recognize what caring for those in the city is, so that it may be present to us in our waking state instead of in a dream?[31] (278e)

28. *Statesman* 277c; see also *Republic* 420c–d, 501a–c.

29. For "earlier" usages, see *Euthyphro* 13c–d and *Meno* 79a–b. We have discussed its significance in the *Republic* in Chapter 4, above. For useful analytical discussions of the philosophical status of *paradeigma* in Plato's metaphysics, see William J. Prior, "The Concept of *Paradeigma* in Plato's Theory of Forms," and Richard Patterson, *Image and Reality in Plato's Metaphysics*. For a treatment of *paradeigma* set by different interpretive questions, see Lane, *Method and Politics in Plato's Statesman*.

30. For a discussion of Plato's attitude toward "false belief," particularly with regard to the *Sophist*, see Michael Frede, "The Literary Form of the *Sophist*," in Gill and McCabe, eds., *Form and Argument in Late Plato*, 135–51.

31. *Statesman* 278e. This and the following translations of passages from the *Statesman* generally follow those of Rowe.

i. Medicine

In the *Statesman,* the art of medicine functions as a *paradeigma* of *politike* nearly as significantly as the ultimate *paradeigma* for *politike,* the art of weaving (on which, see below). The use of the art of medicine as an analogue for the political art is not unique to the *Statesman*—we have seen how it functions in the *Protagoras, Gorgias,* and *Republic*—but its significance for this dialogue is particularly notable.[32]

In general, Plato identifies a number of similarities between medicine and the political art; seven stand out in the *Statesman.* Like medicine, *politike* is (1) a *techne,* that is, a systematic practice informed by knowledge; (2) the competent (not necessarily successful) practice of this art does not depend on its subject, so that the skill of a good doctor or statesman does not depend on the attitude of his patients or citizens, although its practical success may;[33] (3) an inherently ethical practice, that is, it is driven by concern for the good of its subjects. The practices of both *politike* and medicine may be characterized as "therapy," which by definition (for the Greeks) heals rather than harms; however, the practice of *politike* is more directly subject to ethical evaluation.[34] (4) The "cures" by both practitioners may be temporarily painful for their subjects and potentially fatal for "parts" of them.[35] (5) A good statesman, like a good doctor, is free to change the rules, laws, or "prescriptions" he has authorized for his subjects if his judgment of the sickness or problem he faces changes.

(6) The above characteristics of *politike* are potentially compatible with the virtuous practice of democratic politics. However, Plato often refers to *politike* in the *Statesman* (also, at times, in the *Euthydemus*) as "kingship" while comparing it to medicine, thereby indicating how the skill of the practitioner operates on a different and higher level than that of his subjects. Like

---

32. Notably, it did not play the same prominent role in the discussion of perfect justice in the *Republic,* where the socially prevalent practice of law and medicine is regarded as symptomatic of a radically flawed society, and the most significant arts are educative, not remedial—namely, the arts of *gymnastike* and *mousike* (403e–412a), whereas it also plays a prominent role in articulating the practice of politics in the second-best city of Magnesia in the *Laws.* See Chapter 4, Section B, above, and Chapter 5, Section B, below.

33. *Statesman* 293a–b, 296b–d; see also *Republic* 340d–e, 341b.

34. *Statesman* 293b, 296c–d, 297b.

35. *Statesman* 293b–d. Although this passage has been cited in support of Plato as an advocate of antidemocratic, despotic politics, it is no more antidemocratic than a state's authorization of conscription or the death penalty for convicted criminals. Recall *Protagoras* 322d. That is not to say, however, that the act or its effect could be unjust.

specialized *demiourgoi* who are few in relation to the many they serve, practitioners of *politike* amount to a small fraction of the citizenry they serve (297b–c).

(7) Nevertheless, the concern of the practitioners of medicine and the political art differs from that of most other craftsmen in that it characteristically treats their subject "as a whole." In other words, the successful practice of these arts depends on the practitioner's ability to coordinate the effects of their practice with the other dimensions of the life of the subject. Moreover, they are not, as are other arts, subject to the authority of still other arts (except that in certain respects the practice of medicine is affected by *politike*). In this way, both are *technai* of "wholes" rather than particular practical *technai*.[36]

ii. Navigation

To supplement the *paradeigma* of medicine, Plato employs the analogy of seamanship (which he did not use positively in the *Republic*, 488bff, because there were no good seamen to describe):

> Just as a captain (*kubernetes*), always watching out for what is to the benefit of the ship and the sailors, preserves his fellow-sailors not by putting things down in writing but offering his expertise [*techne*] in law, so too in this manner a constitution would be correct, would it not, if it issued from those who are able to rule in this way, offering the strength of their expertise as more powerful than the laws? And is it not the case that there is no mistake for wise rulers, whatever they do, provided that they watch for one great thing, that by always distributing to those in the city what is most just as judged by the intelligent application of their expertise they are able both to preserve them and so far as they can to bring it about they are better than they were?[37]

---

36. For discussions of the art of medicine as a historical practice and conceptual skill in ancient Greece, as well as a term of art in Plato, see Michael Frede, *Essays in Ancient Philosophy*, 225–98; and the collection of articles in *Method, Medicine, and Metaphysics: Studies in the Philosophy of Ancient Science*, ed. R. J. Hankinson. Earlier, helpful treatments of this subject include W. H. S. Jones, *Philosophy and Medicine in Ancient Greece;* and *Ancient Medicine: Selected Papers of Ludwig Edelstein*, ed. Owsei Temkin and C. Lilian Temkin. Also see James Longrigg, *Greek Rational Medicine: Philosophy and Medicine from Alcmaeon to the Alexandrians.*

37. *Statesman* 296e–297b.

The discussion does not deny the existence of an ideal constitution (296e), which remains the standard for "imitation" (297c). Plato's ideal understanding of the political art appears in the *Statesman* as the superiority of the reason of the political art to the typical, practicable rules of law (296c–d, 300c–d). The issue becomes how the "second-best" is to be practically achieved (297e). At this point in the dialogue, the issue of the relative importance of a *politikos* following the laws takes center stage.

b. Measurement

The Eleatic Stranger's assertion of the need for employing *paradeigmata* for successful inquiry into the nature of *politike* does not entirely abandon the previously employed method of division. Rather, it acts as a supplement or specification. Prior to the substantive discussion of *politike* in terms of the art of weaving (on which, see below), he differentiates various kinds of *technai* in order to specify which of these could serve properly as a *paradeigma* for *politike* (279b–281a). The Eleatic Stranger justifies the relevance of *paradeigmata* as "measures" when he spells out the final component of the interpretive framework for defining *politike*—namely, the art of measurement. He defines it as a two-dimensional art; its capacity involves measuring not only with regard to excess and deficiency but also with respect to a fixed standard (283c–284d). (These two notions of measurement do not seem to be unique to the political art but rather indicate the epistemological dimension of all *technai*.[38])

Knowing the political art in terms of a two-dimensional art of measurement enables one to distinguish "according to real forms" (286d; see also 262b), that is, to practice properly the method of division.[39] The Eleatic Stranger (with Young Socrates) now reasserts that their discussion enables them to become better philosophers as well as to discover the meaning of the political art (285d–286a, 286d). The statement does not affirm a philosophi-

---

38. Commentators have pointed out complementary assertions of the significance of this art in the *Sophist* (284b) and *Philebus* (53c, 55c, 57d–e), other "late" dialogues. But the concept of "measure" (so important in mathematical reasoning) was central to Plato's earlier discussions of the political art, particularly in the *Protagoras* and *Gorgias*. The differences between Plato's early and late employments of "measurement" primarily involve their different referents, but they also share likenesses. In the aporetic dialogues, he criticized sophists and rhetoricians in general for presuming to know the political art. From the perspective of the *Statesman*, one might gloss this judgment by arguing that they viewed the political art as an art of measurement only in the first dimension, thus failing to understand the true nature of the art.

39. For a useful, brief discussion of the "forms" of the method of division in relation to other Platonic ideas about forms, see Rowe, *Plato: Statesman*, 4–8.

cal instead of a political purpose for the dialogue.[40] Rather, it illustrates the interdependence of the proper use of philosophical method with the proper understanding of the political art.[41] In general, philosophy is important for critical purposes. Because there are no *paradeigmata* for *politike* among its extant practitioners, relevant *paradeigmata* can be demonstrated only in *logoi* (285d–286a), which requires one to pursue "the longer route" of dialectic (and the method of division).[42]

The new issue facing the definition of *politike* becomes how to employ a fixed measure that also involves judgments of excess and deficiency to define "an art of tendance for the *polis.*" Plato answers with a two-part demonstration. The first is categorical; he distinguishes the political art from the other "arts of the community of citizens" (287b). The basic divide separates "contributory arts" and their exemplars (for instance, slaves, laborers, and merchants) and "directive" arts" and their exemplars (for instance, clerks, soothsayers, priests, sophists, and politicians)—all of whom the Stranger regards as inadequate practitioners of such arts (290a–291c).[43] In so doing, the Stranger asserts a naturalistic order of the arts, and to that extent a natural political order, although no existing political order practically approximates that natural order.[44] The Eleatic Stranger has specified a distinctive niche for *politike.*

4. THE POLITICAL ART AMID IMPERFECT POLITICAL ORDERS

a. Constitutional Categories

Plato initiates his most conclusive definition of *politike* as the bridge between the ideal world of *logoi* and the recalcitrant world of *erga* by discussing the practical framework, or constitutional context (291d), for its exercise. In

---

40. Rowe suggests this. See his Plato, *Statesman,* 3.

41. I wrote this sentence before reading Lane's book, which confirms it by using a different interpretive angle.

42. *Statesman* 286e–287a; see also *Phaedrus* 274a; *Republic* 504bff; see Ostwald, "Introduction," Plato, *Statesman,* xii–xiv.

43. This divide parallels the one between practical and theoretical arts earlier in the dialogue.

44. One might say that this classification indicates the first significant theoretical articulation of "political nature" and, to this extent, anticipates comparable Aristotelian classifications. But, again, it does not presage them according to an immediately coherent teleological scheme. The function assigned to this scheme by the Eleatic Stranger is more critical than descriptive; the "foundation" is clearly in *logoi* alone, not in an Aristotelian deep logical structure of the material world. For Plato, the material aspect of political nature does not potentiate a critical dimension, as it does in Aristotle, which also prevents Plato from ever justifying what exists as inherently good.

the *Republic,* the nature of a just *politeia* was discussed concomitantly with the realization of justice by articulating the ideal political art of philosophical-guardianship, but here *techne* and *politeia* function on two different planes of experience, with the former stemming from the world of *logos* and the latter from the world of *ergon.* This enables the Eleatic Stranger to differentiate constitutional orders without (as was the case in the *Republic*) presupposing the degenerate character of all constitutions other than the ideal one. The first categorization (291d) produces a threefold division, simply defined as rule by one, the few, or the many. This quickly becomes a fivefold division, as the Stranger differentiates correct and deformed manifestations of those constitutional forms. They are to be distinguished along three different axes: whether they are characterized by "violence or consent . . . poverty or riches . . . law-abidingness or disregard of law," thus: kingship/tyranny, aristocracy/oligarchy, democracy/democracy (291e).⁴⁵ (The ambiguity in the definition of democracy is discussed below.) Yet the conceptual form for the practice of genuine *politike* remains the same whatever the constitutional form in which it operates, making its practice compatible with different constitutional principles and practices; and its success (especially given the method of division) ultimately depends on the presence or absence of *episteme* in effecting that operation (292b–d).⁴⁶ Later, this criterion of success or goodness in the political realm becomes whether or not a political order follows the law as a patient might obey the laws of medicine set forth by his doctor and thereby is able to heal itself (302eff).

b. *Politike* and the Rule of Law

In passages reminiscent of the *Republic* and Socrates' trial in the *Apology,* Plato has the Eleatic Stranger paint a mocking portrait of what happens in situations where those unskilled in the arts of navigation and medicine are given responsibility for their practice. He associates such incompetence with the superior authority of *nomoi* over *politike,* in either oligarchies or democracies

---

45. This division of constitutional forms anticipates (but does not inchoately represent) Aristotle's differentiation of constitutional forms into "correct" and "perverted" types. (See *Politics* IV.2).

46. This statement complements one of the Eleatic Stranger's initial statements about *politike,* that one may be a successful practitioner of it regardless of whether one actually exercises power (259b). It also diametrically opposes a principle that informs the ethics of democratic politics, namely, that the wisdom of the decision increases with the proportion of citizens participating in the deliberative process.

(298a–300a). A *politikos*, like a doctor, must be allowed to change his "prescriptions" according to changes in the circumstances to which they would apply (300c–d). Then the Stranger justifies obedience to rules or laws as a second-best solution, where there is no "true constitution" in which a skilled practitioner of *politike* who can imitate it properly has the power to rule (301a–d). *Nomoi* compensate for the absence of genuine *politikoi* and restrain politically unskilled individuals or groups who might transform monarchies into tyrannies, aristocracies into oligarchies. Notably, Plato does not justify obedience to law by appealing to the stability it achieves but rather by arguing that legally authorized standards for political life constitute the best practicable approximation of justice in an ordered, imperfect society. Indeed, the Stranger refers to all imitative constitutions as fundamentally unstable. "They all rest on the sandy foundation of action according to rules and customs without scientific knowledge" (*episteme,* 301e). He justifies attention to second-best solutions and the consideration of imitative constitutions, not because belief in the true constitution has been abandoned, but because the matter of how to deal with imperfection is a crucial political concern. Thus, he asks (302b): "So which of these 'incorrect' constitutions is least difficult to live with, given that they are all difficult, and which the heaviest to bear? Should we take a brief look at this, although a discussion of it will be a side-issue in relation to the subject now set before us? And yet, at any rate in general, perhaps the whole of what we do is for the sake of this sort of thing." This is hardly the remark of a philosopher lost in the bright (or cloudy) sky of idealism.

5. *Politike,* DEMOCRACY, AND THE ART OF WEAVING

Attention now switches to one of the three main categories of constitution, democracy. It stands out among all the others, not only because of its conceptual ambiguity (having the same name regardless of whether the constitution follows or flouts the law) but also because it is regarded as being "at once the hardest to live under and the easiest" (302c).[47] Among the law-abiding

---

47. For the tendency of democracy to violate constitutional form, see Sheldon S. Wolin, "Norm and Form: The Constitutionalizing of Democracy," in Euben et al., eds., *Athenian Political Thought and the Reconstruction of American Democracy,* 29–58, and Chapter 4, above. On the ambiguity of the idea and practice democracy in a relatively ahistorical sense, see William E. Connolly, *Politics and Ambiguity,* 3–9, and idem, *Identity/Difference: Democratic Negotiations of Political Paradox,* x, 200–201.

constitutions, democracy is the worst, but "If all three flout the laws, democracy is the best of them. Thus, if all constitutions are unprincipled, the best thing to do is to live in a democracy. . . . The rule of the multitude is weak in every way; it is not capable of any great good or evil as compared with the other two. This is because in a democracy political authority has been distributed in small portions to many" (303a–b). The democratic distribution of political authority is desirable, according to the Eleatic Stranger, because the politicians of the world are politicians who do not imitate the ideal or correct constitution; they are not *politikoi* but "faction-mongers" who head illusory regimes, "the greatest of imitators and cheats" who should really be regarded as "the greatest of all Sophists" (303c). Given the omnipresence of Sophistic politicians among the ruling classes of all regimes, as well as the fact that Plato provides no practical examples (in this or any other dialogue) of well-ordered, lawful, imitative constitutions—choosing instead to describe the practices of falsely imitative, unjust, and presumably "lawless" regimes—the *Statesman* suggests that Plato may have believed that the democratic political order of the Athenians was the best existing regime.[48]

With these comments about democracy, the Eleatic Stranger states that he has succeeded in isolating "the political art" (303c–d)—and Plato implies that what remains to be done is the work of the reader. The Stranger states that the remaining distinctions are minor, and, indeed, they mostly reaffirm the practical authority of *politike* over other arts and explicate the art of weaving as the best *paradeigma* for *politike*. The first distinction evokes the previous use of *diairesis* to define the political art. Much as the political art as an art of the whole in the aporetic dialogues was an art of "use," not just an art of "production," the political art in the *Statesman* directs the activities of all other arts and determines the proper use of their products. For example, *politike* determines whether and when to use persuasion or force to accomplish a political end, whether and when to fight on behalf of one's *polis* (304a–305a). Appealing to conventional referents that establish the hierarchical superiority of the political art over the arts of rhetoric, war, and strategy (304b–305a), the Eleatic Stranger asserts that the sovereign superiority of the political art with

---

48. This statement may be shocking and may seem to conflict with Socrates' observation in the *Republic* (492a–d) that the multitude in a democratic assembly constitutes "the greatest of all sophists." But, to recall, this statement does not blame democratic institutions so much as it does the rush to judgment fomented by either a crowd or its leaders. On the relation of democracy and injustice in the *Republic,* see Chapter 4, Section C, above.

respect to all other arts stems from its capacity to judge the proper purpose that subordinate arts would serve. The political art, here designated as the kingly art, is not a kind of *praxis* for citizens but a way of ruling the actions of others in positions of power and authority (305c–d), which leads to the Eleatic Stranger's final definition of the political art as an art of weaving.

The determination of weaving as the appropriate *paradeigma* is itself governed by external criteria, that is, by the previously accepted framework for establishing the necessary components of *politike* (279b–283a).[49] "Whereas the one [art] that controls all of these [other arts] and the laws, and cares for every aspect of things in the city, and weaves everything together in the most correct way—this, embracing its capacity with the appellation belonging to the whole, we would, it seems, most appropriately call statesmanship (*politiken*)" (305e). The selection of weaving as a *paradeigma* for *politike* is very much a philosophical judgment that current politicians, Sophists, and rhetoricians are unable to make, but it is nonetheless informed by substantive, practically relevant political values that become manifest as the explication of the art of weaving proceeds.

This art is not inherently a democratic art; that Plato sometimes refers to it as the kingly art is not anomalous. Need it be said, Plato is not simply the political theorist's version of the Protagorean Sophist who associates his discursive art with the deliberative art of democratic citizens; he has no faith in the *demos*. Because democracies are not perfectly just, no democratic art could perfectly signify the true political art. But, as finally depicted in the *Statesman,* the political art is not essentially more anti- than pro-democratic. As a critical standard for political judgment and action, it may be useful for enabling a democratic society to become more virtuous and just.

The Stranger's gloss of the art of weaving supports this point and even suggests a democratic, consensual dimension to *politike.* For much more than the arts of medicine or navigation, the *paradeigma* of the art of weaving emphasizes the importance of conciliation. It promotes cooperation among essentially different components of the social fabric and refuses suppression or domination as its strategic method of choice. It also implies the improbability of achieving political harmony that fully transcends political conflict and

---

49. *Statesman* 283b. On the rationale for not immediately identifying the art of weaving as the appropriate *paradeigma* for *politike,* skipping the series of divisions that preceded its selection, see Ostwald, "Introduction," Plato, *Statesman,* xii–xiv, and Rowe, "Introduction," Plato, *Statesman,* 1–19.

tension, recognizing the significance of second-best solutions for the ordinary conduct of political life.

The conciliatory art of weaving, the political art as an art of leadership, does not fail to adhere to the rigorous ideal standards previously adduced for *politike* in either this dialogue or the *Republic.* Indeed, it will "reject bad material as far as possible and use what is good and serviceable" (308c–309a). Its primary aim is not a practical copy of an ideal blueprint, but generating the best possible product out of the material at one's disposal (308d–e). This done, the *politikos* will have fostered membership in a political community that best approximates justice and happiness.[50] Although the relationship of the weaver to wool is surely hierarchical, it need not imply domination. For all—ordinary citizens or leaders—who think critically about what to do for their political community must, at one level (not all levels), rise "above" the particular situations of themselves and their fellow citizens to imagine ways and means of productively reconciling existing differences.[51] Moreover, as with the skillful practice of the weaver's art, there are many ways to use the same wool—no matter its texture or fabric—to produce an aesthetically pleasing and practically useful piece of clothing.[52]

The aim of the Stranger's ideal of political leadership is to foster a godlike bond of community among the conflicting parts of virtue, "which are diverse in nature and would else be opposing in tendency" (310a); doing so exemplifies the use of the specific drug of medicinal art.[53] The statesman would promote this by skillfully marrying (literally and metaphorically) the elements of courage and moderation in the collectivity, because: "Everything in cities can-

50. Adherence to this critical ideal does not evidence respect for "human rights"—either the inherent dignity of every human being or the individual's political right to be wrong. The Stranger reminds the Young Socrates that a proper statesman will expel from the community all who do not learn from his guidance (308e–309a). But any political community that differentiates criminal from lawful activity and punishes citizens who are judged to have engaged in the former rather than the latter, and even those societies that demonstrate respect for conventionally defined human rights, surely exhibits such differentiation. (One may wonder whether respect for human rights is ever a paramount goal of political action.)

51. For an essay on the art of weaving in Greek culture, see John Scheid and Jesper Svenbro, *The Craft of Zeus—Myths of Weaving and Fabric,* 9–34.

52. I owe this point to Kelli Peduzzi.

53. The association of "nature" with "imperfect"—"conflicting"—conditions marks one way in which the conceptual language of the *Statesman* differs from that of the *Republic*—where "nature" identifies ideas and the ideal. The question of whether this signifies an alteration in Plato's view of what is "natural" is addressed at the beginning of this chapter.

not go well, either on the private or on the public level, unless both of these [traits or groups] are there to give their help" (311b). The design for this political bond is godlike because human beings do not naturally or conventionally know it, which may partly explain why the Eleatic Stranger identifies its producer as "kingly" (see 306aff, 311c). It has a practical, human character, however, and involves a "belief" about values and standards that is shared by "courageous" and "moderate" citizens (310a). Thus does the *paradeigma* of weaving best exemplify the practice and end of the political art. According to the Stranger,

> The weaving together, with regular intertwining, of the disposition of courageous and moderate people, when the kingly expertise brings their life together in agreement making it common between them, completing the most magnificent and best of all fabrics and covering all the other inhabitants of cities, both slave and free, holds them together with this twining and, so far as it belongs to a city to be happy, not falling short of this in any respect, rules and directs. (311b–c)

Young Socrates responds and closes the *Statesman* by saying to the Stranger that he has completed for us (himself and Theodorus) "a most beautiful treatment of the king and statesman." .

A distinctive virtue of *politike* as an art of political leadership in the *Statesman* is its capacity to reconcile virtues that traditionally were regarded as antagonistic: courage and moderation (306b–c). Theoretically reconciled in the idea of justice articulated in the *Republic,* these different virtues are practically reconciled in the *Statesman* through the practice of *politike.* The result assures the avoidance of *stasis* (307c), Plato's overriding political concern. *Politike's* unique capacity stems from the ability to recognize practical corollaries to the absolute standard of measurement, that is, how to conciliate the exercise of these two virtues so that their excess or deficiency with respect to the realization of perfect justice does not harm the political community as a whole (307b–c, 310a–e).

The *Statesman* does not explain the "godlike" design. That appeared in the *Republic.* Nor does it explain what the "beliefs" ought to be. That appears in the *Laws.* What it does is articulate the principal dimensions in *logos* of the political art as a practical art of leadership and rule. In this sense, it operates between the *Republic* and *Laws,* but the continuum does not necessarily mark a theoretical unity or a radical change in political or philosophical perspective as much as it exhibits one crucial dimension of the multifaceted Platonic political art.

B. CONSTITUTIONAL LAWS: ON PLATO'S *Laws*

Probably composed during the last decade of Plato's life, the *Laws* (*Nomoi*) is by far his longest and most likely his last written work. It was "unpublished" at the time of Plato's death, after which his secretary, Philippus of Opus, finalized its form.[54] Although some scholars view the form and content of the dialogue as a degenerate product of creeping senility or another instance of Plato's foolhardy and dangerous political thought, it is generally regarded as one of Plato's most significant achievements.[55] For this author, it marks a major facet of Plato's political thought insofar as it discursively institutionalizes that art in a system of laws for a practicable, yet purely hypothetical, second-best society.

The relative importance of the *Laws* for understanding Plato's political theory and the Platonic political art is a basic issue about which scholarly opinions have been sharply divided. Traditional scholarship has positioned the *Laws* far down the ladder of significance for Plato's political thought, insofar as it merely applies the principles of the *Republic* in a historically limiting way. Whether it lacks the literary color and dialogic drama that characterize most Platonic dialogues or possesses a distinctive literary cast, it fails—so the arguments go—to illuminate any philosophical idea, often summarizing rather than analyzing.[56] This interpretive perspective was reinforced in Great

54. Diogenes Laertius, III.37; see commentary by Guthrie, *A History of Greek Philosophy*, 5:321ff.

55. For the *Laws* as evidence of Plato's literary degeneration in old age, see R. B. Bury, "Introduction," in Plato, *Laws: Books I–VI*, vii, and Laszlo Versenyi, "The Cretan Plato." For derogatory references to the *Laws* in the German tradition of Platonic scholarship, see R. F. Stalley, *An Introduction to Plato's Laws*, 3–4, 9–10. For a recent general appreciation of the value and significance of the *Laws*, see Stalley's book, and P. A. Brunt, "The Model City in Plato's *Laws*," in *Studies in Greek History and Thought*, 245–81.

56. For Irwin, the *Laws* is philosophically inconsequential; he virtually ignores the *Laws* in both *Plato's Moral Theory* and *Plato's Ethics*. Also see Guthrie, *A History of Greek Philosophy*, 5:329—although Guthrie's respect for the contribution of the narrative form of the dialogue to its content qualifies any philosophical derogation of the latter. Andrea Nightingale argues that the *Laws* reflects a distinctive rhetorical strategy, but it is one that suppresses philosophical reflection. See her "Writing/Reading a Sacred Text: A Literary Interpretation of Plato's *Laws*."

Britain and the United States from the 1940s to the early 1980s by the influence of Popper and Strauss. With the epithets "totalitarian" or "theorist of natural law" typically affixed to the political Plato, the foundations of Plato's political theory would have had to have been laid in the *Republic* and only supported in the *Laws*.[57] More recently, this view has been challenged by members of a diverse second group (whose members in other respects may not be affiliated), which includes a new generation of Straussians (guided by Strauss's own statement that the *Laws* "is the most political work of Plato");[58] interpreters from the tradition of Anglo-American analytical philosophy, who see the *Republic* as "moral" or "ethical" and the *Laws* as more clearly and usefully "political;"[59] and proponents of a developmental perspective on Plato's political thought, who typically find inconsistencies or contradictions between the *Republic* and the *Laws*.[60] For members of this group, the *Republic* may be merely a "prelude" or "prolegomenon" to Plato's philosophy about the practice of politics, which is expressed in the *Laws*. The latter is judged to be more politically interesting than the former because of its relative moderation.[61] Less dogmatic interpreters of the *Laws* do not fall neatly into one of these categories. The most important of these are Glenn R. Morrow, in *Plato's Cretan City: A Historical Interpretation of Plato's Laws*, and Andre Laks, in

57. See Karl Popper, *The Open Society and Its Enemies—Vol. 1: The Spell of Plato*, and Strauss's summary of Plato's political philosophy in Strauss and Cropsey, *History of Political Philosophy*, 33–89. Also note how Strauss represents Plato by the *Republic* in *The City and Man*, part 2.

58. Leo Strauss, *The Argument and the Action of Plato's Laws*, 1. See also Thomas Pangle, *The Laws of Plato*, 377. In the first sentence of his "Interpretive Essay," Pangle recognizes the centrality of the political art or "the art of politics" for understanding Plato's *Laws*. However, he does not systematically analyze Plato's treatment of the idea of the political art in the dialogue, and his interpretation of it primarily stems from his overall interpretation of the dialogue as revelatory of the political teachings of "Socrates," who is a somewhat mysterious combination of the historical Socrates and the character of Socrates in Plato's dialogues (375–79).

59. See R. F. Stalley, *An Introduction to Plato's Laws;* see also interpretations of the *Republic* in this tradition (Vlastos, Irwin, Annas, Waterfield), discussed in Chapter 4, above.

60. See, for example, P. Friedlander, *Plato,* 3:419–22; Christopher Bobonich, "Persuasion, Compulsion, and Freedom in Plato's *Laws*"; David Cohen, "Law, Autonomy, and Political Community in Plato's *Laws.*" In "The Unity of Plato's Thought," Timothy Shiell categorizes interpreters of Plato according to whether they find the *Republic* and *Laws* complementary or contradictory. Stalley (p. 9) also mentions a type of interpretation that associates different Platonic dialogues with different audiences. In this perspective, the *Laws* was written for a more "popular" audience than the *Republic*. I don't discuss writers from this group.

61. See Pangle, 377; Stalley, 22; Cohen, and Bobonich (see note 60, above). Also see Christopher Bobonich, "Reading the *Laws*," in Gill and McCabe, eds., *Form and Argument in Late Plato*, 249–82.

a recent article theorizing a particular conceptual relation between the *Republic* and the *Laws.*[62])

Despite their scholarly plausibility, these divergent judgments beg more basic interpretive questions. First, they presuppose a particular understanding of the "political," one that is neither "ethical" nor "philosophical." This understanding may or may not be Plato's, but it is applied to readings of Plato without argument.[63] Second, they presume a particular version of what Plato is doing in writing the *Laws.* For example, he may be either "applying" the "principles" of the *Republic* or "abandoning" them, and the dialogue's central issue may be the tension between "reason" and "revelation" or "philosophy" and "the rule of law." However, if Plato is not spending his career trying either to formulate a systematic philosophy marked by logically correct propositions or to reveal the "limits" of politics, these questions become misleading and indeed moot.

The context of the composition of the *Laws* supports this point. Plato probably began writing the *Laws* in 361, after his final visit to Syracuse, at which time he resumed his position as *scholarchos* of the Academy. His return to academic life, however, did not signal any intellectual or practical withdrawal from political concerns. We know that throughout this period of his leadership of the Academy "students" came to the Academy in antici-

---

62. Morrow's book was first published by Princeton University Press. His splendid book is much more than a historical interpretation of the *Laws* and remains underappreciated for its contribution to the understanding of Plato's political thought. Unfortunately, Charles H. Kahn's otherwise thoughtful preface to the recently issued paperback version of *Plato's Cretan City* does not adequately consider this dimension of Morrow's book. However, Andre Laks usefully does in his article, "Legislation and Demiurgy: On the Relationship Between Plato's *Republic* and *Laws.*" Laks's article has particularly valuable comments on the *Laws* as a philosophical argument about the character of political possibility, which was not explored in the *Republic.* However, Laks tends to follow Morrow in reading the *Laws* as a "projection" of the *Republic,* and this blurs the distinctiveness of his interpretation and those that read the *Laws* as an "application" of the *Republic.* That presupposes a deductive model for Plato's argument in the *Laws,* one that quite possibly obscures the genuinely creative elements in the dialogue, including those that may still be consistent with the ideals of *kallipolis* or the *Republic* more generally. See also Trevor J. Saunders, "Introduction," in Plato, *The Laws,* and idem, "Plato's Later Political Thought," in *The Cambridge Companion to Plato,* ed. Richard Kraut, 464–92 (despite his adherence to Popper's view that Plato's political ideas essentially oppose liberal ideals of democracy and freedom). Finally, see the balanced (if not altogether consistent) commentary by W. K. C. Guthrie in his *A History of Greek Philosophy,* 5:321–82.

63. Moreover, any definition of "political" is itself partly a political answer to a political question, in that it would (at least, temporarily) resolve a contest of power as well as of reason.

pation of, and partly in preparation for, political activity—primarily, although not exclusively, in the form of political counselors. They also came as political dissidents, refugees from their own political regimes.[64] The proportion of politically interested students in the Academy may be uncertain, but their presence raises complex issues about the relation of this long dialogue about the hypothetical city of Magnesia to contemporary actualities and possibilities.

From the perspective employed here, the *Laws* indicates a fresh exploration of issues that Plato previously had not addressed, namely what are the constitutional laws of a *polis* that would best approximate the *logos* of justice. In writing this dialogue, therefore, Plato breaks new ground, for the issue points to a new dimension of his theorization of the political art. The political art articulated in the *Laws* is not a sign of conventional injustice, an expression of justice, or a *logos* of practical political leadership. If one integrates Plato's substantive treatment of the political art in the text with the probably intended effect of the dialogue as a whole, the political art in/of the *Laws* may be read as a philosophical act of political founding that could assist the deliberations of politicians in search of ways to improve their societies. To the extent that Plato's greatest political inspiration was Athens, the *Laws* constitutes the final installment of Plato's conception of how the political art relates critical reason and democracy.

In this treatment of the *Laws*, I again develop my own interpretation of the dialogue of the whole in conjunction with the dialogue's narrative course, paying the most attention to those aspects of the dialogue that address our concerns. Thus, I primarily address Plato's treatment of the political art by attending to the diverse ways in which he articulates both "the political" and "art" and by interpreting the relation of his treatment to democracy, in both its Athenian and contemporary manifestations. But because the relevant material for this treatment is potentially the entirety of this very long dialogue, omitted portions of the dialogue are particularly evident in the application of my method to interpreting the *Laws*.[65] I can only hope that whatever benefits result outweigh the drawbacks of slighting so many parts of this long, rich text.

64. M. Ostwald and John P. Lynch, "The Growth of Schools and the Advance of Knowledge," in *The Cambridge Ancient History*, 6:612–14.

65. But even Morrow's six-hundred-page treatment of the dialogue has lacunae.

I. THE DIALOGIC SETTING: MAGNESIA

The dialogic participants in the *Laws* include three elderly men: an Athenian Stranger, about whom we know nothing; a Cretan named Cleinias, who had family connections to Epimenides the Seer and is said to have encouraged the Athenians in the Persian Wars of the early fifth century (despite the fact that he apparently lived one hundred years earlier); and a Spartan named Megillus, whose family members had been spokesmen for Athenian interests (642d). Although the last two are not Athenian citizens, each is likely to be favorably disposed to Athens and thereby open to *logoi* of an Athenian Stranger.

Unlike most other Platonic dialogues, which are placed in the late fifth century, the *Laws* dramatically transpires in the present, that is, in the mid-fourth century. Given the similarity of the ages of the dialogue's participants, Plato seems to be indicating that *this* political *logos* may be more directly relevant to contemporary political concerns than other dialogues. Indeed, the dialogue opens with the Cretan and the Spartan discussing the primary political features of their cities, notably interpreting these in relation to the intentions of their founders or legislators (*nomothetai,* 625e–626b). Exactly how relevant this discussion is supposed to be to their concerns is not precisely defined. For none of the participants occupies a political office, and the Athenian reiterates throughout the dialogue the purely imaginary form of the hypothetical state of Magnesia they articulate. Nevertheless, the dialogue closes with Cleinias and Megillus still entertaining the project of founding the state of Magnesia and, importantly, still requiring the intellectual counsel of the Athenian (XII, 969c–d). The thrust of the dialogue is therefore more closely related to political possibility than the *logoi* of the *Republic* or the *Statesman.*

What this closeness consists of is not immediately evident. Relative to the *Republic* and *Statesman,* the scope of the *Laws* is confined. As the Athenian says, the focus of their *logos* will not be human nature generally but the virtues and vices of legislators and their legislation (637d). The plurality expressed by the dialogue's title indicates that its contents will not directly provide a pure *logos* of political life, which for Plato has a singular form (thus *Republic* "Constitution"). Still, the *Laws* belongs to the realm of critical *logos* (or critical reasoning) about political fundamentals. Notwithstanding its concern about practicability and its proximity to contemporary political conditions and constraints, the *Laws* is clearly not a piece of descriptive or empirical political sociology, a subject in which Plato evidences no interest.[66] The laws of the *Laws* and the *Laws* itself are constitutional; they would serve as discursive frames for understanding how to reform the politics of an existing society.[67]

Trying to pinpoint the uniquely political character of the *Laws* leads to questions about the relation of Magnesia to Plato's Athens. If the dialogue is more *directly* political than Plato's other dialogues, and Plato composes and discusses it not only after his directly political experience in Syracusan politics, but also in the Academy, what is its relation to current Athenian political practice or Athenian democracy more generally? Glenn Morrow has shed the most light on this topic in *Plato's Cretan City*. He carefully shows how the proposed *nomoi* of Magnesia more closely derive from and resemble those of Athens than they do those of either Crete or Sparta. In other words, Athenian democracy, rather than the oligarchies of Crete or Sparta, has the most to contribute to Plato's theorization of a practicable yet critical political creed.[68] Morrow's answer, however, does not fully answer our question.

To the extent that Morrow is right, the *Laws* ought to be particularly useful for Athenians; however, its differences from the "constitution" and "laws" of Athenian democracy remain too radical to underwrite an oppositional political party. Neither the *Laws* nor its "laws" offer a program for political action. Both operate outside, rather than inside, the ambit of practical political deliberations in Athens. Plato was no fourth-century Solon (even if he had recast himself in the image of his distant relative). Still, the *Laws* could contribute to Athenian political discourse, insofar as it provides reasonable and conceptually clearer criteria for Athenian constitutional ideals than were provided by either practicing politicians such as Demosthenes or political critics

66. Its claims should not be directly compared with those of Aristotle's *Politics*, especially Books III–VI, although more nearly with those of Books VII–VIII. See Ernest Barker, *Greek Political Theory: Plato and His Predecessors*, 444.

67. For a useful comment on how the "laws" of a *polis* (as well as other political communities) were conceptualized both as "the law" and "the laws," see S. C. Todd, *The Shape of Athenian Law*, 18–19.

68. Brunt (259) misreads Morrow (534) when he charges that the latter views Magnesia's basic political structure as thoroughly Athenian. Morrow recognizes many components of Magnesia that radically depart from the Athenian political order; he simply argues that Magnesia has a greater debt to Athenian political practice than it does to the polities of Crete or Sparta. I am not convinced by George Klosko's critique of Morrow via a novel interpretation of the role of the Nocturnal Council in the dialogue. See his "The Nocturnal Council in Plato's *Laws*."

such as Plato's contemporary and intellectual competitor, Isocrates.[69] If we are to understand how these criteria would intersect with the political conventions of mid-fourth-century Athens, we must not only compare the practices of Magnesia to those of Athens but also engage the arguments of the *Laws* itself.

2. THE POLITICAL ART AND MAGNESIA: CONSTITUTIONAL REFORM, EDUCATION, AND THE PROBLEM OF *Stasis*

Given Plato's devotion of most of the *Laws* to articulating the *nomoi* of Magnesia, "the second-best state," the reader may be tempted to turn immediately to Book IV (where their elaboration begins) in order to discover the central ideas of the dialogue.[70] This interpretive tack would be misleading, however, just as would an interpretation of the argument about justice in the *Republic* that ignored Books I–II; or of the relation of rhetoric to goodness in the *Gorgias* that ignored the opening exchanges among Socrates, Gorgias, and Polus; or of the *Protagoras*'s argument about pleasure at the dialogue's end that ignored Protagoras's Great Speech near its beginning. The opening three books of the *Laws* provide the most significant context for understanding the meaning of the Athenian Stranger's subsequent portrayal of Magnesia. They present the problem to which "Magnesia" provides a solution in critical discourse.

Magnesia in the *Laws* would treat the causes and symptoms of civic strife (*stasis*). To this extent, its function parallels that of *kallipolis* in the *Republic*. In the opening description of the purposes of constitutions and laws (629a–c), the Athenian characterizes them as responses to strife, understood as both war between *poleis* and war within a *polis* but with an emphasis on the significance of the latter. He argues that any constitution worthy of consideration in their *logoi* honors a particular conception of "virtue" as the principal means of eliminating *stasis*. The problem of *stasis* functions in the *Laws*,

---

69. In this respect, the *Laws* may well be read, as Friedlander proposes it should be, as exhibiting the combined force of Plato's Solonian and Socratic heritage. See Paul Friedlander, *Plato*, 3:387.

70. Barker ignores the narrative structure of the dialogue in his lengthy interpretation of it, preferring to view it through the lens of twentieth-century subject headings. Thus, in *Greek Political Theory*, he interprets the *Laws* in terms of "its general theory of the state," its "system of social relations" and "system of government," and its "theory of law" and "theory of education."

as in the *Republic,* as Plato's principal concern, and whatever positive suggestion he makes should not be read as abstract propositions generated from the
realm of *logos* alone, but rather as possible solutions to the corrosive effects
of *stasis* on the constitutions of citizens' souls and states. Yet its purpose differs from that of the *Republic* as well. Whereas Plato responded to the problem of *stasis* in Book I of the *Republic* by having "Socrates" critically discuss
hypothetical *logoi* of justice and constitutions, the *Laws* more directly addresses the problem of *stasis* by having an Athenian theorize a practical reformation of extant Greek constitutions and laws; in this respect, the *Laws*
provides a more practical resolution of the conflict between the theoretical requirements of the virtue of justice and the practical requirements of politics—
at least in the context of ancient Greek city-states.

The Athenian's first major point in his discussion of constitutional laws
is how the conceptions of *arete* honored by both Crete and Sparta are too
militaristic, too narrowly gauged toward the promotion of a *part* of virtue,
namely courage and its accompanying *techne* of military expertise. Instead, a
political conception of virtue should reflect the *whole* of virtue, and its accompanying *techne* should exhibit a politics of the common good (630d). Just
as the art of war without guidance by the political art fails to provide collective security (let alone stability or justice) in Plato's rendition of a Protagorean
mythical account of the origins of the political art in the *Protagoras,* the military virtues of Crete and Sparta, which have been cultivated for fighting wars,
do not aid in forestalling *stasis.* For the Athenian Stranger, the virtues of a *polis* need to aim more directly at achieving peace and bringing harmony to the
polis by reconciling conflicting "parties" (628a–b, 630).[71] Indeed, military virtues exercised in an open political context seem to foment *stasis.* Although
they would help their possessor conquer any foe, they may also encourage
him to fight with other citizens and himself (626b–d). Thus, if a (bad) majority vanquishes or "conquers" a (good) minority, a *polis* begins to experience a
war with itself.

---

71. In ancient Athens, there were no organized political parties in the modern sense; instead,
they were groups of political partisans, typically connected to one or a few prominent individuals. On late fifth-century politics, see W. Robert Connor, *The New Politicians of Fifth Century
Athens;* on early fourth-century politics, see Barry Strauss, *Athens After the Peloponnesian War:
Class, Faction and Policy, 403–386* B.C. Also, see the useful overview of fourth-century Athenian
politics and government by P. J. Rhodes, "The Polis and the Alternatives," in *The Cambridge Ancient History,* 6:565–91, esp. 577–79.

Consequently, the Athenian Stranger would construct better criteria for the work of lawgivers. These could be used as part of a framework for rehabilitating the legacies of Lycurgus of Sparta and Minos of Crete (630d–632d). The cardinal virtues of intelligent judgment (*phronesis*), moderation (*sophrosyne*), justice (*dikaiosyne*), and courage (*andreia*) constitute these criteria. The Athenian Stranger designates these as "divine benefits" (*theia agatha*) under the aegis of "mind" (*nous*) and would have the lawgiver instruct his citizens to have these in view whenever they seek "human benefits" (631d). Neither Crete and its lawgiver Minos, nor Sparta and its lawgiver Lycurgus, offer direct models for the theoretical constitution of Magnesia, and the Athenian acknowledges his implicit criticism of their practices (634a–e). The most significant but also most ambiguous basis for the theorization of Magnesia includes Athens and its lawgiver, Solon, as well as the *kallipolis* of the *Republic* and its authors, namely Plato's Socrates and Plato himself. In any event, the issue for the Athenian is not where his ideas come from but how to relate his critical *logos* to the *ergon* of existing or practicable *politeiai* (636a), how to educate a non-ideal city in virtue.

The Athenian now proceeds to define the major features of the virtues and *nomoi* of the *politeia* that a good lawgiver would found (631b–632d). The principal analogue for his intellectual activity again comes from the arts (*technai*), whose practice would promote the health and harmony of the human body. Although no practice should be mechanically followed, the notion of a *techne* remains Plato's principal framework for conceptualizing rational, virtuous activity. The materials for the educational crafting of virtue are pleasure and pain. These are the sensations that accompany the entry of virtue and vice into the soul (653a). As a result, the initial concern of the lawgiver of Magnesia will be the disposition of these "springs of nature" (636d–e) through education (*paideia*); it contributes to the "correct formation of our feelings of pleasure and pain" (653a–c).

The Athenian Stranger asserts the dense interconnections among the emotions, reason, virtue, and education in the following passage:

> I maintain that the earliest sensations that a child feels in infancy are of pleasure and pain, and this is the route by which virtue and vice enter the soul. But for a man to acquire good judgment (*phronesin*), and unshakable correct opinions, however late in life, is a matter of good luck: a man who possesses them and all the benefits they entail is perfected. I call education (*paideian*) the initial acquisition of virtue by the child, when the feelings of pleasure and affection, pain and

hatred, that well up in his soul are channelled in the right courses before he can provide an account (*logon*) of this. Then, when he does understand their concordance these become correct and appropriate habits. The symphony (*xumphonia*) of all these [emotions] is virtue, while the part of it that is rightly trained in respect of pleasures and pains, so as to hate what ought to be hated, right from the beginning up to the very end, and to love what ought to be loved—if you were to mark this part off in your definition (*logo*) and call it "education," you would be giving it, in my opinion, its right name. (653b–c)[72]

To produce virtue, one must develop from childhood onward "a keen desire to become a good and complete citizen who knows how to rule and be ruled with justice" (643e). Ironically, Plato has asserted quintessentially democratic criteria for a *techne* of *logos* and *ergon*, which produces *arete*, understood as the practice of good *citizenship* and the corollary ability of ruling oneself. Conventional versions of this political art were criticized from different perspectives in the *Apology, Crito, Protagoras*, and *Gorgias;* a proper version of the art was theoretically justified and elaborated in the *Republic* and *Statesman;* here, a version is practically spelled out as calculation of what properly and politically regulates pleasure and pain. In the *Laws*, the name for this regulation in the political arena is "law" (644d). The laws are "pharmaceutical," insofar as they affect the capacity to feel pleasure and pain, which in turn involves the ability to fear and feel confidently about the appropriate possibilities and proper "incentives" (*pharmaka*, 647e) for developing these emotions (653a–b). The laws are also essentially political. Plato closes the first book of the *Laws* by characterizing insight into the orientation of the soul toward pleasure and pain as most useful to the *techne* that would nurture the political art (650b). Not unlike its function in other Platonic dialogues, the political art is an art of fostering virtue in the individual and political community. For Plato in the *Laws*, this is an art of educational leadership and self-discipline—no doubt understood to have been practiced by himself in his life as a philosopher and political theorist.

In the practice of this political art, the criterion for its excellent performance cannot be pleasure in itself or pleasure experienced by anybody (658e);

---

72. I combined parts of Bury's translation of this passage in the Loeb edition and Saunders's translation in the Penguin edition to arrive at my rendition of it. I have also done that in other lengthy quotations I have translated from the *Laws*. See Plato, *Laws*, trans. R. G. Bury (Cambridge, Mass.: Harvard University Press, 1926); Plato, *Laws*, trans. T. J. Saunders (Penguin, 1970).

it must be pleasure that accords with the right reason of the law (659d), as interpreted by godlike legislators and statesmen who have bonded to this standard through their years of experience. Here the Athenian turns to Egypt for an example of such standards. They are relatively conservative, for the Athenian believes that most innovations stem from the unmediated desire for pleasure, which he associates with the roars of approval and disapproval that emanate from a crowd of spectators (657b, 659a–b).[73] Egyptian standards, therefore, do not inspire the production of political medicine that encourages change as a potential good. They need the education that laws of a good political order (*politeia*) established by a good lawgiver would provide by cultivating the association of pleasure and justice (660a, 662e–663c). The lawgiver could even use the devices of songs and stories, as well as arguments, to persuade the citizens of these truths (664a). But overall, there must be criteria for *mousike* above and beyond either what a crowd prefers or an indiscriminate principle of equality. (See Bk. VI, 756e–758a.) The Athenian Stranger has little regard for the untutored judgment of the crowd (670b). The only individual who truly has good judgment is the good lawgiver (671c). He understands what to employ for education in virtue, not only with regard to drinking parties, but *mousike* and *gymnastike* more generally (671b–674b).[74]

The aesthetic formation of human sensations of pleasure and pain—*mousike*—exhibits the relative receptivity of a culture to an education in virtue. It also predisposes a society for a particular *politeia*. The Athenian Stranger

73. Such "roars" recall the reactions of the historical Socrates' jurors to his defense. See Plato, *Apology of Socrates* (17c, 20e, 21a, 27b, 30c).

74. Again, this shows Plato's lack of trust in the immediate judgment of ordinary citizens, but, also again, this does not so much evidence an antidemocratic political perspective as it does a rigorous and critical concern about ethical and political dimensions of culture—which no well-functioning democratic society either does or can happily ignore. The plurality of forms of excellent—indeed, potentially virtuous—art and music today makes Plato's argument for a single-gauged standard of critical evaluation hard to stomach. Indeed, there is no way to directly digest it in today's cultural environment. I happen to think that a good way of combining a recognition of the irreducible plurality of excellent forms of music with standards of critical judgment is offered by the professional work of Peter Schickele, who summarizes his philosophy by stating that he is "dedicated to the proposition that all musics are created equal, or, as in the words of Duke Ellington, 'if it sounds good, it is good.'" For a more precise record of Ellington's words, see Mark Tucker, ed., *The Duke Ellington Reader,* 333: "Music itself is a category of sound, but everything that goes into the ear is not music. Music is music, and that's it. If it sounds good, it's good music, and it depends on who's listening *how* good it sounds" (see also 326, 334). No doubt this trust in the ears of the *demos* cannot be said to be Platonic, but reliance on a notion of "goodness" for the interpretation of music certainly is.

does not believe, however, that one can fully explain the nature of a political order or its laws solely by reference to its perceptions of pleasure and pain or its version of *mousike*. To understand them, one must establish a coherent relation between ethics and power—not only grasp the internal disposition of the emotions of citizens but also explain the history of the external structures of practices and institutions. These considerations (at least) lead the Athenian Stranger to define proper *mousike* differently from the way Socrates did in the *Republic*. Here, the Stranger frames his discussion by telling a genealogical tale of external political forms, in which he spells out the reasons for or causes of (*aitiai*) their epochal transformations (676e, 679a–c).

The function of the subsequent mythical and analytical stories parallels Socrates' story in the *Republic* about the origins of *politeia* and the justice that sustains it. In the *Laws*, however, the Athenian Stranger explicitly attempts to make his stories cover historical ground—the realm of *ergon* rather than the realm of *logos*—just as the Eleatic Stranger's *mythos* of the origins of the human race in the *Statesman* concretizes and historicizes the context for defining *politike* and the *politikos*. For each, the aim is to connect a justified critical discourse to a determinate set of actual practices.

Although the specific function of the story of political origins in the *Laws* is uniquely Platonic, it operates within an established genre. That genre consists of the ancient Greek family of myths that were used by intellectuals of various sorts to provide a historical perspective on the present structure of their societies. This genre included Hesiod's account of the successive ages of gold, silver, and bronze in *Theogony* (which Plato transposed in his myth of the metals); Sophocles' Ode to Man in *Antigone*, as well as the Protagorean myth of the origins of the political art, which Plato used in the *Protagoras* as a basis for his critique of democratic sophistry. Each story pinpointed a particular aspect of society that pivotally affected its course, and this is also the case in Plato's story in the *Laws*.

The overall aim of the Athenian Stranger's story is to inform the interlocutors' grasp of a state's historical relation to the achievement of virtue. It includes a division of human history into four stages and most extensively analyzes the weaknesses of two political orders whose experiences are most relevant to any practicable scheme for the cultivation of virtue—monarchy in Persia and democracy in Athens. It also evaluates the relative success of another kind of political order, Spartan oligarchy, whose conception of virtue has already been criticized. In Plato's historical drama, however, the emphasis weighs less heavily on the various societies' dominant conceptions of virtue than it does on their particular ways of practicing the political art.

The first historical stage begins after a cataclysmic flood had destroyed all signs of civilization (677c). All tools as well as all discoveries that had been made in every *techne,* including the political art (as well as any other field of knowledge), had been lost. It was an age without skills or sophistication, but it also was an age of material abundance. Additionally, its members were innocent of the means used in contemporary political orders for exhibiting greed (*pleonexia*) and practicing domination (*philonikias,* 677b). As was the case in the age of Cronus, this era had no lawsuits or factional struggles that disrupted society, and there was no need for a lawgiver. Social life peacefully conformed to ancestral ways (*patrioi nomoi,* 679a–680a).

Subsequent stages display the evolution of the practice of the political art. In the second stage, aristocrats ruled the affairs of extended families in the form of kingships. They iterated the first legal orders and instituted preferences for their own way of life over that of other societies (680e–681d). In the next stage, that of the Trojan War, a number of changeable *politeiai* emerged,[75] but the Athenian Stranger does not specify their character and refers only to a few aspects of the Trojan War (681d–682e). The age of most interest, and the only one for which there are historical records of *nomoi* and *politeiai* available, began generations after the end of the Trojan War. The Athenian Stranger spends the most time discussing this—the fourth era—concentrating on a geographical categorization of its three chief political orders—those of Sparta, Persia, and Athens. It should provide valuable information about the composition of *politeiai* in *ergon,* more useful lessons for their project of founding a political order in Crete than the stories of earlier stages (683e–684a).

In both cases, the Athenian Stranger presumes that the responsibility for the rise and decline of *politeiai* lies with the rulers, not with the people (*demos,* 683e, 690e–691a). (For him, one might say that a political community's "constitution" constitutes a rule for ruling.) The Athenian Stranger states that seven legitimate forms of rule exist, that *stasis* readily arises in all of them, and that legislative "therapy" is needed to eliminate *stasis* as a regular feature of a *politeia* if it is to thrive (690d). In this sense, the second-order character of the rule of a *politeia* complements the second-order character of the art and virtue of justice, whose particular nature involves regulating the educational development and practical functions of all other arts and virtues in the political community.

---

75. Here is an instance of Platonic anachronism—not necessarily deliberate or strategic—in that no record exists of *politeia* in Homer.

This more practical and external account of the relative virtue of Peloponnesian cities demonstrates what the Athenian Stranger had argued before, namely, that these cities not only placed too much emphasis on both war as the aim of the state and military skill and valor as the essence of courage and principal component of virtue as a whole but also inadequately understood both the need for "guidance by virtue as a whole" and the special role of "good judgment" (*phronesis*) in harmonizing "mind" (*nous*) and "belief" (*doxa*) with love and desire (*erotos te kai epithumias*, 688b). He stipulates that only those in whom a concord (or "symphony") between reason and the passions dampens their own potential for discordant behavior are entitled to the power of official political rulers.

Now the Athenian Stranger begins a narrative of the Athenian *politeia*, in which he lauds its ancient ways, where the occupation of some political offices depended on property qualification and the rule of law was revered. As far he is concerned, this *politeia* was still in effect during the first part of the fifth century, throughout the Persian Wars. Insofar as they were mostly fought a generation after Kleisthenes' reforms of 508–507 made the Athenian *politeia* a democracy, the Athenian Stranger has praised a form of democracy (see 701a). During this period, Athenians showed reverence for law and evidenced collective regard for the well-being of the political community as a whole. They also "slavishly" adhered to traditional norms of *mousike*. For the Athenian Stranger, such "slavery" preserved their "freedom."

Problems arose when new criteria were introduced for the conduct of *mousike*. These criteria equally honored the judgment of every citizen and thus "free choice" as an intrinsic value. According to the Athenian Stranger (one may well doubt his historical diagnosis), this led to the embrace of personal pleasure as the only shared criterion for public judgment of aesthetic representations. Where musical standards were once observed by all, the many, understood as "theater-goers," now took their own immediate feelings as sufficient guideposts for judgment and themselves as sufficient judges. This change in cultural standards had dire political consequences. As the Athenian Stranger states:

> Instead of an aristocracy [with respect to aesthetic judgment], a sort of vicious "theatocracy" arose. If [in this musical domain] there had been a democracy of free men, nothing terrible would have occurred. However, music proved to be the starting-point of everyone's belief that he had wisdom and of a general disregard for the law. Freedom [of an unqualified sort] was not far behind. The conviction that

they *knew* made them unafraid, and assurance engendered shame-lessness. For to be fearless of the opinion of a better man, owing to self-confidence, is nothing else than base shamelessness, and it springs from excessive freedom. (701a–b)

He goes on to say that there was a general breakdown of respect for author-ity, whether it was claimed by fathers, mothers, elders, public officials, laws, oaths, promises, or religion in general (701b–c). The irresponsible role of the spectator became the model for the practice of citizenship, and because no ethic of virtue regulated the pursuit of power or pleasure, power and pleasure became ends in themselves.[76] For the Athenian Stranger, the result amounted to a new kind of slavery, the elimination of freedom in the political commu-nity as a whole (702e, 703a, 705e).

This reductive account of the putative corruption of Athenian democracy evidences the way that Plato's ethical and critical concerns merged with anti-democratic sentiments. The Athenian Stranger built his critical perspective around objections to autocratic power, greed, and hedonism. As constitu-tional principles for the conduct of social life, they could not sustain a well-functioning *politeia* or its *nomoi*. In Plato's account of typical political forms, democracy has been reduced to the polar opposite of monarchy. Whereas the latter became corrupt through the overweening power of rulers, the former did so because it lacked any respect for rule. Of course, this account of de-mocracy ignores the political principle that enabled ancient democracies to function as constitutional orders, namely, the regular exercise of citizenship as the office of ruling and being ruled in turn.[77] This principle embeds respect for the rule of law in the activity of citizens freely conducting their public af-fairs as political equals. Any democrat would admit that allowing the ethic of political freedom and equality to be reduced to an ethic of personal pleasure would doom the citizens' capacity to act coherently and purposively as a po-litical community. What Plato must be criticizing in Athenian democracy, therefore, is its inability to sustain consistently a critical standard higher than

---

76. For an interesting analysis of the antidemocratic effects of the ethic of the spectator in recent liberal theory and practice, see Stephen L. Esquith, *Intimacy and Spectacle: Liberal The-ory as Political Education.*

77. The careful reader of Plato should not be surprised by this observation, given the refer-ence in the *Republic* (557e) to a degenerate form of democracy in which the citizens no longer showed any serious interest in exercising their political responsibilities. For the paradigmatic definition of ancient Greek citizenship in terms of "ruling and being ruled" in turn, see Aristotle, *Politics* III.iv (1277b27–28).

pleasure, any ethic that could guide the judgment of citizens and legitimate a just principle of political rule. (In this respect, his criticism comports with his criticism of the "ideal type" of democracy in Book VIII of the *Republic*. See Chapter 4, Section C2, above.)

For Plato, democracy tends toward anarchy, whereas monarchy tends toward tyranny. The former exhibits immoderate power exercised from below; the latter, from above. Whereas the forceful subjectivity of principle-free democrats cannot sustain political authority, tyrannical rulers do not observe any limit on their capacity for domination. Monarchy and democracy may designate types of political order, but neither is a sufficient model for founding a *politeia* characterized by the Athenian Stranger's principles of freedom (*eleutheria*), friendship (*philia*), and critical reason (*noun*) or good judgment (*phronesis*).[78]

Each of the three political orders, the Dorian, the Athenian, and the Persian, was found to be an inadequate model for the task of founding a new colony. What is to be done? The object of the interlocutors' investigations has been "To find out what would be the best way of managing a *polis*, and, in private affairs, how best to lead one's own life" (702a). The Athenian wonders if there is "some test of this that we could set for ourselves." Cleinias fortuitously answers "yes" and now tells his dialogic partners that he has been chosen, along with nine other Cnossans, to help found a Cretan colony by composing a code of laws for it, drawing on local laws found to be satisfactory and on foreign laws as well (702c). He suggests that together they draw from their previous inquiries and "Construct a city in *logos*, as if we were establishing it from the beginning" (702d; see also 702e).

We should recall here that Protagoras was asked by Pericles to help compose the laws for the new pan-Hellenic, Athenian-led colony at Thurii, drawing on the extant laws of any number of Greek cities, and that Plato has him say in the *Protagoras* that he knew what to teach young men: "sound deliberation, both in private matters—how best to manage one's household, and in public matters—how to become most powerful in the *polis* in both speaking and acting," which Socrates transposes by rephrasing this claim as that of teaching "the political art and how to make men into good citizens" (318e–319a). Plato had Socrates expose the inadequacies of Protagoras's understanding of the political art by, inter alia, showing that he could critically defend no

78. 701d; see also 693c–d.

other standard of value than the pleasure of the many. Instead of this standard, he conceptualized an art of measurement that would be able to discriminate among pleasures and determine which ones most likely contributed to an individual's well-being.

That art could not be defended in the *Protagoras*, however, for Plato, at least evidently, had not solved his Socratic Problem. But he did indicate its best solution in a *logos* of justice in the *Republic* and a *logos* of *politike* in the *Statesman*. Now, at the end of his life, Plato has provided criteria for the constitutional laws of a practicable colony. No doubt they are "better" than the laws of Thurii, but, unlike those, Magnesian laws will be founded only in *logos* (703c–d). In this way, Magnesia, a practical product of the Platonic political art, constitutes his final contribution to his reconstruction of the ethical and political principles of Athens.

By the end of Book III, the Athenian Stranger has delineated all of the historical or empirical evidence he takes to be relevant (as a *paradeigma*, 692c) for the construction of a *politeia* by a lawgiver interested in founding a virtuous political community. The political orders of Athens and Persia have provided two extreme points on a compass that would help them estimate a moderate system of rule, but each lacks a critical standard in reason or law for the inculcation of personal or political virtue. The *politeiai* of Sparta and Crete may provide closer approximations of what such a standard might be, but neither practically exemplifies it. Their conceptions of virtue also fail either to forestall *stasis* or to secure the practice of virtue that benefits the political community as a whole.[79]

In the next stage of the discussion, the Athenian Stranger does not derive discursive criteria for virtue from this evidence. All he does is reiterate the ideals of "liberty," "friendship," and "political wisdom" and then invoke the principles and practices that governed the ideal city of the *Republic*. He mentions two of those ideals—"the things of friends are common" (739c–d; see also *Republic* 424a) and the conjunction of philosophic wisdom and political power in an all-powerful individual (or group)—as the simplest way to guide their conception of the political good (709e–711c); then, he uses this conception as his critical standard (*logos*, 712b; see also 858a, 875c–d). These principles remain in the background of their discourse—as a *paradeigma* for their second-best, legal model in *logos* of the instantiation of virtue (739a, 739e, 746b–c). Plato's "second-best" remains both "idealistic" and "unrealis-

---

79. See 702e–703a, 705e, 710e, 712c–713a, 753d.

tic," for the only citizens who can inhabit Magnesia will have been approved by the Athenian Stranger and his friends.[80]

It is important for understanding the critical significance of "Magnesia" that although the Athenian Stranger does not refer to it as a "mixed constitution," it combines constitutional elements that occur in different actual constitutions. This "mixture" is instrumental to achieving a higher critical standard of political freedom, friendship, and wisdom that in some ways is compatible with the ideals of *kallipolis*. Magnesia does not presage either Polybius's conception of a mixed constitution that directly joins features of different *politeiai* without regard to a common critical standard of virtue or eighteenth-century conceptions of a mixed constitution articulated by Montesquieu and Madison, which follow the Polybian precedent.[81] The constitution of Magnesia reflects Plato's effort to create a more immediately practicable guide for making the exercise of political power rational and virtuous than was provided in the *Republic*. But apart from being stipulated as the practically most virtuous society, how do its political values critically relate to contemporary Athenian democracy?

3. MAGNESIA AND DEMOCRACY

a. Rational Persuasion and Political Authority in Magnesia

With regard to the question of how the laws would be enforced and political consensus achieved, the Athenian Stranger has already spelled out an ideal standard, namely the exercise of rule according to law that is accepted "spontaneously and willingly" by its subjects (690c). He recognizes that the actual path to the institutionalization of Magnesian laws will meet resistance. As the Eleatic Stranger asserted in the *Statesman*, he holds that human beings no longer live in the age of Cronus, an age of perfect harmony, when they were guided by tutelary deities; they live in an age when political conflict is unavoidable because the rulers are necessarily men, not gods (713b–e). This does not provide an excuse for coercion. The lawgiver should foster virtuous behavior in the citizenry by generating as little resistance as possible. In the

---

80. The Athenian Stranger seems to recognize this, by (inter alia) mentioning the possibility of a "third-best state" (739b), but he never takes up the task of articulating its features.

81. See Glenn R. Morrow, *Plato's Cretan City*, 521–43. For readings that draw Plato closer to the ambit of these constitutional thinkers, see Harvey Mansfield Jr., *America's Constitutional Soul*, and Thomas Pangle, *The Spirit of Modern Republicanism*.

Republic, he referred to the quickest and easiest path to the institution of his ideal state as the rustication of all citizens in the existing (unjust) *polis* who were over ten years of age. In the *Laws*, however, the ideal of *kallipolis* is not the legislator's aim; a blank canvas is not his context for legislation. Imperfection and conflict characterize this world, and a differentiated unity is his aim. Not surprisingly, his preferred mode for realizing political virtue also differs from the one described in the *Republic*. The primary means for creating harmony in a diverse political community is persuasion.[82]

The art of such persuasion cannot be simply multifarious and pluralistic, replicating the *techne* of poets whose imitations persuade their listeners of the wonders of the Muse; nevertheless, its method is that of dialogic understanding based on mutual respect that enlists the rational approval of citizens rather than imposes an inflexible edict. If ever force must be used, it ought to be "therapeutic" rather than strictly punitive, in accord with the basic character of the legislator's political art (853d, 880d; see also 862d–863e). In order to avoid the kind of dictatorial prescriptions that characterize the work of "slavish doctors," who neither fully understand what they are doing nor consult the patients they treat, the Athenian Stranger recommends that "preambles" be attached to every law (722–23). These would persuasively justify the norms the law prescribes. Such rhetorical tools may seem like euphemistic propaganda (as Popper argues they are), but in the context of Plato's political thought, they more truly indicate Plato's belief that the power of rule both ought to and can become more rational and virtuous than it currently is and that not making the effort to harmonize critical reason, ethical virtue, and power legitimates injustice.

We have seen that belief in such things as "the political community as a whole" and "virtue as a whole" animates the core of Plato's political thought. As citizens of the beginning of the twenty-first century, we have become too well acquainted with how political languages of community, harmony, and solidarity have been used to disguise the oppression of society's weaker elements and to repress the expression of free and critical political speech. But particularly given his allegiance to Socrates, it is hard to believe that fear of free speech drove Plato's critical inquiries, and it is contextually inappropri-

82. As I mentioned at the outset of this chapter, I am not convinced that this represents a change of heart in Plato because the relatively greater intolerance toward opposition in the *Republic* coincides with the way in which unmediated *logos* brooks no quarter. For the alternative view, see the articles by Christopher J. Bobonich listed in the Bibliography, with whose substantive views about the methods of persuasion in the *Laws* I am otherwise in agreement.

ate and interpretively unfair to find in Plato's efforts to improve the ethical character of fourth-century Greek life the seeds of dictatorial behavior in the twentieth century that he surely would have abhorred (Karl Popper notwithstanding). In the context of Plato's own work, one might read the preambles to Magnesian laws, *logoi* for legitimate *nomoi,* as positive counterparts to the tragic justification of "the laws of Athens" provided by Socrates in the *Crito* before he obediently drank the hemlock that the laws had indirectly prescribed.

The problem with Plato's model of political persuasion is not inchoate totalitarianism. Rather, it is its assumption that dialogic understanding must be initiated and ultimately achieved by the rulers rather than the ruled.[83] In the *Laws,* as in the *Republic* and *Statesman,* he continues to believe that the many who would be ruled by a just statesman or legislator cannot provide any guidance for their rulers in the establishment of first principles. To have them do so, according to the Athenian Stranger, is analogous to having a trainee limit the regimens recommended by his trainer or a patient limit the prescriptions of his doctor (684c). The Platonic political art is an art of leadership, not ordinary citizenship, even if it may be useful for ordinary citizens exercising political initiative or making political judgments.[84]

This raises the question of the extent to which Magnesia tolerates change and, correlatively, suppresses dissent. The Athenian Stranger is clearly anxious about change, because he believes that a common standard of virtue is necessary for promoting community in a *polis,* and such a standard cannot undergo radical revision over time and still perform its communitarian function (797d–798d). He points this out in the context of a discussion about

83. I find this point underemphasized in Bobonich.

84. Indeed, the prospect of such utility inspires this study. But Plato does lodge *his* hopes for political reform in the efforts of specially skilled leaders, not the general disposition or judgment of ordinary citizens. Whether this assessment of what the Athenians (or Greeks, more generally) needed is accurate is an important but as yet unanswered question for historians. Whether contemporary democracies particularly need better leadership, citizenship, both, or neither (because less "political" factors are more important) is a subject of much political and theoretical debate. *The Economist* is preoccupied with this problem, as it seeks to provide intellectual and ethical guidance to Western leaders of the juggernaut of global capitalism. A recent installation of its thoughts on "leadership" appears in the issue of 9 December 1995 (23–24). An interesting set of articles by Alan Brinkley, Alan Ryan, and Jacob Heilbrun on the subject of leadership appeared in *The Wilson Quarterly* (Spring 1994): 46–72. The article by Alan Ryan was particularly interesting (55–64). Despite differences between his views of Plato's contribution to this discussion and those offered here, his overall argument about the need for leadership rather than leaders may complement some of my views.

mousike and the need for continuity in the standards for instructing children and states. Endorsement of such continuity, however, does not indicate hostility to any alteration in existing political institutions (as Popper argues); after all, he establishes the law-guardians and Nocturnal Council to authorize changes to the laws. Moreover, the Athenian Stranger recognizes the prominent role of chance or fortune (*tyche*) in all human events—exhibiting a positively postmodern appreciation of contingency (709d). Obviously, Magnesian society is not a paragon of pluralistic toleration of a diversity of moral views, but it is extremely difficult to judge Magnesian restrictions in the same vein as contemporary norms of tolerating (and restricting) "free speech."[85] After all, the disciplinary functions of the capitalist market, state-sanctioned penal institutions, and modern weaponry were not available to Plato as he sought to establish the legal ground-rules for a practical, unified, and just society.

The second guidepost for achieving the differentiated unity of Plato's imaginary city of Magnesia is proportionality; it is his practical version of the principle of moderation or institutionalization of the "second-best" via the art of measurement. The chief principle that informs this art of measurement derives from Plato's major justification of a critical *logos* for a second-best *politeia*. It appears in the form of a myth about the prehistoric age of Cronus in relation to the current age of Zeus, another version of which had appeared in the *Statesman*. Here, Plato associates the myth with a notion of "human nature" (713c). The Athenian Stranger's account and interpretation of the myth run as follows: In the age of Cronus, life was blessedly happy, for they had all things in abundance without effort. The reason or cause is said to be this:

> Cronus was of course aware that human nature, as we've explained [691d] is never able to take complete control of all human affairs without being filled with arrogance and injustice. Bearing this in mind, he appointed kings and rulers for our *poleis;* they were not men, but beings of a superior and more divine order—spirits (*daimonas*). We act [on the same principle] nowadays in dealing with our flocks of sheep and herds of other domesticated animals; we don't make cattle rulers (*archontas*) of cattle or goats [rulers] of goats, but control them ourselves because as a species we are better than them.

---

85. See M. I. Finley, "Censorship in Classical Antiquity," *Times Literary Supplement,* 29 July 1977, pp. 923–25. For provocative, more recent discussions of the general issue of censorship, see Robert C. Post, ed., *Censorship and Silencing.* . . .

So Cronus too, who was well-disposed to man, did the same: he placed us in the care of spirits, a superior order of beings, who were to look after our interests—an easy enough task for them, and a tremendous boon to us, because they produced peace, respect for others (*aidos*), good laws (*eunomian*), and justice (*dikas*) in full measure; faction was absent (*astasiasta*) and happiness (*eudaimona*) reigned among the races of men. The story has a moral (*logos*) for us today, and there is a lot of truth in it: where he who rules a *polis* is not divine but mortal, people have no respite from evil deeds and toil. [The lesson is that] we should make every effort to imitate (*mimeisthai*) [the life men are said to have led] under Cronus; we should run (*dioikein*) our public and private lives, our homes, and our cities, in obedience (*peithomenous*) to what little spark of immortality lies within us, and dignify this distribution of reason with the name of law (*nomon*). (713c–714a)

The critical parts of this passage appear at its beginning and end. At the beginning of the myth, there is a statement about human nature, a necessary truth that constrained even Cronus: Human beings need to be guided by a higher standard than any that they, individually or collectively, can produce themselves, or else their affairs will be marked by arrogance and injustice. This statement drips with irony, of course, because the assertion is produced by human beings. Nevertheless, this irony is not sufficient to condemn it for evidencing a disguised ideological agenda, bad faith, or literary legerdemain. For it mythically validates a rule of reason that is not justifiable solely by reference to established political interests or, in the Thrasymachean language invoked shortly after the Athenian Stranger finishes telling the myth, the interest of the stronger (714c).   ·

In the age of Cronus, this rule was exercised by "spirits." In their own age—so claims the end of the passage—it appears in the rationality of law. For its authority, law relies on a different source than does rule in oligarchies or even democracies. For when these regimes justify their rule on the basis of the rule of law, they do no more than justify rule in the interest of the stronger. A Platonic rule of law, by contrast, does not defend the established order; it functions as a critical standard for reforming it. Moreover, it possesses a feature that essentially informed Plato's *logos* of justice, namely, its capacity to eliminate *stasis* and serve the good of the political community as a whole. The Athenian Stranger says that political orders based on rule by the stronger serve only a part of the political community: "Laws which are not established for the good of the whole *polis* are bogus laws, and when they favor particular sections of the community, they are factional states (*stasioteias*) but not political orders (*politeias*), and the 'justice' (*dikaia*) they ascribe to such laws is empty and vain" (715b).

What distinguishes "law" as a principle of a second-best *politeia* from that of an ideal *politeia* are the practical constraints and assumptions under which it operates, not a judgment about the utopian unreality and uselessness of an ideal *politeia* such as *kallipolis*. First of all, the mythical complement of *kallipolis* in the *Laws*—*arche* in the age of Cronus—serves as an inspiration and source of imitation, "for the best-run of our present-day [*poleis*]" (713b). Second, the ideal of communal property among friends holds for the Athenian Stranger founding Magnesia in the *Laws* as much as it did for Socrates founding *kallipolis* in the *Republic*. But Magnesia has four property classes, unlike *kallipolis*, because enforcing that single standard among the possible colonists of Magnesia would be impractical. The aim of the Magnesian distribution of property nevertheless remains that of *kallipolis*: the elimination of *stasis* (744d). And as was the case for *kallipolis*, the principle informing the construction of Magnesia is providing the best practical safeguard against natural human tendencies toward arrogance and injustice.

Another major difference between *kallipolis* and Magnesia is the far more prominent role allotted to religion in the life of the city; this, too, is justified by the practical constraints under which the lawgivers operate in "founding" Magnesia. Like the preambles to Magnesian laws, religion serves as a persuasive device for lawgivers addressing the new colonists of their city. Given one of the hypothetical presuppositions on which Magnesia is founded, namely the impossibility of the direct rule of reason in the form of philosopher-guardians, religion and faith replace philosophy and reason as the (normally[86]) ultimate authorities in the city. Thus, Plato has the Athenian Stranger promote a variation on the Protagorean slogan (that may have been used by Protagoras in crafting the constitutional laws of Thurii), "Man is the measure of all things," by affirming that God, not man, is "the measure of all things" (716c). "Reason" itself rules indirectly (and imperfectly) via the rule of law (and the activities of the Nocturnal Council).

---

86. The members of the Nocturnal Council, notable for their philosophical training, count as the exceptions to the rule. For more on the role of the Nocturnal Council in Magnesia, see Section 3d, below.

The Stranger's establishment of religion as the ultimate practical guide for political life does not, however, entirely substitute religious for philosophical authority; he does not make *logos* depend on *mythos,* for the *mythos* itself has been justified on the basis of Plato's own critical *logos.* Rather, it exhibits the transposition of critical *logos* from a theoretical ideal to a practicable, but still critical, standard of moderation and measure. After all, the chief task of the Stranger as an adviser to lawgivers is to make reason, rather than power or pleasure, the constitutional ethic of the political community; the "reason" of the virtues of justice and moderation is best suited to dissolve the oppressive character of power (as long as it is properly understood and enacted). If it does not do so completely, nothing else is better suited to enable such dissolution to occur (see 711d). He also presupposes the necessity of a ruling authority (*arche*) for sustaining a *politeia.* The philosopher-guardians in the *Republic* did not technically "rule"; they did not command or exercise *arche.* Authority as domination returns, however, to the political life of Magnesia.

b. Equality and Hierarchy

The Athenian Stranger assumes that seven naturally justified kinds of ruling and being ruled exist in both the *oikos* and *polis:* (1) parents' rule over their children; (2) "high-birth" individuals over "low-birth" individuals; (3) elders' rule over the young; (4) masters' rule over slaves; (5) the rule of the stronger over the weaker, which prevails throughout the animal kingdom; (6) the rule of the wise over the ignorant; and (7) rule by winners of a (political) lottery over its losers. These collectively incompatible but nevertheless natural kinds of rule are realized to varying degrees in extant monarchies, oligarchies, and democracies, but none is completely realized in any of them. Indeed, in themselves these modes of ruling do not legitimate particular constitutional orders; rather, they both deny legitimacy to any *politeia* whose only title to rule is the power of a ruling class and the personal pleasure of its members (Bk. IV, 712e) and provide critical limits for a *politeia* whose rule would be moderate and just. The substantive structure of such a practicable *politeia* of justice and moderation remains to be constructed.

After reminding his interlocutors (near the beginning of Bk. v) of the critical importance of honoring the soul, body, and wealth respectively (742c–744a), the Athenian Stranger offers a "sketch" of the laws of a second-best *politeia* (734e, 768c). Each *politeia* has two basic elements: the manner in which individual citizens become officeholders and exercise authority and the laws by which their power is authorized (735a).

The Athenian Stranger initially interprets the first by characterizing the membership of Magnesia. The fact that discussion of these elements occurs in *logos* rather than *ergon*—that is, as a critical standard for a practicable plan, rather than an actual plan to be carried out immediately by an extant political authority (736b)—allows the Athenian Stranger to screen for citizens. The constraint of practice first appears in his stipulation that there will be four property classes, not because one class for propertyholders is not ideal but because creating it now would require a redistribution of wealth whose "costs" would outweigh its "benefits" (736c–737d). Nevertheless, the Athenian Stranger allows only a factor of four to separate the quantity of wealth owned by the richest and poorest Magnesians (744e). This relatively small gap in the material conditions of rich and poor is necessary to facilitate political action, prevent disputes from arising among citizens, and achieve the greatest possible unity in the *polis* (736e–737b, 739d–e).[87] At the outset, therefore, Plato takes pain to prevent *stasis* resulting from large gaps between rich and poor (see 757a).

This standard, the Athenian Stranger admits, actually indicates an equality involving proportional inequality, typically understood (if not translated) as "proportional equality" (744c). This is no contradiction, because the ideal of equality in Magnesia does not signify absolute equality that results in equality for equals and unequals alike (see *Republic* 558c) but rather "equality of opportunity" (*kairon isotetos*) for the many to obtain honors in the *polis* (744b). Unlike the modern notion of equal opportunity, which actually means the equal opportunity for individuals to become unequal by competitions primarily instituted in civil society, the inequality sanctioned by Magnesian "equality of opportunity" conforms to the Athenian Stranger's conception of the relative virtue citizens actualize in their social-economic-political roles, namely the extent to which they contribute to social peace and justice.[88]

The Athenian Stranger explains this conception of proportional equality when he sets out the *nomoi* for the "first" element of the *politeia*, namely, the elective selection of individuals who rule in the offices of law-guardians (*nomophulakes*) and members of the council (753b–755b).[89] Such elections

<hr />

87. Popper views this aim as evidence of Plato's abhorrence of individualism, which implicitly associates large differences between rich and poor as indicative of individualism.

88. See R. H. Tawney, *Equality*, 103; Michael Young, *The Rise of the Meritocracy, 1870–2033: An Essay on Education and Equality*, 129.

89. On the status of "law-guardians" in Magnesia, see Morrow, *Plato's Cretan City*, 195–215, 238–40, 548–49.

clearly and radically depart from the strictly democratic procedures by which rulers were selected in fourth-century Athens. He states that the selection process (*hairesis*) arrives at a mean between the monarchical and democratic constitutions that he previously said provide the two practical benchmarks for the design of political institutions (756e). He rejects (because he denies) an equality of status between master and slaves or between an honest man and a scoundrel, because they cannot be friends (757a; contrast Aristotle, *Politics* Bk. I.iii–vii). Given the critical standard of "friendship" for Magnesia, that kind of equality would only generate *stasis* (757a), the plague of *politeiai*. He notes approvingly the traditional saying that "equality produces friendliness" and so proceeds to differentiate "two kinds of equality," which in practice are virtual opposites, as a proper gloss on the Greek adage.[90] This crucial passage for understanding the political theory informing the *politeia* of Magnesia deserves quotation at length.

> The first sort of equality [of measures, weights, and numbers] is within the competence of any *polis* and lawgiver (*nomothetes*). That is, one can simply distribute equal awards by lot. But the truest and best equality is not so obvious. It needs the judgment (*krisis*) of Zeus, and only in a limited number of ways does it help the human race; but when *poleis* or individuals do find it profitable, it produces goods for all. It involves granting more to the more virtuous and less to the less virtuous, meaning the allotment of each according to their nature in order to reward virtue with status and to distribute proportionally less to those with less virtue and education. This [second conception of equality] is what for us is itself political justice—and should be what we gaze upon as we bring into being our founded *polis*. The founder of any other [*polis*] should also concentrate on this standard in establishing its laws, not that of the tyrannical few, of one, or of the power of the people (*demos*) but always according to this [standard of] justice (*to dikaion*), which is as we've said, granting equality to unequals, according to nature. None the less, it is necessary for every *polis* at times to employ even this equality to a modified degree, if it is to avoid inciting factional strife (*staseon*) in one part [of the

90. See also 744c, as well as *Gorgias* 508a–b. For the classic discussion of these two kinds of equality, see Aristotle, *Nicomachean Ethics* 1131b27, 1158b30ff, and *Politics* 1301b29ff. The definitive scholarly treatment of this subject in ancient Greek literature is that of F. D. Harvey, "Two Kinds of Equality," *Classica et Mediaevalia* 26:101–47, and 27:99–100.

polis] or another—for the reasonable and considerate, wherever employed, is an infringement of the perfect and exact, as being contrary to strict justice; for the same reason it is necessary to make use also of the equality of the lot, in recognition of the discontent of the many, and in doing so to pray, calling upon God and good luck to have the lot select the most just. Thus it is necessary for us to use both kinds of equality; but we should employ that which requires luck as little as possible. (757b–758a)

In arguing for the use of both kinds of equality, the Athenian Stranger notably does not deprecate the nature of the many as much as he cleaves to the standard of virtue as the basis for political rule. A believer in the possibility of there being a political art of virtue cannot rely on luck for its realization. In any event, he proceeds to identify both election and a lottery as appropriate procedures for appointing most officials (759b).

Despite his predilection for relying on proportional criteria for institutionalizing equality as justice, he authorizes significant democratic powers—the use of the lot in composing membership in the courts and democratic participation in the official procedure for scrutinizing public officials—and promotes the value of political participation by the general citizenry.[91] Toward the end of the *Laws*, the Athenian Stranger restates his belief in the generally competent moral and political judgment of ordinary citizens, observing that "the many" are competent judges of the relative virtue of others, even as they themselves are not its most superior exemplars.[92] (Although clearly less democratic in operation than the Athenian *politeia* of the fourth century, these provisions for the official exercise of political power by the general citizenry notably exceed those existing now in all nominally democratic societies.) Plato believed that his scheme for balancing the political power of various economic classes was the best method of achieving "friendliness" (*philian*) and "concord" (*homonoan*) among the various sections of the citizenry (759b).

In this light, to what extent should we interpret these Magnesian political provisions as antidemocratic? Athens was truly extraordinary in not rely-

---

91. See 759b, 766d, 747e–749c, 767e–768b. To be sure, it is not required of the *demos* as much as it is of the higher property classes, but Magnesia directly involves the *demos* in the authoritative exercise of political power to a greater degree than any twentieth-century democracy.

92. Book XII, 950b. This statement goes at least as far as does Aristotle's more famous justifications in the *Politics* (III.11) for having "the many" participate in deliberations concerning the well-being of the political community as a whole.

ing on elections for authorizing membership in its government or positions of political leadership. During this period, it surely possessed a leadership class, however. The character of its informal membership may have changed somewhat after the death of Pericles, but an elite, not ordinary citizens, continued to compose the pool from which political leaders emerged. They surely were constrained by Athenian democratic ideology, but it is unclear how much such constraint actually served to reduce the gap between rich and poor or to liquefy economic divisions. That ideology maintained the legitimacy of slavery and sharp restrictions on membership in the class of citizens.[93] The relatively antidemocratic character of Magnesian laws (relative to those of the Athenians) does not so much reflect visceral hatred of the *demos* as it does Plato's (perhaps overly) strenuous standards for perfecting a critical *logos* for the political art, as well as his belief that the politics of democratic Athens did not exhibit the highest possibilities of such an art and could not be said to be presumptively or optimally just.

One must keep in mind what Plato is critically evaluating in establishing his preferred set of *nomoi*. For Plato, the task of perfecting a *polis* entailed the perfection of all elements of society, and (as a result) the standards employed had to be comparably comprehensive.[94] His critical perspective embraced much more of social life than what, for fourth-century Athenian democrats, oligarchs, or Aristotle, typically signified "what is in our power to effect in action."[95] That is why it is misleading to associate the arithmetical and geometric conceptions of equality with partisanship for oligarchy or democracy, even though it is logical to point out that democrats primarily used the arithmetical conception and oligarchs used the proportional concept when signifying their preferred conception of political equality.[96] This is also why Plato's views of the place of women in society could be more "progressive"

---

93. On the relationships between the elite and general citizenry in fourth-century Athens, see Josiah Ober, *Mass and Elite in Democratic Athens;* on the restrictions of the class of citizens, M. H. Hansen, *The Athenian Democracy in the Age of Demosthenes,* 52–54, 86–101.

94. The best, if most extreme, example of this view is the Athenian Stranger's following statement in Book VII (790b): "[U]nless private affairs in a *polis* are managed rightly, it is vain to expect that secure laws can be established for public affairs"—which justifies laws regulating the nutrition of pregnant women, as well as marriage, procreation, and common meals. See 781–85, 788a–790a, 793c–d. Such extensive regulation was not abnormal for lawgivers, and Plutarch's *Lives* records comparably extensive regulations authorized by Lycurgus and Solon.

95. See Aristotle, *Nicomachean Ethics* (I.1–3., III.3, VI.1–2, 5) on the relation of political activity to deliberation, which is a function of "what is within our power to effect in action" (III.3, 1112a30–31).

96. See Harvey, "Two Concepts of Equality."

than those of fourth-century democrats, even if they fall short of relatively "more enlightened" nineteenth- and twentieth-century views.[97]

The "equality" championed in contemporary liberal society does not automatically refer to the activities or relationships in civil society. Their inegalitarian character comes under critical review only when it appears to be sanctioned by the state or by some politically determined judgment of the well-being of the political community as a whole. Otherwise, inherently inegalitarian and socially biased principles of merit or profit, which necessarily empower a few over the many, take precedence. In criticizing the "democratic" principle of arithmetical equality, Plato judged it against standards that are not now applied to the evaluation of "democratic" values. Indeed, both Plato and conventional liberals assume that the principles and practices of democracy and virtue do not coincide. However, in Plato's Athens, the presumption was that they did; while today, they presumptively do not.[98]

c. Artisans

The exclusion of artisans (*demiourgoi*) from the role of citizen possibly indicates the most radical departure of the political order of Magnesia from that of Athens. Artisans in fact constituted up to one-fourth of the citizen-population of fourth-century Athens, and the removal of their rights as citizens would certainly have been taken to be an oligarchic attack on the Athenians' democratic way of life.[99] Notably, however, the rationale the Athenian Stranger offers for their exclusion does not derive from any claim about the natural virtue of a privileged class but from the relatively heavy responsibilities of citizenship itself. Performing them competently is itself a vocation, equivalent to a *techne,* a *techne* of political *arete* (846d; see also 847a).[100] Because no one can perform two *technai* well—a variation on Socrates' state-

97. See articles by David Cohen, Susan Okin, and Julia Annas, along with the Vlastos-Lefkowitz debate cited in Chapter 4, above.

98. That explains in part why it is easier for opponents of affirmative action to defend their antiegalitarian and antidemocratic political agenda while rhetorically endorsing equal opportunity, democracy, and virtue. See my "Two Democracies and Virtue," in J. Peter Euben et al., eds., *Athenian Political Thought and the Reconstruction of American Democracy.*

99. Potentially more extreme measures were recommended by Aristotle, and actually more extreme ones were taken by Antipater (who had studied at the Lyceum) in 322, when he established high property qualifications for citizenship. Aristotle, *Politics* VII.9 (1328b39–1329a2); on Antipater's political changes, see Diod. xviii.18.5.

100. In the twentieth century, the most noteworthy treatment of politics as a professional vocation associated its practice exclusively with political leaders, not ordinary citizens. See Max Weber, "Politics as a Vocation," in *From Max Weber: Essays in Sociology,* ed. H. H. Gerth and C. Wright Mills, 77–128.

ment in the *Republic* about the practical conditions for justice: one person, one *techne*—skilled artisans cannot be expected to exercise well the responsibilities of citizenship while also competently practicing their own trade. Manually working *demiourgoi* live throughout the *polis*, but everywhere they are supervised by citizens acting as urban commissioners (848e–849a). Similarly, no farm laborers, retailers, or traders can be citizens, because the constraints of their economic activities prevent them from attending to the vocation of citizenship.

Although this exclusion of artisans certainly marks a departure from democratic practice (and Plato's inclusion of artisans among the citizens of *kallipolis* in the *Republic*), it also illustrates Plato's confidence in the political judgment of ordinary citizens in "second-best" political environs. After all, the political art that was reserved for philosopher-guardians in the *Republic* is vouchsafed (in a less developed form) to all citizens (that is, landed proprietors) in Magnesia.[101] Moreover, the Athenian Stranger singles out *demiourgoi* for praise, highlighting their contribution to the *polis* (920d–e); their location in the city even has religious overtones, indicating Plato's view in the hidden power of their *techne*.[102] Their work is actually paradigmatic of productive work that can benefit the city (so much so that all metics must have a skill if they are to remain in Athens for an extended time, 950a–d).[103] The skill of members of the Nocturnal Council is explained as the skill of a *demiourgos* (965b), which implies that Plato himself is an artisan—albeit of a unique sort.

Plato's ambivalent attitude, both disdainful and fearfully respectful, of the exercise of manual *technai* has deep roots in Greek culture, appearing in the myths of Pandora, Prometheus, Hephaestus, and Athena, Sophocles' "Ode to Man" in *Antigone* (which singles out the miraculous power of the practice of *technai*), as well as the implicit association of Sophocles' Oedipus with the power of an intellectual *techne* operating without adequate ethical control.[104] Moreover, Plato was simply following Greek cultural attitudes in

---

101. To be sure, this is still a far cry from the Protagorean political art, which Zeus gave all citizens—including *demiourgoi*. See Pierre Vidal-Naquet, "A Study in Ambiguity: Artisans in the Platonic City," in *Black Hunter: Forms of Thought and Forms of Society in the Greek World*, 225–26.

102. See Vidal-Naquet, "A Study in Ambiguity: Artisans in the Platonic City."

103. Recall that, at least according to Plutarch, Solon required all citizens to have a *techne* (and did not view citizenship itself as a *techne*). See Plutarch, *Solon* XXII.

104. See Pierre Vidal-Naquet, "A Study in Ambiguity: Artisans in the Platonic City," 224–45.

both valuing the product of *techne* more than its human agent and prizing agriculture over craftsmanship as a more inherently virtuous activity.[105] (His latter view may be said to appear in the words of a founder of modern democratic thought, Thomas Jefferson.[106])

From Plato's philosophical perspective, the ambiguity may be interpreted in the following way: On the one hand, the idea of a *techne* implies the rational control of practice, the ability to shape material or events in accord with

---

105. On the social status of work in relation to workers, see Alison Burford, *Craftsmen in Greek and Roman Society*, 196–212. On the prestige of agriculture over crafts, note Xenophon's comments in his *Oeconomicus* (IV.1–4 and VI.4–8). His comments surely were not universally shared and particularly reflect the biases of the wealthy elite, but it is unlikely that his views do not reflect Athenian society's implicit hierarchy of cultural values. On the Athenians' connection with and devotion to the land, note Thucydides' observations (II.14–17) about how much distress was caused by Pericles' strategic policy of bringing all citizens into the city center in order to salvage their lives, if not their land, in response to Spartan invasions.

106. From Jefferson's *Notes on Virginia:* "Those who labor in the earth are the chosen people of God, if ever He had a chosen people, whose breasts He has made His peculiar deposit for substantial and genuine virtue. It is the focus in which He keeps alive that sacred fire, which otherwise might escape from the face of the earth. Corruption in morals in the mass of cultivators is a phenomenon of which no age nor nation has furnished an example. It is the mark set on those who, not looking up to heaven, to their own soil and industry, as does the husbandman, for their subsistence, depend for it on casualties and caprice of customers. [Of course, advances in marketing skills have sharply reduced *this* dependence.] Dependence begets subservience and venality, suffocates the germ of virtue, and prepares fit tools for the designs of ambition. This, the natural progress and consequence of the arts, has sometimes perhaps been retarded by accidental circumstances; but, generally speaking, the proportion which the aggregate of the other classes of citizens bears in any State to that of its husbandmen, is the proportion of its unsound to its healthy parts, and is a good enough barometer whereby to measure its degree of corruption. While we have land to labor then, let us never wish to see our citizens occupied at a workbench, or twirling a distaff. Carpenters, masons, smiths, are wanting in husbandry; but for the general operations of manufacture, let our workshops remain in Europe. It is better to carry provisions and materials to workmen there, than bring them to the provisions and materials, and with them their manners and principles. The loss by the transportation of commodities across the Atlantic will be made up in happiness and permanence of government. The mobs of great cities add just so much to the support of pure government, as sores do the strength of the human body. It is the manners and spirit of a people which preserve a republic in vigor. A degeneracy in these is a canker which soon eats to the heart of its laws and constitution" (*The Life and Selected Writings of Thomas Jefferson*, ed. Adrienne Koch and William Paden, 280–81). However, Jefferson does seem to praise the *work* of agriculture, whereas the Athenian Stranger consigned heavy agricultural labor to slaves (806d–e). This belief in the natural association of virtue with a particular kind of work represents one of those hard-to-bury prejudices that often appear in otherwise sophisticated thought (and whose significance for the rest of that thought is hard to evaluate). In the century after Jefferson, Marx made a similar mistake, arguing that workers were not only the salt of the earth but the virtuous expression of humanity itself.

deliberate purpose rather than fitful chance (see 709b–d).[107] It was particularly significant in the democratic, sophisticated, and aesthetically oriented culture of the Athenians.[108] On the other hand, it signifies systematic, productive activity; if that activity is not itself regulated by a purpose that conforms to a virtuous end, then the *techne* becomes dangerous, no matter who is the agent. Therefore, a *techne* may be dangerous when practiced by either an unscrupulous Thrasymachus or an uneducated artisan who, lacking time for political education, becomes habituated to a dependent form of life, carrying out projects whose purposes were devised by others.

d. Law-Guardians and the Nocturnal Council

The most plausible evidence for the authoritarian character of Magnesia comes from the prominent role played by the law-guardians and, particularly, the Nocturnal Council, in the governance of the *polis*. Only members of the infantry and cavalry participate in the selection of the law-guardians (753b), and the Nocturnal Council is mostly a small subset of that elite group (961a–b). Although the Athenian Stranger does provide a role for the *demos* in ratifying changes in religious practice (772c–d), the power of ordinary citizens to forestall political changes authorized by the law-guardians was slight. No special segment of the citizenry in fourth-century Athens exercised as extensive political authority as did the two hypothetical political entities of the Magnesian law-guardians and the Nocturnal Council.

The principal source of their independent political power was the ability of the law-guardians to initiate changes in the laws themselves in order to assure the rationality and "salvation" of the *polis* (945b–952c). Yet the extent of the constitutional power of both groups needs to be qualified. Neither is designed to be initiators of political action in the first instance or caretakers of quotidian political business. Rather, they operate as institutional guarantors of the legality and virtue of the political activity undertaken by the people and by other more numerous and democratically constituted sources of leadership.

107. The opposition between *techne* and *tuche* is an important theme for Thucydides. See Lowell Edmunds, *Chance and Intelligence in Thucydides.*

108. For example, the historians M. M. Austin and P. Vidal-Naquet, who refer to Athens as "the city of *techne* par excellence," in their *Economic and Social History of Ancient Greece: An Introduction,* 107. On the social significance of aesthetic life in ancient Greece generally as well as Athens in particular, see J. J. Pollitt, *The Ancient View of Greek Art.*

Plato has the Athenian Stranger locate the seat of ultimate political authority in Magnesia in the Nocturnal Council, a highly select group of mostly older citizens (over fifty years of age) who do not operate amid the light of public scrutiny. Despite many important scholarly treatments of the subject, the answer to the question of who and what guards these guardians of Magnesia remains unknown (except that it is *not* the people themselves).[109] Despite the Athenian Stranger's reference to them as providing the ultimate security for Magnesia (960e), they do not function as a major fount of political power in the Magnesian *polis*.

The Nocturnal Council functions as the guardians of last resort—which comports with the site of their literary appearance, namely at the very end of this lengthy work. Nocturnal Councilors are mostly charged with the task of overseeing the work of others and are preoccupied with theoretical studies about the practical meaning of virtue. As the ones who receive the best possible political education in Magnesia and studiously consider the nature of virtue and the virtues, members of the Nocturnal Council exemplify above all Plato's extraordinary faith in the potential of human beings to understand and actualize guidelines for individual and political virtue. The council primarily operates as the philosophical supplement to the necessary imperfection of the rule-bound laws of Magnesia. It supervises religious beliefs and constitutional laws in a way that provides for the ultimate safety and salvation of the *polis* (960c–962a, 968a, 969c).[110] Although the potential for the abuse of power by such a group is obviously enormous, the Nocturnal Council strikes me (as it has others) as Plato's equivalent for the ancient *polis* of the United States' Supreme Court in that liberal-democratic and capitalist state.[111]

At the end of the *Laws,* Plato, via the Athenian Stranger, has allowed himself to dream once again of the possibility of political excellence and the achievement of political perfection (969b–c). The Nocturnal Council is empowered

---

109. For two contrasting treatments, see Morrow, *Plato's Cretan City,* chap. 9, and George Klosko, "The Nocturnal Council in Plato's *Laws."*

110. In his edition of the *Laws* (515–16), Saunders refers to the Nocturnal Council as being simultaneously a "Council of Legal Studies . . . Philosophical Studies . . . and Propaganda" that performs "legal, philosophical, and didactic" functions.

111. This comparison is not so much an endorsement of the former or criticism of the latter as it is an observation about the relative character of their functions. If it were directly instituted in a twenty-first-century society, a Nocturnal Council would obviously be horrific; but that kind of standard for critical evaluation is uselessly anachronistic.

to have the final word in determining answers for all of the ethical and political questions that preoccupied Plato throughout his philosophical career. Yet we do not learn about how it acquires its wisdom or exercises its power. This question Plato leaves conspicuously unanswered. In the *Laws* the Nocturnal Council primarily marks Plato's belief that skilled deliberation must serve as a prelude to political action that would be just.

AN APPROPRIATION

PART
III

THE PLATONIC POLITICAL ART AND
POSTLIBERAL DEMOCRACY

We have come to the end of Plato's road. Now, we must return to our beginnings, even though our situation has changed. What have we learned? There
are, of course, many ways of learning from Plato's dialogues—just as there
have been and will continue to be many ways of reading them. But any appropriation will not do. We may converse with, interrogate, and appropriate
Plato, but we ought not to exploit him. So, what difference should my interpretation of Plato make "today"? In this chapter, I justify my answer to this
question and deploy Plato in contemporary political arguments. Before doing so, however, I sketch the portrait of Plato I have drawn: Contrary to
Plato's reputation as a radical critic of democracy, I have argued that although
his criticisms of it struck deep at the heart of democracy as an order of justice,
he was not radically antidemocratic. This general claim stems from three aspects of his dialogues that my interpretation of them has shown. First, his critique of democracy was embedded in a critique of the conventional exercise
of political power. Such power was most palpable for Plato in its Athenian,
democratic version, but he was not more hostile to democracy than he was
to other existing forms of government—to the contrary, probably less so.
Second, Plato was not a Platonist. That is, he did not produce an autonomous,
authoritative political theory that would aspire to program political practice.
Third, he produced dialogues on the political art as an art of virtue throughout his life. His notion of the political art always critically engaged relations

between ethics and power, but it did so differentially because of his belief that such an art must be defined differently when employed at various levels of abstraction from convention, in terms of various relations of theory to practice.

This portrait of Plato makes Plato available as a critic who could benefit democracy—particularly, any democrat who admits to gaps between existing democracies and justice and wants to improve the former by achieving the latter. Because the dominant force that drives the current, conventional exercise of political power is, I believe, more hostile than sympathetic to "democracy," understood as the actual exercise of political power by the contemporary equivalent of the *demos* (insofar as such an equivalent exists), the effect of a "Platonic" political discourse today can benefit democracy by educating it, that is, pointing to the obstacles to and conditions for the realization of democratic virtue. Meeting these conditions will foster democratic justice.

The main task of this chapter, however, is to demonstrate how one can make use of my study of Plato's rendition of the political art in contemporary critical discourse and practice. To accomplish this task, three further steps are needed. First, we need to show how to use the method of critical historicism, not as a means of appropriately situating ourselves for reading Plato but in order to resituate his political art in our time. After doing so, we take the second step and discuss the relation of the Platonic political art to contemporary political theory—initially, by noting how the contrast between "the ancients" and "the moderns" affects interpretations of the differences between ancient and modern democracies and then by critically analyzing the new genre of critical discourse that champions "deliberative democracy"—for Plato (technically speaking), an oxymoron. The third step links theory to practice by drawing lessons from the discussion of theories of "deliberative democracy" for critical citizenship and democratic virtue. I address in particular (especially in light of Plato's decision to make the creation of the Academy his most important political legacy) the intellectual and political role of public education—both K–12 and (mostly) higher education—among the major practices and institutions of contemporary democratic societies (although my experience and knowledge of primary, secondary, and higher education in the United States principally informs my judgments).

A. DEHISTORICIZING AND REHISTORICIZING PLATO

By emphasizing the historical and dialogic aspects of Plato's philosophy, my readings of his texts and their contexts might seem to make Plato relatively unavailable to us as a participant in our philosophical, ethical, and political deliberations. But this hardly follows. Unless one thinks that everyone's interest in Plato is completely dominated by the perspective of his current interpreters, the continuing interest in his work attests to the still vital power of Plato's writing. And yet, important questions remain. How does one respect the contingent, historical, and literary aspects of Plato's ideas while tapping them for insight into contemporary problems, particularly those of democracy?

In defining the terms of the legitimate and justifiable dehistoricization and rehistoricization of his political theory or philosophy—that is, the conditions for invoking Plato in contemporary critical discourse as a historical author, not merely a discursive fiction—I shall recall features of the interpretive approach I have employed for reading Plato's texts—critical historicism—an approach that falls between relatively ahistorical and radically historicist approaches. It rejects *both* immediately available (in a naturalist or playfully textualist vein) readings *and* characterizations of his ideas as wholly external and alien to our own.

But then we must ask: How might Plato be dehistoricized without being Platonized, rehistoricized without being bowdlerized?[1] Critical historicism assumes an integral connection between the arguments of historical theorists and their discursive and practical contexts. This suggests that although it may well be pedagogically useful to "test" Plato's political ideas by directly relating them to current problems or wondering "what would Plato allow," such questions will generate answers that can have only a fictive relation to the meaning of Plato's texts (if the critical enterprise is left at that level), one that does not count as an effort in historical understanding.[2] Thus, a proper dehistoricization of Plato does not generate a new kind of neo-Platonism (for

1. These particular questions raise the general question of how properly to employ historical authors in contemporary political and philosophical arguments. If historically understanding a philosopher's context is necessary for a philosophical understanding of the author's work, how does one bridge the gap of historical difference and establish a justifiable, informative, and even instructive relation between the philosopher's past and our present? My answer to this age-old, general question is partial and incomplete, but intentionally so. For I believe that the answer to it should be pluralized, tailored to the historical author in question. The extent to which my answer is generally useful depends on its success in answering the particular question of how to dehistoricize Plato without obliterating the historical specificity of his philosophical identity while making his work interesting and useful for us.

2. For an example of such "testing," see R. H. Crossman, *Plato Today: A Revised Edition*, 9–10; for the phrase "what would Plato allow?" see Jeremy Waldron, "What Would Plato Allow," in Ian Shapiro and Judith Wagner DeCew, eds., *Theory and Practice*, 138–78.

example, to compete with the myriad current forms of neo-Aristotelianism).[3] And yet, the "critical" element of this approach allows an interpreted Platonic discourse to reach our time and minds—and as a discourse rooted in someone other than ourselves.

Employing the history of political theory via critical historicism simply requires anyone who would deploy ideas of the past in the present—anyone dehistoricizing and rehistoricizing Plato—to engage in a complex activity of comparison. Initially, one should establish as best as one can, first, the relation of the theorist's discourse to her or his time; second, the extent to which the effect of her or his thought as an argument in *logos* could apply to circumstances other than his or her own time and place; and, third, the context of our time to which the theorist's *logos* might relate. At each step, this approach highlights the links and discontinuities between *logos* and *ergon* as a historical and philosophical problem; by so doing, it remains faithful to the central problematic of the Platonic political art.[4]

Of course, this task is enormously complex, prone to error, and open-ended—not least because the boundaries between these three intellectual activities are radically porous. It allows neither the problems of ethics and the *polis* nor the discursive solutions Plato offers for them to provide models for our efforts to solve the problems of contemporary societies or political theory. Just as the virtue of the Platonic political art has to be judged in relation to the ethical-practical problems of Athenian democracy and to Greek city-states more generally, so we might usefully adapt the Platonic political art by making a corresponding evaluation of the ethical dispositions, practical conditions, and critical discursive possibilities of existing democracies and political communities. I do not think Plato would be dismayed by this employment of his work, especially because of the way he employed "Socrates" in his dialogues.[5] A historically faithful reading of Plato should not be radically

---

3. For a recent example of a contemporary effort at neo-Platonism, see the recent spate of books by T. K. Seung: *Intuition and Construction; Kant's Platonic Revolution in Moral and Political Philosophy;* and *Plato Rediscovered: Human Value and Social Order.*

4. For an interesting example of this approach to Plato, which is undermined by the insensitivity to the way history constitutes philosophical argument, see Gerald M. Mara, *Socrates' Discursive Philosophy: Logos and Ergon in Platonic Political Philosophy.* In her most recent book, Julia Annas also downplays the historical and political dimensions of Platonic ethics, while nevertheless raising and resolving interesting philosophical questions. See her *Platonic Ethics: Old and New.*

5. I grant that the approach I have employed in crafting these chapters was unavailable, and therefore, to some extent alien, to Plato, but I hope that the resulting claims have been faithful

historicist. Yet this approach forecloses claims that Plato's arguments either defeat or lose out to those of Hobbes or Locke, Rawls or Habermas—or that Plato can resolve debates between liberals and communitarians, poststructuralists and traditionalists, pragmatists and naturalists.

One must accept the fact that whatever the relation between Plato and contemporary concerns, it must be established as much as discovered. For spanning the gap between historical interpretation and contemporary theoretical argument are the choices and values of the interpreter. As a result, the persuasiveness of my employment of Plato for contemporary argument depends less on the evidence I have offered for my interpretation of the Platonic political art than on the authority I earn by conjoining my scholarly arguments to judgments of the practical and discursive conditions in which we live. It is not directly deducible from the previously argued interpretations of Plato and his dialogues. How I employ Plato has a lot to do with my professional view of Plato, but, as an interpreter, it also involves my political identity as a citizen. But at this point the guidance offered by the practice of critical historicism begins to lose its significance. For as one moves from being a historian to a participant in contemporary debates (even if that shift occurs within a single sentence), the center of intellectual responsibility for one's argument subtly shifts away from scholarship and toward politics—just as myriad but not unlimited qualifications intervene in Plato's own connections between *logos* and *ergon*.

Having contributed to an understanding of the Platonic political art in terms of the problems of his own time and determined the boundaries in which a plausible employment of that art for contemporary theorizing should operate, I now more directly politicize the process of critical historicism and engage in the more contestable process of locating a place for "the Platonic political art" in contemporary debates about the relation of critical reason to democracy.[6] These comments are especially open to disagreement

---

enough to Plato as a historical figure that they might elicit his agreement—even if surprise as well—were he to read them today. If one is going to refer to a statement or belief in the dialogues as Platonic in some conceptual sense, the meaning of the statement should not be unrecognizable to its actual author.

6. One might say, then, that the argument of this book has been made in bad faith. For in historical as well as political argument, claims about more than narrowly defined events are essentially contestable. Because present, divergent, political, and intellectual preoccupations cannot be surgically separated from scholarly claims about the historical Plato, there is no bright, shining line to demarcate what evidences the identification of Plato and history from that of ourselves

and criticism, for the relation of the Platonic political art to contemporary problems in discourse and politics depends crucially on the way it is adapted and by whom. Nevertheless, appropriating and deploying Plato amid the contentions of current discourse and practice is not only desirable and unavoidable but also appropriate as a coda for this interpretation of the Platonic political art that emphasizes its internally dynamic tension of *logos* and *ergon*.

B. PLATO IN CONTEMPORARY POLITICAL THEORY

Platonic interventions in contemporary debates in political theory can assume a variety of forms. From the perspective of our interest in the relation of critical reason and democracy, however, two stand out. The first is broad; it involves the different historical character of the ancient and modern (and/or postmodern) contexts—that is, the contrast between "the ancients" and "the moderns." The other is narrower; it involves the contemporary context of political theory and focuses on the various formulations of the idea of deliberative democracy, an idea that would resolve problems that interestingly resemble those that Plato faced. Insofar as the first context sets important practical parameters for the second, we initially address it.

I. PLATO IN THE DEBATE BETWEEN "THE ANCIENTS" AND "THE MODERNS"

The contrast between "the ancients" and "the moderns" consists of practical, institutional comparisons as well as comparative evaluations of the nature and role of political values. The first identifies the ancient-modern contrast in terms of the differences between direct and representative democracy. Its most influential characterization has come from the pen of James Madison, as he defended a new Constitution for the United States as Publius in *The Federalist Papers* of 1787–88. The second interprets the contrast as that of ancient

---

and the present, much as we might try to find it. Moreover, the line becomes increasingly obscured as one emphasizes the contemporary relevance of a historical author. But one should resist the anti-intellectual and antihistorical consequences—which are not the only ones—of this train of thought. For useful treatments, see W. B. Gallie, *Philosophy and the Historical Understanding*, chap. 8, "Essentially Contested Concepts," 157–91, and William E. Connolly, *The Terms of Political Discourse*.

versus modern liberty. Its most notable exponent has been Benjamin Constant, whose 1819 essay, "The Liberty of the Ancients Compared with That of the Moderns," differentiated the rightful and wrongful lessons of ancient societies for postrevolutionary France. In his 1958 inaugural lecture as Chichele Professor of Social and Political theory at Oxford, "Two Concepts of Liberty," Isaiah Berlin glossed Constant's categorical distinctions with the logic of twentieth-century moral philosophy filtered through the experiences of two horrific European wars. The ideas of these writings, if not the writings themselves, have provided the markers for the political theory of twentieth-century liberalism, particularly that which relates to the work of (the presumptively illiberal) Plato.

Madison (and Hamilton) found in the history of Athens examples of most of the serious evils besetting their young American nation. In Pericles, Athens had a leader who fell prey to the lure of prostitutes and pride, who eventually led the city-state into the disastrous Peloponnesian War. Furthermore, the Athenians' direct form of democracy provided no solution to the dangers of demagoguery and majority factions—what Alexis de Tocqueville and John Stuart Mill would later call the (potential) tyranny of the majority. Having little territory, Athens lacked the space for the multiplication of interests, whose existence would discourage the formation of majority factions. As a dominant power in a confederacy, it illustrated the injustice and instability that would mark the conduct of that kind of political association. Characterized as such, democratic Athens served as a useful stand-in for both Federalist criticisms of the existing power of the several states and Federalist arguments for centralizing power in the new republican Constitution of the United States. Need it be said that Madison's analogies were far-fetched and historically inaccurate? Even state legislatures operated via political representation, and Madison admitted that mechanisms of political representation were not entirely alien to the Athenians. But he was convinced that the impetuous and self-destructive tendencies of ancient democracy—also known as the several states—would be replaced by the virtuous conduct of popularly or indirectly elected legislators lodged in a capital district far from their constituents.[7] The orderly operation of republican Constitutional institutions,

---

7. See *The Federalist Papers,* nos. 6, 10, 18, 52, 55, 63. For a recent book that de-emphasizes the differences between the political operation of modern, representative governments and the "directness" of Athenian democracy, see Bernard Manin, *Principles of Representative Government.* For a thorough intellectual history of judgments of Athenian democracy by scholars and politicians who never lived there, see Jennifer Roberts, *Athens on Trial.*

including the checks and balances of the three branches of the federal government, would eliminate the imperfections of democracy and assure the greatest possible production of virtue in American politics.[8]

Madison's criticisms of Athenian political practices did not deny the need for widespread adherence to political virtue; he simply did not believe that it would be naturally displayed by ordinary citizens. In this respect, Madison could be said to have updated Platonic arguments that showcased the inadequacy of the *demos* and its leaders for understanding or practicing civic virtue without abandoning the public interest or intellectual efforts to establish criteria for determining the substance of civic virtue—except for one important difference, namely, that direct democracy was the conventional political norm in Athens whereas it was not in the United States of the 1780s. Despite his anxious suspicions about democracy, however, Madison has been read as a father of "deliberative democracy."[9]

In contrast to Madison's direct employment of the ancients-moderns contrast to resolve contemporary political issues, Benjamin Constant used the contrast to question the very activity of applying ancient standards of civic virtue in contemporary political contexts. Constant was particularly irritated by the appropriation of the Spartan model of civic virtue by French revolutionaries on behalf of Jacobin republicanism, and he blamed the abbé de Mably (and, to a lesser extent, Rousseau) for supposing that such ancient ideas

---

8. See Gordon S. Wood, *The Creation of the American Republic, 1776–1787.* Notably, the republicanism versus democracy conflict, so important for understanding the American Constitution, does not figure in the recent regeneration of republicanism as a political ideal by theorists whose political frameworks are mostly heavily influenced by the history of England, the United Kingdom, and the British Commonwealth. See, for example, J. G. A. Pocock, *The Machiavellian Moment: Florentine Political Thought and the Atlantic Republican Tradition;* Philip Pettit, *Republicanism: A Theory of Freedom and Government;* and Quentin Skinner, *Liberty Before Liberalism.* By contrast, the conflict between republicanism and democracy is both evident and paramount in the work of the American political theorist Sheldon S. Wolin. See his *The Presence of the Past: Essays on the State and the Constitution.*

9. This is one reason that Madison can be used to blur the contemporary (mostly academic) distinction between a supposedly non-virtue based liberalism and virtue-based republicanism. See Stephen Macedo, *Liberal Virtues.* Notably in this regard, Cass Sunstein reincarnates Madisonian republicanism as "deliberative democracy" in, for instance, "Beyond the Republican Revival." For a historical account of Madison as a "deliberative democrat," see Joseph M. Bessette, *The Mild Voice of Reason: Deliberative Democracy and American National Government.* It is hard to say—and it certainly is unjustifiable to do so without argument—that Madison's constitutional mechanisms for improving the political deliberations of "the people" have benefited America's version of the *demos.* But then, again, they were not supposed to.

and practices could be used as paradigmatic models for modern politics.[10] Athens came in for much milder criticism. However, it, too, affirmed the "ancient" as opposed to the "modern" conception of "liberty." Constant's contrast also signified the preference for public over private liberty, the prevalence of war over commerce as the exemplary social practice, and the desire to participate in sharing social power over that of pursuing private pleasures. For Constant, these contrasts evidenced matters of fact, not value, but he used them to justify the detachment of political purpose from education in social virtue—even though Constant himself believed that *more* attention by citizens (not statesmen) to the virtues of ancient, rather than modern, liberty was a most pressing current need.[11]

Constant's preferred synthesis of the values of ancient and modern liberty as the appropriate political perspective on the present anticipated the cultural liberalism of John Stuart Mill. In *On Liberty,* Mill framed his argument by claiming that the contemporary problem of liberty does not involve how to protect it from the abuses of political tyrants—or even (for the most part) from the activities of legislative majorities. The principle enemies of liberty arise from the conformist conventions of social tyranny (exquisitely exemplified, no doubt, in his Victorian culture), whereas the principal object of liberty is the development of a person's "individuality."[12] Because of the cleansing effects of the cold water Mill poured on any institutionalized efforts to inculcate social virtue, his arguments in *On Liberty* have provided intellectual armor for the antagonism of postwar liberal political theory toward Plato—despite Mill's enormous debts to the inspiration of classical Athenian democracy (via George Grote) and Plato (via himself).[13]

Perhaps the most influential twentieth-century Millian has been Isaiah Berlin and his historically informed arguments on behalf of Constant's modern or "negative" liberty over and against "positive" or ancient liberty.[14] His

10. See "The Liberty of the Ancients Compared with That of the Moderns," in Benjamin Constant, *Political Writings,* 307–28.

11. See Stephen Holmes, *Benjamin Constant and the Making of Modern Liberalism,* particularly chap. 1.

12. J. S. Mill, *On Liberty,* ed. Gertrude Himmelfarb (Penguin, 1974), chap. 1, 59–63.

13. For examples, note Mill's review of Grote's *History of Greece* and his readings of various Platonic dialogues. John Stuart Mill, *Essays on Philosophy and the Classics,* ed. J. M. Robson (Toronto: University of Toronto Press, 1978 [*Collected Works, XI*]).

14. See Isaiah Berlin, "Two Concepts of Liberty," in his *Four Essays on Liberty.* In the essay "Political Ideas in the Twentieth Century," which also appears in this volume (48 note, and 49

arguments clearly associate the potential to suppress "negative" liberty with modern democracies (as well as the practical programs of "positive" liberty more generally); they have paved the way for both left- and right-wing liberalism's skepticism about the use of public power on behalf of the common good. The preservation of individual "rights" should take precedence over democratic claims to exercise "power."[15] Because the *demos* and its equivalents have not ruled since antiquity, however, the desire to protect against the tyrannical use of power in every guise tends to privilege the extant exercise of power (as long as it does not violate the exercise of the preferred list of individual rights). Unfortunately, the result adds ethical and political support to antidemocratic forms of power, even as it provides invaluable guardianship for "negative liberty."

Principal bearings of liberal political theory since the nineteenth century, therefore, feature both skepticism about democracy and (unjustified) antagonism toward Plato. The linkage of these two theoretical perspectives has appeared not only in the major postwar scholarly interpretations of Plato (as noted in Chapter 1) but also in the currently most eminent theories of liberal constitutional democracy—those of John Rawls and Jurgen Habermas. We engage their work as we seek to deploy Plato today because it avowedly seeks to promote a kind of deliberative democracy. In this respect, it would resolve

---

note), he finds cause for praise of Karl Popper's critique of historicism in *The Open Society and Its Enemies* (as well as his *The Poverty of Historicism*) without specifically calling attention to his reading of Plato, although Berlin bathes Plato in Popperian light when he cites Plato critically in "Two Concepts of Liberty" (152, 168) and cites Mill against Plato in another essay that appears in this volume, "John Stuart Mill and the Ends of Life" (196). In this context, it is worth noting that Berlin uses a quotation from Constant—which evocatively compares the sacrifice of real beings on behalf of abstract beings to the holocaustal offering of particular people on the altar of "the People"—to lead the 1969 introduction to this volume—and that, in a 1957 talk (first published in the 3 October 1996 issue of *The New York Review of Books,* just thirteen months before his death), Berlin includes Plato among the historical intellectuals who have wanted to endow "scientists" with political authority. See "Political Judgment," reprinted in *The Sense of Reality: Studies in Ideas and Their History,* ed. Henry Hardy, 40–54, at 52. Berlin, like Popper and, to a lesser extent, Constant, reduces the character of the political in the Greek *polis* to its features as a state opposing the citizenry—the very political arrangement that was conspicuously absent in Athenian democracy. They most likely do so because of the pervasive effects of the Jacobin Terror, the Russian Revolution, and the Holocaust on their political views.

For a telling critique of Berlin's dichotomy, especially in terms of the harmful impact it has had on the theorization of liberty, see Quentin Skinner, "The Idea of Negative Liberty," in R. Rorty et al., eds., *Philosophy in History,* 193–221, and Philip Pettit, *Republicanism: A Theory of Freedom and Government,* esp. 17–31.

15. See "Two Concepts of Liberty," 162–66.

the tension between democracy and critical reason that so troubled Plato, motivating much of his critical discourse about democracy, the dialectic of deliberation, and the political art. Does it successfully do so, making a redeployment of Plato unnecessary?

2. THE LIMITS OF "DELIBERATIVE DEMOCRACY"

The mutual implication of deliberation and democracy was first articulated by John Dewey in the 1920s, but "deliberative democracy" and/or "democratic deliberation"—both of which I shall refer to as "DD"—became major terms of art in Western political theory only in the 1990s.[16] The attractiveness of the phrases has both crystallized and increased since the early 1970s, when "participatory democracy" and "liberalism" began to lose their luster as politically and theoretically sufficient critical ideals.

Liberals embraced deliberation as the political form of reasonableness,

---

16. See John Dewey, *The Public and Its Problems,* The following is an incomplete list of monographs and collections of articles that centrally deal with this term: Joshua Cohen, "Deliberation and Democratic Legitimacy," in Alan Hamlin and Philip Pettit, eds., *The Good Polity;* Jürgen Habermas, *Between Facts and Norms: Contributions to a Discourse Theory of Law and Democracy,* originally published in German under the title *Faktizitat und Geltung: Beiträge zur Diskursstheorie des Rechts und des demokratischen Rechtsstaats,* and idem, *The Inclusion of the Other: Studies in Political Theory;* James Fishkin, *Democracy and Deliberation: New Directions for Democratic Reform;* James Bohman, *Public Deliberation: Pluralism, Complexity, and Democracy;* Amy Gutmann and Dennis Thompson, *Democracy and Disagreement,* along with a book of essays about their book, Stephen Macedo, ed., *Deliberative Politics: Essays on Democracy and Disagreement;* James Bohman and William Rehg, eds., *Deliberative Democracy: Essays on Reason and Politics;* Jon Elster, ed., *Deliberative Democracy.* Although John Rawls does not expressly use the term in either *A Theory of Justice* or *Political Liberalism,* his emphasis in both books on applying procedural rules for public political deliberation as a necessary condition for the achievement of justice or "public reason" in contemporary constitutional democracies entitles his work to be included with that of the above. However, he does highlight the phrase as crucially descriptive of the core of his theory in the introduction to the paperback edition of *Political Liberalism* (lviii–lx) and in his last major article, "The Idea of Public Reason Revisited," esp. 771–73. Moreover, the theoretical work of Gutmann and Thompson is deeply indebted to that of Rawls. For a recent statement of Gutmann's debt to Rawls, see her article, "Rawls on the Relationship Between Liberalism and Democracy," in *The Cambridge Companion to Rawls.* Indeed, I am not alone in grouping Rawls and Habermas under this categorical umbrella: See Bohman, *Public Deliberation,* 3–7. For an earlier account of deliberative democracy that is also more patently radical in its critical intent, see Joshua Cohen and Joel Rogers, *On Democracy: Toward a Transformation of American Society.* For a more extensive list of earlier works on "deliberative democracy," see Gutmann and Thompson, *Democracy and Disagreement,* 364, n. 4. For a review essay on recent versions of deliberative democracy (which I saw after writing this section), see Emily Hauptmann, "Deliberation = Legitimacy = Democracy."

and its closeness to contemporary political rhetoric and actual political practice made deliberative liberalism appear more democratic. Participatory democrats liked DD as well, because it differentiated ideally useful and harmful forms of political activism and discourse. Even conservatives have sought to clothe their political views in the terms of DD, often invoking its Aristotelian roots, in which deliberation is categorically an intellectual virtue but also a constitutive component of the thought and action of the morally virtuous man of practical wisdom.[17]

As the notion has achieved academic prominence, however, DD has become an inherently misleading concept. To begin with, it presupposes a liberal, constitutional, and procedural framework for democracy that democracy itself—at least in its original and simplest (Athenian) form—does not. This constraint operates in the principal theoretical works of both Rawls and Habermas, wherein it is taken for granted as an unqualified and democratic good.[18] It should be acknowledged, however, that democracy and constitutionalism are not natural allies, and that valuable democratic ideas and practices may be undermined for the sake of maintaining the ideological alliance known as "constitutional democracy."[19] More important, however, the prevailing discourse of DD elides certain theoretical and political questions so as to obscure extant dynamic relations between ethics and power. A modern deployment of the Platonic political art can more instructively illuminate and question these relations. To make this clear, the basic constituents of DD (at least as understood by Rawls and/or Habermas) need to be spelled out— hardly in every detail, but to the point that a fair and useful dialogue between a rehistoricized Plato and DD can ensue.

17. Rawls, Gutmann, and Thompson exemplify the liberal move to embrace DD in the 1990s. They find company in the work of the legal theorist Cass Sunstein (see note 9, above). Joshua Cohen exemplifies the move by participatory democrats to make DD their own. See the book he co-wrote with Joel Rogers (note 16, above) and his two articles in Bohman and Rehg, eds., *Deliberative Democracy: Essays on Reason and Politics*. George F. Will associated his advocacy of term limits with DD, in *Restoration: Congress, Term Limits, and the Recovery of Deliberative Democracy*.

18. Of course, there are important theoretical differences between Rawls and Habermas, which are highlighted in the exchange between them that occurred in *The Journal of Philosophy* 92 (March 1995): 109–80. (Notably, neither philosopher made any reference during this lengthy exchange to the nationality or historical context of himself or his interlocutor, thereby bracketing any discussion of the possible influence of their practical backgrounds on their theoretical arguments.) Yet many commonalities between them exist, and I point these out below.

19. The tensions and affinities between constitutionalism and democracy are explored by Frank Michelman, in *Brennan and Democracy*.

The procedural move that both Rawls and Habermas take, which establishes constitutive constraints on legitimate political discourse in a democracy, stems from their chief political and philosophical concerns. In Rawls's major work, *A Theory of Justice* (1971), those who would deliberate about justice are asked to assume an "original position" that brackets the distinctive features of their individuality—such as their basic moral commitments and demographic indicators. This is necessary in order to eliminate bias from the deliberative process and create the conditions for a rational consensus. Rawls views this device as an updated discursive equivalent of classical social contract theory—although the theories of Hobbes, Locke, and Rousseau could be said to originate as solutions to hypothetical problems ascribed to a hypothetical "state of nature," whose basic characteristics Rawls also brackets from his theoretical and political deliberations.[20]

Then, beginning with his 1985 article, "Justice as Fairness: Political Not Metaphysical," and crystallizing in his last book, *Political Liberalism* (1993), Rawls finds historical warrant and grounding for his theory in the Anglo-American political tradition's agreement to separate religious conflict from political conflict and to differentiate the practical realms of church and state. Despite the fact that "political liberalism" is what Rawls now calls his theory of justice (rather than "justice as fairness"), he has replaced justice with toleration as the first virtue of social life.[21] Indeed, both "justice as fairness" and "political liberalism" require that fundamental ethical and moral values be kept out of reasonable political discourse, behind a veil of ignorance, in order that we may achieve a political consensus. This consensus is an "overlapping consensus," that is, the shaded area of a Venn diagram where "the

---

20. John Rawls, *A Theory of Justice*, 11–22.

21. I say this despite the pride of place "justice" receives in *A Theory of Justice*, namely, the first word of the first sentence: "Justice is the first virtue of social institutions, as truth is to systems of thought." Liberal political theory achieves coherence by bracketing first-order considerations of the nature of justice, allowing these to result from the deliberation of free and equal citizens. But if the description of those citizens as free and equal is more useful in theory than it is accurate in practice, the results of their deliberations have no clear correlation to a just society. Sandel's initial critique of Rawlsian theory, *Liberalism and the Limits of Justice*, was curiously mislabeled. For the limitations of Rawlsian theory do not stem from "justice" or its prioritization of it; rather, they derive from Rawls's refusal to theorize thoroughly about what justice in late twentieth-century Western democracies might be. Sandel's critique should have been titled "The Limitations of Liberal Justice." (For that matter, Rawls's first book should not have been titled *A Theory of Justice* but rather "A Theory of Liberal Justice" or "A Theory of Justice as Fairness," or, indeed, "Political Liberalism." That it wasn't indicates the relatively self-confident discourse about liberalism that prevailed in the academy during the mid-1960s.)

public" and "the reasonable" (as opposed to "the religious" or "the moral") elements of the diverse political views of citizens intersect. Rawls takes for granted that fundamental conceptions of the good derived from the morality and/or religion of citizens may underlie or motivate their public deliberations, but he does not allow them to pass through the borders that guard political debate among "free and equal citizens," which is informed by "the idea of public reason."[22]

This is not the place to provide another review of the virtues and limits of Rawls's theory (or theories); moreover, I have already made my contribution to it twelve years ago, and the criticisms of Rawls I made there, I daresay, have been often repeated by others and have not been answered to my satisfaction by Rawls.[23] What is appropriate, however, is a critical analysis of how Rawls frames his discussion of democratic deliberation, particularly in contrast to how the characteristics of democracy and deliberation were framed by Plato.

In the introduction to the first edition of *Political Liberalism* (xxi–xxix), Rawls situates his theory of "political liberalism" as a response to a set of peculiarly "modern" problems, problems that (he claims) did not exist in ancient Greek moral philosophy. (Thus, we are presented with another version of the contrast between "the ancients" and "the moderns" discussed in the previous section.) Taking his bearings from Terence Irwin for what were the problems that "Greek philosophy" set out to answer, Rawls notes that it grew out of a response to the inadequacies of Greek civic religion and Homeric justifications for answering the question of what constituted "the reasonable pursuit of true happiness" (xxii) or "the highest good." By contrast, modern philosophy does not pursue this question because the religious dogmas of "modern" religion as it crystallized in the wake of the Reformation answer this question, even as they produced creedal passions that demanded a new

---

22. John Rawls, *Political Liberalism*, 133–72.

23. For an anticipation of these difficulties, see my "Liberals, Communitarians, and the Tasks of Political Theory," esp. 582–90. As of late October 1995, there were over thirty published reviews of Rawls's 1993 book *Political Liberalism*, many of which make this point in one way or another. See, for example, the review by Michael Sandel in the *Harvard Law Review;* Susan Okin's "*Political Liberalism*, Justice, and Gender," as well as her briefer review of *Political Liberalism* in *American Political Science Review;* the pieces by Miriam Galston, Linda Hirshman, Lawrence Mitchell, and Elizabeth Wolgast in *Columbia Law Review* 94, (October 1994); various pieces in *Pacific Philosophical Quarterly* 75 (Sept.–Dec. 1994); Elizabeth Frazer and Nicola Lacey, "Politics and the Public in Rawls' Political Liberalism," *Political Studies* 43 (1995): 233–47. For a more sympathetic and democratic reading of the later Rawls, see Joshua Cohen, "A More Democratic Liberalism."

ethic of toleration. So the question of moral philosophy thus turns to "a problem of political justice, not a problem about the highest good" (xxv), namely, "What are the fair terms of social cooperation between citizens characterized as free and equal yet divided by profound doctrinal conflict? What is the structure and content of the requisite political conception?"

Rawls acknowledges that *this* problem of justice is not the same as "the problem of justice as it arose in the ancient world" (xxv). Unfortunately, he never tells us what that problem was. We are to infer from his account of the origins of ancient Greek moral philosophy, I take it, that the problem of justice for the ancients principally entailed determining a rational account of happiness. But this is to read ancient moral and political philosophy through the lens of a modern moral philosopher (Terence Irwin) whose books on Plato's moral theory and ethics barely mention political issues. Our study of the Platonic political art, including Plato's theoretical formulation of justice as a critical idea, indicates to the contrary that debates about "happiness" did not constitute the essential problems Plato set out to answer. Rather, these problems involved the conflict between "virtue" as a philosophically articulated ethical and political ideal and the power of conventional discourse and practice.

In Plato's *Republic,* this conflict assumes the form of the conflict between Thrasymachus and Socrates as set forth in Books I–II, which Plato's Socrates understands as the problem of *stasis* in the soul and the state. This conflict is born of differing ethical beliefs along with corollary economic, social, and political practices. Indeed, "religious" conflict is not central to the problems Plato addresses. But this is not to say that his concerns about justice are not "political." What differentiates the Platonic and Rawlsian understandings of "the political" is the absence in Rawls's formulation of any systematic linkage between "political" and fundamentally "ethical" or "religious" views. To narrow the political domain in this way, however, is to remove from critical view the ethical or spiritual roots of political conflict along with the political complements of various ethical and spiritual views. This removal has made Rawls's theory of political liberalism particularly irrelevant to the politics of recent times—when ethnic and religious conflicts have played such a large part in political conflicts in southeastern Europe, Africa, and western Asia, whereas in the United States a radical redefinition of the "responsibility" of individuals and citizens (often aided and abetted by corporate interests) has led to the virtual elimination of publicly funded welfare programs, the increased privatization of medical care, and the increasingly troubled state of public schools.

Now Rawls, to be sure, points to such ethnic and political conflicts and bemoans them, saying that they (along with the rise of the Third Reich) evidence what ultimately happens when citizens do not adhere to an idea of public reason. Moreover, he states that the preconditions for the kind of deliberation that is necessary for "deliberative democracy" include full employment and universal health care.[24] So, then, why has this well-intentioned, humane, and "reasonable" political theory fallen on deaf ears outside the academy? I argue that it partially results from the way in which Rawls has framed the principal political problems of our time—which includes his differentiation of "ancient" and "modern" problems of justice. By focusing on the problem raised by the absence of political consensus in post-Reformation Europe as a problem of "doctrinal conflict" as well as the central problem of politics, the reasonable political consensus promoted by "political liberalism" is achieved at the cost of political relevance. By enforcing a boundary between the political and the nonpolitical as he has, he cannot address why citizens may not embrace his idea of public reason or engage in the appropriate kind of political deliberations. By clearly differentiating legitimate "political" conflicts from basic religious and ethical or moral conflicts, much of the energy that drives political debate is overlooked.

We are asked to *begin* by accepting "the fact of reasonable pluralism," even though the ethical (or unethical) content and practical power (or powerlessness) of the component parts of this pluralism energize the political arguments that are to proceed after accepting this "fact." To be sure, the criterion of "public reason" would guide the achievement of this consensus—and Rawls himself emphasizes that the idea of public reason does not endorse stability at any cost[25]—but it could be said that criteria for achieving a practicable consensus within the confines of existing institutions of civil society and the state predetermine the effective meanings for the practical criteria of Rawls's idea of public reason. By taking "the fact of reasonable pluralism" as a politically unproblematic starting point for his theory of justice, Rawlsians will continue to misunderstand the political salience of ethical conflict or the ethical character of political conflict—precisely the kinds of interconnections that Plato highlighted in his dialogues involving the political art. As a result, the "deliberative" character of Rawls's theorization of a legitimate constitutional democracy guided by the idea of public reason will be only marginally

---

24. "Introduction," *Political Liberalism,* paperback ed., lviii–lix.
25. "Introduction," *Political Liberalism* (1996), xxxix.

critical of the status quo—even though one could reasonably argue that the political status quo is guided neither by much public deliberation nor by much democracy.

Now Rawls is surely right to exclude some comprehensive ethical views from direct political debate—at least insofar as they provide no common political or intellectual forum for a deliberative accommodation of differences. Among the views he excludes are those of Thomism, Platonism, and Marxism, each of which asserts a single exclusive conception of the good.²⁶ But— apart from excluding the major sources of social ethics for Catholics and many leftists—this interpretive judgment relies on a faulty view of Plato. What we have found in Plato's dialogues about ethics and politics has been not so much the doctrinal assertion of a single good (or a Madisonian complaint about the excesses of democracy) as the recognition that (1) a background of ethical and political conflict, often fomented by individual and institutional over-reaching, establishes the problematic context for articulating one's conception of justice; (2) one cannot achieve justice without achieving some common conception of the good; and (3) achieving justice and realizing the good require education adapted to individuals' needs. Although a renewed appreciation of Plato can hardly be viewed as a radically innovative political palliative, using the criteria for the practice of the Platonic political art as a baseline for political evaluation might put us in a better position to understand the roots of injustice and the obstacles to justice.²⁷

Habermas's political theory of deliberative democracy stems from a different set of concerns than does Rawls's theory. Not the horrors of religious conflict but the failure of liberal constitutional democracy in his homeland from 1918 to 1945 provides his political, if not his theoretical, problematic. Yet his answer complements Rawls's. As is the case with Rawls, the political substance of the theory emanates from the procedural constraints imposed on legitimate political deliberation. In Habermas's case, however, the proceduralism assumes the form of a theoretical argument about rational and publicly justifiable truth-claims; these claims do not require the bracketing of any particular features of the identity of individual citizens. However, they require acceptance of certain categorical determinations of human experience, including the subsumption of "the moral" under the universalizable rule of

---

26. See "The Idea of Public Reason Revisited," 800, n. 86.

27. For a recent critical perspective on Rawls that notes Plato's questions about justice as useful contrasts (without using the critical baggage of a particular interpretation of Plato), see Glen Newey, "Floating on the LILO: John Rawls and the Content of Justice."

neo-Kantian practical reason and the separation of the universality of "the moral" from the particularity of "the ethical" (the equivalent of conceptions of the good or comprehensive doctrines, according to Rawls). By accepting such categories, Habermas believes that his theory can promote the liberties of *both* "the ancients" *and* "the moderns," liberals *and* republicans, as well as democracy, in ways that Rawls's theory cannot.[28] This becomes clear, he claims, through his analyses of reconstructive procedures of democratic legitimization that are informed by the conditions of rational discourses and negotiations or law and "deliberative politics"—which he argues for in *Between Facts and Norms* and *The Inclusion of the Other*.[29]

Of course, Habermas distances himself from the classical tradition, particularly the "Platonist" metaphysical tradition and the "philosophy of consciousness" associated with Husserl—each of which, he claims, postulated a reality to ideas that was separable from, opposed to, but determinative of, our perceptions and values. For Habermas, the linguistic and pragmatic turn initiated by the theoretical work of Frege and Peirce dissolved these antagonisms.[30] He believes that the practical locus for dissolving these antagonisms is constitutional law in liberal democracies, whose procedural requirements establish the legitimate conditions of political morality.[31] (Achieving political legitimacy, more than justice, most concerns Habermas—as it most bedeviled the Weimar Republic.) Indeed, Habermas's theory matches Rawls's devotion to the U.S. Supreme Court as "the exemplar of public reason" (in *Po-*

28. See Jürgen Habermas, "Reconciliation Through the Public Use of Reason: Remarks on John Rawls's *Political Liberalism*" (which is reprinted in *The Inclusion of the Other;* see also *The Inclusion of the Other,* 258–59).

29. See Habermas, "Reconciliation Through the Public Use of Reason . . . ," 130–31, and idem, "Three Normative Models of Democracy," in *The Inclusion of the Other,* 239–52.

30. See *Between Facts and Norms,* 9–13, 34.

31. This amounts to the practical equivalent of Habermas's previous embrace of the Aristotelian conception of *praxis* as the original locus of ethical politics. See Jürgen Habermas, *Theory and Practice,* 42, where Habermas misrepresents the ancient Greek and Aristotelian conceptions of politics. He regards these as equivalent and tantamount to the "old [ancient Greek] doctrine of politics [that] referred exclusively to *praxis,* in the narrow sense . . . [and that] had nothing to do with *techne,* the skillful production of artifacts and the expert mastery of objectified tasks." According to the argument of this book, the categorical association of ancient Greek or Aristotelian conceptions of politics with *praxis* as opposed to *techne* is radically mistaken and is reflected in the mistaken views of Greek politics held by Hannah Arendt in *The Human Condition.* Habermas seems to realize this in his critique of Arendt, "Hannah Arendt's Communications Concept of Power" but then proceeds to transpose the ideal of conflict-free political practice previously symbolized for Habermas in the notion of *praxis* to the conflict-free discursive notion of the ideal speech situation and its new practical exemplar in the constitutional standards of modern liberal democracies (exemplified by the Basic Law of the Federal Republic).

litical Liberalism) with an implicit belief in the educational powers of the basic law in the Federal Republic. Both men have chosen a practical political example to match a theoretical example, and, for each theorist, these supposedly demonstrate a virtually apolitical, conflict-free standard of evaluation.

Plato would not have accepted these proceduralist conceptions of legitimate political deliberation, but not because of their interest or value. He simply would have noted that the rationality of such deliberation cannot be categorically separated from its ethical component if it would genuinely seek justice and that both exist in a dynamic and dialectical relation to existing forms of power. It is not self-evident (as Rawls seems to presume) that the Westphalian settlement of 1648 marked the principal achievement in the Western march toward justice of the past 350 years; nor is it clear to me (as Habermas has claimed) that Frege and Peirce have satisfactorily resolved the tension between ideas and perceptible reality—one might say between *logos* and *ergon*—of which Plato was keenly aware.

I argue that the failure of twentieth-century liberal political theory (a category that includes the work of Rawls and Habermas) is the insistent refusal to deal with political conflict and tensions. This avoidance is not inherent in liberalism per se. The classical liberal, social contract theories of Hobbes, Locke, and Rousseau legitimated the state by postulating a state of nature marked by conflict, which mirrored their views of the essential social and political conflicts of their time; the establishment of a legitimate state would resolve these conflicts. Rawls begins his theoretical venture by eliminating the causes of basic conflict—either through "the original position" or by reducing the plurality of conflicting views about the good to a "reasonable fact"—before his theory begins even to assume to cut any political mustard. Habermas establishes proceduralist conditions for legitimate public discourse—the ideal speech situation—which presumes that nothing significant for democratic citizens is lost by making their political views pass through that linguistic filter. In both cases, the proceduralist moves are made on behalf of democracy and legitimization, for everyone (hypothetically) is able to adopt the original position or employ the ideal speech situation. But establishing the universal hypothetical access to their theoretical starting points as the foundation of their theoretical projects means that the social conflicts that currently prevent most citizens from happily taking their routes for political deliberation are avoided. In other words, such theories avoid dealing with the actual problematics of justice in contemporary societies.

Platonic justice, as opposed to liberal justice, places such conflicts front and center in making "Socrates" answer Meletus, Protagoras, Gorgias, Polus,

Callicles, Cephalus, Polemarchus, and Thrasymachus (along with his representatives Glaucon and Adeimantus in the first part of Book II of the *Republic*). For Plato, the lack of any adequate conception of the political art or justice stems from the failure of existing ethical discourses or practices of power to resolve basic social conflicts, which stem from over-reaching (*pleonexia*), a sin of the powerful, and from severe economic inequalities. To resolve these problems, Plato finds it necessary to reeducate society, and such reeducation requires a reeducated ruling class. Plato's agreeability to the establishment of a ruling class has always—and rightfully—bothered democrats. And yet no democracy—certainly not the Athenian or American versions—has operated without one. One valuable asset of Platonic theorizing about justice, therefore, is its direct engagement with the question of how the exercise of political power may complement the assertion of justice. Rather than bracketing, naturalizing, or rationalizing conflicts between ethics and power (as liberals, neo-Aristotelians, and sophistic pragmatists do), Plato critically analyzes them and provides a theoretical—not a practical—solution. His conditions of critical reason and just deliberation, therefore, operate in tension with what he takes to be the extant and enduring injustices of law and politics. How might they do so today? Could they do so on behalf of democracy?

C. PLATO AND CRITICAL CITIZENSHIP TODAY

My belief that Plato has much to offer as a partner in political and, in particular, democratic reflections today depends on the truth or validity of some basic assumptions about the features of contemporary politics, particularly those of what I call postliberal democracies. I specify what I take to be defining features of these democracies and then isolate a particular issue, education, which a rehistoricized Platonic political art might usefully address.

I. THE POLITICAL PROBLEMATICS OF POSTLIBERAL DEMOCRACY

I use the term *postliberal democracy* to differentiate our current political condition from that of traditional liberal democracies. Postliberal democracies have three principal elements: (1) There is no accepted consensus about basic ethical or moral values that informs the way in which political problems are conceptualized or treated. (2) The problems themselves do not primarily concern the extension of liberal rights (signified, for instance, by the problem of how to realize the ideal of equal opportunity for all individuals, regardless of their ascriptive social identity) and are not confined to distributive issues that marginally affect the nature of the family or the structure of the economy. At the same time, large inequalities exist in the exercise of political and economic power, and the readily available means for their moderation do not prove to be effective. (3) Nature has become irrelevant or suspect as a category of political understanding, so that our political problems seem to derive less from "human nature" than from existing links between ethics and power that a/effect our efforts to construct nurturing families, educate our children, and compose a life of rewarding work for the citizenry as a whole.

Traditional liberalism relied on the private realm to provide the ethical guideposts for public life. It no longer can do so in a way that facilitates harmony in political life. We live in an age in which the boundaries that divide private and public realms have lost either stability or justification in the realms of ethics, economics, politics, and culture. Thus, in postliberal democracies, (1) governments need to subsidize the activity of parenting, because the financial pressures on many couples force them to rely on costly day-care facilities in order to raise their children; (2) economic "recovery" is marked by a decline in good-paying manufacturing jobs and no increase in the standard of living; (3) there are widespread calls to use the tools of government to regulate the sensationalism of invasive popular media in order to protect children and promote the liberty and equality of women. The result has produced a crisis in our capacity to imagine an ethical political art that would benefit democracy.

This is not to say that in the earlier days of liberal democracy our political lives were much better; for in those days the moral consensus tolerated, if not promoted, racism, sexism, and homophobia (although the human pain produced by the inexorable force of capital accumulation may have been less likely to be viewed as part of the nature of things). It is to say that the political problems we currently experience are not susceptible to traditional liberal solutions or the prevailing alternatives.

2. CRITERIA OF ENLISTING THE PLATONIC POLITICAL ART FOR DEMOCRACY

Plato's "relevance" to postliberal democracies stems primarily from his conception of the political art as a practice of virtue that could justly harmonize the inherently problematic relation of *logos* to *ergon*. Its contribution to democracy derives from the manner in which his conception of the political art transposed connections between ethics and politics from their association with particularly democratic Athenian means of operating political power. Plato's insistence on conceptualizing justice as both the practical aim of philosophy and an ethical political art promoted linkages between critical discourse and practical action, *logos* and *ergon*, which more closely resemble democratic correlations of words and deeds, deliberation and practical action, than do most theoretical projects in the Western philosophical tradition, certainly all of those fundamentally indebted to Aristotle.

Plato surely emphasized oppositions between reality and appearance, *logos* and *ergon*, and he sought to ameliorate the potentially antagonistic character of their relation. But he never argued that they could be—or ever were—stabilized. This is because—in accord with a democratic disposition—their truth-value practically depended on their capacity to respond to and resolve the persistent, unjust conflicts of extant political life. Plato doubted that such harmony could ever be perfectly, practically realized, and he denied that it could be regularly or permanently achieved. In this sense, his political ambition was moderate and his philosophical authority limited. But (unlike Aristotle) he was convinced that it was neither normal nor natural to fail to conceptualize such perfection, to entertain the possibility (not the likelihood) of its realization, and to live one's life in accord with that ideal as much as circumstances permitted. Such a life would be both just and happy, whereas not living such a life implants the seeds of *stasis* in one's self and others.

Of course, Plato's heart did not sing and his brow furrowed when presented with the practices or principles of democracy as he knew it. Platonic questions did not yield democratic answers in his time, and Plato radically differed from most Athenian citizens regarding the extent to which their democracy promoted injustice. Moreover, Plato's conviction that a more critical and ethical understanding of political life could improve its conduct in Athens and other Greek societies led him to establish a new kind of discursive authority for his critical discourse about the political art, one that challenged the actual authority of Athenian democratic practices. He did not, however, directly seek to endow that discourse with practical authority *over* actual democratic practices. So then what authority does it have in relation to democracy?

As it was articulated in the aporetic dialogues and more constructively in the *Republic, Statesman,* and *Laws,* the Platonic political art did not merely possess ironic authority; for Plato, *logos* was to be employed as an instructive, potentially powerful political art. But this art did not signify an art that would dominate extant forms of either discourse or practice. The establishment of the Academy did not require the closure of Isocrates' school or the overthrow of Athenian democracy, even as it would alter one's perspective on their relative value. Plato recognized that the proper exercise of the political art was radically responsive to the actual and ever-changing discursive and practical conditions that occasion its use. To be sure, he did not regard the Academy as a new school for citizens, and his counsel to political leaders did not go to pivotal Athenian politicians but to Dionysius II. However, there was an irreducibly ethical and political dimension to Plato's practice of philosophy from which democracy could benefit.

By staking out new ground for his critical perspective outside the conventional—and primarily democratic—ambits of politics and education, Plato's perspectives on the political art extended intellectual horizons for both justice itself and for more just democracies, asserting stricter criteria for the accommodation of democracy and virtue than had been done in fifth- or fourth-century Athens.[32] In this vein, discussions of the relations of theory and practice in postliberal democracies may invoke the Platonic political art as a significant reference point. This is so particularly if democracy is understood as a form of political life that forever seeks to close the gap between virtue and the political art, requires constant critical evaluation for virtuous citizenship and coherent leadership, and remains skeptical of signs of justice that themselves resist critical evaluation. Plato's treatments of the political art establish benchmarks for nondogmatic harmony among standards of truth in critical discourse, justice in ethical life, and success in politics.

To spell out how an appreciation of the Platonic political art can benefit contemporary theorizing about democracies and their problems, we need to identify more precisely the political dilemmas faced by citizens of postliberal democracies. John Dunn put well one way of viewing them when he said (in 1979), "Democracy is the name for what we cannot have but cannot cease to want."[33] As that which we cannot cease to want, "democracy" signifies a rela-

---

32. Regarding the first point, see Josiah Ober, "How to Criticize Democracy in Late Fifth- and Fourth-Century Athens," in J. Peter Euben et al., eds., *Athenian Political Thought and the Reconstruction of American Democracy,* 149–71.

33. John Dunn, *Western Political Theory in the Face of the Future,* 2d ed., 27.

tively egalitarian sharing of political power, a desire fortified by the belief that it provides the most reliable check on the tyrannical exercise of myriad forms of power (political, economic, religious, and personal). As that which we cannot have, "democracy" signifies the actual exercise of political power by the majority of citizens, a possibility that is radically diminished by the ever more complex and extensive structural arrangements of power by corporations and states. This concern is exacerbated by the widespread prospect (encouraged by corporations and states) of citizens viewing their political responsibilities from the standpoint of their identities as consumers of income, pleasure (preoccupied with themselves, their families, and their own systems of belief), and information—rather than as agents and protectors of their own society and the wider world.

Placed in the context of postliberal democracies, this situation calls for a set of critically justified ethical beliefs that could bolster efforts to limit the power of dominant political majorities while enhancing the social prospects and political agency of ordinary citizens. It calls for a newly variegated understanding of the ethics and politics of democracy in all aspects of social life. In particular, it requires a democratic understanding of current and possible relations between ethics and power and a democratic practice that artfully relates these words to deeds—in the areas of trade, campaign-finance reform, health, education, and welfare (to name a few). These do not now exist in any publicly significant form (which is not to say that many individuals and small institutions are not working to obtain large-scale public hearings for them).[34]

The sense of political *aporia* among democratic theorists is exacerbated by the character of the forces they face. For as the power of private media and corporations in the public realm grows, the boundaries between public and private begin to blur if not dissolve, which increases uncertainty about what constitutes a legitimate, promising realm for public action and political change.[35] In addition, the prospects for increasing prosperity for major

---

34. There are important academic accounts of the theoretical and institutional frameworks for such understandings. For some useful examples, see Joshua Cohen and Joel Rogers, "Secondary Associations and Democratic Governance"; Duncan Kennedy, *Sexy Dressing, etc.;* David Held, *Democracy and the Global Order;* Ian Shapiro, *Democracy's Place;* and idem, *Democratic Justice;* Alain Touraine, *What Is Democracy?* and Ulrich Beck, *The Reinvention of Politics: Rethinking Modernity in the Global Social Order.* Sundry American public officials (such as Paul Wellstone and Bernard Saunders), as well as nascent political parties and their candidates (such as the New Party, Green Party, and Working Families Party), also champion these views.

35. Some look to "civil society" or "culture" both to address these questions and seek their solutions, insofar as they seem to embrace the intersections of ethics and power. These are originally Latin terms for which there is no Greek equivalent. For a defense of the importance of

segments of the citizenry continue to be cloudy (as they have been for over twenty-five years for all but the wealthy and for educated women). The widely noted (but politically unattended) gap between rich and poor is widening in the United States and is larger in the United States than in other advanced industrial societies.[36]

In the consumption-oriented, individualistic, and plutocratic society of the United States, the short-run effect of these trends is to encourage citizens to turn on one another or to blame politicians rather than to encourage one another to think systematically about problems affecting the political community as a whole and constructively act together to solve them. The drumbeat of antigovernment discourse in postliberal democracies for nearly twenty years has eroded the public's faith in the idea of democracy as a political ideal associated with the activity of political involvement and improvement.[37]

Despite these obstacles, there are ever-growing desires for concerted political reform and renewal. Ours is a context that cries out for a comprehensive critical analysis of the power of ethics and the ethics of power in the operation of contemporary democracies. To this extent, it is a context that calls for a Platonic response. A Platonic response preserves the hope for an accommodation of ethics and power while radically and critically exposing the ways in which they currently do not harmonize.

Now the response of Plato himself, although not essentially antagonistic to democracy, certainly motivated critical thinking in an undemocratic direc-

---

"cultural" phenomena, see Judith Butler, "Merely Cultural." For a useful historical and analytical discussion of various German meanings of what gets translated in English as "cultural," see Raymond Geuss, "*Kultur, Bildung, Geist*," *History and Theory*. For a lengthy and sophisticated treatment of various aspects of "civil society," see Jean Cohen and Andrew Arato, *Civil Society and Political Theory*.

36. Relatively recent surveys are Lawrence Mishel et al., *The State of Working America*, 88–103; James A. Auerbach and Richard S. Belous, eds., *The Inequality Paradox: Growth of Income Disparity;* "Pulling Apart: A State-by-State Analysis of Income Trends," *Center on Budget and Policy Priorities* (16 December 1997); Edward N. Wolff, *Top Heavy: The Increasing Inequality of Wealth in America and What Can Be Done About It* (New York: New Press, 1996); Nico Wilterdink, "Increasing Income Inequality and Wealth Concentration in the Prosperous Societies of the West," *Studies in Comparative International Development* 30 (Fall 1995): 3–23. For other sources of primary data, see *The New York Times*, 21 April 1995, pp. A1, A17; 14 August 1995, p. A9; 27 October 1995, p. D2; 19 January 2000, p. B5; *Washington Post National Weekly Edition*, 12–18 June 1995, pp. 6–7. Within Manhattan the difference in average family income between the richest and poorest income tracts rose from 9:1 in 1980 to 12.5:1 in 1990; see *The New York Times*, 20 March 1994, section 13, 6.

37. For a journalist's interesting account of this problem, see E. J. Dionne, *Why Americans Hate Politics* (New York: Simon & Schuster, 1991).

tion because of what he took to be the indissoluble connection between democratic politics and conventional forms of injustice. As such, Plato's critical response to the problems of his democracy belonged to what proved to be a growing tendency to isolate the life of the theorist from the life of politics. No doubt this tendency was fueled by growing faith in leadership from above as the primary means for solving social and political problems, perhaps culminating in the transfiguration of *logos* as an agent of political reform into the *logos* of religious founders as the source of salvation. There are, indeed, three important aspects of the Platonic political art that any democratic employment of it must abjure. I mention them below to clarify what is usefully Platonic (for me) today. What remains is still "Platonic," because I have not found Plato's three democratic deficits central to his philosophical and political project.

First, Plato's view of the preferred means by which his conception of justice would be understood and applied, his practical understanding of the translation of his formal theory of justice into practice, at first glance is clearly antidemocratic. This aspect of his conception appears in the elitist philosophical authority of the guardians, the censorship they impose on the educational life of the citizens, the noble lie they and their citizens must accept in order to motivate the transformation of society, and the image of political reform as painting on a blank canvas, made possible if all one had to deal with was citizens under the age of ten.

These suggestions of the means to realize justice involve particular practical judgments of Plato that do not express the core of his conception of justice; they do not diminish the radically critical potential of the Platonic political art. Recall what I said earlier about the principal character of Plato's problem of justice. That problem essentially derived from the definition of justice in terms of power as domination, a definition that was practically embodied in conventional ethics and politics. Now the conventions he knew best were also, importantly, democratic. Which is to say that the democratic constitution of Athens was the primary carrier of the conception of justice as domination. If Plato was to establish critical distance from the conventional ethics and politics of this time, he must inevitably produce criticisms of democracy. But these criticisms, I have argued, were secondary, rather than primary, features of his conception of justice.

Moreover, Plato's harshest criticisms of democratic political life in this dialogue and others do not focus on ordinary citizens. Rather, they focus on the intellectual and political impostors who presume to know what is best for, who presume to know how to educate and beneficially lead, the ordinary democratic citizens of Athens. Finally, Platonic justice was essentially a *logos* of justice, and Plato believed that there was necessarily a gap between such a *logos* and the actualities of everyday life. Because of that gap, he could not advocate the direct imposition of his conception of justice and the social life of a political community or the psychic life of an individual citizen. Plato's radical political criticism and vaunting ethical idealism immunize his theory from the disease of statism. There would always have to be adjustment to contingency and practical necessity, and efforts at beneficial change would have to embrace persuasion and abjure violence as the method of transformation. Still, Plato did not view democratic deliberation as the preferred means for ending injustice or achieving justice.

The *second* feature of the Platonic political art that detracts from its capacity as a critical aid for democrats today is his tendency to promote belief in the unitary character of political knowledge. Here, all I can say is that fragmentation of political knowledge, for Plato, tended to subordinate it to the power of convention. In Plato's time, political understanding that would promote the well-being of the whole itself had to be whole, for the unitary character of political knowledge was the condition for its capacity to be fully critical. In other contexts, in our societies, political knowledge (if one can call it that) must emanate from a multiplicity of sources (philosophical and poetic, elites and plebs), from various cultures, races, classes, and genders, and to that extent must be pluralistic and democratic to be fully critical. For Plato, these conditions did not foster anticonventional and just political criticism.

The *third* and final worrisome feature of the Platonic political art is his general predilection for political change that begins from the top. With respect to this faith in top-down leadership, all I can say is that it was a sickness that would only spread in the classical world and beyond, and that one should at least compliment Plato for his skepticism that any one person or group of individuals likely to try in his time would be likely to succeed. Moreover, one should recall that in the *kallipolis* of the *Republic* the distribution of wealth would not be sorely unequal—indeed, much less unequal than it was in his time—and his authoritarian rulers would depend for their livelihood on the voluntary, public, and equitable financial contributions of those they ruled— as opposed to the private bribery cloaked as political giving that characterizes the funding of "democratic" elections in the United States today.

These qualifications of the antidemocratic cast of Plato's political thought and the Platonic political art inform my judgment that these aspects of Plato's thought are secondary, not primary. But the main factor for me that validates the utility of Platonic conceptions of the political art involves the different character of contemporary political conventions of our time relative to his. The conventions of injustice in our time are not soldered by democratic institutions. Although rhetorical support for democratic principles and practices still inhabits the center of political discourse, the increasing disparity of income between rich and poor, the growing role of large concentrations of moneyed power in the operation of the economic and social life of American democracy, and the major role played by big donors in the election of public officials actually dissociate advocacy of democracy from endorsement of the conventional social ethics and political power of the day.

If Plato's major concern was as I have argued it to be, namely, the conciliation of virtue and the political art, ethics and power, critical *logos* and practical *ergon*, that concern today is more likely to be reflected in arguments for more rather than less democracy, as long as that is accompanied by more rather than less critical discussion of what virtue might mean in the conduct of the daily lives of citizens. As a result, politics at the beginning of the twenty-first century calls for renewed efforts to accommodate democracy and virtue. This accommodation has not been systematically theorized and only episodically realized in the effective operation of political power. In Athens, it was often occluded by the entanglement of democracy with empire; today, the dominant external forces shaping the postmodern *demos* fragment and pluralize possibilities for their accommodation. Moreover, those who publicly argue for their accommodation tend to be on the reactionary right rather than the democratic left. But this is not the way it has to be, so I argue. In what follows, I offer examples of a critical perspective that might (almost oxymoronically) be called democratically Platonic, a perspective that enlists four features of Plato's conception of the political art as a constituent of justice and democratically relates them to contemporary issues about public education. These issues crystallize the current problems facing concrete efforts to coordinate deliberation and democracy as forms of *logos* and *ergon* in the United States (at least).[38]

38. For compatible formulations of the interconnections among the ideas of critical reason, virtue, democracy, and education, see the work of John Dewey, for instance, *Democracy and Education; The Public and Its Problems; Human Nature and Conduct.* However, Dewey was overly sanguine about "experimentation" and "the public" as sufficient means for achieving harmonious complementarity among the intellectual, ethical, and political dimensions of the individual and society.

3. EDUCATING DEMOCRACY

My argument has been that Plato's theoretical innovations were understandable and useful, given his political and intellectual context, even if they had effectively and undesirably antidemocratic consequences. In our current political context, a redeployed Platonic political art yields politically different—and potentially democratic—results. It can do because (1) the basic features of the Platonic political art—including its indirect link between theory and practice and its dynamic interconnection of ethical issues and political action—evoke crucial components of a conception of democratic virtue, and (2) such a conception is not now occluded by the conflation of democracy with conventional and dominant structures of power (as it was for Plato). In this context, the task of educating democracy, or promoting democratic virtue, is a task for theoretical and political practice. Indeed, democracy is a system of a power, more than an ethical disposition, and as such constantly requires education if it is to most nearly approximate justice. And education needs democracy in order to prevent the successes of education from ossifying into hierarchies that impede equal educational opportunity.

The very idea of "educating democracy," however, requires some elaboration. For I have identified "democracy" as something that (playing off John Dunn's formulation) we do not have but should not cease to want. But if democracy has that character, why is it not a mere phantom, a rhetorical consolation or idyllic fancy amid the insistent (Madisonian) republicanism of American society? How does one make democracy and education compatible, when the former dispenses with a priori privileging of persons or offices, and the latter depends on the justification of distinctions and differentiations? The tasks of educating democracy and identifying what that education entails face formidable challenges.

Any claim to the democratic possibilities of a redeployment of the Platonic political art cannot rest with brief broadsides against the theoretical and political adequacy of major intellectual efforts. It must justify itself by portraying some possibilities of its practical use. The best and simplest practical arena for such a portrait is that of education—for three reasons.

First, Plato's principal, most concerted, and (one might say) political effort during his life was the establishment of the Academy, and Rousseau was not wrong *either* to interpret Plato's *Republic* as "the finest treatise on [pub-

lic] education ever written" or to call (a functioning, perfectly just) democracy a political order for "gods," not "men."[39] So, if we conceptualize a practical corollary or *ergon* to the redeployed *logos* of the Platonic political art, the
contemporary arena of education, particularly public and higher education
that would foster both justice and democracy, naturally appears as a suitable
testing ground.

Second, issues in public education currently attract both politically practical and theoretical attention in the United States.[40] Great anxiety about morality in the political order has been a significant source of renewed academic
and political attention to education and its capacity to cultivate "virtue."[41]
Moreover, the issues involved have economic and legal, as well as ethical, dimensions—as did Plato's conception of education.

Third, one of the greatest anxieties for any democrat about deploying
some aspect of Plato in contemporary argument is the seemingly authoritarian and censorial aspect of his political discourse—its antipathy to any complementarity of the art of deliberation and democracy. It seems difficult to
square such features with a democratic conception of education, and this obstacle must be squarely addressed. How can Platonic questions yield democratic answers in the arena of public education?

Four features of the Platonic political art could be usefully applied to the
understanding and democratic improvement of contemporary education, and
their effects, in turn, could improve and educate democracy: its character as
(1) theoretical, (2) political, (3) realized by a harmonious complementarity of
virtues and skills that can never be fully achieved, and (4) preserved by educational understanding. For Plato, these features of the political art discursively "solved" the problems of *pleonexia* and *stasis* that plagued the souls of
citizens and their political communities. They were to educate power: From
being the mark of domination, it should become the condition of healthy ethical life. In so doing, they would nonreductively link ethics to power and

39. Jean-Jacques Rousseau, *Emile* (London: J. M. Dent, 1780–1938), 8, and *The Social Contract*, Bk. III, chap. iv.

40. Aspects of these surely have implications for other Western and non-Western countries,
but I am unable to state confidently what they are.

41. This should not be surprising. As we have seen, typical liberal conceptions of justice
either bracket considerations of the ethical and political significance of virtue or presuppose
them as part of the liberal theoretical framework. For examples, see Steven Macedo, *Liberal Virtues,* as a centrist-liberal virtue formulation, and Rogers M. Smith, *Civic Ideals,* as a left-liberal
virtue formulation.

power to ethics. Today, they could usefully inform our perspective on educational issues.[42]

How a rehistoricized Platonic political art can contribute to this task becomes clear by reviewing prevailing accounts of how to improve education in American society. Because institutionally sanctioned education should imbue students with necessary and desirable skills for work and citizenship, educational issues raise questions about ethical values and the exercise of power, namely, (1) the ethical or moral content of K–12 and higher education; (2) the economic, social, and intellectual skills educators ought to promote, as well as the measures for evaluating their success (the "standards" and "test" issues); and (3) the relative equality of the funding of K–12 and higher public education—both among public schools and between public and private/independent or religious/parochial schools. Education has become America's "civil rights" issue today. (Indeed, the theoretical conflict between conservative and democratic liberals [for example, between Milton Friedman or William F. Buckley and John Dewey or Ralph Nader] or between liberals and communitarians now takes place at the practical level, and the issue of convergence is education. It is a natural focus for communitarians and conservatives, because there is no great leap from emphasizing greater attention to virtue to focusing on the state of education. But because liberals now presuppose the importance of theorizing the conditions for sustaining liberalism, it preoccupies them, too.)

These three issues ought to be treated together as dynamic elements of the interrelation of ethics and power in the political realm and considered in terms of democratic virtue. Yet the ethical and political dimensions of these issues are usually treated in isolation from one another. When dealing with education, liberal, conservative, and communitarian political theorists instead tend to avoid dealing with issues of power and inequality in order to focus on matters of "rights" and "virtue" as ethical issues, typically as they concern the role of religion in public education and the role of public education in promoting the many religious and cultural traditions in which American citizens are raised. To justify this claim, let us look directly at exemplary liberal treatments of contemporary education.

Liberals once shied away from talking about education in public virtue as

42. Such contributions, however, do not require the study of Plato or my interpretation of the Platonic political art; if they did, I would be presenting a neo-Platonist argument, and I believe in neither "Platonism" nor its subsequent variations.

essential for (liberal) democracy. Now, however, that amounts to the order of the day.[43] Recognizing that cultural conditions, and educational conditions in particular, must foster the political and intellectual habits that liberal democracy requires, these theorists have attended to the economic and social conditions that would foster intellectual autonomy, civic participation, and nonchauvinistic patriotism. Yet liberals rarely discuss how noneducational institutions and ideologies (such as the behemoth of global capitalism) constitute the boundaries of "education" or how they generate major obstacles to the realization of the liberal ideals and programs. Recently, liberals have defended affirmative action as an asset to social harmony, and one that does not significantly discriminate against more "meritorious" candidates. However, they do not deny that "merit" is being partially compromised, on behalf of the common good. Because they do not challenge the ideological underpinnings of the conservative attack on affirmative action, because they do not question how basic categories of ethical evaluation are themselves thoroughly political, their criticisms may be rhetorically reassuring but practically ineffective.[44]

Many conservative, as opposed to democratic, liberals have focused on "tests," "standards," and the indisputable standard of "merit" as ethically neutral, "equal opportunity" baselines of excellence that all citizens ought to be judged against. However, standardized multiple-choice tests, as well as quantitatively measured standards of achievement, are deeply political. By "political," I do not mean that such tests are necessarily or intentionally biased or reflect a politicized process but rather that they systematically favor certain intellectual skills over other ones. The advancement of students via tests naturally stratifies them, and the political cost of *this* kind of bias is rarely discussed. More often than not, high-stakes tests apportion merit without our fully comprehending or justifying the relative merit of the tests being used. In

43. For good examples of liberal treatments of democratic or civic virtue as it pertains to education, see Amy Gutmann, *Democratic Education;* Eamon Callan, *Creating Citizens;* Alan Ryan, *Liberal Anxieties and Liberal Education;* and Stephen Macedo, *Diversity and Distrust: Civic Education in a Multicultural Democracy.* For a more thoroughly democratic (but still fundamentally liberal) educational agenda, see Benjamin Barber, *An Aristocracy of Everyone: The Politics of Education and the Future of America.*

44. For these new liberal arguments for affirmative action, see William G. Bowen and Derek Bok, *The Shape of the River: Long-Term Consequences of Considering Race in College and University Admissions.* Also see the recent spate of articles by Nathan Glazer, in which he justifies his change from opponent to advocate of affirmative action. The initial, major articulation of this view appeared in *The New Republic* 60, no. 2, 6 April 1998, pp. 18–23.

effect, they deplete democracy even as they would equalize opportunities for various kinds of education.[45] (Indeed, liberals should be more worried than they are, for the discriminatory impact and flawed character of most testing schemes in use have been validated by a recently completed, Congressionally mandated study.[46])

Conservatives and communitarians do not reject the virtues now highlighted by liberals as essential for education and citizenship. However, as in the case of the conservative public intellectual William J. Bennett, conservatives tend to emphasize the inculcation of moral virtue from the private, rather than the public, realm—from family, religion, and business, rather than from officially public institutions.[47] The political position of communitarians is more ambiguous than that of either liberals or conservatives, because they (1) do not radically (or predictably) criticize the protection of individual rights provided by liberal institutions; (2) emphasize a collective dimension to the inculcation of moral virtue for a political community that liberals typically shy away from; and (3) criticize the power of capitalist-market forces from a "moral" point of view.[48] Thus, communitarians, often buttressed by a version of neo-Aristotelianism, account for the ethical dimensions of politics, but they invariably promote a critical discourse that fails to fully recognize

45. The antidemocratic effects of equal opportunity, measured educationally in terms of quantifiable test scores, have been noted (albeit ignored) for years. See Michael Young, *The Rise of the Meritocracy, 1870–2033;* John H. Schaar, "Equality of Opportunity, and Beyond," in *Equality,* ed. J. Roland Pennock and John W. Chapman, 228–49. For some recent discussions of the problematic effects of testing and standardized measures of educational success on democracy, see Nicholas Lemann, *The Big Test: The Secret History of the American Meritocracy;* and the more theoretically oriented discussion, "Do We Need Educational Standards?" in the New Democracy Forum of *Boston Review,* which is led by Deborah Meier's piece, "Educating a Democracy," 24, no. 6 (December 1999–January 2000): 4–20. An earlier but still useful discussion of the "standardized testing" issue appears in Diane Ravich, ed., *Debating the Future of American Education: Do We Need National Standards and Assessments?* and Diane Ravitch, *National Standards in American Education: A Citizen's Guide.* Any recognition of the potentially antidemocratic effects of accepting socially dominant conceptions of merit as ethically and politically neutral remains notably unnoticed in the works by Gutmann and Ryan cited above.

46. See Jay P. Heubert and Robert M. Hauser, eds., *High Stakes: Testing for Tracking, Promotion, and Graduation.*

47. William J. Bennett, *The Devaluing of America: The Fight for Our Culture and Our Children.*

48. See Michael J. Sandel, *Liberalism and the Limits of Justice,* and idem, *Democracy's Discontent: America in Search of a Public Philosophy,* along with the book essays on the latter, *Debating Democracy's Discontent,* ed. Anita L. Allen and Milton C. Regan Jr.; William A. Galston, *Liberal Purposes: Goods, Virtues, and Diversity in the Liberal State;* and Amitai Etzioni, *The Spirit of Community: Rights, Responsibilities, and the Communitarian Agenda.*

the effects of conflicts stemming from the powerful and hubristic tendencies of racism, nationalism, capitalism, technological developments, or electoral government. Consequently, they at best seek to cage these conflicts rather than actively resolve them.[49] Instead, they focus on more media-friendly, readily comprehensible problems, such as the increasingly explicit treatment of and engagement with sexuality, the self-destructive and socially murderous effects of drug addiction, and the decline of the two-parent family as principal sources of decay in primary and secondary education in America.

Significant differences separate liberals, conservatives, and communitarians, but from our perspective their similarities stand out. None of them makes central to their own thinking economic questions about the amount of money devoted to education, compared with other sectors of state and federal budgets. More crucially, none addresses the corrosive effects of the positive social value associated with economic consumption or capital accumulation *as factors that constitutively affect* the character and merits of their theoretical conceptions. "Civic republicanism" is one idea; digitalized global capitalism is another. In other words, ethical questions are treated as if they are not crucially shaped by political considerations, whereas power issues do not appear to have basically ethical features. Liberals, conservatives, and communitarians downplay the role of anti-intellectual forces fostered by the cultural image of American success as the product of individualistic, self-made grit and determination or the role of money as the primary, common coin of America's ethical diversity.[50]

---

49. For a more extensive discussion of the critical limits of neo-Aristotelianism, see my "Contemporary Aristotelianism." For recent Straussian incarnations of neo-Aristotelianism—many of which make important points—see Thomas L. Pangle, *The Ennobling of Democracy: The Challenge of the Postmodern Age;* and Harvey Mansfield Jr., *America's Constitutional Soul.* For an attempt by a neo-Straussian to construct an Aristotelian conception of the political art for contemporary societies out of the resources of ancient Greek thought, see Arlene W. Saxonhouse, *Fear of Diversity: The Birth of Political Science in Ancient Greek Thought,* esp. 232. But note her recent, more nuanced interpretation of democracy in ancient Greek thought: *Athenian Democracy: Modern Mythmakers and Ancient Theorists.* Perhaps the latest installment of the Straussian, neo-Aristotelian attempt to invest liberal political discourse with a particular, relatively conservative discourse of virtue is that of Peter Berkowitz, *Virtue and the Making of Modern Liberalism.* For a neo-Aristotelian and quasi-Straussian critique of "deliberative democracy," see Miriam Galston, "Taking Aristotle Seriously: Republican-Oriented Legal Theory and the Moral Foundation of Deliberative Democracy."

50. See Richard Hofstadter, *Anti-Intellectualism in American Life.* For a recent account of the cultural and intellectual aspects of the political history of the United States, see Robert H. Wiebe, *Self-Rule: A Cultural History of American Democracy.*

The failure to see the full ethical and power-political dimensions of education appears in many current discussions about educational vouchers as a method of school financing. In its most extreme and widely discussed form, this policy allows taxpayers to spend their tax dollars for K–12 education on either public or private schools.[51] Although this policy would have devastating effects on the public realm and has been criticized vigorously on these grounds by many Democrats, it does have the "practical" virtue of linking the ethics of excellence and individualism with the powerful allure of market capitalism. It raises the flag of "standards" to promote "excellence" and to reward the meritorious performance of "individuals" without spending more public monies to realize these goals.[52] In this respect, advocates of vouchers can legitimately employ the otherwise liberal rhetorical banner of "equal educational opportunity."

At the college level, education is less a public burden, and so "the public" is less politically involved—even though college education is now regarded as a prerequisite for attaining secure membership in the great, amorphous American middle class. Here, "conservatism" assumes negative forms—such as the opposition to affirmative action (for instance, at the University of California) and remediation (for example, at the City University of New York)— on behalf of "merit," and positive forms—such as belief in mass-produced multiple-choice tests as objective guides to the intellectual merit of applicants (for instance, at both the University of California and the City University of New York), as well as the belief in a seemingly "given" (or unjustified) set of shared values that resist the decentering effects of multicultural education.

The rhetoric of "standards" has informed the harsh, recent criticisms of

51. This policy was initially promoted by Milton Friedman. See his *Capitalism and Freedom*, 93 and generally 85–107.

52. Remarkably, advocates of these policies promote them by claiming that they will improve education for the economically disadvantaged—and the policies often receive support from parental members of these groups who want almost anything that promises quick improvements in the education their children currently receive in public schools—when some of the primary rationales for these policies involve the destruction of teachers' unions, one of the last and strongest bastions of the union movement in the United States. See the more recent work of Caroline Hoxby. On the benefits of school vouchers for students from disadvantaged backgrounds, see her piece, "Are Efficiency and Equity in School Finance Substitutes or Complements?"; on the need to dismantle teachers' unions in order to improve education, see her piece, "How Teachers' Unions Affect Education Production." Her work has received favorable notice from both conservative and traditionally liberal weeklies. See *The Economist (US)* 341, no. 7988, 19 October 1996, pp. 33–34, and John Cassidy, "Annals of Education: Schools Are Her Business," *The New Yorker*, 18 and 25 October 1999, pp. 144–61.

the City University of New York voiced by New York City Mayor Rudolph Giuliani, Herman Badillo, chair of the Board of Trustees of the City University of New York, and Benno Schmidt, ex-president of Yale University, director of the for-profit schools organization owned by Chris Whittle, and vice-chair of the Board of Trustees of CUNY. Here the process of making educational policy has been not only "political" in the previous sense but has also been politicized.[53] More generally, recent accounts by senior professors of the troubles besetting American academia have associated its putative decline with both cultural nihilism and "democratization." They claim that Truth and Beauty, along with other eternal verities of Western civilization, are under attack and that the more democratic demographics of university faculty express an elective affinity with criticism of revered texts that harbors no respect for either "the classics" or truth (not to mention Truth).[54]

53. Their rabid criticism over the past three years has been chronicled in *The New York Times* by Karen W. Arenson. Benno Schmidt was hired by Mayor Giuliani to compile a report on the City University of New York, which (not surprisingly) validated the views of Mr. Badillo and himself—and led to his appointment as the (unpaid) Vice-Chair of CUNY's Board of Trustees. His report, *CUNY—An Institution Adrift*, has been roundly and publicly criticized by educational researchers, such as David Lavin, dozens of CUNY faculty from all disciplines, and the Association of the Bar of the City of New York, in an important study, titled "Remediation and Access: To Educate the 'Children of the Whole People'" (October 1999). Popular misconceptions about CUNY have also been fostered by the highbrow, imbalanced account of the City College of New York (and CUNY more generally) by James Traub, *City on a Hill: Testing the American Dream at City College*, and the lowbrow journalism of the Manhattan Institute writer Heather MacDonald.

54. This argument was most widely circulated over ten years ago by the Straussian Allan Bloom (whose initial claim to scholarly fame involved translating Plato's *Republic* and endorsing Leo Strauss's view of that dialogue as a relatively apolitical work, except insofar as it argued against political idealism). See Allan Bloom, *The Closing of the American Mind*. Two recent salvoes by retiring academics also express these viewpoints: Gertrude Himmelfarb, *One Nation, Two Cultures*, and Alvin Kernan, *In Plato's Cave*. From the latter (299–300): "[T]he democratic tendencies in higher education, while praiseworthy in many ways, have gone too far . . . [when] we begin to say something like 'words can have *no* meaning' . . . 'all great books of the past were written by men to put women down.'" Thus, there is a great need "for a more effective educational system." The great antagonist of Truth is, of course, Richard Rorty, who also finds roots of this evil in Plato and Platonism (oddly and glibly defined by him in his most recent book— noted below—as "the idea that great works of literature all, in the end, say the same thing"). He, like the conservatives, is very negative about the present university and pessimistic about its future. However, he likes to define his politics as social democratic. Nonetheless, his critique of Truth has not clearly cut any mustard on behalf of truth—at least insofar as it affects (his) political analyses of American society and culture. For example, see his analysis of the best in American cultural history as a source of political rhetoric for the left, namely, *Achieving Our Country*,

The liberal, conservative, and communitarian conceptualizations of a political morality for education, however, miss the effects of conventional forms of power on the composition of social moralities and their educational equivalents. For no school's brick walls or university's ivory towers can create safe havens today for the life of the mind or spirit. In the 1960s, the free speech movement and the antiwar movement argued that universities had to recognize their political character. At the beginning of the twenty-first century, the political character of the university is no longer in doubt. Because that character is less immediately supportive of the cultural status quo than it was in the 1960s, conservative politicians have sought to defund and more strictly regulate public universities—which educate 80 percent of American college students—in order to reduce the power of faculty to determine what education consists of!

Democratic opposition to conservative proposals, however, is notably fragmented in both theory and practice. With regard to K–12 public schooling, progressives of various stripes call for increased public spending on education. But in the progressive version of democratic realism, there is a peculiar silence about the relevance of ethical motivations to political programs—involving education or anything else.[55] On the other hand, major democratic liberals long for cultural monism, even as they do not (as conservatives are more wont to do) ground ethical education in religious dogma.[56] Other liberals or progressives transpose this sense of unity to the globe in order to incorporate the ethics of different cultures; they rename it "humanity." But such justifications of multiculturalism at the level of human rights and cosmopolitanism, although certainly worthwhile, are often ethically and politically vague or implicitly presumptuous about what non-Westerners want and need.[57]

---

135 for the quotation, 135–38 for his dumping on Plato, 125–38 for his discussion of intellectual life in the academy, and 3–124 for his attempt to revive the left with the cultural ethics of Walt Whitman and John Dewey.

55. See the otherwise illuminating work of Ian Shapiro, in *Democracy's Place,* dedicated to a previous, theoretical advocate of democratic realism, and *Democratic Justice.*

56. For a traditional American liberal's treatment of the necessary unity that should structure educational discourse, see Arthur M. Schlesinger Jr., *The Disuniting of America.* On the essentially religious character of morality, and the importance of allowing greater space for it in American education, see Michael Perry, *Religion in Politics: Constitutional and Moral Perspectives.*

57. For an insightful example of the former, see Jeremy Waldron, "Multiculturalism and Melange," in the excellent collection of essays edited by Robert K. Fullinwider, *Public Education in a Multicultural Society.* For a good example of the latter, see Martha C. Nussbaum, *Cultivating Humanity: A Classical Defense of Reform in Liberal Education.*

As for poststructuralists, the norm for them is to criticize the hegemony of any and all educational disciplines. To be sure, "education" often involves socialization and is not always synonymous with the most dialectical forms of learning; moreover, poststructuralist discourse often has the virtue of exposing the underside of all educational programs as unholy alliances of ethics and power that advance the agenda of white, male, global corporatism. But *it* lacks a complementary ethical or political vision for education at the postsecondary level and is woefully irrelevant to the task of K–12 public education, where the challenge is to ingrain discipline without punishment.[58] As for neo-Marxists, they may attend to the powerful effects of corporate and technologically driven activities on world affairs in general and education in particular, but they too often pay insufficient attention either to the importance of individual motivation or to what can maintain the simultaneously critical and constructive role of educational institutions in society.[59] These various wings of the democratic left fly in contradictory directions.

The limitations of these perspectives are enforced by the absorption of Plato into Platonism and the blacklisting of Plato as a resource for democrats. In this age of postliberal democracy, the major critical political discourses either do not speak to the problems that beset us or identify them primarily in negative terms. They do not adequately address how the exercise of power and its relations to social ethics potentially harm the fabric of political community and the possibilities of justice. None offers the means by which we might educate power for the benefit of the people as a whole. And yet, amid the overtly antidemocratic tendencies of global capitalism and mass culture, universities can become intellectual havens for educating democracy.

In this light, Plato's aspiration for a rational and virtuous political art can be used to nourish an intellectual disposition that would enhance rather than harm democracy, by enriching and perfecting it, rather than limiting it. The Platonic political art does not automatically generate a particular political ideology, policy, strategy, or tactic. But it can, I think, lead us to ask the right questions—which then can point us in directions that might lead to the best answers.

---

58. At the same time, I highly recommend the poststructuralist criticism of the contemporary university as presented by Bill Readings, *The University in Ruins.*

59. For a new book that reflects this perspective, see Stanley Aronowitz, *The Knowledge Factory.*

Such sketchy criticisms may well seem uncharitable, glib, and dismissive, especially because I am not in a position here to provide a novel political theory or set of practical policies. Obviously, I have no silver bullet. But then again, neither did Plato. Indeed, one of the chief lessons to be learned, I should think, from Plato's dialogues on the political art (and especially the *Republic*) involves the necessity of theoretical and political idealism, their practical insufficiency, and the absence of any direct and systematic compatibility of these idealisms to a successful and ethical political program. There have been virtually no "Platonic" political movements in history—which speaks volumes about the virtues and limitations of Plato's political legacy. Hence, my aim is simply to use my critical perspective to attend to the dynamic interplay of ethics and power in educational issues in order to enhance democratic virtue. This should expose the nature of the opposition to democratic improvement in the conduct of education—that is, education that would facilitate a more democratic and just distribution of power in society (and societies) while promoting intellectual development for all. The current makeup of critical discourse in political theory—which pits ethically oriented liberals, conservatives, and communitarians on one side and power-oriented democratic realists, poststructuralists, and neo-Marxists on the other—forecloses this perspective, a perspective inspired by having redeployed the Platonic political art in today's postliberal democracies.

That said, I cannot escape making at least a meager effort to connect theory to practice. Thus, if one *were* to venture some practical suggestions from this perspective, they would utilize the four features of the Platonic political art mentioned above.

1. With regard to the importance of enhancing educational understanding, a democratic Platonist would suggest that we spend more on the enlightenment of the souls of citizens than we do on their incarceration and that we do so through the strengthening of public education rather than its privatization and commercialization.

2. With regard to the complementarity of virtues and skills, a democratic Platonist would loosen the ties Plato drew between these two, enhancing public participation in order to promote a wider commonality of political virtues amid the differentiating skills and ethics called for by the economic and bureaucratic divisions of labor. In terms of education, this would mean (1) redoubling efforts to equalize and enhance educational opportunities, and (2) supporting efforts by university faculty and administrators to maintain or

increase institutional autonomy in the face of increasing efforts to muffle the university as a source of critical discourse about the arts, literature, society, nature, and the professions. However, relative to the liberal separation of virtues and skills, a democratic Platonist would recognize that the prominence of the ethics/power nexus in social discourse and practices requires a greater complementarity of virtues and skills.

3. With regard to the political field of operation for a redeployed version of the Platonic political art, a democratic Platonist would initially note its supposedly distinct "ethical" and "practical-power" dimensions. For example, she would suggest that the teaching of religious ethics should not be excluded from public education, as long as its inclusion does not drain resources from public education or inhibit any children from freely developing their own ability to understand and act on what is morally good for themselves and their political community. This suggests a blurring of the line between the secular and religious when it comes to moral education in the public schools. But it also would not allow religiously devout parents to have the right to censor public school curricula.[60] In terms of educational issues that pertain to national and international power, a democratically Platonic perspective would insist that the supposed imperatives of economic growth in a competitive global economy not be taken as given—goals to be met by technical management of the interest of capitalists, rather than workers—but as political interpretations of the meaning of justice, malleable goals that need to be harnessed for the well-being of individuals, societies, and environmental ecologies.

4. Finally, with regard to the theoretical character of the political art, a democratic Platonist would have little tolerance for the "politically correct," at least as interpreted by Catherine MacKinnon in *Only Words*, not because she rejects the ideals of equality or lacks sensitivity to the problems of injustice that political correctness identifies, but because of the danger inherent in formally institutionalizing at the levels of public law or elementary, secondary, and higher education the discursive means by which political ideals might be realized.[61] Along with Socrates, Plato radically problematized the

---

60. Here, I am endorsing the Appeals Court view in *Mozert v. Hawkins*, 827 F. 2nd 1058, and disagreeing with the Kansas Supreme Court's view of the teaching of evolution in Kansas's secondary schools. See *The New York Times*, 10 August 1999, p. A1.

61. Catherine MacKinnon, *Only Words*.

very notion of belief. To substitute any conventional practice of justice or the interest of any natural human group as a sufficient embodiment of justice tends to reduce the meaning of justice to that of convention and the meaning of power to that of domination, thus eliminating the possibility of justice as the power of ethics in community. And because democracy requires continuous criticism in order to limit its own Michelsian tendencies to generate oligarchically ruled hierarchies, this problematization is also crucially democratic.

In discussing the Platonic political art in postliberal democracies, we have come upon, then, a remarkable irony. For Plato established his conception of the political art in opposition to the ethical and political conventions of his day, which were importantly democratic. To this extent, Plato was regarded as a foe of democracy. In contemporary postliberal democracy, where political equality is marginal to, rather than constitutive of, the conduct of public life, where power is not in the hands of the many but rather jealously guarded by the few, where democratic power, in short, does not define the conventions of justice, the critical discourse of the Platonic political art can become a democratic asset.

Despite the fact that his discussion of the incompatibility of democracy and virtue has traditionally done more to suggest their incompatibility than the work of any other political theorist, Plato is a most useful dialogic partner for critical democrats today. Indeed, it is the argument of this book that this tradition is mistaken. Plato's political theory and the Platonic political art are certainly critical of democracy (and to that extent antidemocratic). But I have argued that the major thrust behind this theoretical stance was an interest in the critical accommodation of virtue and the political art, the belief that in the necessary effort to critically understand and practically promote justice one cannot automatically assume that any political order, including a democratic one, actually provides it. In my view, no democrat should be averse to such a concern. Plato's usefulness stems from the scope of his critical reflections and the extent of his ethical aspirations for the conduct of political life. His conception of the political art may be particularly useful for those who believe in democracy, not only because it effectively limits political power but also because it points to the most promising forces for its ethical improvement. Were Plato able to read about this use of his political art, the irony would not be lost on this most famous student of Socrates.

BIBLIOGRAPHY

With a few exceptions, this bibliography includes only references cited in the body of the book. It represents the building blocks of the narrative and argument; it does not approximate the range of sources consulted. Also not included are classic texts in political theory or philosophy written before 1900.

Adam, James, ed. *The Republic of Plato,* vol. 1. 2d ed. Cambridge: Cambridge University Press, 1969.

Adkins, A. W. H. *Merit and Responsibility: A Study in Moral Values.* Chicago: University of Chicago Press, 1960.

———. "*Arete, Techne,* Democracy, and Sophists: *Protagoras* 316b–328d." *Journal of Hellenic Studies* 93 (1973): 3–12.

Allen, Anita L., and Milton C. Regan Jr., eds. *Debating Democracy's Discontent.* New York: Oxford University Press, 1998.

Allen, James. "Failure and Expertise in the Ancient Conception of Art." In Tamara Horowitz and Allen I. Janis, eds., *Scientific Failure,* 81–108. Lanham, Md.: Rowman & Littlefield, 1994.

Allen, R. E. *Plato's "Euthyphro" and the Earlier Theory of Forms.* New York: Humanities Press, 1980.

———. *Socrates and Legal Obligation.* Minneapolis: University of Minnesota Press, 1980.

Anderson, Warren D. *Ethos and Education in Greek Music: The Evidence of Poetry and Philosophy.* Cambridge, Mass.: Harvard University Press, 1966.

———. *Music and Musicians in Ancient Greece.* Ithaca: Cornell University Press, 1994.

Andersson, Torseten J. *Polis and Psyche—A Motif in Plato's* Republic. Stockholm, 1971.

Andrew, Edward. "Equality of Opportunity as the Noble Lie." *History of Political Thought* 10 (1989): 577–95.

Annas, Julia. "Plato's *Republic* and Feminism." *Philosophy* 51 (1976): 307–321.

———. "Plato and Common Morality." *Classical Quarterly* n.s. 28 (1978): 437–51.

———. *An Introduction to Plato's* Republic. Oxford: Oxford University Press, 1981.

———. *Platonic Ethics: Old and New.* Ithaca: Cornell University Press, 1999.
———. "Plato the Sceptic." In James Klagge and Nicholas Smith, eds., *Methods of Interpreting Plato and His Dialogues: Oxford Studies in Ancient Philosophy—Supplementary Volume, 1992,* 43–72. Oxford: Clarendon Press, 1992.
Arendt, Hannah. *The Human Condition.* Chicago: University of Chicago Press, 1958.
———. *Between Past and Future: Eight Exercises in Political Thought.* New York: Viking Press, 1968.
Armstrong, C. B. "Plato's Academy." *Proceedings of the Leeds Philosophical and Literary Society* 7 (1953).
Aronowitz, Stanley. *The Knowledge Factory.* Boston: Beacon Press, 2000.
Asmis, Elisabeth. "Plato on Poetic Creativity." In Kraut, ed., *The Cambridge Companion to Plato,* 338–64.
Austin, J. L. *How to Do Things with Words.* 2d ed. Cambridge, Mass.: Harvard University Press, 1975.
Austin, M. M., and P. Vidal-Naquet. *Economic and Social Analysis of Ancient Greece: An Introduction.* Berkeley and Los Angeles: University of California Press, 1977.
Ball, Terence. "Plato and Aristotle: The Unity Versus the Autonomy of Theory and Practice." In Ball, ed., *Political Theory and Praxis,* 57–69.
Ball, Terence, ed. *Political Theory and Praxis: New Perspectives.* Minneapolis: University of Minnesota Press, 1977.
Bambrough, Renford. "Plato's Political Analogies" (1956). In Vlastos, ed., *Plato: A Collection of Critical Essays, vol. 2: Ethics, Politics, and Philosophy of Art and Religion,* 187–205.
———. "Plato's Modern Friends and Enemies." *Philosophy* 140 (1962): 97–113.
Bambrough, Renford, ed. *Plato, Popper, and Politics.* Cambridge: Heffer, 1967.
Barber, Benjamin. *An Aristocracy of Everyone: The Politics of Education and the Future of America.* New York: Ballantine, 1992.
Barker, Ernest. *Greek Political Theory: Plato and His Predecessors.* London: Methuen, 1960 (1918).
Beck, Ulrich. *The Reinvention of Politics: Rethinking Modernity in the Global Social Order.* Trans. Alan Ritter. Oxford: Polity Press, 1997.
Bennett, William J. *The Devaluing of America: The Fight for Our Culture and Our Children.* New York: Simon & Schuster, 1992.
Benson, Hugh, ed. *Essays in the Philosophy of Socrates.* Oxford: Oxford University Press, 1992.
Berger, Harry, Jr. "Levels of Discourse in Plato's Dialogues." In Anthony J. Cascardi, ed., *Literature and the Question of Philosophy,* 77–100. Baltimore: Johns Hopkins University Press, 1986.
Berkowitz, Peter. *Virtue and the Making of Modern Liberalism.* Princeton: Princeton University Press, 1999.
Berlin, Isaiah. "Two Concepts of Liberty" (1958). In Isaiah Berlin, *Four Essays on Liberty,* 118–72. London: Oxford University Press, 1969.
———. "Political Judgment." *New York Review of Books,* 3 October 1996, p. 26–30. Reprinted in Isaiah Berlin, *The Sense of Reality: Studies in Ideas and Their*

History, ed. Henry Hardy, 40–54. New York: Farrar, Straus and Giroux, 1996.

Bessette, Joseph M. *The Mild Voice of Reason: Deliberative Democracy and American National Government.* Chicago: University of Chicago Press, 1994.

Bloom, Allan. "Interpretive Essay." In *Plato's Republic,* trans. Allan Bloom. New York: Basic Books, 1968.

———. *The Closing of the American Mind.* New York: Basic Books, 1987.

Bluck, R. S. *Plato's Life and Thought.* London: Routledge & Kegan Paul, 1949.

Bluck, R. S., ed. *Plato's* Meno. Cambridge: Cambridge University Press, 1961.

Bobonich, Christopher. "Persuasion, Compulsion, and Freedom in Plato's *Laws.*" *Classical Quarterly* 41 (1991): 365–88.

———. "Akrasia and Agency in Plato's *Laws* and *Republic.*" *Archiv für Geschichte der Philosophie* 76 (1994): 3–36.

———. "The Virtues of Ordinary People in Plato's *Statesman.*" In Rowe, ed., *Reading the* Statesman, 313–29.

Boedeker, Deborah, and Kurt Raaflaub, eds. *Democracy, Empire, and the Arts in Fifth-Century Athens.* Cambridge, Mass.: Harvard University Press, 1998.

Boegehold, Alan L., and Adele C. Scafuro, eds. *Athenian Identity and Civic Ideology.* Baltimore: Johns Hopkins University Press, 1994.

Bohman, James. *Public Deliberation: Pluralism, Complexity, and Democracy.* Cambridge, Mass.: MIT Press, 1996.

Bohman, James, and William Rehg, eds. *Deliberative Democracy: Essays on Reason and Politics.* Cambridge, Mass.: MIT Press, 1997.

Bowen, William G., and Derek Bok. *The Shape of the River: Long-Term Consequences of Considering Race in College and University Admissions.* Princeton: Princeton University Press, 1998.

Brandwood, Leonard. *The Chronology of Plato's Dialogues.* Cambridge: Cambridge University Press, 1990.

Brickhouse, Thomas C., and Nicholas D Smith. *Socrates on Trial.* Princeton: Princeton University Press, 1989.

Brunt, P. A. "The Model City in Plato's *Laws.*" In P. A. Brunt, *Studies in Greek History and Thought,* 245–81. Oxford: Clarendon Press, 1993.

———. "Plato's Academy and Politics" In P. A. Brunt, *Studies in Greek History and Thought,* 282–342. Oxford: Clarendon Press, 1993.

Burford, Alison. *Craftsmen in Greek and Roman Society.* Ithaca: Cornell University Press, 1972.

Burkert, Walter. *Greek Religion.* Trans. John Raffan. Cambridge, Mass.: Harvard University Press, 1985.

Burnet, John. *Plato's* Phaedo. Oxford, 1911.

———. *Plato's* Euthyphro, Apology of Socrates, *and* Crito. Oxford: Clarendon Press, 1924.

Burnyeat, Myles F., "Sphinx Without a Secret." *New York Review of Books.* 30 May 1985, p. 30–36.

Bury, R. B. "Introduction." In Plato, *Laws: Books I–VI.* Cambridge, Mass.: Harvard University Press, 1926.

Butler, Judith. "Merely Cultural." *New Left Review,* no. 227 (1998): 33–44.

Calder, W. M., and S. T. Trzaskoma, eds. *George Grote Reconsidered.* Weidmann, 1997.

Calhoun, G. M. *Athenian Clubs in Politics and Litigation.* Austin: University of Texas Press, 1913.

Caliagero, Guido. "Gorgias and the Socratic Principle: *Nemo Sua Sponte Peccat.*" In C. J. Classen, ed., *Sophistik,* 408–42. Darmstadt, 1976.

Callan, Eamon. *Creating Citizens.* Oxford: Oxford University Press, 1997.

Calvert, Brian. "The Politicians of Athens in the *Gorgias* and *Meno.*" *History of Political Thought* 5 (1984): 1–9.

Campbell, Blair. "Constitutionalism, Rights, and Religion: The Athenian Example." *History of Political Thought* 7 (1986): 243–67.

Carter, L. B. *The Quiet Athenian.* Oxford: Clarendon Press, 1986.

Cartledge, Paul. *Sparta and Lakonia: A Regional History.* London: Routledge & Kegan Paul, 1979.

———. *Agesilaos and the Crisis of Sparta.* Baltimore: Johns Hopkins University Press, 1987.

———. *The Greeks: A Portrait of Self and Others.* Oxford: Oxford University Press, 1993.

Cherniss, Harold. *Aristotle's Criticism of Plato and the Academy,* vol. 1. Baltimore: Johns Hopkins University Press, 1944.

———. *The Riddle of the Early Academy.* Berkeley and Los Angeles: University of California Press, 1945.

Chroust, Anton-Hermann. *Socrates—Man and Myth: The Two Socratic Apologies of Xenophon.* London: Routledge & Kegan Paul, 1957.

———. "Plato's Academy: The First Organized School of Political Science in Antiquity." *Review of Politics* 29 (1967): 25–40.

Cleary, John H., and Gary M. Gurtler S.J. *Proceedings of the Boston Area Colloquium in Ancient Philosophy,* vol. 13. Lanham, Md.: University Press of America, 1999.

Cohen, David. "Law, Autonomy, and Political Community in Plato's *Laws.*" *Classical Philology* 8 (1993): 301–17.

Cohen, Joshua, and Joel Rogers. *On Democracy: Toward a Transformation of American Society.* New York: Penguin, 1983.

———. "Deliberation and Democratic Legitimacy." In Hamlin and Pettit, eds., *The Good Polity,* 17–34.

———. "Secondary Associations and Democratic Governance." *Politics and Society* 20 (1992): 393–472.

———. "A More Democratic Liberalism." *Michigan Law Review* 92 (1994): 1503–46.

Cole, A. T. "*Anonymous Iamblichi* and His Place in Greek Political Theory." *Harvard Studies in Classical Philosophy* LXV (1961): 127–63.

———. *Democritus and the Sources of Greek Anthropology.* American Philological Association, Philological Monographs, no. 24. Chapel Hill, N.C.: Press of Western Reserve University, 1967.

———. *The Origins of Rhetoric in Ancient Greece.* Baltimore: Johns Hopkins University Press, 1991.

Collingwood, R. C. *Autobiography.* Oxford: Clarendon Press, 1939.

Connolly, William E. *The Terms of Political Discourse.* 2d ed. Princeton: Princeton University Press, 1983.

———. *Politics and Ambiguity.* Madison: University of Wisconsin Press, 1987.

———. *Identity/Difference: Democratic Negotiations of Political Paradox.* Ithaca: Cornell University Press, 1991.

———. "Beyond Good and Evil: The Ethical Sensibility of Michel Foucault." *Political Theory* 21 (1993): 365–89.

Connor, W. Robert. *The New Politicians of Fifth Century Athens.* Princeton: Princeton University Press, 1973.

Constant, Benjamin. "The Liberty of the Ancients Compared with That of the Moderns." In Benjamin Constant, *Political Writings,* trans. Biancamaria Fontana, 307–28. Cambridge: Cambridge University Press, 1988.

Cooper, John M. *Reason and Human Good.* Cambridge, Mass.: Harvard University Press, 1975.

———. "The Psychology of Justice in Plato." *American Philosophical Quarterly* 14 (1977): 151–57.

———. "Introduction." In Plato, *Complete Works,* ed. John M. Cooper, vii–xxvi. Indianapolis: Hackett, 1997.

Cornford, F. M. "Athenian Philosophical Schools." In J. B. Bury et al., eds., *Cambridge Ancient History, vol. 6: Macedon, 401–301 B.C.,* 302–51. Cambridge: Cambridge University Press, 1927.

———. "Introduction." *The* Republic *of Plato,* trans. F. M. Cornford, xv–xxix. New York: Oxford University Press, 1941, 1945.

———. *The Unwritten Philosophy and Other Essays.* Cambridge: Cambridge University Press, 1950.

Cross, R. C., and A. D. Woozley. *Plato's Republic: A Philosophical Commentary.* London, 1964.

Crossman, R. H. *Plato Today: A Revised Edition.* London: George Allen & Unwin, 1937 (1959).

Davies, J. K. *Athenian Propertied Families.* Oxford, 1971.

———. *Democracy and Classical Athens.* London: Thames and Hudson, 1978.

———. *Wealth and the Power of Wealth in Classical Athens.* New York: Oxford University Press, 1981.

Derrida, Jacques, "Plato's Pharmacy." In Jacques Derrida, *Dissemination,* trans. Barbara Johnson, 65–171. Chicago: University of Chicago Press, 1981 (1968).

———. *Limited, Inc.* Chicago: University of Chicago Press, 1988.

Devereux, Daniel T. "Separation and Immanence in Plato's Theory of Forms." *Oxford Studies in Ancient Philosophy* 12 (1994): 63–90.

Dewey, John. *Democracy and Education.* New York: Macmillan, 1916.

———. *The Public and Its Problems.* New York: Swallow Press, 1954 (1927).

———. *Human Nature and Conduct.* New York: Modern Library, 1954 (1932).

Diels, Hermann, with Walther Kranz, eds. Die *Fragmente der Vorsokratiker: Griechisch und deutsch.* 7th ed. Berlin: Weidmann, 1951, 1954. (Cited in text as Diels-Kranz.)

Dionne, E. J. *Why Americans Hate Politics.* New York: Simon & Schuster, 1991.

Dodds, E. R. *The Greeks and the Irrational.* Berkeley and Los Angeles: University of California Press, 1968 (1951).

──────. "The Ancient Concept of Progress." In E. R. Dodds, ed., *The Ancient Concept of Progress, and Other Essays on Greek Literature and Belief,* 1–25. Oxford: Clarendon Press, 1973.

Dodds, E. R., ed. *Plato: Gorgias: A Revised Text with Introduction and Commentary.* Oxford: Clarendon Press, 1959.

Dover, K. J. *Greek Popular Morality in the Time of Plato and Aristotle.* Berkeley and Los Angeles: University of California Press, 1974.

──────. "The Freedom of the Intellectual in Greek Society." *Talanta* 7 (1976): 1–27.

Dunn, John. *Western Political Theory in the Face of the Future.* Cambridge: Cambridge University Press, 1979.

──────. *Political Obligation in Its Historical Context.* Cambridge: Cambridge University Press, 1980.

──────. *Rethinking Modern Political Theory.* Cambridge: Cambridge University Press, 1985.

──────. *Interpreting Political Responsibility.* Princeton: Princeton University Press, 1990.

──────. *The History of Political Theory and Other Essays.* Cambridge: Cambridge University Press, 1996.

Dunn, John, ed. *Democracy: The Unfinished Journey, 508 BC–1993 AD.* Oxford: Oxford University Press, 1992.

Eagleton, Terry. *Ideology: An Introduction.* London: Verso, 1991.

Easterling, P. E., and J. V. Muir, eds. *Greek Religion and Society.* Cambridge: Cambridge University Press, 1985.

Edelstein, Ludwig. *Plato's Seventh Letter.* Leiden: E. J. Brill, 1966.

──────. *Ancient Medicine: Selected Papers of Ludwig Edelstein.* Ed. Owsei Temkin and C. Lilian Temkin. Baltimore: Johns Hopkins University Press, 1967.

Edmunds, Lowell. *Chance and Intelligence in Thucydides.* Cambridge, Mass.: Harvard University Press, 1975.

Ehrenberg, Victor, "The Origins of Democracy." *Historia* 1 (1950): 515–47.

──────. *The People of Aristophanes: A Sociology of Old Attic Comedy.* 2d ed. Oxford: Basil Blackwell, 1951.

──────. *The Greek State.* 2d ed. London: Methuen, 1969 (1960).

Elster, Jon, ed. *Deliberative Democracy.* Cambridge: Cambridge University Press, 1998.

Esquith, Stephen. *Intimacy and Spectacle: Liberal Theory as Political Education.* Ithaca: Cornell University Press, 1994.

Etzioni, Amitai. *The Spirit of Community: Rights, Responsibilities, and the Communitarian Agenda.* New York: Crown, 1993.

Euben, J. Peter. "Creatures of a Day: Thought and Action in Thucydides." In Ball, ed., *Political Theory and Praxis,* 28–56.

──────. "The Philosophy and Politics of Plato's *Crito.*" *Political Theory* 6 (1978): 149–72.

──────. "The Battle of Salamis and the Origins of Political Theory." *Political Theory* 14 (1986): 359–90.

————. *The Tragedy of Political Theory: The Road Not Taken.* Princeton: Princeton University Press, 1990.

————. "Democracy and Political Theory: A Reading of Plato's *Gorgias.*" In Euben et al., *Athenian Political Thought and the Reconstruction of American Democracy.*

————. *Corrupting Youth.* Princeton: Princeton University Press, 1997.

Euben, J. Peter, with John R. Wallach and Josiah Ober, eds. *Athenian Political Thought and the Reconstruction of American Democracy.* Ithaca: Cornell University Press, 1994.

Eucken, Christopher. *Isokrates: Seine Positionen in der Auseinandersetzung mit den zeitgenössichen Philosophen.* Berlin: De Gruyter, 1983.

Evans, Richard J. *In Defense of History.* New York: Norton, 1999.

Farness, Jay. *Missing Socrates: Problems of Plato's Writing.* University Park, Pa.: The Pennsylvania State University Press, 1991.

Farrar, Cynthia. *The Origins of Democratic Thinking.* Cambridge: Cambridge University Press, 1988.

————. "Ancient Greek Political Theory as a Response to Democracy." In Dunn, ed. *Democracy: The Unfinished Journey, 508 BC–1993 AD,* 17–39.

Ferrari, G. R. F. *Listening to the Cicadas: A Study of Plato's* Phaedrus. Cambridge: Cambridge University Press, 1987.

————. "Plato and Poetry." In George A. Kennedy, ed., *The Cambridge History of Literary Criticism, vol. 1: Classical Criticism,* 92–148. Cambridge: Cambridge University Press, 1989.

————. "Introduction." In Plato, *The Republic,* ed. G.R.F. Ferrari and trans. Tom Griffith. Cambridge: Cambridge University Press, 2000.

Field, G. C. *Plato and His Contemporaries,* 3d ed. London: Methuen, 1967.

Fine, Gail. "Separation." *Oxford Studies in Ancient Philosophy* 2 (1984): 31–87.

————. "Immanence." *Oxford Studies in Ancient Philosophy* 4 (1986): 71–97.

————. *On Ideas: Aristotle's Criticism of Plato's Theory of Forms.* Oxford: Clarendon Press, 1993.

Finley, Moses I. *The Ancient Greeks: An Introduction to Their Life and Thought.* Penguin, 1991 (1963).

————. *The Ancestral Constitution: An Inaugural Lecture.* London: Cambridge University Press, 1971.

————. *Democracy Ancient and Modern.* Rev. ed. New Brunswick: Rutgers University Press, 1973, 1985.

————. "Censorship in Classical Antiquity." *Times Literary Supplement,* 29 July 1977, p. 923–25.

————. *Politics in the Ancient World.* Cambridge: Cambridge University Press, 1983.

Fishkin, James. *Democracy and Deliberation: New Directions for Democratic Reform.* New Haven: Yale University Press, 1992.

Forrest, W. G. *A History of Sparta, 950–192 B.C.* New York: Norton, 1968.

Foster, M. B. "A Mistake of Plato's in the *Republic.*" *Mind* n.s. 46 (1937): 386–93.

Foucault, Michel. *The Foucault Reader.* Ed. Paul Rabinow. New York: Pantheon, 1984.

————. *The Use of Pleasure—The History of Sexuality,* vol. 2. New York: Random House, 1985.

————. *Discourse and Truth: The Problematization of Parrhesia.* Ed. Joseph Pearson. Unpublished manuscript, 1985.

Fowler, D. H. *The Mathematics of Plato's Academy.* Oxford: Clarendon Press, 1987.

Frankfurt, Harry. "Freedom of the Will and the Concept of the Person." In Harry Frankfurt, *The Importance of What We Care About—Philosophical Essays,* 11–25. Cambridge: Cambridge University Press, 1988 (1971).

Frazer, Elizabeth, and Nicola Lacey. "Politics and the Public in Rawls' Political Liberalism." *Political Studies* 43 (1995): 233–47.

Frede, Dorothea. "The Impossibility of Perfection: Socrates' Criticism of Simonides' Poem in the *Protagoras.*" *Review of Metaphysics* 39 (1986): 729–53.

Frede, Michael. *Essays in Ancient Philosophy.* Minneapolis: University of Minnesota Press, 1987.

————. "Plato's Arguments and the Dialogue Form." In James Klagge and Nicholas Smith, eds., *Methods of Interpreting Plato and His Dialogues: Oxford Studies in Ancient Philosophy—Supplementary Volume, 1992,* 201–19. Oxford: Clarendon Press, 1992.

————. "The Literary Form of the *Sophist.*" In Gill and McCabe, eds., *Form and Argument in Late Plato,* 135–51.

Friedlander, Paul. *Plato: The Dialogues, II.* Trans. Hans Meyerhoff. New York: Bollingen, 1964.

————. *Plato,* vol. 3. Princeton: Princeton University Press, 1969.

Friedman, Milton. *Capitalism and Freedom.* Chicago: University of Chicago Press, 1962.

Fritz, Kurt von. *Platon in Sizilien und des Problem der Philosophenherrschaft.* Berlin, 1968.

Fuks, Alexander. *The Ancestral Constitution.* London: Routledge & Kegan Paul, 1953.

————. *Social Conflict in Ancient Greece.* Leiden: E. J. Brill, 1984.

Gadamer, Hans-Georg. *Truth and Method.* New York: Seabury Press, 1975 (1965).

————. "Plato and the Poets" and "Plato's Educational State." In *Dialogue and Dialectic—Eight Hermeneutical Studies on Plato,* trans. P. Christopher Smith, 39–72 and 73–92. New Haven: Yale University Press, 1980 (1934, 1942).

————. *The Idea of the Good in Platonic-Aristotelian Philosophy.* New Haven: Yale University Press, 1986 (1978).

————. "Gadamer on Gadamer." A 1989 interview in *Gadamer and Hermeneutics,* ed. Hugh J. Silverman, 13–19. New York: Routledge, 1991.

Gagarin, Michael. "The Purpose of Plato's *Protagoras.*" *Transactions of the American Philological Association* 100 (1970): 133–64.

Gaiser, Kurt. *Platons Ungeschriebene Lehre: Studien zur systematischen und geschichtlichen Begründung der Wissenschaften in der platonischen Schule.* Stuttgart, 1963.

————. "Plato's Enigmatic Lecture, 'On the Good.'" *Phronesis* 25 (1980): 5–37.

Gallie, W. B. *Philosophy and the Historical Understanding.* London: Chatto and Windus, 1964.

Galston, Miriam. "Taking Aristotle Seriously: Republican-Oriented Legal Theory and the Moral Foundation of Deliberative Democracy." *California Law Review* 82 (1994): 329–99.

Galston, William A. *Liberal Purposes: Goods, Virtues, and Diversity in the Liberal State.* Cambridge: Cambridge University Press, 1991.

Garland, Robert. *Introducing the New Gods.* Ithaca: Cornell University Press, 1992,

Geuss, Raymond. *The Idea of a Critical Theory.* Cambridge: Cambridge University Press, 1981.

———. "Kultur, Bildung, Geist." *History and Theory* 35 (1996): 151–64.

Gill, Christopher. "Rethinking Constitutionalism in *Statesman* 291–303." In Rowe, ed., *Reading the Statesman,* 292–305.

———. "Afterword: Dialectic and the Dialogue Form in Late Plato." In Gill and McCabe, eds., *Form and Argument in Late Plato.*

Gill, Christopher, and Mary Margaret McCabe, eds. *Form and Argument in Late Plato.* Oxford: Clarendon Press, 1996.

Glazer, Nathan. "In Defense of Preference." *New Republic* 60, April 6, 1998, pp. 18–23.

Gonzales, Francisco J. *The Third Way: New Directions in Platonic Studies.* Lanham, Md.: Rowman & Littlefield, 1995.

Gould, John. *The Development of Plato's Ethics.* New York: Russell & Russell, 1972 (1956).

Gouldner, Alvin. *Enter Plato: Classical Greece and the Origins of Social Theory.* New York: Basic Books, 1965.

Graham, Daniel. "Socrates and Plato." *Phronesis* 37 (1992): 141–65.

Green, Donald and Ian Shapiro. *The Pathologies of Rational Choice.* New Haven: Yale University Press, 1994.

Grene, David. *Greek Political Theory: The Image of Man in Plato and Thucydides.* Chicago: University of Chicago Press, 1950 (1967).

Griswold, Charles. "The Ideas and the Criticism of Poetry in Plato's *Republic,* Book x." *Journal of the History of Philosophy* 19 (1981): 135–50.

Griswold, Charles, ed. *Platonic Writings/Platonic Readings.* Forthcoming as a reissued paperback, with a new preface and updated bibliography. University Park, Pa.: The Pennsylvania State University Press, 2001 (1988).

Grote, George, *Plato and Other Companions of Socrates,* vol. 4. London, 1888.

Gulley, Norman. *The Philosophy of Socrates.* London: Routledge & Kegan Paul, 1968.

Guthrie, W. K. C. *A History of Greek Philosophy, vol. 1: The Earlier Presocratics.* Cambridge: Cambridge University Press, 1962.

———. *A History of Greek Philosophy, vol. 2: The Presocratic Tradition from Parmenides to Democritus.* Cambridge: Cambridge University Press, 1965.

———. *A History of Greek Philosophy, vol. 3: The Fifth-Century Enlightenment.* Cambridge: Cambridge University Press, 1969.

———. *Socrates.* Cambridge: Cambridge University Press, 1971.

———. *A History of Greek Philosophy, vol. 4: Plato—The Man and His Dialogues, Earlier Period.* Cambridge: Cambridge University Press, 1975.

———. *A History of Greek Philosophy, vol. 5: The Later Plato and the Academy.* Cambridge: Cambridge University Press, 1978.

———. *A History of Greek Philosophy, vol. 6: Aristotle, an Encounter.* Cambridge: Cambridge University Press, 1981.

Gutmann, Amy. *Democratic Education.* Princeton: Princeton University Press, 1987.

———. "Rawls on the Relationship Between Liberalism and Democracy." In *The Cambridge Companion to Rawls.* Cambridge: Cambridge University Press, in press.

Gutmann, Amy, and Dennis Thompson. *Democracy and Disagreement.* Cambridge, Mass.: Harvard University Press, 1996.

Habermas, Jürgen. *Theory and Practice.* Trans. John Viertel. Boston: Beacon Press, 1974.

———. "Hannah Arendt's Communications Concept of Power." *Social Research* 44 (1977): 3–24.

———. *Between Facts and Norms: Contributions to a Discourse Theory of Law and Democracy.* Trans. William Rehg. Cambridge, Mass.: MIT Press, 1996 (1992).

———. "Reconciliation Through the Public Use of Reason: Remarks on John Rawls's *Political Liberalism*" (with reply by Rawls). *Journal of Philosophy* 92 (1995): 109–80.

———. *The Inclusion of the Other: Studies in Political Theory.* Ciaran Cronin and Pablo De Greiff, eds. Cambridge, Mass.: MIT Press, 1998.

Hackforth, R. *The Authorship of the Platonic Epistles.* Manchester: University Press, 1913.

———. *The Composition of Plato's* Apology. Cambridge: Cambridge University Press, 1933.

Hall, Robert W. *Plato and the Individual.* The Hague: Martinus Nijhoff, 1963.

———. "*Techne* and Morality in the *Gorgias.*" In J. P. Anton and G. L. Kustas, eds., *Essays in Ancient Greek Philosophy,* 202–18. Albany: State University of New York Press, 1971.

———. *Plato.* London: George Allen, 1981.

Halliwell, S. "Introduction." *Plato: Republic 10.* Warminster: Aris & Phillips, 1988.

Halliwell, S., ed. *Plato: Republic 5.* Warminster: Aris & Phillips, 1993.

Hamlin, Alan, and Philip Pettit, eds. *The Good Polity.* Oxford: Blackwell, 1989.

Hankinson, R. J. *Method, Medicine, and Metaphysics: Studies in the Philosophy of Ancient Science.* Edmonton: Academic Printing and Publishing, 1988.

Hansen, Mogens Herman. "The Athenian 'Politicians,' 403–322 B.C." *Greek, Roman, and Byzantine Studies* 24 (1983): 33–55.

———. *The Athenian Assembly in the Age of Demosthenes.* Oxford: Basil Blackwell, 1987.

———. "Solonian Democracy in Fourth-Century Athens." *Classica et Mediaevalia* 40 (1989): 71–100.

———. *The Athenian Democracy in the Age of Demosthenes.* Oxford: Basil Blackwell, 1991.

Harvey, F. D. "Literacy in the Athenian Democracy." *Revue des Études Grecques* 79 (1966): 586–35.

———. "Two Kinds of Equality." *Classica et Mediaevalia*. 26 (1966): 101–47, and 27 (1967): 99–100.

Harward, J., ed. *The Platonic Epistles*. New York: Arno Press, 1976.

Hauptmann, Emily. "Deliberation = Legitimacy = Democracy." *Political Theory* 27 (1999): 857–72.

Havelock, E. A. *The Liberal Temper in Greek Politics*. New Haven: Yale University Press, 1957.

———. *Preface to Plato*. New York: Grosset & Dunlap, 1963.

———. "*Dikaiosune:* An Essay in Greek Intellectual History." *Phoenix* 23 (1969): 46–70.

———. *The Greek Concept of Justice*. Cambridge, Mass.: Harvard University Press, 1978.

———. *The Literate Revolution in Ancient Greece and Its Cultural Consequences*. Princeton: Princeton University Press, 1982.

Hegel, G. W. F. *The Philosophy of History*. Trans. J. Sibree. New York: Dover, 1956.

Heidegger, Martin. "Letter on Humanism." In *Basic Writings of Heidegger*, ed. David F. Krell, 193–242. New York: Harper & Row, 1977 (1947).

———. "The Self-Assertion of the German University." In Gunther Neske and Emil Kettering, eds., *Martin Heidegger and National Socialism: Questions and Answers*, 5–13. New York: Paragon House, 1990 (1933).

Heinimann, F. "Eine vorplatonische Theorie der *Techne.*" *Museum Helveticum* 18 (1961): 105–30.

Held, David. *Democracy and the Global Order*. Stanford: Stanford University Press, 1995.

Heubert, Jay P., and Robert M. Hauser, eds. *High Stakes: Testing for Tracking, Promotion, and Graduation*. Washington, D.C.: National Academy Press, 1999.

Himmelfarb, Gertrude. *One Nation, Two Cultures*. New York: Random House, 2000.

Hoerber, R. G. *The Theme of Plato's Republic*. St. Louis, 1944.

Hofstadter, Richard. *Anti-Intellectualism in American Life*. New York, 1963.

Howland, Jacob. "Re-reading Plato: The Problem of Platonic Chronology." *Phoenix* 45 (1991): 189–214.

Hoxby, Caroline. "How Teachers' Unions Affect Education Production." *Quarterly Journal of Economics* 111 (1996): 671–718.

———. "Are Efficiency and Equity in School Finance Substitutes or Complements?" *Journal of Economic Perspectives* 10 (1996): 51–72.

Huntington, Samuel. "The United States." In *The Crisis of Democracy: Report on the Governability of Democracies to the Trilateral Commission*. New York: New York University Press, 1975.

Hurley, S. N. *Natural Reasons: Personality and Polity*. New York: Oxford University Press, 1989.

Hutter, Horst. *Politics and Friendship: The Origins of Classical Notions of Politics in the Theory and Practice of Friendship*. Waterloo, Ont.: Wilfried Laurier University Press, 1978.

Inwood, M. J. Review of Trampedach, *Platon. . . . Classical Review* 47 (1997): 335–38.

Irwin, Terence. *Plato's Moral Theory: The Early and Middle Dialogues.* Oxford: Clarendon Press, 1977.

———. *Plato's Ethics.* Oxford: Clarendon Press, 1995.

Jaeger, Werner. *Paideia: The Ideals of Greek Culture, vol. 1: Archaic Greece/The Mind of Athens.* Trans. G. Highet. New York: Oxford University Press, 1939 (1945).

———. *Paideia: The Ideals of Greek Culture, vol. 2: In Search of the Divine Centre.* Trans. G. Highet. New York: Oxford University Press, 1943.

———. *Paideia: The Ideals of Greek Culture, vol. 3: The Conflict of Cultural Ideals in the Age of Plato.* New York: Oxford University Press, 1944.

———. "On the Origin and Cycle of the Philosophic Ideal of Life" (1928). Reprinted in Werner Jaeger, *Aristotle: Fundamentals of the History of his Development,* 2d ed., 426–61. London: Oxford University Press, 1967 (1927, 1934).

Janaway, Christopher. "Arts and Crafts in Plato and Collingwood." *Journal of Aesthetics and Art Criticism* 50 (1992): 45–54.

———. *Images of Excellence: Plato's Critique of the Arts.* Oxford: Clarendon Press, 1995.

Jefferson, Thomas, "Notes on Virginia." In *The Life and Selected Writings of Thomas Jefferson,* ed. Adrienne Koch and William Paden. New York: Modern Library, 1944.

Jonas, Hans. *The Gnostic Religion: The Message of the Alien God and the Beginnings of Christianity.* 2d ed., rev. Boston: Beacon Press, 1963.

Jones, A. H. M. "Athenian Democracy and Its Critics." In A. H. M. Jones, *Athenian Democracy,* 41–72. Oxford: Basil Blackwell, 1957.

———. *Sparta.* Oxford: Basil Blackwell, 1967.

Jones, W. H. S. *Philosophy and Medicine in Ancient Greece.* Baltimore: Johns Hopkins Press, 1946.

Joseph, H. W. B. *Ancient and Modern Philosophy.* Oxford, 1935.

Kahn, Charles H. "Drama and Dialectic in Plato's *Gorgias.*" In *Oxford Studies in Ancient Philosophy,* vol. 1, ed. J. Annas, 75–121. Oxford: Clarendon Press, 1983.

———. "On the Relative Date of the *Gorgias* and the *Protagoras.*" In *Oxford Studies in Ancient Philosophy,* vol. 6, ed. J. Annas, 69–102. Oxford: Clarendon Press, 1988.

———. "Proleptic Composition in the *Republic,* or Why Book 1 Was Never a Separate Dialogue." *Classical Quarterly* n.s. 43 (1993): 131–42.

———. Foreword. In Glenn R. Morrow, ed., *Plato's Cretan City: A Historical Interpretation of the Laws,* xvii–xxvii. Princeton: Princeton University Press, 1993.

———. *Plato and the Socratic Dialogue: The Philosophical Use of a Literary Form.* Cambridge: Cambridge University Press, 1996.

Kennedy, Duncan. *Sexy Dressing, etc.* Cambridge, Mass.: Harvard University Press, 1993.

Kennedy, George A. *The Art of Persuasion in Greece.* Princeton: Princeton University Press, 1963.

Kerferd, G. B. "Protagoras' Doctrine of Justice and Virtue." *Journal of Hellenic Studies* 73 (1953): 42–45.

———. *The Sophistic Movement.* Cambridge: Cambridge University Press, 1981.

Kerford, G. B., ed. *The Sophists and Their Legacy.* Wiesbaden, 1981.

Kernan, Alvin. *In Plato's Cave.* New Haven: Yale University Press, 1999.

Klosko, George. *The Development of Plato's Political Theory.* New York: Methuen, 1986.

———. "The Nocturnal Council in Plato's *Laws.*" *Political Studies* 36 (1988): 74–88.

Korsgaard, Christine M. *Creating the Kingdom of Ends.* Cambridge: Cambridge University Press, 1996.

Kramer, H. J. "Die grundsatzlichen Fragen der Indirekten Platonüberlieferung." *Idee und Zahl* (1968): 106–50.

———. *Arete bei Platon und Aristoteles: Zum Wesen und zur Geschichte der platonischen Ontologie.* Abhandlungen der Heidelberger Akademie der Wissenschaft, Philosophisch-historische Klasse, 1959, 6. Heidelberg, 1969.

———. *Plato and the Foundation of Metaphysics.* Ed. and trans. John M. Catan. Albany: State University of New York Press, 1990.

Kraut, Richard. *Socrates and the State.* Princeton: Princeton University Press, 1984.

———. "The Defense of Justice in Plato's *Republic.*" In Kraut, ed., *The Cambridge Companion to Plato.*

Kraut, Richard, ed. *The Cambridge Companion to Plato.* Cambridge: Cambridge University Press, 1992.

———. *Plato's Republic: Critical Essays.* Lanham, Md.: Rowman & Littlefield, 1997.

Kube, Jorge. *Techne und Arete.* Berlin, 1969.

Laks, Andre. "Legislation and Demiurgy: On the Relationship Between Plato's *Republic* and *Laws.*" *Classical Antiquity* 9 (1990): 209–29.

Lane, Melissa. *Method and Politics in Plato's* Statesman. Cambridge: Cambridge University Press, 1998.

Larsen, J. A. O. "Cleisthenes and the Development of Greek Democracy at Athens." In *Essays in Political Theory Presented to George H. Sabine,* 1–16. Ithaca: Cornell University Press, 1948.

Laslett, Peter, ed. *Philosophy, Politics, and Society.* Oxford: Basil Blackwell, 1956.

Lavin, David E., and David Hyllegard. *Changing the Odds: Open Admissions and the Life Chances of the Disadvantaged.* New Haven: Yale University Press, 1996.

Lear, Jonathan. "Inside and Outside the *Republic.*" *Phronesis* 37 (1992): 184–215.

———. *Open-Minded.* Cambridge, Mass.: Harvard University Press, 1998.

Lefkowitz, Mary. "Only the Best Girls Get to." *Times Literary Supplement,* 5–11 May 1989, pp. 484, 497.

Lemann, Nicholas. *The Big Test: The Secret History of the American Meritocracy.* New York: Farrar Straus Giroux, 1999.

Levinson, Sanford. *Constitutional Faith.* Princeton: Princeton University Press, 1988.

Lewis, D. M., et al. *The Cambridge Ancient History, vol. 6: The Fourth Century.* Cambridge: Cambridge University Press, 1994.

Leys, Wayne. "Was Plato Non-Political." In Vlastos, ed., *Plato: A Collection of Critical Essays, vol. 2: Ethics, Politics, and Philosophy of Art and Religion.*

Lloyd, G. E. R. *Polarity and Analogy.* Cambridge: Cambridge University Press, 1966.

———. *Magic, Reason, and Experience.* Cambridge: Cambridge University Press, 1979.

Loenen, Dirk. *Protagoras and the Greek Community.* Amsterdam, 1940.

———. *Stasis.* Amsterdam, 1953.

Longrigg, James. *Greek Rational Medicine: Philosophy and Medicine from Alcmaeon to the Alexandrians.* London: Routledge, 1993.

Loraux, Nicole. *The Invention of Athens: The Funeral Oration in the Classical City.* Trans. Alan Sheridan. Cambridge, Mass.: Harvard University Press, 1986 (1981).

———. "Reflections of the Greek City on Unity and Division." In Anthony Molho, Kurt Raaflaub, and Julia Emlen, eds., *City States in Classical Antiquity and Medieval Italy,* 33–51. Ann Arbor: University of Michigan Press, 1991.

Lynch, John P. *Aristotle's School.* Berkeley and Los Angeles: University of California Press, 1974.

Macdowell, Douglas. *The Law in Classical Athens.* Ithaca: Cornell University Press, 1978.

Macedo, Stephen. *Liberal Virtues.* Oxford: Clarendon Press, 1990.

———. *Diversity and Distrust: Civic Education in a Multicultural Democracy.* Cambridge, Mass.: Harvard University Press, 2000.

Macedo, Stephen, ed. *Deliberative Politics: Essays on Democracy and Disagreement.* New York: Oxford University Press, 1999.

MacIntyre, Alasdair. *After Virtue: A Study in Moral Theory.* Notre Dame: University of Notre Dame Press, 1981, 1984.

———. *Whose Justice? Whose Rationality?* Notre Dame: University of Notre Dame Press, 1988.

MacKinnon, Catherine. *Only Words.* Cambridge, Mass.: Harvard University Press, 1993.

MacLachlan, Bonnie. "The Harmony of the Spheres: *Dulcis Sonus.*" In *Harmonia Mundi—Musica e filosofia nell'antichita/Music and Philosophy in the Ancient World,* ed. Robert W. Wallace and Bonnie MacLachlan, 7–19. Rome: Edizioni dell'Ateneo, 1991.

Manin, Bernard. *Principles of Representative Government.* Cambridge: Cambridge University Press, 1997.

Mansfield, Harvey, Jr. *America's Constitutional Soul.* Baltimore: Johns Hopkins University Press, 1993.

Mara, Gerald M. *Socrates' Discursive Democracy: Logos and Ergon in Platonic Political Philosophy.* Albany: State University of New York Press, 1997.

Marrou, H. I. *A History of Education in Antiquity.* Trans. George Lamb. Madison: University of Wisconsin Press, 1956 (1948).

Meier, Christian. *Die Entstehung des Politischen bei dem Griechen.* Trans. as *The Greek Discovery of Politics.* Cambridge, Mass.: Harvard University Press, 1990.

Meiggs, R. *The Athenian Empire.* Oxford: Clarendon Press, 1972.

Merlan, Philip. "Form and Content in Plato's Philosophy." *Journal of the History of Ideas* 8 (1947): 406–30.

Michelman, Frank. *Brennan and Democracy*. Princeton: Princeton University Press, 1999.

Miller, Mitchell H., Jr. *The Philosopher in Plato's Statesman*. The Hague: Martinus Nijhoff, 1980.

Mishel, Lawrence, et al. *The State of Working America*. Ithaca: Cornell University Press, 1999.

Momigliano, Arnaldo. *The Development of Greek Biography*. Cambridge, Mass.: Harvard University Press, 1971.

Monoson, S. Sara. "Frank Speech, Democracy, and Philosophy: Plato's Debt to a Democratic Strategy of Civic Discourse." In Euben et al., eds., *Athenian Political Thought and the Reconstruction of American Democracy*, 172–97.

———. *Plato's Democratic Entanglements*. Princeton: Princeton University Press, 2000.

Moravcsik, Julius. *Plato and Platonism*. Oxford: Blackwell, 1992.

Morgan, Michael L. *Platonic Piety: Philosophy and Ritual in Fourth-Century Athens*. New Haven: Yale University Press, 1990.

Morris, Ian, and Kurt Raaflaub, eds. *Democracy 2500? Questions and Challenges*. Dubuque: Kendall/Hunt Publishing, 1998.

Morrison, Donald. "Professor Vlastos' Xenophon." *Ancient Philosophy* 7 (1987): 9–22.

Morrison, J. S. "The Origins of Plato's Philosopher-Statesman." *Classical Quarterly* n.s. 8 (1958): 198–218.

Morrow, Glenn R., ed. *Plato's Epistles*. Indianapolis: Bobbs-Merrill, 1962 (1935).

———. *Plato's Cretan City: A Historical Interpretation of the Laws*. Princeton: Princeton University Press, 1993.

Mosse, Claude. *Athens in Decline, 404–86 B.C.* London: Routledge & Kegan Paul, 1974.

Murphy, N. R. *The Interpretation of Plato's Republic*. Oxford, 1951.

Murray, Oswyn. "Cities of Reason." In O. Murray and S. Price, eds., *The Greek City from Homer to Alexander*, 1–25. Oxford: Clarendon Press, 1995.

Nagy, Gregory. *The Best of the Achaeans: Concepts of the Hero in Archaic Greek Poetry*. Rev. ed. Baltimore: Johns Hopkins University Press, 1999.

Nehamas, Alexander. "Plato on Imitation and Poetry in *Republic* 10." In *Plato on Beauty, Wisdom, and the Arts*, ed. J. Moravcsik and P. Temko, 47–78. Totowa, N.J.: Rowman & Littlefield, 1982.

———. "Meno's Paradox and Socrates as a Teacher." *Oxford Studies in Ancient Philosophy*, vol. 3, ed. J. Annas, 1–30. Oxford: Clarendon Press, 1985.

———. "Socratic Intellectualism." In *Proceedings of the Boston Area Colloquium on Ancient Philosophy*, vol. 2, 275–316. Lanham, Md.: University Press of America, 1986.

———. "Plato and the Mass Media." *The Monist* 71 (1988): 214–34.

———. "Eristic, Antilogic, Sophistic, Dialectic: Plato's Demarcation of Philosophy from Sophistry." *History of Philosophy Quarterly* 7 (1990): 3–16.

———. "What Did Socrates Teach and to Whom Did He Teach It?" *Review of Metaphysics* 46 (1992): 279–306.

———. *The Virtues of Authenticity.* Princeton: Princeton University Press, 1998. (Includes all the above articles.)

———. *The Art of Living: Socratic Reflections from Plato to Foucault.* Berkeley and Los Angeles: University of California Press, 1998.

Nettleship, R. L. *Lectures on the* Republic *of Plato.* Ed. G. R. Benson. London, 1898.

Newey, Glen. "Floating on the LILO: John Rawls and the Content of Justice." *Times Literary Supplement,* 10 September 1999, pp. 9–10.

Nightingale, Andrea. "Writing/Reading a Sacred Text: A Literary Interpretation of Plato's *Laws.*" *Classical Philology* 88 (1993): 279–300.

North, Helen. *Sophrosyne: Self-Knowledge and Self-Restraint in Greek Literature.* Ithaca: Cornell University Press, 1966.

Nussbaum, Martha C. *The Fragility of Goodness: Luck and Ethics in Greek Tragedy and Philosophy.* Cambridge: Cambridge University Press, 1986.

———. *Cultivating Humanity: A Classical Defense of Reform in Liberal Education.* Cambridge, Mass.: Harvard University Press, 1997.

Oakeshott, Michael. "Rationalism in Politics." In Michael Oakeshott, *Rationalism in Politics and Other Essays,* 1–36. London: Methuen, 1962.

Ober, Josiah. *Mass and Elite in Democratic Athens: Rhetoric, Ideology, and the Power of the People.* Princeton: Princeton University Press, 1989.

———. "What Democracy Meant." *History Today* (January 1994), 22–27.

———. "How to Criticize Democracy in Late Fifth- and Fourth-Century Athens." In Euben et al., *Athenian Political Thought and the Reconstruction of American Democracy,* 149–71.

———. *The Athenian Revolution: Essays on Ancient Greek Democracy and Political Theory.* Princeton: Princeton University Press, 1996.

———. *Political Dissent in Democratic Athens: Intellectual Critics of Popular Rule.* Princeton: Princeton University Press, 1998.

Ober, Josiah, and Charles Hedrick, eds. *Demokratia: A Conversation on Democracies, Ancient and Modern.* Princeton: Princeton University Press, 1996.

Ober, Josiah, and Catherine Vanderpool. "Athenian Democracy." *Prologue: Quarterly of the National Archives* 25 (1993): 127–35.

O'Brien, Michael J. "The Unity of the *Laches.*" In *Yale Classical Studies* 18, ed. Lawrence Richardson Jr., 133–47. New Haven: Yale University Press, 1963.

———. *The Socratic Paradoxes and the Greek Mind.* Chapel Hill: University of North Carolina Press, 1967.

Okin, Susan M. "Philosopher Queens and Private Wives: Plato on Women and the Family." *Philosophy and Public Affairs* 6 (1977): 345–69.

———. "*Political Liberalism,* Justice, and Gender." *Ethics* 105 (1994): 23–43.

———. Review of Rawls's *Political Liberalism. American Political Science Review* 87 (1993): 1010–11.

Osborne, Catherine. "The Repudiation of Representation in Plato's *Republic* and Its Repercussions." *Proceedings of the Cambridge Philological Society* 33 (1987): 53–73.

Ostwald, Martin. *Nomos and the Beginnings of Athenian Democracy.* Oxford: Clarendon Press, 1986.

————. *From Popular Sovereignty to the Rule of Law.* Berkeley and Los Angeles: University of California Press, 1986.

————. "Introduction." *Plato's* Statesman. Trans. J. B. Skemp. Indianapolis: Hackett, 1992.

Ostwald, Martin, and John P. Lynch. "The Growth of Schools and the Advance of Knowledge." In D. M. Lewis et al., eds., *Cambridge Ancient History, vol. 6: The Fourth Century B.C.,* 2d ed., 592–633. Cambridge: Cambridge University Press, 1994.

Pangle, Thomas. "Interpretive Essay." In *The* Laws *of Plato,* ed. Thomas Pangle. New York: Basic Books, 1980.

————. *The Spirit of Modern Republicanism: The Moral Vision of the American Founders and the Philosophy of Locke.* Chicago: University of Chicago Press, 1988.

————. *The Ennobling of Democracy: The Challenge of the Postmodern Age.* Baltimore: Johns Hopkins University Press, 1991.

Parker, Robert. *Athenian Religion: A History.* Oxford: Clarendon Press, 1996.

Parry, Adam. *Logos and Ergon in Thucydides.* Salem, N.H.: Ayer Publishers, 1988 (1957).

Parry, Richard P. "The Craft of Justice." In F. J. Pelletier and J. King-Farlow, eds., *New Essays on Plato: Canadian Journal of Philosophy,* Supplement, 9 (1983): 19–38.

Patterson, Richard. *Image and Reality in Plato's Metaphysics.* Indianapolis: Hackett, 1985.

Patzer, A., ed. *Der Historische Sokrates.* Darmstadt, 1987.

Perlman, S. "The Politicians in the Athenian Democracy of the Fourth Century B.C." *Athenaeum* 41 (1963): 327–55.

————. "Political Leadership in Athens in the Fourth Century B.C." *La Parola del Passato* 22 (1967): 173–75.

Perry, Michael. *Religion in Politics: Constitutional and Moral Perspectives.* New York: Oxford University Press, 1997.

Pettit, Philip. *Republicanism: A Theory of Freedom and Government.* Oxford: Oxford University Press, 1997.

Pocock, J. G. A. *The Machiavellian Moment: Florentine Political Thought and the Atlantic Republican Tradition.* Princeton: Princeton University Press, 1975.

Polansky, Ronald. "Foundationalism in Plato?" In Tom Rockmore and Beth J. Singer, eds., *Antifoundationalism Old and New,* 41–55. Philadelphia: Temple University Press, 1992.

Pollitt, J. J. *Art and Experience in Classical Greece.* Cambridge: Cambridge University Press, 1972.

————. *The Ancient View of Greek Art.* New Haven: Yale University Press, 1974.

————. *The Art of Ancient Greece: Sources and Documents.* Cambridge: Cambridge University Press, 1990.

Popper, Karl. *The Poverty of Historicism.* New York: Harper & Row, 1961.

————. *The Open Society and Its Enemies, vol. 1: The Spell of Plato.* Princeton: Princeton University Press, 1965 (1943).

Post, Robert C., ed. *Censorship and Silencing: Practices of Cultural Regulation*. Los Angeles: Getty Research Institute, 1998.

Press, Gerald A., ed. *Plato's Dialogues: New Studies and Interpretations*. Lanham, Md.: Rowman & Littlefield, 1993.

Prior, William J. "The Concept of *Paradeigma* in Plato's Theory of Forms." *Apeiron* 17 (1983): 33–42.

Pritchett, W. Kendrick. *The Greek State at War*, part 2. Berkeley and Los Angeles: University of California Press, 1974.

Raaflaub, Kurt. "Democracy, Oligarchy, and the Concept of the 'Free Citizen' in Late Fifth-Century Athens." *Political Theory* 11 (1983): 517–44.

———. "Contemporary Perceptions of Democracy in Fifth-Century Athens." *Classica et Mediaevalia* 40 (1989): 33–70.

———. "Democracy, Power, and Imperialism in Fifth-Century Athens." In Euben et al., eds., *Athenian Political Thought and the Reconstruction of American Democracy*, 103–46.

———. "The Transformation of Athens in the Fifth Century." In *Democracy, Empire, and the Arts in Fifth-Century Athens*, ed. Boedeker and Raaflaub, 15–41.

Ravitch, Diane, ed. *Debating the Future of American Education: Do We Need National Standards and Assessments?* Washington, D.C.: Brookings Institution, 1995.

———. *National Standards in American Education: A Citizen's Guide*. Washington, D.C., Brookings Institution, 1995.

Rawls, John. *A Theory of Justice*. Cambridge, Mass.: Harvard University Press, 1971.

———. *Political Liberalism*. New York: Columbia University Press, 1993 (1996).

———. "The Idea of Public Reason Revisited." *University of Chicago Law Review* 64 (1997): 765–807.

Readings, Bill. *The University in Ruins*. Cambridge, Mass.: Harvard University Press, 1996.

Reeve, C. D. C. *Philosopher-Kings*. Princeton: Princeton University Press, 1988.

———. *Socrates in the* Apology: *An Essay on Plato's* Apology of Socrates. Indianapolis: Hackett, 1989.

Rhodes, P. J. "Athenian Democracy After 403 B.C." *Classical Journal* 74 (1980): 319–20.

———. "The Polis and the Alternatives." In D. M. Lewis et al., eds., *The Cambridge Ancient History, vol. 6: The Fourth Century*, 565–91. Cambridge: Cambridge University Press, 1994.

Robb, Kevin. *Literacy and Paideia in the Ancient Greece*. New York: Oxford University Press, 1994.

Roberts, Jennifer. *Athens on Trial: The Antidemocratic Tradition in Western Thought*. Princeton: Princeton University Press, 1994.

Robertson, Martin. *A History of Greek Art*. Cambridge: Cambridge University Press, 1975.

Robinson, Richard. *Plato's Earlier Dialectic*. 2d ed. Oxford: Clarendon Press, 1953.

Romilly, Jacqueline de. *The Great Sophists of Periclean Athens*. Oxford: Oxford University Press, 1992.

Roochnik, David. "Socrates' Use of the *Techne*-Analogy." *Journal of the History of Philosophy* 24 (1986): 295–310.

———. *Of Art and Wisdom: Plato's Understanding of Techne.* University Park, Pa.: The Pennsylvania State University Press, 1996.

Rorty, Richard. *Philosophy and the Mirror of Nature.* Princeton: Princeton University Press, 1979.

———. *Achieving Our Country.* Cambridge, Mass.: Harvard University Press, 1998.

Rosen, Stanley. *Plato's Statesman: The Web of Politics.* New Haven: Yale University Press, 1995.

Ross, W. D. *Plato's Theory of Ideas.* Oxford, 1951.

Rowe, Christopher J. *Plato.* New York: St. Martin's, 1984.

Rowe, Christopher J., ed. *Reading the* Statesman: *Proceedings of the III Symposium Platonicum.* International Plato Studies 4. Sankt Augustin, Germany: Academia Verlag, 1995.

Rutherford, R. B. *The Art of Plato.* Cambridge, Mass.: Harvard University Press, 1995.

Ryan, Alan. *Liberal Anxieties and Liberal Education.* New York: Hill and Wang, 1998.

Ryle, Gilbert. *Plato's Progress.* Cambridge: Cambridge University Press, 1966.

Sachs, David. "A Fallacy in Plato's *Republic.*" *Philosophical Review* 72 (1963): 141–58. Reprinted in Vlastos, ed., *Plato: A Collection of Critical Essays, vol. 2: Ethics, Politics, and Philosophy of Art and Religion.*

Sagan, Eli. *The Honey and the Hemlock: Democracy and Paranoia in Ancient Athens and Modern America.* Princeton: Princeton University Press, 1991.

Sandel, Michael J. *Liberalism and the Limits of Justice.* Cambridge: Cambridge University Press, 1982.

———. Review of John Rawls, *Political Liberalism. Harvard Law Review* 107 (1994): 1765–94.

———. *Democracy's Discontent: America in Search of a Public Philosophy.* Cambridge, Mass.: Harvard University Press, 1996.

Santas, Gerasimos. *Socrates: Philosophy in Plato's Early Dialogues.* London: Routledge, 1979.

Sartorius, Rolf. "Fallacy and Political Radicalism in Plato's *Republic.*" *Canadian Journal of Philosophy* 3 (1974): 349–63.

Saunders, Trevor J. "Introduction." In Plato, *The Laws.* Penguin, 1970.

———. "'The RAND Corporation of Antiquity'? Plato's Academy and Greek Politics." In J. H. Betts et al., eds., *Studies in Honor of T. B. L. Webster,* vol. 1, 200–210. Bristol: Classical Press, 1986.

———. "Plato's Later Political Thought." In R. Kraut, ed., *The Cambridge Companion to Plato,* 464–92. Cambridge: Cambridge University Press, 1992.

Saunders, Trevor J., ed. *Early Socratic Dialogues.* Penguin, 1987.

Sayre, Kenneth. *Plato's Literary Garden: How to Read a Platonic Dialogue.* Notre Dame: University of Notre Dame Press, 1995.

Saxonhouse, Arlene. "The Philosopher and the Female in the Political Thought of Plato." *Political Theory* 4 (1976): 195–212.

————. *Fear of Diversity: The Birth of Political Science in Ancient Greece.* Chicago: University of Chicago Press, 1992.

————. *Athenian Democracy: Modern Mythmakers and Ancient Theorists.* Notre Dame: University of Notre Dame Press, 1996.

————. "Democracy, Equality, and Eide: A Radical View of Book 8 of Plato's *Republic.*" *American Political Science Review* 92 (1998): 273–83.

Schaar, John H. "Equality of Opportunity, and Beyond." In *Equality,* ed. J. Roland Pennock and John W. Chapman, *Nomos* 9, 228–49. New York: Atherton Press, 1967.

Scheid, John, and Jesper Svenbro. *The Craft of Zeus—Myths of Weaving and Fabric.* Trans. Carol Volk. Cambridge, Mass.: Harvard University Press, 1996.

Schiappa, Edward. *Protagoras and Logos.* Columbia: University of South Carolina Press, 1991.

Schleiermacher, Friedrich. "Introduction." In Friedrich Schleiermacher, *Introductions to the Dialogues of Plato,* trans. William Dobson, 1–47. Cambridge: J. & J. J. Deighton, 1836.

Schlesinger, Arthur M., Jr. *The Disuniting of America.* New York: Norton, 1992.

Schmitt, Carl. *The Concept of the Political.* Trans. G. Schwab. New Brunswick: Rutgers University Press, 1976 (1927).

Scodel, H. R. *Diairesis and Myth in Plato's Statesman. Hypomnemata* 85. Göttingen, 1987.

Sealey, Raphael. "Callistratos of Aphidna and His Contemporaries." *Historia* 5 (1956): 178–203.

————. "The Origins of Demokratia." *California Studies in Classical Antiquity* 6 (1973): 253–95.

Seung, T. K. *Intuition and Construction.* New Haven: Yale University Press, 1993.

————. *Kant's Platonic Revolution in Moral and Political Philosophy.* Baltimore: Johns Hopkins University Press, 1994.

————. *Plato Rediscovered: Human Value and Social Order.* Lanham, Md.: Rowman & Littlefield, 1995.

Shapiro, Ian. *Democracy's Place.* Ithaca: Cornell University Press, 1996.

————. *Democratic Justice.* New Haven: Yale University Press, 1999.

Shiell, Timothy. "The Unity of Plato's Thought." *History of Political Thought* 12 (1991): 377–90.

Shorey, Paul. "The Idea of Good in Plato's *Republic.*" *Classical Philology* 1 (1895): 188–239.

————. "Introduction." Plato, *The Republic.* Rev. ed. Loeb Classical Library, Plato, *Works,* 5–6. Cambridge, Mass.: Harvard University Press, 1969–1970 (1930, 1937).

————. *What Plato Said.* Chicago: University of Chicago Press, 1933.

Sinclair, R. K. *Democracy and Participation in Athens.* Cambridge: Cambridge University Press, 1988.

Skemp, J. B. "Introduction." In J. B. Skemp, *Plato's Statesman.* London: Routledge & Kegan Paul, 1952.

————. *Plato.* Oxford, 1976.

Shklar, Judith N. *The Faces of Injustice.* New Haven: Yale University Press, 1990.
Skinner, Quentin. "Meaning and Understanding in the History of Ideas" (1969). Reprinted in Tully, ed., *Meaning and Context: Quentin Skinner and His Critics,* 64–107.
———. "The Idea of Negative Liberty." In R. Rorty et al., eds., *Philosophy in History,* 193–221. Cambridge: Cambridge University Press, 1984.
———. "A Reply to My Critics." In Tully, ed., *Meaning and Context: Quentin Skinner and His Critics,* 231–88.
———. *Liberty Before Liberalism.* Cambridge: Cambridge University Press, 1998.
Smith, Rogers M. *Civic Ideals.* New Haven: Yale University Press, 1997.
Snell, Bruno. *The Discovery of the Mind.* New York: Harper & Row, 1960.
Solmsen, F. Review of Edelstein's *Plato's Seventh Letter. Gnomon* 41 (1969): 29–34.
Sprague, Rosamond Kent. *The Older Sophists.* Columbia: University of South Carolina Press, 1972.
———. *Plato's Philosopher-King: A Study of the Theoretical Background.* Columbia: University of South Carolina Press, 1976.
Stalley, R. F. *An Introduction to Plato's* Laws. Oxford: Basil Blackwell, 1983.
Ste. Croix, G. E. M. de. *Class Struggle in the Ancient Greek World.* Ithaca: Cornell University Press, 1981.
Stone, I. F. *The Trial of Socrates.* Boston: Little, Brown, 1988.
Strauss, Barry S. *Athens After the Peloponnesian War: Class, Faction, and Policy, 403–386 B.C.* Ithaca: Cornell University Press, 1987.
———. *Fathers and Sons in Athens: Ideology and Society in the Era of the Peloponnesian War.* Princeton: Princeton University Press, 1993.
Strauss, Leo. *Persecution and the Art of Writing.* Glencoe: Free Press, 1952.
———. "Plato." In Leo Strauss and Joseph Cropsey, eds., *History of Political Philosophy,* 33–89. Chicago: University of Chicago Press, 1963.
———. *On Tyranny.* Rev. and enlarged ed. of Xenophon's *Hiero.* Ithaca: Cornell University Press, 1963.
———. *The City and Man.* Chicago: University of Chicago Press, 1964.
———. *Socrates and Aristophanes.* New York: Basic Books, 1966.
———. *What Is Political Philosophy.* Westport: Greenwood Press, 1973.
———. *The Argument and the Action of Plato's* Laws. Chicago: University of Chicago Press, 1975.
———. *Studies in Platonic Philosophy.* Ed. Thomas Pangle. Chicago: University of Chicago Press, 1983.
Sunstein, Cass. "Beyond the Republican Revival." *Yale Law Journal* 97 (1988): 1539–90.
Tate, J. "'Imitation' in Plato's *Republic.*" *Classical Quarterly* 22 (1928): 16–23.
———. "Plato and 'Imitation.'" *Classical Quarterly* 26 (1932): 161–69.
Tawney, R. H. *Equality.* With intro. by Richard Titmuss. London: Unwin Books, 1964 (1931–52).
Taylor, A. E. *Plato, The Man and His Work.* London, 1926.
———. "Aeschines of Sphettus" (1928). In A. E. Taylor, *Philosophical Papers,* 1–28. London: Macmillan, 1934.

Thesleff, Holger. *Studies in the Chronology of Plato's Dialogues.* Helsinki: Societas Scientiarum Fennica, 1982.

Thomas, Rosalind. *Literacy and Orality in Ancient Greece.* Cambridge: Cambridge University Press, 1992.

Thompson, Dennis F. See Gutmann, Amy.

Thompson, W. H. "On the Philosophy of Isocrates, and His Relation to the Socratic Schools." In *The Phaedrus of Plato,* ed. W. H. Thompson, 170–83. London, 1868.

Thorson, Thomas L., ed. *Plato: Totalitarian or Democrat?* Englewood Cliffs, N.J.: Prentice-Hall, 1963.

Tigerstedt, E. N. *Interpreting Plato.* Uppsala: Almqvist & Wiksell, 1977.

Tiles, J. E. "*Techne* and Moral Expertise." *Philosophy* 59 (1984): 49–66.

Todd, S. C. *The Shape of Athenian Law.* Oxford: Clarendon Press, 1993.

Too, Yung Lee. *The Rhetoric of Identity in Isocrates: Text, Power, Pedagogy.* Cambridge: Cambridge University Press, 1995.

Touraine, Alain. *What Is Democracy?* Boulder: Westview Press, 1997.

Trampedach, Kai. *Platon, Die Akademie, und Die Zeitgenössische Politik.* Stuttgart, 1994.

Traub, James. *City on a Hill: Testing the American Dream at City College.* Reading, Mass.: Addison-Wesley, 1994.

Tuana, Nancy, ed. *Feminist Interpretations of Plato.* University Park, Pa.: The Pennsylvania State University Press, 1994.

Tully, James, ed. *Meaning and Context: Quentin Skinner and His Critics.* Princeton: Princeton University Press, 1988.

Vernant, Jean-Pierre. *The Origins of Greek Thought.* Ithaca: Cornell University Press, 1982 (1962).

———. *Myth and Thought Among the Greeks.* London: Routledge & Kegan Paul, 1983 (1965).

Versenyi, Laszlo. "The Cretan Plato." *Review of Metaphysics* 15 (1961–1962): 67–80.

———. *Socratic Humanism.* New Haven: Yale University Press, 1963.

Vidal-Naquet, Pierre. "Plato's Myth of the *Statesman:* The Ambiguities of the Golden Age and History." *Journal of Hellenic Studies* 98 (1978): 132–41.

———. "A Study in Ambiguity: Artisans in the Platonic City." In Pierre Vidal-Naquet, *Black Hunter: Forms of Thought and Forms of Society in the Greek World,* 224–45. Baltimore: Johns Hopkins University Press, 1986 (1981).

Vlastos, Gregory, "Slavery in Plato's Thought" (1941). Reprinted in Vlastos, *Platonic Studies,* 147–63, and in Vlastos, *Studies in Greek Philosophy,* vol. 1.

———. "Solonian Justice." *Classical Philology* 41 (1946): 65–83. Reprinted in Vlastos, *Studies in Greek Philosophy,* vol. 1.

———. "Equality and Justice in Early Greek Cosmology." *Classical Philology* 42 (1947): 156–78. Reprinted in Vlastos, *Studies in Greek Philosophy,* vol. 1.

———. "*Isonomia Politike*" (1964). Reprinted in Vlastos, *Platonic Studies,* 164–203, and in Vlastos, *Studies in Greek Philosophy,* vol. 1.

———. "Introduction: The Paradox of Socrates." In Vlastos, ed., *The Philosophy of Socrates,* 1–22.

———. "The Unity of the Virtues in the *Protagoras*" (1972). Reprinted in Vlastos, *Platonic Studies*, 221–69, and in Vlastos, *Studies in Greek Philosophy*, vol. 2.

———. "The Theory of Social Justice in the *Polis* in Plato's *Republic.*" In Helen North, ed., *Interpretations of Plato*, 1–40. Leiden: E. J. Brill, 1977, and in Vlastos, *Studies in Greek Philosophy*, vol. 2.

———. *Platonic Studies*. 2d ed. Princeton: Princeton University Press, 1981.

———. "The Socratic *Elenchus.*" In J. Annas, ed., *Oxford Studies in Ancient Philosophy*, vol. 1, 27–58. Oxford: Clarendon Press, 1983, and in Vlastos, *Socratic Studies*.

———. "The Historical Socrates and Athenian Democracy." *Political Theory* 11 (1983): 495–516. Also in Vlastos, *Socratic Studies*.

———. "Was Plato a Feminist?" *Times Literary Supplement*, 17–23 March 1989, pp. 276, 288–289, and *Times Literary Supplement*, 15–21 December 1989, p. 1393. Reprinted in Vlastos, *Studies in Greek Philosophy*, vol. 2.

———. *Socrates: Ironist and Moral Philosopher*. Cambridge: Cambridge University Press, 1991.

———. *Socratic Studies*. Ed. Myles Burnyeat. Cambridge: Cambridge University Press, 1994.

———. *Studies in Greek Philosophy, vol. 1: The Presocratics*. Ed. Daniel W. Graham. Princeton: Princeton University Press, 1995.

———. *Studies in Greek Philosophy, vol. 2: Socrates, Plato, and Their Tradition*. Ed. Daniel W. Graham. Princeton: Princeton University Press, 1995.

Vlastos, Gregory, ed. *Plato: A Collection of Critical Essays, vol. 2: Ethics, Politics, and Philosophy of Art and Religion*. Garden City, N.Y.: Doubleday, 1971.

———. *The Philosophy of Socrates: A Collection of Critical Essays*. Garden City, N.Y.: Anchor Books, 1971.

Waerdt, Paul Van Der, ed. *The Socratic Movement*. Ithaca: Cornell University Press, 1994.

Waldron, Jeremy. "What Would Plato Allow." In Ian Shapiro and Judith Wagner De-Cew, eds., *Theory and Practice*, 138–78. New York: New York University Press, 1995.

———. "Multiculturalism and Melange." In Robert K. Fullinwider, ed., *Public Education in a Multicultural Society*. Cambridge: Cambridge University Press, 1996.

Wallace, Robert W. *The Areopagos Council, to 307 B.C.* Baltimore: Johns Hopkins University Press, 1989.

Wallach, John R. Review of Alasdair Macintyre's *After Virtue: A Study in Moral Theory*. *Telos*, no. 57 (1983): 233–40.

———. Review of M. I. Finley's *Politics in the Ancient World*. *Political Theory* 12 (1984): 302–7.

———. "Liberals, Communitarians, and the Tasks of Political Theory." *Political Theory* 15 (1987): 581–611.

———. "Socratic Citizenship." *History of Political Thought* 9 (1988): 393–418.

———. Review of Cynthia Farrar's *The Origins of Democratic Thinking*. *American Political Science Review* 83 (1989): 1362–64.

———. "Contemporary Aristotelianism." *Political Theory* 20 (1992): 613–41.
———. "Two Democracies and Virtue." In Euben et al., eds., *Athenian Political Thought and the Reconstruction of American Democracy*, 319–40.
———. Review of Eli Sagan, *The Honey and the Hemlock. Polis* 14 (1995): 189–97.
———. "Plato's Socratic Problem, and Ours." *History of Political Thought* 18 (1997): 377–98.
Walsh, John. "The Dramatic Dates of Plato's *Protagoras* and the Lessons of *Arete*." *Classical Quarterly* 34 (1984): 101–6.
Weber, Max. "Politics as a Vocation." In *From Max Weber: Essays in Sociology*, ed. H. H. Gerth and C. Wright Mills, 77–128. New York: Oxford University Press, 1958.
Weiss, Roslyn. *Socrates Dissatisfied: An Analysis of Plato's Crito*. New York: Oxford University Press, 1998.
Westlake, H. D. "Dion and Timoleon." In Lewis et al., eds., *The Cambridge Ancient History, 2d ed., vol. 6: The Fourth Century B.C.*, 693–722.
White, Hayden. *Tropics of Discourse: Essays in Cultural Criticism*. Baltimore: Johns Hopkins University Press, 1978.
———. *The Content of the Form: Narrative Discourse and Historical Representation*. Baltimore: Johns Hopkins University Press, 1987.
———. "Historical Emplotment and the Problem of Truth." In Saul Friedlander, ed., *Probing the Limits of Representation: Nazism and the "Final Solution."* Cambridge, Mass.: Harvard University Press, 1992.
———. "Writing in the Middle Voice." *Stanford Literary Review* 9 (Fall 1992): 179–87.
———. "Response to Arthur Marwick." *Journal of Contemporary History* 30 (1995): 233–46.
White, Nicholas P. "Rational Prudence in Plato's *Gorgias*." In Dominic J. O'Meara, ed., *Platonic Investigations*, 139–62. Washington, D.C.: Catholic University of America, 1985.
———. "The Rulers' Choice." *Archiv für Geschichte der Philosophie* 68 (1986): 22–46.
———. *A Companion to Plato's Republic*. Indianapolis: Hackett, 1979.
Whitehead, Alfred North. *Process and Reality*. Ed. David Ray Griffin and Donald W. Sherburne. New York: Free Press, 1978.
Wiebe, Robert H. *Self-Rule: A Cultural History of American Democracy*. Chicago: University of Chicago Press, 1995.
Will, George F. *Restoration: Congress, Term Limits, and the Recovery of Deliberative Democracy*. New York: Free Press, 1992.
Williams, Bernard. "The Analogy of City and Soul in Plato's *Republic*." In E. N. Lee et al., eds., *Exegesis and Argument: Studies in Greek Philosophy Presented to Gregory Vlastos*, 196–206. Assen: Van Gorcum, 1973.
———. *Ethics and the Limits of Philosophy*. Cambridge, Mass.: Harvard University Press, 1985.
———. *Shame and Necessity*. Berkeley and Los Angeles: University of California Press, 1993.

Wittgenstein, Ludwig. *Culture and Value.* Ed. G. H. von Wright. Chicago: University of Chicago Press, 1980.

Wolff, Edward. *Top Heavy: The Increasing Inequality of Wealth in America and What Can Be Done About It.* New York: New Press, 1996.

Wolin, Sheldon S. *Politics and Vision.* Boston: Little, Brown, 1960.

———. "Political Theory as a Vocation" (1969). Reprinted in M. Fleisher, ed., *Machiavelli and the Nature of Political Thought,* 23–75. New York: Atheneum, 1972.

———. *The Presence of the Past: Essays on the State and the Constitution.* Baltimore: Johns Hopkins University Press, 1989.

———. "Norm and Form: The Constitutionalizing of Democracy." In Euben et al., eds., *Athenian Political Thought and the Reconstruction of American Democracy,* 29–58.

Wood, Ellen, and Neal Wood. *Class Ideology and Ancient Political Theory—Socrates, Plato, and Aristotle in Social Context.* New York: Oxford University Press, 1978.

———. "Socrates and Democracy: A Reply to Gregory Vlastos." *Political Theory* 14 (1986): 55–82.

Wood, Gordon S. *The Creation of the American Republic, 1776–1787.* New York: Norton, 1972.

Woodbury, Leonard. "Simonides on *Arete.*" *Transactions of the American Philological Association* 84 (1953): 135–63.

Worthington, Ian, ed. *Voice into Text: Orality and Literacy in Ancient Greece.* Leiden: E. J. Brill, 1996.

Young, Michael. *The Rise of the Meritocracy, 1870–2033: An Essay on Education and Equality.* Penguin, 1961 (1958).

Young, Robert, ed. *Untying the Text: A Post-Structuralist Reader.* Boston: Routledge & Kegan Paul, 1981.

Yunis, Harvey. *Taming Democracy: Political Rhetoric in Classical Athens.* Ithaca: Cornell University Press, 1996.

INDEX

The nouns, proper nouns, and names listed below are intended as bookmarks for the narrative, subjects, arguments, and discussions in the main text and footnotes of the book. The index itself is not an exhaustive account of the book's topics or citations.